Attribution of Non-State Actor Conduct During Armed Conflict

THE LIEBER STUDIES

The *Lieber Studies* is the flagship publication of the Lieber Institute for Law and Warfare. It is designed to provide scholars, practitioners, and students with in-depth and critical analysis of the most challenging legal issues related to warfare in the twenty-first century. Established by the Department of Law and Philosophy of the United States Military Academy at West Point, the mission of the Lieber Institute is to foster a deeper understanding of the complex and evolving relationship between law and warfare to educate and empower current and future combat leaders. It does so through global academic engagement and advanced interdisciplinary research. As such, it lies at the crossroads of scholarship and practice by bringing together scholars, military officers, government legal advisers, and members of civil society from around the world to collaboratively examine the role and application of the law of armed conflict in current and future armed conflicts, as well as that of other regimes of international law in situations threatening international peace and security.

Lieber Institute for Law and Warfare
The Lieber Studies

Volume 12

Attribution of Non-State Actor Conduct During Armed Conflict

General Editors

PROFESSOR MICHAEL N. SCHMITT

PROFESSOR SEAN WATTS

Managing Editor

PROFESSOR ROBERT LAWLESS

Author

JENNIFER MADDOCKS

OXFORD
UNIVERSITY PRESS

OXFORD
UNIVERSITY PRESS

Oxford University Press is a department of the University of Oxford.
It furthers the University's objective of excellence in research, scholarship,
and education by publishing worldwide. Oxford is a registered trade mark of
Oxford University Press in the UK and in certain other countries.

Published in the United States of America by Oxford University Press
198 Madison Avenue, New York, NY 10016, United States of America.

Library of Congress Cataloging-in-Publication Data
Names: Maddocks, Jennifer author
Title: Attribution of non-state actor conduct during armed conflict / Jennifer Maddocks.
Description: New York : Oxford University Press, 2026. | Series: Lieber studies series |
Includes bibliographical references and index.
Identifiers: LCCN 2025048972 (print) | LCCN 2025048973 (ebook) | ISBN 9780197842652 hardback |
ISBN 9780197842669 epub | ISBN 9780197842676 updf | ISBN 9780197842683 online
Subjects: LCSH: Government liability (International law) | War (International law) |
Non-state actors (International relations)
Classification: LCC KZ4080 .M33 2026 (print) | LCC KZ4080 (ebook)
LC record available at https://lccn.loc.gov/2025048972
LC ebook record available at https://lccn.loc.gov/2025048973

DOI: 10.1093/oso/9780197842652.001.0001

Printed by Integrated Books International, United States of America

The manufacturer's authorized representative in the EU for product safety is
Oxford University Press España S.A. of Parque Empresarial San Fernando de Henares,
Avenida de Castilla, 2 – 28830 Madrid (www.oup.es/en or product.safety@oup.com).
OUP España S.A. also acts as importer into Spain of products made by the manufacturer.

CONTENTS

FOREWORD

It is both a professional privilege and a personal pleasure to introduce Dr. Jennifer Maddocks' cutting-edge work, *Attribution of Non-State Actor Conduct During Armed Conflict*. The book represents the culmination of years of rigorous research, analysis, and reflection on one of the most complex and consequential topics in contemporary international law—the attribution to States of conduct by non-State actors that occurs during armed conflicts. It is a topic that is both fascinating and of enormous practical relevance to the work of international law practitioners globally.

The book is an expanded and revised version of Dr. Maddocks' PhD dissertation, completed at the University of Reading under my supervision. She began her work while assigned as a British Army officer on the faculty of the United States Naval War College's Stockton Center for International Law. Dr. Maddocks brought extensive operational experience to the task, experience that deepened even further in postings following that assignment. The result is a work that is not only academically sound and highly original but also one that is uniquely sensitive to international law's actual application in practice. As her supervisor and as the General Editor of the *Lieber Studies* series, I am delighted to see this work published in a forum dedicated to advancing high-level, policy-relevant scholarship on the relationship between international law and warfare.

With conflicts involving non-State actors raging on multiple continents, the publication of *Attribution of Non-State Actor Conduct During Armed Conflict* could not be timelier. The last several decades have witnessed a growing number of armed groups, militias, private military and security companies (PMSCs), cyber actors, and other non-State entities becoming involved in armed conflicts around the world. In many cases, one or more States assist them by providing financial, logistical, operational, or even ideological support, while operating outside formal State structures.

The presence of these non-State actors on the modern battlefield poses fundamental challenges to the normative architecture of international law, which is predominantly State-centric. With some notable exceptions, such as international criminal law, international law is primarily about the rights and obligations of

States. This is the case regarding the law of armed conflict. Individuals commit war crimes, but only States violate the law of armed conflict, either because their forces breach an obligation the State shoulders or because the conduct of another State, a non-State group, or a private individual is attributable to the State.

In this impressive work, Dr. Maddocks takes a deep dive into the attribution of non-State actor conduct to a State such that the State is responsible under the law of State responsibility for the former's actions. When, and under what conditions, must a non-State entity's actions be treated as the acts of a State as a matter of law? How do the six key rules of attribution that bear on non-State actor conduct operate individually and collectively? What voids or asymmetries remain in the existing legal framework that allow States to benefit from proxy relationships while evading accountability? How should shortfalls in the law be remedied?

Not only does Dr. Maddocks' comprehensive and in-depth survey of the key attribution rules bearing on the actions of non-State actors during armed conflict distinguish this work, but so too does the lens through which she examines them. The analysis is built around three detailed case studies—the conflicts in Syria, Ukraine, and the Democratic Republic of the Congo. They are conflicts involving diverse non-State groups that have multifaceted relationships with external States and have repeatedly violated the laws of armed conflict. Accordingly, all three represent fertile ground for assessing attribution in practice. Dr. Maddocks masterfully integrates them into her doctrinal analysis, enabling readers to appreciate the real-world implications of abstract legal rules.

It is a work marked by clarity and precision, one that will become essential reading for those concerned with the international legal regulation of contemporary conflict. For international lawyers, it offers a masterful doctrinal exploration of attribution in the law of State responsibility. Legal policymakers and military legal advisers will find this book to be an invaluable resource in informing their interpretive choices and assessing the implications of those choices for accountability. For international relations scholars focusing on conflict, it offers a nuanced analysis of a legal framework intended to hold States accountable for their actions, including during warfare, as well as the fault lines resident within that framework.

It is rare to encounter a work that combines doctrinal depth, methodological rigor, normative insight, and practical understanding in equal measure. *Attribution of Non-State Actor Conduct During Armed Conflict* is such a work. I am confident that it will become a seminal reference in both academic and professional discussions of State accountability in modern conflict. I applaud Dr. Maddocks for producing this superb volume and thank her for the honor and pleasure of having served as her PhD supervisor.

Michael N. Schmitt
Professor of Law, University of Reading
Professor Emeritus, U.S. Naval War College

ACKNOWLEDGMENTS

I commenced this research in late 2016, while serving in the British Army Legal Services. At that time, I was very fortunate to be posted to the Stockton Center for International Law at the U.S. Naval War College to undertake a postgraduate research degree under the supervision of Professor Michael Schmitt. I completed my PhD in early 2022, while still in service with the British Army. I then carried out the additional research required to produce this book while working as an Assistant Professor at the United States Military Academy, West Point.

I owe thanks to many people for their invaluable assistance in completing this work. First and foremost, I am profoundly grateful to Professor Schmitt for his wise counsel, guidance, and patience throughout the drafting process. He has been incredibly generous with his time, reviewing and providing advice on numerous draft chapters. This book, together with all my academic writing, owes much to Professor Schmitt's intellectual rigor, sage advice, and continued support.

Second, I would like to thank my former colleagues in the British Army Legal Services for providing the opportunity to commence this research and for their assistance along the way. In particular, I owe thanks to Alex Taylor for his support when I initially expressed an interest in the Stockton Center role, to Amanda Brown for suggesting attribution as a potential topic to focus on in my research, and to Phil Oram for his understanding and flexibility as I completed the final stages of my PhD. I am also grateful for the operational opportunities my role as an Army lawyer provided. After leaving the Stockton Center, I deployed to Iraq as part of the counter-ISIS fight, then worked as a legal adviser in an operational headquarters. Both roles provided insights into States' relationships with non-State actors during armed conflict that I would not otherwise have gained.

Third, I would like to thank my West Point colleagues for their considerable support and friendship over the past three years. Specific thanks must go to Sean Watts for his continued advice and guidance, including reviews of several draft chapters, and to Rob Lawless for his thorough appraisal of the entire manuscript in his role as Managing Editor of the *Lieber Studies* series.

In addition, I owe thanks to Katharine Fortin for her valuable comments on an earlier draft of the chapter relating to Article 9 and to Liisi Adamson for her assistance regarding the cover image.

Finally, I am grateful to my niece Eleanor for her help in finalizing the footnotes, and to all my family for their unstinting support.

Jennifer Maddocks
July 2025

TABLE OF CASES

ARBITRAL TRIBUNALS AND CLAIMS COMMISSIONS

American and British Claims Arbitration Tribunal

American-Venezuela Mixed Claims Commission

British-Mexican Claims Commission

British-Venezuela Mixed Claims Commission

European Court of Human Rights

Franco-Italian Commission

French-Mexican Mixed Claims Commission

General Claims Commission

International Centre for Settlement of Investment Disputes (ICSID)

International Court of Arbitration of the International Chamber of Commerce

International Court of Justice

International Criminal Court

International Criminal Tribunal for the former Yugoslavia

Iran-U.S. Claims Tribunal

Italy-Venezuela Mixed Claims Commission

Mexico-United States Mixed Claims Commission

Mixed Claims Commission (U.S. & Germany)

Permanent Court of Arbitration

Permanent Court of International Justice

Spanish Zone of Morocco Claims

United Nations Commission On International Trade Law

United States–Great Britain Claims Commission

United States–El Salvador Arbitration Tribunal

NATIONAL COURTS

Italy

Netherlands

United Kingdom

United States

TABLE OF TREATIES, LEGISLATION, AND INTERNATIONAL DOCUMENTS

TREATIES AND CONVENTIONS

INTERNATIONAL LAW COMMISSION DOCUMENTS

UNITED NATIONS DOCUMENTS

Other Documents

ACRONYMS AND ABBREVIATIONS

AP I	Additional Protocol I to the Geneva Conventions
AP II	Additional Protocol II to the Geneva Conventions
ARSIWA	Articles on the Responsibility of States for Internationally Wrongful Acts
CAR	Central African Republic
CIA	Central Intelligence Agency
CNDP	National Congress for the Defense of the People (DRC)
DNR	Donetsk People's Republic (Ukraine)
DRC	Democratic Republic of the Congo
ECHR	European Convention on Human Rights
ECtHR	European Court of Human Rights
FARDC	Armed Forces of the Democratic Republic of the Congo
FRY	Federal Republic of Yugoslavia
FSA	Free Syrian Army
GRU	The Russian General Staff Main Intelligence Directorate
HTS	Hayat Tahrir al-Sham (Syria)
ICC	International Criminal Court
ICJ	International Court of Justice
ICRC	International Committee of the Red Cross
ICTY	International Criminal Tribunal for the former Yugoslavia
IHL	International humanitarian law
IHRL	International human rights law
ILC	International Law Commission
IRGC	Islamic Revolutionary Guard Corps
ISIS	Islamic State in Iraq and Syria
LNR	Luhansk People's Republic (Ukraine)
M23	Movement of 23 March (DRC)
MLC	Congo Liberation Movement (DRC)
NATO	North Atlantic Treaty Organization
NDF	National Defense Force (Syria)
NIAC	Non-international armed conflict
NSA	Non-State actor
OSCE	Organization for Security and Cooperation in Europe

PKK	Kurdistan Workers' Party
PMF	Popular Mobilization Forces (Iraq)
PMSC	Private military and security company
RDF	Rwandan Defense Force
SDF	Syrian Democratic Forces
SFOR	Stabilization Force in Bosnia and Herzegovina
SNA	Syrian National Army
UN	United Nations
VRS	Army of the Republika Srpska (Bosnia and Herzegovina)
YPG	Kurdish People's Protection Units

PART ONE

Introduction

1

Introduction

1.1 INTRODUCTION

Armed conflicts are replete with examples of States acting through private partners or proxies. It is necessary to look no further than the hostilities in Syria to find a plethora of non-State actors (NSA) on the battlefield,[1] many of which received at least some degree of State support. In the early stages of the conflict, for instance, the Syrian regime used local militias to repress the protests.[2] Shi'a militia groups, including Hezbollah, later bolstered the regime's forces, with backing from Iran.[3] Once Russia became involved in the fight, it employed private military companies such as the Wagner Group to reinforce the regime.[4] Turkey acted through Syrian militias in its operations against the Kurds in the north of the country.[5] The United States and its allies assisted, first, the rebels

1. One study estimated that the forces opposing the Syrian government in the early years of the conflict comprised 1,500 armed groups. *See* Christopher M. Blanchard et al., *Armed Conflict in Syria, Overview and U.S. Response*, 5 Current Pol. & Econ. of the Middle East 237, 243 (2014).

2. Brian M. Jenkins, RAND, The Dynamics of Syria's Civil War 6–7 (2014), www.rand.org/pubs/perspectives/PE115.html.

3. Michael Knights, *Iran's Foreign Legion: The Role of Iraqi Shiite Militias in Syria*, Wash. Inst. (June 27, 2013), www.washingtoninstitute.org/policy-analysis/irans-foreign-legion-role-iraqi-shiite-militias-syria; Marisa Sullivan, Inst. for the Study of War, Hezbollah in Syria (Apr. 2014), http://www.understandingwar.org/sites/default/files/Hezbollah_Sullivan_FINAL.pdf.

4. Metin Gurcan, *Private Military Companies: Moscow's Other Army in Syria*, Al-Monitor (Nov. 29, 2017), www.al-monitor.com/pulse/originals/2017/11/turkey-russia-private-army-in-syria.html.

5. Sarah El Deeb & Joseph Krauss, *Money, Hatred for the Kurds Drives Turkey's Syrian Fighters*, AP News (Oct. 15, 2019), https://apnews.com/7386b1149d2642afb3258e3d07d167dc.

Attribution of Non-State Actor Conduct During Armed Conflict. Jennifer Maddocks, Oxford University Press.
 DOI: 10.1093/oso/9780197842652.003.0001

opposing the government[6] before switching focus to the fight against ISIS, conducted in large part via another NSA, the Syrian Democratic Forces.[7] And in late 2024, the rebel group Hay'at Tahrir al-Sham (HTS) launched a surprise offensive against Syrian regime forces, ultimately taking control of Damascus and toppling President Assad.[8]

The situation in Syria exemplifies several common features of contemporary armed conflict: the diversity of the NSAs on the battlefield; the varied relationships between those NSAs and the States involved in the conflict; and the prevalence of conduct that potentially violates international law. Abuses against civilians were rife in Syria,[9] as they are in other conflicts around the world.[10] And frequently, the acts during armed conflict that violate international humanitarian law (IHL) are committed by NSAs that receive State support.[11]

This reality presents challenges to the traditional framework of international law, which assumes that States are the predominant actors on the world stage with a monopoly on the use of force. It raises questions, moreover, regarding accountability for the harms caused, including the issue of when an NSA's conduct in violation of IHL can be attributed to a State. Although much has been written regarding attribution in the law of State responsibility, the precise circumstances in which private conduct is attributable to a State remain unclear. Adding clarity to that issue, in situations of armed conflict, is the primary goal of this book.

6. Mark Mazzetti & Matt Apuzzo, *U.S. Relies Heavily on Saudi Money to Support Syrian Rebels*, N.Y. Times (Jan. 23, 2016), www.nytimes.com/2016/01/24/world/middleeast/us-relies-heavily-on-saudi-money-to-support-syrian-rebels.html?_r=1; John Walcott, *Trump Ends CIA Arms Support for Anti-Assad Syria Rebels: U.S. Officials*, Reuters (July 19, 2017), www.reuters.com/article/us-mideast-crisis-usa-syria-idUSKBN1A42KC.

7. Aron Lund, *Origins of the Syrian Democratic Forces: A Primer*, New Humanitarian (Jan. 22, 2016), https://deeply.thenewhumanitarian.org/syria/articles/2016/01/22/origins-of-the-syrian-democratic-forces-a-primer; William Rosenau & Zack Gold, CNA, "The Cheapest Insurance in the World"? The United States and Proxy Warfare 29–40 (July 2019), www.cna.org/CNA_files/PDF/DRM-2019-U-020227-1Rev.pdf.

8. William Christou, *Syrian Rebels Reveal Year-Long Plot That Brought Down Assad Regime*, The Guardian (Dec. 13, 2024), https://www.theguardian.com/world/2024/dec/13/syrian-rebels-reveal-year-long-plot-that-brought-down-assad-regime.

9. *See, e.g.*, *Open Letter to the Leaders of the Syrian Opposition Regarding Human Rights Abuses by Armed Opposition Members*, Hum. Rts. Watch (Mar. 20, 2012), https://www.hrw.org/news/2012/03/20/open-letter-leaders-syrian-opposition.

10. *See, e.g.*, International Committee of the Red Cross (ICRC), 2024 ICRC Report on IHL and the Challenges of Contemporary Armed Conflicts (2024), https://www.icrc.org/en/report/2024-icrc-report-ihl-challenges.

11. *See infra* ch. 2, sec. 2.3.

1.2 ACCOUNTABILITY FOR IHL VIOLATIONS INVOLVING NON-STATE ACTORS

NSAs' involvement in armed conflicts raises challenging issues of accountability. Of course, the fighters responsible for any conduct in violation of IHL might be criminally liable for committing a war crime.[12] Individual criminal responsibility, however, cannot address the wider culpability of the entity for which the fighter was acting, and it might provide limited means of redress for any victims.[13]

If the NSA that committed the relevant acts is an organized armed group, it could theoretically be held to account for violating its own IHL obligations.[14] Yet in practice, it is extremely difficult for those harmed by an NSA's conduct to bring claims against it. Armed groups exist only temporarily: they fragment, they are defeated, or occasionally they meet with success and become the government. Any claim against the NSA as an entity must be brought while it still exists. In reality, such claims are extremely rare and unlikely to succeed.[15] Often, therefore, the only realistic option for those harmed by an NSA's conduct is to invoke the responsibility of a State.

State responsibility is a critical means of redress for victims of international law violations involving NSAs. The law of State responsibility was codified by the International Law Commission (ILC) in its 2001 Draft Articles on the Responsibility of States for Internationally Wrongful Acts (ARSIWA).[16] It provides that when conduct in violation of a State's international law obligations is attributable to that State, it amounts to an internationally wrongful act, engaging the State's international responsibility.[17] Certain legal consequences then follow, including an obligation on the responsible State to cease its harmful conduct and to

12. For example, Finland commenced proceedings against the leader of a Russian NSA for war crimes committed in Ukraine. *See Finnish Prosecutor Charges Russian Ultranationalist Leader with War Crimes*, RADIO FREE EUROPE RADIO LIBERTY (Oct 31, 2024), https://www.rferl.org/a/finland-russia-torden-petrovsky-war-crimes-ukraine/33182169.html. The International Criminal Court has also prosecuted members of NSAs for war crimes. *See, e.g.*, Prosecutor v. Thomas Lubanga Dyilo, Case No. ICC-01/04-01/06-2842, Judgment (Mar. 14, 2012) [hereinafter *Lubanga*].

13. *See, e.g.*, Conor McCarthy, *Victim Redress and International Criminal Justice: Competing Paradigms, or Compatible Forms of Justice?* 10 J. INT'L CRIM. JUST. 351 (2012).

14. *See, e.g.*, Jann Kleffner, *The Applicability of International Humanitarian Law to Organized Armed Groups*, 93 INT'L REV. RED CROSS 443 (2011).

15. *See, e.g.*, PATRICK DUMBERRY, REBELLIONS AND CIVIL WARS 204–9 (2022).

16. Draft Articles on Responsibility of States for Internationally Wrongful Acts, with commentaries *in* Int'l Law Comm'n, Rep. on the Work of its Fifty-Third Session, U.N. Doc. A/56/10 (2001), *reprinted in* [2001] 2 Y.B. INT'L L. COMM'N 31, U.N. Doc. A/CN.4/SER.A/2001/Add.1 (Part 2) [hereinafter ARSIWA]. For further discussion regarding ARSIWA, including the articles' development and their status in customary international law, *see infra* ch. 3.

17. ARSIWA, *supra* note 16, arts. 1–2.

make reparation for any injury or damage caused.[18] The application of the law of State responsibility can therefore lead to more effective remedies for victims than either international criminal law or attempts to hold NSAs directly to account. It also ensures that States bear responsibility for breaches of their international legal obligations committed by those persons and entities that act on the State's behalf.

Attribution is critical to the law of State responsibility. A State only bears international responsibility if the conduct in question is attributable to it.[19] If the relevant acts are not attributable to a State, they remain private in character and cannot lead to State responsibility. When a State participates in an armed conflict via its own armed forces, the position on attribution is clear: any conduct on the part of those armed forces that violates IHL is clearly attributable to the State.[20] When, however, it is an NSA that commits the relevant acts, the attribution analysis becomes far more complex.

In such cases, it is necessary to assess whether there is any basis on which the conduct in question could be attributed to a State. It may be the case, for example, that the NSA performed the relevant acts on the State's instructions, or under its control.[21] The role of determining when conduct performed by a private actor should be elevated to the public domain and attributed to a State is performed by the six rules of attribution expressed in ARSIWA. These six rules are the focus of this book.

1.3 RESEARCH OVERVIEW

The ILC's work on the law of State responsibility highlights the difficulties that arise when seeking to determine States' responsibility for the conduct of actors that fall outside the structure of the State. These difficulties are particularly apparent during armed conflict, when distinguishing between public conduct that is attributable to a State and private conduct that is not.[22] Determining where the relevant thresholds for attribution should lie leads to tensions between competing interests.

In conflict situations, accountability concerns call for less stringent rules of attribution to ensure that States bear international responsibility when the NSAs that act on their behalf violate international law. But counter to this is the principle that States should bear responsibility only for conduct that can be truly categorized as their own.[23] Holding States accountable for a wide range of private

18. *Id.* arts. 30–31, 34–39.

19. For further discussion regarding attribution, *see infra* ch. 3, sec. 3.4.

20. ARSIWA, *supra* note 16, art. 4. *See also infra* ch. 4, sec. 4.3.

21. ARSIWA, *supra* note 16, art. 8. *See also infra* ch. 6.

22. For further discussion of this public–private divide, *see infra* ch. 3, sec. 3.4; ch. 7, sec. 7.2.3.1.

23. *See* Application of the Convention on the Prevention and Punishment of the Crime of Genocide (Bosn. & Herz. v. Serb. & Montenegro), Judgment, 2007 I.C.J. Rep. 43, ¶ 406 (Feb. 26).

conduct, with which they might be only marginally involved, would extend States' responsibility too far, particularly in situations of armed conflict in which NSAs often act with considerable autonomy and with varying levels of State support. A delicate balance must therefore be struck.

1.3.1 Objectives and Scope

This study explores that balance, seeking to ascertain whether it is correctly poised or tips too far in one direction. The book's first objective is to clarify the precise circumstances in which NSA conduct is attributable to a State during armed conflict. While some of the rules that determine when conduct is attributable to a State have been the subject of considerable scholarship,[24] others have received minimal academic attention.[25] Notwithstanding this disparity, ambiguity remains regarding the meaning of all the rules of attribution reflected in ARSIWA that relate to NSA conduct. The book's primary purpose is thus to shed light on when the respective rules apply, using examples from armed conflict.

The book's second objective is to evaluate the sufficiency of the rules of attribution related to NSA conduct to assess the extent to which they satisfy their object and purpose in situations of armed conflict. This question is addressed individually, in respect of each rule of attribution,[26] and also collectively with regard to the rules related to State organs and agents.[27] Regarding these latter three rules of attribution, expressed in Articles 4, 5, and 8 ARSIWA, the book identifies a gap in accountability that allows States to act via proxy in a manner that they could not lawfully act via their own organs.[28] A third aim of the book, therefore, is to assess how these inadequacies in the law of State responsibility should be remedied.[29]

In terms of scope, the book's focus is the application of the law of State responsibility to NSA conduct during armed conflict. In other words, the book considers the responsibility of States for acts committed by NSAs that breach the State's international legal obligations. The book does not address States' responsibility for their own conduct in assisting an NSA, which may breach a primary norm of international law that is binding on the State.[30] For example, regarding Russia's

24. The rule that has been the subject of most scholarship is reflected in art. 8 ARSIWA. *See infra* ch. 6.

25. Out of the six rules of attribution addressed in this book, art. 9 ARSIWA has received the least attention from legal scholars and international courts and tribunals. *See infra* ch. 8.

26. *See infra* chs. 4–6, 8–10.

27. ARSIWA, *supra* note 16, arts. 4, 5, 8. *See also infra* ch. 7.

28. *See infra* ch. 7, sec. 7.2.3.

29. *See infra* ch. 4, sec. 4.4.3; ch. 5, sec. 5.4.4; ch. 6, sec. 6.4.7; ch. 7, sec. 7.3.

30. Regarding the distinction between primary and secondary norms, *see infra* ch. 3, sec. 3.2.

support to rebels operating in eastern Ukraine from 2014,[31] the book considers Russia's potential responsibility for the rebels' acts in violation of IHL, such as their indiscriminate attacks.[32] It does not assess Russia's potential violation of the prohibition on the use of force[33] due to its own State officials' support to the rebels.[34]

Regarding the law of State responsibility, the book focuses on the six rules reflected in ARSIWA that relate to the attribution of NSA conduct to a State.[35] Articles 4, 5, and 8 ARSIWA address the conduct of State organs and agents; these are the most important rules when considering the attribution of NSA conduct to a State during armed conflict.[36] When considering these three rules of attribution, the book also addresses Article 7 ARSIWA, which determines when NSA conduct performed in excess of authority or in contravention of instructions is attributable to a State.[37] The final three rules that the book examines are those expressed in Articles 9, 10, and 11 ARSIWA. These are exceptional rules of attribution that are only rarely invoked by States or by international courts and tribunals.[38]

The remaining attribution standards within ARSIWA fall outside the scope of this work because they relate to the conduct of States rather than NSAs.[39] However, the book does briefly address Article 16 ARSIWA, which relates to a State's complicity in the internationally wrongful conduct of another State.[40] The purpose is to assess the potential application of this provision to States' aid or assistance to NSAs, in circumstances when none of the rules of attribution apply.[41]

Notwithstanding the focus on armed conflict, the book does not engage in any analysis of whether the conflicts it examines are international or non-international

31. *See infra* ch. 2, sec. 2.4.2.

32. *See, e.g.*, *Ukraine: Horror of Civilian Bloodshed in Indiscriminate Attacks*, AMNESTY INT'L (Feb. 2, 2015), https://www.amnesty.org/en/latest/news/2015/02/ukraine-horror-civilian-bloodshed-indiscriminate-attacks/.

33. U.N. Charter art. 2(4).

34. For a legal analysis that illustrates this distinction in the context of Hamas's attacks on Israel on Oct. 7, 2023, *see* Jennifer Maddocks, *Israel-Hamas 2023 Symposium—Iran's Responsibility for the Attack on Israel*, ARTICLES OF WAR (Oct. 20, 2023), https://lieber.westpoint.edu/irans-responsibility-attack-israel/.

35. ARSIWA, *supra* note 16, arts. 4, 5, 8, 9–11.

36. *See infra* chs. 4–7.

37. ARSIWA, *supra* note 16, art. 7. *See also infra* ch. 4, sec. 4.5; ch. 5, sec. 5.5.

38. *See infra* chs. 8–10.

39. ARSIWA, *supra* note 16, arts. 6, 17, 18. For a brief discussion of art. 6 in the context of State organs, *see infra* ch. 4, sec. 4.3.3.

40. ARSIWA, *supra* note 16, art. 16.

41. *See infra* ch. 7, sec. 7.3.1.

in character.[42] Nevertheless, this is relevant to the issues of attribution that the book addresses. First, the nature of the conflict impacts the IHL obligations that are binding on the conflict parties. In this respect, the analysis in later chapters gives examples of NSA conduct that could breach IHL as a means to illustrate its conclusions on attribution. It does not conduct a detailed examination of the specific IHL obligations that apply or whether the conduct in question actually violated IHL.

Second, the precise point at which a non-international armed conflict (NIAC) commences is often unclear.[43] Thus, the book addresses situations that could fall below the armed conflict threshold, such as the early stages of the disturbances in Syria and Ukraine.[44] In this context, given that IHL may not apply, the analysis also considers NSA conduct that could violate the State's international human rights law (IHRL) obligations.

Third, a State's support to an NSA engaged in hostilities could internationalize the conflict, transforming a conflict that is non-international in character into one that is international.[45] Much has been written regarding the appropriate test to determine internationalization of conflicts and whether this should be the same as the test to regulate attribution under the law of State responsibility. This issue is discussed in detail later in this book.[46]

The analysis in subsequent chapters centers primarily on violent acts committed during hostilities that potentially violate IHL. It is increasingly common, however, for NSAs to engage in harmful conduct in the cyber domain. When cyber operations are linked to armed conflict, as occurred during Russia's conflict with Ukraine,[47] these fall within the book's scope. Given the growing consensus among States that international law, including the law of State responsibility, applies to cyberspace,[48] the book proceeds on the basis that the rules of attribution reflected in ARSIWA are equally applicable to this domain.

42. Regarding the classification of the conflict in Ukraine, *see, e.g.*, Michael N. Schmitt, *Ukraine Symposium—Classification of the Conflict(s)*, ARTICLES OF WAR (Dec. 14, 2022), https://lieber.westpoint.edu/classification-of-the-conflicts/.

43. Two criteria must be met before disturbances are classified as a NIAC: the hostilities must reach a minimum level of intensity; and the NSAs involved in the conflict must be sufficiently organized. *See* Prosecutor v. Tadić, Case No. IT-94-1-AR-72, Decision on the Defence Motion for Interlocutory Appeal on Jurisdiction, ¶ 70 (Int'l Crim. Trib. for the former Yugoslavia Oct. 2, 1995). *See also* SANDESH SIVAKUMARAN, THE LAW OF NON-INTERNATIONAL ARMED CONFLICT 155–211 (2012).

44. *See infra* ch. 2, secs. 2.4.1, 2.4.2.

45. *See generally* KUBO MAČÁK, INTERNATIONALIZED ARMED CONFLICTS IN INTERNATIONAL LAW (2018).

46. *See infra* ch. 6, sec. 6.4.

47. *See infra* ch. 2, sec. 2.4.2.2.

48. Rep. of the Group of Governmental Experts on Advancing Responsible State Behaviour in Cyberspace in the Context of International Security 18, ¶ 71(g), U.N. Doc. A/76/135

NSAs are defined in the negative, namely, as any person, group, or entity falling outside the structure of a State. During armed conflict, therefore, the term encompasses a broad spectrum of actors, ranging from armed groups to private military companies to individual hackers engaged in hostile cyber operations. This study considers States' relationships with all categories of NSA engaged in conflict, whether the NSA is based within or outside the State's own territory.[49] It does not, however, consider States' potential responsibility for the conduct of commercial entities that provide support to one or more of the belligerents, such as Microsoft or Starlink.[50] Also, it does not address the potential responsibility of NSAs for their own conduct,[51] or the individual criminal responsibility of an NSA's members.[52]

While the relationships between States and NSAs involve a minimum of two actors, they are often more complex.[53] It is common, for instance, for armed groups involved in conflict to receive support from more than just one State.[54] These multifaceted relationships raise important issues of shared responsibility between States, as well as the potential for shared responsibility between States and NSAs.[55] Although highly relevant, such issues are beyond the scope of this work.

Finally, this book focuses solely on legal attribution, which is the process of determining when conduct in violation of international law is attributable to a

(July 14, 2021). *See also* TALLINN MANUAL 2.0 ON THE INTERNATIONAL LAW APPLICABLE TO CYBER OPERATIONS rr. 14–30 (Michael N. Schmitt ed., 2017).

49. This contrasts with much of the scholarship relating to "proxy warfare," which focuses solely on external States' support to actors involved in conflict. *See, e.g.*, ANDREW MUMFORD, PROXY WARFARE 11, 45 (2013); GERAINT HUGHES, MY ENEMY'S ENEMY: PROXY WARFARE IN INTERNATIONAL POLITICS 11 (2014).

50. *See, e.g.*, *Microsoft Threat Report: How Russia's War on Ukraine Is Impacting the Global Cybersecurity Community*, DARK READING (Jan. 31, 2024), https://www.darkreading.com/threat-intelligence/microsoft-threat-report-how-russia-s-war-on-ukraine-is-impacting-the-global-cybersecurity-community; Nick Paton Walsh et al., *Ukraine Relies on Starlink for Its Drone War. Russia Appears to Be Bypassing Sanctions to Use the Devices Too*, CNN (Mar. 26, 2024), https://www.cnn.com/2024/03/25/europe/ukraine-starlink-drones-russia-intl-cmd/index.html.

51. *See, e.g.*, Kleffner, *supra* note 14, Andrew Clapham, *Human Rights Obligations of Non-State Actors in Conflict Situations*, 88 INT'L REV. RED CROSS 491 (2006).

52. For an example of a rebel leader found guilty of war crimes, *see Lubanga*, *supra* note 12.

53. MUMFORD, *supra* note 49, at 103.

54. For example, the rebel group M23 received substantial support from both Rwanda and Uganda. *See infra* ch. 2, sec. 2.4.3.

55. *See, e.g.*, Jean d'Aspremont et al., *Sharing Responsibility Between Non-State Actors and States in International Law: Introduction*, 62 NETHERLANDS INT'L L. REV. 49 (2015); Veronika Bilkova, *Armed Opposition Groups and Shared Responsibility*, 62 NETHERLANDS INT'L L. REV. 69 (2015); André Nollkaemper et al., *Guiding Principles on Shared Responsibility in International Law*, 31 EUR. J. INT'L L. 15 (2020).

State under the law of State responsibility. The term "attribution" also has other meanings. For example, it can refer to technical attribution in the cyber domain, which involves identifying the source of a malicious cyberattack.[56] It can also refer to political attribution, when States publicly attribute conduct in violation of international law to another State.[57] While both technical and political attribution can be relevant to the legal analysis to ascertain a State's international responsibility, neither is conclusive in this respect. Legal attribution of NSA conduct to a State is determined via the six rules of attribution reflected in ARSIWA that are the focus of this book.[58]

1.3.2 Methodology

This book predominantly comprises a doctrinal study of the norms governing States' international responsibility.[59] Its primary concern is the customary international law reflected in ARSIWA and its commentaries, including the underlying sources of law upon which the individual articles are based. The jurisprudence of the International Court of Justice (ICJ) and other international courts and tribunals on the issue of attribution and the academic scholarship relating to that jurisprudence are of particular importance.

The research applies the rules of attribution reflected in ARSIWA to three case studies. While the law of State responsibility is of general application, understanding its impact in situations of armed conflict requires a focus on specific hostilities. The use of recent conflicts as case studies provides a means to illustrate how the respective rules of attribution might apply to real-world examples of NSA conduct, thereby amplifying the rules' meaning and scope.[60]

The book focuses on the hostilities in Syria that commenced in 2011, the conflict in Ukraine that began in 2014, and the conflict in the Democratic Republic of Congo (DRC) involving the rebel group M23, which started in 2012 and reignited in late 2021. Several reasons justify the selection of these conflicts as case studies. First, they each involved NSAs that acted with State support.

56. *See generally* Herbert Lin, *Attribution of Malicious Cyber Incidents: From Soup to Nuts*, 70 J. Int'l Aff. 75 (2016).

57. *See, e.g.*, Kristen E. Eichensehr, *The Law and Politics of Cyberattack Attribution*, 67 UCLA L. Rev. 520 (2020).

58. *See infra* chs. 4–10.

59. On the meaning of this categorization of legal research, *see, e.g.*, Terry Hutchinson & Nigel Duncan, *Defining and Describing What We Do: Doctrinal Legal Research*, 17 Deakin L. Rev. 83, 101–5 (2012).

60. For further discussion regarding case study research, *see, e.g.*, Helena Harrison et al., *Case Study Research: Foundations and Methodological Orientations*, 18 Forum: Qualitative Soc. Res. 1 (2017).

Second, they each featured numerous acts by the relevant NSAs that potentially violate international law. And third, the three conflicts occurred in diverse geographical regions, thereby highlighting the global character of the issues this book seeks to address.

The analysis in the chapters that follow focuses on events occurring during the three conflicts until January 2025. The book, therefore, does not address more recent developments that may be pertinent to the issue of attribution. It is also worth noting that some chapters refer to other conflicts to illustrate the attribution analysis. Thus, although the three case studies provide the book's primary illustrative tool, the study also uses examples from other armed conflicts when appropriate.

The book principally concerns the law of State responsibility. However, it also addresses other bodies of international law. Given the focus on armed conflict, one particularly important area of law is IHL. Attribution of conduct to a State only leads to that State's international responsibility if the acts in question violate an international legal obligation that is binding on the State. Such obligations can derive from either treaty law or customary international law. In armed conflict scenarios, it is most likely that the acts would violate IHL. Some chapters additionally address potential breaches of a State's IHRL obligations.

The primary focus of the study is on what the law is (*lex lata*) as opposed to what the law should be (*lex ferenda*).[61] While admitting that this distinction is "in large measure a false dichotomy,"[62] the research considers the existing norms within the law of State responsibility that are relevant to the issue of attribution and the proper interpretation of those norms to meet the law's object and purpose.[63] In so doing, the research adopts the widely held view that although the ILC sought to codify the law of State responsibility as it stood in 2001, that law is not inflexible and must continue to adapt to meet the challenges of the modern world, including those arising during armed conflict.[64]

61. The book considers *lex ferenda* principally in relation to the ways in which international law could develop to hold States to account in respect of their support to NSAs when the rules of attribution do not apply. *See infra* ch. 7, sec. 7.3.

62. Rosalyn Higgins, Problems and Process: International Law and How We Use It 10 (1995).

63. Although not strictly applicable to the interpretation of customary international law, the study's interpretive approach is based on the relevant rules of the Vienna Convention on the Law of Treaties. *See* Vienna Convention on the Law of Treaties art. 31(1), May 23, 1969, 1155 U.N.T.S. 331. This approach is consistent with that taken by other legal scholars. *See, e.g.*, Panos Merkouris, Interpretation of Customary International Law (2024).

64. *See, e.g.*, Merkouris, *supra* note 63, at 9, 12 (discussing the evolutive interpretation of customary international law).

1.3.3 Structure

The book is structured into five parts. Part Two sets the scene for the later legal analysis, focusing first on States' relationships with NSAs during armed conflict. Chapter 2 highlights not only the prevalence of States' support to NSAs but also the varied connections that exist between States and NSAs during armed conflict and the propensity of those NSAs to act in a manner that violates IHL. The chapter then outlines the three case studies, namely, the conflicts in Syria, Ukraine, and the DRC. These hostilities demonstrate the diverse relationships between States and NSAs in conflict situations and provide countless examples of harmful conduct on the part of NSAs. Chapter 3 introduces the law of State responsibility, considering the development of the ILC's draft articles, the attribution regime reflected within, and the status of ARSIWA in customary international law.

Part Three of the book focuses on the three rules of attribution reflected in Articles 4, 5, and 8 ARSIWA.[65] These are the rules most likely to apply in attributing NSA conduct to a State during armed conflict, and their status in customary international law is clear. They relate to the activities of State organs and agents, meaning those persons or entities through which the State chooses to act to achieve its conflict goals. In each case, attribution of conduct to the State is deemed appropriate due to the factual or the legal relationship that exists between the NSA and the State at the time the NSA acts in a manner that potentially violates international law.

Chapter 4 relates to State organs (Article 4 ARSIWA), Chapter 5 focuses on persons or entities empowered to perform public functions on the State's behalf (Article 5), and Chapter 6 addresses the attribution to a State of conduct performed under its instructions, direction, or control (Article 8). These chapters seek to clarify the practical meaning of the respective rules of attribution by applying them to examples of NSA conduct from the case studies outlined in Chapter 2. In addition, the three chapters assess the sufficiency of the rules in this context to determine whether they adequately meet their object and purpose. This analysis leads to a conclusion that the three rules of attribution, as interpreted by authoritative bodies such as the ILC and the ICJ, fail to hold States properly to account for the conduct of NSAs that act on their behalf.

Chapter 7 completes Part Three by drawing together the analysis of Articles 4, 5, and 8 ARSIWA. It examines the effectiveness of the attribution regime that these three rules represent, concluding that each of the rules would better meet its object and purpose if interpreted more flexibly, thereby attributing more NSA conduct to the supporting State. Even with a more flexible interpretation of the three rules of attribution, however, an accountability gap would remain. Attribution is appropriate only when the NSA performed the relevant conduct on a State's behalf. There are many situations during armed conflict, however, when

65. *See infra* chs. 4–7.

NSAs act on their own account, meaning that attribution is not appropriate, but with significant State support.

Frequently, States provide intelligence, training, or other assistance to NSAs without also exercising a high degree of control over their conduct. ARSIWA includes no mechanism through which a State can bear international responsibility for its own contribution to an NSA's conduct in violation of international law. Chapter 7 concludes by examining, in brief, potential ways in which international law could develop to hold States to account in respect of their support to NSAs when the rules of attribution do not apply. These include the potential evolution of the complicity rule reflected in Article 16 ARSIWA[66] to encompass States' aid or assistance to NSAs.[67]

Part Four of the book focuses on the remaining three rules of attribution related to NSA conduct, expressed in Articles 9, 10, and 11 ARSIWA.[68] They differ from the rules examined in Part Three in that they can attribute conduct to a State even if there are no factual or legal links between the State and the NSA at the time the latter acts in potential violation of international law. Thus, these rules do not address the conduct of State organs or agents of the State. Rather, they deal with certain exceptional situations in which attribution of NSA conduct to a State is deemed to be appropriate.

During armed conflict, it is far more likely that the rules examined in Part Three will apply to attribute an NSA's conduct to a State, as opposed to the rules assessed in Part Four. Articles 9, 10, and 11 ARSIWA are rarely invoked by States, international courts and tribunals, or humanitarian bodies, and doubts remain regarding their status in customary international law. Additional ambiguity surrounds the rules' application. Part Four of the book seeks to shed light on their respective meanings and scope of application, again through the use of the case studies outlined in Chapter 2 and other conflicts. In addition, it assesses the rules' utility in holding States to account for potential international law violations involving NSAs.

Chapter 8 focuses on the rule reflected in Article 9 ARSIWA. This may apply when NSAs perform public tasks in the absence or default of the official authorities, such as occurred during the vacuum of authority caused by Russia's 2022 invasion of Ukraine. Chapter 9 then turns to examine Article 10 ARSIWA, which addresses the attribution of a successful insurrectional movement's conduct to the territorial State. Finally, Chapter 10 assesses the rule expressed in Article 11 relating to NSA conduct that a State chooses to acknowledge and adopt as its own.

The conclusion in Part Five, Chapter 11, provides final reflections on the entire attribution regime expressed in ARSIWA. It highlights the importance of effective mechanisms, in both the law of State responsibility and other bodies of

66. ARSIWA, *supra* note 16, art.16.

67. *See infra* ch. 7, sec. 7.3.1.

68. *See infra* chs. 8–10.

international law, to ensure that States are properly held to account when they choose to achieve their conflict aims via NSAs. The future of warfare is unlikely to see any diminution in either the power and autonomy of NSAs or of States' desire to defend their interests without becoming directly embroiled in conflict.[69] States will, in all likelihood, continue to "externalize the burden of warfare,"[70] particularly as their focus shifts toward great power competition and the necessity to compete while avoiding direct confrontation.[71] Meanwhile, future hostilities that involve NSAs are likely to continue to feature numerous IHL violations.

As such, the need to hold States to account for their contributions to the harms perpetrated by NSAs remains paramount. While concurrent developments in international law to hold NSAs directly responsible for their own conduct are critical, they must be accompanied by the effective accountability of States. Despite NSAs' increasing power and influence in international affairs, it is State support that frequently enhances not only their authority but also their ability to cause harm. The law of State responsibility must therefore evolve to reflect that reality.

69. *See, e.g.*, Andreas Krieg, *Externalising the Burden of War: The Obama Doctrine and U.S. Foreign Policy in the Middle East*, 92 Int'l Affairs 97, 107–8 (2016).

70. Andreas Krieg & Jean-Marc Rickli, *Surrogate Warfare: The Art of War in the 21st Century?* 18 Def. Stud. 113, 114 (2018).

71. ICRC, Allies, Partners and Proxies: Managing Support Relationships in Armed Conflict to Reduce the Human Cost of War 19 (Mar. 2021), www.icrc.org/en/publication/4498-allies-partners-and-proxies-managing-support-relationships-armed-conflict-reduce.

PART TWO

Setting the Scene

2

States and Non-State Actors in Armed Conflict

2.1 INTRODUCTION

States are abstract entities, and, as such, they must always act through human beings. During armed conflict, it is often the State's own organs, such as its military forces, that act on the State's behalf. In this situation, it is usually straightforward to conclude that any conduct performed by those organs that violates the State's international legal obligations is attributable to the State and engages its international responsibility.[1] In other scenarios, however, the position may be more complex. States sometimes choose to achieve their national security goals via persons or entities that have a more informal, ambiguous relationship with the State. This is particularly common during armed conflict. Examples abound of States opting to achieve their conflict aims via non-State actors (NSA) that fall outside the structure of the State.[2]

This chapter begins by examining the varied relationships that may exist between States and NSAs during armed conflict. In so doing, it aims to set the scene for the attribution analysis that follows. To determine whether an NSA's conduct is attributable to a State, it is first necessary to understand the relationship between them. The chapter considers the different forms such relationships may take, as well as some of the reasons why States use NSAs to achieve their conflict aims. It additionally examines why NSAs engaged in conflict so frequently act in a manner that violates international humanitarian law (IHL). Thereafter, it outlines the three case studies used in later chapters to illustrate the attribution analysis. These are the conflicts in Syria, Ukraine, and the Democratic Republic of the Congo (DRC).

1. For further discussion regarding organs of State, *see infra* ch. 4.

2. *See infra* sec. 2.4.

Attribution of Non-State Actor Conduct During Armed Conflict. Jennifer Maddocks, Oxford University Press.
 DOI: 10.1093/oso/9780197842652.003.0002

2.2 STATES' RELATIONSHIPS WITH NON-STATE ACTORS IN ARMED CONFLICT

The number of NSAs on the battlefield has increased dramatically in recent years. In 2018, the International Committee of the Red Cross reported that more armed groups had emerged in the previous six years than in the preceding six decades.[3] Meanwhile, the character of certain NSAs has changed, particularly in terms of their power and autonomy. ISIS is a clear example; the group was able to exert its authority over large swathes of Syria and Iraq from 2014 until it lost control of its remaining stronghold in March 2019.[4] Hezbollah also illustrates the trend. Since its formation in the early 1980s, the group has played an increasingly important role not only in Lebanese politics[5] but also in conflicts across the region.[6]

While in the past territorial competition occurred principally between States, today it is NSAs that more frequently challenge States for control over elements of their geography and their people.[7] In 2017, for example, the Syrian regime was estimated to exert control over less than 20 percent of its territory, with the vast majority of the remainder controlled by NSAs including ISIS, the Syrian Democratic Forces (SDF), and various rebel and Islamic factions.[8] In late 2024,

3. Peter Maurer, Moving from Outrage to Action on Civilian Suffering, ICRC President's Speech to UNGA Event on the Protection of Civilians and Respect for IHL (Sept. 26, 2018), www.icrc.org/en/document/moving-outrage-action-civilian-suffering. *See also* ICRC, The Roots of Restraint in War 13 (Dec. 2018), www.icrc.org/en/publication/4352-roots-restraint-war [hereinafter Roots of Restraint]; Int'l Comm. Red Cross, Allies, Partners and Proxies: Managing Support Relationships in Armed Conflict to Reduce the Human Cost of War 16–17 (Mar. 2021), www.icrc.org/en/publication/4498-allies-partners-and-proxies-managing-support-relationships-armed-conflict-reduce [hereinafter Allies, Partners and Proxies].

4. BBC News, *Islamic State Group Defeated as Final Territory Lost, US-Backed Forces Say* (Mar. 23, 2019), www.bbc.com/news/world-middle-east-47678157.

5. Counter Extremism Project, Hezbollah's Influence in Lebanon (Apr. 2018), www.counterextremism.com/sites/default/files/Hezbollah%20Influence%20in%20Lebanon_043018.pdf.

6. *See, e.g.*, Marisa Sullivan, Inst. for the Study of War, Hezbollah in Syria (Apr. 2014), http://www.understandingwar.org/sites/default/files/Hezbollah_Sullivan_FINAL.pdf; Matthew Levitt, *Waking Up the Neighbors: How Regional Intervention Is Transforming Hezbollah*, Wash. Inst. (July 23, 2015), www.washingtoninstitute.org/policy-analysis/view/waking-up-the-neighbors-how-regional-intervention-is-transforming-hezbollah [hereinafter Levitt, *Waking Up the Neighbors*].

7. Michael von der Schulenburg, *The Era of Armed Non-State Actors – Risks of Global Chaos*, Changing Character of Conflict Platform (last visited Jan. 5, 2025), https://conflictplatform.ox.ac.uk/cccp/research/michael-von-der-schulenburg-the-era-of-armed-non-state-actors-risks-of-global-chaos.

8. *A Year on Astana Agreement, the Winners Are Iranians, Russians, Turks, the Regime*, Syrian Observatory for Hum. Rts. (May 4, 2018), www.syriahr.com/en/91151/.

one of those Islamist groups, Hay'at Tahrir al-Sham (HTS), succeeded in ousting President Assad and taking control over the Syrian government.[9]

The situation in Syria illustrates the increased power and importance of NSAs as well as the State-like role they often play.[10] This is particularly apparent in contemporary conflict, where non-international armed conflicts involving NSAs predominate over State-on-State conflict.[11] Most of the armed conflicts taking place in the world today are internal in character, featuring militias, insurrectional movements, paramilitary groups, and armed bands, fighting either against the established government or among themselves.[12]

Yet despite their increased prominence, NSAs rarely act with complete autonomy. Often, to achieve their aims, NSAs rely to a greater or lesser extent on the support of one or more States.[13] And from the States' perspective, they often perceive a distinct advantage in participating indirectly in conflict via NSAs rather than committing their own forces to the fight.[14]

2.2.1 States' Support to Non-State Actors

Acting through NSAs is an ancient technique of foreign policy, used by States throughout history to further their national interests. As early as the Peloponnesian War, the Spartans and the Athenians each provided support to local rebellions

9. William Christou, *Syrian Rebels Reveal Year-Long Plot That Brought Down Assad Regime*, The Guardian (Dec. 13, 2024), https://www.theguardian.com/world/2024/dec/13/syrian-rebels-reveal-year-long-plot-that-brought-down-assad-regime.

10. Shane R. Reeves & Ronald Alcala, *Five Legal Takeaways from the Syrian War*, Harv. Nat'l Sec. J. 1, 4–6 (Sept. 30, 2019). *See also infra* sec. 2.4.1.

11. *See, e.g.*, Annyssa Bellal, Geneva Acad., The War Report: Armed Conflicts in 2018, at 19 (Apr. 2019), www.geneva-academy.ch/joomlatools-files/docman-files/The%20War%20Report%202018.pdf; ACLED, Global Conflicts Double over the Past Five Years (Dec. 2024), https://acleddata.com/conflict-index/.

12. *Today's Armed Conflicts*, Geneva Acad. (last visited Jan. 5, 2025), https://geneva-academy.ch/galleries/today-s-armed-conflicts.

13. Idean Salehyan et al., *External Rebel Sponsorship and Civilian Abuse: A Principal-Agent Analysis of Wartime Atrocities*, 68 Int'l Org. 633, 634 (2014).

14. For discussion why this is the case, *see, e.g.*, Richard D. Newton, Joint Special Operations U. Rep. 09-3, The Seeds of Surrogate Warfare (Feb. 2009); Joseph L. Votel & Eero R. Keravuori, *The By-With-Through Operational Approach*, Joint Force Q. 89 (Apr. 12, 2018); Daniel L. Byman, *Why Engage in Proxy War? A State's Perspective*, Brookings (May 21, 2018), www.brookings.edu/blog/order-from-chaos/2018/05/21/why-engage-in-proxy-war-a-states-perspective/; Andreas Krieg & Jean-Marc Rickli, *Surrogate Warfare: The Art of War in the 21st Century?* 18 Def. Stud. 113, 124–26 (2018).

against their enemies.[15] The trend did not diminish in the centuries that followed and examples of States' support to NSAs abound. These range from French assistance to patriots during the American Revolution[16] to support provided by the Allies to resistance movements in occupied Europe during World War II.[17]

States' use of NSAs to promote their foreign policy goals became increasingly prevalent after 1945. During the Cold War, inter-State rivalries were rife but numerous factors, including the ever-present threat of nuclear confrontation, militated against the outbreak of large-scale war.[18] States accordingly looked for means other than State-on-State conflict to achieve their aims, often intervening in smaller, regional conflicts, such as independence struggles against colonial rule.[19] Rebel movements fighting against the Portuguese in Angola, for instance, received significant external assistance, causing the conflict to escalate and descend into civil war.[20]

Today, surrogate warfare remains a prominent feature of States' management of violence.[21] Iran, for instance, established a network of proxies across the Middle East that it supports to maintain a strategic advantage over Israel and other adversaries.[22] Russia makes extensive use of private military and security companies (PMSC) and other NSAs to fight on its behalf in the conflict in Ukraine and elsewhere.[23] And the United States and its allies support the SDF in northeast Syria as a way to indirectly influence the fight against ISIS.[24]

15. Max Boot, *Countering Hybrid Warfare, in* The Armed Conflict Survey 2015 at 11, 11–12 (Nigel Inkster ed., 2015).

16. *See, e.g.*, Neil Longley York, Turning the World Upside Down: The War of American Independence and the Problem of Empire 118–20 (2003).

17. Travis L. Homiak, Joint Special Operations U. Rep. 09-3, Expanding the American Way of War: Working "Through, With, or By" Non-U.S. Actors 27–28 (Feb. 2009); Boot, *supra* note 15, at 16–17.

18. Andrew Mumford, Proxy Warfare 38–44 (2013).

19. Newton, *supra* note 14; Geraint Hughes, My Enemy's Enemy: Proxy Warfare in International Politics 21 (2014).

20. Hughes, *supra* note 19, at 62–86.

21. Krieg & Rickli, *supra* note 14, at 116.

22. Diane M. Zorri et al., Joint Special Operations U. Rep. 20-5, Iranian Proxy Groups in Iraq, Syria, and Yemen: A Principal-Agent Comparative Analysis 4–5 (Dec. 2020), https://apps.dtic.mil/sti/pdfs/AD1146327.pdf.

23. Ryan Bauer & Erik E. Mueller, *Ukraine Is a Breeding Group for Russian PMCs*, RAND (June 14, 2023), https://www.rand.org/pubs/commentary/2023/06/ukraine-is-a-breeding-ground-for-russian-pmcs.html; Charles Clover et al., *Russia Recruits Yemeni Mercenaries to Fight in Ukraine*, Fin. Times (Nov. 24, 2024), https://www.ft.com/content/da966006-88e5-4c25-9075-7c07c4702e06.

24. Aron Lund, *Origins of the Syrian Democratic Forces: A Primer*, New Humanitarian (Jan. 22, 2016), https://deeply.thenewhumanitarian.org/syria/articles/2016/01/22/origins-of-the-syrian-democratic-forces-a-primer [hereinafter Lund, *Syrian Democratic Forces*].

States' motives for employing proxies in conflict situations are both simple and compelling: "Rather than bearing the political, financial, and military burden of direct intervention, States can in effect hire surrogate forces to fight and die on their behalf."[25] Proxy intervention thus allows States to influence a conflict's outcome while minimizing the associated political and military risks.[26] This is particularly attractive to States wishing to shape a conflict in which their key national interests are not at stake,[27] or in which they wish to avoid direct hostilities with an adversary. Avoiding escalation is therefore a key goal for States choosing to act via proxy.

Acting indirectly via NSAs additionally provides a means to counter adversaries that are militarily superior, against which the State's conventional forces cannot compete.[28] Iran's support to insurgents in Iraq after 2003, for example, allowed the State to frustrate and defeat the aims of the United States and its allies without the costs of committing its own forces to the fight.[29] Proxy networks can also bolster States' deterrence strategies,[30] and preserve or enhance States' spheres of influence.[31] This is evident not only with regard to Iran, but also in Russia's interactions with NSAs in regions that formed part of the former Soviet Union.[32]

In Ukraine, for instance, between 2014 and 2022, Moscow sought to preserve its regional hegemony by providing significant support to the rebels fighting against the pro-Western regime in Kiev.[33] Russia's intervention in the conflict additionally offered an opportunity to support NSAs with which it shared significant

25. William Rosenau & Zack Gold, CNA, "The Cheapest Insurance in the World"? The United States and Proxy Warfare 1 (July 2019), www.cna.org/CNA_files/PDF/DRM-2019-U-020227-1Rev.pdf. *See also* Jack Watling & Nick Reynolds, Royal United Servs. Inst., War by Others' Means 10–27 (2020); Zorri et al., *supra* note 22.

26. Mumford, *supra* note 19, at 8. *See also* Krieg & Rickli, *supra* note 14, at 116.

27. Mumford, *supra* note 19, at 2; Hughes, *supra* note 19, at 3–4; Andreas Krieg, *Externalising the Burden of War: The Obama Doctrine and U.S. Foreign Policy in the Middle East*, 92 Int'l Aff. 97, 102, 107–8 (2016); Krieg & Rickli, *supra* note 14, at 117–18.

28. Mumford, *supra* note 19, at 51.

29. Mumford, *supra* note 19, at 51–53; Hughes, *supra* note 19, at 14; Zorri et al., *supra* note 22, at 1–2, 19.

30. Hughes, *supra* note 19, at 26–27, 140; Ariane Tabatabai, *The Fruits of Iran's Victory in Syria*, Lawfare (Apr. 15, 2018), www.lawfareblog.com/fruits-irans-victory-syria; Jack Watling, Royal United Servs. Inst., Iran's Objectives and Capabilities: Deterrence and Subversion 16–17 (Feb. 2019), https://rusi.org/explore-our-research/publications/occasional-papers/irans-objectives-and-capabilities-deterrence-and-subversion.

31. Hughes, *supra* note 19, at 31; Ariane M. Tabatabai et al., RAND, The Iran Threat Network: Four Models of Iran's Nonstate Client Partnerships (2021), www.rand.org/pubs/research_reports/RR4231.html.

32. Hughes, *supra* note 19, at 31.

33. *See infra* sec. 2.4.2.

cultural ties, expressed through a common language, history, religion, and customs.[34] Thus, it is common for States to back NSAs with which they share national, ethnic, or ideological links.[35] Religious ties, for example, were important to Iran when mobilizing Shi'a Muslims from across the region to fight in Syria in support of the Assad regime.[36]

Intervening covertly additionally offers plausible deniability.[37] This is clearly illustrated by Russia's use of PMSCs such as the Wagner Group to promote its interests in the conflicts in Syria, Ukraine, and across the globe.[38] When members of the Wagner Group attacked U.S. forces in Syria in February 2018, Moscow denied all knowledge of their activities.[39] The Kremlin furthermore avoided the domestic criticism it would have received had an equivalent number of its soldiers died in battle.[40] Members of a PMSC or any other NSA are expendable in a way that a State's own service personnel are not.[41]

2.2.2 States' Outsourcing of Functions to Non-State Actors

Russia's use of the Wagner Group to achieve its foreign policy goals exemplifies States' propensity to outsource combat-related functions to NSAs. The trend is also evident in Turkey's use of Syrian militias to fight in the Libyan conflict[42] and in Iran's deployment of members of the Afghan Hazara minority to fight on its

34. Anna Matveeva, Through Times of Trouble: Conflict in Southeastern Ukraine Explained from Within 9, 24–34 (2018).

35. Mumford, *supra* note 19, at 34–38; Hughes, *supra* note 19, at 25–26, 29–30; Tim Maurer, *"Proxies" and Cyberspace*, 21 J. Conflict & Sec. L. 383, 387 (2016).

36. Ben Farmer & Akhtar Makoii, *Thirsty for Martyrdom and a Living Wage: Why Thousands of Afghans Signed up to Iran's Shadowy War in Syria*, The Telegraph (Jan. 26, 2020), www.telegraph.co.uk/news/2020/01/26/thirsty-martyrdom-living-wage-thousands-afghans-signed-irans/.

37. Hughes, *supra* note 19, at 15–16; Krieg, *supra* note 27, at 102.

38. Kimberley Marten, *Russia's Use of Semi-State Security Forces: The Case of the Wagner Group*, 35 Post-Soviet Aff. 181 (2019); Mike Giglio, *Inside the Shadow War Fought by Russian Mercenaries*, Buzzfeed (Apr. 17, 2019), https://www.buzzfeednews.com/article/mikegiglio/inside-wagner-mercenaries-russia-ukraine-syria-prighozhin.

39. Tomas Gibbons-Neff, *How a 4-Hour Battle Between Russian Mercenaries and US Commandos Unfolded in Syria*, N.Y. Times (May 24, 2018), www.nytimes.com/2018/05/24/world/middleeast/american-commandos-russian-mercenaries-syria.html.

40. *Id. See also* Marten, *supra* note 39, at 193; Giglio, *supra* note 38.

41. Mumford, *supra* note 19, at 76; Hughes, *supra* note 19, at 25; Krieg & Rickli, *supra* note 14, at 121–22; Watling & Reynolds, *supra* note 25, at 22–26.

42. Anchal Vohra, *It's Syrian vs. Syrian in Libya*, Foreign Pol'y (May 5, 2020), https://foreignpolicy.com/2020/05/05/libya-civil-conflict-syrian-mercenaries-turkey-russia-gna-haftar/.

behalf in Syria.[43] These scenarios differ from situations in which States choose to assist an NSA that is engaged in its own fight against an adversary. When States outsource tasks to an NSA, the latter performs the relevant public functions in the place of the State's own organs. In each case, the NSA does not fight on its own account, to achieve its own conflict aims. Instead, the State empowers the NSA to engage in conflict on the State's behalf, to promote the State's own foreign policy objectives.

These relationships are often informal and may be denied by the States concerned. Nevertheless, they bear similarities to the contractual outsourcing relationships that States often enter with private entities during armed conflict.[44] For instance, the United States and its allies have made prolific use of PMSCs during combat operations since the end of the Cold War.[45] African States similarly utilize PMSCs to provide a range of services in their conflicts against armed groups.[46] And China uses private contractors to protect its people and assets in zones of conflict.[47]

The common feature of all such arrangements is that the State tasks an NSA to perform one or more governmental functions in place of the State's own armed forces or other organs of State. Thus, the function the NSA performs on the State's behalf is public in character, but it does not necessarily involve active combat.[48] In practice, private entities perform a range of tasks for States during armed conflict, which may be loosely divided into four categories.[49]

43. Farmer & Makoii, *supra* note 36; Phillip Smyth, *Iran's Afghan Shiite Fighters in Syria*, WASH. INST. (June 3, 2014), https://www.washingtoninstitute.org/policy-analysis/irans-afghan-shiite-fighters-syria.

44. *See generally* SEAN MCFATE, MERCENARIES AND WAR: UNDERSTANDING PRIVATE ARMIES TODAY (Dec. 2019), https://apps.dtic.mil/sti/pdfs/AD1115550.pdf.

45. *Id.* at 18–23. *See also* Juan Carlos Zarate, *The Emergence of a New Dog of War: Private International Security Companies, International Law, and the New World Disorder*, 34 STAN. J. INT'L L. 75 103–15 (1998).

46. Mucahid Durmaz & Murtala Abdullahi, *"White Hands": The Rise of Private Armies in African Conflicts*, AL JAZEERA (Apr. 28, 2022), https://www.aljazeera.com/features/2022/4/28/white-hands-the-rise-of-private-militaries-in-african-conflict.

47. Alessandro Arduino, *Chinese Private Security Firms Are Growing Their Presence in Africa: Why It Matters*, THE CONVERSATION (Aug 8, 2022), https://theconversation.com/chinese-private-security-firms-are-growing-their-presence-in-africa-why-it-matters-187309.

48. *See, e.g.*, IAN RALBY & HANNAH TONKIN, CHATHAM HOUSE, REGULATION OF PRIVATE MILITARY SECURITY COMPANIES IN ARMED CONFLICT (2011), www.chathamhouse.org/sites/files/chathamhouse/public/Research/ International%20Law/071011ralby%26tonkin.pdf; FRAUKE RENZ, STATE RESPONSIBILITY AND NEW TRENDS IN THE PRIVATIZATION OF WARFARE 5–8 (2020).

49. Henrik Heidenkamp & ROYAL UNITED SERVS. INST., SUSTAINING THE UK'S DEFENCE EFFORT: CONTRACTOR SUPPORT TO OPERATIONS MARKET DYNAMICS 4 (2012), https://rusi.org/explore-our-research/publications/whitehall-reports/sustaining-the-uk%E2%80%99s-defence-effort-contractor-support-to-operations-market-dynamics.

First, contractors frequently provide services in support of personnel working in deployed locations. In the relatively stable environment of the Balkans, for instance, contractors provided a range of base operations support services to the U.S. military, including food and waste management and recreational services.[50]

Second, contractors commonly provide equipment and logistical support services, such as maintaining and servicing weapons systems and other equipment. The growing sophistication of technology on the battlefield means that specialist contract support to operations is increasingly important.[51]

Also critical to military operations is the third category of activity: the provision of security. Particularly in volatile environments, contractors often engage in security tasks that previously fell within the exclusive purview of the armed forces. Such functions include the physical protection of individuals and convoys traveling through unsecured areas, as well as the protection of fixed assets such as military facilities or government buildings.[52]

The fourth and final category of function encompasses roles with a direct operational effect. In contrast with the other three categories, contractors performing such roles contribute directly to the State's military operations. The U.S. use of contractors to undertake operational roles such as interrogation, the operation of military equipment, and intelligence analysis falls within this category.[53] It also encompasses States' use of NSAs to engage in combat operations, as illustrated by Angola and Sierra Leone's use of the PMSCs Executive Outcomes and Sandline International in the 1990s.[54]

Today, while States rarely acknowledge PMSCs' engagement in combat operations, reporting reveals contractors' direct participation in hostilities across the globe, including in Syria, Yemen, and many parts of Africa.[55] As noted previously,

50. U.S. Gov't Accountability Off., GAO-03-695, Military Operations: Contractors Provide Vital Services to Deployed Forces but are not adequately Addressed in DOD Plans 7 (2003).

51. Michael E. Guillory, *Civilianizing the Force: Is the United States Crossing the Rubicon?* 51 Air Force L. Rev. 111, 123–26 (2001).

52. Ralby & Tonkin, *supra* note 48, at 4.

53. Heidenkamp & Royal United Servs. Inst., *supra* note 49, at 4; James Risen & Mark Mazzetti, *Blackwater Guards Tied to Secret C.I.A. Raids*, N.Y. Times (Dec. 10, 2009), www.nytimes.com/2009/12/11/us/politics/11blackwater.html.

54. Ralby & Tonkin, *supra* note 48, at 3. *See also* Zarate, *supra* note 45, at 93–103; McFate, *supra* note 44, at 17–18.

55. *See, e.g.*, Durmaz & Abdullahi, *supra* note 46; Marten, *supra* note 39, at 182–83 (2019); Emily Hager & Mark Mazzetti, *Emirates Secretly Sends Colombian Mercenaries to Yemen Fight*, N.Y. Times (Nov. 25, 2015), www.nytimes.com/2015/11/26/world/middleeast/emirates-secretly-sends-colombian-mercenaries-to-fight-in-yemen.html?_r=0; Matthew Hill & Borges Nhamirre, *Mercenaries Fighting Insurgents in Mozambique Set to Exit*, Bloomberg (Mar. 31, 2021), https://www.bloomberg.com/news/articles/2021-03-31/military-contractor-fighting-mozambique-militants-set-to-exit; Benoit Faucon & Kejal Vyas, *The Hottest Job in a World at*

it is not only PMSCs that States employ for this purpose; they also use armed groups. The Libyan conflict in 2021 illustrates the trend.[56] While Syrian militias supported by Turkey reinforced the Government of National Accord, a diverse coalition of forces bolstered the Libyan National Army on the other side of the hostilities. This included Syrian militias backed by Russia, a contingent from the Wagner Group, PMSCs based in the United Arab Emirates, and militias from Chad and Sudan.[57]

States' outsourcing of combat functions to NSAs is likely to remain a prominent feature of conflict in the years to come. Moreover, as technology develops, this tendency is increasingly evident in nonphysical domains of warfare. States often outsource tasks to NSAs in the cyber domain, leading to a reliance by States on the private sector both to defend their networks and to act offensively.[58] For example, Russia reportedly recruits cybercriminals to conduct offensive operations in support of its war aims in Ukraine.[59] Iran similarly uses hacker groups to launch harmful cyber operations against its adversaries, including Saudi Arabia and the United States.[60]

In contrast with the contractual arrangements that may be evident when States outsource functions to PMSCs, individuals acting on States' behalf in the cyber domain frequently have an informal, ill-understood relationship with the State.[61] In this context, therefore, it may be particularly difficult to ascertain whether the State outsourced the relevant functions to an NSA or whether the individuals concerned were private citizens, choosing to act entirely of their own accord.

War: Gun-for-Hire, WALL ST. J. (Feb. 17, 2025), https://www.wsj.com/world/the-hottest-job-in-a-world-at-war-gun-for-hire-360ab035.

56. *See generally* JAVIER MARTÍN, LIBYA: THE FIRST TOTALLY PRIVATIZED WAR IN MODERN HISTORY (2020), www.ohchr.org/Documents/issues/Mercenaries/WG/OtherStakeholders/shockmonitor_submission.pdf.

57. Final Rep. of the Panel of Experts on Libya Established Pursuant to Security Council Resolution 1973 (2011) 7–8, ¶¶ 16–23, 30–33, ¶¶ 86–100, U.N. Doc S/2021/229 (Mar. 8, 2021); Nathan Vest & Colin P. Clarke, *Is the Conflict in Libya a Preview of the Future of Warfare?* DEF. ONE (June 2, 2020), www.defenseone.com/ideas/2020/06/conflict-libya-preview-future-warfare/165807/; Vohra, *supra* note 42; MARTÍN, *supra* note 56; Alia Brahimi, *Libya Has a Mercenaries Problem. It's Time for the International Community to Step Up*, ATLANTIC COUNCIL (May 21, 2021), www.atlanticcouncil.org/blogs/menasource/libya-has-a-mercenaries-problem-its-time-for-the-international-community-to-step-up/.

58. Kristen E. Eichensehr, *Public-Private Cybersecurity*, 95 TEX. L. REV. 467, 501 (2017).

59. Tom Uren, *Russia's GRU Thugs Double Down on Recruiting Cybercrooks*, LAWFARE (Oct. 18, 2024), https://www.lawfaremedia.org/article/russia's-gru-thugs-double-down-on-recruiting-cybercrooks.

60. Annie Fixler, *The Cyber Threat from Iran After the Death of Soleimani*, 13 CTC SENTINEL 20, 23 (Feb. 2020), https://ctc.westpoint.edu/cyber-threat-iran-death-soleimani/.

61. Eichensehr, *supra* note 58, at 510.

2.2.3 Civilians' Involvement in Armed Conflict

The conflict in Ukraine vividly demonstrates the increasing role that civilians can play in armed conflict. This is evident in the cyber domain, as well as in the physical domains of warfare. Consider, for example, the actions of Ukraine's "IT Army" following Russia's invasion in February 2022.[62] According to news reports, thousands of Ukrainian technology workers launched cyber operations targeting Russia's government, media, and financial institutions.[63] While some may have responded to a public appeal by a government minister,[64] the extent to which they were acting independently or further to a tasking by the State remains unclear.

Ukrainian civilians also contributed more directly to the efforts to defend their State against Russia's aggression. For instance, they manufactured and threw Molotov cocktails at enemy forces,[65] they offered poisoned cakes to Russian soldiers,[66] and they used applications on their phones to notify nearby air defense units of incoming missiles and drones.[67] As with Ukraine's "IT Army," however, the extent to which the government influenced or endorsed these citizens' actions remains unclear.

Other States are similarly preparing to use civilians to bolster their defense efforts. Russia's aggression against Ukraine prompted States located near Russia's borders to look critically at their national defense strategies and adopt a policy of "total defense."[68] This involves a "whole of society" approach to national security,

62. Sam Schechner, *Ukraine's "IT Army" Has Hundreds of Thousands of Hackers, Kyiv Says*, WALL ST. J. (Mar. 4, 2022), www.wsj.com/livecoverage/russia-ukraine-latest-news-2022-03-04/card/ukraine-s-it-army-has-hundreds-of-thousands-of-hackers-kyiv-says-RfpGa5zmLtavrot27OWX; Kate Conger & Adam Satariano, *Volunteer Hackers Converge on Ukraine Conflict with No One in Charge*, N.Y. TIMES (Mar. 4, 2022), www.nytimes.com/2022/03/04/technology/ukraine-russia-hackers.html.

63. Schechner, *supra* note 62; Conger & Satariano, *supra* note 62.

64. Schechner, *supra* note 62; Frank Bajak, *Ukraine Digital Army Brews Cyberattacks, Intel and Infowar*, ABC NEWS (Mar. 5, 2022), https://abcnews.go.com/Politics/wireStory/ukraine-digital-army-brews-cyberattacks-intel-infowar-83265880.

65. Eleanor Sly, *Ukrainians Hurl Molotov Cocktails at Russian Tank from Window of Passing Car in Drive-by Attack*, THE INDEPENDENT (Mar. 1, 2022), www.independent.co.uk/news/world/europe/ukraine-molotov-cocktails-russia-tanks-b2025849.html.

66. Rachel Scully, *Two Russian Soldiers Killed, 28 in Hospital After Being Poisoned by Ukrainian Civilians: Officials*, THE HILL (Apr. 3, 2022), https://thehill.com/policy/international/3257737-two-russian-soldiers-killed-28-in-hospital-after-being-poisoned-by-ukrainian-civilians-officials/.

67. Dan Sabbagh, *Ukrainians Use Phone App to Spot Deadly Russian Drone Attacks*, THE GUARDIAN (Oct. 29, 2022), www.theguardian.com/world/2022/oct/29/ukraine-phone-app-russia-drone-attacks-eppo.

68. *See, e.g.*, STEPHEN J. FLANAGAN ET AL., RAND, DETERRING RUSSIAN AGGRESSION IN THE BALTIC STATES THROUGH RESILIENCE AND RESISTANCE (Apr. 15, 2019), https://www.rand.org/pubs/research_reports/RR2779.html; James Kenneth Wither, *Back to the Future? Nordic Total Defence Concepts*, 20 DEF. STUD. 61 (2020).

meaning that in the event of conflict, civilians act in coordination with the security services to defend their homeland. Nordic and Baltic States, for instance, have prepared for resistance as part of their defense strategies. This would involve the civilian population working in tandem with State security forces and civilian branches of government to undertake a range of tasks including sabotage and unconventional intelligence collection.[69]

Acts of resistance on the part of the civilian population may similarly feature in conflicts outside Europe, for instance, in the event of hostilities on the island of Taiwan.[70] Some of the individuals involved in such defensive efforts might be military reservists, such as members of a National Guard, in which case their relationship with the State is clear.[71] Others, however, might belong to small civilian resistance cells and therefore have more ambiguous links to the State in which they operate.[72]

2.2.4 The Varied Relationships Between States and Non-State Actors

The preceding analysis demonstrates the wide range of relationships that may exist between States and NSAs engaged in conflict. At one end of the spectrum, an NSA might depend wholly upon a State sponsor to survive and operate, and act entirely at that State's bidding.[73] At the other, the links between an NSA and a State might be difficult to discern. For example, an NSA might act voluntarily in furtherance of the State's interests but without the State's knowledge or support.

Frequently, the relationships between States and NSAs during armed conflict fall somewhere between these two extremes. In many cases, the State will provide assistance to the NSA. This can range from nonlethal assistance, such as the communications and medical equipment the Obama administration provided to Syrian rebels in the early stages of the conflict,[74] to extensive military aid. Often, States provide NSAs with material support, such as arms, ammunition,

69. Flanagan et al., *supra* note 68, at 6.

70. *See, e.g.*, Jeremiah Lumbaca, *Every Taiwan Citizen a Resistance Member: Preparing for a Chinese Occupation*, Modern War Inst. (Sept. 14, 2023), https://mwi.westpoint.edu/every-taiwan-citizen-a-resistance-member-preparing-for-a-chinese-occupation/. *See also* Singapore Ministry of Defence, Total Defence, https://www.mindef.gov.sg/defence-matters/defence-topic/total-defence.

71. *See infra* ch. 4.

72. Flanagan et al., *supra* note 68, at 18.

73. For discussion of de facto State organ status, *see infra* ch. 4, sec. 4.4.

74. Mark Hosenball, *Exclusive: Obama Authorizes Secret Support for Syrian Rebels*, Reuters (Aug. 1, 2012), www.reuters.com/article/us-usa-syria-obama-order/exclusive-obama-authorizes-secret-u-s-support-for-syrian-rebels-idUSBRE8701OK20120801.

equipment, and finance. But States' assistance can also take the form of training, the provision of intelligence, or messaging in the information environment.[75] Alternatively, States might offer a safe haven from which an NSA can operate, as the Taliban government in Afghanistan did to Al Qaeda prior to the terrorist attacks on September 11, 2001.[76]

Sometimes States intervene directly in a conflict alongside their support to an NSA. In Libya in 2011, for instance, certain NATO States engaged in an air campaign to directly assist rebel forces fighting the Gaddafi regime while simultaneously supplying equipment and other support to the rebels.[77] States may, alternatively, intervene in conflicts solely by providing assistance to NSAs. For example, Iran bolsters the Houthis in Yemen not through the deployment of its conventional military forces but rather via the provision of financial, military, and political aid.[78]

The nature and extent of support a State provides to an NSA influences the relationship between the parties. In general, the more the NSA relies on the State for assistance, the greater the degree of control the State can exercise over the NSA's conduct. If an NSA has other sources of support, it is more likely to pursue objectives that run counter to those of the State.[79] To maintain their local legitimacy, NSAs often go to great lengths to preserve their independence, distancing themselves from their State sponsor or playing competing sponsors off against each other.[80] Thus, although foreign sponsorship implies some degree of State authority over the recipient, the levels of dependence and control in the relationships between States and NSAs vary widely.[81]

The terminology used to describe States' relationships with NSAs, such as the term "proxy" or references to NSAs acting as a State's "agent," is therefore not always accurate. These terms imply an unequal affiliation, in which a powerful State sponsors a weaker NSA.[82] But while such hierarchical relationships undoubtedly abound during armed conflict, they do not typify all interactions between States and NSAs. One study found, for instance, that while Iran maintains a "network

75. *See infra* sec. 2.4. Regarding States' support to NSAs in the information environment, *see* Mumford, *supra* note 19, at 68–69.

76. *See* S.C. Res. 1378 (Nov. 14, 2001).

77. Mark Urban, *Inside Story of the UK's Secret Mission to Beat Gaddafi*, BBC News (Jan. 19, 2012), www.bbc.co.uk/news/magazine-16573516; Mumford, *supra* note 19, at 25–26.

78. Zorri et al., *supra* note 22, at 86–89.

79. Tyrone Groh, *The Utility of Proxy War*, Lawfare (Apr. 28, 2019), www.lawfareblog.com/utility-proxy-war.

80. *Id.*; A.B.A., Ctr. for Hum. Rts. & Rule of L. Initiative, The Legal Framework Regulating Proxy Warfare 16 (Dec. 2019), www.americanbar.org/content/dam/aba/administrative/human_rights/chr-proxy-warfare-report-2019.pdf.

81. Maurer, *supra* note 35, at 395–97.

82. *Id.* at 387.

of influence" with regional NSAs, it does not uniformly control or orchestrate their activities.[83] Instead, Iran's relationships with NSAs vary across a spectrum; although some Shi'a militia groups are dependent on Iranian support to survive, other NSAs, such as the Houthis in Yemen, would continue to pursue their objectives, albeit with diminished resources, if Tehran ceased its assistance.[84]

Other features of the relationships between States and NSAs are similarly diverse. While some rebel groups are almost entirely the creation of their external sponsor, others originate from grass-roots political movements, only later receiving State support.[85] Some alliances, such as Iran's relationship with Hezbollah, endure for decades,[86] while others last for no longer than is necessary for the State to issue instructions to the NSA to perform a task on its behalf.[87] The means and the degree of contact between the State and the NSA may also fluctuate. While in some cases, members of the State's armed forces might be co-located with the NSA to provide direct advice and support, in others, the State might provide training or other assistance remotely, without any physical contact with the NSA.[88]

Another area of significant divergence relates to the character of the NSA. Although many of the NSAs involved in armed conflict are armed groups, States task myriad different individuals and groups to act on their behalf, ranging from warlords to criminal gangs.[89] States employ PMSCs to secure and promote their interests in conflicts across the globe,[90] and use private hackers to project their power and influence through cyberspace.[91] Proxy strategies are particularly

83. Int'l Inst. for Strategic Stud., Iran's Networks of Influence in the Middle East (Nov. 2019), https://www.iiss.org/publications/strategic-dossiers/iran-dossier/. *See also* Tabatabai et al., *supra* note 32.

84. Int'l Inst. for Strategic Stud., *supra* note 83.

85. Salehyan et al., *supra* note 13, at 638.

86. *See generally* Matthew Levitt, Hezbollah: The Global Footprint of Lebanon's Party of God (2013).

87. *See infra* ch. 6, sec. 6.3.

88. Cordula Droege & David Tuck, *Fighting Together: Obligations and Opportunities in Partnered Warfare*, Humanitarian L. & Pol'y (Mar. 27, 2017), https://blogs.icrc.orgcom/law-and-policy/fighting-together-obligations-and-opportunities-in-partnered-warfare/.

89. *See, e.g.*, Daniel Byman & Israa Saber, *A Foreign Policy Toward Warlords*, Lawfare (Mar. 30, 2020), www.lawfareblog.com/foreign-policy-toward-warlords.

90. Mumford, *supra* note 19, at 8–9, 80–81; Krieg & Rickli, *supra* note 14, at 121; McFate, *supra* note 44.

91. Maurer, *supra* note 35, at 383–84. *See also* George H. Wittman, *China's Cyber Militia*, Am. Spectator (Oct. 21, 2011), https://spectator.org/36718_chinas-cyber-militia/; Dorothy Denning, *Following the Developing Iranian Cyberthreat*, The Conversation (Dec. 12, 2017), https://theconversation.com/following-the-developing-iranian-cyberthreat-85162; Ed Caesar, *The Incredible Rise of North Korea's Hacking Army*, New Yorker (Apr. 19, 2021), www.newyorker.com/magazine/2021/04/26/the-incredible-rise-of-north-koreas-hacking-army.

attractive to States in the cyber domain, given the technical challenges of determining the origin of harmful cyber operations and the increased opportunities for plausible deniability.[92]

The character of the NSA, the nature and extent of the State's support, and other features in States' relationships with NSAs are all pertinent to the degree to which a State can influence an NSA's activities.[93] A State is more likely to exercise a high degree of control if it maintains a close, enduring, alliance with an NSA, in which the NSA is highly dependent on the State for its continued operations. But a State's control over an NSA's activities cannot be assumed. Sometimes, States assist NSAs without exerting any degree of control over their activities.[94] In other cases, NSAs exhibit significant autonomy, despite receiving long-standing and extensive State support.[95] Moreover, while State control is more likely if members of the State's armed forces operate alongside an NSA, it does not automatically follow in such circumstances that the State commands the NSA's operations.[96]

In reality, working with NSAs necessarily involves some relinquishment of control.[97] States rarely have the same level of confidence in the conduct of an NSA as they would in their own armed forces. Regardless of the degree of cooperation between a State and an NSA, surrogates are autonomous actors with their own agenda to pursue.[98] State sponsorship of NSAs can therefore lead to unintended consequences that undermine the sponsor's goals, including the diversion of weapons and the emergence of criminal organizations.[99] It can also lead to the empowerment of NSAs and an increase in the prevalence and severity of the abuses they perpetrate against the civilian population.[100]

92. Mumford, *supra* note 19, at 86–90.

93. Allies, Partners and Proxies, *supra* note 3, at 25.

94. *See, e.g.*, Michael Knights, *The Houthi War Machine: From Guerrilla War to State Capture*, CTC Sentinel (Sept. 2018), https://ctc.usma.edu/houthi-war-machine-guerrilla-war-state-capture/; Bruce Riedel, *In Yemen, the Houthi Strategy has Promise and Risk*, Brookings (May 16, 2019), www.brookings.edu/blog/order-from-chaos/2019/05/16/in-yemen-the-houthi-strategy-has-promise-and-risk/.

95. This is true of Hezbollah. *See* Levitt, *Waking Up the Neighbors*, *supra* note 6.

96. *See infra* ch. 6, sec. 6.4.

97. Hughes, *supra* note 19, at 144; Melissa Dalton et al., Ctr. for Strategic & Int'l Stud. Civilians and "By, With, and Through": Key Issues and Questions related to Civilian Harm and Security Partnership 3 (Apr. 2018), www.csis.org/analysis/civilians-and-and-through.

98. Krieg, *supra* note 27, at 109; Dalton et al., *supra* note 97, at 7.

99. A.B.A, *supra* note 80, at 5–7; Mumford, *supra* note 19, at 108–10; Hughes, *supra* note 19, at 143–44.

100. Dalton et al., *supra* note 97, at 3.

2.3 NON-STATE ACTORS' INVOLVEMENT IN INTERNATIONAL LAW VIOLATIONS

Violence against civilians is a prominent feature of conflict, and often, this is perpetrated by NSAs in receipt of State support.[101] As one report relating to the Syrian conflict noted, "introducing new, as well as more sophisticated and/or more powerful weapons, into a civil war—increasingly being fought in urban areas in some cases by people with very little or no formal training—will almost certainly increase risks to civilians."[102] Thus, States' provision of material assistance, such as arms and ammunition, frequently delivers the means through which an NSA can cause significant harm.[103] State sponsorship can additionally increase the likelihood that NSAs will target civilians, on the basis that the external support they receive reduces their reliance on the local population.[104]

Unlike State armed forces, many NSAs in receipt of State support are not formally trained in IHL and remain unaware of its key principles.[105] One study found that in Syria, while defectors from the regime's military forces understood the distinction between civilians and combatants due to their prior military training, many other rebels did not.[106] Instead, the study found that many fighters perceived themselves as civilians and some viewed civilians belonging to the Alawite religious sect as legitimate military targets, a perception that was heightened by the Assad regime's use of Alawite proxy militias.[107]

Rebel groups and other NSAs in receipt of State support frequently lack not only legal training, but also the discipline and control that typically characterizes a State's armed forces.[108] This reality further contributes to the number of abuses

101. Salehyan et al., *supra* note 13, at 637; Rosenau & Gold, *supra* note 25, at 45.

102. Ctr. for Civilians in Conflict, Issue Brief: Civilian Protection in Syria 1 (Dec. 2012), https://civiliansinconflict.org/wp-content/uploads/2017/09/Syria-2012-Brief.pdf.

103. Droege & Tuck, *supra* note 88.

104. Salehyan et al., *supra* note 13, at 639.

105. A.B.A., *supra* note 80, at 27; Allies, Partners and Proxies, *supra* note 3, at 38–39.

106. Ctr. for Civilians in Conflict, *supra* note 102, at 5–6.

107. *Id.* at 5.

108. A.B.A., *supra* note 80, at 27; Ctr. for Civilians in Conflict, *supra* note 102, at 5–6. Regarding the indiscipline of NSAs operating in Syria, *see* Saskia Baas, Small Arms Survey, Syria's Armed Opposition: A Spotlight on the Moderates 10 (Jan. 2016), https://www.smallarmssurvey.org/resource/syrias-armed-opposition-spotlight-moderates-sana-dispatch-5. Regarding rebels in Libya, *see* Robin Wigglesworth, *Libyan Rebels' Limitations Hinder Progress*, Fin. Times (Apr. 25, 2011), www.ft.com/content/abd48080-6f5a-11e0-952c-00144feabdc0; Al Jazeera, *Evidence of Mass Murder After Gaddafi's Death* (Oct. 17, 2012), www.aljazeera.com/news/2012/10/17/evidence-of-mass-murder-after-gaddafis-death.

committed by NSAs engaged in hostilities.[109] For instance, although opposition groups in Syria signed codes of conduct to address allegations of abuse, such as the mistreatment of detainees, enforcement was difficult in the absence of an effective chain of command.[110] States' empowerment of armed groups through the provision of weapons and other support therefore entails a clear risk that the NSA will act abusively, outside the remit of the State's control, with little prospect of responsible disarmament and demobilization.[111]

Some States address this risk by imposing intrusive monitoring and reporting requirements on their interactions with NSAs.[112] The United States, for instance, vetted opposition fighters in Syria before providing them with material support.[113] Such measures are, however, time-consuming and expensive and reduce States' ability to plausibly deny their activity.[114] Given these drawbacks, States often choose instead to maintain distance from the beneficiary of their assistance, thereby reducing their authority or control over the NSA's conduct.[115] This practice can make it difficult to identify where responsibility for any harmful conduct should lie,[116] a challenge that becomes particularly apparent when seeking to determine the potential responsibility of a State.

2.4 CASE STUDIES

To understand when private conduct may be attributed to a State in situations of armed conflict, it is helpful to apply the law to specific acts performed by NSAs. To that end, this book focuses on three conflicts in which NSAs played a prominent role: the hostilities in Syria that commenced in 2011; the conflict in Ukraine that began in 2014; and the conflict in the DRC involving the rebel group M23, which started in 2012 and reignited in late 2021.

109. Graham Cronogue, *Rebels, Negligent Support, and State Accountability: Holding States Accountable for the Human Rights Violations of Non-State Actors*, 23 Duke J. Comp. & Int'l L. 365, 366 (2013).

110. Ctr. for Civilians in Conflict, *supra* note 102, at 7–8.

111. Droege & Tuck, *supra* note 88.

112. For a detailed discussion of the control measures introduced by the United States when working with NSAs, *see* Erica L. Gaston, Illusions of Control (2024).

113. Watling & Reynolds, *supra* note 25, at 30–31; Gaston, *supra* note 112, ch. 3.

114. Byman, *supra* note 14; Stephen Biddle et al., *Small Footprint, Small Payoff: The Military Effectiveness of Security Force Assistance*, 41 J. Strategic Stud. 89, 101–2 (2018), Gaston, *supra* note 112.

115. Erica D. Borghard, *Proxy War Can Have Dangerous Consequences*, Wash. Post (July 25, 2014), www.washingtonpost.com/news/monkey-cage/wp/2014/07/25/proxy-war-can-have-dangerous-consequences/; Groh, *supra* note 80; Roots of Restraint, *supra* note 3, at 14–15.

116. Droege and Tuck, *supra* note 88.

These three case studies vividly illustrate the varied ways in which States engage with NSAs during armed conflict.[117] They also demonstrate NSAs' propensity to act in a manner that could violate IHL.[118] This chapter outlines the relevant facts of each conflict, focusing on the relationships between the various States and NSAs involved. The attribution analysis in later chapters then elaborates on some of these examples to illuminate when and how the different rules of attribution could apply to conduct on the part of the NSAs that potentially violates international law.

2.4.1 Syria

The Syrian civil war began in early 2011, with largely peaceful protests against the government of Bashar al-Assad.[119] Government forces responded with violence, and in the ensuing months, armed conflict broke out in parts of the country.[120] The hostilities then evolved into a complex, sectarian war, involving numerous armed groups, frequent violations of international law, and significant State intervention.[121]

Various States initially rallied behind the forces opposing President Assad.[122] But with the rise of ISIS in 2014, the focus of many States shifted from regime change to counterterrorism. From that time on, the United States and its allies prioritized their support to NSAs involved in the fight against ISIS, principally the Kurdish People's Protection Units (YPG).[123] Turkey, however, perceived the YPG's rise as a threat due to the Kurds' links to the terrorist group the PKK. Ankara therefore used the Syrian opposition forces for its own ends, to seize control of territory held by the Kurds along its southern border.[124]

Myriad forces also supported the Syrian government. These included not only the Iranian and Russian militaries but also Hezbollah and other Shi'a militia groups, which benefited from significant aid from Iran.[125] From late 2015, the

117. *See supra* sec. 2.2.4.

118. *See supra* sec. 2.3.

119. *See generally* Brian M. Jenkins, RAND, The Dynamics of Syria's Civil War 8 (2014), www.rand.org/pubs/perspectives/PE115.html; Christopher M. Blanchard et al., *Armed Conflict in Syria, Overview and U.S. Response*, 5 Current Pol. & Econ. of the Middle East 237 (2014).

120. Jenkins, *supra* note 119; Blanchard et al., *supra* note 119.

121. Jenkins, *supra* note 119; Blanchard et al., *supra* note 119, at 243.

122. Baas, supra note 108, at 3–4.

123. *See infra* sec. 2.4.1.3.

124. *See infra* sec. 2.4.1.4.

125. Int'l Inst. for Strategic Stud., *supra* note 83.

Wagner Group, a Russian PMSC, additionally bolstered pro-regime forces with backing from Moscow.[126]

In early 2015, a Jihadist coalition of forces opposing the Assad regime took control of Idlib province in northwest Syria.[127] Syrian forces succeeded in regaining some of this territory, but a stalemate ensued following a 2020 ceasefire.[128] In the years that followed, one of the extremist groups, Hay'at Tahrir al-Sham (HTS), became the dominant force in northwest Syria.[129] In late 2024, HTS launched a surprise offensive against Syrian regime forces, ultimately taking control of Damascus and toppling President Assad.[130]

This mélange of ever-evolving State and non-State participants in the hostilities is a distinct feature of the Syrian conflict. Another is the parties' propensity to violate international law.[131] During the first year of the conflict, the UN Human Rights Council established a Commission of Inquiry, mandated to investigate all alleged international human rights law (IHRL) violations in Syria.[132] The Commission produced numerous reports, documenting countless abuses involving all parties to the hostilities.[133]

To aid in the subsequent attribution analysis, this chapter highlights four groups of NSAs involved in the Syrian conflict: the rebels opposing the Assad regime, NSAs bolstering Syrian government forces, Kurdish groups involved in the fight against ISIS, and militias acting with Turkish support.

126. Marten, *supra* note 38, at 193–96.

127. Thomas Joscelyn, *Jihadist Coalition Claims Control of Idlib*, Long War J. (Mar. 28, 2015), https://www.longwarjournal.org/archives/2015/03/jihadist-coalition-claims-control-of-idlib.php.

128. Christou, *supra* note 9.

129. *Id.*

130. *Id*; Chrsitina Goldbaum, *Rebel Leader Who Overthrew al-Assad Is Declared Syria's President* (Jan. 29, 2025), https://www.nytimes.com/2025/01/29/world/middleeast/syria-leader-al-shara-government.html.

131. *See generally* Beth Van Schaack, Imagining Justice for Syria (2020); Syria Justice & Accountability Centre, The State of Justice: Syria 2021 (Mar. 2021), https://syriaaccountability.org/new-report-the-state-of-justice-in-syria-2021/.

132. U.N. Human Rights Council Res. S-16/1, ¶ 7 (May 4, 2011); Rep. of the Indep. Int'l Comm'n of Inquiry on the Syrian Arab Republic 4, ¶ 4, U.N. Doc A/HRC/S-17/2/Add-1 (Nov. 23, 2011) [U.N. Nov. 2011 Rep.].

133. *See, e.g.*, U.N. Nov. 2011 Rep., *supra* note 132; Rep. of the Indep. Int'l Comm'n of Inquiry on the Syrian Arab Republic, U.N. Doc. A/HRC/19/69 (Feb. 22, 2012); Rep. of the Indep. Int'l Comm'n of Inquiry on the Syrian Arab Republic, U.N. Doc. A/HRC/22/59 (Feb. 5, 2013) [hereinafter U.N. Feb. 2013 Rep.]; Rep. of the Indep. Int'l Comm'n of Inquiry on the Syrian Arab Republic, U.N. Doc. A/HRC/34/64 (Feb. 2, 2017); Rep. of the Indep. Int'l Comm'n of Inquiry on the Syrian Arab Republic, U.N. Doc. A/HRC/39/65 (Aug. 9, 2018) [hereinafter U.N. Aug. 2018 Rep.]; Rep. of the Indep. Int'l Comm'n of Inquiry on the Syrian Arab Republic, U.N. Doc. A/HRC/46/55 (Mar. 2, 2021).

2.4.1.1 Rebels Fighting the Assad Regime

Following the initial protests, increasing numbers of the Syrian regime's military forces defected, leading to the establishment of the Free Syrian Army (FSA) in July 2011.[134] The FSA's members comprised a vast array of insurgents, with widely varying capabilities, ideology, and political goals.[135] Rebel groups would frequently amalgamate and divide, transferring their loyalties on a regular basis.[136] Thus, despite efforts to create a central command, the FSA remained little more than a "brand name" under which the various factions would fight.[137]

From the early days of the conflict, Turkey allowed FSA members to use its territory for planning and established cross-border rebel supply lines.[138] Meanwhile, Saudi Arabia and Qatar supplied significant quantities of weaponry to rebel fighters,[139] and the United States provided them with "nonlethal" aid, such as communications equipment.[140] In addition, the U.S. Central Intelligence Agency (CIA) operated covertly, arming and training the rebels in conjunction with international partners.[141]

Overall, however, the CIA scheme was ineffective. Its highly bureaucratic approach, together with stringent vetting and weapons-tracking requirements,

134. Joshua Landis, *Free Syrian Army Founded by Seven Officers to Fight the Syrian Army*, Syria Comment (July 29, 2011), www.joshualandis.com/blog/free-syrian-army-established-to-fight-the-syrian-army/; Joseph Holliday, Inst. for the Study of War, Syria's Armed Opposition (Mar. 2012), www.understandingwar.org/sites/default/files/Syrias_Armed_Opposition.pdf.

135. Baas, *supra* note 108, at 3; Van Schaack, *supra* note 131, at 27–28.

136. Jenkins, *supra* note 119, at 8.

137. U.N. Feb. 2013 Rep, *supra* note 133, at 8, ¶ 25. *See also* Elizabeth O'Bagy, Inst. for the Study of War, The Free Syrian Army (Mar. 2013), www.understandingwar.org/sites/default/files/The-Free-Syrian-Army-24MAR.pdf.

138. Liam Stack, *In Slap at Syria, Turkey Shelters Anti-Assad Fighters*, N.Y. Times (Oct. 27, 2011), https://www.nytimes.com/2011/10/28/world/europe/turkey-is-sheltering-antigovernment-syrian-militia.html; Faysal Itani & Aaron Stein, Atlantic Council, Turkey's Syria Predicament 1, 3 (May 2016), https://www.atlanticcouncil.org/in-depth-research-reports/issue-brief/turkey-s-syria-predicament/.

139. Roula Khalaf & Abigail Fielding-Smith, *How Qatar Seized Control of the Syrian Revolution*, Fin. Times (May 17, 2013), www.ft.com/content/f2d9bbc8-bdbc-11e2-890a-00144feab7de.

140. Mark Hosenball, *Exclusive: Obama Authorizes Secret U.S. Support for Syrian Rebels*, Reuters (Aug. 1, 2012), https://www.reuters.com/article/world/obama-authorizes-secret-support-for-syrian-rebels-idUSBRE8701OK/.

141. Eric Schmitt, *CIA said to Aid in Steering Arms to Syrian Opposition*, N.Y. Times (June 21, 2012), https://www.nytimes.com/2012/06/21/world/middleeast/cia-said-to-aid-in-steering-arms-to-syrian-rebels.html; C. J. Chivers & Eric Schmitt, *Arms Airlift to Syria Rebels Expands, with Aid from CIA*, N.Y. Times (Mar. 24, 2013), https://www.nytimes.com/2013/03/25/world/middleeast/arms-airlift-to-syrian-rebels-expands-with-cia-aid.html; Greg Miller, *CIA Ramping Up Covert Training Program for Moderate Syrian Rebels*, Wash. Post (Oct. 2, 2013), https://www.washingtonpost.com/world/national-security/cia-ramping-up-covert-training-program-for-moderate-syrian-rebels/2013/10/02/a0bba084-2af6-11e3-8ade-a1f23cda135e_story.html.

slowed the volume and pace of assistance to such an extent that it undermined the FSA's fighting capacity.[142] Moreover, the moderate rebels, who aligned ideologically with the United States and its allies, were frequently the weakest.[143] Western-backed rebels lost considerable ground to better-organized, better-funded Islamist groups.[144] Concurrently, the priorities of the rebels' State backers turned from toppling President Assad to stemming the flow of refugees from Syria and combatting terrorism. Acknowledging this reality, the United States announced the conclusion of the CIA program in July 2017.[145]

2.4.1.2 Non-State Actors Fighting in Support of the Syrian Regime

The considerable combat losses, desertions, and defections suffered by the Syrian Army forced the government to rely increasingly upon NSAs, including Hezbollah and other Shi'a militia groups.[146] Hezbollah played a critical role in bolstering Assad's forces from 2013,[147] with its fighters and commanders leading battles and training countless Shi'a militia fighters.[148] Although it operated with considerable autonomy, Hezbollah became involved in the Syrian conflict at Iran's instigation, and received significant support from both Iran and Syria.[149]

Iran dispatched members of the Islamic Revolutionary Guard Corps (IRGC), a parallel arm of Iran's military that reports directly to the Supreme Leader, to guide pro-government military efforts and manage its network of proxies in Syria.[150]

142. Gaston, *supra* note 112, at 111–15.

143. Baas, *supra* note 108, at 2.

144. *Id.* at 7–8.

145. John Walcott, *Trump Ends CIA Arms Support for Anti-Assad Syria Rebels: US Officials*, Reuters (July 19, 2017), www.reuters.com/article/us-mideast-crisis-usa-syria-idUSKBN1A42KC.

146. Jeffrey White, *Hezbollah's Declaration of War in Syria: Military Implications*, Wash. Inst. (May. 29, 2013), www.washingtoninstitute.org/policy-analysis/view/hezbollahs-declaration-of-war-in-syria-military-implications; Sullivan, *supra* note 6, at 4; Nadav Pollak, *The Transformation of Hezbollah by Its Involvement in Syria*, Wash. Inst., (Aug. 4, 2016), www.washingtoninstitute.org/policy-analysis/transformation-hezbollah-its-involvement-syria.

147. Samia Nakhoul, *Special Report: Hezbollah Gambles All in Syria*, Reuters (Sept. 26, 2013), www.reuters.com/article/us-syria-hezbollah-special-report/special-report-hezbollah-gambles-all-in-syria-idUSBRE98P0AI20130926; Sullivan, *supra* note 6, at 14; Levitt, *Waking up the Neighbors*, *supra* note 6.

148. Pollak, *supra* note 146.

149. Nakhoul, *supra* note 147; Levitt, *supra* note 86, at 12; Watling, *supra* note 30, at 17.

150. Dexter Filkins, *The Shadow Commander*, New Yorker (Sept. 23, 2013), www.newyorker.com/magazine/2013/09/30/the-shadow-commander; Paul Bucala & Frederick W. Kagan, Critical Threats, Iran's Evolving Way of War: How the IRGC Fights in Syria 12–13 (Mar. 2016), www.criticalthreats.org/wp-content/uploads/2016/07/imce-imagesIrans_Evolving_Way_of_War_IRGC_in_Syria_FINAL-1.pdf.

These included numerous Shi'a militias recruited from across the region, including from Lebanon, Iraq, Pakistan, and Afghanistan.[151] Iran supplied the groups with training and equipment, enabling them not only to fight in the conflict but also to secure key supply routes and extend Tehran's regional influence.[152]

Syrian paramilitary groups also bolstered government forces. One of these, known as the Shabbiha or "ghost" forces, played a critical role in crushing the protests during the early stages of the conflict and assisted in controlling territory after it was secured by Syrian security forces.[153] These forces derived from local criminal gangs and reportedly included ex-convicts, released from prison in exchange for loyalty to the Assad regime.[154]

Russia's intervention in support of the Syrian regime, from 2015, included the State's direct participation in the conflict via its own armed forces and also its indirect involvement through the Wagner Group.[155] The group received significant assistance from Russia, particularly from the State's military intelligence service, the GRU.[156] For much of its existence, the full extent of the Wagner Group's links to Moscow remained unclear, obfuscated by factors such as the involvement of the oligarch Yevgeny Prigozhin in the group's funding and establishment.[157] However, in 2023, President Putin admitted the group's close ties to the Kremlin.[158]

151. Zorri et al., *supra* note 22, at 53–54, 69.

152. *Id.*; Michael Knights, *Iran's Foreign Legion: The Role of Iraqi Shiite Militias in Syria*, Wash. Inst. (June 27, 2013) www.washingtoninstitute.org/policy-analysis/irans-foreign-legion-role-iraqi-shiite-militias-syria; Farzin Nadimi, *Iran's Afghan and Pakistani Proxies: In Syria and Beyond?* Wash. Inst. (Aug. 22, 2016), www.washingtoninstitute.org/policy-analysis/irans-afghan-and-pakistani-proxies-syria-and-beyond; Farmer & Makoii, *supra* note 36.

153. U.N. Nov. 2011 Rep., *supra* note 132; at 6, ¶ 20; Aron Lund, *Who Are the Pro-Assad Militias?* Carnegie Endowment for Int'l Peace (Mar. 2, 2015), https://carnegieendowment.org/middle-east/diwan/2015/03/who-are-the-pro-assad-militias?lang=en [hereinafter Lund, *Pro-Assad Militias*]. *See also* Expert Report of Ewan Brown 61–66, ¶¶ 126–37, Colvin et al. v. Syrian Arab Republic, No. 1:16-cv-01423-ABJ (D.D.C. Mar. 22, 2018), https://cja.org/wp-content/uploads/2018/04/17-Expert-Report-of-Ewan-Brown-dated-March-2-2018_Redacted.pdf.

154. Jenkins, *supra* note 119, at 6; Lund, *Pro-Assad Militias*, *supra* note 153.

155. Marten, *supra* note 38.

156. *Id.* at 187, 192; Giglio, *supra* note 38.

157. Marten, *supra* note 38, at 182, 187.

158. Nicolas Camut, *Putin Admits Kremlin Gave Wagner Nearly $1 Billion in the Past Year*, Politico (June 27, 2023), https://www.politico.eu/article/vladimir-putin-yevgeny-prigozhin-russia-kremlin-gave-wagner-group-nearly-1-billion-in-the-past-year/.

2.4.1.3 Non-State Actors Supported by the U.S.-led Coalition in the Fight Against ISIS

From 2014 onward, the principal focus of the United States and its allies shifted from opposing the Assad regime to combatting terrorism.[159] The U.S.-led coalition began air strikes against ISIS in Syria[160] and the U.S. Congress approved a new program to train and equip Syrian rebels to fight the Islamists on the ground.[161] The scheme ran into difficulties, however, training only a handful of rebels.[162] The United States therefore suspended the program in October 2015.[163]

The same month, a new military coalition formed, known as the Syrian Democratic Forces (SDF).[164] The alliance was established with Pentagon assistance, aimed at defeating ISIS and providing information to support U.S. airstrikes.[165] Although it included rebels of diverse ethnicity and religion, the Kurdish YPG were the predominant force.[166]

The United States' assistance to the SDF included air and artillery support, transporting SDF fighters across enemy lines, and the supply of weaponry and equipment.[167] Moreover, the Obama administration authorized U.S. forces to deploy to Syria, principally to act in an advisory role.[168] According to a military spokesman, U.S. forces were "advising the Syrian fighters on the ground" but were "not involved in direct, front-line combat."[169]

159. Aaron Stein, Atlantic Council, Partner Operations in Syria (July 2017), www.atlanticcouncil.org/in-depth-research-reports/report/partner-operations-in-syria/; Van Schaack, *supra* note 131, at 31–33.

160. Statement by the President on Airstrikes in Syria (Sept. 23, 2014), https://obamawhitehouse.archives.gov/the-press-office/2014/09/23/statement-president-airstrikes-syria.

161. H.R.J. Res. 124, 113th Cong. (2014) § 149. *See also* Christopher M. Blanchard & Amy Belasco, Cong. Res. Serv., Train and Equip Program for Syria: Authorities, Funding and Issues for Congress 36–39 (June 9, 2015), https://fas.org/sgp/crs/natsec/R43727.pdf; Gaston, *supra* note 112, at 127–35.

162. Gaston, *supra* note 112, at 127–35.

163. Michael D. Shear et al., *Obama Administration Ends Effort to Train Syrians to Combat ISIS*, N.Y. Times (Oct. 9, 2015), www.nytimes.com/2015/10/10/world/middleeast/pentagon-program-islamic-state-syria.html?_r=0.

164. Lund, *Syrian Democratic Forces, supra* note 24; Rosenau & Gold *supra* note 25, at 29–40.

165. Lund, *Syrian Democratic Forces, supra* note 24; Gaston, *supra* note 112, at 139–48.

166. Lund, *Syrian Democratic Forces, supra* note 24.

167. *Id.*; Rosenau & Gold, *supra* note 25, at 34–36; Michael R. Gordon & Anne Barnard, *U.S. Airlifts Hundreds of Militia Fighters in Attack to Cut Off Raqqa, Syria*, N.Y. Times (Mar. 22, 2017), www.nytimes.com/2017/03/22/world/middleeast/us-airlift-raqqa-syria.html.

168. John Ismay, *U.S. Says 2,000 Troops are in Syria, a Fourfold Increase*, N.Y. Times (Dec. 6, 2017), www.nytimes.com/2017/12/06/world/middleeast/us-troops-syria.html.

169. Gordon & Barnard, *supra* note 167.

Other States also assisted the SDF's counter-ISIS mission, although their support was largely restricted to airstrikes.[170] These efforts successfully displaced ISIS in large areas of northern Syria.[171] As the SDF gained control over areas previously held by the terrorist group, it detained ISIS fighters and their families in makeshift camps and prisons.[172] The numbers within these facilities increased dramatically after the fall of ISIS's last stronghold in March 2019.[173]

The United States and its allies assisted the SDF to detain ISIS fighters, funding security measures such as fencing, the installation of bars on windows, and the construction of new facilities.[174] The coalition additionally assisted in securing the perimeter of Al-Hawl camp, housing numerous ISIS women and children, and supported the Kurdish administration to identify individuals within the camp via biometric enrolment.[175]

2.4.1.4 Militias Fighting on Turkey's behalf

Turkey strongly opposed the U.S.-led coalition's support to the SDF due to the group's links to the terrorist group, the PKK.[176] Given the SDF's success in holding territory taken from ISIS, Ankara's priority evolved from toppling President Assad to preventing the emergence of an autonomous Kurdish region, linked to the PKK, on its southern border.[177] In 2016, Turkey supported a Syrian rebel

170. Anthony Dworkin, Eur. Council on Foreign Rel., Europe's New Counter-Terrorism Wars 5–10 (Oct. 2016), https://ecfr.eu/archive/page/-/ECFR192_-_EUROPES_NEW_COUNTER-TERROR_WARS_FINAL.pdf.

171. *Timeline: The Rise, Spread, and Fall of the Islamic State*, Wilson Ctr. (Oct. 28, 2019), www.wilsoncenter.org/article/timeline-the-rise-spread-and-fall-the-islamic-state.

172. Eric Schmitt, *Pentagon Wades Deeper into Detainee Operations in Syria*, N.Y. Times, (Apr. 5, 2018), www.nytimes.com/2018/04/05/world/middleeast/pentagon-detainees-syria-islamic-state.html [hereinafter Schmitt, *Pentagon Wades Deeper*].

173. *Hundreds of ISIL Fighters Surrender in Syria's Baghouz: SDF*, Al Jazeera (Mar. 7, 2019), www.aljazeera.com/news/2019/3/7/hundreds-of-isil-fighters-surrender-in-syrias-baghouz-sdf; Elizabeth Dent, *The Unsustainability of ISIS Detentions in Syria*, Middle East Inst. (Mar. 2019), https://www.mei.edu/publications/unsustainability-isis-detentions-syria.

174. Schmitt, *Pentagon Wades Deeper*, *supra* note 172; Van Schaack, *supra* note 131, at 278–79; Katie Bo Williams, *Coalition Plans to Expand Giant ISIS Prison in Syria*, Def. One (Feb. 24, 2021), www.defenseone.com/policy/2021/02/coalition-plans-expand-giant-isis-prison-syria/172270/.

175. Louisa Loveluck, *In Syrian Camp for Women and Children Who Left ISIS Caliphate, a Struggle Even to Register Names*, Wash. Post (June 28, 2020), www.washingtonpost.com/world/middle_east/syria-al-hol-annex-isis-caliphate-women-children/2020/06/28/80ddabb4-b71b-11ea-9a1d-d3db1cbe07ce_story.html.

176. Lund, *Syrian Democratic Forces*, *supra* note 24; Nicholas Norberg, *U.S. Syria Withdrawal Impact on Kurdish Partners*, Lawfare (Jan. 8, 2019), www.lawfareblog.com/us-syria-withdrawal-impact-kurdish-partners.

177. Itani & Stein, *supra* note 138, at 6; Engin Yüksel, Strategies of Turkish Proxy Warfare in Northern Syria: Back With a Vengeance 1, 3 (Nov. 2019), www.clingend

offensive against ISIS militants, aiming not only to defeat ISIS but also to prevent the SDF from creating a zone along Turkey's southern border from which the PKK could operate.[178]

By the end of 2017, the disparate militia groups acting for Turkey had unified, becoming known as the Syrian National Army (SNA).[179] SNA fighters participated in two further operations alongside Turkish armed forces, each of which gained control over additional areas of Syrian territory along Turkey's southern border.[180] Turkey provided significant support to the militias, including training, salaries, and weapons.[181] It additionally encouraged new recruits to join the SNA, including Syrian refugees located in Turkey, with the offer of cash stipends.[182]

Having taken control of areas of northern Syria, Turkey put in place new governance structures.[183] In areas such as Afrin, local councils linked to the SNA governed on a day-to-day basis, but the "real authority" lay with Turkish governors.[184] Turkey paid the salaries of all local civilian and military personnel,[185] Turkish-trained police officers provided security, and local officials collaborated closely with Ankara.[186]

Turkey also supported Syrian rebels to resist advances by the Syrian regime in Idlib province in northwest Syria.[187] Ankara reached agreements with the

ael.org/sites/default/files/2019-11/strategies-turkish-proxy-warfare-in-northern-syria.pdf; Asli Aydintaşbaş, *A New Gaza: Turkey's Border Policy in Northern Syria*, EUR. COUNCIL ON FOREIGN REL. (May 28, 2020), https://ecfr.eu/publication/a_new_gaza_turkeys_border_policy_in_northern_syria/.

178. STEIN, *supra* note 159, at 13–15; Aydintaşbaş, *supra* note 177.

179. Dilara Hamit & Erdogan Çagatay Zontur, *Free Syrian Army Transforms into Syrian National Army*, ANADOLU AGENCY (Oct. 9, 2019), www.aa.com.tr/en/middle-east/free-syrian-army-transforms-into-syrian-national-army/1607384; Elizabeth Tsurkov, *Who Are Turkey's Proxy Fighters in Syria?* N.Y. REV. (Nov. 27, 2019), https://www.nybooks.com/online/2019/11/27/who-are-turkeys-proxy-fighters-in-syria/.

180. U.N. Aug. 2018 Rep., *supra* note 133, at 3, 5, ¶¶ 4, 14; Rep. of the Indep. Int'l Comm'n of Inquiry on the Syrian Arab Republic 4, 10, ¶¶ 12, 45–47, U.N. Doc. A/HRC/43/57 (Jan. 28, 2020).

181. Tsurkov, *supra* note 179; Aydintaşbaş, *supra* note 177.

182. Aaron Stein et al., *Post Conflict Stabilization: Turkey and the End of Operation Euphrates Shield*, ATLANTIC COUNCIL (July 13, 2017), https://www.atlanticcouncil.org/blogs/syriasource/post-conflict-stabilization-turkey-and-the-end-of-operation-euphrates-shield/; Tsurkov, *supra* note 179.

183. Stein et al., *supra* note 182; U.N. Aug. 2018 Rep., *supra* note 133, at 6, 7, ¶¶ 25, 29.

184. Aydintaşbaş, *supra* note 177.

185. *Id.*; Tsurkov, *supra* note 179.

186. *See, e.g.*, Rep. of the Indep. Int'l Comm'n of Inquiry on the Syrian Arab Republic 13, ¶ 60, U.N. Doc. A/HRC/45/31 (Aug. 14, 2020).

187. Orhan Coskun & Suleiman Al-Khalidi, *Turkish-Backed Rebels Say They Seized Town in Syria's Idlib in First Advance*, REUTERS (Feb. 25, 2020), www.reuters.com/article/us-syria-security/turkish-backed-rebels-say-they-seized-town-in-syrias-idlib-in-first-advance-idUSKCN20J0SO.

dominant rebel group in the region, HTS, on matters such as border crossings and the delivery of humanitarian aid.[188] Turkey's indirect support for HTS served to increase the group's legitimacy while also allowing Turkey to exert some influence over the group's conduct.[189] Turkey thus benefited from its relationship with the group when HTS succeeded in toppling the Assad regime and taking power in late 2024.[190]

2.4.2 Ukraine

In common with the Syrian hostilities, the conflict in Ukraine began with largely peaceful protests in the State's capital, Kiev.[191] Known as the Euro-Maidan, the wave of demonstrations that commenced in November 2013 was triggered by the government's decision to prioritize closer ties with Russia rather than the European Union.[192] Ukrainian security forces responded to the protests with excessive force, thereby escalating the demonstrations into violent clashes and further radicalizing the protest movement.[193] President

188. Aydintaşbaş, *supra* note 177; Yüksel, *supra* note 177, at 13; Sultan Al Kanj, *Reviewing the Turkey-HTS Relationship*, Chatham House (May 2019), https://kalam.chathamhouse.org/articles/reviewing-the-turkey-hts-relationship/.

189. Gonul Tol, *How Turkey Won the Syrian Civil War*, Foreign Aff. (Dec. 11, 2024), https://www.foreignaffairs.com/turkey/how-turkey-won-syrian-civil-war.

190. *Id.*

191. *See generally* Steven Woehrel, Cong. Res. Serv., Ukraine: Current Issues and U.S. Policy (Mar. 24, 2014) https://www.everycrsreport.com/files/20140324_RL33460_6e1a9ce87fec19677515812c4af16d3bc8529723.pdf [hereinafter Woehrel Rep. Mar. 2014]; Int'l Crim. Ct. Off. Prosecutor, Rep. on Preliminary Examination Activities 34–37 (Nov. 14, 2016), www.icc-cpi.int/iccdocs/otp/161114-otp-rep-PE_ENG.pdf [hereinafter ICC Rep. 2016); Michael Kofman et al., RAND, Lessons from Russia's Operations in Crimea and Eastern Ukraine 33–45 (2017), www.rand.org/content/dam/rand/pubs/research_reports/RR1400/RR1498/RAND_RR1498.pdf; Matveeva, *supra* note 34; Thomas de Waal, Carnegie Europe, Uncertain Ground: Engaging with Europe's de facto States and Breakaway Territories 61–70 (Dec. 3, 2018), https://carnegieeurope.eu/2018/12/03/uncertain-ground-engaging-with-europe-s-de-facto-states-and-breakaway-territories-pub-77823; Sabine Fischer, The Donbas Conflict: Opposing Interests and Narratives, Difficult Peace Process, German Inst. for Int'l & Sec. Aff. (Apr. 2019), www.swp-berlin.org/10.18449/2019RP05/.

192. Woehrel Rep. Mar. 2014, *supra* note 191, at 8; ICC Rep. 2016, *supra* note 191, at 34; Kofman et al., *supra* note 196, at 1; Matveeva, *supra* note 34, at 34–36.

193. Rep. on the Human Rights Situation in Ukraine 3 (Apr. 15, 2014), https://reliefweb.int/sites/reliefweb.int/files/resources/Ukraine_Report_15April2014.pdf; Steven Woehrel, Cong. Res. Serv., Ukraine: Current issues and U.S. Policy 1 (Sept. 4, 2014), www.everycrsreport.com/files/20140904_RL33460_ac8f6d5380c670426d952dc39e784d173dac9739.pdf [hereinafter Woehrel Rep. Sept. 2014]; Matveeva, *supra* note 34, at 36–40.

Yanukovych fled to Russia in February 2014, leading to the establishment of a new government.[194]

The formation of a pro-Western regime in Ukraine posed a significant threat to Russia's regional hegemony.[195] Following the collapse of the Soviet Union and Ukraine's attainment of independence in 1991, Russia had retained considerable influence over its neighbor, particularly in eastern and southern Ukraine where Russian is the first language of many inhabitants.[196] The east also retained economic ties to Russia,[197] while the stationing of the Black Sea Fleet on the Crimean peninsula preserved an important Russian military foothold on Ukrainian territory.[198]

While international attention focused on Russia's covert operation to gain control over Crimea,[199] a political protest movement gathered pace in the eastern Donbas region.[200] Anti-government demonstrators waving Russian flags seized administrative buildings and the protest leaders declared themselves "people's mayors" and "people's governors."[201] In April 2014, local Donbas leaders declared the establishment of the Donetsk People's Republic (DNR) and the Luhansk People's Republic (LNR), followed in each case by a referendum on self-rule.[202]

The Ukrainian government deployed forces to the east of the country in an "anti-terror operation" aimed at regaining control of the Donbas.[203] This involved the nation's security forces and also a number of volunteer battalions.[204] The latter, committed to fighting for the unity of Ukraine, stepped in to fill the void left by

194. Woehrel Rep. Mar. 2014, *supra* note 191, at 8; ICC Rep. 2016, *supra* note 191, at 34; Kofman et al., *supra* note 191, at 1.

195. Franklin Holcomb, Inst. for the Study of War, The Kremlin's Irregular Army: Ukrainian Separatist Order of Battle 7 (Sept. 2017), https://www.understandingwar.org/backgrounder/kremlin%E2%80%99s-irregular-army-ukrainian-separatist-order-battle.

196. Woehrel Rep. Sept. 2014, *supra* note 193, at 6; Kofman et al., *supra* note 191, at 49.

197. Woehrel Rep. Sept. 2014, *supra* note 193, at 6; Kofman et al., *supra* note 191, at 49.

198. Luke Harding, *Ukraine Extends Lease for Russia's Black Sea Fleet*, The Guardian (Apr. 21, 2010), www.theguardian.com/world/2010/apr/21/ukraine-black-sea-fleet-russia.

199. Kofman et al., *supra* note 191, at 5–12; Matveeva, *supra* note 34, at 57–66.

200. Kofman et al., *supra* note 191, at 33–45.

201. *Id.* at 33.

202. Woehrel Rep. Sept. 2014, *supra* note 193, at 3; Matveeva, *supra* note 34, at 102–6, 111–13; Fischer, *supra* note 191, at 9.

203. *Ukraine Says Donetsk "Anti-Terror Operation" Under Way*, BBC News (Apr. 16, 2014), www.bbc.com/news/world-europe-27035196.

204. Rep. on the Human Rights Situation in Ukraine 3, ¶ 3 (July 15, 2014), https://www.ohchr.org/sites/default/files/Documents/Countries/UA/Ukraine_Report_15July2014.pdf.

the Donbas-based security forces.[205] Russia, meanwhile, aided the rebels in their fight against the Ukrainian government and also deployed the Wagner Group to bolster rebel forces.

2.4.2.1 Russian Support to Rebels in the Donbas

Despite assertions within Ukraine and the wider international community that responsibility for the insurgency in the Donbas lay solely with Moscow,[206] the conflict's origins were predominantly local.[207] The majority of demonstrators were Donbas residents who felt threatened by recent developments within their country, such as the decision to repeal the official status of the Russian language.[208] It remains unclear whether the Kremlin had any involvement in the initial assaults on government buildings.[209] However, Moscow's influence over the rebel campaign became apparent when individuals linked to Russia were appointed to positions of authority within the rebel administrations.[210] A Russian citizen, Aleksander Borodai, was proclaimed Prime Minister of the DNR, while a former Russian intelligence operative known as Strelkov took command of rebel fighters.[211]

The rebel forces were diverse, with paramilitary groups, local recruits from the Donbas, and defectors from the Ukrainian security services fighting alongside each other.[212] They included volunteers from Russia, who joined the fight with the open encouragement of the government.[213] Russia directly supported rebel

205. Woehrel Rep. Sept. 2014, *supra* note 193, at 3; Rosaria Puglisi, Istituto Affari Internazionali, Heroes or Villains? Volunteer Battalions in Post-Maidan Ukraine 5 (Mar. 8, 2015), www.iai.it/sites/default/files/iaiwp1508.pdf; Matveeva, *supra* note 34, at 123–26.

206. *See, e.g.*, Lina Kushch & Thomas Grove, *Pro-Russia Protesters Seize Ukraine Buildings, Kiev Blames Putin*, Reuters (Apr. 6, 2014), www.reuters.com/article/us-ukraine-crisis-storm-idUSBREA350B420140406; Ivo Daalder et al., Brookings, Preserving Ukraine's Independence, Resisting Russian Aggression: What the United States and NATO Must Do 2 (Feb. 2015), www.brookings.edu/wp-content/uploads/2016/06/UkraineReport_February2015_FINAL.pdf; Holcomb, *supra* note 195, at 7.

207. Matveeva, *supra* note 34, at 1–16, 80–88, 93, 271–79.

208. Kofman et al., *supra* note 191, at 33; Matveeva, *supra* note 34, at 27–30.

209. Kofman et al., *supra* note 191, at 39.

210. *Id.* at 38; Aric Toler & Melinda Haring, *Russia Funds and Manages Conflict in Ukraine, Leaks Show*, Atlantic Council (Apr. 24, 2017), www.atlanticcouncil.org/blogs/ukrainealert/russia-funds-and-manages-conflict-in-ukraine-leaks-show.

211. Kofman et al., *supra* note 191, at 38–40, 57–58, 60; Holcomb, *supra* note 195, at 7; Matveeva, *supra* note 34, at 95–96, 106–7, 132–33.

212. Kofman et al., *supra* note 191, at 53.

213. Matveeva, *supra* note 34, at 96–99; Fischer, *supra* note 191, at 15.

operations, firing artillery from Russian territory into Ukraine.[214] Furthermore, Moscow supplied the rebels with funding as well as sophisticated military equipment including tanks, rocket launchers, and other heavy weapons.[215] This included the Buk surface-to-air missile system that the rebels used to bring down Malaysia Airlines Flight MH17 in July 2014.[216]

Meanwhile, Ukraine's "anti-terror" campaign continued, initially meeting with considerable success.[217] By August 2014, the rebels were "on the precipice of failure."[218] But failure was not an outcome that Moscow could tolerate.[219] It therefore changed its approach to one of more direct intervention by sending in its regular forces, increasing supplies of military equipment, and coordinating the rebels' military strategy.[220]

Russian troops in eastern Ukraine not only participated in the hostilities but also acted in a command role.[221] By January 2015, large numbers of Russian military and GRU (military intelligence) officers were in the Donbas serving as advisers and trainers.[222] Moscow further strengthened command and control by reorganizing the rebel units into a formal military structure, with Russian officers in command from battalion level upwards.[223] Russia additionally conducted a purge of rebel leaders, aiming to

214. Maksymilian Czuperski et al., Atlantic Council, Hiding in Plain Sight: Putin's War in Ukraine 5 (May 2015), www.atlanticcouncil.org/in-depth-research-reports/report/hiding-in-plain-sight/; Matveeva, *supra* note 34, at 155.

215. Czuperski et al., *supra* note 214, at 5; Daalder et al., *supra* note 206, at 8; Matveeva, *supra* note 34, at 127, 150–51.

216. Matveeva, *supra* note 34, at 157–58. *See also* Marko Milanović, *The Netherlands and Australia Attribute the Downing of MH17 to Russia*, EJIL:Talk! (May 25, 2018), www.ejiltalk.org/the-netherlands-and-australia-attribute-the-downing-of-mh17-to-russia/.

217. Czuperski et al., *supra* note 214, at 5; Matveeva, *supra* note 34, at 150–54, 161–63.

218. Kofman et al., *supra* note 191, at 57.

219. Matveeva, *supra* note 34, at 215.

220. Czuperski et al., *supra* note 214, at 5; Igor Sutyagin, Royal United Servs. Inst., Russian Forces in Ukraine 4 (Mar. 2015), https://static.rusi.org/201503_bp_russian_forces_in_ukraine.pdf; ICC Rep. 2016, *supra* note 191, at 37, ¶ 166; Holcomb, *supra* note 195, at 9; Matveeva, *supra* note 34, at 163–66.

221. Sutyagin, *supra* note 220, at 9.

222. Daalder et al., *supra* note 206, at 10; McDermott, *supra* note 208, at 26–27.

223. Daalder et al., *supra* note 206, at 10; Int'l Crisis Group, Russian and the Separatists in Eastern Ukraine 8 (Feb. 5, 2016), https://www.crisisgroup.org/europe-central-asia/eastern-europe/ukraine/russia-and-separatists-eastern-ukraine; McDermott, *supra* note 208, at 20.

remove those commanders who refused to integrate into the new command structure.[224]

Russia's actions resulted in the swift defeat of Ukrainian forces, adding urgency to the peace negotiations in Minsk, Belarus.[225] A ceasefire was agreed in September 2014[226] but renewed fighting led to a fresh round of negotiations and a second Minsk accord, concluded in February 2015.[227] Thereafter, Russian intelligence officers known as "curators" controlled the ceasefire.[228] Moscow's influence in the Donbas persisted until its full-scale invasion in February 2022. Later the same year, Russia purported to annex certain areas of Ukraine's territory, including the Donbas.[229] From this time on, any remaining doubts regarding Russia's authority over the region disappeared.

2.4.2.2 State Support to Non-State Actors Operating in the Cyber Domain

Any overview of NSAs' involvement in the conflict in Ukraine would be incomplete without reference to the many cyberattacks that accompanied the hostilities.[230] Cyber operators supporting both Moscow and Kiev were active from the early stages of the conflict,[231] with the number and severity of cyberattacks rising in parallel with ongoing political events.[232] In the early years of the conflict,

224. Anders Åslund, *Putin Moves to Direct Rule in the Donbass*, Newsweek (June 1, 2016), www.newsweek.com/putin-moves-direct-rule-donbas-412411; Int'l Crisis Group, *supra* note 223, at 3–4; Matveeva, *supra* note 34, at 180–81, 216–17, 279–80.

225. Matveeva, *supra* note 34, at 164–66, 169–70.

226. *Ukraine Ceasefire: The 12-Point Plan*, BBC News (Feb. 9, 2015), www.bbc.co.uk/news/world-europe-29162903.

227. *Ukraine Ceasefire: New Minsk Agreement Key Points*, BBC News (Feb. 12, 2015), www.bbc.co.uk/news/world-europe-31436513.

228. Int'l Crisis Group, *supra* note 223, at 3, 12; Matveeva, *supra* note 34, at 180; Fischer, *supra* note 191, at 24.

229. Laris Karklis & Erin Cunningham, *Three Maps That Explain Russia's Annexations and Losses in Ukraine*, Wash. Post (Sept. 30, 2022), https://www.washingtonpost.com/world/2022/09/30/map-ukraine-regions-annexation-russia/.

230. Except where otherwise indicated, the use of the term "cyberattack" or "attack" in this section refers to a cyber operation in the generic sense, rather than an attack within the meaning of IHL.

231. Tim Maurer, *Cyber Proxies and the Crisis in Ukraine*, *in* Cyber War in Perspective: Russian Aggression Against Ukraine 85 (Kenneth Geers ed., 2015).

232. Nikolay Koval, *Revolution Hacking*, *in* Cyber War in Perspective: Russian Aggression Against Ukraine 55 (Kenneth Geers ed., 2015); Conger & Satariano, *supra* note 63

however, it was Ukraine that suffered the most significant barrage of hostile cyber activity.[233]

From the conflict's commencement, "a plague of cyberattacks" hit Ukrainian companies and government agencies.[234] The nexus between these incidents and the armed conflict is evident not only from the timing of the attacks but also their nature; they were plainly designed to weaken and destabilize the new government, while promoting a pro-Russian agenda.[235]

In some cases, the sophistication of the cyber weapon employed against Ukraine implied some degree of State involvement in the operation.[236] For instance, the complex malware Snake, believed to have been developed in Russia, infected dozens of Ukrainian computer networks in the early stages of the conflict.[237] Later, sophisticated cyberattacks targeted the Ukrainian power network. The first occurred in December 2015, involving significant power outages.[238] Cyber security experts subsequently assessed that the Russian hacker group known as Sandworm was responsible.[239]

Sandworm was identified prior to the power network attack as the hacker team responsible for planting BlackEnergy malware on wide-ranging targets, both within and outside Ukraine.[240] BlackEnergy was employed against varying targets including government ministries and the Ukrainian railway.[241] In December 2016, a year after the first attack on the Ukrainian power grid, the network was hit again; this time with a more sophisticated cyber weapon.[242] Experts again traced the attack to Sandworm.[243]

233. Laurens Cerulus, *How Ukraine Became a Test Bed for Cyberweaponry*, POLITICO (Feb. 14, 2019), www.politico.eu/article/ukraine-cyber-war-frontline-russia-malware-attacks/.

234. ANDY GREENBERG, SANDWORM: A NEW ERA OF CYBERWAR AND THE HUNT FOR THE KREMLIN'S MOST DANGEROUS HACKERS 2 (2019). *See also id.* at 136–37.

235. Koval, *supra* note 232, at 56; MICHAEL CONNELL & SARAH VOGLER, CNA, RUSSIA'S APPROACH TO CYBER WARFARE 19 (Mar. 2017), www.cna.org/cna_files/pdf/DOP-2016-U-014231-1Rev.pdf.

236. Vincent L. Morelli, CONG. RES. SERV., UKRAINE: CURRENT ISSUES AND U.S. POLICY 20 (Jan. 3, 2017), https://fas.org/sgp/crs/row/RL33460.pdf.

237. Sam Jones, *Cyber Snake Plagues Ukraine Networks*, FIN. TIMES (Mar. 7, 2014), www.ft.com/content/615c29ba-a614-11e3-8a2a-00144feab7de.

238. GREENBERG, *supra* note 234, at 51–52.

239. DRAGOS, CRASHOVERRIDE: ANALYSIS OF THE THREAT TO ELECTRIC GRID OPERATIONS 10 (June 13, 2017), https://nsarchive.gwu.edu/sites/default/files/documents/3869008/Dragos-CRASHOVERRIDE-Analyzing-the-Threat-to.pdf; GREENBERG, *supra* note 234, at 52.

240. GREENBERG, *supra* note 234, at 5–34.

241. MORELLI, *supra* note 236, at 20; GREENBERG, *supra* note 234, at 126.

242. DRAGOS, *supra* note 239, at 11; GREENBERG, *supra* note 234, at 128–33, 141–45.

243. DRAGOS, *supra* note 239, at 4.

The effects of a subsequent ransomware attack directed against Ukraine in June 2017 were yet more profound.[244] The NotPetya worm shut down much of the government, as well as power companies, hospitals, banks, and airports, and extended beyond Ukraine's borders to disable companies across the globe.[245] Although disguised as a criminal enterprise, experts concluded that this was an intentional attack targeting Ukraine.[246] Once again, Sandworm was implicated.[247] Some months later, several States formally attributed the attack to Russia.[248]

In October 2018, the British government went further, asserting that the GRU was associated not only with Sandworm, but also with "BlackEnergy Actors" and other named hacking groups.[249] The National Cyber Security Centre assessed with "high confidence" that the GRU was "almost certainly responsible" not only for NotPetya, but also other cyberattacks.[250] Yet, as with many government statements, the pronouncement did not include details of the supporting facts. It remains unclear, for instance, whether all the individuals involved in the cyberattacks worked directly for the GRU, or whether some were NSAs acting in support of the GRU's activities. It is not known whether just one group carried out the operations targeting Ukraine or if a range of individuals were involved, with varying relationships to the State.[251] Thus, notwithstanding States' assertions regarding Russia's responsibility for the cyberattacks, ambiguity remains.

244. Nicholas Weaver, *Thoughts on the NotPetya Ransomware Attack*, LAWFARE (June 28, 2017), https://www.lawfareblog.com/thoughts-notpetya-ransomware-attack.

245. GREENBERG, *supra* note 234, at 180–89.

246. Mark Landler & Scott Shane, *U.S. Condemns Russia for Cyberattack, Showing Split in Stance on Putin*, N.Y. TIMES (Feb. 15, 2018), www.nytimes.com/2018/02/15/us/politics/russia-cyberattack.html.

247. GREENBERG, *supra* note 234, at 207.

248. Pavel Polityuk, *Ukraine Points Finger at Russian Security Services in Recent Cyber Attack*, REUTERS (July 1, 2017), www.reuters.com/article/us-cyber-attack-ukraine-idUSKBN19M39P; Ellen Nakashima, *Russian Military Was Behind "NotPetya" Cyberattack in Ukraine, CIA Concludes*, WASH. POST, (Jan. 12, 2018), www.washingtonpost.com/world/national-security/russian-military-was-behind-notpetya-cyberattack-in-ukraine-cia-concludes/2018/01/12/048d8506-f7ca-11e7-b34a-b85626af34ef_story.html; Phil Muncaster, *Five Eyes Nations United in Blaming Russia for NotPetya*, INFO SEC. (Feb. 19, 2018), www.infosecurity-magazine.com/news/five-eyes-united-blaming-russia/; Landler and Shane, *supra* note 246; GREENBERG, *supra* note 234, at 243–45.

249. U.K. National Cyber Security Centre, Reckless Campaign of Cyber Attacks by Russian Military Intelligence Service Exposed (Oct. 3, 2018), www.ncsc.gov.uk/news/reckless-campaign-cyber-attacks-russian-military-intelligence-service-exposed.

250. *Id.*

251. GREENBERG, *supra* note 234, at 277–79.

2.4.3 The Democratic Republic of the Congo

In contrast with the conflicts in Ukraine and Syria, the decades-long hostilities in the DRC began in the 1990s, triggered in part by the reverberating effects of the genocide in neighboring Rwanda.[252] From the outset, the conflict was characterized by the participation of numerous armed groups, acting with the benefit of significant external State support, and the commission of egregious abuses against the civilian population.[253] This book focuses on just one small aspect of the wider conflict in the DRC, involving the rebel group M23.

M23's full name is the Movement of 23 March, a reference to an agreement formalized on that date in 2009.[254] This provided for senior officers from another armed group, the National Congress for the Defense of the People (CNDP), to be granted the status of a political party and appointed to key positions within the DRC's national army, the FARDC.[255] In early 2012, two ex-CNDP officers, General Ntaganda and Colonel Makenga, founded M23, arguing that the DRC government had failed to live up to the terms of the 2009 deal.[256]

With extensive support from the governments of Rwanda and Uganda, M23 rapidly gained territory in eastern DRC.[257] For the remainder of 2012, violence escalated, and the group ultimately gained control of Goma, the provincial capital

252. *See generally* Emizet F. Kisangani, *Conflict in the Democratic Republic of Congo: A Mosaic of Insurgent Groups*, 20 INT'L J. WORLD PEACE 51 (2003); Phoebe Okawa, *Congo's War: The Legal Dimension of a Protracted Conflict*, 77 BRIT. Y.B. INT'L L. 203 (2006); Christopher Williams, *Explaining the Great War in Africa: How Conflict in the Congo Became a Continental Crisis*, 37 FLETCHER F. OF WORLD AFF. 81 (2013).

253. *See, e.g.*, DEMOCRATIC REPUBLIC OF THE CONGO 1993-2003: REPORT OF THE MAPPING EXERCISE DOCUMENTING THE MOST SERIOUS VIOLATIONS OF HUMAN RIGHTS AND INTERNATIONAL HUMANITARIAN LAW COMMITTED WITHIN THE TERRITORY OF THE DEMOCRATIC REPUBLIC OF THE CONGO BETWEEN MARCH 1993 AND JUNE 2003 (Aug. 2010), https://www.ohchr.org/Documents/Countries/CD/DRC_MAPPING_REPORT_FINAL_EN.pdf.

254. JASON STEARNS, RIFT VALLEY INST., FROM CNDP TO M23: THE EVOLUTION OF AN ARMED MOVEMENT IN EASTERN CONGO 44–45 (2012), https://riftvalley.net/wp-content/uploads/2018/06/RVI-Usalama-Project-1-CNDP-M23.pdf.

255. STEARNS, *supra* note 254, at 41; Cathy Nangini et al., *Visualizing Armed Groups: The Democratic Republic of the Congo's M23 in Focus*, 3 INT'L J. SEC. & DEV. 1, 3 (2014).

256. STEARNS, *supra* note 254, at 44; Nangini et al., *supra* note 255, at 3–4; Add. to the Interim Rep. of the Group of Experts on the Democratic Republic of the Congo Concerning Violations of the Arms Embargo and Sanctions Regime by the Government of Rwanda 26–27, ¶¶ 103–7, U.N. Doc. S/2012/348/Add.1 (June 27, 2012) [hereinafter U.N. June 2012 Rep.].

257. STEARNS, *supra* note 254, at 44–45; Final Rep. of the Group of Experts on the Democratic Republic of the Congo 19–27, U.N. Doc. S/2012/843 (Nov. 15, 2012) [hereinafter U.N. Nov. 2012 Rep.].

bordering Rwanda.[258] The NSA later weakened following a split into factions and was defeated in late 2013.[259]

At that time, most M23 fighters fled to Uganda and Rwanda.[260] The group then reemerged in November 2021, conducting a raid on Congolese army positions.[261] M23's attacks continued and the group again won control over significant territory in eastern DRC,[262] including the key city of Goma in January 2025.[263] As with its previous military campaign, the group acted with support from both Rwanda and Uganda[264] and committed numerous acts in potential violation of international law.[265]

2.4.3.1 Rwandan Support to M23

Rwanda assisted armed groups within eastern DRC from the early days of the conflict.[266] Kigali's principal rationale was its distrust of the Congolese authorities'

258. Pete Jones & David Smith, *Congo Rebels Take Goma with Little Resistance and to Little Cheer*, The Guardian (Nov. 20, 2012), www.theguardian.com/world/2012/nov/20/congo-rebel-m23-take-goma.

259. Midterm Rep. of the Group of Experts on the Democratic Republic of the Congo 8–9, ¶¶ 27–29, U.N. Doc S/2013/433 (19 July 2013) [hereinafter U.N. July 2013 Rep.]; Nicholas Bariyo, *M23 Rebels Call Halt to Congolese Insurgency*, Wall St. J. (Nov. 5, 2013), www.wsj.com/articles/SB10001424052702303936904579179181600437224.

260. *Easing the Turmoil in the Eastern DR Congo and Great Lakes*, Int'l Crisis Group (May 25, 2022), https://www.crisisgroup.org/africa/great-lakes/democratic-republic-congo-uganda-burundi-rwanda/easing-turmoil-eastern-dr-congo.

261. *Id*; Congo Res. Group, The Resurgence of the M23 (Aug. 2024), https://files.ebuteli.org/assets/9152943b-ca84-455d-8c00-a0f3e020cb1a.

262. Midterm Rep. of the Group of Experts on the Democratic Republic of the Congo, 9–13, U.N. Doc. S/2022/967 (Dec. 16, 2022), https://documents.un.org/doc/undoc/gen/n22/757/86/pdf/n2275786.pdf [hereinafter U.N. Dec. 2022 Rep.]; Final Rep. of the Group of Experts on the Democratic Republic of the Congo 12–14, U.N. Doc. S/2023/431 (June 13, 2023), https://documents.un.org/doc/undoc/gen/n23/123/80/pdf/n2312380.pdf [hereinafter U.N. June 2023 Rep.]; Midterm Rep. of the Group of Experts on the Democratic Republic of the Congo 10–11, U.N. Doc. S/2024/969 (Dec. 27, 2024), https://documents.un.org/doc/undoc/gen/n24/373/37/pdf/n2437337.pdf [hereinafter U.N. Dec. 2024 Rep.]; Joseph Winter & Will Ross, *Rwanda-Backed Rebels Seize Key Town in DR Congo*, BBC News (Jan. 5, 2025), https://www.bbc.com/news/articles/c9wlzg7xn0no.

263. Caleb Kabanda & Ruth Maclean, *Rebels Backed by Rwanda Announce Capture of Key City in Eastern Congo*, N.Y. Times (Jan. 27, 2025), https://www.nytimes.com/2025/01/27/world/africa/rebels-capture-goma-congo.html#.

264. U.N. June 2023 Rep., *supra* note 262, at 15–17.

265. *See, e.g.*, Hum. Rts. Watch, M23 Rebels Kill, Rape Civilians (July 22, 2013), https://www.hrw.org/news/2013/07/22/dr-congo-m23-rebels-kill-rape-civilians; Amnesty Int'l, DR Congo: Rwandan-Backed M23 Rebels Perpetrating Summary Killings and Rapes (Feb. 17, 2023), https://www.amnesty.org/en/latest/news/2023/02/dr-congo-rwandan-backed-m23-rebels-perpetrating-summary-killings-and-rapes/.

266. Okawa, *supra* note 252, at 206–7; Williams, *supra* note 252, at 86–87.

ability to adequately secure the border and protect Rwanda from the threat posed by Hutu militias.[267] The State's involvement in the region intensified further with the commencement of the M23 rebellion in 2012.[268] The same year, the U.N. Group of Experts tasked with examining the situation in the DRC produced two detailed and damning reports regarding Rwandan involvement in the conflict.[269] The Group documented systematic State support for M23, finding that "Rwandan officials . . . coordinated the creation of the rebel movement and its major military operations . . . ."[270]

The Rwandan Defense Force (RDF) provided significant aid to M23, including uniforms and military equipment, even prior to the group's establishment.[271] The RDF instructed recruits at M23's four training camps[272] and RDF commanders established a network of recruiters operating for M23 in many villages in western Rwanda, as well as in refugee camps.[273] RDF soldiers then escorted the new recruits to the border and sent them into the DRC.[274]

Rwandan forces additionally provided direct combat support to M23.[275] During M23's first military campaign, the RDF reinforced all major rebel operations and deployed permanently alongside the NSA to assist in controlling territory.[276] Rwandan officers and special forces units, supposedly deployed with the FARDC, also supplied covert support and intelligence to M23 operations.[277] The Group of Experts concluded in 2012 that "Rwandan officials [exercised] overall command and strategic planning for M23," with Ntaganda and Makenga receiving "direct military orders from the Chief of Staff of the [RDF] who in turn acted on instructions from the Minister of Defence . . . ."[278]

When M23 split into factions in early 2013, Rwanda backed the faction headed by Makenga.[279] The group reemerged under Makenga's leadership in late 2021, acting

267. STEARNS, *supra* note 254, at 14–15.

268. *Id.* at 44.

269. U.N. June 2012 Rep., *supra* note 256; U.N. Nov. 2012 Rep., *supra* note 257.

270. U.N. Nov. 2012 Rep., *supra* note 257, at 6, ¶ 4.

271. U.N. June 2012 Rep., *supra* note 256, at 4–7, ¶¶ 8–13.

272. U.N. Nov. 2012 Rep., *supra* note 257, at 11, ¶ 25. *See also* HUM. RTS. WATCH, *supra* note 265.

273. U.N. Nov. 2012 Rep., *supra* note 257, at 138.

274. U.N. June 2012 Rep., *supra* note 256, at 7–8, ¶¶ 16–18; U.N. Nov. 2012 Rep., *supra* note 257, at 11, ¶¶ 22–23.

275. U.N. June 2012 Rep., *supra* note 256, at 14–16, ¶¶ 31–32; HUM. RTS. WATCH, *supra* note 265; U.N. June 2023 Rep., *supra* note 262, at 15–17; U.N. Dec. 2024 Rep., *supra* note 262, at 12, ¶ 49.

276. U.N. Nov. 2012 Rep., *supra* note 257, at 7, ¶ 8.

277. *Id.* at 8, ¶¶ 11–12, 138.

278. U.N. Nov. 2012 Rep., *supra* note 257, at 13, ¶ 32.

279. U.N. July 2013 Rep., *supra* note 259, at 4, ¶ 10, 7, ¶ 21.

once again alongside RDF forces and with substantial Rwandan assistance.[280] For instance, UN reports assert that the RDF "provided troop reinforcements to M23 with the aim of seizing or reinforcing strategic areas"[281] and employed advanced military equipment in support of the rebels' operations.[282]

2.4.3.2 Ugandan Support to M23

In common with its neighbor, Rwanda, Uganda's support to rebels in eastern DRC spanned decades.[283] Through its interventions, Uganda sought to minimize the threat from hostile armed groups operating near its western border and also profited economically from the DRC's vast mineral wealth.[284] Although Uganda's support to M23 was less significant than that provided by Rwanda, the authorities in Kampala played a critical role in facilitating M23's activities.[285]

During M23's first military campaign, Ugandan officials permitted the group to establish a permanent presence in Kampala and provided the group with political advice and technical assistance.[286] In addition, the Ugandan military assisted with M23's recruitment,[287] participated in the planning of its operations, and provided military advice.[288] Furthermore, Ugandan troops intervened directly in the conflict alongside M23 fighters, they provided fire support to the group's operations,[289] and assisted the group logistically.[290]

When the conflict reignited in 2021, Uganda again assisted the group by allowing M23 fighters to freely move across its territory.[291] In addition, the UN experts found that officials from the Ugandan military and military intelligence

280. U.N. Dec. 2022 Rep., *supra* note 262, at 11–12; U.N. June 2023 Rep., *supra* note 262, at 15–17; U.N. Dec. 2024 Rep., *supra* note 262, at 12, ¶ 49; Lucy Fleming & Didier Bikorimana, *Two Armies Accused of Backing DR Congo's Feared Rebels*, BBC News (July 9, 2024), https://www.bbc.com/news/articles/c134kgdpd6do.

281. U.N. June 2023 Rep., *supra* note 262, at 16, ¶ 57.

282. U.N. Dec. 2024 Rep., *supra* note 262, at 12–13.

283. The issue of Uganda's support to armed groups in the DRC came before the ICJ in the *Armed Activities* case. *See* Armed Activities on the Territory of the Congo (Dem. Rep. Congo v. Uganda), Judgment, 2005 I.C.J. Rep. 168 (Dec. 19).

284. *Id.* ¶¶ 35–41, 237–50.

285. U.N. Nov. 2012 Rep., *supra* note 257, at 6, ¶ 4.

286. *Id.* at 17–18, ¶¶ 48–50.

287. *Id.* at 16–17, ¶¶ 44–47.

288. *Id.* at 13, ¶ 35, 18, ¶¶ 51–54.

289. *Id.* at 14, ¶¶ 38–40.

290. *Id.* at 15, ¶¶ 42–43.

291. U.N. Dec. 2022 Rep., *supra* note 262, at 12.

provided more active support for the group, including by hosting meetings attended by M23's leaders.[292]

2.5 CONCLUSION

Any legal analysis regarding the attribution of NSA conduct to a State during armed conflict must focus not only on the law but also on the facts surrounding the relationship between the relevant State and NSA. This chapter sets the scene for the subsequent analysis by highlighting pertinent facts regarding States' relationships with NSAs engaged in conflict. Later chapters will draw upon the three case studies and use examples from these and other conflicts to demonstrate the meaning and scope of application of the six rules of attribution. First, however, it is pertinent to introduce the law of State responsibility more broadly.

292. Fleming & Bikorimana, *supra* note 280; Sonia Rolley, *Uganda Provided Support to M23 Rebels in Congo, UN Report Says*, Reuters (July 8, 2024), https://www.reuters.com/world/africa/uganda-provided-support-m23-rebels-congo-un-report-says-2024-07-08/.

3

Introduction to the Law of State Responsibility

3.1 INTRODUCTION

A State's potential responsibility in connection with non-State actor (NSA) conduct is determined by the law of State responsibility. This body of law regulates when States bear responsibility for conduct that international law deems to be wrongful and the consequences that flow from that responsibility.[1] Its primary purpose, therefore, is to ensure the enforcement of, and compliance with, States' international legal obligations.[2]

The starting point for any contemporary study of the law of State responsibility is the work on the subject by the International Law Commission (ILC) in its Draft Articles on Responsibility of States for Internationally Wrongful Acts (ARSIWA).[3] While the topic formed the subject of significant prior scholarship and codification efforts,[4] the ILC's comprehensive work on the issue constitutes the benchmark for any critical analysis of the field.

1. *See* Christine Chinkin, *A Critique of the Public/Private Dimension*, 10 Eur. J. Int'l L. 387, 395 (1999).

2. Alan Nissel, *The ILC Articles on State Responsibility: Between Self-Help and Solidarity*, 38 N.Y.U. J. Int'l L. & Pol. 355, 355–56, 369 (2006).

3. Draft Articles on Responsibility of States for Internationally Wrongful Acts, with commentaries *in* Int'l Law Comm'n, Rep. on the Work of its Fifty-Third Session, U.N. Doc. A/56/10 (2001), *reprinted in* [2001] 2 Y.B. Int'l L. Comm'n 31, U.N. Doc. A/CN.4/SER.A/2001/Add.1 (Part 2) [hereinafter ARSIWA].

4. For a summary of prior codification efforts, *see* Roberto Ago (Special Rapporteur), First Rep. on State Responsibility—Review of Previous Work on Codification of the Topic of the International Responsibility of States, U.N. Doc. A/CN.4/217 and Add.1 (1969). *See also* Louis B. Sohn & R.R. Baxter, *Convention on the International Responsibility of States for Injuries to Aliens*, 55 Am. J. Int'l L. 548 (1961); Pierre-Marie Dupuy, *Dionisio Anzilotti and the Law of International Responsibility of States*, 3 Eur. J. Int'l L. 139 (1992); Daniel M. Bodansky & John R. Crook, *Symposium on the ILC's State Responsibility Articles: Introduction and Overview*, 96 Am. J. Int'l

Attribution of Non-State Actor Conduct During Armed Conflict. Jennifer Maddocks, Oxford University Press.
 DOI: 10.1093/oso/9780197842652.003.0003

This chapter introduces the law of State responsibility to set the scene for the attribution analysis that follows. It considers the articles' drafting history within the ILC and the place of the six rules of attribution within the broader law of State responsibility reflected in ARSIWA. It also addresses ARSIWA's status in customary international law, concluding that although the articles are often treated as binding law, they are neither a complete nor a perfect representation of the law of State responsibility.

3.2 THE DEVELOPMENT OF THE DRAFT ARTICLES

The ILC's role, in accordance with Article 13 of the UN Charter, is to "initiate studies and make recommendations for the purpose of . . . encouraging the progressive development of international law and its codification."[5] Thus, the ILC does not create international law. Its dual roles are to codify existing customary international law and to advance the law's progressive development. During its first session in 1949, the ILC selected State responsibility as one of the initial topics for codification.[6] ARSIWA and its commentaries were finally complete in 2001, the product of nearly five decades of work involving five different Special Rapporteurs.[7]

The ILC's work on the law of State responsibility was initially slow to progress.[8] Roberto Ago's appointment as Special Rapporteur from 1969, however, gave the project new momentum. Under Ago's leadership, the ILC made the key decision

L. 773, 776–77 (2002); Jan Arno Hessbruegge, *The Historical Development of the Doctrines of Attribution and Due Diligence in International Law*, 36 N.Y.U. J. INT'L L. & POL. 265 (2004); Lucie Laithier, *Private Codification Efforts*, *in* THE LAW OF INTERNATIONAL RESPONSIBILITY 53 (James Crawford et al. eds., 2010); JAMES CRAWFORD, STATE RESPONSIBILITY: THE GENERAL PART 3–35 (2013).

5. U.N. Charter art. 13. *See also* Int'l Law Comm'n, Summary Records and Documents of the First Session including the Rep. of the Comm'n to the General Assembly (1949), *in* [1949] 1 Y.B. INT'L L. COMM'N 9, ¶¶ 2–3, U.N. Doc. A/CN.4/SR.1-38 [hereinafter ILC Y.B. 1949 vol. 1]; Fernando Lusa Bordin, *Reflections of Customary International Law: The Authority of Codification Conventions and ILC Draft Articles in International Law*, 63 INT'L & COMP. L.Q. 535, 555 (2014).

6. ILC Y.B. 1949 vol. 1, *supra* note 5, at 49–50.

7. The five rapporteurs were Garcia Amador, Roberto Ago, Willem Riphagen, Gaetano Arangio-Ruiz, and James Crawford. For a summary of their respective work as Special Rapporteur, *see, e.g.*, James Crawford, *State Responsibility*, *in* MAX PLANCK ENCYCLOPEDIA OF PUBLIC INTERNATIONAL LAW ¶¶ 6–15 (Rüdiger Wolfrum ed., 2015) [hereinafter Crawford, *State Responsibility*]; Bodansky & Crook, *supra* note 4, at 777–79. For a critique of the ILC's work, *see* Philip Allott, *State Responsibility and the Unmaking of International Law*, 29 HARV. INT'L L.J. 1 (1988).

8. *See, e.g.*, Bodansky & Crook, *supra* note 4, at 777; James Crawford, *Revising the Draft Articles on State Responsibility*, 10 EUR. J. INT'L L. 435, 436 (1999) [hereinafter Crawford, *Revising the Draft Articles*].

to no longer address contentious issues surrounding the scope of States' international obligations, as articulated within substantive or "primary" norms. Instead, the ILC focused exclusively on codifying general or "secondary" rules, meaning the principles that govern States' responsibility when they violate a primary norm.[9]

To illustrate, when States are party to an armed conflict, they are bound by primary obligations, including those arising under international humanitarian law (IHL) such as the rule prohibiting indiscriminate attacks.[10] It is the secondary law of State responsibility, however, that determines when an IHL violation engages the State's responsibility, as well as the legal consequences of that breach.[11] These secondary rules apply to all substantive areas of international law, regardless of the primary norm that is violated, the nature of the obligation, or the identity of the State or other actor to which the duty is owed.[12] Their key characteristic is, therefore, their generality of application across all substantive areas of international law.[13]

Although the division between primary and secondary norms is not always clear,[14] the ILC's change in focus allowed its State responsibility project to progress. During his time as Special Rapporteur, Ago completed work on the general conditions relevant to State responsibility, including the draft rules of attribution.[15] Adopted in 1980,[16] the first draft articles form the basis of the law of State responsibility now reflected in ARSIWA.[17] The first reading of the ILC's work, including a full set of draft articles, was then completed in 1996.[18]

9. *See* Roberto Ago (Special Rapporteur), Second Rep. on State Responsibility—The Origin of International Responsibility 178, ¶ 7, U.N. Doc. A/CN.4/233 (1970).

10. Protocol Additional to the Geneva Conventions of 12 August 1949, and Relating to the Protection of Victims of International Armed Conflicts arts. 48, 51, June 8, 1977, 1125 U.N.T.S. 3 [hereinafter AP I]; 1 Customary International Humanitarian Law, rr. 1, 11, 12 (Jean-Marie Henckaerts & Louise Doswald-Beck eds., 2005) [hereinafter Customary IHL].

11. ARSIWA, *supra* note 3, general cmt. ¶ 1.

12. *Id.* ¶ 5. The position is different, however, when special rules of international law govern responsibility. *See id.* art. 55.

13. Bodansky & Crook, *supra* note 4, at 780–81.

14. *See, e.g.*, ARSIWA, *supra* note 3, general cmt. to ch. iv, ¶ 7.

15. Crawford, *supra* note 4, at 36.

16. Text of the Articles of Part 1 of the Draft Adopted by the Commission on First Reading, *in* Int'l Law Comm'n, Rep. of the Comm'n to the General Assembly on the Work of its Thirty-Second Session (1980), *reprinted in* [1980] 2 Y.B. Int'l L. Comm'n 30–34, U.N. Doc. A/CN.4/SER.A.1980/Add.1 (Part 2) [hereinafter ILC Y.B. 1980 vol. II].

17. ARSIWA, *supra* note 3, general cmt. ¶ 2; Hessbruegge, *supra* note 4, at 269.

18. *See* Draft Articles on State Responsibility with Commentaries thereto Adopted by the ILC on First Reading, pt. 1 ch. 2 (1996), *in* Int'l Law Comm'n, Rep. on the Work of its Forty-Eighth Session, U.N. Doc. A/51/10, *reprinted in* [1996] 2 Y.B. Int'l L. Comm'n 59, U.N. Doc. A/CN.4/SER.A/1996/Add.1 (Part 2).

James Crawford was nominated Special Rapporteur in 1997 with a mandate to complete a final draft of the project by 2001. In the second reading from 1998 to 2001, Crawford succeeded in resolving the most controversial outstanding issues including those relating to countermeasures, the settlement of disputes, and the notion of State crimes.[19] The substance of the rules of attribution, however, remained largely unaltered from Ago's time.[20]

3.3 ELEMENTS OF AN INTERNATIONALLY WRONGFUL ACT

The basic principle that underpins ARSIWA is articulated in its foundational rule: "Every internationally wrongful act of a State entails the international responsibility of that State."[21] The term "international responsibility" refers to the new legal relations arising under international law pursuant to a State's internationally wrongful act.[22] These include obligations on the responsible State to cease its harmful conduct and to make reparation for any injury or damage caused.[23]

There are two elements to an internationally wrongful act, as articulated in Article 2 ARSIWA.[24] First, the conduct in question is attributable to the State under international law, and second, the conduct breaches an international obligation of that State.[25]

The requirement for attribution provides the "human link" between the conduct in potential violation of international law and the artificial entity of the State.[26] As States are abstract entities, they "can act only by and through their agents and representatives."[27] Therefore, to determine whether a State's international responsibility is engaged, it is necessary to ascertain whether the conduct in question is characterized as an act of the State.[28] This is decided via various

19. *Id.* at 39–41.

20. Crawford, *Revising the Draft Articles*, *supra* note 8, at 438–39.

21. ARSIWA, *supra* note 3, art. 1.

22. *Id.* art. 1, cmt. ¶ 1. *See also id.* arts. 28–41.

23. *Id.* arts. 30–31, 34–39.

24. *Id.* art. 2.

25. *Id. See also* Brigitte Stern, *The Elements of an Internationally Wrongful Act*, *in* The Law of International Responsibility 193, 200–18 (James Crawford et al. eds., 2010). The International Court of Justice (ICJ) confirmed these two requirements in its jurisprudence. *See, e.g.*, United States Diplomatic and Consular Staff in Tehran (U.S. v. Iran), Judgment, 1980 I.C.J. Rep. 3 ¶ 56 (May 24).

26. Chinkin, *supra* note 1, at 395.

27. Questions relating to Settlers of German Origin in Poland, Advisory Opinion, 1923 P.C.I.J. (ser. B) No. 6 ¶ 34 (Sept. 10).

28. ARSIWA, *supra* note 3, art. 2, cmt. ¶ 5.

rules of attribution. If one of these rules applies, the relevant individual or group is considered "a tool of the State" for the purposes of the law of State responsibility.[29] But if the conduct in question is not attributable to a State, it remains private in character and cannot constitute an internationally wrongful act.[30]

The second element of an internationally wrongful act is the violation of any international obligation that is binding on the responsible State, whether this arises under treaty or customary international law.[31] As the ARSIWA commentary makes clear, "What matters for these purposes is not simply the existence of a rule but its application in the specific case to the responsible State."[32] In the context of an armed conflict, for instance, a State might breach its IHL obligations if members of its armed forces direct their attacks against the civilian population.[33] In such circumstances, the attacks violate the State's obligations under IHL, and those acts are attributable to the State because they were committed by the State's armed forces.[34] Therefore, the two elements of an internationally wrongful act are satisfied and the State's responsibility is engaged.

Omissions can also constitute internationally wrongful acts.[35] Responsibility arises in such circumstances when the State is under a positive duty to act but fails to do so. For example, a State's responsibility might be engaged if its organs fail to exercise due diligence to stop an armed group's activities within its territory from causing harm to other States.[36]

A further requirement of an internationally wrongful act, not expressly stated in Article 2, is the absence of any circumstances precluding wrongfulness.[37] The six circumstances articulated in ARSIWA provide "a shield against an otherwise well-founded claim for the breach of an international obligation."[38] These include,

29. Luigi Condorelli & Claus Kress, *The Rules of Attribution: General Considerations*, *in* The Law of International Responsibility 221 (James Crawford et al. eds., 2010).

30. ARSIWA, *supra* note 3, art. 2. *See also id.* chapeau to pt. 1 ch. II, cmt. ¶ 3.

31. *Id.* art. 2, cmt. ¶ 7; *id.* art. 12, cmt. ¶ 3. *See also* Stern, *supra* note 25, at 210–12.

32. ARSIWA, *supra* note 3, art. 2, cmt. ¶ 13. The duties to which States are bound vary from one State to the next due to their varying treaty commitments. *See* Crawford, *State Responsibility*, *supra* note 7, ¶ 2.

33. AP I, *supra* note 10, arts. 48, 51; Customary IHL, *supra* note 10, r. 1.

34. ARSIWA, *supra* note 3, art. 4.

35. *Id.* art. 2. *See also* Gordon Christenson, *Attributing Acts of Omission to the State*, 12 Mich. J. Int'l L. 312 (1991); Franck Latty, *Actions and Omissions*, *in* The Law of International Responsibility 355, 357–63 (James Crawford et al. eds., 2010).

36. For discussion regarding States' due diligence obligations, *see, e.g.*, Riccardo Pisillo-Mazzeschi, *The Due Diligence Rule and the Nature of the International Responsibility of States*, 35 German Y.B. Int'l L. 9 (1992).

37. Condorelli & Kress, *supra* note 29, at 224; Stern, *supra* note 25, at 217.

38. ARSIWA, *supra* note 3, chapeau to pt. 1 ch. v, cmt. ¶ 1. *See also id.* arts. 20–25.

for example, lawful acts of self-defense in accordance with the UN Charter[39] and acts performed within the limits of another State's consent.[40]

A State's responsibility can be engaged even if no damage or injury results from its breach of an international obligation.[41] For instance, a State might bear responsibility for conducting indiscriminate attacks in an armed conflict even in the absence of evidence that civilians were harmed.[42] The law of State responsibility also includes no requirement for "fault" in terms of a particular level of knowledge or intent on the part of a State, beyond that required by the particular primary norm that is breached.[43] Instead, a State's responsibility might arise irrespective of the subjective intention of the actor responsible for the conduct potentially violating international law.[44] When assessing a State's potential responsibility for conduct in breach of its international obligations, therefore, a key question to answer relates not to the aims of the actor concerned but rather the actor's relationship with the State.

3.4 THE ATTRIBUTION OF CONDUCT TO A STATE

The concept of State responsibility rests upon a strict division between the public and private domains. Conduct is either attributable to a State, in which case it is public in character and can constitute an internationally wrongful act, or it is private and cannot lead to State responsibility.[45] References to attribution thus denote "the operation of attaching a given action or omission to a State."[46] Or as Caron put it, the rules of attribution "delineate the edge of State Responsibility,

39. *Id.* art. 21. *See also* U.N. Charter, art. 51.

40. ARSIWA, *supra* note 3, art. 20. Consent precludes the wrongfulness of the conduct only in relation to the consenting State. *Id.* The other circumstances precluding wrongfulness are countermeasures, *force majeure*, distress, and necessity. *See id.* arts. 22–25.

41. James Crawford (Special Rapporteur), First Rep. on State Responsibility 28–29, U.N. Doc. A/CN.4/490 and Add.1–7 (1998), https://legal.un.org/ilc/documentation/english/a_cn4_490.pdf [hereinafter Crawford's First Rep. on State Responsibility]. Note, however, that certain primary norms are only violated if damage is caused. *See* ARSIWA, *supra* note 3, art. 2, cmt. ¶ 9; CRAWFORD, *supra* note 4, at 54–60.

42. CUSTOMARY IHL, *supra* note 10, r. 1. However, the level of damage or injury will impact the nature and quantum of any reparations owed to the injured state. *See* ARSIWA, *supra* note 3, arts. 31, 34–38.

43. Crawford's First Rep. on State Responsibility, *supra* note 41, at 29–30. *See also* Crawford, *Revising the Draft Articles*, *supra* note 8, at 438.

44. Stern, *supra* note 25, at 209–10.

45. ARSIWA, *supra* note 3, art. 2.

46. *Id.* cmt. ¶ 12.

separating the public realm for which the State may be held responsible from the private realm" for which it is not.[47]

The principle that underlies the attribution standards reflected in ARSIWA is that States should bear responsibility only for conduct that can properly be categorized as their own.[48] Earlier versions of the ILC's work included a specific article to this effect that was later deleted.[49] The intent of that article, however, is firmly embedded in the remaining rules of attribution. Thus, the fact that a particular act takes place within a State's territory or by one of its nationals is not sufficient to attribute the relevant conduct to the State.[50] Instead, a far stronger link must exist between the State and the private conduct at issue.

That link can be established by either the factual relationship between the State and the NSA, or by their legal relationship under the State's domestic law. A primary question when considering the issue of attribution is whether the relevant individual or group is characterized as a State organ under the terms of the State's domestic law. If it is, the person or entity is a de jure State organ and the State bears responsibility for all its conduct when acting in that capacity, as reflected in Article 4 ARSIWA.[51] Examples of actors that fall within this category are soldiers within a State's armed forces, police officers, and government ministers.

Article 4 applies equally to the conduct of de facto State organs.[52] This term refers to those persons or entities that are not labeled as organs of State by domestic law but are nonetheless analogous to State organs as a matter of fact, due to their complete dependence on the State and their lack of autonomy.[53] This status could apply, for instance, to a militia group that acts as a State police force if the required levels of dependence and control are met.

47. David D. Caron, *The Basis of Responsibility: Attribution and Other Trans-Substantive Rules of State Responsibility*, *in* The Iran-United States Claims Tribunal: Its Contribution to the Law of State Responsibility 109, 110 (Richard B. Lillich & Daniel B. Magraw eds., 1998) [hereinafter Caron, *Basis of Responsibility*]. *See also* Chinkin, *supra* note 1, at 387.

48. ARSIWA, *supra* note 3, chapeau to pt. 1 ch. II, cmt. ¶ 2. *See also* Crawford's First Rep. on State Responsibility, *supra* note 41, at 33, ¶ 154; Tal Becker, Terrorism and the State: Rethinking the Rules of State Responsibility 24–42 (2006); Condorelli & Kress, *supra* note 29, at 224; Olivier de Frouville, *Attribution of Conduct to the State: Private Individuals*, *in* The Law of International Responsibility 257, 260–61 (James Crawford et al. eds., 2010).

49. Draft art. 11 provided: "The conduct of a person or a group of persons not acting on behalf of the State shall not be considered as an act of the State under international law." *See* ILC Y.B. 1980 vol. II, *supra* note 16, at 31.

50. Crawford's First Rep. on State Responsibility, *supra* note 41, at 33, ¶ 154. *See also* Caron, *Basis of Responsibility*, *supra* note 47, at 127.

51. ARSIWA, *supra* note 3, art. 4. For detailed analysis of this basis of attribution, *see infra* ch. 4.

52. ARSIWA, *supra* note 3, art. 4, cmt. ¶ 11. For analysis of *de facto* State organ status, *see infra* ch. 4, sec. 4.4.

53. ARSIWA, *supra* note 3, art. 4, cmt. ¶ 11.

Control is also a key factor when considering attribution under the rule reflected in Article 8. This applies when an NSA acts on the State's instructions, or under its direction or control.[54] The broad purpose of the rule is to attribute to a State private conduct that, in fact, is performed on the State's behalf. For instance, if a State tasks an armed group to assault a village and during that operation the NSA targets civilians, the NSA's conduct in violation of IHL may be attributable to the State.[55]

In contrast to Article 8, the presence or absence of State control over an entity's activities is irrelevant to the issue of attribution under the rule reflected in Article 5.[56] This rule applies when States empower NSAs, via their domestic law, to exercise public functions on the States' behalf. For instance, if a State delegates the task of interrogating individuals detained during an armed conflict to a private military and security company (PMSC) and the contractors working for that PMSC mistreat detainees, their conduct in potential violation of IHL is attributable to the State.[57]

The remaining rules of attribution relating to NSA conduct, reflected in Articles 9, 10, and 11 ARSIWA, address certain exceptional scenarios that may arise during armed conflict.[58] These are the subject of Part Three of this book.[59] They differ from the rules expressed in Articles 4, 5, and 8 in that they can attribute private conduct to a State even if there is no factual or legal relationship between the State and the NSA at the time the latter acts in violation of international law. Also, in contrast with the other rules of attribution, they are rarely invoked by States, humanitarian organizations, or international courts and tribunals, and their status in customary international law remains subject to doubt.[60]

The rule expressed in Article 9 applies to conduct that is "called for" in the absence or default of the official authorities.[61] In other words, when NSAs step in to undertake essential governmental tasks due to the absence of State officials, the rule might attribute their conduct to the territorial State.

Article 10 reflects another unusual basis of attribution. This applies when an insurrectional movement that challenges the government's authority succeeds in taking power either in the whole of the State's territory or in part, thereby creating

54. *Id.* art. 8. For detailed analysis of this basis of attribution, *see infra* ch. 6.

55. Customary IHL, *supra* note 10, r. 1. For discussion of attribution based on State instructions, *see infra* ch. 5, sec. 5.3.

56. ARSIWA, *supra* note 3, art. 5. *See also id.* cmt. ¶ 7.

57. Regarding the protections IHL affords to detainees, *see* Customary IHL, *supra* note 10, rr. 87–90. For a detailed analysis of this basis of attribution, *see infra* ch. 5.

58. ARSIWA, *supra* note 3, arts. 9–11.

59. *See infra* chs. 8–10.

60. *Id.*

61. ARSIWA, *supra* note 3, art. 9. For a detailed analysis of this basis of attribution, *see infra* ch. 8.

a new State.[62] The rationale for attribution in these circumstances is the continuity that exists between the personnel and the organizational structures of the insurrectional movement and those of the new government it creates once it succeeds in taking power.[63]

Finally, the rule reflected in Article 11 applies when a State acknowledges and adopts an NSA's prior conduct as its own. For instance, the conduct of an armed group that launches an attack against civilians, in violation of IHL, could be attributed to a State if its officials subsequently acknowledge and adopt the NSA's conduct as the State's own.[64]

More than one of the rules of attribution expressed in ARSIWA could potentially apply to the same factual scenario. The attack against civilians referred to in the context of Article 11, for example, could equally be attributable to the State based on the rule reflected in Article 8, because the NSA acted under the State's control at the relevant time.[65] Thus, the rules are cumulative, but they are also limitative, in the sense that States bear responsibility for an NSA's conduct only if the threshold for attribution relevant to one or more of those rules is satisfied.[66]

If none of the rules of attribution apply, the relevant conduct remains private in character and cannot lead to State responsibility.[67] The rules, therefore, serve a critical purpose: to determine which side of the public–private divide particular conduct should fall. Yet, the strict categorization of acts that results from the process of attribution does not reflect the realities of armed conflict.[68] During hostilities, there is often no clear delineation between public and private conduct.[69] For instance, States frequently provide critical assistance to armed groups without also controlling their behavior, meaning that none of the rules of attribution are likely to apply.

In its lengthy discussions regarding the law of State responsibility, the ILC did not specifically address States' contributions to private wrongs as a potential basis of responsibility. Special Rapporteur Ago raised this in passing but dismissed the possibility of a State's complicity in NSA conduct on the basis that "those persons

62. ARSIWA *supra* note 3, art. 10. For a detailed analysis of this basis of attribution, *see infra* ch. 9.

63. ARSIWA *supra* note 3, art. 10, cmt. ¶ 4.

64. *Id.* art. 11. For a detailed analysis of this basis of attribution, *see infra* ch. 10.

65. ARSIWA, *supra* note 3, art. 8. *See infra* ch. 6, sec. 6.4.

66. Crawford's First Rep. on State Responsibility, *supra* note 41, at 34, ¶ 155.

67. ARSIWA, *supra* note 3, art. 2. *See also* Chinkin, *supra* note 1.

68. This is evident in the three case studies, outlined *supra* in ch. 2, sec. 2.4.

69. *See generally* Chinkin, *supra* note 1; Robert H. Mnookin, *The Public/Private Dichotomy: Political Disagreement and Academic Repudiation*, 130 U. Pa. L. Rev. 1429 (1982); Gurpreet Mahajan, *Reconsidering the Private-Public Distinction*, 12 Critical Rev. of Int'l Soc. & Pol. Phil. 133 (2009); Constantijn van Aartsen, *The End of the Public-Private Divide*, Maastricht U. (Sept. 14, 2016), www.maastrichtuniversity.nl/blog/2016/09/end-public-private-divide.

cannot be regarded as separate subjects of international law."[70] Thus, because NSAs lack international legal personality, ARSIWA does not provide any mechanism by which States can bear responsibility for their contributions to international legal violations perpetrated by NSAs.[71]

This omission raises questions regarding the adequacy of the law of State responsibility, as reflected in ARSIWA, to address the realities of States' involvement in modern warfare. It also invites scrutiny of ARSIWA's status in customary international law.[72] More than twenty years have passed since ARSIWA's adoption, during which time NSAs have played an increasingly important role in conflicts across the globe. Questions arise, therefore, whether ARSIWA reflected customary international law at the time of the articles' adoption in 2001, and also whether the law of State responsibility has continued to evolve since that date.

3.5 ARSIWA'S STATUS IN CUSTOMARY INTERNATIONAL LAW

After the ILC finalized and adopted ARSIWA in 2001, the UN General Assembly took note of the draft articles and commended them to governments.[73] The Resolution postponed future consideration of the articles, leaving open the question whether these should be addressed in a subsequent convention.[74] States that commented on this possibility largely expressed reservations, arguing that taking steps towards adopting a treaty would risk undermining the broad consensus that had been reached regarding ARSIWA's content and scope.[75]

70. Int'l Law Comm'n, Documents of the Twenty-Seventh Session Including the Rep. of the Comm'n to the General Assembly (draft art. 11, cmt. ¶ 11) (1975), *in* [1975] 2 Y.B. INT'L L. COMM'N 73, U.N. Doc. A/CN.4/SER.A/1975/Add.1 73.

71. For further discussion regarding NSAs' status under international law, *see, e.g.*, Jan Klabbers, *(I Can't Get No) Recognition: Subjects Doctrine and the Emergence of Non-State Actors, in* NORDIC COSMOPOLITANISM: ESSAYS IN INTERNATIONAL LAW FOR MARTTI KOSKENNIEMI 365 (Jarna Petman & Jan Klabbers eds., 2003); Andrea Bianchi, *The Fight for Inclusion: Non-State Actors and International Law, in* FROM BILATERALISM TO COMMUNITY INTEREST: ESSAYS IN HONOUR OF BRUNO SIMMA 39 (Ulrich Fastenrath et al. eds., 2011).

72. James Crawford, *The ILC's Articles on Responsibility of States for Internationally Wrongful Acts: A Retrospect*, 96 AM. J. INT'L L. 874, 888 (2002) [hereinafter Crawford, *A Retrospect*].

73. G.A. Res. 56/83, U.N. Doc. A/RES/56/83 (Dec. 12, 2001).

74. *Id.* ¶ 4.

75. *See, e.g.*, Responsibility of States for Internationally Wrongful Acts: Comments and Information Received from Governments 6, ¶ 7 (comments of the United Kingdom), U.N. Doc. A/62/63 (Mar. 9, 2007) [hereinafter Government Comments]; U.S. Dep't of State, Draft Articles on State Responsibility: Comments of the Government of the United States of America 1–2 (Mar. 1, 2001), https://2009-2017.state.gov/documents/organization/28993.pdf. For an outline of opposing views on the issue see, for example, David D. Caron, *The ILC Articles on State Responsibility: The Paradoxical Relationship Between Form and Authority*, 96 AM. J. INT'L L.

Notwithstanding ARSIWA's continued status as draft articles, which are not binding on States,[76] the ILC's work is considered "the most authoritative statement available on questions of State responsibility."[77] As the United Kingdom put it:

> States generally have accepted the draft articles in their current form. At present, the draft articles reflect an authoritative statement of international law and have been referred to by international courts and tribunals, writers and, more recently, domestic courts . . . . [S]ince 2001 the draft articles have gained widespread recognition and approval. Many States, including the United Kingdom, regularly turn to the draft articles and the commentaries as guidance on issues of State responsibility that arise in day-to-day practice.[78]

ARSIWA is thus widely accepted and is generally considered to have codified well-established rules of customary international law.[79] During the period from 1973 to 2022, international courts, tribunals, and other bodies referred to the articles and their commentaries (both in their form prior to and following their adoption in 2001) a total of 453 times.[80] However, a review of the relevant practice reveals that these frequent citations are not always accompanied by a quality of reasoning or approval in State practice.[81] As Caron observed, "when there is a 'legal vacuum' of authority relevant to an issue, courts and arbitral panels will turn to whatever is available. In that situation, a set of articles adopted by the ILC will be quite influential, perhaps even more influential than a treaty."[82]

857, 862–66 (2002) [hereinafter Caron, *The ILC Articles*]; James Crawford & Simon Olleson, *The Continuing Debate on a U.N. Convention on State Responsibility*, 54 INT'L & COMP. L. Q. 959 (2005); CRAWFORD, *supra* note 4, at 90-92; Federica L. Paddeu, *To Convene or Not to Convene? The Future Status of the Articles on State Responsibility: Recent Developments*, 21 MAX PLANCK Y.B. U.N. L. 83 (2018); Arman Sarvarian, *The Ossified Debate on a U.N. Convention on State Responsibility*, 70 INT'L & COMP. L.Q. 769 (2021).

76. ARSIWA represents a "subsidiary means for the determination of rules of law." *See* Statute of the International Court of Justice art. 38(1), June 26, 1945, 59 Stat. 1055, 33 U.N.T.S. 993. *See also* Caron, *The ILC Articles, supra* note 75, at 867–68; Bordin, *supra* note 5, at 537.

77. Government Comments, *supra* note 75, at 3, ¶ 2 (comments of Norway on behalf of the Nordic countries).

78. *Id.* at 6, ¶ 5 (comments of the United Kingdom).

79. *Id.* at 3, ¶ 2 (comments of Norway on behalf of the Nordic countries); *id.* at 17, ¶ 40 (comments of Germany). *See also* CRAWFORD, *supra* note 4, at 43; TALLINN MANUAL 2.0 ON THE INTERNATIONAL LAW APPLICABLE TO CYBER OPERATIONS at 79 (Michael N. Schmitt ed., 2017).

80. Materials on the Responsibility of States for Internationally Wrongful Acts viii, U.N. Doc. ST/LEG/SER B/25/Rev.1 (2023).

81. Martins Paparinskis, *The Once and Future Law of State Responsibility*, 114 AM. J. INT'L L. 618, 624–25 (2020).

82. Caron, *The ILC Articles, supra* note 75, at 866. *See also* Allott, *supra* note 7, at 11; Robert Rosenstock, *The ILC and State Responsibility*, 96 AM. J. INT'L L. 792, 792 (2002); Bordin, *supra*

When considering the status of the work, it is important to recall that ARSIWA's adoption followed a period of "intense negotiation and compromise" with the result that "the text of the draft articles in its entirety is not wholly satisfactory to any State."[83] The ILC necessarily made legal and policy judgments when finalizing the work, particularly in light of the numerous pressures to which it was subject.[84] As such, ARSIWA is not a complete or perfect representation of the law of State responsibility; it is the best depiction of the law that the ILC was able to agree upon at that time.[85]

There is, moreover, a danger that the process of codification undertaken by the ILC entailed a process of simplification and compromise that fails to reflect the true complexity of this body of law.[86] The alacrity with which international courts and tribunals have sought to "apply" the articles illustrates ARSIWA's appeal but also, perhaps, masks the more nuanced interpretations of the law that might have been made in the articles' absence.

Each of ARSIWA's provisions, therefore, should be treated not as binding law but rather as evidence of the particular international rule upon which it is founded.[87] Given the ILC's dual mandates of codification and progressive development, there are inevitably elements of each within the text.[88] While many provisions are uncontroversial and clearly reflective of customary international law,[89] others remain in a state of development.[90] The status of any one article therefore cannot be assumed and in some cases, it may be far from straightforward to ascertain whether a provision is customary in nature or representative of *lex ferenda*.[91]

note 5; Georgio Gaja, *Interpreting Articles Adopted by the International Law Commission*, 85 BRIT. Y.B. INT'L L. 10, 11 (2015).

83. Government Comments, *supra* note 75, at 6, ¶ 4 (comments of the United Kingdom). *See also* U.S. Dep't of State, *supra* note 75.

84. *See* Crawford, *A Retrospect*, *supra* note 72, at 888. *See also* CRAWFORD, *supra* note 4, at 3–44.

85. For a summary of some of the issues raised by States and legal scholars, *see* CRAWFORD, *supra* note 4, at 85–90.

86. Nissel, *supra* note 2, at 358 n. 13.

87. Bodansky & Crook, *supra* note 4, at 775; Bordin, *supra* note 5, at 560.

88. ARSIWA, *supra* note 3, general cmt. ¶ 1. *See also* U.S. Dep't of State, *supra* note 75.

89. Art. 4 ARSIWA falls into this category. *See* Application of the Convention on the Prevention and Punishment of the Crime of Genocide (Bosn. & Herz. v. Serb. & Montenegro), Judgment, 2007 I.C.J. Rep. 43, ¶ 385 (Feb. 26).

90. The legal regime relating to serious breaches of peremptory norms falls into this category. *See* ARSIWA, *supra* note 3, art. 41, cmt. ¶ 14. *See also* U.S. Dep't of State, *supra* note 75, at 7–8.

91. Gilbert Guillaume, *Overview of Part One of the Articles on State Responsibility*, *in* THE LAW OF INTERNATIONAL RESPONSIBILITY 187, 188 (James Crawford et al. eds., 2010).

A further factor impacting upon ARSIWA's status is the continued development of the law of State responsibility.[92] This is a particularly pertinent consideration in the context of armed conflict given the articles' State-centric focus, founded on the international legal order's recognition of States as the primary bearers of rights and obligations.[93] Both prior to and since ARSIWA's adoption, the world has witnessed an increased complexity of international actors, including a multiplicity of powerful NSAs.[94] This reality is not adequately addressed within ARSIWA.[95] But the possibility cannot be excluded that the customary law of State responsibility that underlies the ILC's work is already adapting in response to this change.[96]

3.6 CONCLUSION

The ILC's work on the law of State responsibility is extremely thorough and comprehensive. The reliance that States and judicial bodies have placed on ARSIWA since the articles' adoption is largely well-founded and bolsters their status as an authoritative restatement of customary international law. However, as the analysis in this chapter demonstrates, care must be taken when considering the interpretation and status of each individual article. There are ambiguities inherent in each of the rules of attribution reflected in ARSIWA, as will become apparent in the chapters that follow.

92. Caron, *The ILC Articles*, *supra* note 75, at 859. The ILC's work on the responsibility of international organizations reflects the continuing development of the law in this area. *See* Draft Articles on the Responsibility of International Organizations, with commentaries, *in* Int'l Law Comm'n, Rep. of the ILC on its Sixty-Third Session (2011), *reprinted in* [2011] 2 Y.B. Int'l L. Comm'n, U.N Doc A/CN.4/SER.A/2011/Add.1 (Part 2).

93. Bianchi, *supra* note 71, at 39–40.

94. Caron, *The ILC Articles*, *supra* note 75, at 859; Krieg & Rickli, *supra* note 15, at 120.

95. Edith Brown Weiss, *Invoking State Responsibility in the Twenty-First Century*, 96 Am. J. Int'l L. 798, 799 (2002); Bodansky & Crook, *supra* note 4, at 790.

96. The articles' endorsement by the General Assembly as opposed to their adoption as a convention purposively allows for flexibility in the law's further development. *See* Crawford, *supra* note 4, at 90–91.

PART THREE

State Organs and Agents

4

Organs of State

4.1 INTRODUCTION

As a general rule, States bear responsibility only for their own conduct, namely, the acts of those persons or entities that qualify as organs of government, or otherwise act as agents of the State.[1] The first principle of attribution formulated by the International Law Commission (ILC) in the Draft Articles on Responsibility of States for Internationally Wrongful Acts (ARSIWA) accordingly relates to the conduct of State organs.[2] Although this basis of attribution appears to be of no relevance to the activities of private individuals or groups, in certain circumstances, the rule is broad enough to encompass the conduct of entities that appear, at first glance, to be non-State actors (NSA).

Article 4 ARSIWA provides:

> 1. The conduct of any State organ shall be considered an act of that State under international law, whether the organ exercises legislative, executive, judicial or any other functions, whatever position it holds in the organization of the State, and whatever its character as an organ of the central Government or of a territorial unit of the State.
> 2. An organ includes any person or entity which has that status in accordance with the internal law of the State.[3]

1. Draft Articles on Responsibility of States for Internationally Wrongful Acts, with commentaries, general cmt. to ch. II, ¶ 2, *in* Int'l Law Comm'n, Rep. on the Work of its Fifty-Third Session, U.N. Doc. A/56/10 (2001), *reprinted in* [2001] 2 Y.B. Int'l L. Comm'n 31, 38, U.N. Doc. A/CN.4/SER.A/2001/Add.1 (Part 2) [hereinafter ARSIWA].

2. *Id.* art. 4.

3. *Id.*

Attribution of Non-State Actor Conduct During Armed Conflict. Jennifer Maddocks, Oxford University Press.
 DOI: 10.1093/oso/9780197842652.003.0004

This rule has been described by the International Court of Justice (ICJ) as "one of the cornerstones of the law of State responsibility."[4] Given its general acceptance by States, as well as by international courts and tribunals,[5] there is little doubt that the ICJ was correct to describe the rule as "one of customary international law."[6]

Those persons and entities that qualify as organs of State are decided primarily by the State itself. Nations are free, by virtue of their sovereignty, to organize themselves as they wish and to determine those organs that make up the machinery of State.[7] The status of an entity under the State's own internal legal regime is, therefore, the most important factor when determining whether the rule reflected in Article 4 applies to attribute the entity's conduct to the State.[8] But that is not the end of the matter. If it were, a State could avoid responsibility simply by choosing not to designate an entity that forms part of the State's structure as one of its organs.[9]

There are thus two forms of State organ within the meaning of the rule reflected in Article 4: de jure organs, which are characterized as organs of the State under the State's domestic law, and de facto organs, which have that status because of their exceptional relationship with the State. This chapter examines each category of State organ in turn before exploring the circumstances in which a State organ is deemed to be acting in its official capacity, meaning that the rule of attribution applies. First, however, the chapter considers the rule of attribution in general terms, briefly outlining its drafting history and the features of the rule that apply to both categories of State organ.

4. Application of the Convention on the Prevention and Punishment of the Crime of Genocide (Bosn. & Herz. v. Serb. & Montenegro), Judgment, 2007 I.C.J. Rep. 43, ¶ 385 (Feb. 26) [hereinafter *Bosnian Genocide*]. *See also* ARSIWA, *supra* note 1, art. 4, cmt. ¶ 13.

5. ARSIWA, *supra* note 1, art. 4, cmt. ¶¶ 3–4.

6. *Bosnian Genocide, supra* note 4, ¶ 385. *See also* Difference Relating to Immunity from Legal Process of a Special Rapporteur of the Commission on Human Rights, Advisory Opinion, 1999 I.C.J. Rep. 62, ¶ 62 (Apr. 29); Armed Activities on the Territory of the Congo (Dem. Rep. Congo v. Uganda), Judgment, 2005 I.C.J. Rep. 168, ¶ 213 (Dec. 19) [hereinafter *Armed Activities*]; 1 CUSTOMARY INTERNATIONAL HUMANITARIAN LAW r. 149 (Jean-Marie Henckaerts & Louise Doswald-Beck eds., 2005) [hereinafter CUSTOMARY IHL].

7. Military and Paramilitary Activities in and against Nicaragua (Nicar. v. U.S.), Judgment, 1986 I.C.J. Rep. 14, ¶ 205 (June 27) [hereinafter *Nicaragua*]. *See also* Djamchid Momtaz, *Attribution of Conduct to the State: State Organs and Entities Empowered to Exercise Elements of Governmental Authority*, *in* THE LAW OF INTERNATIONAL RESPONSIBILITY 237, 239 (James Crawford et al. eds., 2010).

8. ARSIWA, *supra* note 1, art. 4. *See also* David D. Caron, *The Basis of Responsibility: Attribution and Other Trans-Substantive Rules of State Responsibility*, *in* THE IRAN-UNITED STATES CLAIMS TRIBUNAL: ITS CONTRIBUTION TO THE LAW OF STATE RESPONSIBILITY 109, 130 (Richard B. Lillich & Daniel B. Magraw eds., 1998).

9. ARSIWA, *supra* note 1, art. 4, cmt. ¶ 11.

4.2 ATTRIBUTION PURSUANT TO ARTICLE 4

4.2.1 Drafting History

The principle that a State is responsible for the conduct of its own organs is uncontroversial and well established.[10] For example, in the *Salvador Commercial Company* case in 1902, the arbitrators noted that "a State is responsible for the acts of its rulers, whether they belong to the legislative, executive, or judicial department of the Government, so far as the acts are done in their official capacity."[11] This principle is reflected in the preparatory work for the 1930 Hague Conference for the Codification of International Law,[12] as well as the 1929 and 1961 Harvard Draft Conventions on State responsibility.[13]

Special Rapporteur Ago conducted an extensive review of the law underlying the principle[14] and suggested three draft articles to encompass the various elements of the rule now expressed in Article 4.[15] These were replicated in similar form in the draft articles adopted by the Commission on first reading.[16] Meanwhile, a fourth draft article made clear that the conduct of a State organ, acting in that capacity, was considered an act of State even if that organ exceeded its competence

10. James Crawford, State Responsibility: The General Part 116–17 (2013).

11. Claim of the Salvador Commercial Company, 15 R.I.A.A. 467, 477 (U.S.-El Salvador Arb. Trib., 1902), https://legal.un.org/riaa/cases/vol_XV/467-479.pdf.

12. Bases of Discussion Drawn up in 1929 by the Preparatory Committee of the Conference for the Codification of International Law, Basis of Discussion No. 7, 12 (The Hague, 1930), *reprinted in* Int'l Law Comm'n, Documents of the Eighth Session Including the Rep. of the Comm'n to the General Assembly (1956), *in* [1956] 2 Y.B. Int'l L. Comm'n 223, U.N. Doc, A/CN.4/SER.A/1956/Add.1.

13. Harvard Draft Convention on Responsibility of States for Damage Done in Their Territory to the Person or Property of Foreigners, arts. 3, 7 (1929), *reprinted in* Int'l Law Comm'n, Documents of the Eighth Session Including the Rep. of the Comm'n to the General Assembly (1956) *in* [1956] 2 Y.B. Int'l L. Comm'n 229, U.N. Doc, A/CN.4/SER.A/1956/Add.1; Harvard Draft Convention on the International Responsibility of States for Injuries to Aliens, arts. 15–17 (1961), *reprinted in* Int'l Law Comm'n, Documents of the Twenty-First Session Including the Rep. of the Comm'n to the General Assembly (1969), *in* [1969] 2 Y.B. Int'l L. Comm'n 142, 145–46, U.N. Doc A/CN.4/SER.A/1969/Add.1.

14. Roberto Ago (Special Rapporteur), Third Rep. on State Responsibility—the Internationally Wrongful Act of the State, Source of International Responsibility, U.N. Doc A/CN.4/246 and Add.1–3 (1971), *in* [1971] 2 Y.B. Int'l L. Comm'n 199, 233–62, U.N. Doc. A/CN.4/SER.A/1971/Add.1 (Part 1) [hereinafter Ago's Third Rep. on State Responsibility].

15. *Id.* at 243 (draft art. 5), 253 (draft art. 6), 262 (draft art. 7).

16. Text of the Articles of Part 1 of the Draft Adopted by the Commission on First Reading, *in* Int'l Law Comm'n, Rep. of the Comm'n to the General Assembly on the Work of its Thirty-Second Session (1980), *in* [1980] 2 Y.B. Int'l L. Comm'n 30, 31 (draft arts. 5, 6, 7), U.N. Doc. A/CN.4/SER.A/1980/Add.1 (Part 2).

or contravened instructions.[17] This latter provision is now enshrined in Article 7 ARSIWA and is the focus of section 4.5 of this chapter.[18]

After Crawford was appointed Special Rapporteur, he reviewed the draft articles relating to the conduct of State organs and concluded that they should be combined into one single article.[19] He additionally noted that there was a problem with the proposed reliance on a State's internal laws to determine whether a person or entity qualified as an organ of State.[20] Earlier versions of Article 4 provided only for the conduct of de jure State organs to be attributable to the State.[21] Crawford observed, however, that "internal law was not always sufficient for determining such status."[22] The fact that a State's police are not characterized as a State organ by domestic law, for example, "cannot mean that for international law purposes they are not organs of the State."[23]

The version of Article 4 that was ultimately adopted provides in its second paragraph that "An organ *includes* any person or entity which has that status in accordance with the internal law of the State."[24] This indicates that domestic law is the most important, but not the only factor to be taken into account. The ARSIWA commentary explains that "a State cannot avoid responsibility for the conduct of a body which does in truth act as one of its organs merely by denying it that status under its own law."[25] This wording leads to the distinct categories of de jure and de facto State organs, which are discussed in turn in Sections 4.3 and 4.4.

4.2.2 General Features of the Attribution Standard

Although the methods of establishing whether an entity qualifies as a de jure or a de facto State organ are very different,[26] the two categories of State organ share

17. *Id.* (draft art. 10).

18. ARSIWA, *supra* note 1, art. 7. For further discussion regarding Article 7, *see infra* sec. 4.5.

19. James Crawford (Special Rapporteur), First Rep. on State Responsibility 34–39, U.N. Doc. A/CN.4/490 and Add.1–7 (1998) [hereinafter Crawford's First Rep. on State Responsibility].

20. *Id.* at 34, ¶ 163.

21. Ago's Third Rep. on State Responsibility, *supra* note 14, at 243 (draft art. 5). *See also* Crawford's First Rep. on State Responsibility, *supra* note 19, at 34.

22. Int'l Law Comm'n, Summary Records of the Meetings of the Fiftieth Session (1998), *in* [1998] 1 Y.B. Int'l L. Comm'n 229, ¶ 3, U.N. Doc. A/CN.4/SER.A/1998 [hereinafter ILC Y.B. 1998 vol. I].

23. ARSIWA, *supra* note 1, art. 4, cmt. ¶ 11. Certain States raised the same concern in their comments on the draft articles. *See* Int'l Law Comm'n, Comments and Observations Received by Governments 105–6, U.N. Doc A/CN.4/488 and Add.1–3 (1998).

24. ARSIWA, *supra* note 1, art. 4 (emphasis added).

25. *Id.*, art. 4, cmt. ¶ 11.

26. *See infra* secs. 4.3, 4.4.

identical qualities. First, the reference to a State organ is intended in "the most general sense," irrespective of an organ's function, location, or position in the State hierarchy.[27] It includes local government entities as well as all the individual and collective entities that make up the organization of the State and act on its behalf.[28] During armed conflict, therefore, any activity undertaken by the military, intelligence, security, or other State agencies engages the State's international responsibility if it violates an international legal obligation that is binding on the State.[29]

For the purposes of the rule reflected in Article 4, there is no distinction between the activities of the various government entities, such as police officers, military personnel, or members of the judiciary.[30] It does not matter, for instance, that under a State's Constitution the judiciary is independent of the other branches of government; a judge could still violate the State's international obligations, for example, by a denial of justice that breaches the State's duties under international human rights law.[31] The level at which the organ operates within the State's structure is also irrelevant. Thus, in the case of a State's military, the actions of the lowest-ranking private soldier bind the State in the same manner as those of its most senior generals.[32]

Importantly, the rule reflected in Article 4 attributes all the organ's conduct performed in an official capacity to the State.[33] This means that the rule has wider effects than the other attribution standards reflected in ARSIWA.[34] Once an entity is designated as a de jure or de facto organ of State, all its official conduct is attributable to the State, regardless of whether this was performed under the State's authority or in accordance with its instructions.[35] Thus, the rule reflected in Article 4 attributes State organs' conduct to the State irrespective of the State's exercise of control over their behavior.[36] It is only a State organ's private conduct, performed in a personal capacity, that is not so attributable. This is a key feature of the rule

27. ARSIWA, *supra* note 1, art. 4, cmt. ¶ 6.

28. *Id.* cmt. ¶ 1.

29. *Id.* art. 2.

30. Momtaz, *supra* note 7, at 239.

31. Ago's Third Rep. on State Responsibility, *supra* note 14, at 245, ¶ 142; Crawford, *supra* note 10, at 121–23; Robert Kolb, The International Law of State Responsibility 77 (2018).

32. Ago's Third Rep. on State Responsibility, *supra* note 14, at 243–44, ¶ 138; *Armed Activities*, *supra* note 6, ¶ 213.

33. For discussion regarding the distinction between official and private conduct, *see infra* sec. 4.5.1.

34. For discussion regarding the respective effects of attribution of the rules reflected in Articles 4, 5, and 8 ARSIWA, *see* infra ch. 7, sec. 7.2.1.

35. ARSIWA, *supra* note 1, art. 7. For discussion of *ultra vires* conduct, *see infra* sec. 4.5.

36. ARSIWA, *supra* note 1, art. 4, cmt. ¶ 13. Note that a State's exercise of control is, nevertheless, critical to a person or entity's qualification as a *de facto* State organ. *See infra* sec. 4.4.

reflected in Article 4 that explains, to some extent, the strict test for de facto State organ status examined in Section 4.4.

4.3 DE JURE STATE ORGANS

When a State's internal law characterizes an entity as an organ of State, the State bears responsibility for that entity's conduct from the date of its incorporation into the State's structure.[37] Thus, the Islamic Revolutionary Guard Corps (IRGC), established in the early days of the Iranian Revolution, was officially recognized as an organ of the Iranian State by a decree issued by the Supreme Leader, Ayatollah Khomeini, in May 1979.[38] The IRGC's conduct from this date is therefore attributable to Iran,[39] including any acts in breach of Iran's international legal obligations committed during its operations in Syria and elsewhere.[40]

Russia similarly bears responsibility for the conduct of its de jure State organs, including the actions of the State's military intelligence agency, the GRU. Accordingly, the harmful cyber operations mounted by certain GRU officers against Ukraine are attributable to Russia[41] and potentially constitute internationally wrongful

37. The only exception to this principle is when the State organ is not acting in its public capacity at the relevant time. *See infra* sec. 4.5.

38. *See* Kenneth P. Yeager v. Islamic Republic of Iran, Award No. 324-10199-1, ¶ 40 (Iran-U.S. Claims Trib., 1987) [hereinafter *Yeager*]. *See also* Kenneth Katzman, The Warriors of Islam: Iran's Revolutionary Guard 51 (1993). The IRGC's role in the Iranian State was subsequently enshrined in the Iranian constitution. *See* Const. of Islamic Republic of Iran, art. 150 (1979), www.constituteproject.org/constitution/Iran_1989.pdf?lang=en (last visited July 2, 2025).

39. *See* William L. Pereira Associates v. Islamic Republic of Iran, Award No. 116-1-3, ¶ 130 (Iran-U.S. Claims Trib., 1984). *See also* Caron, *supra* note 8, at 139–40.

40. For discussion of the IRGC's role in the Syrian conflict, *see, e.g.*, Amir Toumaj, *Array of Pro-Syrian Government Forces Advances in Aleppo*, FDD's Long War J. (Dec. 9, 2016), www.longwarjournal.org/archives/2016/12/array-of-pro-syrian-government-forces-advance-in-aleppo.php; Paul Bucala & Frederick W. Kagan, Critical Threats, Iran's Evolving Way of War: How the IRGC Fights in Syria 12–13 (Mar. 2016), www.criticalthreats.org/wp-content/uploads/2016/07/imce-imagesIrans_Evolving_Way_of_War_IRGC_in_Syria_FINAL-1.pdf. Regarding potential international law violations involving the IRGC in Syria and elsewhere, *see, e.g.*, Amnesty International, Report 2017/18: The State of the World's Human Rights 351 (2018), www.amnesty.org.uk/files/2018-02/annualreport2017.pdf; Andrew Hanna & Garrett Nada, *Timeline: Iran's Assassinations and Plots*, U.S. Inst. for Peace (Sept. 16, 2020), https://iranprimer.usip.org/blog/2020/sep/16/timeline-iran-assassinations-and-plot.

41. *See supra* ch. 2, sec. 2.4.2.3. *See also* U.K. National Cyber Security Centre, Reckless Campaign of Cyber Attacks by Russian Military Intelligence Service Exposed (Oct. 3, 2018), www.ncsc.gov.uk/news/reckless-campaign-cyber-attacks-russian-military-intelligence-service-exposed; Samantha Fry & Samuel Rebo, *Summary: Justice Department Charges Six Russian GRU Officers,*

acts.[42] The same is true in respect of the downing of Malaysia Airlines Flight MH17 in July 2014 due to the direct involvement of Russian officials in the incident.[43]

4.3.1 Qualification as a de Jure State Organ

Although an entity's status as a de jure State organ is normally clear from a review of the State's internal law, it is, on occasion, the subject of dispute. For instance, in 2006, Israel alleged before the UN Security Council that Hezbollah's actions in attacking Israeli territory and kidnapping two Israeli soldiers were attributable to Lebanon due to the group's participation in the Lebanese government.[44] However, as Ruys observes, the fact that Hezbollah at the time held a small number of seats in the Lebanese Parliament and two minister posts in the Cabinet was insufficient to conclude that all Hezbollah militants were organs of the State.[45] That might have been the case had Hezbollah been leading the government, in which case its military wing might have become part of the government's security apparatus,[46] but with such a small representation in government and failing attribution on other grounds, the fighters remained NSAs.

The ICJ examined the question of when entities qualify as de jure State organs in the context of the genocide committed in Srebrenica.[47] While the applicant in the case, Bosnia and Herzegovina, argued that the perpetrators of the genocide were de jure organs of the Federal Republic of Yugoslavia (FRY), the respondent

LAWFARE (Oct. 20, 2020), www.lawfareblog.com/summary-justice-department-charges-six-russian-gru-officers.

42. *See* Michael N. Schmitt, *"Below the Threshold" Cyber Operations: The Countermeasures Response Option and International Law*, 54 VA. J. INT'L L. 697, 707–08 (2014); Michael Schmitt & Jeffrey Biller, *The NotPetya Cyber Operation as a Case Study of International Law*, EJIL:TALK! (July 11, 2017), www.ejiltalk.org/the-notpetya-cyber-operation-as-a-case-study-of-international-law/#more-15401.

43. Marko Milanović, *The Netherlands and Australia Attribute the Downing of MH17 to Russia*, EJIL:TALK! (May 25, 2018), www.ejiltalk.org/the-netherlands-and-australia-attribute-the-downing-of-mh17-to-russia/ [hereinafter Milanović, *Downing of MH17*]; Sophie Tanno, *Dutch Court Finds Two Russians, One Ukrainian Separatist Guilty over Downing of Flight MH17*, CNN (Nov. 17, 2022), https://www.cnn.com/2022/11/17/europe/mh17-trial-verdict-intl/index.html.

44. Permanent Representative of Israel to the United Nations, Identical Letters Dated 12 July 2006 from the Permanent Representative of Israel to the United Nations Secretary-General and the President of the Security Council, U.N. Doc. S/2006/515 (July 12, 2006). *See also* Ehud Olmert, Israeli Prime Minister, Press Conference: Lebanon Is Responsible and Will Bear the Consequences (July 12, 2006), https://www.gov.il/en/pages/pm-olmert-lebanon-is-responsible-and-will-bear-the-consequences-12-jul-2006.

45. Tom Ruys, *Crossing the Thin Blue Line: An Inquiry into Israel's Recourse to Self-Defense Against Hezbollah*, 43 STAN. J. INT'L L. 265, 276–77 (2007).

46. *Id.*

47. *Bosnian Genocide*, *supra* note 4, ¶ 386.

contested this characterization.[48] To assess the ICJ's judgment in the case, it is helpful to outline the facts.

The genocide in Srebrenica occurred following the breakup of the former Yugoslavia and the emergence of several new sovereign States. Within Bosnia and Herzegovina, the Republika Srpska had de facto control over significant territory, as well as the loyalty of many Bosnian Serbs.[49] The Republika Srpska never attained international recognition as a sovereign State, but it did have its own army, the VRS, from May 1992.[50] In the same month, the Yugoslav army officially withdrew from Bosnia and Herzegovina. Most of its units, however, remained in place, transferring into the VRS together with their weapons and equipment.[51] Moreover, VRS officers continued to be administered from Belgrade, and their salaries and pensions were paid by the FRY.[52]

Bosnia and Herzegovina argued before the ICJ that in light of these factors, VRS officers remained de jure organs of the FRY.[53] The ICJ disagreed, finding no evidence that such individuals were officers of the FRY's army under the terms of that State's internal law.[54] Further, the ICJ emphasized that the payment of salaries and other benefits to some officers of the VRS did not automatically make them organs of the FRY.[55]

The ICJ's conclusion is consistent with Article 4 ARSIWA and the commentary thereto.[56] For an entity to constitute a de jure organ of State, nothing less than that status under the State's internal law will suffice.[57] Attribution on this basis is, nevertheless, relevant when considering irregular actors' conduct during armed conflict. On occasion, States choose to formally incorporate irregular or local forces into the structures of the State. Despite their formal status, such groups might

48. *Id.* ¶ 387.

49. *Id.* ¶ 235. *See also* André J. J. de Hoogh, *Articles 4 and 8 of the 2001 ILC Articles on State Responsibility, The Tadić Case and Attribution of Acts of Bosnian Serb Authorities to the Federal Republic of Yugoslavia*, 72 Brit. Y.B. Int'l L. 255, 258–60 (2002); Vojin Dimitrijević & Marko Milanović, *The Strange Story of the Bosnian Genocide Case*, 21 Leiden J. Int'l L. 65, 67 (2008).

50. *Bosnian Genocide*, *supra* note 4, ¶¶ 235, 238.

51. Prosecutor v. Tadić, Case No. ICTY IT-94-1-T, Opinion and Judgment, ¶ 115 (Int'l Crim. Trib. for the former Yugoslavia, May 7, 1997); *Bosnian Genocide*, *supra* note 4, ¶ 238.

52. *Id.*

53. *Bosnian Genocide*, *supra* note 4, ¶ 387.

54. *Id.* ¶¶ 386, 388. *But see id.* dissenting opinion of Judge Mahiou, ¶ 108.

55. *Bosnian Genocide*, *supra* note 4, ¶¶ 386, 388.

56. ARSIWA, *supra* note 1, art. 4, cmt. ¶¶ 1–13. *See also* Marko Milanović, *State Responsibility for Genocide: A Follow-Up*, 18 Eur. J. Int'l L. 669, 674 (2007) [hereinafter Milanović, *State Responsibility for Genocide: A Follow-Up*].

57. *See* Stefan Talmon, *The Responsibility of Outside Powers for Acts of Secessionist Entities*, 58 Int'l & Comp. L.Q. 493, 495 (2009).

continue to resemble NSAs in terms of their degree of organization and their subservience to State control.[58] Yet from the time of their integration into the State, the forces' conduct becomes attributable to the State under the rule reflected in Article 4.

4.3.2 Non-State Actors That Become De Jure State Organs

One example of an NSA attaining the status of a de jure State organ arose in 1997, in the context of Papua New Guinea's attempts to quash an internal rebellion.[59] The government entered a contract with the private military company, Sandline International, in which it authorized the entity to support its armed forces in suppressing the uprising.[60] To circumvent the provisions of the country's constitution, which prohibited paramilitary and mercenary activities, the contract provided for the enrolment of all Sandline personnel into Papua New Guinea's national police force as "special constables."[61] Therefore, for the short period of time prior to the contract's termination, Sandline personnel were de jure State organs and any conduct on their part that violated Papua New Guinea's international legal obligations engaged the responsibility of the State.[62]

A more recent example of an NSA's incorporation into a State's armed forces arose in Syria. In early 2013, the local Shabbiha and Jaysh al-Shaabi paramilitary groups were reorganized into a National Defense Force (NDF) and placed under the command of the Syrian military.[63] Reporting indicates that the NDF was established in accordance with Syrian law as a branch of the Syrian Arab

58. Erica L. Gaston, Illusions of Control 19 (2024).

59. Virginia Newell & Benedict Sheehy, *Corporate Militaries and States: Actors, Interactions, and Reactions*, 41 Tex. Int'l L.J. 67, 74–75 (2006); Oliver R. Jones, *Implausible Deniability: State Responsibility for the Actions of Private Military Firms*, 24 Conn. J. Int'l L. 239, 274 (2009); Hannah Tonkin, State Control over Private Military and Security Companies in Armed Conflict 85 (2011).

60. Newell & Sheehy, *supra* note 59, at 74–75; Jones, *supra* note 59, at 274; Tonkin, *supra* note 59, at 85.

61. Agreement for the Provision of Military Assistance Between the Independent State of Papua New Guinea and Sandline International (Jan. 31, 1997), *available at* www.michie.net/pnginfo/sandline-c.html (last visited July 2, 2025).

62. This position is reflected in the Montreux Document, agreed by seventeen States in 2008. *See* Montreux Document on Pertinent International Legal Obligations and Good Practices for States Related to Operations of Private Military and Security Companies during Armed Conflict 12, ¶ 7 (Sept. 17, 2008), https://www.montreuxdocument.org/pdf/document/en.pdf.

63. Carter Ctr., Syria: Pro-Government Paramilitary Forces 8 (Nov. 5, 2013), www.cartercenter.org/resources/pdfs/peace/conflict_resolution/syria-conflict/pro-governmentparamilitaryforces.pdf.

Army.[64] If that is correct, the group's status as a de jure State organ means that from the date of its incorporation into the State's structure, Syria bears responsibility for all the violations of its international law obligations involving NDF fighters, including the alleged massacres of civilians committed in the town of al-Bayda in May 2013.[65] Moreover, the NDF's conduct is attributable to Syria irrespective of any reported indiscipline on the part of its fighters.[66] The rule reflected in Article 4 requires only that the conduct in question was committed by an organ of State acting in its official capacity, not that the acts were committed under the State's control.[67]

This is particularly pertinent when considering Ukraine's responsibility for the conduct of the volunteer battalions that fought on the State's behalf during the early stages of the conflict in eastern Ukraine.[68] These militia groups emerged in April 2014 to protect their neighborhoods from rebel forces but were later integrated into the structure of the Ukrainian State and placed under the authority of the Ukrainian government.[69] From that date on the battalions were de jure organs of State, meaning that Ukraine bears responsibility for the many international law violations they committed while acting in their official capacity, notwithstanding Kiev's apparent lack of control over the groups' activities.[70]

64. *Insight: Battered by War, Syrian Army Creates Its Own Replacement*, Reuters (Apr. 21, 2013), www.reuters.com/article/us-syria-crisis-paramilitary-insight-idUSBRE93K02R20130421; Abdullah Al-Jabassini, Eur. U. Inst., From Insurgents to Soldiers: The Fifth Assault Corps in Daraa, Southern Syria 5 (May 14, 2019), https://cadmus.eui.eu/bitstream/handle/1814/62964/RR_2019_09_EN.pdf?sequence=1&isAllowed=y.

65. Hum. Rts. Watch, "No One's Left": Summary Executions by Syrian Forces in al-Bayda and Baniyas (Sept. 13, 2013), www.hrw.org/report/2013/09/13/no-ones-left/summary-executions-syrian-forces-al-bayda-and-baniyas.

66. Carter Ctr., *supra* note 63, at 6.

67. ARSIWA, *supra* note 1, art. 4, cmt. ¶ 13; *id.* art. 7.

68. Ilmari Käihkö, *A Nation in the Making, in Arms: Control of Force, Strategy and the Ukrainian Volunteer Battalions*, 18 Def. Stud. 147 (2018); Rosaria Puglisi, Istituto Affari Internazionali, Heroes or Villains? Volunteer Battalions in Post-Maidan Ukraine 5 (Mar. 8, 2015), www.iai.it/sites/default/files/iaiwp1508.pdf.

69. Rep. on the Human Rights Situation in Ukraine 15, ¶ 74 (July 15, 2014), https://www.ohchr.org/sites/default/files/Documents/Countries/UA/HRMMUReport15June2014.pdf; Rep. on the Human Rights Situation in Ukraine 4, ¶ 10 (Aug. 17, 2014), https://www.ohchr.org/sites/default/files/Documents/Countries/UA/Ukraine_Report_15July2014.pdf; Human Rights Violations and Abuses and International Humanitarian Law Violations Committed in the Context of the Ilovaisk Events in August 2014, at 1 n. 5, 8 n. 52 (Aug. 1, 2018), https://www.ohchr.org/sites/default/files/Documents/Countries/UA/ReportOnIlovaisk_EN.pdf [hereinafter Ilovaisk Events]; Käihkö, *supra* note 68, at 159.

70. *See, e.g.*, Amnesty Int'l, Ukraine: Abuses and War Crimes by the Aidar Volunteer Battalion in the North Luhansk Region (Sept. 8, 2014), www.amnesty.org/en/documents/EUR50/040/2014/en/ [hereinafter Amnesty Int'l, Aidar Volunteer Battalion]; Ilovaisk Events, *supra* note 69, at 10–16.

Reporting similarly indicates that members of the Wagner Group became de jure State organs of Russia following the NSA's attempted mutiny in the summer of 2023.[71] Elements of the Wagner Group in Ukraine were subsumed by the Rosgvardia, or National Guard, while its fighters in Africa became part of Russia's so-called Africa Corps.[72] From the date of their change of status, the fighters' acts in potential violation of international law are attributable to Russia. These might include, for instance, the fighters' alleged killings of civilians in the Central African Republic in October 2023.[73]

The same is true of the Popular Mobilization Forces (PMF) in Iraq.[74] These groups initially emerged in 2014 in response to a call by clerics to support Iraq's collapsing security forces in the fight against ISIS.[75] Two years later, the Iraqi government formally integrated the PMF into the State's structure as "an independent military formation and a part of the Iraqi armed forces."[76] Some factions remained under considerable Iranian influence, however, leading the Iraqi government to issue further decrees ordering PMF units to relinquish any political or external affiliations and come under the full control of the Prime Minister.[77] Despite this,

71. Kimberly Marten, *Where's Wagner Now? One Year After the Mutiny*, Ponars Eurasia (June 21, 2024), https://www.ponarseurasia.org/wheres-wagner-now-one-year-after-the-mutiny/; Matt Murphy, *A Year After Mutiny, Kremlin Controls Wagner Remnants*, BBC (June 23, 2024), https://www.bbc.com/news/articles/c4nn1p81q59o. The same is true of the rebels in the Donbas following Russia's annexation of the territory in September 2022. *See* Ukraine and the Netherlands v. Russia, App. Nos. 8019/16, 28525/20 and 11055/22, ¶ 364 (2025) (ECtHR) [hereinafter *ECtHR Ukraine Merits Judgment*].

72. Marten, *supra* note 71; Murphy, *supra* note 71; John A. Lechner, *Is Africa Corps a Rebranded Wagner Group?* Foreign Pol'y (Feb. 7, 2024), https://foreignpolicy.com/2024/02/07/africa-corps-wagner-group-russia-africa-burkina-faso/; Marcel Plichta et al., *The Wagner Group Lives on in Africa*, Lawfare (July 21, 2024), https://www.lawfaremedia.org/article/the-wagner-group-lives-on-in-africa.

73. Philip Obaji Jr., *Putin's Private Army Accused of Massacring Dozens to Seize Gold Mine*, Daily Beast (Dec. 23, 2023), https://www.thedailybeast.com/putins-private-army-accused-of-massacring-dozens-to-seize-gold-mine.

74. Kirk H. Sowell, *The Rise of Iraq's Militia State*, Carnegie Endowment for Int'l Peace (Apr. 23, 2015), https://carnegieendowment.org/sada/2015/04/the-rise-of-iraqs-militia-state?lang=en; Garrett Nada & Mattisan Rowan, *Pro-Iran Militias in Iraq*, U.S. Inst. for Peace (Nov. 10, 2021), https://iranprimer.usip.org/blog/2021/nov/10/profiles-pro-iran-militias-iraq.

75. Bill Roggio & Amir Toumaj, *Iraq's Prime Minister Establishes Popular Mobilization Forces as a Permanent "Independent Military Formation,"* FDD's Long War J. (July 28, 2016), www.longwarjournal.org/archives/2016/07/iraqs-prime-minister-establishes-popular-mobilization-front-as-a-permanent-independent-military-formation.php; Nada & Rowan *supra* note 74.

76. Roggio & Toumaj, *supra* note 75. *See also* Nada & Rowan, *supra* note 74; Crispin Smith & Jacques Singer-Emery, *Servants of Two Masters: The Risks Inherent in Iraq's Hashd Al-Sha'abi Legislation*, 52 N.Y.U. J. Int'l L. & Pol. 167 (2019).

77. Ali Mamouri, *Iraq Orders Militia to Fully Integrate into State Security Forces*, Al-Monitor (July 2, 2019), www.al-monitor.com/pulse/originals/2019/07/iraq-pmu-iran-abdul-mahdi-shi

certain militias continued to ignore Baghdad's authority, engaging in human rights abuses against peaceful protestors and targeting coalition forces in rocket attacks.[78] Yet assuming such conduct was performed in the militias' official capacity, it is attributable to Iraq by virtue of the rule reflected in Article 4, even if it was unauthorized.[79]

Given Tehran's considerable influence over some PMF factions, questions arise whether any of their acts in breach of Iraq's international legal obligations are attributable to Iran[80] or whether responsibility should be shared between the two States.[81] Such considerations are beyond this chapter's scope. However, the ICJ addressed a related issue in the *Bosnian Genocide* case, namely, where responsibility should lie when a de jure State organ acts not on behalf of another State, but for a non-State public authority. According to the Court, the State organ's conduct in such circumstances is attributable not to the State to which it belongs but rather to the NSA for which it acts.[82]

4.3.3 State Organs that Act on Behalf of a Non-State Public Authority

In the *Bosnian Genocide* case, the ICJ examined the status of a paramilitary unit involved in the Srebrenica genocide, known as the Scorpions.[83] Bosnia and Herzegovina claimed that the group was incorporated into the FRY's armed forces and was therefore a de jure State organ. Rejecting this submission due to insufficient evidence, the ICJ noted that "in any event the act of an organ placed by a

ite-militias.html; Michael Knights, *Normalizing Security in the Nineveh Plains*, Wash. Inst. (July 5, 2019), www.washingtoninstitute.org/policy-analysis/view/normalizing-security-in-the-nineveh-plains.

78. Michael Georgy, *Exclusive: Iran-Backed Militias Deployed Snipers in Iraq Protests—Sources*, Reuters (Oct. 17, 2019), www.reuters.com/article/us-iraq-protests-iran-snipers-exclusive/exclusive-iran-backed-militias-deployed-snipers-in-iraq-protests-sources-idUSKBN1WW0B1. *See also* Amnesty Int'l, Iraq: Turning a Blind Eye: The Arming of the Popular Mobilization Units (2017), www.amnestyusa.org/files/iraq_report_turning_a_blind_eye.pdf; Smith & Singer-Emery, *supra* note 76, at 188–91.

79. Smith & Singer-Emery, *supra* note 76, at 200–202; Crispin Smith, *It's Time Iraq Accepts Legal Responsibility for Its Iran-Backed Militias*, Just Sec. (Mar. 23, 2020), www.justsecurity.org/69273/its-time-iraq-accepts-legal-responsibility-for-its-iran-backed-militias/. *See also infra* sec. 4.5.

80. ARSIWA, *supra* note 1, art. 17.

81. *Id.*, art. 47. *See also* André Nollkaemper & Dov Jacobs, *Shared Responsibility in International Law: A Conceptual Framework*, 34 Mich. J. Int'l L. 359 (2013); André Nollkaemper et al., *Guiding Principles on Shared Responsibility in International Law*, 31 Eur. J. Int'l L. 15 (2020).

82. *Bosnian Genocide*, *supra* note 4, ¶ 389.

83. *Id.*

State at the disposal of another public authority shall not be considered an act of that State if the organ was acting on behalf of the public authority at whose disposal it had been placed."[84] The relevant public authority in this case was an NSA, namely, the Republika Srpska.

Through this passing comment, the ICJ seems to refer to the rule of attribution reflected in Article 6 ARSIWA, according to which the conduct of an organ of one State that performs governmental functions for another State is attributable to the latter rather than the former.[85] But the ICJ broadens Article 6's scope so that it applies when a State places one of its organs at the disposal of a "public authority," even if that authority is an NSA with no legal personality of its own.[86] Had the evidence established that the Scorpions were a de jure organ of the FRY, their conduct would not have been attributable to the State because they were acting on behalf of the Republika Srpska.

The ICJ's approach thus limits Article 4's application in situations where a State organ acts on behalf of a public authority outside the structure of the State. To illustrate, consider the early years of the conflict in eastern Ukraine when Russian troops reportedly acted alongside rebel forces.[87] If the Russian military personnel were ordered by their chain of command to participate in the conflict, they were acting in their official capacity as de jure State organs notwithstanding the absence of any Russian insignia on their uniforms at the time. As such, Russia bears responsibility for any international law violations with which they were involved.[88] But if Russia placed the troops at the disposal of one of the administrations in eastern Ukraine, the ICJ's approach may mean that they were acting on behalf of another public authority, with the result that Russia would bear no responsibility for their conduct.

Such a conclusion appears anomalous. Nevertheless, assuming that the ICJ's approach would not change the other elements of the rule reflected in Article 6, these would limit its scope of application. Thus, attribution would only be appropriate if the State organ acts under the "exclusive direction and control" of the local administration rather than "on instructions from the sending State."[89] Given the reporting indicating Russian control over key military decisions in the

84. *Id. See also* Milanović, *State Responsibility for Genocide: A Follow-Up*, *supra* note 56, at 675; Talmon, *supra* note 57, at 495.

85. ARSIWA, *supra* note 1, art. 6.

86. Milanović, *State Responsibility for Genocide: A Follow-Up*, *supra* note 56, at 676; Simon Olleson, Brit. Inst. Int'l & Comp. L., The Impact of the ILC's Articles on Responsibility of States for Internationally Wrongful Acts 25–26 (Oct. 10, 2007), www.biicl.org/files/3107_impactofthearticlesonstate_responsibilitypreliminarydraftfinal.pdf.

87. *See supra* ch. 2, sec. 2.4.2.

88. This might include, for example, violations related to the downing of Flight MH17. *See* Milanović, *Downing of MH17*, *supra* note 43.

89. ARSIWA, *supra* note 1, art. 6, cmt. ¶ 2.

Donbas and the probability that Moscow retained authority over its military personnel,[90] the threshold for attribution seems unlikely to be met.

The same is likely to be true in many other armed conflict situations. Although States frequently bolster local administrations,[91] any of the supporting State's organs that are placed at the disposal of the NSA would normally retain their own autonomy and status and continue to act, at least in part, for the State to which they belong.[92] In most cases, the evidence will not support a conclusion that State officials are completely subject to the NSA's direction and control, meaning that their conduct is still attributable to the State.[93]

Nonetheless, in the unlikely event that a State organ truly acts "under the authority of and for the purposes of" a non-State public authority,[94] the question remains whether the ICJ's approach limits the scope of the rule reflected in Article 4. It is notable, first, that ICJ's position seems to accord with Article 4's commentary. This asserts that the reference to a State organ covers all the entities that make up the organization of the State "and act on its behalf."[95] If an entity acts on behalf of another public authority, doubt arises whether attribution pursuant to the rule reflected in Article 4 is appropriate.

But there remains a distinction between attributing a State organ's conduct to another State, as envisaged by Article 6 ARSIWA, and attributing it to an NSA. Although non-State public authorities increasingly resemble States in the way they act and the powers they exercise, they do not possess international legal personality in the same manner as States. It is very difficult to hold NSAs directly to account for their conduct in violation of international law. The ICJ's approach therefore exposes a clear gap in accountability: If the State is not responsible for the conduct of its own organs when they act for an NSA, it is likely that no entity will be held to account when those organs violate international law.[96]

There are, accordingly, clear policy grounds for the continued application of the rule reflected in Article 4. A State should not be absolved of responsibility if it chooses to place its organs at the disposal of a de facto administration, particularly if that administration is closely linked to the State and only survives by virtue

90. Int'l Crisis Group, Russia and the Separatists in Eastern Ukraine, 8 (Feb. 5, 2016), https://www.crisisgroup.org/sites/default/files/b79-russia-and-the-separatists-in-eastern-ukraine.pdf.

91. Regarding Russian influence in eastern Ukraine, *see, e.g.*, Thomas de Waal, Carnegie Europe, Uncertain Ground: Engaging with Europe's de facto States and Breakaway Territories 61–70 (Dec. 3, 2018), https://carnegieeurope.eu/2018/12/03/uncertain-ground-engaging-with-europe-s-de-facto-states-and-breakaway-territories-pub-77823.

92. *See* ARSIWA, *supra* note 1, art. 6, cmt. ¶ 4.

93. *Id.* cmt. ¶ 2. *See also* Talmon, *supra* note 57, at 495–96.

94. ARSIWA, *supra* note 1, art. 6 cmt. ¶ 2.

95. *Id.* art. 4, cmt. ¶ 1.

96. Milanović, *State Responsibility for Genocide: A Follow-Up*, *supra* note 56, at 676.

of the State's support. Moreover, it is highly questionable whether this isolated observation by the ICJ, in the absence of any legal analysis or justification, reflects customary international law.[97] It remains to be seen whether the scope of the rule expressed in Article 6 will expand in the future to address situations in which State organs are placed at the disposal of non-State public authorities. But for the time being, the rule reflected in Article 4 should continue to apply to attribute State organs' conduct to the State to which they belong.

4.4 DE FACTO STATE ORGANS

While de jure State organs are generally easy to identify through an examination of the State's internal law, the same is not true of those entities that, de facto, amount to an organ of State. The latter form part of the machinery of government because of their actual relationship with the State, rather than their characterization by domestic law. But the ARSIWA commentary does not provide any guidance regarding the specific relationship that must exist between the State and an entity for the latter to qualify as a de facto organ.[98] Further assistance regarding this issue derives, instead, from the jurisprudence of the ICJ.

4.4.1 Guidance Provided by the ICJ

4.4.1.1 NICARAGUA

The *Nicaragua* case concerned U.S. responsibility for the activities of opposition groups fighting against the Nicaraguan government, known as the *contras*.[99] In its judgment, the ICJ assessed the relationship between the United States and the NSA, finding that the State:

(i) financed, organized, trained, supplied, equipped, and armed the *contras*;[100]
(ii) provided the *contras* with intelligence, including information on the location and movements of government troops;[101]
(iii) provided the *contras* with aircraft suitable for supply-dropping and reconnaissance;[102]

97. *Id.*

98. ARSIWA, *supra* note 1, art. 4, cmt. ¶¶ 1–13. *See also* de Hoogh, *supra* note 49, at 289–90.

99. *Nicaragua*, *supra* note 7.

100. *Id.* ¶¶ 99–101, 106–8, 112, 115.

101. *Id.* ¶¶ 101, 104, 106.

102. *Id.* ¶¶ 101, 104, 106, 115.

(iv) decided and planned, or at least closely collaborated in deciding and planning, some of the *contras*' military and paramilitary operations;[103]
(v) devised and directed specific strategies and tactics, for example regarding when to seize and hold Nicaraguan territory;[104]
(vi) selected some of the *contras*' military and paramilitary targets;[105]
(vii) selected, installed, and paid the *contras*' leaders;[106] and
(viii) provided operational support to the *contras*.[107]

Taking these factual findings into account, the ICJ examined whether the *contras*' conduct in violation of international law was attributable to the United States. The Court identified that the first question it needed to answer was whether "the relationship of the *contras* to the United States Government was so much one of dependence on the one side and control on the other that it would be right to equate the *contras*, for legal purposes, with an organ of the United States Government. . . ."[108] Thus, the two essential elements for an NSA to qualify as a de facto State organ are the NSA's dependence on the State and the State's exercise of control over the NSA's activities.

In regard to the dependence requirement, the ICJ found that the *contras* could not initially conduct their most important military and paramilitary activities without the wide-ranging support provided by the United States.[109] However, this was not true in later years, when the *contras* were able to continue their activities despite the cessation of State support.[110] The Court concluded, therefore, that although the assistance provided to the *contras* by the United States had been "crucial to the pursuit of their activities," it was "insufficient to demonstrate their complete dependence on United States aid."[111]

Regarding the control element of the test, the ICJ found that a "potential for control" was inherent in the *contras*' high level of dependence on the State.[112] Nonetheless, the Court considered that the evidence before it was insufficient to reach a finding on whether the U.S. government made use of that potential.[113] In

103. *Id.* ¶¶ 106, 112, 115.

104. *Id.* ¶ 104.

105. *Id.* ¶¶ 112, 115.

106. *Id.* ¶ 112.

107. *Id.* ¶¶ 112, 115.

108. *Id.* ¶ 109.

109. *Id.* ¶¶ 110–11.

110. *Id.* ¶ 110.

111. *Id.* ¶ 110.

112. *Id.* ¶¶ 109–10.

113. *Id.* ¶ 110.

sum, the Court determined that there was "no clear evidence of the United States having actually exercised such a degree of control in all fields as to justify treating the *contras* as acting on its behalf."[114] Therefore, the Court was "unable to determine that the *contra* force may be equated for legal purposes with the forces of the United States."[115]

4.4.1.2 Bosnian Genocide

The ICJ elaborated on the test for establishing de facto State organ status in the *Bosnian Genocide* case. Here, it framed the relevant question as "whether it is possible in principle to attribute to a State conduct of persons—or groups of persons—who, while they do not have the legal status of State organs, in fact act under such strict control by the State that they must be treated as its organs. . . ."[116] The Court then clarified that to achieve this status, the persons or groups must:

> in fact . . . act in "complete dependence" on the State, of which they are ultimately merely the instrument. In such a case, it is appropriate to look beyond legal status alone, in order to grasp the reality of the relationship between the person taking action, and the State to which he is so closely attached as to appear to be nothing more than its agent . . . .[117]

The ICJ applied this test of "complete dependence" and "strict control" to the facts of the FRY's relationship with the Bosnian Serb forces that perpetrated the genocide in Srebrenica. On the evidence put forward in the case, the Court found that:

> (i) close ties existed between the FRY and the authorities of the Republika Srpska, both of a political and financial nature and also relating to the administration and control of Bosnian Serb forces;[118]
> (ii) the FRY conceived and shared with the Republika Srpska the vision of a "Greater Serbia";[119]
> (iii) troops of Bosnian Serb origin within the Yugoslav Peoples' Army were transformed into, or joined, the Bosnian Serb forces;[120]

114. *Id.* ¶ 109.

115. *Id.* ¶ 110.

116. *Bosnian Genocide*, *supra* note 4, ¶ 391.

117. *Id.* ¶ 392.

118. *Id.* ¶ 237.

119. *Id.* ¶ 237.

120. *Id.* ¶ 238.

(iv) from 1993 onwards, about 1,800 officers within the Bosnian Serb forces were "administered" from Belgrade, including in relation to their pay, promotions, and pensions;[121]
(v) Bosnian Serb forces were armed and equipped by the FRY;[122] and
(vi) the economies of the FRY and Republika Srpska were integrated through the creation of a single economic entity, thus enabling the FRY government to finance the Bosnian Serb forces.[123]

Notwithstanding the extremely close relationship between Bosnian Serb forces and the State, the ICJ concluded that those forces could not be regarded as "mere instruments through which the FRY was acting, and as lacking any real autonomy."[124] While the relations between the parties had been "strong and close in previous years . . . and these ties undoubtedly remained powerful," at the time of the genocide, they were "not such that the Bosnian Serbs' political and military organizations should be equated with organs of the FRY."[125] Therefore, the requirements for attribution relevant to the rule reflected in Article 4 ARSIWA were not satisfied.

4.4.1.3 A Test of "Complete Dependence and Control"

The ICJ's judgments reveal several factual circumstances that may assist in determining whether the relationship between a State and an NSA is sufficiently strong for the latter to qualify as a de facto State organ. No one factor is, by itself, decisive, but each of the following may point to a conclusion that an entity, in fact, acts as an organ of State:

(i) the State created the entity;[126]
(ii) the State selected, installed, and paid the group's political leaders;[127]
(iii) the State devised the entity's strategy and directed its tactics;[128] and
(iv) the support provided by the State, in areas such as the organization, training and equipping of the force, the planning of operations and the choosing of targets, was crucial to the pursuit of the entity's activities.[129]

121. *Id.* ¶ 283.

122. *Id.* ¶ 239.

123. *Id.* ¶ 240.

124. *Id.* ¶ 394.

125. *Id.*

126. *Nicaragua*, *supra* note 7, ¶¶ 93–94; *Armed Activities*, *supra* note 6, ¶¶ 158–60. *See also* Talmon, *supra* note 57, at 499.

127. *Nicaragua*, *supra* note 7, ¶ 112.

128. *Id.* ¶ 110; *Bosnian Genocide*, *supra* note 4, ¶ 394.

129. *Nicaragua*, *supra* note 7, ¶ 112.

Additional criteria may also be relevant, including the entity's performance of governmental functions and its degree of integration into the State. While the ICJ did not specifically address these factors, arbitral tribunals have taken them into account when examining entities' potential status as de facto State organs.[130] And their significance is clear. If the purpose of de facto State organ status is to attribute to a State the conduct of entities that, in fact, act as its organs, those entities' integration into the State's structures and their performance of functions that are normally accomplished by State organs must be of relevance.[131]

The factors outlined above all feed into an assessment of the key question at issue, namely, whether the relationship between the parties is one of complete dependence and control.[132] Regarding the first element of the test, if an NSA has "some qualified, but real, margin of independence" from the State, such as an ability to express differences over strategic options, this indicates the NSA is not completely dependent on the State.[133] The entity must have no real autonomy of its own but rely wholly on the State in all areas of its activity.[134] In other words, the NSA cannot conduct its activities without the State's support and the cessation of aid would result in the end of these activities.[135] An NSA might demonstrate this high degree of dependence by acting consistently in accordance with the State's wishes for fear that if it failed do so, the State would withdraw the support upon which the NSA relies for its continued operations.[136]

130. Emilio Agustín Maffezini v. The Kingdom of Spain, Case No. ARB/97/7, Decision of the Tribunal on Objections to Jurisdiction, ¶¶ 75–89 (Int'l Ctr for Settlement of Inv. Disp., Jan. 25, 2000) [hereinafter *Maffezini*]; Flemingo Duty Free Shop Private Limited v. The Republic of Poland, Arbitral Award, ¶¶ 418–35 (Perm. Ct. Arb., Aug. 12, 2016) [hereinafter *Flemingo Duty Free Shop*].

131. For further discussion regarding governmental functions, *see infra* ch. 5, sec. 5.3.

132. For commentary regarding this test, *see* de Hoogh, *supra* note 49, at 269–74; Marko Milanović, *State Responsibility for Genocide*, 17 Eur. J. Int'l L. 553, 576–77 (2006) [hereinafter Milanović, *State Responsibility for Genocide*]; Olivier Corten, *L'Arrêt rendu par la CIJ dans l'affaire du Crime de génocide (Bosnie-Herzégovine c. Serbie): vers un assouplissement des conditions permettant d'engager la responsabilité d'un État pour génocide?*, 53 Annuaire Français de Droit Int'l 249, 265–67 (2007); Olleson *supra* note 86, at 26–29; Marko Milanović, *State Responsibility for Acts of Non-State Actors: A Comment on Griebel and Plücken*, 22 Leiden J. Int'l L. 307, 315–18 (2009) [hereinafter Milanović, *A Comment on Griebel and Plücken*]; Talmon, *supra* note 57, at 497–502; Tonkin, *supra* note 59, at 93–95; Crawford, *supra* note 10, at 124–26.

133. *Bosnian Genocide*, *supra* note 4, ¶ 394. *See also* Corten, *supra* note 132, at 266; Vladyslav Lanovoy, Complicity and its Limits in the Law of International Responsibility, 313 (2016).

134. *Bosnian Genocide*, *supra* note 4, ¶ 391; *Nicaragua*, *supra* note 7, ¶ 109.

135. Talmon, *supra* note 57, at 499–500.

136. Corten, *supra* note 132, at 267.

In the event that the "complete dependence" threshold is met, the potential for control that exists as a result of that dependence must actually be exercised by the State, to "a particularly great degree," in all the entity's fields of activity.[137] This does not mean, however, that State control must be demonstrated over the particular act or omission that amounts to a breach of the State's international legal obligations.[138] Instead, a more general appraisal is required, assessing the level of control exercised by the State over the entire range of the entity's activities at the relevant time. If that assessment reveals a consistent freedom of action in certain areas of the entity's operations, thereby indicating an absence of "strict control" by the State, the second element of the ICJ's test is not satisfied.[139]

The preceding analysis demonstrates the stringency of the test to establish de facto State organ status. To date, only one international court or tribunal has applied this test and concluded that an NSA qualifies as a de facto organ of State.[140] Given that this status serves to attribute all the entity's conduct to the State, even if it acts outside the scope of its authority or contravenes instructions,[141] it is right that de facto State organ status should be "exceptional" in nature and arise only rarely.[142] However, the test formulated by the ICJ is so demanding that some scholars have questioned whether a State's relationship with an NSA could ever satisfy this high threshold.[143] Further clarity regarding the test and its utility may be gained by applying it to examples of NSA conduct during armed conflict.

4.4.2 Application of the ICJ Guidance to Armed Conflict

Of the NSAs considered in the case studies outlined in Chapter 2, the rebel group M23 had particularly close ties with a supporting State.[144] Both Rwanda and Uganda sustained M23's activities, but the group's relationship with the Rwandan

137. *Nicaragua*, *supra* note 7, ¶ 110; *Bosnian Genocide*, *supra* note 4, ¶ 393.

138. In this respect, the test for de facto State organs differs from the test relevant to art. 8 ARSIWA. *See infra* ch. 6, sec. 6.4. *See also* Talmon, *supra* note 57, at 501.

139. *Bosnian Genocide*, *supra* note 4, ¶ 391.

140. *See ECtHR Ukraine Merits Judgment*, supra note 71, ¶¶ 363–64. For discussion of this judgment, *see infra* sec. 4.4.2. Arbitral tribunals have found entities to qualify as *de facto* State organs based on a looser test. *See Maffezini*, *supra* note 130, ¶¶ 75–89; *Flemingo Duty Free Shop*, *supra* note 130, ¶¶ 418–35.

141. ARSIWA, *supra* note 1, art. 7. *See also infra* sec. 4.5.

142. *Bosnian Genocide*, *supra* note 4, ¶ 393.

143. Talmon, *supra* note 57, at 501; Jörn Griebel & Milan Plücken, *New Developments Regarding the Rules of Attribution? The International Court of Justice's Decision in Bosnia v. Serbia*, 21 Leiden J. Int'l L. 601, 613 (2008). *But see* Milanović, *A Comment on Griebel and Plücken*, *supra* note 132, at 317–18.

144. *See supra* ch. 2, sec. 2.4.3.

government was exceptionally strong. Officials in Kigali were involved in planning the M23 rebellion and in April 2012, the Rwandan government took overt steps to aid the group's establishment.[145] The Rwandan Defense Force (RDF) provided M23 fighters with uniforms and military equipment and also facilitated their transportation within Rwanda, then back into the Democratic Republic of the Congo (DRC) to launch the rebellion.[146] In light of such activity, the Group of Experts determined that "Rwandan officials . . . coordinated the creation of the rebel movement."[147] These circumstances therefore point to M23's status as a de facto State organ of Rwanda.[148]

A further factor that supports this conclusion is the Rwandan government's involvement in the selection and installation of the group's leaders.[149] The UN Group of Experts found that "Rwandan officials nominated the political leadership and government of M23," with the Rwandan Minister of Defense unilaterally appointing the group's political coordinator and the individual members of its governing body.[150] In addition, senior Rwandan officials assisted the group to obtain funding by mobilizing financial backers.[151]

Following the group's establishment, Rwandan authorities played a significant role in M23's operations, with regular meetings taking place between M23 commanders and RDF officers.[152] RDF units commonly operated alongside M23, acting as force multipliers in all major rebel operations.[153] According to the UN Group of Experts, M23's military leaders received orders from the RDF's Chief of Staff, who himself acted on the instructions of the Rwandan Minister

145. Jason Stearns, Rift Valley Inst., from CNDP to M23: The Evolution of an Armed Movement in Eastern Congo 44 (2012), https://riftvalley.net/publication/cndp-m23/; Add. to the Interim Rep. of the Group of Experts on the Democratic Republic of the Congo Concerning Violations of the Arms Embargo and Sanctions Regime by the Government of Rwanda 4–7, U.N. Doc. S/2012/348/Add.1 (June 27, 2012) [hereinafter U.N. June 2012 Rep.]. *See also supra* ch. 2, sec. 2.4.3.

146. U.N. June 2012 Rep., *supra* note 145, at 4–7.

147. Final Rep. of the Group of Experts on the Democratic Republic of the Congo 6, U.N. Doc. S/2012/843 (Nov. 15, 2012) [hereinafter U.N. Nov. 2012 Rep.].

148. *Nicaragua*, *supra* note 7, ¶¶ 93–94; *Armed Activities*, *supra* note 6, ¶¶ 158–60.

149. *Nicaragua*, *supra* note 7, ¶ 112.

150. U.N. Nov. 2012 Rep., *supra* note 147, at 12. *See also* Stearns, *supra* note 145, at 44–45.

151. U.N. June 2012 Rep., *supra* note 145, at 11.

152. *Id.* at 17.

153. U.N. Nov. 2012 Rep., *supra* note 147, at 7; Midterm Rep. of the Group of Experts on the Democratic Republic of the Congo 12, ¶ 49, U.N. Doc. S/2024/969 (Dec. 27, 2024), https://documents.un.org/doc/undoc/gen/n24/373/37/pdf/n2437337.pdf [hereinafter U.N. Dec. 2024 Rep.].

of Defense.[154] Rwandan officials additionally oversaw the provision of logistical support to M23,[155] furnishing significant quantities of equipment to the group, with increased deliveries of heavy weapons and ammunition prior to specific operations.[156] By virtue of such findings, the Group of Experts concluded in 2012 that "Rwandan officials [exercised] overall command and strategic planning for M23."[157]

Rwandan support for M23 was thus crucial to its operations.[158] Rwanda not only supported the group logistically, with significant supplies of military and nonmilitary equipment, but also mobilized political and financial support, supplied the group with intelligence, organized a systematic recruitment campaign on M23's behalf, and provided training for those recruits.[159] In accordance with the ICJ's jurisprudence, therefore, these factors are all indicative of M23's status as a de facto State organ of Rwanda.[160]

But those circumstances, alone, are insufficient to conclude that M23 attained that status. According to the ICJ, a relationship of complete dependence and control must also be established, meaning that M23 was entirely dependent upon Rwanda, with no real autonomy of its own.[161] Thus, M23 can only qualify as a de facto State organ if it was, in all respects other than its legal status, effectively a branch of the Rwandan armed forces, subject to the same degree and quality of State control as the RDF, both in terms of its subjection to orders and its reliance on the State.[162]

While in many respects it appears that this stringent threshold is met, other factors point away from that conclusion. In particular, within the detailed reports compiled by the UN Group of Experts, there is nothing to indicate that Rwanda paid salaries to any M23 leaders or fighters. Indeed, reporting indicates that the

154. U.N. Nov. 2012 Rep., *supra* note 147, at 13. More recent reporting refers to a similarly high degree of Rwandan control over M23 operations. *See* U.N. Dec. 2024 Rep., *supra* note 153, at 12, ¶ 49 ("Every M23 unit was supervised and supported by RDF special forces").

155. U.N. Nov. 2012 Rep., *supra* note 147, at 13.

156. *Id.* at 9–10; U.N. Dec. 2024 Rep., *supra* note 153, at 12-13.

157. U.N. Nov. 2012 Rep., *supra* note 147, at 13, ¶ 32. Regarding M23's more recent operations, *see* Michelle Nichols, *Exclusive: Rwanda Exercises Command and Control over M23 Rebels, Say UN Experts*, Reuters (July 2, 2025), https://www.reuters.com/world/africa/rwanda-exercises-command-control-over-m23-rebels-say-un-experts-2025-07-02/.

158. *See Nicaragua*, *supra* note 7, ¶ 112.

159. U.N. June 2012 Rep., *supra* note 145, at 9–11; U.N. Nov. 2012 Rep., *supra* note 147, at 8, 11, 138; John Emerson, *DR Congo: M23 Rebels Committing War Crimes*, Hum. Rts. Watch (Sept. 11, 2012), www.hrw.org/news/2012/09/11/dr-congo-m23-rebels-committing-war-crimes.

160. *See supra* sec. 4.4.1.

161. *Bosnian Genocide*, *supra* note 4, ¶ 391; *Nicaragua*, *supra* note 7, ¶ 109.

162. ARSIWA, *supra* note 1, art. 4, cmt. ¶ 11. *See also* Milanović, *State Responsibility for Genocide*, *supra* note 132, at 577, 587.

group had other sources of income, for example from taxation, smuggling, and the illegal exploitation of natural resources.[163] The group also received substantial support from Uganda.[164] These facts suggest that M23's dependence upon Rwanda was not "complete."[165] On balance, therefore, despite the significant support provided by the Rwandan government to M23 and the high level of control Kigali exercised over M23's operations, it is far from certain that the group qualifies as a de facto State organ of Rwanda.

It is nevertheless instructive to assess whether the position is any different in respect of the other NSAs involved in the conflicts addressed in Chapter 2. In Syria, for instance, the Shabbiha militia had very close links to the Assad regime prior to the group's incorporation into the NDF. Thus, the UN Commission of Inquiry examining the conflict in Syria described the Shabbiha as "de facto agents" of the State,[166] while the U.S. Treasury Department asserted that the group "operated as a direct action arm of the Government of Syria and its security forces."[167]

In common with these assessments, certain factors point to a conclusion that, de facto, the Shabbiha qualified as an organ of the Syrian State. First, the Assad regime effectively created the entity, transforming it from a criminal gang into a loyal defender of the government.[168] Second, Syrian officials paid, armed, and informally organized the Shabbiha.[169] Third, the group frequently acted in concert with government forces, leading the UN Commission of Inquiry to repeatedly refer to "government forces and *Shabbiha*" when addressing the issue of those responsible for the numerous international law violations referenced in its reports.[170] Given these factors, it is possible that the "complete dependence" element of the test for de facto State organ status is satisfied.

163. U.N. Nov. 2012 Rep., *supra* note 147, at 140–41; Midterm Rep. of the Group of Experts on the Democratic Republic of the Congo 10-11, U.N. Doc S/2013/433 (July 19, 2013); *The M23 "Version 2"—Local Stakes, Motivations, Perceptions, and Impacts*, INT'L PEACE INFORMATION SERVICE (Apr. 4, 2024), https://ipisresearch.be/publication/the-m23-version-2-local-stakes-motivations-perceptions-and-impacts/.

164. *See supra* ch. 2, sec. 2.4.3.2.

165. *See Bosnian Genocide*, *supra* note 4, ¶ 394.

166. Rep. of the Indep. Int'l Comm'n of Inquiry on the Syrian Arab Republic 17, ¶ 93, U.N. Doc. A/HRC/19/69 (Feb. 22, 2012) [hereinafter U.N. Feb. 2012 Rep.].

167. U.S. Dep't of the Treasury, Treasury Sanctions Al-Nusrah Front Leadership in Syria and Militias Supporting the Asad Regime (Dec. 11, 2012), www.treasury.gov/press-center/press-releases/pages/tg1797.aspx.

168. BRIAN M. JENKINS, RAND CORPORATION, THE DYNAMICS OF SYRIA'S CIVIL WAR 6 (2014), www.rand.org/pubs/perspectives/PE115.html; Aron Lund, *Who Are the Pro-Assad Militias?*, CARNEGIE MIDDLE EAST CTR. (Mar. 2, 2015), http://carnegie-mec.org/diwan/59215?lang=en.

169. U.N. Feb. 2012 Rep., 2012, *supra* note 166, at 17, ¶ 93.

170. *See, e.g.*, Rep. of the Indep. Int'l Comm'n of Inquiry on the Syrian Arab Republic 1–2, U.N. Doc. A/HRC/21/50 (Aug. 16, 2012); Rep. of the Indep. Int'l Comm'n of Inquiry on the Syrian

There remains some doubt, however, whether the Assad regime exercised sufficient control over the Shabbiha's activities for the group to be considered a de facto organ of State. The Shabbiha reportedly acted with a sense of impunity, with no real limits on how its members behaved.[171] The decision to create the NDF in 2013 is also indicative of an absence of State control. This has been described as an attempt to "reinstitutionalize a chaotic militia movement" and connect the militias more firmly to the central government.[172] Although heavily reliant on the Assad regime, therefore, the group's freedom of action appears too great for it to constitute a de facto arm of the nation's security forces.[173]

Turning to the hostilities in Ukraine, the European Court of Human Rights (ECtHR) conducted a detailed analysis of Russia's relationship with rebels in the east of the country in its decision on jurisdiction and admissibility in *Ukraine and the Netherlands v. Russia*.[174] In its subsequent judgment on the merits, the Court concluded that "from 11 May 2014, the relationship of the separatists to the Russian Federation was so much one of dependence on the one side and control on the other that it would be right to equate the separatists in the 'DPR' and the 'LPR' with *de facto* organs of the Russian Federation, within the meaning of Article 4 ARSIWA."[175]

In reaching this conclusion, the ECtHR found that Russia's relationship with rebel forces in the east of the country intensified as the conflict progressed.[176] While Russia initially provided varying degrees of support to the armed rebel groups, by the time of the "referendums" on May 11, 2014, "the separatist operation as a whole was being managed and coordinated by the Russian Federation."[177] From this date, Moscow selected, installed, and paid the rebels' political leaders, replacing members of the local administrations' leadership as necessary to ensure that individuals sufficiently loyal to Moscow were in post.[178] The ECtHR noted

Arab Republic, annex iv, ¶ 4, U.N. Doc. A/HRC/22/59 (Feb. 5, 2013) [hereinafter U.N. Feb. 2013 Rep.].

171. U.N. Feb. 2013 Rep., *supra* note 170, annex v, ¶ 6; Salwa Amor & Ruth Sherlock, *How Bashar al-Assad Created the Feared Shabiha Militia: An Insider Speaks*, THE TELEGRAPH (Mar. 23, 2014), www.telegraph.co.uk/news/worldnews/middleeast/syria/10716289/How-Bashar-al-Assad-created-the-feared-shabiha-militia-an-insider-speaks.html.

172. Lund, *supra* note 168.

173. *Nicaragua*, *supra* note 7, ¶ 109.

174. Ukraine and the Netherlands v. Russia, App. No. 8019/16, 43800/14 & 28525/20 (2022) (ECtHR) [hereinafter *ECtHR Ukraine Admissibility Judgment*].

175. *ECtHR Ukraine Merits Judgment*, supra note 71, ¶ 363.

176. *ECtHR Ukraine Admissibility Judgment*, *supra* note 174, ¶¶ 690–93.

177. *Id.*

178. *Id.* ¶¶ 671–73, 693. *See also* Anders Åslund, *Putin Moves to Direct Rule in the Donbass*, NEWSWEEK (June 1, 2016), www.newsweek.com/putin-moves-direct-rule-donbas-412411; INT'L CRISIS GROUP, *supra* note 90, at 3, 12; DONALD N. JENSEN, NATO DEFENCE COLLEGE,

that this marked a critical step in the transition of the array of irregular armed groups into a single "separatist administration."[179]

From the summer of 2014, the rebels were highly dependent on Russia. The significant funding provided by Moscow, amounting to potentially 90 percent of the local administrations' budgets, together with the considerable quantities of equipment and weaponry supplied, suggests that the rebel movement could not survive and function without Russian support.[180] This conclusion is supported by the fact that the rebels were on the verge of defeat before Russia intervened in the conflict in late July 2014.[181] It seems unsurprising, therefore, that the ECtHR concluded that the "complete dependence" element of the test for de facto State organ status was satisfied.

Russia also took steps to exercise increased levels of control over the rebels' activities.[182] The ECtHR found that following the "referendums" and the formation of the separatist administration, "there was a decision to exert authority over the entirety of the area under separatist control and to bring separatist groups which had, until that point, been allowed for tactical reasons to operate somewhat independently back under a centralised command."[183] Moscow reorganized the rebels into a formal military structure commanded by Russian officers, seeking to eliminate those battalions and commanders who refused to toe the line.[184]

Higher-level decision making regarding the separatists' military operations was thus the responsibility of Russian State organs, or those acting on their behalf.[185] The ECtHR found that the rebels' senior leadership received orders from Russia and in the event of differing views as to military strategy, Moscow's orders were obeyed.[186] The U.S. Secretary of State similarly concluded in July 2017

Moscow in the Donbas: Command, Control, Crime and the Minsk Peace Process 7–8 (Mar. 2017), www.ndc.nato.int/news/news.php?icode=1029.

179. *ECtHR Ukraine Admissibility Judgment*, *supra* note 174, ¶ 693.

180. *Id.* ¶¶ 630–39, 689. *See also* Int'l Crisis Group, *supra* note 90, at 7; Michael Kofman et al., RAND Corporation, Lessons from Russia's Operations in Crimea and Eastern Ukraine xiii (2017), www.rand.org/content/dam/rand/pubs/research_reports/RR1400/RR1498/RAND_RR1498.pdf.

181. *ECtHR Ukraine Admissibility Judgment*, *supra* note 174, ¶ 632; Anna Matveeva, Through Times of Trouble: Conflict in South Eastern Ukraine Explained from Within, 161–66 (2018).

182. *See supra* ch. 2, sec. 2.4.2.

183. *ECtHR Ukraine Admissibility Judgment*, *supra* note 174, ¶ 693.

184. *Id.* ¶ 611; Int'l Crisis Group, *supra* note 90, at 8; Matveeva, *supra* note 184, at 175; Jensen, *supra* note 181, at 10.

185. *ECtHR Ukraine Admissibility Judgment*, *supra* note 174, ¶¶ 590–91, 602, 693; Int'l Crisis Group, *supra* note 90, at 8.

186. *ECtHR Ukraine Admissibility Judgment*, *supra* note 174, ¶¶ 619–20.

that Moscow exercised "complete control" over the separatists.[187] For the ECtHR, therefore, both elements of the ICJ's test were satisfied and "whatever their legal status, the separatists were . . . ultimately, a mere instrument of [the Russian] State."[188]

This decision is significant as it represents the first occasion on which an international court has applied the ICJ's test and found it to be satisfied. Nonetheless, certain factors that the ECtHR did not specifically address in its judgments raise questions regarding the rebels' status as de facto State organs. First, the rebel movement in eastern Ukraine was local in its origins; Moscow did not create it.[189] Second, reporting indicates a level of indiscipline and infighting on the part of rebel leaders that appears incompatible with Russia's exercise of "strict control."[190] Some fighters reportedly operated in "rogue" units, not under Russian command.[191] Furthermore, certain areas of the rebels' activities, such as their relationships with local politicians and oligarchs, remained outside the scope of Russian influence.[192]

These factors cast doubt on whether all the Donbas rebels may be regarded as integral to the apparatus of the Russian State and "mere instruments through which [Russia] was acting."[193] The ECtHR's judgments reflect a willingness on the part of the Court to view the separatists as one cohesive group, operating under a consistently high degree of Russian control, rather than as individual rebel units with varying relationships to the Russian State.[194] While the Court's ruling ensures Russia's accountability for the separatists' actions in violation of international law, its conclusions on de facto State organ status stand apart from those of other international courts and tribunals to date. It remains to be seen whether judicial bodies will follow the ECtHR's lead in the future and find that the ICJ's strict test can be satisfied in different factual circumstances.

This inquiry is pertinent not only to States' relationships with armed groups but also to the cyber domain.[195] When States act through cyber operators such as

187. *Tillerson Praises Turks for Standing Up to Coup Plotters, Delivers Blunt Message to Russia on Ukraine*, Radio Free Europe Radio Liberty (July 9, 2017), www.rferl.org/a/tillerson-ukraine-poroshenko-kyiv-united-states/28604023.html.

188. *ECtHR Ukraine Merits Judgment*, *supra* note 71, ¶ 363.

189. Kofman et al., *supra* note 183, at 33, 57–59; Matveeva, *supra* note 184, at 93–117.

190. Jensen, *supra* note 181, at 9.

191. Ivo Daalder et al., Atlantic Council, Preserving Ukraine's Independence, Resisting Russian Aggression: What the United States and NATO Must Do 12 (Feb. 2015), www.brookings.edu/wp-content/uploads/2016/06/UkraineReport_February2015_FINAL.pdf.

192. Jensen, *supra* note 181, at 9–10.

193. *Bosnian Genocide*, *supra* note 4, ¶ 394.

194. *ECtHR Ukraine Admissibility Judgment*, *supra* note 174; *ECtHR Ukraine Merits Judgment*, supra note 71, ¶ 363.

195. *See supra* ch. 2, sec. 2.4.2.3.

private hackers, the same attribution thresholds must be met but in practice, the requisite evidence is more difficult to gather. Even if technical attribution is possible, meaning that an injured State is able and willing to identify the particular individual or group of cyber operators responsible for a harmful operation, any links between those cyber operators and a State are often indistinct.[196] Thus, de facto State organ status is likely to be of limited relevance in the cyber domain due to the considerable challenge of obtaining the requisite evidence to prove a relationship of complete dependence and control between a particular cyber operator and the State.[197]

4.4.3 A More Effective Test to Assess de Facto State Organ Status

The preceding analysis reveals the limited practical utility of the ICJ's test of complete dependence and control in situations of conflict. On the one hand, the stringency of the test makes sense; de facto State organ status should arise only in exceptional circumstances, given that all the conduct of an entity with that status is attributable to the State. But on the other hand, the test's strictness and inflexibility exclude relationships in which the NSA exercises any degree of autonomy or obtains resources from any source other than the State.

Given the test's stringency, States can easily evade international responsibility simply by acting via a person or entity that is not designated as a State organ by its internal law. Moreover, States' structures differ considerably around the world. The test's limited scope of application, therefore, leads to inconsistency in the attribution of conduct between different States.[198] While acts in violation of international law committed by an entity that one State designates as its organ would lead to that State's international responsibility, the same conduct that an equivalent entity performs on behalf of another State, which is not so designated, would not.

The impacts of the test are particularly apparent when considering situations of armed conflict. If the ICJ's test cannot be satisfied in respect of M23's relationship with Rwanda, or the Shabbiha's affiliation with Syria, very few relationships between States and NSAs engaged in conflict will be sufficiently close to satisfy both elements of the test. The cumulative requirements of the entity's complete dependence on the State, plus the State's exercise of a high degree of control over

196. Tim Maurer, Cyber Mercenaries: The State, Hackers, and Power 22–25 (2018).

197. For commentary regarding de facto State organ status in the cyber domain see, for example, Tallinn Manual 2.0 on the International Law Applicable to Cyber Operations, r. 15, cmt. ¶¶ 3–4 (Michael N. Schmitt ed., 2017); Michael N. Schmitt, *"Virtual" Disenfranchisement: Cyber Election Meddling in the Grey Zones of International Law*, 19 Chi. J. Int'l L. 30, 60 (2018); Nicholas Tsagourias & Michael Farrell, *Cyber Attribution: Technical and Legal Approaches and Challenges*, 31 Eur. J. Int'l L. 941, 952 (2020).

198. Kolb, *supra* note 31, at 78.

the entire scope of the entity's activities, potentially exclude militias such as M23 from qualifying as de facto State organs, without permitting an examination of their wider relationship with the State to assess whether it parallels that of a de jure organ. This outcome appears inconsistent with the ILC's aim in broadening the scope of Article 4 to encompass those entities that act, in truth, as part of the machinery of government.[199]

To meet that aim, a less stringent test is required that assesses the reality of the overall relationship between the State and the NSA without requiring the extant levels of dependence and control to be "complete" in nature. While an NSA's level of dependence on the State and the State's degree of control over the entity's wider activities are both highly relevant considerations when making this assessment, they should not predominate over other pertinent factors. Instead, all the features of the relationship between the State and the NSA should be considered, including the factual circumstances identified by the ICJ as indications of de facto State organ status.[200] In addition to the respective levels of dependence and control, these might include:

1. State involvement in the NSA's creation;[201]
2. Shared goals or ideology between the State and the NSA;
3. The public character of the functions performed by the NSA;[202]
4. State involvement in all fields of the NSA's activities;[203]
5. State involvement in devising the NSA's overall strategy;[204]
6. State organs acting alongside or in concert with the NSA;
7. The State's selection of the NSA's political or military leaders;[205]
8. State involvement in the planning of the NSA's operations and the selection of its targets;[206]
9. State involvement in the NSA's recruitment practices;
10. The State's payment of salaries to leaders and/or members of the NSA.

Consideration of a range of factors, tailored to the situation at issue, would allow a fairer and less rigid assessment of the true relationship between a State and an NSA. A similar approach has been followed by certain arbitral tribunals, which

199. ARSIWA, *supra* note 1, art. 4, cmt. ¶ 11.

200. *See supra* sec. 4.4.1.

201. *Nicaragua, supra* note 7, ¶¶ 93–94. *See also, Armed Activities, supra* note 6, ¶¶ 158–60.

202. *Maffezini, supra* note 130, ¶¶ 75–89; *Flemingo Duty Free Shop, supra* note 130, ¶¶ 418–35.

203. *Nicaragua, supra* note 7, ¶ 109.

204. *Id.* ¶ 110; *Bosnian Genocide, supra* note 4, ¶ 394.

205. *Nicaragua, supra* note 7, ¶ 112.

206. *Id.*

found entities to qualify as de facto State organs without requiring evidence of complete dependence and control.[207]

When applied to Iran's relationship with Hezbollah, for example, the shared ideology between the State and the NSA is a factor of particular importance. This leads Hezbollah to consistently act in furtherance of Iranian interests without a need for the State to exercise a high degree of control over its activities. The group's intimate relationship with one particular organ of the Iranian State, the IRGC, is also of relevance.[208] A further indication of Hezbollah's place within the wider architecture of the Iranian State is the group's significance to Tehran's overall concept of defense and deterrence.[209] These elements, however, must be weighed against factors that point away from Hezbollah's status as a de facto State organ. These include the considerable autonomy the group demonstrates when conducting military operations,[210] the support it received from other States such as Syria,[211] and the important domestic role it plays within Lebanon.[212]

Given that attribution pursuant to Article 4 ARSIWA means that all the NSA's conduct is attributable to the State, irrespective of the degree of State involvement in the activity concerned, a conclusion that Hezbollah qualifies as a de facto State organ of Iran appears inappropriate. As the ICJ noted, de facto State organ status is "exceptional" in nature.[213] Thus, the status should arise only when a particularly close relationship exists between the State and the NSA that extends to all the NSA's fields of activity.[214]

207. *Maffezini*, *supra* note 130, ¶¶ 75–89; *Flemingo Duty Free Shop*, *supra* note 130, ¶¶ 418–35.

208. *See, e.g.*, Ben Hubbard, *Iran Out to Remake Mideast with Arab Enforcer: Hezbollah*, N.Y. Times (Aug. 27, 2017), www.nytimes.com/2017/08/27/world/middleeast/hezbollah-iran-syria-israel-lebanon.html?rref=collection%2Fsectioncollection%2Fworld&action=click&contentCollection=world.

209. Ariane Tabatabai, *The Fruits of Iran's Victory in Syria*, Lawfare (Apr. 15, 2018), www.lawfareblog.com/fruits-irans-victory-syria; Jack Watling, Royal United Servs. Inst., Iran's Objectives and Capabilities: Deterrence and Subversion 16–17 (Feb. 2019), https://www.rusi.org/explore-our-research/publications/occasional-papers/irans-objectives-and-capabilities-deterrence-and-subversion.

210. Marisa Sullivan, Inst. for the Study of War, Middle East Security Report 19: Hezbollah in Syria 4 (Apr. 2014), www.understandingwar.org/sites/default/files/Hezbollah_Sullivan_FINAL.pdf.

211. Mohanad Hage Ali, *Power Points Defining the Syria-Hezbollah Relationship*, Carnegie Middle East Ctr. (Mar. 29, 2019), https://carnegie-mec.org/2019/03/29/power-points-defining-syria-hezbollah-relationship-pub-78730.

212. Counter Extremism Project, Hezbollah's Influence in Lebanon (Apr. 2018), www.counterextremism.com/sites/default/files/Hezbollah%20Influence%20in%20Lebanon_043018.pdf; Matthew Levitt, *Hezbollah Shadow Governance in Lebanon*, Wash. Inst. (Aug. 6, 2024), https://www.washingtoninstitute.org/policy-analysis/hezbollah-shadow-governance-lebanon.

213. *Bosnian Genocide*, *supra* note 4, ¶ 393.

214. *Nicaragua*, *supra* note 7, ¶ 109.

But to achieve its object and purpose and to prevent States from using their internal laws to evade responsibility, this status must apply more broadly than the "complete dependence and control" test allows. A more flexible interpretation of the rule of attribution might, for example, lead to a conclusion that, despite the Assad regime's lack of strict control over the Shabbiha's harmful activities, when the relationship is viewed as a whole, the group nevertheless qualifies as a de facto organ of Syria.[215] Such an approach would better meet the object and purpose of the rule reflected in Article 4 and act as a disincentive to States to act via proxy in a manner that they cannot lawfully act via their de jure State organs.

4.5 *ULTRA VIRES* ACTS

In the unlikely event that an NSA qualifies as a de facto State organ, it is no different from one established in law.[216] This means that the entirety of the organ's conduct, performed in its official capacity, is attributable to the State.[217] Or as Milanović puts it, "the mere identity of the actor as a State organ suffices for attribution to occur."[218] The principle is reflected in Article 7 ARSIWA: "The conduct of an organ of State . . . shall be considered an act of the State under international law if the organ . . . acts in that capacity, even if it exceeds its authority or contravenes instructions."[219]

The rationale behind the rule is teleological. If an injured State had to prove that a State organ was acting within the scope of its authority at the time it committed an act in potential violation of international law, this would afford States "a ready loop-hole by which to evade responsibility" and place an impossible burden on injured States.[220] Moreover, the rule expressed in Article 7 enhances compliance with international law by encouraging States to oversee their organs' conduct and

215. *See supra* sec. 4.4.2.

216. Crawford, *supra* note 10, at 126.

217. Theodore Meron, *International Responsibility of States for Unauthorized Acts of Their Officials*, Brit. Y.B. Int'l L. 85 (1957).

218. Milanović, *A Comment on Griebel and Plücken*, *supra* note 132, at 315.

219. ARSIWA, *supra* note 1, art. 7. For a review of judicial pronouncements regarding Article 7, *see* Olleson, *supra* note 86, at 76–81.

220. Int'l Law Comm'n, Documents of the Twenty-Fourth Session Including the Rep. of the Comm'n to the General Assembly (1972), *in* [1972] 1 Y.B. Int'l L. Comm'n 79 ¶ 19, U.N. Doc. A/CN.4/SER.A/1972/Add.1 [hereinafter ILC Y.B. 1972 vol. II]. *See also* Int'l Law Comm'n, Documents of the Thirty-Eighth Session (1986), *in* [1986] 1 Y.B. Int'l L. Comm'n, 12, ¶ 5 (comments of Special Rapporteur Mr. Willem Riphagen), U.N. Doc. A/CN.4/SER.A/1986/Add.1 (Part 1) [hereinafter ILC Y.B. 1986 vol. II]; Meron *supra* note 217, at 88–89; Olivier de Frouville, *Attribution of Conduct to the State: Private Individuals*, *in* The Law of International Responsibility 257, 263–64 (James Crawford et al. eds., 2010); Tonkin, *supra* note 59, at 98.

ensure that they abide by the State's international legal obligations.[221] If a State fails in this respect, it bears responsibility for all the legal violations committed, whether or not the organ was acting under the State's authority or control at the relevant time.

Activities of this nature, performed in excess of authority but nevertheless attributable to the State, are described as *ultra vires* acts. In the *Union Bridge Company* case, for example, Great Britain was held responsible for the *ultra vires* conduct of one of its officers who was authorized to seize belligerent property during the Boer War, but who mistakenly appropriated material belonging to a neutral party.[222] In a similar manner, if members of Ukraine's volunteer battalions violated IHL after their integration into Ukraine's armed forces,[223] their conduct is attributable to Ukraine even if they were acting contrary to specific State instructions. The position would only be different if the battalions' members were acting in a private capacity at the relevant time.[224]

4.5.1 The Distinction Between *Ultra Vires* and Private Acts

The key consideration when characterizing conduct as either *ultra vires* or private is whether the individuals concerned were acting in their capacity as organs of State.[225] In the case of a de jure organ, this assessment focuses on the range of powers that the entity is granted by the State's internal law.[226] De facto State organs, in contrast, have no official function or capacity in accordance with domestic law, nor, in all likelihood, any rules governing their conduct or operations. Accordingly, it may be more challenging when considering the latter's activities to determine whether these were performed in exercise of authority granted by the State.[227]

The General Claims Commission considered the distinction between private and *ultra vires* conduct in the *Mallén* case, concerning two assaults by an American

221. Monica Hakimi, *Toward a Legal Theory on the Responsibility to Protect*, 39 Yale J. Int'l L. 247, 264 (2014).

222. Union Bridge Co. (United States) v. Great Britain, 6 R.I.A.A. 138, 141–42 (Am.-Brit. Arb. Trib., 1924). *See also* Meron, *supra* note 217, at 94, 96.

223. *See* Käihkö, *supra* note 68; Amnesty Int'l, Aidar Volunteer Battalion, *supra* note 70.

224. ARSIWA, *supra* note 1, art. 7.

225. ARSIWA, *supra* note 1, art. 7, cmt. ¶ 7. *See also* Caron, *supra* note 8, at 136.

226. Crawford, *supra* note 10, at 136.

227. Vladislav Lanovoy, *The Use of Force by Non-State Actors and the Limits of Attribution of Conduct*, 28 Eur. J. Int'l L. 563, 576 (2017).

police officer on a Mexican national.[228] The first assault was considered "a malevolent and unlawful act of a private individual who happened to be an official."[229] This, therefore, was not attributable to the United States. But the Commission's assessment was different regarding the second assault. Although this seemed "a private act of revenge," it was attributable to the United States on the basis that the perpetrator showed his badge, thereby asserting his official capacity, and took Mallén to jail following the assault.[230]

Similar considerations arose in the *Caire* case, in which Mexico was found to be internationally responsible for the acts of two of its army officers who unlawfully shot a French national after he refused to give them a sum of money.[231] Taking into account the officers' use of their insignia when carrying out the arrest, the arbitration panel concluded that they "acted under cover of their status as officers and used means placed at their disposal on account of that status."[232] Despite the fact that the officers were seeking private gain at the time of the incident, the ILC cites this decision with approval.[233] A more recent judgment indicates, however, that if the officers had been clearly off duty and out of uniform at the relevant time, the opposite conclusion may have been appropriate.

In *Makuchyan and Minasyan v. Azerbaijan and Hungary*, the ECtHR concluded that a member of the Azerbaijani armed forces was "not acting in the exercise of his official duties" when he killed one member of the Armenian military and attempted to kill another during a NATO-sponsored course.[234] The Court concluded that "the crimes were committed as a result of [the perpetrator's] private decision to kill during the night and outside of training hours . . . because [the Armenian participants] had allegedly previously mocked and provoked him."[235] While the Court did not engage in its judgment with the rules reflected in Articles 4 or 7 ARSIWA,[236] its overall conclusion in this respect is sound. The murder and

228. Francisco Mallén (United Mexican States) v. U.S.A., 4 R.I.A.A. 173 (Gen. Claims Comm., 1927).

229. *Id.* at 174–75.

230. *Id.* at 177. *See also* Meron, *supra* note 217, at 109–11.

231. Estate of Jean-Baptiste Caire (France) v. The United Mexican States, 5 R.I.A.A. 516 (French-Mexican Mixed Claims Comm., 1929).

232. *Id.* at 531. *See also* Meron, *supra* note 217, at 109–10.

233. ARSIWA, *supra* note 1, art. 7, cmt. ¶ 5.

234. Makuchyan & Minasyan v. Azerbaijan & Hungary, App. No. 17247/13, ¶ 111 (2020) (ECtHR).

235. *Id.*

236. For a critique of this aspect of the judgment, *see* Marko Milanović, *Attribution, Jurisdiction, Discrimination, Decapitation: A Comment on Makuchyan and Minsyan v. Azerbaijan and Hungary*, EJIL:TALK! (July 10, 2020), https://www.ejiltalk.org/attribution-jurisdiction-discrimination-decapitation-a-comment-on-makuchyan-and-minasyan-v-azerbaijan-and-hungary/.

attempted murder were clearly private acts rather than official acts carried out contrary to orders, therefore the rule reflected in Article 4 does not attribute them to Azerbaijan.[237]

Each case will turn on its own facts. But as the *Mallén* and the *Caire* cases illustrate, it is the perception that the State organ creates through its actions that is key, rather than the purpose for which it acts.[238] The ARSIWA commentary reflects this principle, providing that whenever a State organ acts in "an apparently official capacity, or under colour of authority," such actions are attributable to the State even if the person or entity concerned had ulterior or improper motives or was abusing public power.[239] It follows that if NDF fighters in Syria used the official identification cards with which they were issued to facilitate looting or other potential IHL violations,[240] such activity is likely to be attributable to the State even if the fighters' motivation was personal gain.

The use of equipment provided by the State is not, however, sufficient to prove that conduct is public rather than private in character.[241] Thus, if a member of the NDF used a weapon issued by the Syrian government to kill a foreign national during a private dispute, that fact alone is insufficient to attribute the act to Syria. The key issue, instead, is whether the NDF fighter exploited his official position to make it appear to the victim that he was "cloaked with governmental authority."[242] Depending on the context, this may be far from easy to establish. If a State organ operates covertly, for example, it might display no outward manifestation of the authority under which it acts.[243]

237. *Id.* For a discussion of the case in the context of Article 11 ARSIWA, *see infra* ch. 10, sec. 10.2.3.

238. ILC Y.B. 1972 vol. II, *supra* note 220, 93, ¶ 55. *But see Yeager*, *supra* note 38, ¶¶ 64–66. For a critique of the tribunal's judgment in *Yeager*, *see* Caron, *supra* note 8, at 136–38.

239. ARSIWA, *supra* note 1, art. 4, cmt. ¶ 13. *See also* Int'l Law Comm'n, Rep. of the Comm'n to the General Assembly (1975), *in* 2 Y.B. INT'L L. COMM'N 67 (draft art. 10, cmt. ¶ 17), U.N. Doc. A/CN.4/SER.A/1975/Add.1 [hereinafter ILC Y.B. 1975 vol. II]; ILC Y.B. 1986 vol. II, *supra* note 220, at 12, ¶ 5; Crawford's First Rep. on State Responsibility, *supra* note 19, at 48, ¶ 240; Meron, *supra* note 217, at 93; de Frouville, *supra* note 220, at 263–64.

240. CARTER CTR., *supra* note 63, at 6, 8; Sam Dagher, *Syria's Alawite Force Turned Tide for Assad*, WALL ST. J. (Aug. 26, 2013), www.wsj.com/articles/syrias-alawite-force-turned-tide-for-assad-1377568628.

241. ILC Y.B. 1975 vol. II, *supra* note 239, at 69–70 (draft art. 10, cmt. ¶ 26). *But see* Meron, *supra* note 217, at 113.

242. Petrolane Inc. v. Islamic Republic of Iran, Award No. 518-131-2, ¶¶ 82–83 (Iran-U.S. Claims Trib., 1991). *See also* ARSIWA, *supra* note 1, art. 7, cmt. ¶ 7.

243. KIMBERLY N. TRAPP, STATE RESPONSIBILITY FOR INTERNATIONAL TERRORISM 35 (2011).

The distinction between official and private conduct is particularly pertinent when de jure State organs rebel against the State. Syrian soldiers, for instance, began defecting from the regime's armed forces in mid-2011, leading to the formation of the Free Syrian Army.[244] If those soldiers were still de jure members of the State's armed forces at the time of their involvement in potential international law violations,[245] the question arises whether their acts are attributable to Syria.

The International Court of Arbitration addressed this issue in *Cengiz v. Libya*, relating to attacks conducted during the Libyan conflict from 2011 and 2014.[246] The Tribunal concluded that it was irrelevant whether the troops that conducted the attacks were loyal to Libya's former leader, Muammar Gaddafi, or to the new government: "The Libyan State must assume responsibility for the looting performed by its regular armed forces—independently of purpose or political affiliation."[247] This conclusion, however, appears anomalous. As Dumberry observes, at the time of the attacks, the troops were no longer acting in their official capacity as organs of State but rather as rebels.[248] As such, they were acting in a private capacity at the relevant time and Article 4 should not attribute their conduct to the State.[249]

The ARSIWA commentary highlights one exception to the normal distinction between *ultra vires* and private behavior. If an organ's private conduct is systematic, to the extent that the State knew or should have known about it and taken appropriate preventative steps, then attribution is appropriate notwithstanding the private nature of the relevant acts.[250] Therefore, even if members of Syria's NDF were acting in a private capacity when they first engaged in looting,[251] their subsequent acts of looting in violation of Syria's IHL or human rights obligations are attributable to the State due to Syrian officials' knowledge of the militias' behavior and their failure to prevent its reoccurrence.

244. Charles Lister, Brookings, The Free Syrian Army: A Decentralized Insurgent Brand 5 (Nov. 2016), www.brookings.edu/wp-content/uploads/2016/11/iwr_20161123_free_syrian_army.pdf.

245. *See, e.g.*, U.N. Feb. 2012 Rep., *supra* note 166, at 20–21.

246. Cengiz Construction, Industry & Trade Company v. Libya, Case No. 21537/ZF/AYZ, Final Award, ¶ 428 (Int'l Ct. Arb. of the Int'l Chamber of Commerce, 2018).

247. *Id.*

248. Patrick Dumberry, Rebellions and Civil Wars, 162–63 (2022). *See also* Michael Akehurst, *State Responsibility for the Wrongful Acts of Rebels—An Aspect of the Southern Rhodesian Problem*, 43 Brit. Y.B. Int'l L., 49, 63 (1968-1969).

249. For further discussion of the Cengiz case in the context of Article 10 ARSIWA, *see infra* ch. 9, sec. 9.3.1.

250. ARSIWA, *supra* note 1, art. 7, cmt. ¶ 8.

251. The Carter Ctr., *supra* note 63, at 6, 8.

4.5.2 The Conduct of a State's Armed Forces

As the preceding examples illustrate, the principle reflected in Article 7 ARSIWA is particularly relevant when considering the behavior of a State's armed forces, or militias that qualify as State organs. Although conduct in breach of the State's IHL obligations is invariably committed in disobedience to orders, international courts and tribunals have consistently held States accountable for their troops' conduct on the basis that this is *ultra vires* rather than private behavior.[252] Moreover, even if the actions of military personnel can properly be characterized as private, it is arguable that in conflict situations, the entirety of the armed forces' conduct is attributable to the State.

This results from Article 3 of the 1907 Fourth Hague Convention and Article 91 of the 1977 First Additional Protocol to the Geneva Conventions (AP I).[253] According to both provisions, in international armed conflicts, a State is responsible for "all acts committed by persons forming part of its armed forces."[254] This principle has been described by the ICJ as "a well-established rule of a customary nature."[255] Yet ambiguity persists regarding its precise meaning and effects.[256]

In the *Armed Activities* case, the ICJ noted when referring to Articles 3 and 91 that it was "irrelevant for the attribution of their conduct to Uganda whether [Ugandan armed forces] acted contrary to the instructions given or exceeded their authority."[257] This wording reflects the principle set out in Article 7 ARSIWA and does not obviously ascribe any broader meaning to those provisions. Similarly, the commentaries to Article 91 AP I and Article 7 ARSIWA indicate that only *ultra vires* acts, not private acts, of a State's armed forces are attributable to the State.[258]

252. *See, e.g.*, Thomas H. Youmans (U.S.A.) v. United Mexican States, 4 R.I.A.A. 110, 116 (Gen. Claims Comm'n., 1926); D. Earnshaw & Others (Great Britain) v. U.S., 6 R.I.A.A. 160, 162 (Am.-Brit. Arb. Trib., 1925). *See also* IAN BROWNLIE, STATE RESPONSIBILITY: PART 1 146–47 (1983); Meron, *supra* note 217.

253. Convention No. IV Respecting the Laws and Customs of War on Land, art. 3, Oct. 18, 1907, 36 Stat. 2227, T.S. No. 539; Protocol Additional to the Geneva Conventions of 12 August 1949, and Relating to the Protection of Victims of International Armed Conflicts, art. 91, June 8, 1977, 1125 U.N.T.S. 3 [hereinafter AP I].

254. *Id.*

255. *Armed Activities, supra* note 6, ¶ 214. *But see id.* dissenting opinion of Judge ad hoc Kateka, ¶ 54.

256. *See generally* Frits Kalshoven, *State Responsibility for Warlike Acts of the Armed Forces: From Article 3 of Hague Convention IV of 1907 to Article 91 of Additional Protocol I of 1977 and Beyond*, 40 INT'L & COMP. L.Q. 827 (1991).

257. *Armed Activities, supra* note 6, ¶ 214.

258. COMMENTARY ON THE ADDITIONAL PROTOCOLS OF 8 JUNE 1977 TO THE GENEVA CONVENTIONS OF 12 AUGUST 1949, ¶ 3660 (Yves Sandoz, Christophe Swinarski & Bruno Zimmermann eds., 1987) [hereinafter COMMENTARY ON THE ADDITIONAL PROTOCOLS]; ARSIWA, *supra* note 1, art. 7, cmt. ¶ 4.

The *opinio juris* of the United States supports this construction.[259] But many commentators consider that in situations of international armed conflict, Articles 3 and 91 operate more broadly than the principle reflected in Article 7.[260] The ILC, in its earlier deliberations, also regarded these IHL provisions as forming an exception to the general rule now expressed in Article 7.[261] And the ICTY referred to Article 91 as establishing "a special regime of State responsibility" under which the acts of armed forces are attributable to a State during armed conflict, whether or not they act in a private capacity.[262]

To illustrate the distinction, consider the conduct of Ukraine's volunteer battalions. As discussed in Section 4.3.1, these became de jure State organs in 2014 and were implicated in numerous IHL violations. It is possible that the battalions' members committed some of these abuses in their private capacity, particularly given that they were operating in home territory. Individuals might have committed acts of theft, for instance, while on leave from their official duties.[263] In such circumstances, neither the rule reflected in Article 4 nor any of the other rules of attribution outlined in ARSIWA would attribute their conduct to Ukraine.[264] But if the conflict was international in character at the relevant time[265] and Article 91 AP I operates as an exception to the general principle reflected in Article 7 ARSIWA, the volunteer battalions' private conduct is nevertheless attributable to Ukraine.

This broader interpretation of Article 91 is likely to be most significant when the relevant conflict occurs in the State's own territory. Often, when a State participates in an international armed conflict its forces are deployed away from

259. Customary IHL, *supra* note 6, r. 149.

260. *See, e.g.*, Kalshoven, *supra* note 256, at 837–38, 853; Marco Sassòli, *State Responsibility for Violations of International Humanitarian Law*, 84 Int'l Rev. Red Cross, 401, 405–6 (2002); Luigi Condorelli, *The Imputability to States of Acts of International Terrorism*, 19 Israel Y.B. Hum. Rts. 233, 236 (1989); Tonkin, *supra* note 59, at 95–97; Lindsey Cameron & Vincent Chetail, Privatizing War: Private Military and Security Companies Under Public International Law 163–64 (2013).

261. Int'l Law Comm'n, Summary Records of the Twenty-Seventh Session (1975), *in* [1975] 1 Y.B. Int'l L. Comm'n, 16, ¶ 4 (comments of Special Rapporteur Ago), U.N. Doc. A/CN.4/SER.A/1975; *id.* at 7, ¶ 5 (comments of Mr. Reuter).

262. Prosecutor v. Tadić, Case No. IT-94-1-A, Appeals Chamber Judgment, ¶ 98 n. 117 (Int'l Crim. Trib. for the former Yugoslavia, July 15, 1999).

263. Amnesty Int'l, Aidar Volunteer Battalion, *supra* note 70.

264. ARSIWA, *supra* note 1, art. 7; *id.* art. 4, cmt. ¶ 13; *id.* art. 8, cmt. ¶ 8.

265. For discussion regarding the character of the conflict in Ukraine, *see, e.g.*, International Criminal Court, Office of the Prosecutor, Rep. on Preliminary Examination Activities 2016, at 37 (Nov. 14, 2016), www.icc-cpi.int/iccdocs/otp/161114-otp-rep-PE_ENG.pdf; Amnesty Int'l, Ukraine: Mounting Evidence of War Crimes and Russian Involvement (Sept. 7, 2014), www.amnesty.org/en/latest/news/2014/09/ukraine-mounting-evidence-war-crimes-and-russian-involvement/.

home, meaning that their presence in the conflict zone is due solely to the role they perform for the State.[266] In such circumstances, military personnel would rarely act in a truly private capacity.[267] Instead, throughout their deployment, military personnel typically act in exercise of their official functions, leading to the attribution of their conduct to the State.[268] The differing interpretations of Article 91 AP1 appear, therefore, to be of minimal practical import.

The rule's impact is potentially greater regarding the conduct of NSAs. Some scholars argue that when read in light of the definition of a State's armed forces in Article 43 AP I,[269] Article 91 operates as a *lex specialis* rule of attribution.[270] In other words, in conflicts to which AP I applies, the acts of all groups acting under a State's responsible command within the meaning of Article 43, and therefore forming part of its armed forces, are attributable to the State.[271] Applied to the conflict in the DRC,[272] this would mean that if M23 fighters acted on Rwanda's behalf and subordinated themselves to the State's command within the meaning of Article 43, the many IHL violations involving M23 fighters are attributable to Rwanda.[273] This would be the case even if the relevant acts are not attributable to Rwanda under any of the rules reflected in ARSIWA.[274]

266. Sassòli, *supra* note 260, at 405–6; Tonkin, *supra* note 59, at 95–98.

267. One exception might be if military personnel commit private acts whilst on leave from their duties in occupied territory. *See* Kalshoven, *supra* note 256.

268. Sassòli, *supra* note 260, at 405–6; Tonkin, *supra* note 59, at 95–98.

269. AP I, *supra* note 253, art. 43. *See also* Commentary on the Additional Protocols, *supra* note 258, ¶¶ 1672–81; Kubo Mačák, Internationalized Armed Conflicts in International Law, 179–80 (2018).

270. Kalshoven, *supra* note 256, at 847–48; Knut Ipsen, *Combatants and Non-Combatants, in* The Handbook of International Humanitarian Law 85 (Dieter Fleck ed., 2008); Carsten Hoppe, *Passing the Buck: State Responsibility for Private Military Companies*, 19 Eur. J. Int'l L. 989, 1005–12 (2008); Tonkin, *supra* note 59, at 82–84; Frauke Renz, State Responsibility and New Trends in the Privatization of Warfare 106–10, 216–17 (2020). In addition, the 2008 Montreux Document uses the language of art. 43 AP I when addressing a hiring State's responsibility for a private military and security company's violations of international law. *See* Montreux Document, *supra* note 62, pt. 1, ¶ 7. *But see* Katherine Del Mar, *The Requirement of "Belonging" Under International Humanitarian Law*, 21 Eur. J. Int'l L. 105, 120–21 (2010).

271. Marko Milanović, *Special Rules of Attribution of Conduct in International Law*, 96 Int'l L. Stud., 295, 324–29 (2020) [hereinafter Milanović, *Special Rules of Attribution*].

272. *See supra* ch. 2, sec. 2.4.3.

273. *See, e.g.*, Human Rts. Watch, M23 Rebels Kill, Rape Civilians (July 22, 2013), https://www.hrw.org/news/2013/07/22/dr-congo-m23-rebels-kill-rape-civilians; Amnesty Int'l, DR Congo: Rwandan-Backed M23 Rebels Perpetrating Summary Killings and Rapes (Feb. 17, 2023), https://www.amnesty.org/en/latest/news/2023/02/dr-congo-rwandan-backed-m23-rebels-perpetrating-summary-killings-and-rapes/.

274. ARSIWA, *supra* note 1, arts. 4, 5, 8–11.

It is far from certain, however, that Article 91 has that effect. While the International Committee of the Red Cross (ICRC) *Study of Customary IHL* supports the broad interpretation of a State's armed forces in Article 43,[275] it does not translate this into a special rule of attribution.[276] Instead, when addressing the issue of responsibility, the ICRC replicates ARSIWA's attribution framework without any modification to the rule reflected in Article 4.[277]

The commentary to Article 91 also makes no reference to the provision's operation as a special rule of attribution.[278] Instead, this refers to the general rules reflected in Articles 4 and 7 ARSIWA and, in the context of damage caused by individuals who are not members of the State's armed forces, it indicates that States might bear responsibility for their own organs' failure to exercise due diligence to prevent such acts from occurring.[279] The more authoritative view of Article 91, therefore, is that it is not a *lex specialis* rule of attribution, but that it merely refers to a State's responsibility for acts that are attributable to it in accordance with the general rules reflected in ARSIWA.[280]

4.6 CONCLUSION

Notwithstanding its application to organs of State, the rule reflected in Article 4 ARSIWA is of clear relevance to the issue of State responsibility for the conduct of NSAs. During armed conflict, the rule applies primarily when NSAs are integrated into a State's structure via the State's internal laws. While not a frequent occurrence, several conflict parties have incorporated militia groups into their State apparatus, as illustrated by the NDF in Syria and the Ukrainian volunteer battalions. Once these entities gain the status of de jure State organs, the entirety of their conduct in that capacity is attributable to the State, even if it is *ultra vires*. The rule outlined in Article 7 ARSIWA thus performs an important function. It holds States to account for the acts of their organs, even if a State fails to exert sufficient control over an organ's conduct to ensure the latter's compliance with international law.

The principle expressed in Article 7 should, in theory, apply equally to entities that attain the status of State organs due to the strength of their de facto relationship with the State. In practice, however, it is questionable whether an entity with sufficient autonomy to commit *ultra vires* acts could ever qualify as a de facto State

275. Customary IHL, *supra* note 6, r. 4.

276. *Id.* r. 149.

277. *Id. See also* Milanović, *Special Rules of Attribution*, *supra* note 271, at 329.

278. Commentary on the Additional Protocols, *supra* note 258, ¶ 3660.

279. *Id. See also* Del Mar, *supra* note 270, at 121–23; Milanović, *Special Rules of Attribution*, *supra* note 271, at 328–29.

280. Milanović, *Special Rules of Attribution*, *supra* note 271, at 329.

organ.[281] The requirement for the State to exercise "strict control" over the entity's conduct, in all its fields of activity, likely excludes this possibility.[282]

Even if evidence of a high degree of State control is available, an entity only constitutes a de facto State organ if it also exhibits "complete dependence" on the State. As the examples in this chapter illustrate, however, these dual requirements are rarely satisfied. The test formulated by the ICJ potentially excludes militias such as M23 from qualifying as de facto State organs, without any opportunity to assess whether their overall relationship with the State mirrors that of a de jure organ.

Such an outcome appears inconsistent with the ILC's aims in broadening the wording of Article 4 ARSIWA to encompass de facto State organs, as well as the comments of governments upon which this change was based.[283] Although an NSA's conduct might be attributable to a State on other grounds if the criteria relevant to Article 4 are not met,[284] each of the rules of attribution reflected in ARSIWA is designed to address a different set of circumstances. When an NSA is integrated into a State's apparatus and acts for the State in all its fields of activity, the rule reflected in Article 4 should apply to attribute its conduct performed in an official capacity to the State.

The ICJ acknowledged the importance of de facto State organ status in the *Bosnian Genocide* case, noting that a restriction of the rule of attribution to de jure State organs "would allow States to escape their international responsibility by choosing to act through persons or entities whose supposed independence would be purely fictitious."[285] However, the inflexibility of the test relevant to de facto State organ status deprives it of practical significance and potentially requires a State to maintain a closer relationship with an NSA than it sustains with its de jure organs. A more effective test is therefore required that examines the entirety of the relationship between the State and the NSA without requiring the extant levels of dependence and control to be "complete" in nature.[286]

De facto State organ status should nevertheless remain "exceptional" in character because of its effects, attributing all the entity's official conduct to the State.[287] If an entity does not act for the State in all its fields of activity, attribution might be appropriate on another basis. It may be that the NSA was acting under the State's instructions, direction, or control.[288] Alternatively, if the entity was exercising governmental functions at the relevant time, the attribution standard reflected in Article 5 ARSIWA may apply. This is the focus of Chapter 5.

281. *See* ILC Y.B. 1972 vol. II, *supra* note 220, at 72 n. 4.

282. de Frouville, *supra* note 220, at 268.

283. Crawford's First Rep. on State Responsibility, *supra* note 19, at 35; ILC Y.B. 1998 vol. I, *supra* note 22, at 229, ¶ 3. *See also* ILC Y.B. 1975 vol. II, *supra* note 239, at 80, ¶ 32.

284. ARSIWA, *supra* note 1, arts. 5, 8, 9–11.

285. *Bosnian Genocide*, *supra* note 4, ¶ 392.

286. *See supra* sec. 4.4.3.

287. *Bosnian Genocide*, *supra* note 4, ¶ 393.

288. ARSIWA, *supra* note 1, art. 8. *See infra* ch. 6.

5

Persons or Entities Exercising Elements of Governmental Authority

5.1 INTRODUCTION

It is common today for non-State actors (NSAs) to carry out activities that, in years past, were considered governmental in nature. Privatization and outsourcing have increased markedly across all sectors of government, including in military-related activities in combat zones.[1] The trend is equally apparent in the cyber domain, where private actors not only play a significant role in upholding cybersecurity but also engage in hostile operations on States' behalf.[2] Meanwhile, States such as Russia and Iran have increasingly used private entities like the Wagner Group or local militias to fight in conflicts on their behalf.[3]

This blurring of the boundaries between public- and private-sector activity has led to concerns regarding accountability for the wrongful behavior of the private entities concerned. The abuses committed by members of the Wagner Group in the conflicts in Syria, Ukraine, and elsewhere are a case in point.[4] While the

1. *See supra* ch. 2, sec. 2.2.2

2. *See, e.g.*, Dustin Volz, *U.S. Blames North Korea for "WannaCry" Cyber Attack*, REUTERS (Dec. 18, 2017), https://www.reuters.com/article/us-usa-cY.B.er-northkorea-idUSKBN1ED00Q/; Paulina Rios Maya, *Who Is Lazarus Group: A Deep-Dive into the North Korean Cyber Gang*, EM360 (Nov. 27, 2024), https://em360tech.com/tech-article/who-is-lazarus-group.

3. Kimberley Marten, *Russia's Use of Semi-State Security Forces: The Case of the Wagner Group*, 35 POST-SOVIET AFF. 181 (2019); ARIANE M. TABATABAI ET AL., RAND, THE IRAN THREAT NETWORK: FOUR MODELS OF IRAN'S NONSTATE CLIENT PARTNERSHIPS 14–16 (2021), www.rand.org/pubs/research_reports/RR4231.html.

4. *See, e.g.*, Amy MacKinnon, *New Report Exposes Brutal Methods of Russia's Wagner Group*, FOREIGN POL'Y (June 11, 2020), https://foreignpolicy.com/2020/06/11/russia-wag

Attribution of Non-State Actor Conduct During Armed Conflict. Jennifer Maddocks, Oxford University Press.
 DOI: 10.1093/oso/9780197842652.003.0005

individual fighters are personally liable under criminal law for their misconduct, the question of State responsibility remains.[5]

This chapter assesses the circumstances in which States bear responsibility for the conduct of NSAs they authorize to perform governmental functions on their behalf. The applicable rule, enshrined in Article 5 of the Draft Articles on Responsibility of States for Internationally Wrongful Acts (ARSIWA), is commonly considered to reflect customary international law.[6] It provides:

> The conduct of a person or entity which is not an organ of the State under article 4 but which is empowered by the law of that State to exercise elements of the governmental authority shall be considered an act of the State under international law, provided the person or entity is acting in that capacity in the particular instance.[7]

The commentary to Article 5 sets out three conditions that must be satisfied for the rule to apply.[8] First, the NSA's conduct must amount to an exercise of governmental authority. Second, the private actor must be empowered by the domestic law of the State to exercise such authority. And third, the private actor must in fact exercise those public powers, rather than acting in a private capacity, at the relevant time.[9]

ner-group-methods-bouta-killing-report/; Sean McFate, *The Mercenaries Behind the Bucha Massacre*, WALL ST. J. (Apr. 12, 2022), https://www.wsj.com/articles/mercenaries-behind-bucha-massacre-russia-ukraine-putin-attack-terror-brutality-wagner-group-moscow-geneva-convention-war-crimes-atrocities-11649797041.

5. *See* Jennifer Maddocks, *Russia, The Wagner Group, and the Issue of Attribution*, ARTICLES OF WAR (Apr. 28, 2021), https://lieber.westpoint.edu/russia-wagner-group-attribution/; Jennifer Maddocks, *Putin Admits to Funding the Wagner Group: Implications for Russia's State Responsibility*, ARTICLES OF WAR (June 30, 2023), https://lieber.westpoint.edu/putin-admits-funding-wagner-group-implications-russias-state-responsibility/.

6. *See, e.g.*, 1 CUSTOMARY INTERNATIONAL HUMANITARIAN LAW r. 149 (Jean-Marie Henckaerts & Louise Doswald-Beck eds., 2005); Official Compendium of Voluntary National Contributions on the Subject of How International Law Applies to the Use of Information and Communications Technologies by States Submitted by Participating Governmental Experts at the Group of Governmental Experts on Advancing Responsible State Behavior in Cyberspace in the Context of International Security Established Pursuant to General Assembly Resolution 73/266, U.N. Doc. A/76/136* at 21, 39, 78–79, 90, 141 (July 13, 2021) (positions of Brazil, Estonia, Germany, Romania, Switzerland, and United States) [hereinafter Official Compendium]. *See infra* sec. 5.4.3 for discussion whether the "empowered by law" element of the rule reflects customary international law.

7. Draft Articles on Responsibility of States for Internationally Wrongful Acts, with commentaries, art. 5, *in* Int'l Law Comm'n, Rep. on the Work of Its Fifty-Third Session, U.N. Doc. A/56/10 (2001), *reprinted in* [2001] 2 Y.B. INT'L LAW COMM'N 31, 42, U.N. Doc. A/CN.4/SER.A/2001/Add.1 (Part 2) [hereinafter ARSIWA].

8. *Id.* cmt. ¶ 2.

9. *Id.*

Although these criteria appear straightforward, doubts remain about Article 5's application. This is largely due to uncertainty as to the types of activity that fall within the sphere of governmental authority, as well as ambiguity regarding the nature of the delegation that is required for an entity to be empowered by the law of the State. This chapter seeks to add clarity to such issues. It commences by reviewing the rule's drafting history and general features before moving to address, in turn, each of the three criteria relevant to its application.

5.2 ATTRIBUTION PURSUANT TO ARTICLE 5

5.2.1 Drafting History

The principle that States should bear responsibility for the conduct of entities that perform public functions on their behalf is evident in the preparatory work for the 1930 Hague Conference relating to the Codification of International Law.[10] The International Law Commission (ILC) then began to examine this as a potential basis of attribution in 1971. Special Rapporteur Ago noted that there are situations "in which an individual or even a group of individuals having no official status under the internal legal order does in fact have occasion to perform a function which should normally be performed by an organ of the State administration . . . without thereby acquiring the status of a State official."[11]

In such circumstances, Ago observed that the relevant conduct "should be considered as acts of the State from the viewpoint of international law."[12] He referred to certain case law in support including the *Zafiro* case, which concerned the attribution to the United States of acts performed by the crew of a merchant

10. Bases of Discussion Drawn up in 1929 by the Preparatory Committee of the Conference for the Codification of International Law, Basis of Discussion No. 16 (The Hague, 1930), *reprinted in* Int'l Law Comm'n, Documents of the Eighth Session Including the Rep. of the Comm'n to the General Assembly 223, 223 (1956), *in* [1956] 2 Y.B. INT'L LAW COMM'N, U.N. Doc. A/CN.4/SER.A/1956/Add.1. *See also* ARSIWA, *supra* note 7, art. 5, cmt. ¶ 4. The principle did not, however, appear in the 1929 or 1961 Harvard Draft Conventions on State responsibility. *See* Harvard Draft Convention on Responsibility of States for Damage Done in Their Territory to the Person or Property of Foreigners (1929), *reprinted in* Int'l Law Comm'n, Documents of the Eighth Session Including the Rep. of the Comm'n to the General Assembly 229 (1956), *in* [1956] 2 Y.B. INT'L LAW COMM'N, U.N. Doc. A/CN.4/SER.A/1956/Add.1; Harvard Draft Convention on the International Responsibility of States for Injuries to Aliens (1961), *reprinted in* Int'l Law Comm'n, Documents of the Twenty-First Session Including the Rep. of the Comm'n to the General Assembly 142, 145–46 (1969), *in* [1969] 2 Y.B. INT'L LAW COMM'N, U.N. Doc. A/CN.4/SER.A/1969/Add.1.

11. Roberto Ago (Special Rapporteur), Third Rep. on State Responsibility—the Internationally Wrongful Act of the State, Source of International Responsibility, U.N. Doc. A/CN.4/246 and Add.1–3 (1971), *in* [1971] 2 Y.B. INT'L LAW COMM'N 199, 262, ¶ 187, U.N. Doc. A/CN.4/SER.A/1971/Add.1 (Part 1) [hereinafter Ago's Third Rep. on State Responsibility].

12. *Id.* at 263, ¶ 188.

vessel.[13] The United States argued that the *Zafiro* must be regarded as a merchant ship; not a public vessel for whose conduct the State was liable.[14] The Arbitral Tribunal disagreed, finding that "the liability of the State for [the *Zafiro*'s] actions must depend upon the nature of the service in which she is engaged and the purpose for which she is employed."[15] Irrespective of the legal regime under which the vessel operated, the tribunal concluded that the *Zafiro* functioned as a supply ship for the U.S. Navy, under the command of the officer on board.[16] Therefore, due to the public character of the tasks performed, the United States was responsible for the crew's actions.[17]

Ago additionally referred to the "pseudo-volunteers" sent to Spain by some States during the 1936 to 1939 civil war.[18] He quoted with approval the remarks of the Mexican delegate at the League of Nations, who observed that had these individuals been true volunteers, they would have acted in breach of their respective States' criminal laws. Instead, they were treated as heroes. The reality of the situation was that they were acting on behalf of their respective States, meaning their conduct was governmental in character and engaged the States' responsibility.[19]

The draft article Ago formulated to reflect this basis of attribution was general in character, also encompassing the rules now expressed in Articles 8 and 9 ARSIWA.[20] Regarding the principle now enshrined in Article 5, the draft referred only to the performance of public functions; it did not require the State to empower the NSA to act.[21] Three years later, the ILC Drafting Committee proposed a new draft article, which included the three elements of the rule now reflected in Article 5.[22] Thus, in addition to the requirement to exercise public functions, the draft also articulated the need for empowerment by law and for the entity to be acting in a public capacity at the relevant time.[23]

13. *Id.* at 264, ¶ 192, citing D. Earnshaw & Others (Great Britain) v. U.S.A., 6 R.I.A.A. 160, 162 (Am.-Brit. Arb. Trib., 1925) [hereinafter *Zafiro* case].

14. *Zafiro* case, *supra* note 13, at 162.

15. *Id.*

16. *Id.* at 163.

17. *Id.* at 160.

18. Ago's Third Rep. on State Responsibility, *supra* note 11, at 264, ¶ 192.

19. *Id.*

20. *Id.* at 267 (draft art. 8). For discussion and analysis of arts. 8 and 9 ARSIWA, *see infra* chs. 6, 8.

21. Ago's Third Rep. on State Responsibility, *supra* note 11, at 267 (draft art. 8).

22. Int'l Law Comm'n, Rep. of the Comm'n to the General Assembly (draft art. 7(2)) (1974), *in* [1974] 2 Y.B. INT'L LAW COMM'N 277, U.N. Doc. A/CN.4/SER.A/1974/Add.1 (Part One) [hereinafter ILC Y.B. 1974 vol. II].

23. *Id.*

The ILC considered this basis of attribution again upon Crawford's appointment as Special Rapporteur.[24] At that time, the relevant draft article referred not only to entities empowered to exercise elements of the government authority but also to territorial governmental entities within federal States.[25] Crawford noted that the latter are State organs, meaning they fall within the scope of the rule now reflected in Article 4.[26] However, "parastatals" that exercise government functions require a separate basis of attribution.[27] Crawford observed that this should encompass "such persons as private security guards acting as prison warders, to the extent that they exercise public powers such as powers of detention and discipline pursuant to a judicial sentence or to prison regulations."[28]

The version of Article 5 that was ultimately adopted does not differ substantially from the draft the ILC Drafting Committee proposed in 1974. After the removal of the language related to territorial governmental entities, the rule that remains refers to the three elements outlined above. These are discussed, in turn, in Sections 5.3 to 5.5. The commentary to the rule additionally highlights certain general features of the attribution standard.

5.2.2 General Features of the Attribution Standard

The commentary to Article 5 ARSIWA indicates that the rule "is intended to take account of the increasingly common phenomenon of parastatal entities, which exercise elements of governmental authority in place of State organs, as well as situations where former State corporations have been privatized but retain certain public or regulatory functions."[29] Thus, the commentary recognizes the prevalence of outsourcing and its potential impacts on a State's international responsibility. In such circumstances, if a State chooses to delegate governmental functions to a private entity and that entity acts in a manner that violates the State's international legal obligations, the rule reflected in Article 5 attributes the relevant violations to the State.[30]

It follows that the object and purpose of the rule is to attribute conduct to States, and ensure that they cannot avoid responsibility, when they choose to outsource

24. James Crawford (Special Rapporteur), First Rep. on State Responsibility 38–39, U.N. Doc. A/CN.4/490 and Add.1–7 (1998) [hereinafter Crawford's First Rep. on State Responsibility].

25. *Id.*

26. *Id.* ¶¶ 186–88. *See also* ARSIWA, *supra* note 7, art. 4.

27. Crawford's First Rep. on State Responsibility, *supra* note 24, at 39, ¶ 189.

28. *Id.*

29. ARSIWA, *supra* note 7, art. 5, cmt. ¶ 1.

30. *Id.* art. 5. *See also* Int'l Law Comm'n, Summary Records of the Meetings of the Fiftieth Session (comments of Special Rapporteur James Crawford) (1998), *in* [1998] 1 Y.B. INT'L LAW COMM'N 228, U.N. Doc. A/CN.4/SER.A/1998 [hereinafter ILC Y.B. 1998 vol. I].

or privatize functions that are traditionally performed by the State's own organs.[31] To illustrate, the ARSIWA commentary cites the German government's comments prior to the 1930 Hague Conference: "From the point of view of international law, it does not matter whether a State polices a given area with its own police or entrusts this duty, to a greater or less extent, to autonomous bodies."[32] In either case, the State should bear responsibility for any international law violations committed during the performance of those governmental functions.[33]

The same principle holds true in conflict situations. For example, if a State delegates the management of a detention facility in a conflict zone to a private company and that company's employees commit acts in breach of the State's obligations under international humanitarian law (IHL), the rule reflected in Article 5 operates to attribute the employees' conduct to the State.

In contrast with the rule reflected in Article 4 ARSIWA,[34] the rule expressed in Article 5 does not attribute all the entity's conduct to the State. The acts to which Article 5 applies might be performed by persons or groups that undertake a range of tasks; some for the State, and some for one or more private entities. For example, in a conflict location, the same private military and security company (PMSC) might guard a military base on behalf of a State and also work for a private company, protecting its mining business. The rule reflected in Article 5 applies only to the governmental tasks the NSA performs for the State. It therefore represents a narrower basis of attribution than Article 4.[35]

The commentary makes clear that the identity or character of the NSA that undertakes the relevant public tasks is immaterial to the rule's application.[36] Provided it does not qualify as an organ of State under the State's domestic law, the NSA's attributes and status are not relevant for the purposes of attribution.[37] Thus, the NSAs to which the rule applies may be totally or partially State-owned or State-funded, or entirely private, such as commercial companies specializing in cybersecurity or operating as PMSCs.[38] They may equally be private individuals

31. ARSIWA, *supra* note 7, chapeau to pt. I, ch. II, cmt. ¶ 7; ILC Y.B. 1998 vol. I, *supra* note 30, at 228 (comments of Special Rapporteur James Crawford).

32. ARSIWA, *supra* note 7, art. 5, cmt. ¶ 4, citing League of Nations, Conference for the Codification of International Law, Bases of Discussion for the Conference drawn up by the Preparatory Committee, vol. 3: Responsibility of States for Damage Caused in their Territory to the Person or Property of Foreigners 90 (1929).

33. *Id.*

34. ARSIWA, *supra* note 7, art. 4. For discussion regarding Article 4, *see supra* ch. 4.

35. For further discussion regarding how the rules of attribution relate to each other, *see infra* ch. 7, sec. 7.2.

36. ARSIWA, *supra* note 7, art. 5, cmt. ¶¶ 2, 3.

37. *Id.* For discussion regarding organs of State, *see supra* ch. 4.

38. ARSIWA, *supra* note 7, art. 5, cmt. ¶¶ 2, 3.

or groups, such as an individual contractor, a militia group, or a loose association of hackers.

The presence or absence of State control over an entity's activities is equally irrelevant to the rule's application.[39] In this respect, the ARSIWA commentary makes clear that "an entity is covered even if its exercise of authority involves an independent discretion or power to act; there is no need to show that the conduct was in fact carried out under the control of the State."[40] From an evidentiary perspective, therefore, it may be easier for an injured State to prove attribution on this basis than pursuant to the rule reflected in Article 8, which requires proof of State instructions, direction, or control.[41] Unlike the rule of attribution expressed in Article 8, however, Article 5 applies only to conduct that is governmental in character.

5.3 ELEMENTS OF GOVERNMENTAL AUTHORITY

The text of Article 5 makes clear that for the rule of attribution to apply, the NSA concerned must be exercising "elements of the governmental authority" at the time it acts in violation of the State's international legal obligations.[42] The commentary describes this notion as encompassing "functions of a public character normally exercised by State organs."[43] The emphasis is therefore upon those functions performed in the public interest that are conventionally carried out by government bodies or agencies, as opposed to by private entities.

It is, however, far from easy to identify the precise activities that a State traditionally performs.[44] The ARSIWA commentary provides limited guidance in this respect, stating that "[b]eyond a certain limit, what is regarded as 'governmental' depends on the particular society, its history and traditions."[45] To exacerbate the issue, there is no common understanding in international law regarding what

39. *Id.* cmt. ¶ 7.

40. *Id.*

41. *Id.* art. 8. For discussion regarding this rule of attribution, *see infra* ch. 6.

42. ARSIWA, *supra* note 7, art. 5.

43. *Id.* cmt. ¶ 2. *See also* Int'l Law Comm'n, Draft Articles on State Responsibility with Commentaries Thereto Adopted by the Int'l Law Comm'n on First Reading, art. 7, cmt. ¶ 18 (Jan. 1997).

44. *See* David D. Caron, *The ILC Articles on State Responsibility: The Paradoxical Relationship Between Form and Authority*, 96 Am. J. Int'l L. 857, 861 (2002).

45. ARSIWA, *supra* note 7, art. 5, cmt. ¶ 6. The ILC did not intend to define the scope of governmental authority. *See* Crawford's First Rep. on State Responsibility, *supra* note 24, at 39, ¶ 190; ILC Y.B. 1998 vol. I, *supra* note 30, at 229; Int'l Law Comm'n, Summary Records of the Meetings of the Fifty-Third Session (2001), *in* [2001] 1 Y.B. Int'l Law Comm'n 92, ¶ 21, U.N. Doc. A/CN.4/SER.A/2001.

constitutes a governmental or public act.[46] Such ambiguity engenders uncertainty regarding the scope of the rule reflected in Article 5 and potentially leads to the arbitrary application of the rules of attribution. As Special Rapporteur Ago noted, "If the same public function were performed in one State by organs of the State proper and in another by para-State institutions, it would indeed be absurd if the international responsibility of the State were engaged in one case and not in the other."[47] For instance, it would make little sense to attribute armed security activities to one State on the basis that these acts are normally performed by military personnel, but not to another where the function is commonly outsourced.

Further difficulties arise due to the prevalence of outsourcing in recent years.[48] As public functions are increasingly privatized, activities that were historically performed by the State may cease to serve as relevant indicators of what is truly governmental in nature.[49] If States continue to outsource functions to private entities, the range of activities that are considered governmental may steadily diminish, leading to further ambiguity regarding the scope of Article 5 and a reduction in States' responsibility.[50]

A better approach, therefore, is to identify factors that apply to all States, irrespective of their individual outsourcing practices, and apply them to an evaluation of the functions that States empower NSAs to perform. This provides greater certainty regarding the meaning of governmental activity and bypasses the difficulties arising from States' varying attitudes toward privatization.

5.3.1 Guidance Within the ARSIWA Commentary

The ARSIWA commentary identifies four factors that are of particular importance when determining whether a function performed by an NSA falls within

46. Noble Ventures Inc. v. Romania, Case No. ARB/01/11, ¶ 82 (Int'l Ctr. for Settlement of Inv. Disp., Oct 12, 2005). *See also* Crawford's First Rep. on State Responsibility, *supra* note 24, at 33–34; U. Ctr. for Int'l Humanitarian L., Expert Meeting on Private Military Contractors: Status and State Responsibility for their Actions 18–20 (Aug. 29–30, 2005), www.ucihl.org/communication/Private_Military_Companies_report.pdf.

47. Int'l Law Comm'n, Summary Records of the Twenty-Sixth Session (1974), *in* [1974] 1 Y.B. Int'l Law Comm'n 8, ¶ 17, U.N. Doc. A/CN.4/SER.A/1974 [hereinafter ILC Y.B. 1974 vol. I].

48. *See supra* ch. 2, sec. 2.2.2.

49. Hannah Tonkin, State Control over Private Military and Security Companies in Armed Conflict, 101 (2011); James Crawford, State Responsibility: The General Part 129 (2013). In 1971, for example, Special Rapporteur Ago included "public transport" and "postal communications" within the examples he gave of public tasks; functions that, today, are unlikely to be considered governmental in nature. *See* Ago's Third Rep. on State Responsibility, *supra* note 11, at 263, ¶ 190.

50. Christine Chinkin, *A Critique of the Public/Private Dimension*, 10 Eur. J. Int'l L. 387, 390 (1999); U. Ctr. for Int'l Humanitarian L., *supra* note 46, at 18–19; Frauke Renz, State Responsibility and New Trends in the Privatization of Warfare 253 (2020).

the sphere of governmental authority. These are (1) the content of the powers, (2) the way they are conferred on an entity, (3) the purposes for which the powers are to be exercised, and (4) the extent to which the entity is accountable to the government in the exercise of the powers.[51]

The content of the powers delegated to an NSA is key to determining the public or private status of a particular function. This analysis focuses on the activities that the State empowers the entity to perform and, in particular, whether those activities are normally reserved to the State or can be freely carried out by private individuals.[52] For instance, the exercise of powers involving the use of force or the right to constrain or control the activities of private individuals strongly indicates that the function concerned is governmental in nature.[53]

The third criterion related to the purpose of the powers also assists in this assessment. The exercise of security functions, for example, will be governmental if the purpose is to guard a military base in a combat zone, but not if the aim of the powers is to protect the facilities of a commercial mining company. The fact that delegated powers are to be exercised in the public interest might therefore indicate a governmental nexus. However, a public purpose does not always equate to governmental status. Some powers, such as those related to education and the postal service, serve the public interest but do not amount to an exercise of governmental authority.[54] The purpose of the powers should thus be considered alongside other factors.

The remaining two criteria outlined in the ARSIWA commentary are of more limited assistance. The way in which the powers are conferred relates to the "empowered by the law" requirement, discussed in Section 5.4. In this respect, the fact that a State has empowered an NSA to perform a particular function might be a clear indication of its governmental status.[55] However, the manner of the delegation is less important to this determination. For example, a State might enact legislation authorizing the delegation of a particular function to a PMSC, thereby indicating the importance of its decision and perhaps a likelihood that the delegated task is governmental. But that might equally be the case if a lesser means of empowerment is used, such as a contract. Thus, the way the powers are conferred to an NSA has little bearing on the status of the delegated activity.

51. ARSIWA, *supra* note 7, art. 5, cmt. ¶ 6.

52. Crawford, *supra* note 49, at 129–30. *See also infra* sec. 5.3.2.

53. Alexis P. Kontos, *"Private" Security Guards: Privatized Force and State Responsibility Under International Human Rights Law*, 4 Non-State Actors & Int'l L. 199, 221–22 (2004); Alexander Kees, *Responsibility of States for Private Actors*, *in* Max Planck Encyclopedia of Public Int'l L. ¶ 12 (Rüdiger Wolfrum ed., 2011); Renz, *supra* note 50, at 131–33.

54. Lindsey Cameron & Vincent Chetail, Privatizing War: Private Military and Security Companies under Public International Law 174 (2013).

55. *See infra* the discussion of the overall context in sec. 5.3.3.

The final factor referred to in the commentary relates to accountability, in terms of government supervision over the delegated activity.[56] This criterion captures the premise that States may wish to exercise greater control over private entities performing governmental functions than those that are not. But the fact that an NSA is not accountable to the government does not automatically mean that it is not performing public functions. The commentary to Article 5 makes clear that there is no requirement for State control over the activities in question for the rule to apply.[57] Indeed, if accountability were given too much weight when assessing potential attribution on this basis, it could undermine the rule's entire application.[58] As Tonkin writes in the context of PMSCs, "it is precisely in those cases where the government authorises a PMSC to carry out a particular function, and yet fails to hold that PMSC accountable for its actions, that the rationale for the attribution of PMSC misconduct to the State is the strongest."[59]

The content and purpose of the powers are therefore the most helpful criteria among those identified in the ARSIWA commentary. Other factors may also assist when assessing whether a particular activity amounts to an exercise of governmental authority.[60] These include the overall context in which the functions are performed,[61] and whether the delegated powers can be classified as "quintessentially governmental" in character.

5.3.2 Quintessentially Governmental Functions

The powers that a State delegates to an NSA may be described as quintessentially governmental if they are typically performed by the State and they are central to the nature and purposes of government.[62] Thus, the levying of taxes, the conduct

56. ARSIWA, *supra* note 7, art. 5, cmt. ¶ 6. *See also* Crawford, *supra* note 49, at 131.

57. ARSIWA, *supra* note 7, art. 5, cmt. ¶ 7.

58. Chia Lehnardt, *Private Military Companies and State Responsibility*, *in* From Mercenaries to Market: The Rise and Regulation of Private Military Companies 139, 145 (Simon Chesterton & Chia Lehnardt eds., 2007); Cameron & Chetail, *supra* note 54, at 55, 174; Tonkin, *supra* note 49, at 103.

59. Tonkin, *supra* note 49, at 103. *See also* Lehnardt, *supra* note 58, at 145.

60. The ARSIWA commentary indicates that the four factors are of "particular importance" but not the only criteria to be considered. *See* ARSIWA, *supra* note 7, art. 5, cmt. ¶ 6.

61. *See infra* sec. 5.3.3.

62. There is no definition in international law of those functions that are inherently governmental. However, guidance as to the meaning of the term may be found in the domestic law and policy of States. *See, e.g.*, Publication of the Office of Federal Procurement Policy (OFPP) Policy Letter 11-01, Performance of Inherently Governmental and Critical Functions, Fed. Reg. 176, 56,227 (Sept. 12, 2011), www.gpo.gov/fdsys/pkg/FR-2011-09-12/pdf/2011-23165.pdf. *See also* Lindsay Windsor, *James Bond, Inc.: Private Contractors and Covert Action*, 101 Geo. L.J. 1427, 1431–40 (2013); James R. Lisher, *Outsourcing Cyberwarfare: Drawing the Line*

of foreign affairs, and the enactment of laws are all inherently governmental. But identifying the full range of tasks falling within this category is increasingly complex. As one scholar noted:

> When private companies are now rendering logistical support for military operations, running prisons and conducting interrogations, providing armed escort for personnel and convoys, doing general policing work, and carrying out surveillance, it is becoming more and more difficult, without offending either logic or common sense, to insist on maintaining that a particular activity is "quintessentially sovereign" or "typically private."[63]

The assessment is particularly problematic in the cyber domain where, due to the novelty of cyber operations and the proliferation of NSAs, it appears challenging to identify any functions that are traditionally reserved to the State.

Nonetheless, if the focus remains on the content and purpose of the relevant functions, certain activities qualify as inherently governmental irrespective of the domain in which they are undertaken. The ARSIWA commentary identifies several government functions that fall within this category, including "powers of detention and discipline pursuant to a judicial sentence . . . identification of property for seizure"[64] and the activities of the police.[65] It follows that the law enforcement functions performed by the Shabbiha militia in support of the Assad regime during the early stages of the Syrian conflict were quintessentially governmental.[66]

Offensive combat also falls within this category, as a corollary of the State monopoly on the legitimate use of force.[67] Accordingly, the PMSCs that participated in the conflicts in Sierra Leone and Angola were engaged in governmental activity, as were members of the Wagner Group when they fought on Russia's behalf in Ukraine, Syria, and elsewhere.[68] Similarly, the Syrian militias that Turkey

for Inherently Governmental Functions in Cyberspace, J. CONT. MGMT. 7, 8–10 (Fall 2014); Frédéric Mégret, *Are There "Inherently Sovereign Functions" in International Law?* 115 AM. J. INT'L L. 452 (2021).

63. ZIAODONG YANG, STATE IMMUNITY IN INTERNATIONAL LAW, 59–60 (2012).

64. ARSIWA, *supra* note 7, art. 5, cmt. ¶ 2.

65. *Id.* chapeau to pt. I ch. II, cmt. ¶ 6.

66. *See supra* ch. 2, sec. 2.4.1.

67. Rep. of the Working Group on the Use of Mercenaries as a Means of Violating Human Rights and Impeding the Exercise of the Right of Peoples to Self-Determination 13, U.N. Doc. A/HRC/15/25 (July 2, 2010). *See also* Katja Nieminen, *Rules of Attribution and the Private Military Contractors at Abu Ghraib: Private Acts or Public Wrongs?* 15 FINNISH Y.B INT'L L. 289, 291 (2004); Mégret, *supra* note 62, at 471–74; Nigel D. White, *Symposium of Frédéric Mégret, "Are There 'Inherently Sovereign Functions' in International Law?" Outsourcing Military and Security Functions*, 115 AM. J. INT'L L. UNBOUND 317 (2021).

68. IAN RALBY & HANNAH TONKIN, CHATHAM HOUSE, REGULATION OF PRIVATE MILITARY SECURITY COMPANIES IN ARMED CONFLICT 3 (2011), www.chathamhouse.org/sites/files/chathamhouse/public/Research/ International%20Law/071011ralby%26tonkin.pdf; Marten, *supra* note 3; Metin Gurcan, *Private Military Companies: Moscow's Other Army in Syria*, AL-MONITOR

employed to promote its foreign policy goals in the conflicts in northern Syria, Libya, and Nagorno-Karabakh exercised elements of Ankara's governmental authority.[69] The same is true of private individuals or groups tasked by States to undertake covert missions on their behalf, provided these involve the use of offensive force.[70]

Purely defensive functions may equally qualify as inherently governmental. For instance, an armed contractor protecting a military base against enemy attack in the context of an ongoing conflict is exercising public powers; this is clear from the content of the powers, which involve the use of force, and the purpose for which they are performed: to protect the State's military base.[71] In such circumstances, it may be helpful to assess whether the person or entity concerned is directly participating in hostilities within the meaning of IHL.[72] Although controversy remains as to the precise activities that amount to a direct participation in hostilities,[73] any conduct on the part of an NSA that meets this threshold is so closely associated with the hiring State's military operations that it is inherently governmental in nature.[74]

The same is true of all PMSC activities with a direct operational effect, such as providing convoy security for military operations, interrogating detainees, or operating military equipment.[75] In addition, the running of prisoner-of-war camps

(Nov. 29, 2017), https://www.al-monitor.com/pulse/originals/2017/11/Turkey-russia-private-army-in-syria.html.

69. Ben Hubbard et al., *Syrian Arab Fighters Backed by Turkey Kill Two Kurdish Prisoners*, N.Y. Times (Oct. 12, 2019), https://www.nytimes.com/2019/10/12/world/middleeast/turkey-invasion-syria-kurds.html; Tom Allinson & Abderrahmane Ammar, *Erdogan's Syrian Mercenaries in Libya*, Deutsche Welle (Feb. 11, 2020), www.dw.com/en/libya-are-Turkeys-syrian-mercenaries-a-new-threat/a-52329943; Dror Zeevi, *Turkey Fuels Nagorno-Karabakh Conflict: Drones, Mercenaries and Dreams of Imperial Resurgence*, Just Sec. (Oct. 16, 2020), https://www.justsecurity.org/72910/turkey-fuels-nagorno-karabakh-conflict-drones-mercenaries-and-dreams-of-imperial-resurgence/.

70. Ago's Third Rep. on State Responsibility, *supra* note 11, at 263, ¶ 190.

71. *See* ARSIWA, *supra* note 7, art. 5, cmt. ¶ 6.

72. *See* Nils Melzer, Int'l Committee of the Red Cross, Interpretive Guidance on the Notion of Direct Participation in Hostilities under International Humanitarian Law 38 (May 2009), www.icrc.org/eng/assets/files/other/icrc-002-0990.pdf.

73. *See, e.g.*, Michael N. Schmitt, *Deconstructing Direct Participation in Hostilities: The Constitutive Elements*, 42 N.Y.U. J. Int'l L. & Pol. 697 (2010); Bill Boothby, *"And for Such Time As": The Time Dimension to Direct Participation in Hostilities*, 42 N.Y.U. J. Int'l L. & Pol. 741 (2010).

74. For example, Renz notes that the analysis of tactical intelligence amounts to a direct participation in hostilities and is therefore governmental in nature, whereas the analysis of strategic intelligence is not. *See* Renz, *supra* note 50, at 217–18, 220–21.

75. Lehnardt, *supra* note 58, at 146; Tonkin, *supra* note 49, at 101; Cameron & Chetail, *supra* note 54, at 200–201.

or places of civilian internment in international armed conflict is quintessentially governmental, as treaty obligations prohibit States from outsourcing such tasks.[76]

Equivalent functions performed in the cyber domain also qualify as inherently governmental. Therefore, if in the context of an armed conflict, a State empowers an NSA to undertake certain cyber activities in support of the State's kinetic operations, the entity's conduct in this respect amounts to an exercise of governmental authority. The 2022 cyber operations against the satellite company, Viasat, timed to coincide with and support Russia's full-scale invasion of Ukraine, fall within this category.[77] Equally, an offensive cyber operation that results in physical damage to or a loss in functionality of the target's governmental cyber infrastructure is public in character due to its potential to breach the State's international legal obligations and thus implicate its foreign policy.[78] In cases such as these, it may assist to enquire whether the relevant function is normally performed only by persons or entities that act with government authorization.[79] Or, in other words, if the functions are performed without such authority, they would amount to criminal acts.

To summarize, if a State empowers an NSA to perform functions such as law enforcement or the conduct of foreign affairs, these activities should properly be considered as an exercise of governmental authority. When assessing the functions performed by any private entity, however, it is important to disaggregate the various tasks the NSA carries out and address the issue of attribution separately in each case.[80] For instance, if a PMSC performs a range of tasks within a detention facility located in a combat zone, its conduct in interrogating detainees should be considered separately from its other functions, such as cleaning or feeding the troops. While the former is quintessentially governmental in nature, the latter tasks are not.

76. Geneva Convention (III) relative to the Treatment of Prisoners of War art. 39, Aug. 12, 1949, 6 U.S.T. 3316, 75 U.N.T.S. 135; Geneva Convention (IV) relative to the Protection of Civilian Persons in Time of War art. 99, Aug. 12, 1949, 6 U.S.T. 3516, 75 U.N.T.S. 287. *See also* U. Ctr. for Int'l Humanitarian L., *supra* note 46, at 7, 19–20.

77. Sam Cohen, *Acid Rain Malware and Viasat Network Downtime in Ukraine: Assessing the Cyber War Threat*, Just Sec. (Sept. 12, 2022), www.justsecurity.org/83021/acidrain-malware-and-viasat-network-downtime-in-ukraine-assessing-the-cyber-war-threat/.

78. Tallinn Manual 2.0 on the International Law Applicable to Cyber Operations rr. 4, 66, 68, 69 (Michael N. Schmitt ed., 2017) [hereinafter Tallinn Manual 2.0]. For further examples of inherently governmental functions in the cyber domain see, for example, Michael N. Schmitt & Liis Vihul, *Proxy Wars in Cyberspace: The Evolving International Law of Attribution*, Fletcher Sec. Rev. 54, 62 (2014); Michael N. Schmitt, *"Below the Threshold" Cyber Operations: The Countermeasures Response Option and International Law*, 54 Va. J. Int'l L. 697, 709 (2014).

79. Crawford, *supra* note 49, at 169.

80. *See* Bosh International Inc. & B&P Ltd. Foreign Investments Enterprise v. Ukraine, Case No. ARB/08/11, Award ¶ 176 (Int'l Ctr. for Settlement of Inv. Disp., 2012) [hereinafter *Bosh International*].

But the fact that activities like cleaning are not inherently governmental does not automatically exclude them from amounting to an exercise of governmental authority. Instead, further enquiry is required to determine whether these functions nevertheless have a sufficient governmental nexus to fall within the scope of the rule expressed in Article 5.

5.3.3 The Overall Context

If the powers a State delegates to an NSA are not inherently governmental, they may nevertheless qualify as public in character due to their strong nexus to governmental activity. This may be judged by considering the wider context in which the relevant functions are performed. English courts adopted a similar approach when considering the distinction between sovereign and private powers for the purposes of State immunity.[81] The courts concluded that, when viewed in context, the provision of educational and medical services for military personnel located at U.S. air bases in the United Kingdom was sovereign in nature.[82] Lord Hoffman stated, "I do not think that there is a single test or 'bright line' by which cases on either side can be distinguished. Rather, there are a number of factors which may characterize the act as nearer to or further from the central military activity."[83] He went on to articulate the most important considerations when making this determination, including the location where the relevant activities are conducted, whom they involve, and the nature of the act.[84]

Assessing tasks in context may prove particularly helpful when determining the status of PMSC activities that are not inherently governmental, such as the provision of armed guarding services or logistical support. Functions performed by a PMSC in a combat zone are more likely to amount to governmental activity than those carried out in a benign environment. However, the location itself is not determinative. For example, the activities of armed security guards protecting a private oil field within an area of combat are not governmental in nature.[85] Conversely, private contractors operating unmanned aerial systems in support of combat operations are engaged in governmental activity, even if they are far removed from the battlefield.[86]

81. I Congresso del Partido [1983] 1 AC 244, 267 (Eng.); Littrell v. U.S.A. (No. 2) [1995] 1 WLR 82 at 91, 94–95 (Eng.); Holland v. Lampen-Wolfe [2000] 1 WLR 1573 at 1577 (Eng.). *See also* YANG, *supra* note 63, at 105–7.

82. Littrell v. U.S.A. (No. 2) [1995] 1 WLR 82 at 91, 94–95; Holland v. Lampen-Wolfe [2000] 1 WLR 1573 at 1577.

83. Littrell v. U.S.A. (No. 2) at 95 (per Hoffman, L.J.).

84. *Id.*

85. TONKIN, *supra* note 49, at 101–2, 108.

86. RENZ, *supra* note 50, at 212–43.

Further factors therefore need to be considered, including the identity of the personnel for whose benefit the function is performed. In the guarding context, if the assets or personnel of a private company are protected, the activity is not governmental in nature. Alternatively, if the intent is to protect military assets or civilian officials, the activity is for the benefit of the State and is more likely to fall within the sphere of governmental authority. Finally, it may be relevant to consider the nature of any equipment provided to PMSC personnel for use in the performance of their duties, such as firearms. While not conclusive alone, when considered together, these factors may assist in determining whether the PMSC is exercising elements of governmental authority.

A gray area nevertheless remains, particularly regarding those PMSC functions with the weakest nexus to military action such as the delivery of goods. An assessment whether such activities are governmental in character is especially difficult in contemporary conflicts, in which armed groups often fail to discriminate between military and nonmilitary targets.[87] Thus, in recent combat environments, even functions with a weak military nexus have drawn contractors into hostilities, as illustrated by the deaths of four Blackwater employees in Fallujah, Iraq, while collecting nonmilitary equipment.[88]

This development tends to expand the range of circumstances in which a contractor's activities within a combat zone may amount to an exercise of governmental authority. The decisions of the English courts relating to the provision of medical and educational services on a military base also support a more inclusive interpretation of the scope of governmental functions.[89] Although determinations as to the status of contractors' activities will be fact-specific, many services provided by a PMSC in a conflict zone, for the benefit of State armed forces or government officials, may therefore fall within the scope of governmental authority.[90]

In the cyber domain, the context in which an activity is performed is equally relevant when considering its public or private character. While cyber operations can be carried out remotely, rendering the location potentially immaterial, other contextual factors may assist in this determination. Any tools or information a government provides in connection with a cyber operation, such as malware or intelligence, may point to its governmental nature.[91] Furthermore, the nexus between a cyber operation and government activity is of particular importance. For example, although the maintenance of computer networks is not an inherently

87. Lehnardt, *supra* note 58, at 148.

88. David Barstow, *The Struggle for Iraq: The Contractors; Security Firm Says Its Workers Were Lured into Iraqi Ambush*, N.Y. Times (Apr. 9, 2004), www.nytimes.com/2004/04/09/world/struggle-for-iraq-contractors-security-firm-says-its-workers-were-lured-into.html.

89. Littrell v. U.S.A. (No. 2); Holland v. Lampen-Wolfe [2000] 1 WLR 1573.

90. Tonkin, *supra* note 49, at 107–8. *See also* Cameron & Chetail, *supra* note 54, at 202.

91. Sam Jones, *Cyber Crime: States Use Hackers to Do Digital Dirty Work*, Fin. Times (Sept. 4, 2015), www.ft.com/content/78c46db4-52da-11e5-b029-b9d50a74fd14.

governmental function, if a private company is tasked with maintaining and defending the computer network that supports a State's integrated air defense system, the close nexus between this function and the State's military activity is likely to lead to the conclusion that it falls within the scope of governmental authority.

5.3.4 Powers Conferred on Ordinary Citizens

As the preceding examples illustrate, conduct that is closely linked to military activity generally amounts to an exercise of governmental authority. Similarly, powers that involve the use of force are normally governmental in nature. The ARSIWA commentary, however, includes one important caveat in this respect, stating that Article 5 "does not extend to cover . . . situations where internal law authorizes or justifies certain conduct by way of self-help or self-defense; i.e. where it confers powers upon or authorizes conduct by citizens or residents generally."[92] The use of force by NSAs acting purely to defend themselves, or to exercise a power of citizen's arrest in accordance with domestic law, therefore falls outside the scope of the rule reflected in Article 5.

Notwithstanding this limitation, if a State delegates a function to a private entity and authorizes that entity to exercise specific powers in the performance of the task, the entity's conduct is likely to fall within Article 5's scope.[93] Clarity may be gained in such circumstances by assessing whether the powers exercised by the NSA are greater than those at the disposal of ordinary citizens under the State's domestic law. That may be the case if the delegated activity involves, for example, a power to constrain, supervise, regulate, or control the activities of private individuals, if necessary, using force.[94]

Consider, in this respect, the decision taken by various States in 2011 to authorize their merchant vessels to carry weapons for the purpose of countering the threat from Somali-based pirates.[95] At that time, a number of governments "reversed longstanding legal bans or serious restrictions on the direct arming of merchant ships," thereby allowing armed crew members or guards to forcefully prevent an illegal boarding.[96] While the use of force by such individuals was governed by national laws of self-defense, the authorization to carry and

92. ARSIWA, *supra* note 7, art. 5, cmt. ¶ 7.

93. Kontos, *supra* note 53, at 221; CAMERON & CHETAIL, *supra* note 54, at 170–71.

94. CAMERON & CHETAIL, *supra* note 54, at 198.

95. William Marmon, *Merchant Ships Starting to Carry Armed Guards Against Somali Pirates*, EUR. INST. (Nov. 2011), www.europeaninstitute.org/index.php/ei-blog/137-november-2011/1471-merchant-ships-start-to-carry-armed-guards-against-somali-pirates-1122.

96. *Id.*

potentially use firearms for this purpose was provided by the State in which the vessel was registered.[97] It follows that if guards on board a merchant vessel used their firearms in a manner that breached the flag State's international legal obligations, that conduct could amount to an exercise of governmental authority for the purposes of Article 5. Although the guards acted in accordance with national laws of self-defense, they exercised powers (namely, the authority to use firearms on board the vessels) that were granted by the flag State and were greater than the powers of ordinary citizens. As such, their conduct was public in character and could potentially engage the responsibility of the State.[98]

5.3.5 Conclusions as to the Scope of Governmental Authority

In summary, governmental authority for the purposes of the rule enshrined in Article 5 ARSIWA encompasses those traditional powers that undergird the State's existence as a public authority.[99] But in practice, it is far from easy to identify exactly where the boundaries lie. When assessing whether a delegated function is public or private in character, the first requirement is to identify the specific powers involved and to disaggregate them if appropriate. The following questions may then assist in evaluating whether an activity that a State delegates to an NSA amounts to an exercise of governmental authority:

1. Is the function quintessentially governmental, involving, for example, law enforcement or the use of force?
2. In what context will the function be performed? Relevant factors include:
   a. The location where the activity is carried out;
   b. Its nexus to military or other governmental activity;
   c. The identity of the personnel for whose benefit the activity is performed; and
   d. The nature of any tools, equipment, or information that the State provides to the entity for use in connection with the function's performance.

97. *See, e.g.*, Dep't for Transport, Interim Guidance to UK Flagged Shipping on the Use of Armed Guards (updated Dec. 1, 2015) (U.K.), www.gov.uk/government/publications/interim-guidance-to-uk-flagged-shipping-on-the-use-of-armed-guards-to-defend-against-the-threat-of-piracy-in-exceptional-circumstances/dddd.

98. Such conduct would only be attributable to the flag State pursuant to the rule reflected in Article 5 if the State empowered the entity to act in accordance with its domestic laws and the entity was acting in its public capacity at the relevant time. *See infra* secs. 5.4, 5.5.

99. Nwamaka R. Okany, *State Delegation of Functions to Private and Autonomous Entities: A Basis for Attribution Under the Rules of State Responsibility*, *in* State Responsibility and the Individual 327, 335 (Kalliopi Koufa ed., 2006).

3. Does the activity involve greater powers than those at the disposal of ordinary citizens? For example, does it involve a power to constrain, supervise, regulate, or control the activities of private individuals, if necessary, by force?
4. Is the activity carried out in the public interest?

While a positive answer to the first question might conclusively indicate that the relevant activity falls within the scope of governmental authority, a negative response to this question is merely indicative of the contrary conclusion. Further inquiry into the matter is then required, including consideration of the issues raised in questions 2 to 4. Once all the questions are addressed, it may be clear that the conduct in question either is, or is not, an exercise of governmental authority. But ambiguity may remain in relation to some borderline activities. If courts or tribunals are called upon to determine the issue of attribution in such marginal cases, the outcome is likely to depend upon the weight the court gives to the various factors outlined above. In addition, the court will need to assess whether the entity was properly empowered by the State to perform the activities concerned.

5.4 EMPOWERED BY THE LAW

The ILC included a specific requirement within Article 5 that the person or entity exercising governmental functions must be "empowered by the law of that State" to do so.[100] ARSIWA thus incorporates an express condition referring to a State's domestic law, without which responsibility will not arise. In the view of one ILC member, the inclusion of this requirement was justified because "the entities in question were not part of the formal structure of the State, and only internal law could authorize them to exercise elements of the governmental authority."[101] However, the ILC's deliberations and the ARSIWA commentary do not specify what form the relevant legal authorization must take.

5.4.1 The Nature of the Empowerment Requirement

Specific legislation authorizing a State to delegate elements of its governmental authority to an NSA clearly meets the empowerment requirement articulated within Article 5.[102] But the question remains whether any other basis will suffice. Writing after ARSIWA's adoption, former Special Rapporteur Crawford

100. ARSIWA, *supra* note 7, art. 5. *See also id.* cmt. ¶ 7.

101. ILC Y.B. 1998 vol. I, *supra* note 30, at 236, ¶ 23 (comments of Mr. Herdocia Sacasa).

102. *See, e.g.*, Phillips Petroleum Co. Iran v. Islamic Republic of Iran, Award No. 425-39-2, ¶ 89 n. 22 (Iran-U.S. Claims Trib., 1989); Flemingo Duty Free Shop Private Limited v. The Republic of Poland, Arbitral Award, ¶¶ 436–39 (Perm. Ct. Arb., Aug. 12, 2016).

stated that this criterion "requires that the capacity to exercise authority be derived from the law of the state."[103] He further clarified that "[i]f such functions are lawfully conferred by public contract, then the empowering law would qualify for the purposes of an Article 5 delegation."[104] Thus, the ARSIWA commentary gives the example of private security firms "contracted to act as prison guards" to demonstrate the circumstances when the rule reflected in Article 5 might apply.[105] In this situation, the entity to which the powers are delegated is "empowered by law" for the purposes of Article 5, provided that the contract is concluded in accordance with the State's domestic law. Given the prevalence of contractual arrangements between governments and PMSCs, this clarification is important.

To illustrate, consider the actions of the Wagner Group in Syria.[106] Reporting indicates that from January 2018, members of the PMSC acted to defend Syria's oil fields pursuant to a contract agreed between a Russian company, Evro Polis, and the Syrian Energy Ministry.[107] The terms of this agreement reflected an earlier Memorandum of Understanding signed in 2016, which could not be enforced until a new Syrian law was passed to recognize it.[108] Assuming that the requisite law was in effect in 2018, it seems that the Wagner Group was properly empowered by Syrian domestic law to protect oil fields on the State's behalf, meaning that any of the NSA's actions when performing those functions that violated Syria's international legal obligations are attributable to the State.[109]

The nature of the legal authorization required to enable a delegation of governmental authority varies according to the domestic legal traditions of the country concerned. For instance, while the UK government may conclude contracts with private persons without statutory authority, as an exercise of its executive powers,[110] other States require specific legislation for such contractual

103. Crawford, *supra* note 49, at 132.

104. *Id.* at 131. *See also* Nicholas Tsagourias & Michael Farrell, *Cyber Attribution: Technical and Legal Approaches and Challenges*, 31 Eur. J. Int'l L. 941, 952–53 (2020).

105. ARSIWA, *supra* note 7, art. 5, cmt. ¶ 2.

106. *See supra* ch. 2, sec. 2.4.1.

107. Marten, *supra* note 3, at 194; Irina Malkova et al., *Russian Mercenary Army Financier Made an Oil Deal with Syria Just Before Clash with U.S. Troops*, The Bell (Feb. 27, 2018), https://thebell.io/en/russian-mercenary-army-financier-made-oil-deal-syria-just-clash-u-s-troops/.

108. Marten, *supra* note 3, at 194.

109. *See generally* Michael A. Rizzotti, *Russian Mercenaries, State Responsibility and Conflict in Syria: Examining the Wagner Group Under International Law*, 37 Wis. Int'l L.J. 569, 599–604 (2020).

110. For discussion regarding UK prerogative powers, *see, e.g.*, David Torrance, UK House of Commons Library, The Royal Prerogative and Ministerial Advice (July 8, 2024), https://researchbriefings.files.parliament.uk/documents/CBP-9877/CBP-9877.pdf.

arrangements to be lawful.[111] Empowerment by law may thus take varying guises. It could be established via a statutory or executive order, for example. Equally, it could be founded through other domestic legal instruments such as regulations, bylaws, or administrative acts, or via delegations made thereunder, including contracts, charters, operating licenses, and concessions.[112] In essence, any form of delegation that complies with the requirements of the relevant State's domestic law will suffice.

Ambiguity remains, however, regarding the level of detail that must be included within the relevant legal authorization. In particular, it is unclear whether a contract that specifies a broad delegated function will suffice, or whether the instrument must articulate the precise activities that the NSA is authorized to carry out in performance of that function. Article 5's commentary suggests that the delegated public powers must be specified within the authorization.[113] But in Crawford's opinion, there is no requirement that the empowering law should comprehensively define the entity's roles and responsibilities.[114] This latter view is persuasive, as otherwise few delegations of authority would likely be detailed enough to lead to attribution. For instance, a contract delegating guarding functions to a PMSC might specify the categories of personnel or facilities to be protected, the equipment that contractors may use for this purpose, and whether they are entitled to use force. However, it would not normally include details such as day-to-day patrolling requirements or the rules of engagement under which the contractors operate.[115]

Questions also arise regarding the attribution of conduct to a State when the relevant government functions are performed not by the entity to which they are delegated but by a different NSA. If the contract or other legal instrument specifically provides for the entity to subcontract the functions concerned to another NSA, the actions of the subcontractor when exercising those powers are attributable to the State.[116] If, however, the contract or other form of legal authorization does not envisage a right to subcontract, the issue of attribution is less clear.

For example, if a State grants PMSC A authorization to operate military equipment and PMSC A then subcontracts those functions to PMSC B without the

111. For example, France has enacted legislation relating to the outsourcing of public functions. *See, e.g.*, V. Capdevielle, *The Regulatory Context of Private Military and Security Services in France*, PRIV-WAR REPORT–FRANCE, NATIONAL REPORTS SERIES 11/09 (May 21, 2009), https://iow.eui.eu/wp-content/uploads/sites/40/2013/11/nr-11-09-FRA.pdf.

112. CRAWFORD, *supra* note 49, at 130; CAMERON & CHETAIL, *supra* note 54, at 168; Okany, *supra* note 99, at 336. *See also Bosh International*, *supra* note 80, at 173.

113. ARSIWA, *supra* note 7, art. 5, cmt. ¶ 7 ("The internal law in question must specifically authorize the conduct as involving the exercise of public authority . . .").

114. CRAWFORD, *supra* note 49, at 132.

115. Regarding the development of PMSCs' rules of engagement, *see* RENZ, *supra* note 50, at 163.

116. U. CTR. FOR INT'L HUMANITARIAN L., *supra* note 46, at 22; TONKIN, *supra* note 49, at 111.

State's consent, the State has not directly empowered PMSC B to exercise elements of its governmental authority.[117] It seems, therefore, that any acts committed by PMSC B when operating that equipment are not attributable to the State. That is particularly the case if the State acts, as soon as it becomes aware of the unauthorized subcontracting, to prevent the continued operation of the equipment by PMSC B. The position may be different, however, if the State is aware of, and tolerates, PMSC B's performance of the function, or authorizes PMSC B's conduct in a way that does not accord with the State's domestic law. In such circumstances, the State's empowerment of PMSC B is effectuated not by law but rather via informal means, through its implicit acceptance or authorization of PMSC B's activities.

5.4.2 Empowerment by Means Other Than Law

The position of PMSC B in the preceding example is comparable to that of NSAs, such as militia groups, that engage in governmental activities on a State's behalf without any formal delegation of authority via the State's domestic law. Consider, for instance, the Shabbiha militias that fought on behalf of the Syrian regime during the early stages of the conflict.[118] These groups were armed by the government and acted alongside the State's national security forces, using violence to crush peaceful demonstrations.[119] Although such forces were integrated into the government in early 2013,[120] their status prior to that date is unclear. It may be that they qualified as de facto State organs of the Syrian regime, pursuant to Article 4 ARSIWA,[121] or they acted under the State's instructions, direction, or control for the purposes of Article 8.[122] But it may equally be the case that the requirements

117. It may also be the case that the original contractor acted outside the terms of the contract when sub-contracting, meaning that its conduct is *ultra vires*. For discussion of *ultra vires* conduct, *see infra* sec. 5.5.

118. *See supra* ch. 2, sec. 2.4.1. *See also* Expert Report of Ewan Brown 61–66, ¶¶ 126–37, Colvin et al. v. Syrian Arab Republic, No. 1:16-cv-01423-ABJ (D.D.C., Mar. 22, 2018), https://cja.org/wp-content/uploads/2018/04/17-Expert-Report-of-Ewan-Brown-dated-March-2-2018_Redacted.pdf.

119. Rep. of the Indep. Int'l Comm'n of Inquiry on the Syrian Arab Republic 6, ¶ 20, U.N. Doc. A/HRC/S-17/2/Add.1 (Nov. 23, 2011). *See also* U.S. Dep't of the Treasury, Treasury Sanctions Al-Nusrah Front Leadership in Syria and Militias Supporting the Asad Regime (Dec. 11, 2012), www.treasury.gov/press-center/press-releases/pages/tg1797.aspx.

120. Carter Ctr., Syria Pro-Government Paramilitary Forces 8 (Nov. 5, 2013), www.cartercenter.org/resources/pdfs/peace/conflict_resolution/syria-conflict/pro-governmentparamilitaryforces.pdf.

121. *See supra* ch. 4, sec. 4.4.

122. *See infra* ch. 6.

of neither of these rules is satisfied, particularly given that the group reportedly acted with a sense of total impunity.[123]

The Shabbiha clearly exercised public powers in Syria prior to 2013 in that they acted alongside State security forces, conducting law enforcement functions on behalf of the regime.[124] It appears, however, that the requisite authority to do so was not delegated to the Shabbiha in accordance with Syrian law. Instead, in early 2011, the Syrian regime reportedly "began to use money and services to buy the allegiance of unemployed youth, to distribute guns, cars, and security clearances to trusted loyalists and their families, essentially weaponizing the vast web of client networks constructed over four decades of Assad family rule."[125] In this way, it seems that the regime empowered the Shabbiha to act but did not do so by law, meaning that the rule reflected in Article 5 would not apply to attribute the Shabbiha's conduct to the State.

The situation of the Shabbiha is by no means unique. Also in Syria, Shi'a militia groups, including Hezbollah, augmented government forces on the battlefield with the apparent sanction of the Syrian regime, but with no clear legal authority to do so.[126] In some cases, Hezbollah fighters even exerted tactical control over Syrian soldiers on the battlefield;[127] an undisputable exercise of Syria's governmental authority. Turkey similarly employed militias to fight on its behalf in the north of Syria, without openly formalizing this arrangement via its internal law.[128] And Russia has made prolific use of NSAs such as the Wagner Group to enhance its strategic interests in Syria and elsewhere,[129] while prohibiting the use of PMSCs in its domestic legal regime.[130]

123. Rep. of the Indep. Int'l Comm'n of Inquiry on the Syrian Arab Republic, annex v, ¶ 6, U.N. Doc. A/HRC/22/59 (Feb. 5, 2013).

124. *See supra* sec. 5.3.2.

125. Aron Lund, *Who Are the Pro-Assad Militias?* CARNEGIE ENDOWMENT FOR INT'L PEACE (Mar. 2, 2015), https://carnegieendowment.org/middle-east/diwan/2015/03/who-are-the-pro-assad-militias?lang=en.

126. *See, e.g.*, Michael Knights, *Iran's Foreign Legion: The Role of Iraqi Shiite Militias in Syria*, WASH. INST. (June 27, 2013), www.washingtoninstitute.org/policy-analysis/view/irans-foreign-legion-the-role-of-iraqi-shiite-militias-in-syria; NICHOLAS BLANFORD, CTC SENTINEL, THE BATTLE FOR QUSAYR: HOW THE SYRIAN REGIME AND HIZB ALLAH TIPPED THE BALANCE 18–22 (Aug. 2013), https://ctc.westpoint.edu/the-battle-for-qusayr-how-the-syrian-regime-and-hizb-allah-tipped-the-balance/; MARISA SULLIVAN, INST. FOR THE STUDY OF WAR, HEZBOLLAH IN SYRIA (Apr. 2014), http://www.understandingwar.org/sites/default/files/Hezbollah_Sullivan_FINAL.pdf.

127. BLANFORD, *supra* note 126, at 19–20.

128. Hubbard et al., *supra* note 69. Turkey also employed the same Syrian militias to fight on its behalf in Libya and in Nagorno-Karabakh. *See* Allinson & Ammar, *supra* note 69; Zeevi, *supra* note 69.

129. Marten, *supra* note 3; Gurcan, *supra* note 68; Michelle Nichols, *Up to 1,200 Deployed in Libya by Russian Military Group: UN Report*, REUTERS (May 6, 2020), www.reuters.com/article/us-libya-security-sanctions/up-to-1200-deployed-in-libya-by-russian-military-group-un-report-idUSKBN22I2XW.

130. Marten, *supra* note 3, at 184–88; Sabra Ayres, *Russia's Shadowy World of Military Contractors: Independent Mercenaries, or Working for the Kremlin?* LOS ANGELES TIMES

In all such cases, it appears likely that the respective States' use of NSAs to fight on their behalf was authorized at the highest levels of government. Such approvals might, therefore, satisfy the "empowered by law" requirement within Article 5. But given that States commonly prefer their dealings with NSAs to remain covert, details of any domestic authorizations rarely enter the public domain. Consider, for example, U.S. engagements with NSAs that support or facilitate its special operations forces' counterterrorism operations.[131] While the relevant fiscal authority is in the public domain,[132] any operations conducted in reliance of this authorization remain classified.[133] As such, it would not be apparent to any parties injured by the relevant NSAs' conduct whether those NSAs were properly empowered to act in accordance with U.S. law.

The same is likely to be true when States task proxies to act on their behalf in the cyber domain. In contrast with the contractual relationships common between States and PMSCs, "the public-private collaborations in cybersecurity are informal, de facto partnerships, operating outside a contractual framework."[134] As such, the relationships that exist between cyber operators and the State are frequently nebulous and ill-understood.[135] Within China, for example, private individuals, companies and civilian agencies are all involved in

(Feb. 18, 2018), www.latimes.com/world/europe/la-fg-russia-mercenaries-20180218-story.html; Nathaniel Reynolds, *Putin's Not-So-Secret Mercenaries: Patronage, Geopolitics, and the Wagner Group*, Carnegie Endowment for Int'l Peace (July 8, 2019), https://carnegieendowment.org/2019/07/08/putin-s-not-so-secret-mercenaries-patronage-geopolitics-and-wagner-group-pub-79442.

131. Wesley Morgan, *Behind the Secret U.S. War in Africa*, Politico (July 2, 2018), www.politico.com/story/2018/07/02/secret-war-africa-pentagon-664005; Daniel R. Mahanty & Elias Youssef, Ctr. for Civilians in Conflict, Exception(s) to the Rule(s): Civilian Harm, Oversight, and Accountability in the Shadow Wars 13–14 (Nov. 2020), www.stimson.org/wp-content/uploads/2020/11/CIVIC_US_Report_ETR-FINAL1.pdf.

132. 10 U.S.C. § 127e–Support of Special Operations to Combat Terrorism, https://uscode.house.gov/view.xhtml?req=granuleid:USC-prelim-title10-section127e&num=0&edition=prelim. *See also* U.S. Deputy Secretary of Def., Directive-Type Memorandum 18-005–Authority for Support of Special Operations for Irregular Warfare (Aug. 3, 2018), https://fas.org/irp/doddir/dod/dtm-18-005.pdf.

133. *See* Nick Turse & Alice Speri, *How the Pentagon Uses a Secretive Program to Wage Proxy Wars*, The Intercept (July 1, 2022), https://theintercept.com/2022/07/01/pentagon-127e-proxy-wars/; Charlie Savage & Eric Schmitt, *Rules for Pentagon Use of Proxy Forces Shed Light on a Shadowy War Power*, N.Y. Times (May 14, 2023), https://www.nytimes.com/2023/05/14/us/politics/military-proxy-niger-somalia-human-rights.html.

134. Kristen E. Eichensehr, *Public-Private Cybersecurity*, 95 Tex. L. Rev. 467, 510 (2017).

135. Tim Maurer, Cyber Mercenaries 16–18 (2018).

cyber activity for the benefit of the State, with variable levels of government involvement in their actions.[136] In such circumstances, even if it is possible to establish that the State empowered a particular hacker group to act, the likelihood of proving that this was done in accordance with the State's domestic law appears extremely slim.

It is possible, of course, that if the criteria relevant to Article 5 are not satisfied, another rule might attribute the NSA's conduct to the State, particularly the rule expressed in Article 8 ARSIWA relating to a State's instructions, direction, or control.[137] When a State authorizes an NSA to perform governmental functions on its behalf, however, Article 8 may not be the most appropriate basis of attribution. For instance, when the militias in Syria switched focus at Turkey's behest to fight against the Kurds rather than President Assad, they abandoned their own goals and acted purely for Turkey.[138] From that time on, they were exercising combat functions on Ankara's behalf and their conduct should be attributable to Turkey, regardless of the State's issuance of instructions, or its exercise of direction or control. States should not be able to hide behind the covert or informal manner in which they empower NSAs to avoid attribution. Viewed in light of States' contemporary use of proxies in conflict situations, therefore, the requirement for legal empowerment overly restricts the application of the rule expressed in Article 5 and in some cases, deprives it of practical effect.

5.4.3 The "Legal" Aspect of the Empowerment Requirement

This limitation to Article 5's scope of application does not accord well with the object and purpose of the rules of attribution and the wider law of State responsibility.[139] While the ARSIWA commentary acknowledges the relevance of States' internal laws when assessing responsibility, it also emphasizes the primacy of international law: "States cannot use their internal law as a means of escaping international responsibility."[140] The focus of international law, moreover, is upon the reality of a situation, rather than the apparent structures created by a State's

136. Mara Hvistendahl, *China's Hacker Army*, Foreign Pol'y (Mar. 3, 2010), http://foreignpolicy.com/2010/03/03/chinas-hacker-army/. *See also* Maurer *supra* note 135, at 107–19; FireEye, Red Line Drawn: China Recalculates its Use of Cyber Espionage 15 (June 2016), https://infocon.org/mirrors/vx%20underground%20-%202025%20June/APTs/2016/2016.06.21%20-%20RPT%20China/Paper/RPT%20China.pdf.

137. ARSIWA, *supra* note 7, art. 8. *See also infra* ch. 6.

138. Sam Heller, *Turkey's "Turkey First" Syria Policy*, Century Found. (Apr. 12, 2017), https://tcf.org/content/report/turkeys-turkey-first-syria-policy/.

139. *See* ARSIWA, *supra* note 7, chapeau to pt. I, ch. II, cmt. ¶ 7.

140. *Id.* art. 3, cmt. ¶ 8.

domestic law.[141] Thus, "States are not allowed on the one hand to act *de facto* through individuals and on the other to disassociate themselves from such conduct when these individuals breach international law."[142] Although this observation by the International Criminal Tribunal for the former Yugoslavia related to attribution pursuant to the rule reflected in Article 8 ARSIWA, it would be anomalous if the same principle did not apply to the rule expressed in Article 5.

A State should not be able to delegate elements of its governmental functions in a manner that does not accord with the requirements of its domestic law and thereby evade international responsibility for any unlawful acts committed by that entity.[143] Instead, there is force in the argument made by the government of Japan that "an internal law is only a presumptive factor in determining whether an act of an entity is attributed to the State."[144] Under this rationale, the definitive factor is the exercise of elements of governmental authority. As Cameron and Chetail argue, a State should bear responsibility where outsourcing is carried out contrary to or in the absence of authorizing national laws, on the basis that it has either interpreted its domestic legal regime to allow for the delegation or it has knowingly derogated from such laws.[145]

Such a loosening of the requirement for legal empowerment does not align with the wording of Article 5 ARSIWA but is nevertheless consistent with certain case law on the issue, as well as the earlier work of the ILC. In the *Armed Activities* and *Bosnian Genocide* cases, the International Court of Justice failed to mention any need for empowerment through domestic law in the context of Article 5.[146] An arbitral tribunal concluded in 2006 that an NSA's conduct was attributable to Egypt based on the rule expressed in Article 5, "even if [the entity] has not been officially empowered by law to exercise elements of the governmental authority."[147] And the ILC did not initially consider legal empowerment to be a prerequisite for attribution, emphasizing the significance of the public nature of the functions carried out by the private entity as opposed to the formal relationship

141. Dame Mossé Case, 13 R.I.A.A. 486, 493 (Franco-Italian Comm'n, 1953); Prosecutor v. Tadić, Case No. IT-94-1-A, Appeals Chamber Judgment ¶ 121 (Int'l Crim. Trib. for the former Yugoslavia, July 15, 1999) [hereinafter *Tadić*].

142. *Tadić*, *supra* note 141, ¶ 117. *See also* Kenneth P. Yeager v. Islamic Republic of Iran, Award No. 324-10199-1, ¶ 45 (Iran-U.S. Claims Trib., 1987).

143. Kees, *supra* note 53, ¶ 13.

144. Int'l Law Comm'n, Comments and Observations Received from Governments 48–49, U.N. Doc. A/CN.4/515 and Add.1–3 (2001), https://legal.un.org/ilc/documentation/english/a_cn4_515.pdf.

145. Cameron & Chetail, *supra* note 54, at 169–70.

146. Armed Activities on the Territory of the Congo (Dem. Rep. Congo v. Uganda), Judgment, 2005 I.C.J. Rep. 168, ¶ 160 (Feb. 14); Application of the Convention on the Prevention and Punishment of the Crime of Genocide (Bosn. & Herz. v. Serb. & Montenegro), Judgment, 2007 I.C.J. Rep. 43, ¶ 414 (Feb. 26) [hereinafter *Bosnian Genocide*].

147. Helnan International Hotels A/S v. The Arab Republic of Egypt, Case No. ARB 05/19, Award ¶ 93 (Int'l Ctr. for Settlement of Inv. Disp., 2006).

between that entity and the State.[148] As Special Rapporteur Ago stated in 1971, "[I]t is logical that the act of a private person who, in one way or another, is performing a function or task of an obviously public character should be considered as an act attributable to the community and should engage the responsibility of the State at the international level."[149]

Notably, one of the examples Ago used to illustrate the principle now expressed in Article 5 ARSIWA related to the conduct of individuals who may have acted in breach of their respective States' internal laws.[150] Thus, the "pseudo-volunteers" that fought in the Spanish Civil War were not empowered to act in a manner that accorded with their States' domestic laws; their actions, instead, may have violated those States' criminal laws. Nevertheless, because they were "sent" by their States to fight, Ago considered that their conduct was governmental in character and engaged the responsibility of the relevant States.[151]

The draft article Ago formulated to express this basis of attribution made no reference to any requirement for the entity exercising public functions to be empowered by law.[152] When, three years later, the wording of the draft article changed to incorporate a requirement for legal empowerment, the ILC did not clearly articulate the basis for this amendment, or cite any precedents in its support.[153] The ILC then considered the draft article's formulation again in 1998. At that time, Special Rapporteur Crawford concluded that the reference to internal law should be retained owing to the "exceptional nature" of the situations addressed, noting further that "all the situations in which a non-State entity was not authorized by internal law would then come under article 8."[154]

The analysis in Chapter 6, however, highlights the stringent attribution thresholds applicable to Article 8 and the difficulty injured States face in proving that an NSA acted under a State's instructions, direction, or control.[155] Furthermore, in some circumstances, a State's issuance of instructions, or its exercise of direction or control, is not the most appropriate basis of attribution. While it is right to focus on the State's influence over an NSA's conduct when that NSA plays its own role in the conflict, and acts in pursuance of its own independent goals, the position

148. Ago's Third Rep. on State Responsibility, *supra* note 11, at 264, ¶ 191.

149. *Id.*

150. *Id.* at 264, ¶ 192.

151. *Id.*

152. *Id.* at 267 (draft art. 8).

153. ILC Y.B. 1974 vol. II, *supra* note 22, at 277. *See also* ILC Y.B. 1974 vol. I, *supra* note 47, at 36 (comments of Mr. Tsuruoka); *id.* at 38 (comments of Mr. Pinto); ILC Y.B. 1974 vol. II, *supra* note 22, at 282 (draft art. 7, cmt. ¶ 18).

154. ILC Y.B. 1998 vol. I, *supra* note 30, at 246 (comments of Mr. Crawford). *See also* Crawford's First Rep. on State Responsibility, *supra* note 24, at 56 (draft art. 7, cmt. ¶ 4).

155. *See infra* ch. 6.

is different when the NSA concerned is fighting purely for the State. Turkey's evolving relationship with Syrian militias illustrates the point. Initially, Turkey provided support to these groups in their fight against the Assad regime in the early stages of the Syrian conflict.[156] Later, however, Turkey diverted these groups away from their goal of toppling President Assad and empowered them to fight instead against the Syrian Kurds.[157] Later still, Turkey used these same militias to promote its interests in the conflicts in Libya and Nagorno-Karabakh.[158]

In the latter circumstances, the militias were not acting on their own account; they were acting solely for Turkey. The same is true of some of the Shi'a militia groups that fought for Iran in the Syrian conflict, such as the Afghan Fatemiyoun.[159] It is also true of the Wagner Group and other Russian PMSCs when they acted to promote Moscow's foreign policy objectives overseas.[160] In the Central African Republic, for instance, Russia reportedly signed a military cooperation agreement with the government, the terms of which were fulfilled not by Russia's own armed forces but by PMSCs.[161] In essence, Moscow authorized the PMSCs to satisfy its obligations under the agreement and thereby perform public functions on the State's behalf. It is wholly appropriate, therefore, for the NSAs' conduct to be attributed to the State pursuant to the rule reflected in Article 5 ARSIWA.

The ILC's inclusion of a requirement for "empowerment by law," however, precludes Article 5's application to circumstances such as this. In response to allegations of war crimes in the Central African Republic,[162] Moscow used the fact

156. Heller, *supra* note 138; Faysal Itani & Aaron Stein, Atlantic Council, Turkey's Syria Predicament (May 2016), https://www.atlanticcouncil.org/in-depth-research-reports/issue-brief/turkey-s-syria-predicament/; Engin Yüksel, Netherlands Inst. of Int'l Rel., Strategies of Turkish Proxy Warfare in Northern Syria: Back with a Vengeance (Nov. 2019), www.clingendael.org/sites/default/files/2019-11/strategies-turkish-proxy-warfare-in-northern-syria.pdf.

157. Heller, *supra* note 138; Itani & Stein, *supra* note 156; Yüksel, *supra* note 156.

158. Allinson & Ammar, *supra* note 69; Zeevi, *supra* note 69.

159. Farzin Nadimi, *Iran's Afghan and Pakistani Proxies: In Syria and Beyond?* Wash. Inst. (Aug. 22, 2016), www.washingtoninstitute.org/policy-analysis/irans-afghan-and-pakistani-proxies-syria-and-beyond; Ben Farmer & Akhtar Makoii, *Thirsty for Martyrdom and a Living Wage: Why Thousands of Afghans Signed up to Iran's Shadowy War in Syria*, The Telegraph (Jan. 26, 2020), www.telegraph.co.uk/news/2020/01/26/thirsty-martyrdom-living-wage-thousands-afghans-signed-irans/; Tabatabai et al., *supra* note 3.

160. Marten, *supra* note 3.

161. Joint Enquiry of the Special Procedures of the Human Rights Council on the Alleged Activities of Russian Private Military and Security Companies in the Central African Republic, Ref. AL RUS 5/2021 (Mar. 24, 2021), https://spcommreports.ohchr.org/TMResultsBase/DownLoadPublicCommunicationFile?gId=26305.

162. *See, e.g.*, Declan Walsh, *Russian Mercenaries Are Driving War Crimes in Africa, UN Says*, N.Y. Times (June 27, 2021), https://www.nytimes.com/2021/06/27/world/asia/russia-mercenaries-central-african-republic.html.

that PMSCs are not authorized under Russian domestic law to bolster its denial of responsibility in connection with the NSAs' activities.[163] Thus, Russia effectively bypasses responsibility for any abuses its PMSCs commit by enabling the groups' participation in the conflict through informal means, falling outside the State's domestic legal regime.[164] The outcome is that the rule reflected in Article 5, as interpreted by the ILC, would not attribute to Russia the many international law violations committed by members of the Wagner Group in the Central African Republic and elsewhere.[165]

This result defeats the object and purpose of the rule of attribution, allowing States to use their internal law to sidestep international responsibility.[166] It would be less problematic if the NSAs' conduct could be attributed to Russia on other grounds, such as pursuant to the State's instructions, direction, or control, as reflected in Article 8 ARSIWA.[167] Indeed, one commentator suggests that the illegal status of PMSCs in Russia is actually a means of control; if contractors are operating unlawfully, they can be threatened with prosecution for illegal behavior at any time.[168] But when a State effectively outsources the role of its armed forces to an NSA, that NSA's conduct should be attributable to the State, irrespective of the State's exercise of control, and irrespective of the means through which the NSA is empowered to act.

It is arguable, therefore, that the requirement for legal empowerment included within the ILC's formulation of Article 5 is not reflective of customary international law.[169] This conclusion is supported by the *opinio juris* of some States in their national statements regarding the application of international law to the

163. Permanent Mission of the Russian Federation to the U.N., Response to the Joint Enquiry of the Special Procedures of the Human Rights Council on the Alleged Activities of Russian Private Military and Security Companies in the Central African Republic (Apr. 28, 2021), https://spcommreports.ohchr.org/TMResultsBase/DownLoadFile?gId=36281.

164. The setting up of "armed units" and "mercenarism" is prohibited under the terms of Russia's constitution and criminal code. *See* CONST. OF THE RUSSIAN FEDERATION, Dec. 12, 1993, arts. 13(5), 71, http://www.constitution.ru/en/10003000-02.htm (last visited July 3, 2025); Criminal Code of the Russian Federation No. 63-Fz, art. 359 (June 13, 1996), https://www.wipo.int/edocs/lexdocs/laws/en/ru/ru080en.pdf.

165. *See, e.g.*, Walsh, *supra* note 162; HUM. RTS. Watch, CENTRAL AFRICAN REPUBLIC: ABUSES BY RUSSIA-LINKED FORCES (May 3, 2022), https://www.hrw.org/news/2022/05/03/central-african-republic-abuses-russia-linked-forces.

166. *See* ARSIWA, *supra* note 7, chapeau to pt. I, ch. II, cmt. ¶ 7.

167. *Id.* art. 8. For further discussion of Article 8, *see infra* ch. 6.

168. Marten, *supra* note 3, at 181, 188, 191, 199.

169. There is little State practice or *opinio juris* to demonstrate States' views regarding this basis of attribution. Governments did not raise objections to draft art. 5, although several States sought greater clarification as to its terms. *See* Crawford's First Rep. on State Responsibility *supra* note 24, at 38–39; Comments and Observations Received from Governments *supra* note 144, at 48–49; Kees, *supra* note 53, ¶ 13.

cyber domain, which make no mention of any requirement for empowerment by law in the context of the rule of attribution reflected in Article 5.[170] In the absence of such a requirement, it follows that all forms of State authorization, whether they accord with the domestic legal regime or not, should be considered when examining whether the State has empowered an NSA to perform governmental functions.[171]

If one accepts this principle, there is nevertheless a need to consider how far it extends. State empowerment remains a clear requirement of the attribution standard, implying a necessity for positive action by the State in delegating public functions, rather than a simple failure to prevent the exercise of such powers.[172] Accordingly, evidence of a clear link between the State and the NSA must exist; the mere performance of governmental functions without such evidence is insufficient to lead to attribution on this basis. The following section assesses the types of State behavior that should suffice to empower an NSA to perform governmental functions on its behalf for the purposes of Article 5.

5.4.4 A More Effective Way to Assess "Empowerment"

Examples from contemporary armed conflict, such as Russia's use of the Wagner Group to perform combat functions on its behalf, demonstrate States' willingness to delegate governmental functions to private entities via means that are often covert and may not accord with the State's domestic law. The rule of attribution reflected in Article 5 would better meet its object and purpose, therefore, if it required only that the State empowers an NSA to exercise elements of its governmental authority without any need to prove that such empowerment was effectuated by law. This would enable all forms of State authorization to be considered when assessing the issue of attribution.

This loosening of the "empowerment" criterion would not affect the remaining two requirements of the rule reflected in Article 5. Thus, attribution on this basis would arise only in respect of conduct on the part of an NSA that can be classified as governmental in nature, and only if the NSA is acting in that public capacity at

170. *See, e.g.*, Official Compendium, *supra* note 6, at 21, 78–79, 90 (positions of Brazil, Romania, Switzerland); Jeppe Mejer Kjelgaard & Ulf Melgaard, *Denmark's Position Paper on the Application of International Law in Cyberspace*, 92 Nordic J. Int'l L. 446, 452 (2023); Position Paper of the Republic of Austria: Cyber Activities and International Law 8 (2024), https://perma.cc/W49Q-C2RS (last visited June 26, 2025). Other States, however, do refer to the empowerment by law criterion. *See, e.g.*, Official Compendium *supra* note 6, at 39, 141 (positions of Germany, United States).

171. Such a conclusion seems to be supported by certain comments made by Crawford in 1998. *See* ILC Y.B. 1998 vol. I, *supra* note 30, at 243.

172. If an NSA exercises governmental functions without State empowerment, the rule of attribution reflected in art. 9 ARSIWA could apply. *See* ARSIWA, *supra* note 7, art. 9. For discussion regarding this basis of attribution, *see infra* ch. 8.

the time it commits the acts in potential breach of international law.[173] Moreover, some form of positive action on the part of the State would still be necessary to "empower" the NSA to perform the relevant function; a mere failure to prevent the exercise of such powers would not suffice. As such, the attribution standard would remain distinct from the rule reflected in Article 9 ARSIWA, which relates to an NSA's performance of governmental functions in the absence or default of the official authorities.[174]

The key question, therefore, is to determine the types of State behavior that should suffice to empower an NSA to perform governmental functions on its behalf in the absence of authorization under the State's domestic law. A clear link between the State and the NSA is required, but the rule should not be too prescriptive in this respect, to allow consideration of all the relevant facts and circumstances. Evidence of the following factors may be of relevance:

1. State involvement in the entity's creation;
2. Connections between State organs and the NSA's leadership;
3. The NSA acting alongside or in concert with State organs;
4. Instructions or orders from State organs to the NSA to perform the relevant function;
5. The issuance of guidance or direction by State organs in relation to the manner in which the NSA should perform the function;
6. Payments by the State to the NSA; and
7. The State's provision of assistance, equipment, or training to the NSA that enables its performance of the function.

If such factors were relevant to the issue of empowerment, as suggested, an additional question key to this assessment is who the NSA is acting for at the relevant time.[175] If the NSA is acting in pursuit of its own goals in the conflict, the criteria for attribution under the rule reflected in Article 5 would not normally be met. Thus, when Turkey first assisted the rebels fighting the Assad regime in Syria, Article 5 was not an appropriate basis on which to attribute the NSAs' conduct to the State. At that time, the rebels were acting principally on their own account with Turkey's assistance; they were not exercising elements of Turkey's governmental authority.[176] But if an NSA is clearly performing public functions for a State and would not be conducting the operations concerned without that State's authorization, attribution pursuant to Article 5 may be appropriate. When the

173. *See supra* sec. 5.3; *see infra* sec. 5.5.

174. ARSIWA, *supra* note 7, art. 9. *See also infra* ch. 8.

175. In the *Bosnian Genocide* case, for instance, the ICJ concluded that the Bosnian Serbs were acting for the Republika Srpska, not on behalf of the Federal Republic of Yugoslavia. *See Bosnian Genocide, supra* note 146, ¶ 388.

176. Itani & Stein, *supra* note 156; Heller, *supra* note 138.

rebels in Syria switched focus at Turkey's behest to fight against the Kurds, and later to participate in the conflicts in Libya and Nagorno-Karabakh, they were performing combat functions on Turkey's behalf.[177] In such circumstances, the rule reflected in Article 5 should attribute their conduct when performing those functions to the State, including their acts in potential violation of international law.[178]

Interpreted in this broader manner, the rule of attribution reflected in Article 5 potentially captures other harmful conduct by NSAs in conflict situations. For example, the fact that Syria reportedly armed the Shabbiha and used the group to crush the protests in Syria alongside State security forces[179] might demonstrate that the Assad regime authorized the NSA to perform law enforcement functions on its behalf. The close association between the Wagner Group and the Russian military intelligence service, the GRU, together with the role the PMSC played in support of Moscow's strategic aims in conflicts across the globe[180] and significant State funding[181] might point toward Russia's empowerment of the group to act as an unofficial combat arm of the State. But Iran's provision of weapons to the Houthis appears insufficient to constitute empowerment. Reporting indicates that the Houthis' objectives and actions were not influenced by Iran and would continue unchanged in the absence of Iranian support.[182] Thus, rather than exercising elements of Iranian governmental authority, the Houthis acted on their own account, with assistance from Tehran.[183]

As these examples illustrate, a more relaxed construction of the empowerment requirement would entail fact-based assessments to determine the rule's

177. Itani & Stein, *supra* note 156; Heller, *supra* note 138; Elizabeth Tsurkov, *Who Are Turkey's Proxy Fighters in Syria?* N.Y. Rev. (Nov. 27, 2019), https://www.nybooks.com/online/2019/11/27/who-are-turkeys-proxy-fighters-in-syria/; Zeevi, *supra* note 69.

178. *See, e.g.*, Amnesty Int'l, Syria: Damning Evidence of War Crimes and Other Violations by Turkish Forces and their Allies (Oct. 18, 2019), https://www.amnesty.org/en/latest/press-release/2019/10/syria-damning-evidence-of-war-crimes-and-other-violations-by-turkish-forces-and-their-allies/.

179. Lund, *supra* note 125.

180. Mike Giglio, *Inside the Shadow War Fought by Russian Mercenaries*, Buzzfeed (Apr. 17, 2019), https://www.buzzfeednews.com/article/mikegiglio/inside-wagner-mercenaries-russia-ukraine-syria-prighozhin; Kimberly Marten, *Semi-State Security Actors and Russian Aggression*, Lawfare (July 8, 2018), www.lawfareblog.com/semi-state-security-actors-and-russian-aggression.

181. Nicolas Camut, *Putin Admits Kremlin Gave Wagner Nearly $1 Billion in the Past Year*, Politico (June 27, 2023), https://www.politico.eu/article/vladimir-putin-yevgeny-prigozhin-russia-kremlin-gave-wagner-group-nearly-1-billion-in-the-past-year/.

182. Jack Watling, Royal United Servs. Inst., Iran's Objectives and Capabilities: Deterrence and Subversion 24–25 (Feb. 2019), https://static.rusi.org/20190219_op_irans_objectives_and_capabilities_web.pdf; Tabatabai et al., *supra* note 3, at 13–14.

183. Watling, *supra* note 182, at 24–25; Tabatabai et al., *supra* note 3, at 13–14.

application. The facts surrounding the NSA's activities would similarly be relevant when assessing the extent of the NSA's conduct that should be attributed to the State. In the case of Hezbollah, for instance, the rule would only attribute the group's actions in potential breach of international law to Iran when the NSA performs extraterritorial combat functions on Tehran's behalf; not when it acts in any other capacity, such as in a political role in Lebanon.[184] Hezbollah's actions in Syria might meet this test given that the group first became involved in the conflict at Iran's behest, it coordinated its actions closely with the Islamic Revolutionary Guard Corps, and operated with the benefit of considerable Iranian support.[185]

Some of the factors that might be relevant to the issue of empowerment, if interpreted more broadly, could also lead to attribution on other grounds. State officials' instructions to an NSA, for instance, are equally pertinent when considering attribution under the rule expressed in Article 8.[186] This does not negate, however, the importance of the attribution standard reflected in Article 5. First, when a State empowers a private entity to perform public functions on its behalf, all the NSA's conduct in that capacity is attributable to the State, even if it is *ultra vires*.[187] In contrast, Article 8 does not attribute to a State conduct performed outside the scope of the State's instructions, direction, or control.[188] Second, if the criteria for attribution under Article 5 are met, there is no requirement to prove that the State exerted any degree of control over the NSA's conduct. A more flexible interpretation of the "empowerment" criterion could, accordingly, play a critical role in holding States to act when they choose to act via NSAs. Moreover, it could act as an incentive to States to ensure that the NSAs they authorize to perform public functions on their behalf comply with international law.

5.5 DISTINGUISHING PUBLIC AND PRIVATE ACTS

Once it is determined that a State has empowered an NSA to exercise elements of its governmental authority, the third criterion for attribution under the rule expressed in Article 5 requires that the entity was, in fact, acting in that capacity at the time it committed the act in question. There is no additional requirement that

184. *See, e.g.*, Cong. Res. Serv., Lebanese Hezbollah (May 10, 2024), https://crsreports.congress.gov/product/pdf/IF/IF10703.

185. Samia Nakhoul, *Special Report: Hezbollah Gambles All in Syria*, Reuters (Sept. 26, 2013), www.reuters.com/article/us-syria-hezbollah-special-report/special-report-hezbollah-gambles-all-in-syria-idUSBRE98P0AI20130926; Seth G. Jones, *The Escalating Conflict with Hezbollah in Syria*, Ctr. for Strategic & Int'l Stud. (June 20, 2018), www.csis.org/analysis/escalating-conflict-hezbollah-syria.

186. *See infra* ch. 6, sec. 6.3.

187. ARSIWA, *supra* note 7, art. 7. *See also infra* sec. 5.5.

188. ARSIWA, *supra* note 7, art. 7.

the State must direct or control how the delegated task is carried out.[189] Instead, the public powers exercised by an NSA may involve "an independent discretion or power to act,"[190] meaning that the entity makes its own decisions regarding its day-to-day conduct, without governmental oversight.

A State may bear international responsibility even if the entity's conduct was *ultra vires*, meaning that it was carried out in excess of authority or in contravention of any instructions given by the State. This position is reflected in Article 7 ARSIWA, which articulates the general rule regarding States' responsibility for *ultra vires* acts.[191] But the principle holds true only if, during the incident in question, the entity was performing governmental functions. It is therefore necessary to distinguish between conduct that is deemed "official," in exercise of the delegated public tasks, and that which is "private," and carried out either in an entity's personal capacity or on behalf of a client other than the State.

This distinction may be illustrated by the abuses committed by contractors working for PMSCs during the armed conflict in Iraq. Legal commentators have raised considerable concerns regarding the issue of accountability for legal breaches involving PMSCs, such as the detainee abuse at Abu Ghraib.[192] When working in combat zones, contractors have additionally been involved in incidents involving civilian deaths such as the killing of seventeen Iraqis by Blackwater employees escorting a U.S. convoy.[193] Despite the frequency with which PMSC misconduct occurs, it is rare for such activity to be authorized by the hiring State. It is therefore necessary to determine whether the abuses committed were private acts that are not attributable to the State, or *ultra vires* activities carried out in the contractors' official capacity, leading to State responsibility.

The determination whether particular conduct relates to an exercise of governmental authority is a question of fact in each case.[194] As the ARSIWA commentary makes clear, "If it is to be regarded as an act of the State for purposes of international responsibility, the conduct of an entity must . . . concern governmental activity and not other private or commercial activity in which the entity

189. *Id.* art. 5, cmt. ¶ 7.

190. *Id.*

191. *Id.* art. 7. *See supra* ch. 4, sec. 4.5 for discussion regarding art. 7 in the context of art. 4 ARSIWA.

192. *See, e.g.*, Nieminen, *supra* note 67; Michael Hurst, *After Blackwater: A Mission-Focused Jurisdictional Regime for Private Military Contractors during Contingency Operations*, 76 GEO. WASH. L. REV. 1308 (2008); Charles Tiefer, *No More Nisour Squares: Legal Control of Private Security Contractors in Iraq and After*, 88 ORE. L. REV. 745 (2009); Kontos, *supra* note 53.

193. Hurst, *supra* note 192; Tiefer, *supra* note 192. *See also* Michael Safi, *Trump Pardons Blackwater Contractors Jailed for Massacre of Iraq Civilians*, THE GUARDIAN (Dec. 23, 2020), www.theguardian.com/world/2020/dec/23/trump-pardons-blackwater-contractors-jailed-for-massacre-of-iraq-civilians.

194. ARSIWA, *supra* note 7, art. 7, cmt. ¶¶ 7–8.

may engage."[195] A clear disaggregation of the activities carried out by an entity assists in this respect. It must then be determined whether the act in question was connected to the performance of public functions, or to another task carried out either for the State, or for another beneficiary.

When a company acts pursuant to private contracts entirely distinct from the public functions performed for the State, such conduct will not lead to State responsibility.[196] Therefore, if a PMSC provides armed security to protect a military base in a combat zone as well as security services for a mineral extraction company operating in the region, only its activities in relation to the former are attributable to the State. Similarly, if a cybersecurity company that is empowered to conduct cyber defense of military networks also performs information security services for private clients, its conduct in respect of the latter is not attributable to the State.[197]

Likewise, activities carried out in a contractor's personal capacity do not engage the State's responsibility. To be considered private in nature, the relevant conduct must be "so removed from the scope of [the individual's] official functions that it should be assimilated to that of private individuals, not attributable to the State."[198] Accordingly, an offense committed by PMSC contractors when they are off duty and away from their place of work is unlikely to engage the responsibility of the State. Equally, if the employees of a cybersecurity company performing digital forensics functions on behalf of the State engage in activities that are unrelated to the government mandate, such as cybercrime, the State bears no responsibility for their conduct.[199]

Where, however, the conduct in question is "carried out by persons cloaked with governmental authority,"[200] it is attributable to the State, even if it exceeds the scope of the delegated powers. Consider, for instance, the detainee abuse committed by interrogators working for CACI International Inc. at Abu Ghraib.[201] While such conduct was not authorized by the U.S. government and may have been specifically prohibited under the terms of the contract, it was undoubtedly carried out in the exercise of delegated governmental authority because the mistreatment was incidental to the contractors' official role as interrogators within the prison.[202] Therefore, the IHL violations involving private contractors at Abu

195. *Id.* art. 5, cmt. ¶ 5.

196. *Id.* art. 7, cmt. ¶ 7. *See also* Simon Olleson, *Attribution in Investment Treaty Arbitration*, 31 I.C.S.I.D. Rev. 457, 472–73 (2016).

197. Tallinn Manual 2.0, *supra* note 78, r. 15, cmt. ¶ 11.

198. ARSIWA, *supra* note 7, art. 7, cmt. ¶ 7.

199. Tallinn Manual 2.0, *supra* note 78, r. 15, cmt. ¶ 12.

200. ARSIWA, *supra* note 7, art. 7, cmt. ¶ 7, *citing* Petrolane Inc. v. Islamic Republic of Iran, Award No. 518-131-2, 64 at 92 (Iran-U.S. Claims Trib., 1991).

201. *See* Nieminen, *supra* note 67.

202. Tonkin, *supra* note 49, at 113.

Ghraib in 2003 are attributable to the United States.[203] The same reasoning applies to the killings in Baghdad's Nisour Square by Blackwater employees, committed while the contractors were acting in their official capacity, providing convoy security.[204]

Equivalent considerations apply in the cyber domain. Thus, the *Tallinn Manual 2.0* gives the example of a State that empowers a private company to use passive measures in defense of governmental cyber infrastructure.[205] If the company also engages in active defense, by "hacking back" in excess of the delegated governmental authority, such *ultra vires* conduct is attributable to the State as it is incidental to the company's activities in defending the government networks.[206]

A corresponding analysis is also appropriate regarding the conduct of certain militia groups in the event that they were appropriately empowered to perform combat functions on a State's behalf.[207] Consider, for instance, the atrocities perpetrated by Syrian militias during Turkey's October 2019 operation to take control of territory previously held by the Kurds in northern Syria.[208] If the other elements of the rule reflected in Article 5 can be satisfied, the abuses the militias committed were clearly *ultra vires* acts and attributable to the State, rather than conduct performed in the fighters' private capacities. The same is true of any violations of Russia's international legal obligations committed by members of the Wagner Group during the Syrian conflict, such as the alleged torture and killing of a detainee.[209]

The distinction between public and private acts is not, however, always clear. For example, the UK government raised a query with the ILC regarding the conduct of a private security firm empowered to act as railway police.[210] The facts of that example may apply equally to a PMSC that is authorized to use force in guarding a facility within a military base in a combat zone. Consider the position

203. *Id.*

204. Tiefer, *supra* note 192.

205. Tallinn Manual 2.0, *supra* note 78, r. 15, cmt. ¶ 12.

206. *Id.*

207. *See supra* sec. 5.4.

208. Hubbard et al., *supra* note 69; Stephanie Nebehay, *U.N. Urges Turkey to Investigate Executions in Syria*, Reuters (Oct. 15, 2019), https://www.reuters.com/article/syria-security-turkey-un-idUKL5N2702GQ/; Amnesty Int'l, *Syria: Damning Evidence of War Crimes and Other Violations by Turkish Forces and Their Allies* (Oct. 18, 2019), www.amnesty.org/en/latest/news/2019/10/syria-damning-evidence-of-war-crimes-and-other-violations-by-turkish-forces-and-their-allies/.

209. Marc Bennetts, *Investigators Say Man Filmed Beheading Syrian Is Russian Mercenary*, The Times (Nov. 22, 2019), www.thetimes.co.uk/article/man-in-syrian-torture-video-identified-as-wagner-group-mercenary-fqss9q2qm.

210. Int'l Law Comm'n, Documents of the Fiftieth Session (1998), *in* [1998] 2 Y.B. Int'l Law Comm'n 109, ¶ 4, U.N. Doc. A/CN.4/SER.A/1998/Add.1 (Part 1).

if contractors working for the PMSC act, while in uniform, in excess of the authority granted by the State by using force to detain an individual whose conduct does not threaten the security of the facility. The question arises whether that would be an example of an *ultra vires* act attributable to the State, or conduct committed in the individuals' private capacity.

In this situation, further information would be required to determine whether the contractors were "purportedly or apparently carrying out their official functions" at the time of the incident.[211] If at the relevant time they were on duty and relied upon their uniforms or the appearance of authority that this bestowed upon them when detaining the individual, thereby giving the impression that they were acting in their official capacity, their actions are likely to be attributable to the State.[212] If, however, they were off duty, located away from the military facility, and detained the individual with no reliance upon their uniforms or other insignia as an indication of authority, their actions may be considered those of ordinary citizens and not attributable to the State.[213]

According to the ARSIWA commentary, the distinction between official and private acts "may be avoided if the conduct complained of is systematic or recurrent, such that the State knew or ought to have known of it and should have taken steps to prevent it."[214] This can, again, be illustrated through the example of the PMSC empowered to guard an installation on a military base. Consider, for instance, the situation if contractors working for the PMSC exceed their authority on a regular basis by repeatedly using unauthorized violence against civilians seeking to enter the site. If such conduct should have come to the attention of the State but the State did nothing to address it, attribution is appropriate. That is the case even if, on a one-off basis, it is found that the contractors concerned were acting in a private capacity, rather than in the exercise of public powers.[215]

Examples such as these illustrate the difficulty, in certain cases, in determining whether an NSA exercises public powers at the time it commits an act potentially engaging the State's responsibility. This is a question of fact in each case that rests largely on the nexus between the activity concerned and the relevant governmental function. It also depends, to an extent, upon how broadly the notion of an entity's capacity, when exercising such public functions, is defined. But although its application can be problematic, the rule expressed in Article 7 ARSIWA is a necessary means to exclude private conduct from the scope of the attribution standard. It also ensures that any conduct that forms part of an NSA's exercise of governmental functions is properly attributable to the State.

211. ARSIWA, *supra* note 7, art. 7, cmt. ¶ 8.

212. Estate of Jean-Baptiste Caire (France) v. United Mexican States, 5 R.I.A.A. 516 (Fr.-Mex. Mixed Claims Comm'n, 1929).

213. *Id. See also supra* ch. 4, sec. 4.5.

214. ARSIWA, *supra* note 7, art. 7, cmt. ¶ 8.

215. *Id.*

5.6 CONCLUSION

The privatization of military and security functions in recent years is symptomatic of an ongoing shift in international relations, whereby States are no longer the sole and predominant actors on the international stage. This development has blurred the lines between public and private activity, leading to difficulties in identifying "elements governmental authority" for the purposes of Article 5 ARSIWA, particularly in new domains such as cyber.

Nonetheless, some functions, such as offensive combat and law enforcement, retain an inherently governmental character. Other conduct that is not quintessentially public in nature may also fall within the scope of governmental authority when viewed in its wider context. In respect of the latter, it may assist to consider factors such as the location where the relevant activities are carried out and the identity of the persons for whose benefit they are performed. Although such considerations may bring a broader range of functions within the scope of governmental authority, it is only those activities that amount to a breach of the State's international obligations that engage the responsibility of the State. In respect of PMSC conduct, this is far more likely to arise in the context of armed security or functions with a direct operational effect than it is in relation to tasks performed in support of personnel or equipment, such as maintenance or cleaning.

In the cyber domain, equivalent considerations apply when determining whether a private cyber operator's conduct amounts to an exercise of governmental authority. Cyber activity undertaken in support of military operations, as well as law enforcement functions undertaken by cybersecurity companies, are likely to be governmental in nature. The scope of Article 5 regarding activities in the cyber domain may thus be wider than commonly perceived. The *Tallinn Manual 2.0*, for example, includes scenarios within the commentary relating to Article 8 ARSIWA that may equally fall within the scope of Article 5.[216] These involve the defense of government computer networks, offensive cyber operations against another State, or cyber support to ongoing military operations;[217] activities that are all likely to amount to an exercise of governmental authority.

In addition to a requirement that the conduct concerned was governmental in character, the ARSIWA commentary provides for attribution pursuant to Article 5 only if the entity acts in its public capacity at the relevant time and the State empowered the entity to exercise the relevant functions. Regarding the latter criterion, a primary consideration is whether the relevant powers were delegated in accordance with the State's internal law. In this respect, any form of legal empowerment will suffice, whether this is effectuated through legislation, regulation, contract, or any other means permitted under the domestic legal regime. In the absence of legal empowerment, however, this chapter argues that other forms of State authorization should become relevant. Provided the State positively

216. TALLINN MANUAL 2.0, *supra* note 78, r. 17, cmt. ¶¶ 4, 7, 12, 14.

217. *Id.*

empowered the NSA to act, even if in a manner inconsistent with the State's domestic laws, the conduct of the entity should be attributable to the State. The contrary conclusion runs counter to the spirit of ARSIWA and incentivizes States to outsource public functions in an illegitimate manner.

A more inclusive interpretation of the basis of attribution reflected in Article 5 is justified in view of the nature of the functions concerned, which are traditionally reserved to the State and frequently affect the rights of individuals. Moreover, this construction of the attribution standard closes, to some extent, the accountability gap that emerges when considering the activities of NSAs such as the Shabbiha and the Wagner Group. As the rule of attribution expressed in Article 5 does not require State supervision over the entity's activities, a State may bear responsibility for the actions of an NSA exercising public functions, even in the absence of evidence of any degree of State control. This is particularly relevant in the contemporary conflict environment, in which States frequently fail to ensure that NSAs acting on their behalf comply with the State's international legal obligations. If, however, the requirements of Article 5 are not met, the issue of State control becomes paramount. This is discussed further in Chapter 6.

6

Persons or Entities Acting on the State's Instructions or Under Its Direction or Control

6.1 INTRODUCTION

It has long been recognized as a principle of international law that a State should bear responsibility for the conduct of those persons who act on its behalf.[1] In 1927, for example, the U.S.–Mexico Claims Commission found Mexico responsible for the conduct of a private citizen who shot and killed a U.S. national.[2] The Commission concluded, "It is difficult to determine with precision the status of these guards . . . but at any rate they were 'acting for' Mexico or for its political subdivisions."[3] The International Law Commission (ILC) took authorities such as this into account when formulating the rule now reflected in Article 8 of the Draft Articles on Responsibility of States for Internationally Wrongful Acts (ARSIWA).[4]

Article 8 provides that "[t]he conduct of a person or group of persons shall be considered an act of a State under international law if the person or group of persons is in fact acting on the instructions of, or under the direction or control

1. Draft Articles on Responsibility of States for Internationally Wrongful Acts, with commentaries, art. 8, cmt. ¶ 2, *in* Int'l Law Comm'n, Rep. on the Work of its Fifty-Third Session, U.N. Doc. A/56/10 (2001), *reprinted in* [2001] 2 Y.B. INT'L L. COMM'N 31, 47, U.N. Doc. A/CN.4/SER.A/2001/Add.1 (Part 2) [hereinafter ARSIWA].

2. Charles S. Stephens and Bowman Stephens (U.S.A.) v. United Mexican States, 4 R.I.A.A. 265 (Gen. Claims Comm'n, 1927).

3. *Id.* at 267.

4. *See, e.g.*, Roberto Ago (Special Rapporteur), Third Rep. on State Responsibility—the Internationally Wrongful Act of the State, Source of International Responsibility, U.N. Doc A/CN.4/246 and Add.1–3 (1971), *in* [1971] 2 Y.B. INT'L L. COMM'N 199, 264, ¶ 192, U.N. Doc. A/CN.4/SER.A/1971/Add.1 (Part 1) [hereinafter Ago's Third Rep. on State Responsibility].

Attribution of Non-State Actor Conduct During Armed Conflict. Jennifer Maddocks, Oxford University Press.
 DOI: 10.1093/oso/9780197842652.003.0006

of, that State in carrying out the conduct."[5] This basis of attribution is widely considered to reflect customary international law.[6] It is a residual rule, meaning that it applies only if an assessment has first been made that the person or entity concerned is not a State organ for the purposes of Article 4 ARSIWA and it is not empowered to exercise elements of governmental authority within the meaning of Article 5.[7]

By referring to the conduct of a person or group, Article 8 looks to the State's influence over the particular behavior that amounts to a breach of the State's international legal obligations. This is in contrast with Article 4, which focuses on the wider relationship between the State and the non-State actor (NSA).[8] To determine attribution in the context of Article 8, therefore, a detailed assessment is required as to the State's influence over, or involvement in, the specific acts committed by the NSA that violate the State's international legal obligations.

The rule of attribution reflected in Article 8 has been the subject of considerable academic comment.[9] This has largely addressed the conflicting jurisprudence of

5. ARSIWA, *supra* note 1, art. 8.

6. *See* 1 Customary International Humanitarian Law, r. 149 (Jean-Marie Henckaerts & Louise Doswald-Beck eds., 2005) [hereinafter Customary IHL]; Application of the Convention on the Prevention and Punishment of the Crime of Genocide (Bosn. & Herz. v. Serb. & Montenegro), Judgment, 2007 I.C.J. Rep. 43, ¶ 398 (Feb. 26) [hereinafter *Bosnian Genocide*]. This basis of attribution is also supported by the *opinio juris* of certain States in the context of attribution in the cyber domain. *See, e.g.*, Official Compendium of Voluntary National Contributions on the Subject of How International Law Applies to the Use of Information and Communications Technologies by States Submitted by Participating Governmental Experts at the Group of Governmental Experts on Advancing Responsible State Behavior in Cyberspace in the Context of International Security Established Pursuant to General Assembly Resolution 73/266, U.N. Doc. A/76/136* at 10, 21, 28, 39–40, 47, 61, 71, 79, 90, 117, 141 (July 13, 2021) (positions of Australia, Brazil, Estonia, Germany, Japan, the Netherlands, Norway, Romania, Switzerland, United Kingdom, and United States) [hereinafter Official Compendium].

7. For discussion regarding Articles 4 and 5 ARSIWA, *see supra* chs. 4, 5.

8. For discussion regarding the relationship between the rules reflected in Articles 4, 5, and 8 ARSIWA, *see infra* Ch. 7, sec. 7.2.

9. *See*, e.g., André J. de Hoogh, *Articles 4 and 8 of the 2001 ILC Articles on State Responsibility, The Tadić Case and Attribution of Acts of Bosnian Serb Authorities to the Federal Republic of Yugoslavia*, 72 Brit. Y.B. Int'l L. 255 (2002); Marko Milanović, *State Responsibility for Genocide*, 17 Eur. J. Int'l L. 553 (2006); Davis B. Tyner, *Internationalization of War Crimes Prosecutions: Correcting the International Criminal Tribunal for the Former Yugoslavia's Folly in Tadic*, 18 Florida J. Int'l L. 843 (2006); Marina Spinedi, *On the Non-Attribution of the Bosnian Serbs' Conduct to Serbia*, 5 J. Int'l Crim. Just. 829 (2007); Antonio Cassese, *The Nicaragua and Tadić Tests Revisited in Light of the ICJ Judgment on Genocide in Bosnia*, 18 Eur. J. Int'l L. 649 (2007); Stefan Talmon, *The Responsibility of Outside Powers for Acts of Secessionist Entities*, 58 Int'l & Comp. L. Q. 493 (2009); Olivier de Frouville, *Attribution of Conduct to the State: Private Individuals*, *in* The Law of International Responsibility 257 (James Crawford et al. eds., 2010); Hannah Tonkin, State Control over Private Military and Security Companies in Armed Conflict 113–21 (2011); Lindsey Cameron & Vincent Chetail, Privatizing

the International Court of Justice (ICJ) and the International Criminal Tribunal for the former Yugoslavia (ICTY) regarding the appropriate control threshold.[10] But despite the significant attention the issue has received, the precise meaning of control in this context remains unclear. There is, moreover, additional ambiguity regarding the concepts of State instructions and direction. These elements of the rule have received relatively little attention from legal scholars in comparison with the notion of control, and, in practice, the three terms are often conflated. This chapter seeks to add clarity regarding the meaning of all three bases of attribution encompassed within Article 8, examining their potential application in situations of armed conflict. It begins with an examination of the rule's drafting history.

6.2 ATTRIBUTION PURSUANT TO ARTICLE 8

6.2.1 Drafting History

The first version of the rule of attribution now reflected in Article 8 ARSIWA was proposed by Special Rapporteur Roberto Ago in the 1970s. This provided that the conduct of persons or groups of persons who "in fact . . . act on behalf of the State" should be considered an act of State in international law.[11] The intent was to encompass "groups which, though not belonging to the regular army of the State, carried out military activities in times of war."[12] Ago gave the example of "private persons who exceptionally performed the functions of auxiliaries of the regular armed forces, as the Paris taxi drivers had done in World War I during the battle of the Marne" and also "the 'volunteers' which certain Powers sent, or allowed to

WAR: PRIVATE MILITARY AND SECURITY COMPANIES UNDER PUBLIC INTERNATIONAL LAW 204–25 (2013); JAMES CRAWFORD, STATE RESPONSIBILITY: THE GENERAL PART 141–65 (2013); Kubo Mačák, *Decoding Article 8 of the International Law Commission's Articles on State Responsibility: Attribution of Cyber Operations by Non-State Actors*, 21 J. CONFLICT & SEC. L. 405 (2016) [hereinafter Mačák, *Decoding Article 8*]; Remy Jorritsma, *Where General International Law Meets International Humanitarian Law: Attribution of Conduct and the Classification of Armed Conflicts*, 23 J. CONFLICT & SEC. L. 405 (2018).

10. Military and Paramilitary Activities in and against Nicaragua (Nicar. v. U.S.), Judgment, 1986 I.C.J. Rep. 14, ¶ 115 (June 27) [hereinafter *Nicaragua*]; Prosecutor v. Tadić, Case No. ICTY IT-94-1-A, Appeals Chamber Judgment, ¶¶ 115–62 (Int'l Crim. Trib. for the former Yugoslavia, July 15, 1999) [hereinafter *Tadić Appeals Chamber*]; *Bosnian Genocide*, *supra* note 6, ¶¶ 396–406. *See also infra* sec. 6.4.

11. Ago's Third Rep. on State Responsibility *supra* note 4, at 267 (draft art. 8). *See also* Int'l Law Comm'n, Rep. of the Comm'n to the General Assembly (1974), *in* [1974] 2 Y.B. INT'L L. COMM'N 283, U.N. Doc. A/CN.4/SER.A/1974/Add.1 (Part One) [hereinafter ILC Y.B. 1974 vol. II]. The ILC adopted all the draft articles relating to attribution in 1996. *See* Int'l Law Comm'n, Rep. of the Comm'n to the General Assembly on the Work of its Forty-Eighth Session (1996), *in* [1996] 2 Y.B. INT'L L. COMM'N 59, U.N. Doc. A/CN.4/SER.A/1996/Add.1 (Part Two).

12. Int'l Law Comm'n, Summary Records of the Twenty-Sixth Session (1974), *in* [1974] 1 Y.B. INT'L L. COMM'N 32, ¶ 5, U.N. Doc. A/CN.4/SER.A/1974.

go, to countries where a civil war was in progress."[13] In addition, the ILC referred in this context to "abductions carried out in foreign territory by private persons acting, in fact, on behalf of the State,"[14] noting that "if the persons in question could be proved to have acted in concert with and at the instigation of the organs of a State, the action of abduction must be regarded as an act of that State."[15]

The ILC's choice of language indicates that it envisaged the rule applying when a State establishes an agency relationship with an NSA, during which the State directs the NSA to perform a particular act on its behalf.[16] Thus, the commentary to the initial draft article stipulated: "it must be genuinely proved that the person or group of persons were actually appointed by organs of the State to discharge a particular function or to carry out a particular duty, that they performed a given task at the instigation of those organs."[17]

Other ILC comments in the 1970s, however, suggest a potentially broader conception of the rule. These refer to States bearing responsibility for the conduct of groups formed with State encouragement, which the State provides with financial assistance, training, and weapons, and with which the State coordinates its own forces' operations.[18] The ILC asserted that such groups:

> cease to be individuals from the standpoint of international law. They become formations which act in concert with, and at the instigation of, the State, and perform missions authorized by or even entrusted to them by that State. They then fall into the category of persons or groups which are linked, in fact if not formally, with the State machinery . . . .[19]

Special Rapporteur Crawford addressed the ambiguity inherent in the attribution standard when, in 1998, the ILC again considered the rule's formulation. Crawford noted that "as a matter of ordinary language, a person may be said to act 'on behalf of' another person without any actual instruction or mandate from that other person."[20] Taking into account the ICJ's judgment in *Nicaragua*, in which the

13. *Id.* at 32, ¶¶ 5, 7.

14. *Id.* at 32–33, ¶ 7.

15. ILC Y.B. 1974 vol. II, *supra* note 11, at 284.

16. James Crawford (Special Rapporteur), First Rep. on State Responsibility 34, ¶ 158, U.N. Doc. A/CN.4/490 and Add.1–7 (1998) [hereinafter Crawford's First Rep. on State Responsibility]. *See also* Mačák, *Decoding Article 8*, *supra* note 9, at 414–15.

17. ILC Y.B. 1974 vol. II, *supra* note 11, at 284–85 (draft art. 8, cmt. ¶ 8).

18. Int'l Law Comm'n, Documents of the Twenty-Seventh Session Including the Rep. of the Comm'n to the General Assembly (1975), *in* [1975] 2 Y.B. INT'L L. COMM'N 80, ¶ 32, U.N. Doc. A/CN.4/SER.A/1975/Add.1.

19. *Id.* at 80 (draft art. 11, cmt. ¶ 32).

20. Crawford's First Rep. on State Responsibility, *supra* note 16, at 40, ¶ 197.

Court envisaged attribution based on the State's exercise of "effective control,"[21] Crawford considered the extent to which the language of Article 8 should encompass a State's de facto control over a person or group, in addition to cases of "express agency" involving an "actual instruction or mandate" from the State.[22] Crawford proposed revised wording whereby the conduct of persons or groups "in fact acting on the instructions of, or under the direction and control of" the State should be considered an act of state under international law.[23] While this change could be viewed as a mere elucidation of the nebulous concept of an entity acting "on behalf of" a State,[24] it also expands, to a limited extent, the scope of the rule by encompassing less formal associations between States and NSAs.[25]

The final development in Article 8's evolution was a minor change to Crawford's proposed wording made by the ILC Drafting Committee. The latter amended Crawford's reference to "direction and control," using instead the disjunctive "or."[26] The Drafting Committee thus emphasized that the requirements for direction or control are alternative, not cumulative.[27] This drafting history perhaps explains the inconsistency in the commentary to Article 8, which, on the one hand, refers to direction and control together as a single attribution standard[28] but, on the other, indicates that it is sufficient to establish either one of these criteria.[29] The disjunctive formulation was subsequently included in the text adopted by the General Assembly in 2001.[30]

21. *Nicaragua*, *supra* note 10, ¶ 115. *See also infra* sec. 6.4.1.1.

22. Crawford's First Rep. on State Responsibility, *supra* note 16, at 40, ¶ 197.

23. *Id.* at 56 (draft art. 8(a)). *See also id.* at 43, ¶¶ 212–13.

24. *See* Int'l Law Comm'n, Summary Records of the Meetings of the Fiftieth Session (1998), *in* [1998] 1 Y.B. INT'L L. COMM'N 230, ¶ 8 (comments of Mr. Crawford), U.N. Doc. A/CN.4/SER.A/1998 [hereinafter ILC Y.B. 1998 vol. I].

25. In his separate opinion in *Nicaragua*, Judge Ago criticized the majority for referring to "control" in the context of attribution, viewing this as a "less precise" basis on which to attribute private conduct to a State. *See Nicaragua*, *supra* note 10, Separate Opinion of Judge Ago ¶ 18 n. 1. *See also* ILC Y.B. 1998 vol. I, *supra* note 24, at 289, ¶ 79 (comments of Mr. Simma); Claus Kress, *L'Organe de facto en Droit International Public: Réflexions sur l'Imputation a l'État de l'Acte d'un Particulier à la Lumière des Développements Récents*, 105 REVUE GÉNÉRALE DE DROIT INTERNATIONAL PUBLIC 93, 119–20 (2001); Mačák, *Decoding Article 8*, *supra* note 9, at 414.

26. ILC Y.B. 1998 vol. I, *supra* note 24, at 289, ¶ 79; Int'l Law Comm'n, Rep. of the Comm'n to the General Assembly on the Work of its Fifty-Second Session (2000), *in* [2000] 2 Y.B. INT'L L. COMM'N 65, U.N. Doc. A/CN.4/SER.A/2000/Add.1 (Part 2)/Rev.1 [hereinafter ILC Y.B. 2000 vol. II].

27. ILC Y.B. 1998 vol. I, *supra* note 24, at 289, ¶ 79.

28. ARSIWA, *supra* note 1, art. 8, cmt. ¶ 1.

29. *Id.* art. 8, cmt. ¶ 7.

30. *Id.* art. 8. *See also* G.A. Res. 56/83, Responsibility of States for Internationally Wrongful Acts (Jan. 28, 2002).

6.2.2 General Features of the Attribution Standard

While Article 8's text indicates that a State's instructions, direction, and control are separate and distinct grounds of attribution, several factors are common to all three. First, there must exist a "specific factual relationship" amounting to "a real link between the person or group performing the act and the State machinery."[31] Article 8 is not concerned with formal or legal associations between a private entity and the State, but instead the connections that exist, in fact, as a result of the State's decision to act via an NSA.[32] Thus, private conduct is not attributable to a State solely due to an NSA's behavior, but rather due to the actions of a State organ in interacting with that NSA, namely, by issuing it with instructions, or exercising direction or control over its activities.[33]

Second, the relationship between the NSA and the State must be hierarchical in nature, meaning that the entity is subordinate to the State and does its bidding. This may be demonstrated by the fact that the entity accepts the instructions given and agrees to act upon them or conducts itself in compliance with the State's direction or control.[34] Such a relationship must exist at the time at which the instructions are issued, or the direction or control over the relevant operation is exercised.[35] Accordingly, a horizontal alliance between partners, such as one arising from the provision of training and support, will not lead to attribution.[36]

Third, in contrast with the test relating to de facto State organs considered in Chapter 4,[37] the links between the entity and the State must pertain to the specific conduct at issue. It is not sufficient for the purposes of Article 8 for the State to issue general instructions, or to exercise broad control over an entity in respect of the entire range of its activities. Instead, "the instructions, direction or control must relate to the conduct which is said to have amounted to an internationally wrongful act."[38] This specific focus is also reflected in the effects of attribution; only conduct performed under the State's instructions, direction, or control is attributable to the State.

31. ARSIWA, *supra* note 1, art. 8, cmt. ¶ 1.

32. de Frouville, *supra* note 9, at 271.

33. Gordon A. Christenson, *Attributing Acts of Omission to the State*, 12 Mich. J. Int'l L. 312, 346 (1990); Talmon, *supra* note 9, at 502.

34. Mačák, *Decoding Article 8*, *supra* note 9, at 415.

35. Cameron & Chetail, *supra* note 9, at 205.

36. Mačák, *Decoding Article 8*, *supra* note 9, at 427.

37. *See supra* ch. 4, sec. 4.4.

38. ARSIWA, *supra* note 1, art. 8, cmt. ¶ 7.

Fourth, an NSA's status or identity is irrelevant to attribution on this basis.[39] The rule applies to the conduct of private individuals and groups, as well as to the activities of corporate and other entities, irrespective of whether they have legal personality.[40] Furthermore, the rule potentially applies to any form of conduct.[41] In contrast with attribution arising under the rule reflected in Article 5, there is no requirement for the NSA's acts to involve governmental activity.[42] Instead, a State may bear responsibility for any type of conduct, provided this was performed on the State's instructions, or under its direction or control.

If, however, an NSA acts outside the scope of the State's instructions, direction, or control, that behavior is not normally attributable to the State. The rule reflected in Article 7 ARSIWA, relating to the attribution of *ultra vires* conduct to the State, applies only to State organs and to entities empowered to exercise elements of governmental authority.[43] When dealing with NSAs falling outside these categories, the State will not normally assume the risk that its instructions or direction will be followed in an internationally wrongful manner.[44] However, that is not the end of the matter. The ARSIWA commentary provides that the State may nevertheless bear responsibility for unauthorized conduct if this was "incidental to the mission" and did not clearly exceed its scope.[45] The practical implications of this guidance are considered later in this chapter.[46]

Despite the supposedly disjunctive nature of instructions, direction, and control,[47] the latter two terms are ordinarily considered together, as a single attribution standard. Accordingly, direction and control have several features in common. One such shared characteristic is that both require an ongoing relationship between the entity and the State that endures for an undefined period. Thus, according to the *Tallinn Manual 2.0*, "the two terms refer to a continuing process of exercising authority over an activity such as a cyber operation."[48] Additionally, for conduct to be attributable to a State on the basis of direction or control, a "core relationship of subordination" must exist between the State and its agent.[49]

39. *Id.* art. 8, cmt. ¶ 2.

40. *Id.* cmt. ¶ 9.

41. *Id.* cmt. ¶ 2.

42. *Id.* art. 5. *See also supra* ch. 5, sec. 5.3.

43. ARSIWA, *supra* note 1, art. 7. *See also supra* ch. 4, sec. 4.5; ch. 5, sec. 5.5.

44. ARSIWA, *supra* note 1, art. 8, cmt. ¶ 8.

45. *Id.*

46. *See infra* secs. 6.3.1.2, 6.4.3.2.

47. ARSIWA, *supra* note 1, art. 8, cmt. ¶ 7.

48. Tallinn Manual 2.0 on the International Law Applicable to Cyber Operations r. 17, cmt. ¶ 5 (Michael N. Schmitt ed., 2017) [hereinafter Tallinn Manual 2.0].

49. Crawford, *supra* note 9, at 146.

In contrast, instructions may be issued on a one-off basis, meaning that the NSA remains a "free agent" and the relationship between the entity and the State might endure only for the limited period in time during which the instructions are issued.[50]

6.3 STATE INSTRUCTIONS

6.3.1 The Meaning of Instructions

When a State's organs instruct an NSA to perform an act that violates the State's international legal obligations, that act is attributable to the State.[51] To illustrate the principle, the ARSIWA commentary replicates the ILC's earlier references to individuals "employed as auxiliaries or . . . sent as 'volunteers' to neighbouring countries, or . . . instructed to carry out particular missions abroad."[52] Thus, the conduct of the NSAs that committed acts of sabotage in the United States on the orders of the German government during World War I, in violation of the laws of neutrality, was attributable to Germany.[53] Similarly, if the individual responsible for the 2024 killing of a Russian General in Moscow was acting on the instructions of Ukraine's security services, the assassination is attributable to Ukraine.[54]

As these examples illustrate, the essence of "instructions" as a basis of attribution is the issuance of some form of order or command by a State organ to an NSA that prompts the NSA to act in a manner that violates the State's international legal obligations.[55] There is no requirement for the State to also supervise the NSA's conduct at the time it acts upon those instructions.[56] It suffices if the State engages with the NSA prior to the event and thereby causes the

50. *Id. See also* de Frouville, *supra* note 9, at 271. For further discussion regarding the distinction between instructions and control, *see infra* sec. 6.4.3.3.

51. ARSIWA, *supra* note 1, art. 8, cmt. ¶¶ 1–2.

52. *Id.* cmt. ¶ 2. *See also supra* sec. 6.2.1.

53. *See* Lehigh Valley R.R. Co. & others (United States) v. Germany (Sabotage Cases) 8 R.I.A.A. 225 (Mixed Claims Comm'n, 1939). *See also* Dayna L. Kaufman, *Don't Do What I Say, Do What I Mean!: Assessing a State's Responsibility for the Exploits of Individuals Acting in Conformity with a Statement from a Head of State*, 70 FORDHAM L. REV. 2603, 2623–25 (2002).

54. For legal analysis of this incident, *see* Michael N. Schmitt, *Killing General Kirillov: Questions and Answers*, ARTICLES OF WAR (Dec. 24, 2024), https://lieber.westpoint.edu/killing-general-kirillov-questions-answers/.

55. Kress, *supra* note 25, at 126; FRAUKE RENZ, STATE RESPONSIBILITY AND NEW TRENDS IN THE PRIVATIZATION OF WARFARE 138 (2020).

56. U. Ctr. for Int'l Humanitarian L., EXPERT MEETING ON PRIVATE MILITARY CONTRACTORS: STATUS AND STATE RESPONSIBILITY FOR THEIR ACTIONS 20–21 (Aug. 29–30, 2005), www.ucihl.org/communication/Private_Military_Companies_report.pdf.

NSA to act in the manner complained of. For example, if the individual who killed the Russian general in Moscow was acting on Ukraine's instructions,[57] that act is attributable to Ukraine even if State officials did not also oversee the assassination.

It is insufficient, however, if an NSA simply acts in accordance with a common goal it shares with the State. For instance, the conduct of patriotic hackers who act of their own accord in launching malicious cyber operations against a perceived enemy of the State does not lead to attribution.[58] It is also doubtful whether the online guidance Ukrainian officials provided to members of the "IT Army" regarding Russian targets and the software they should use amounts to State instructions.[59] This information not directed to an identifiable NSA, but rather offered to any volunteers who might be willing to act.[60] The commentary to Article 8 refers to the need for "a specific factual relationship between the person or entity engaging in the conduct and the State;"[61] a relationship that would not exist in the case of an ever-changing group of volunteer hackers.

To lead to attribution, therefore, the State must positively assign the task in question to a specific NSA.[62] But the NSA's motivation for following the State's instructions is immaterial; it might act for financial gain or solely out of patriotism.[63] Equally, it is not important what form the instructions take. These could be incorporated into the terms of a contract with a private military and security company (PMSC), for example, or issued as orders in the field.[64] The content of the instruction, however, is key to determining whether the State's responsibility is engaged.

57. Schmitt, *supra* note 54.

58. Regarding patriotic hackers acting against Estonia in 2007, *see* ENEKEN TIKK ET AL., INTERNATIONAL CYBER INCIDENTS: LEGAL CONSIDERATIONS 31–32 (2010), https://ccdcoe.org/uploads/2018/10/legalconsiderations_0.pdf.

59. Yuriy Zaliznyak, *Ukraine's Volunteer "IT Army" Responds to Russian Hackers, Minister Says*, ABC NEWS (Aug. 25, 2022), https://abcnews.go.com/International/ukraines-volunteer-army-responds-russian-hackers-minister/story?id=88651955.

60. *Id.*

61. ARSIWA, *supra* note 1, art. 8, cmt. ¶ 1.

62. For example, the U.S. Justice Department charged two Russian intelligence officers with directing private hackers to steal large quantities of data. *See* Vindu Goel & Eric Lichtblau, *Russian Agents Were Behind Yahoo Hack, U.S. Says*, N.Y. TIMES (Mar. 15, 2017), https://www.nytimes.com/2017/03/15/technology/yahoo-hack-indictment.html.

63. Michael N. Schmitt, *"Virtual" Disenfranchisement: Cyber Election Meddling in the Grey Zones of International Law*, 19 CHI. J. INT'L L. 30, 61–61 (2018) [hereinafter Schmitt, *"Virtual" Disenfranchisement*].

64. TONKIN, *supra* note 9, at 114–17; CRAWFORD, *supra* note 9, at 145; CAMERON & CHETAIL, *supra* note 9, at 206.

6.3.1.1 The Content of the Instruction

Often, evidence of State instructions is simply not available.[65] For this reason, few courts or tribunals have found that conduct is attributable to a State on this basis.[66] One exception is the *Nicaragua* case, in which the ICJ concluded that the actions of a group of NSAs known as Unilaterally Controlled Latino Assets, or UCLAs, were attributable to the United States because they acted "on the direct instructions" of U.S. officials when laying mines in Nicaraguan ports.[67]

In the same case, the ICJ also heard evidence that U.S. officials issued instructions to another group of NSAs, the *contras*.[68] For example, members of the U.S. Central Intelligence Agency (CIA) were "urging" the NSA to launch an offensive to take and hold Nicaraguan territory and after the offensive failed, the CIA "told" the group to keep fighting.[69] However, the ICJ deemed this insufficient to lead to attribution and focused instead on the U.S. exercise of control.[70] The Court's reasoning is not clearly stated in the judgment, but it could relate to the specificity of the instructions concerned.[71]

It is apparent from the ICJ's earlier jurisprudence relating to the 1979 Iranian revolution that a broad pronouncement from the State is insufficient to amount to "instructions" for the purposes of attribution.[72] Thus, Ayatollah Khomeini's general call on the youth of Iran to "expand with all their might their attacks against the United States and Israel" did not amount to "an authorization from the State to undertake the specific operation of invading and seizing the United States Embassy."[73] The ICJ affirmed that for attribution to arise, the relevant

65. The ILC acknowledged this during its discussions regarding art. 8. *See* Crawford's First Rep. on State Responsibility, *supra* note 16, at 43, ¶ 212; ILC Y.B. 1998 vol. I, *supra* note 24, at 289, ¶ 79. *See also* ARSIWA, *supra* note 1, art. 7, cmt. ¶ 3.

66. In the *Bosnian Genocide* case, for instance, the ICJ found that "The Applicant has not proved that instructions were issued by the federal authorities in Belgrade, or by any other organ of the FRY, to commit the massacres." *See Bosnian Genocide*, *supra* note 6, ¶¶ 398, 413.

67. *Nicaragua*, *supra* note 10, ¶ 75. *See also id.* ¶ 80.

68. For discussion regarding the United States' relationship with the *contras*, *see supra* ch. 4, sec. 4.4.1.1. *See also infra* sec. 6.4.1.1.

69. *Nicaragua*, *supra* note 10, ¶ 104. *See also* Kaufman, *supra* note 53, at 2642–45.

70. *Nicaragua*, *supra* note 10, ¶ 109. *See also infra* sec. 6.4.1.1.

71. This was the view taken by the ICTY Appeals Chamber. *See Tadić Appeals Chamber*, *supra* note 10, ¶ 114. It is also possible that the ICJ took the *contras*' level of autonomy into account if this enabled the NSA to choose whether to follow the State's instructions. *See Nicaragua*, *supra* note 10, ¶¶ 108–9.

72. United States Diplomatic and Consular Staff in Tehran (U.S. v. Iran), Judgment, 1980, I.C.J. Rep. 3, ¶¶ 57–59 (May 24) [hereinafter *Tehran Hostages*]. *See also* Alfred Short v. Islamic Republic of Iran, Award No. 312-11135-3, ¶ 35 (Iran-U.S. Claims Trib., 1987); Saint-Gobain Performance Plastics Europe v. Bolivarian Republic of Venezuela, Case. No. ARB/12/13, ¶¶ 447–52 (Int'l Ctr. for Settlement of Inv. Disp., Dec. 30, 2016).

73. *Tehran Hostages*, *supra* note 72, ¶ 59.

instruction must specify the course of conduct it wants the NSA to pursue, thereby demonstrating that "in fact, on the occasion in question the militants acted on behalf of the State, having been charged by some competent organ of the Iranian State to carry out a specific operation."[74]

It is unclear, however, whether the ICJ applied this same test when addressing Iran's responsibility for the second phase of events, following the initial seizure of the Embassy.[75] In this context, the Court noted that numerous Iranian authorities expressed approval for the militants' actions[76] and cited a decree issued by Ayatollah Khomeini in which he declared that Iran would not give permission for the majority of hostages to be released until the United States had handed over the former Shah for trial.[77] The ICJ concluded that this policy, announced by Ayatollah Khomeini, was sufficient "fundamentally to transform the legal nature of the situation" so that "[t]he militants, authors of the invasion and jailers of the hostages, had now become agents of the Iranian State for whose acts the State itself was internationally responsible."[78] While the Court did not fully articulate the basis for this conclusion, it may be that the specificity of the instruction was key.[79] Thus, a vague call to unspecified individuals to act in a particular manner will not give rise to attribution but a more precise direction to particular persons or groups, who then act in accordance with that instruction, engages the State's responsibility.[80]

The ICJ confirmed the requirement for specific instructions in its later judgment in the *Bosnian Genocide* case. Here, the Court stipulated that instructions must be given "in respect of each operation in which the alleged violations occurred, not generally in respect of the overall actions taken by the persons or groups of persons having committed the violations."[81] The practical meaning of this requirement is somewhat ambiguous, however, resting as it does upon the concept of an "operation," which may be broadly or more narrowly defined.[82]

74. *Id.* ¶ 58. *See also* Kress, *supra* note 25, at 102; Kaufman, *supra* note 53, at 2621–25; Nicholas Tsagourias & Michael Farrell, *Cyber Attribution: Technical and Legal Approaches and Challenges*, 31 Eur. J. Int'l L. 941, 954–55 (2020).

75. *Tehran Hostages*, *supra* note 72, ¶¶ 69–75. *See also* Kress, *supra* note 25, at 102.

76. *Tehran Hostages*, *supra* note 72, ¶ 71.

77. *Id.* ¶ 73.

78. *Id.* ¶ 74. For discussion of the case in the context of Article 11 ARSIWA, *see infra* ch. 10, sec. 10.2.3.

79. Luigi Condorelli, *The Imputability to States of Acts of International Terrorism*, 19 Israel Y.B. on Hum. Rts. 233, 238 (1989); Kaufman, *supra* note 53, at 2622–23.

80. The judgment of the ICTY Appeals Chamber in the *Tadić* case supports this conclusion. *See Tadić Appeals Chamber*, *supra* note 10, ¶ 133.

81. *Bosnian Genocide*, *supra* note 6, ¶ 400. *See also Tehran Hostages*, *supra* note 72, ¶ 58.

82. Crawford, *supra* note 9, at 145.

In general, an operation is deemed to consist of a number of constituent acts,[83] any one of which could amount to a violation of the State's international legal obligations. But whether the State's instructions should relate to the operation as a whole or to the individual acts committed within that operation remains unclear.

To illustrate, consider the conduct of the Syrian militias involved in Turkey's incursion into areas of northeast Syria in October 2019.[84] Reporting indicates that the militias were acting on the orders of Turkish officials.[85] But while Turkey's instructions clearly encompassed the militias' broader conduct in taking control of territory previously held by the Syrian Democratic Forces (SDF), it seems unlikely that Turkey ordered the militias to carry out the particular atrocities during those operations that violated Turkey's obligations under international humanitarian law (IHL).[86] Indeed, the militias' reported lawlessness and lack of discipline suggests that such abuses occurred of the NSAs' own volition rather than under Turkey's orders.[87] The question therefore arises whether Turkey's responsibility is engaged pursuant to its broad instructions to the militias to participate in the operation, if those instructions did not also include orders relating to the specific acts committed in the course of the operation that violated international law.

The ARSIWA commentary appears to answer this question in the negative. This declares that Article 8 applies if an NSA acts "on the instructions of the State in carrying out the wrongful conduct"[88] and later stipulates that the State's instructions "must relate to the conduct which is said to have amounted to an internationally wrongful act."[89] It seems that from the ILC's perspective, therefore, attribution is appropriate only if the State specifically charges the NSA to act a way that breaches the State's international legal obligations. This strict interpretation also finds support in the ICJ's jurisprudence.[90] But the ILC commentary

83. NATO defines operations as "a sequence of coordinated actions with a defined purpose which are military and contribute to a broader approach including non-military actions." *See* NATO, Allied Joint Doctrine for the Conduct of Operations, AJP-3 (ed. C, version 1) 1–2, ¶ 1.4 (Feb. 2019), https://www.coemed.org/files/stanags/01_AJP/AJP-3_EDC_V1_E_2490.pdf.

84. *See supra* ch. 2, sec. 2.4.1.4.

85. Elizabeth Tsurkov, *Who Are Turkey's Proxy Fighters in Syria?* N.Y. Rev. (Nov. 27, 2019), www.nybooks.com/daily/2019/11/27/who-are-turkeys-proxy-fighters-in-syria/.

86. Amnesty Int'l, Syria: Damning Evidence of War Crimes and Other Violations by Turkish Forces and Their Allies (Oct. 18, 2019), www.amnesty.org/en/latest/news/2019/10/syria-damning-evidence-of-war-crimes-and-other-violations-by-turkish-forces-and-their-allies/; Martin Chulov, *Syria: Videos of Turkey-Backed Militias Show "Potential War Crimes,"* The Guardian (Oct. 26, 2019), https://www.theguardian.com/world/2019/oct/26/syria-turkey-arab-videos-torture-kurdish-bodies-militia.

87. Tsurkov, *supra* note 85.

88. ARSIWA, *supra* note 1, art. 8, cmt. ¶ 1.

89. *Id.* ¶ 7.

90. *Tehran Hostages*, *supra* note 72, ¶ 58.

nevertheless recognizes that some borderline cases may arise.[91] Such cases may be clarified further by examining the notion of *ultra vires* acts.

6.3.1.2 State Instructions and *Ultra Vires* Acts

While affirming that a State will not generally assume the risk that its instructions will be performed in an internationally unlawful manner, the ARSIWA commentary recognizes that an NSA's harmful conduct might be so closely linked to the mission it undertakes on the State's behalf that the State's responsibility should be engaged.[92] Thus, according to the ILC, cases involving potentially *ultra vires* acts "can be resolved by asking whether the unlawful or unauthorized conduct was really incidental to the mission or clearly went beyond it."[93] But determining, in practice, where the line should be drawn between acts that are attributable to a State and those which are *ultra vires* may prove problematic. For instance, were the Syrian militias' actions in executing Kurdish prisoners[94] incidental to the mission they were tasked by Turkey to perform, or did they clearly go beyond it?

This is a question of fact, to be determined considering all the relevant circumstances. It seems, in this case, that the most likely conclusion is that the militias' actions went beyond the scope of the mission, meaning that the abuses were *ultra vires* and not attributable to Turkey. Certainly, the militias' conduct did not assist in the accomplishment of the operation; it was not necessary for them to act in this manner to comply with Turkey's instructions.[95] Thus, notwithstanding moral and policy arguments that the militias' abuses should engage Turkey's responsibility, there is considerable doubt whether they are attributable to Turkey based on the State's instructions.[96]

The position may be clearer in other scenarios involving States' instructions to NSAs. For instance, if contractors working for a PMSC are instructed to interrogate detainees on behalf of a State and mistreat the detainees during an interrogation, that mistreatment is attributable to the State in view of the close link between

91. ARSIWA, *supra* note 1, art. 8, cmt. ¶ 8.

92. *Id.*

93. *Id.*

94. Ben Hubbard et al., *Syrian Arab Fighters Backed by Turkey Kill Two Kurdish Prisoners*, N.Y. Times (Oct. 12, 2019), https://www.nytimes.com/2019/10/12/world/middleeast/turkey-invasion-syria-kurds.html; Martin Chulov & Mohammed Rasool, *Kurdish Politician Among Nine Civilians Shot Dead by Pro-Turkey Forces in Syria*, The Guardian (Oct. 13, 2019), https://www.theguardian.com/world/2019/oct/13/female-kurdish-politician-among-nine-civilians-killed-by-pro-turkey-forces-in-syria-observers-say; Stephanie Nebehay, *U.N. Urges Turkey to Investigate Executions in Syria*, Reuters (Oct. 15, 2019), www.reuters.com/article/us-syria-security-turkey-un/un-urges-turkey-to-investigate-executions-in-syria-idUSKBN1WU19W.

95. Cameron & Chetail, *supra* note 9, at 207.

96. For discussion whether the militias' abuses were conducted under Turkey's effective control, *see infra* sec. 6.4.4. For analysis regarding the potential attribution of the militias' conduct to Turkey based on the rule reflected in Article 5 ARSIWA, *see supra* ch. 5.

the abuse and the task the PMSC was instructed to undertake.[97] But when the connection between the State's instructions and the NSA's misconduct is more attenuated, greater ambiguity arises. For instance, if the State's instructions relate solely to the capture of an individual but do not address the manner in which the detainee should be treated thereafter, the question arises whether any subsequent detainee abuse engages the State's responsibility.[98]

One possible answer is that the abuse is not attributable to the State, because the State's instructions did not relate to the specific conduct that amounts to the potential internationally wrongful act.[99] Moreover, the detainee abuse occurred after the capture mission was complete and therefore did not assist in its accomplishment.[100] But all the facts should be considered before reaching a conclusion in this respect. For instance, how soon after the capture did the detainee abuse take place? Was this perpetrated by the same individuals who conducted the capture mission? Did State officials know that the NSA was likely to abuse the detainee but turn a blind eye to this possibility when issuing instructions? Ultimately, the closer the connection between the mission the State tasks the NSA to undertake and the potential violation of international law, the greater the likelihood of attribution. However, if the State expressly instructs the NSA to treat detainees humanely and the NSA breaches that instruction, its acts are *ultra vires* and therefore not attributable to the State.[101]

It may be particularly difficult to determine whether an NSA's acts fall within the scope of a State's instructions when those instructions are ambiguous in scope. To illustrate, consider the indiscriminate attacks conducted by rebels in eastern Ukraine during the 2015 Debaltseve offensive.[102] If evidence is available to prove that Russian officials commanded the rebels to attack the city in this manner, the rebels' conduct in violation of IHL is attributable to the State. However, if Russia's instructions were broader in nature, the legal position is less clear. For example, Russian officers might have ordered the rebels to take control of the city without

97. ARSIWA, *supra* note 1, art. 8, cmt. ¶ 8. *See also* Katja Nieminen, *Rules of Attribution and the Private Military Contractors at Abu Ghraib: Private Acts or Public Wrongs?*, 15 Finnish Y.B. Int'l L. 289, 317–18 (2004).

98. de Hoogh, *supra* note 9, at 284–85.

99. ARSIWA, *supra* note 1, art. 8, cmt. ¶¶ 1, 7.

100. Cameron & Chetail, *supra* note 9, at 207.

101. ARSIWA, *supra* note 1, art. 8, cmt. ¶ 8; Kress, *supra* note 25, at 136. For a contrary view, *see Tadić Appeals Chamber, supra* note 10, ¶¶ 119, 121.

102. Amnesty Int'l, Ukraine: Horror of Civilian Bloodshed in Indiscriminate Attacks (Feb. 2, 2015), www.amnesty.org/en/press-releases/2015/02/ukraine-horror-civilian-bloodshed-indiscriminate-attacks/ [hereinafter Amnesty Int'l, Civilian Bloodshed]; Joanne Mariner, *Dabaltseve Under Fire*, Huffpost (Feb. 14, 2015), www.huffpost.com/entry/debaltseve-under-fire_b_6684642; Rep. on the Human Rights Situation in Ukraine 18, ¶ 83 (Feb. to May 2015), www.ohchr.org/Documents/Countries/UA/10thOHCHRreportUkraine.pdf [hereinafter Ukraine Rep. 2015].

issuing any tactical direction as to how this should be done. In that situation, it is doubtful whether the relevant orders were sufficiently precise to lead to attribution.[103] Alternatively, Russia might have given more detailed directions that implicitly authorized the rebels' use of indiscriminate attacks, in which case the rebels' conduct should be attributable to the State.[104] But a third possibility is that Russia's commands were ambiguous, in that they could have been interpreted either lawfully, by directing attacks only at military objectives, or unlawfully, by targeting the city indiscriminately.[105]

Determining attribution in this context depends on the particular facts. It is also helpful to consider the rule's object and purpose, namely, to hold States to account for the conduct of those persons and entities that act on their behalf, as their agents.[106] To accord with this aim, a general instruction that leaves open the method of fulfilling the State's directive should suffice to engage the State's responsibility.[107] Given that there is no requirement for a State to exercise control over the way in which its instructions are carried out once issued,[108] the opposite conclusion provides an incentive to States to issue vague instructions and thereby evade responsibility.[109] As noted in Chapter 2, States often choose to act via NSAs to enhance plausible deniability and to minimize the risks associated with the use of their own armed forces.[110] But when they do so, States should bear the risk that their instructions are interpreted in an unlawful manner and take feasible steps to ensure that in executing those instructions, the NSA acts in accordance with the State's international legal obligations.

6.3.2 State Instructions to NSAs During Armed Conflict

Evidence that a State instructed an NSA to act in an internationally wrongful manner is rare. As the case studies in Chapter 2 illustrate, the available evidence

103. *See* ARSIWA, *supra* note 1, art. 8, cmt. ¶¶ 1, 7; *Tehran Hostages*, *supra* note 72, ¶ 58. For discussion whether Russia exercised effective control over the rebels, *see infra* sec. 6.4.4.

104. Tonkin, *supra* note 9, at 115–16.

105. Protocol Additional to the Geneva Conventions of 12 August 1949, and Relating to the Protection of Victims of International Armed Conflicts arts. 51, 52, June 8, 1977, 1125 U.N.T.S. 3 [hereinafter AP I]; Customary IHL, *supra* note 6, rr. 7, 11–12.

106. *See supra* sec. 6.2.1; ARSIWA, *supra* note 1, chapeau to pt. I, ch. II, cmt. ¶ 2.

107. Crawford, *supra* note 9, at 145; Kress, *supra* note 25, at 136; Oliver R. Jones, *Implausible Deniability: State Responsibility for the Actions of Private Military Firms*, 24 Conn. J. Int'l L. 239, 271 (2009).

108. This follows from the disjunctive nature of instructions and control. *See* ARSIWA, *supra* note 1, art. 8, cmt. ¶ 7. *See also* U. Ctr. for Int'l Humanitarian L., *supra* note 56, at 20–21.

109. U. Ctr. for Int'l Humanitarian L., *supra* note 56, at 21-22.

110. *See supra* ch. 2, sec. 2.2.1.

typically relates to the State's provision of material or other support to the NSA, not to its issuance of instructions.[111] Nonetheless, a few examples in the case studies illustrate the potential for attribution on this basis.

During the conflict in the Democratic Republic of the Congo (DRC), for example, Rwanda provided support not only to the rebel group M23 but also to other armed groups.[112] In 2012, the UN Group of Experts reported that Rwandan officials were in direct contact with the commander of one armed group, Nduma Defence of Congo, and entrusted him with the task of killing the leader of a rival group.[113] Once he had completed the task, the commander surrendered to the DRC's armed forces and Rwanda's head of military intelligence arranged for his evacuation to Rwanda.[114] If accurate, this reporting provides a clear example of a private individual acting on the instructions of a State, in a manner that potentially violates the State's international legal obligations. Accordingly, the killing is attributable to Rwanda.

Moving to the Syrian conflict, it appears that the Syrian regime issued instructions to members of the Shabbiha to act on its behalf. According to one report, President Assad's brother, Maher al-Assad, organized a meeting in July 2011 during which he charged individuals with responsibility for leading the Shabbiha in different parts of the country, briefing the commanders that the NSA "should set out to terrify protesters."[115] The intention was reportedly to "create a paramilitary group to do the dirty work" so that the Syrian army would not be viewed on world media shooting at protesters.[116] One of the Shabbiha commanders who was present claimed that specific instructions were issued: "[T]hey told us to kill protesters, armed or unarmed, and torture those you capture."[117] Commanders across the country would then report back to Maher al-Assad regarding their activities and were sometimes given "hit lists" of people to assassinate.[118]

111. *See id.* sec. 2.4.

112. *Id.* sec. 2.4.3.

113. Add. to the Interim Rep. of the Group of Experts on the Democratic Republic of the Congo Concerning Violations of the Arms Embargo and Sanctions Regime by the Government of Rwanda 18, ¶ 36, U.N. Doc. S/2012/348/Add.1 (June 27, 2012) [hereinafter U.N. June 2012 Rep.].

114. *Id.*

115. Salwa Amor & Ruth Sherlock, *How Bashar al-Assad Created the Feared Shabiha Militia: An Insider Speaks*, Souria Houria (Mar. 24, 2014), : https://souriahouria.com/how-bashar-al-assad-created-the-feared-shabiha-militia-an-insider-speaks-by-salwa-amor-ruth-sherlock-in-gaziantep/.

116. *Id.*

117. *Id.*

118. *Id.*

While this report is unsubstantiated, the United States[119] and the European Union[120] both imposed sanctions on Maher al-Assad, the latter describing him as the "principal overseer of violence against demonstrators."[121] This lends some weight to the allegations. If the reporting is correct and assuming Maher al-Assad was an organ of the Syrian State at the time of the meeting,[122] the abuses committed pursuant to such orders are attributable to Syria. This includes not only the actions of the commanders to whom the instructions were issued, but also the conduct of any members of the Shabbiha who acted on those commanders' orders.

The instructions that Maher-al-Assad is alleged to have issued are quite explicit. But evidence also exists of more ambiguous orders promulgated to paramilitary groups in the early stages of the Syrian conflict. For example, in August 2011, the Syrian National Security Bureau reportedly issued an instruction to NSAs to "maintain control" of areas that had been previously "cleansed of wanted persons" during security operations.[123] These groups subsequently committed numerous atrocities against civilians.[124]

For such conduct to be attributable to Syria based on the instructions element of Article 8, further evidence would be required to establish a link between the order to "maintain control" and the subsequent behavior of the NSAs. It may be that, considering all the relevant circumstances, the instruction implicitly authorized the NSAs to act in a manner that violated Syria's human rights obligations. But when examining an ongoing relationship, such as the Syrian regime's associations with paramilitary groups, it may be more appropriate to consider the broader context in which the relevant conduct was performed and in particular, whether the entity was acting under the State's direction or control.

119. Exec. Order No. 13572 of Apr. 29, 2011, Blocking Property of Certain Persons with respect to Human Rights Abuses in Syria, 76 Fed. Reg. no. 85 (May 3, 2011), www.gpo.gov/fdsys/pkg/FR-2011-05-03/pdf/2011-10910.pdf.

120. Council of the European Union, Decision Concerning Restrictive Measures Against Syria and Repealing Decision 2011/782/CFSP, 2012/739/CFSP, annex 1 (Nov. 29, 2012), https://eur-lex.europa.eu/legal-content/EN/TXT/PDF/?uri=CELEX:32012D0739&from=GA.

121. *Id.* This reference could simply refer to Maher al-Assad's role in overseeing violence committed by government forces. However, a conclusion that the Syrian State played a role in the Shabbiha's activities is supported by the findings of the U.N. Commission of Inquiry. *See* Rep. of the Indep. Int'l Comm'n of Inquiry on the Syrian Arab Republic 21–22, ¶ 133, U.N. Doc. A/HRC/21/50 (Aug. 16, 2012).

122. ARSIWA, *supra* note 1, art. 4. *See also supra* ch. 4.

123. Expert Report of Ewan Brown 65–66, Colvin et al. v. Syrian Arab Republic, No. 1:16-cv-01423-ABJ (D.D.C., Mar. 22, 2018), https://cja.org/wp-content/uploads/2018/04/17-Expert-Report-of-Ewan-Brown-dated-March-2-2018_Redacted.pdf.

124. *Id.* at 66.

6.4 STATE DIRECTION OR CONTROL

6.4.1 Guidance Provided by the ICJ and ICTY

Despite the indication within the ARSIWA commentary that direction and control are distinct grounds of attribution,[125] courts and tribunals applying the rule reflected in Article 8 have focused largely on the notion of control. The requisite type and degree of State control to satisfy the rule have generated considerable debate. This commenced with the ICJ's 1986 judgment in *Nicaragua.*[126]

6.4.1.1 NICARAGUA

In its *Nicaragua* judgment, the ICJ examined U.S. support to a rebel group known as the *contras.*[127] U.S. officials provided substantial assistance to the NSA, including involvement in planning the *contras*' operations and developing the group's strategies and tactics.[128] In light of such support, the ICJ considered, first, whether the *contras*' activities were attributable to the United States on the basis that the group amounted to a de facto State organ.[129] Having decided the issue in the negative,[130] the Court moved on to consider the potential application of the rule now reflected in Article 8.

In this context, the ICJ stated:

All the forms of United States participation mentioned above, and even the general control by the respondent State over a force with a high degree of dependency on it, would not in themselves mean, without further evidence, that the United States directed or enforced the perpetration of the acts contrary to human rights and humanitarian law alleged by the applicant State. Such acts could well be committed by members of the *contras* without the control of the United States. For this conduct to give rise to legal responsibility of the United States, it would in principle have to be proved that that State had effective control of the military or paramilitary operations in the course of which the alleged violations were committed.[131]

This paragraph of the ICJ's judgment gave rise to the oft-debated "effective control" test. While the Court went on to find that the test was not satisfied in respect

125. ARSIWA, *supra* note 1, art. 8, cmt. ¶ 7.

126. *Nicaragua, supra* note 10. While the ICJ had previously considered the rule of attribution now reflected in art. 8 in *Tehran Hostages*, its judgment in that case focused on the "instructions" element of the rule; it did not mention direction or control. *See Tehran Hostages, supra* note 72, ¶¶ 57–60. *See also supra* sec. 6.3.1.

127. For a summary of U.S. support to the *contras, see supra* ch. 4, sec. 4.4.1.1.

128. *Nicaragua, supra* note 10, ¶¶ 104, 106, 112.

129. *See supra* ch. 4, sec. 4.4.1.

130. *Nicaragua, supra* note 10, ¶ 110.

131. *Id.* ¶ 115.

of U.S. support to the *contras*, it did not clearly set out the basis for this conclusion.[132] It may be founded on a lack of evidence to indicate a direct link between U.S. assistance to the *contras* and the latter's commission of acts in violation of the State's international legal obligations. But this is far from clear, particularly given the Court's earlier conclusion that the conduct of another NSA, the UCLAs, was attributable to the United States.[133] Here, the ICJ established that U.S. personnel participated "in the planning, direction, support and execution of the [UCLAs'] operations"[134] but failed to clarify why, in contrast with its conclusion regarding the *contras*, such participation was sufficient to attribute the UCLAs' conduct to the State.

It may be that, in the ICJ's view, the United States exercised effective control over the UCLAs' conduct in launching attacks against Nicaragua.[135] It is equally possible, however, that the ICJ reached this conclusion on a different basis.[136] Additional questions arise due to the dearth of legal reasoning to substantiate the Court's position, a point that Judge Ago commented on in his separate opinion in the case.[137] In Ago's view, State responsibility is appropriate only when a State specifically authorizes the conduct in potential violation of international law,[138] as reflected in the earlier version of Article 8 that he was responsible for drafting when Special Rapporteur.[139] Ago noted the imprecision and "apparent contradictions" resulting from the way in which the ICJ majority addressed the notion of control.[140] Such deficiencies have contributed to the debate surrounding the effective control test and have led to varying interpretations of the Court's conclusions in subsequent case law and academic commentary.

132. *Id.* ¶ 116.

133. *Id.* ¶¶ 80, 86. *See also supra* sec. 6.3.1.1.

134. *Nicaragua*, *supra* note 10, ¶ 86.

135. Cameron & Chetail, *supra* note 9, at 213; Nieminen, *supra* note 97, at 307.

136. Judge Ago, for instance, concluded that the UCLAs' conduct was attributable to the United States on the basis that they belonged "to public entities empowered within its domestic legal order to exercise certain elements of the governmental authority." *See Nicaragua*, *supra* note 10, Separate Opinion of Judge Ago, ¶ 15. Cassese considered that U.S. responsibility was engaged because the UCLAs were "totally dependent" on the State. *See* Cassese, *supra* note 9, at 652. The ICTY Appeals Chamber, meanwhile, determined that attribution was appropriate because the UCLAs acted on the United States' instructions. *See Tadić Appeals Chamber*, *supra* note 10, ¶ 114.

137. *Nicaragua*, *supra* note 10, Separate Opinion of Judge Ago ¶ 18. *See also* Cassese, *supra* note 9, at 653.

138. *Nicaragua*, *supra* note 10, Separate Opinion of Judge Ago ¶ 16. *See also* Crawford's First Rep. on State Responsibility, *supra* note 16, at 40, ¶ 200.

139. *See supra* sec. 6.2.1.

140. *Nicaragua*, *supra* note 10, Separate Opinion of Judge Ago ¶ 18; *id.* at n. 1.

6.4.1.2 *Tadić*

In the *Tadić* case, both the Trial Chamber[141] and the Appeals Chamber[142] of the ICTY conducted an extensive review of the ICJ's judgment in *Nicaragua*. The case concerned Duško Tadić, a guard in one of the Bosnian internment camps in Bosnia and Herzegovina who was involved in the massacre of numerous individuals. To determine whether he was guilty of grave breaches of the Geneva Conventions, the ICTY needed to consider whether the conflict during which the offenses were committed was international in character. This was relevant to the issue of jurisdiction. If the forces that committed the atrocities were acting on behalf of the Federal Republic of Yugoslavia (FRY), Tadić could be tried under Article 2 of the ICTY Statute for breaching the Fourth Geneva Convention.[143] If, however, the forces were not acting on the FRY's behalf, meaning that the conflict was non-international in character, the ICTY had no jurisdiction to consider such charges.

Trial Chamber Judgment. To determine the correct classification of the conflict, the ICTY Trial Chamber concluded that the applicable legal test was whether the acts of the Bosnian Serb forces, in committing the atrocities, could be attributed to the FRY. This, in turn, depended upon the level of control exercised by the FRY over the Bosnian Serb forces.[144]

The Trial Chamber reviewed the judgment in *Nicaragua* and concluded that the ICJ had set just one test of effective control. Thus, the Chamber considered that the Court's reference to "dependence on the one side and control on the other" related directly to the threshold set for effective control, rather than setting a separate test relevant to de facto State organs.[145] Applying that threshold, the Trial Chamber concluded that the requisite level of control was not reached due to a lack of evidence that the Bosnian Serbs "were anything more than mere allies, albeit highly dependent allies," of the FRY.[146]

Presiding Judge McDonald dissented, finding that the Bosnian Serb forces were indeed dependent upon and controlled by the FRY, meaning that the conflict was international in character.[147] In Judge McDonald's view, *Nicaragua* established two distinct tests for attribution, or two bases upon which the actions of

141. Prosecutor v. Tadić, Case No. ICTY IT-94-1-T, Opinion and Judgment (Int'l Crim. Trib. for the former Yugoslavia, May 7, 1997) [hereinafter *Tadić Trial Chamber*].

142. *Tadić Appeals Chamber*, *supra* note 10.

143. Statute of the International Criminal Tribunal for the former Yugoslavia, art. 2, S.C. Res. 827 (May 25, 1993), adopting The Secretary-General Report Pursuant to Paragraph 2 of Security Council Resolution 808; Convention IV relative to the Protection of Civilian Persons in Time of War, Aug. 12, 1949, 6 U.S.T. 3516, 75 U.N.T.S. 287 [hereinafter GC IV].

144. *Tadić Trial Chamber*, *supra* note 141, ¶ 584.

145. *Id.* ¶ 585.

146. *Id.* ¶ 606.

147. *Id.* Separate and Dissenting Opinion of Judge McDonald Regarding the Applicability of Article 2 of the Statute ¶ 34.

the Bosnian Serb forces could be attributed to the FRY.[148] She concluded that an agency relationship existed between the FRY and the Bosnian Serb forces under the more stringent test of complete dependence and control, meaning that there was no need to consider attribution under the subsidiary effective control test.[149]

Appeals Chamber Judgment. When the ICTY Appeals Chamber considered the issue, it departed both from the view of the Trial Chamber majority and that of Judge McDonald. The Appeals Chamber again looked for guidance to the ICJ's judgment in *Nicaragua* and concluded that the same test should apply to determine both the attribution of acts to the State for the purposes of State responsibility and the classification of the conflict as international or non-international.[150] The Chamber rejected the submission of the Prosecution, following the dissenting judgment of Judge McDonald, that the ICJ had put forward two bases of attribution.[151]

Instead, the Appeals Chamber considered that the ICJ had distinguished between three categories of individuals: those with the status of officials (namely members of government administration or armed forces); those who acted in the pay and on the direct instructions and under the supervision of State personnel (the UCLAs); and those who fall into neither of the previous categories (the *contras*).[152] Like the Trial Chamber, the Appeals Chamber considered that the ICJ's reference to effective control amounted to an elaboration of the dependence and control test that it had previously articulated.[153] However, in a clear departure from the Trial Chamber, the Appeals Chamber rejected that test and instead put forward one of its own: overall control.

The Appeals Chamber considered the version of Article 8 adopted by the ILC in 1998 and concluded that a high threshold of control is not required in every situation.[154] Instead, the degree of control might vary according to the factual circumstances of each case. Regarding the conduct of a private individual or unorganized group, the Chamber considered it necessary to show that the State issued specific instructions concerning the commission of the breach of international law.[155] But with regard to the acts of individuals in an organized and hierarchically structured group, a standard of "overall control" is sufficient.[156] In this respect, after setting out the grounds on which it considered that the ICJ's

148. *Id.* ¶¶ 22–25.

149. *Id.* ¶ 34.

150. *Tadić Appeals Chamber*, *supra* note 10, ¶¶ 99–104.

151. *Id.* ¶¶ 106–7, 111–12.

152. *Id.* ¶ 109.

153. *Id.* ¶ 112.

154. *Id.* ¶¶ 117–20.

155. *Id.* ¶¶ 120, 132.

156. *Id.* ¶¶ 116–23.

judgment in *Nicaragua* was at variance with judicial and State practice,[157] the Appeals Chamber stated:

> [I]n order to attribute the acts of a military or paramilitary group to a State, it must be proved that the State wields overall control over the group, not only by equipping and financing the group, but also by coordinating or helping in the general planning of its military activity. Only then can the State be held internationally accountable for any misconduct of the group. However, it is not necessary that, in addition, the State should also issue, either to the head or to members of the group, instructions for the commission of specific acts contrary to international law.[158]

The focus of the overall control test is therefore the overarching control by the State over the NSA, rather than the State's control over any specific act. The Appeals Chamber went on to clarify that for this threshold to be met, the State must have "a role in organising, coordinating or planning the military actions of the military group, in addition to financing, training and equipping or providing operational support to that group."[159] There are thus two essential requirements: Not only must the State provide support to the NSA, it must also participate in the planning or coordination of its military activity.[160] If these conditions are fulfilled, then according to the ICTY, the conduct of the group may be regarded as "acts of *de facto* State organs," regardless of any specific instruction given by the State regarding the commission of particular acts.[161]

In the Appeal Chamber's view, therefore, both tests formulated by the ICJ in *Nicaragua* should be subsumed into one, much looser, test of overall control.[162] The Appeals Chamber concluded that the FRY did exercise overall control over the Bosnian Serb forces, noting that it was not necessary to show that the particular operations carried out by such forces, during which the alleged crimes were committed, were specifically ordered or planned by the FRY.[163] Accordingly, the conflict was international in character.

The ICTY did not make a specific finding as to the FRY's responsibility for the Bosnian Serbs' actions, as that issue was not within its mandate. It may, however, be inferred from the judgment that in the Appeals Chamber's opinion, overall control is the appropriate test for the purposes of both conflict classification and

157. *Id.* ¶¶ 124–30.

158. *Id.* ¶ 131.

159. *Tadić Appeals Chamber*, *supra* note 10, ¶ 137.

160. The ICTY confirmed these dual requirements in its subsequent jurisprudence. *See, e.g.*, Prosecutor v. Kordić and Čerkez, Appeals Chamber Judgment, ICTY IT-95-14/2-A (2004) ¶ 361 [hereinafter *Kordić Appeals Chamber*].

161. *Tadić Appeals Chamber*, *supra* note 10, ¶ 137.

162. Talmon, *supra* note 9, at 506–7.

163. *Tadić Appeals Chamber*, *supra* note 10, ¶ 156.

State responsibility.[164] Therefore, given the overall control exercised by the FRY, the State should bear responsibility for all the Bosnian Serbs' conduct.

Reactions to Tadić. The Appeals Chamber's judgment in *Tadić* has been the subject of considerable academic comment: some positive,[165] but much of it negative.[166] Those who criticize the judgment point out that in formulating just one test to determine the issues of both conflict classification and attribution, the ICTY has conflated the secondary rules of State responsibility with the primary rules international law.[167] This was an unnecessary step for the Tribunal to take when classifying the conflict.[168] In addition, as an international criminal tribunal with a jurisdiction limited to individuals, the ICTY was not competent to tackle issues of State responsibility.[169]

This latter critique is implied in the commentary to Article 8 ARSIWA, which highlights that the legal issue facing the ICTY was individual criminal responsibility, not State responsibility.[170] However, the commentary does not directly

164. *Id.* ¶¶ 103, 117–23.

165. *See, e.g.*, *Bosnian Genocide*, *supra* note 6, dissenting opinion of Vice President Al-Khasawneh; *id.* (dissenting opinion of Judge ad hoc Mahiou); Cassese, *supra* note 9; Spinedi, *supra* note 9; Luigi Condorelli & Claus Kress, *The Rules of Attribution: General Considerations*, *in* The Law of International Responsibility 221, 234–35 (James Crawford et al. eds., 2010); Scott J. Shackelford & Richard B. Andres, *State Responsibility for Cyber Attacks: Competing Standards for a Growing Problem*, 42 Ga. J. Int'l L. 971, 984–88 (2010); Kimberly N. Trapp, State Responsibility for International Terrorism 40–45 (2011); Tom Gal, *Unexplored Outcomes of Tadić*, 12 J. Int'l Crim. Just. 59, 63–64 (2014); Robert Heinsch, *Conflict Classification in Ukraine: The Return of the "Proxy War"?*, 91 Int'l L. Stud. 323 (2015); Jorritsma, *supra* note 9; Tsagourias & Farrell, *supra* note 74, at 962–65.

166. *See, e.g.*, Theodor Meron, *Classification of Armed Conflict in the Former Yugoslavia: Nicaragua's Fallout*, 92 Am. J. Int'l L. 235 (1998); Kaufman, *supra* note 53, at 2650–52; Tyner, *supra* note 9, at 852; Milanović, *State Responsibility for Genocide*, *supra* note 9, at 583; Talmon, *supra* note 9, at 506–7; Katherine Del Mar, *The Requirement of "Belonging" Under International Humanitarian Law*, 21 Eur. J. Int'l L. 105 (2010); Tonkin, *supra* note 9, at 118-19; Dapo Akande, *Classification of Armed Conflicts: Relevant Legal Concepts*, *in* International Law and the Classification of Conflicts 32, 57–62 (Elizabeth Wilmshurst ed., 2012); Djemila Carron, *When Is a Conflict International? Time for New Control Tests in IHL*, 98 Int'l Rev. Red Cross 1019, 1025–28 (2016); Kubo Mačák, Internationalized Armed Conflicts in International Law 43–47 (2018).

167. *See, e.g.*, Meron, *supra* note 166, at 237; Tyner, *supra* note 9, at 852; Milanović, *State Responsibility for Genocide*, *supra* note 9, at 583; del Mar, *supra* note 166, at 108–9; Tonkin, *supra* note 9, at 118–19; Sandesh Sivakumaran, The Law of Non-International Armed Conflict 227 (2012); Mačák, *supra* note 166, at 44. For contrary views, *see* Marco Sassòli, *State Responsibility for Violations of International Humanitarian Law*, 84 Int'l Rev. of the Red Cross 401, 408 (2002); Spinedi, *supra* note 9, at 832–33; Jorritsma, *supra* note 9.

168. *Tadić Appeals Chamber*, *supra* note 10, Separate Opinion of Judge Shahabuddeen ¶ 17.

169. Milanović, *State Responsibility for Genocide*, *supra* note 9, at 578; Crawford, *supra* note 9, at 150; Carron, *supra* note 166, at 1025–26.

170. ARSIWA, *supra* note 1, art. 8, cmt. ¶ 5.

pronounce upon the applicability or appropriateness of overall control as opposed to effective control, instead asserting that the extent of State control should be assessed on the facts of each case.[171] Both control standards, therefore, are arguably consistent with the wording of Article 8 and the commentary thereto.[172]

But the ARSIWA commentary makes no reference to the ICTY's assertion that there should be a different control test depending upon the nature of the controlled entity.[173] This omission indicates that in the ILC's view, the same standard of control should apply whether the NSA concerned is an individual or a nonorganized group on the one hand, or an organized group on the other.[174] The basis for this distinction, as set out by the Appeals Chamber, is that

> an organised group differs from an individual in that the former normally has a structure, a chain of command and a set of rules as well as the outward symbols of authority. Normally a member of the group does not act on his own but conforms to the standards prevailing in the group and is subject to the authority of the head of the group. Consequently, for the attribution to a State of acts of these groups it is sufficient to require that the group as a whole be under the overall control of the State.[175]

As Crawford points out, however, this distinction loses its force when the ICTY's rationale is applied to an individual, such as a single terrorist.[176] If the actions of an organized group can be attributed to a State further to that State's exercise of overall control over the group, the same logic should apply if a State exerts an equivalent level of control over the actions of a single terrorist,[177] or an unorganized group of hackers acting for a State in the cyber domain.[178]

The Appeals Chamber also faced criticism due to its misinterpretation of the judgment in *Nicaragua*, illustrated by its failure to distinguish between the test applicable to de facto State organs relevant to Article 4 ARSIWA and the test to determine attribution under the rule reflected in Article 8.[179] The ICTY is not alone

171. *Id.* cmt. ¶¶ 4, 5. For a critique of the ILC's stance, *see* Tyner, *supra* note 9, at 876.

172. Trapp, *supra* note 165, at 42; Heinsch, *supra* note 165, at 348.

173. ARSIWA, *supra* note 1, art. 8, cmt. ¶¶ 1–9.

174. Kaufman, *supra* note 53, at 2651; Crawford, *supra* note 9, at 153–54.

175. *Tadić Appeals Chamber*, *supra* note 10, ¶ 120.

176. Crawford, *supra* note 9, at 153–54. *See also* Kress, *supra* note 25, at 130–31; Kaufman, *supra* note 53, at 2650–51.

177. Crawford, *supra* note 9, at 153–54.

178. Tsagorias & Farrell, *supra* note 74, at 964.

179. Milanović, *State Responsibility for Genocide*, *supra* note 9, at 581; Olivier Corten, *L'arrêt rendu par la CIJ dans l'affaire du Crime de Génocide (Bosnie-Herzégovine c Serbie): vers un assouplissement des conditions permettant d'engager la responsabilité d'un état pour génocide?* 53 Annuaire Français de Droit International 249, 267 (2007); Talmon, *supra* note 9, at 506–7; Akande, *supra* note 166, at 59; Crawford, *supra* note 9, at 152.

in failing to make this differentiation; notably, the ILC also conflated the two tests in its commentary to Article 8.[180] The distinction is important, however, due to its impact on the effects of attribution. If an entity qualifies as a de facto State organ, all its conduct performed in that capacity is attributable to the State.[181] In contrast, if a State exerts effective control over an NSA's conduct, the resulting attribution relates only to the specific acts that were performed under the State's control. The overall control test's focus on the wider relationship between an entity and a State renders this distinction nugatory and significantly lowers the level of control necessary for a State's responsibility to be engaged. This, in turn, has given rise to further criticism, on the basis that a State's legal responsibility should arise only in relation to acts carried out that are really its own.[182]

Finally, legal scholars have criticized the Appeals Chamber's judgment due to its reliance on facts and precedents that do not fully support its conclusions.[183] Sassòli and Olson point out that most of the cases on which the Chamber relies relate to a State's control over armed groups operating on its own territory, where territorial control may have been the decisive factor.[184] A further case relied on, the decision of the European Court of Human Rights (ECtHR) in *Loizidou v. Turkey*, relates to occupied territory where the armed forces of the occupying power were present, and specific IHL rules applied regarding that power's responsibilities.[185] Here, the ECtHR's references to Turkey's exercise of "effective overall control"[186] related not to control over persons, but to control over territory.[187] Moreover, the use of control tests in the human rights context is aimed primarily at determining whether

180. *See* ARSIWA, *supra* note 1, art. 8, cmt. ¶ 4.

181. *See supra* ch. 4.

182. Marko Milanović, *From Compromise to Principle: Clarifying the Concept of State Jurisdiction in Human Rights Treaties*, 8 Hum. Rts. L. Rev. 411, 440 (2008) [hereinafter Milanović, *From Compromise to Principle*]; Akande, *supra* note 166, at 60.

183. Marco Sassòli & Laura M. Olson, *Prosecutor v. Tadić (Judgement) Case No. IT-94-1-A 38 ILM 1518 (1999)*, 94 Am. J. Int'l L. 571, 575 (2000); Marco Sassòli, *The Legal Qualification of the Conflict in the Former Yugoslavia: Double Standards or New Horizons for International Humanitarian Law? in* International Law in the Post-Cold War World: Essays in Memory of Li Haopei 307, 327 (Sienho Yee & Wang Tieya eds., 2001); Mačák, *supra* note 166, at 43; Tatyana Jane Eatwell, State Responsibility for the Unlawful Conduct of Armed Groups (Ph.D. dissertation, University of Cambridge) 40–48 (2019), www.repository.cam.ac.uk/bitstream/handle/1810/302004/Eatwell%20Thesis%20May%202020%20updated%20Electronic%20Final.pdf?sequence=8&isAllowed=y.

184. Sassòli & Olson, *supra* note 183, at 575. *But see Tadić Appeals Chamber*, *supra* note 10, ¶ 138.

185. Sassòli & Olson, *supra* note 183, at 327. *See also* Loizidou v. Turkey, App. No. 15318/89, ¶¶ 56–57 (Dec. 18, 1996) (ECtHR).

186. *Loizidou v. Turkey*, *supra* note 185, ¶¶ 49, 56.

187. Corten, *supra* note 179, at 268; Milanović, *From Compromise to Principle*, *supra* note 182, at 444–45; Eatwell, *supra* note 183, at 44–48.

persons within the relevant territory fall within the State's jurisdiction.[188] That is an entirely separate issue to the attribution of private conduct to the State.[189]

So far as international courts and tribunals are concerned, the ICTY continued to apply the overall control test in its subsequent cases.[190] The International Criminal Court (ICC) additionally followed the *Tadić* approach, but without explaining whether its use of the test was grounded in the secondary law of State responsibility or the primary rules of IHL.[191] In all such jurisprudence, the ICTY and the ICC adopted the overall control test for the purpose only of determining conflict classification. The appropriate threshold of control was then considered again by the ICJ, in the context of State responsibility, in the *Armed Activities* case.[192]

6.4.1.3 *Armed Activities*

One of the issues to be determined by the ICJ in *Armed Activities* was the nature of the support Uganda provided to a rebel group opposing the DRC's government. The DRC alleged that Uganda was closely involved in the recruitment, training, and supplying of the Congo Liberation Movement, or MLC, and its military wing.[193] In addition, it contended that Ugandan troops acted in close cooperation with MLC fighters in battles against the Congolese army and provided them with tactical support, including artillery cover.[194] Uganda, for its part, admitted providing political and military assistance to the MLC but denied any role in the group's formation and asserted that its aid was limited to the requirements of self-defense.[195]

The ICJ concluded that there was no credible evidence that Uganda created the MLC, or that Uganda controlled or could control the way the assistance it

188. Milanović, *From Compromise to Principle*, *supra* note 182, at 441, 447.

189. *Id.* at 446; de Frouville, *supra* note 9, at 269.

190. *See, e.g.*, Prosecutor v. Aleksovski, Case No. ICTY IT-95-14/I-A, Appeals Chamber Judgment, ¶¶ 120–34 (Int'l Crim. Trib. for the former Yugoslavia, Mar. 24, 2000) [hereinafter *Aleksovski Appeals Chamber*]; Prosecutor v. Blaškić, Case No. ICTY IT-95-14/T, Judgment, ¶¶ 96–101 (Int'l Crim. Trib. for the former Yugoslavia, Mar. 3, 2000) [hereinafter *Blaškić Trial Chamber*]; *Kordić Appeals Chamber*, *supra* note 160, ¶¶ 296–361; Prosecutor v. Delalić et al., Case No. ICTY IT-96-21-A, Appeals Chamber Judgment, ¶¶ 14–26 (Int'l Crim. Trib. for the former Yugoslavia, Feb. 20, 2001) [hereinafter *Delalić Appeals Chamber*].

191. Prosecutor v. Thomas Lubanga Dyilo, Case No. ICC-01/04-01/06-2842, Judgment, ¶ 541 (Mar. 14, 2012). *See also* Marko Milanović, *Special Rules of Attribution of Conduct in International Law*, 96 Int'l L. Stud. 295, 320–21 (2020) [hereinafter Milanović, *Special Rules of Attribution*].

192. Armed Activities on the Territory of the Congo (Dem. Rep. Congo v. Uganda), Judgment, 2005 I.C.J. Rep. 168 (Dec. 19).

193. *Id.* ¶ 32.

194. *Id.* ¶ 32.

195. *Id.* ¶ 41.

provided was used.[196] Furthermore, the Court found that there was no probative evidence upon which to conclude that the MLC acted on the instructions or under the direction or control of Uganda.[197]

In reaching this conclusion, the ICJ did not mention effective control or discuss the relevant attribution threshold. The court referred to its earlier judgment in *Nicaragua* but made no reference to the ICTY Appeal Chamber's judgment in *Tadić*.[198] In so doing, the ICJ implicitly rejected the ICTY's approach, but did not do so explicitly until two years later in its judgment in the *Bosnian Genocide* case.[199]

6.4.1.4 *Bosnian Genocide*

In *Bosnian Genocide*, the Court considered the issue of State responsibility in relation to the massacres at Srebrenica.[200] The ICJ first assessed whether the Bosnian Serb forces of the Republika Srpska were acting as de jure or de facto organs of the FRY. Having reached a negative conclusion,[201] the court went on to consider whether the massacres had been committed by persons acting on the FRY's instructions, or under its direction or control. Referring to Article 8 ARSIWA and to its earlier judgment in *Nicaragua*, the Court emphasized that it had previously put forward two separate tests for attribution and highlighted the differences between them.[202] With regard to effective control, the ICJ asserted that this must be exercised, "in respect of each operation in which the alleged violations occurred, not generally in respect of the overall actions taken by the persons or groups of persons having committed the violations."[203]

The ICJ then addressed the judgment of the ICTY Appeals Chamber in *Tadić*. Conceding that the test of overall control might be suitable to determine the issue of conflict characterization, the court stressed the ICTY's lack of jurisdiction to rule on questions of State responsibility and described the test as "unpersuasive" in that context.[204] In the ICJ's view, there is no requirement for the same test to be adopted to determine these very different issues, and the concept of overall control is far too broad to determine attribution for the purposes of State responsibility.[205]

196. *Id.* ¶ 160.

197. *Id.*

198. For a critique of this omission, *see id.* Separate Opinion of Judge Kooijmans ¶ 25.

199. *Bosnian Genocide*, *supra* note 6.

200. For further discussion regarding the background to the case, *see supra* ch. 4, sec. 4.4.1.2.

201. *Bosnian Genocide*, *supra* note 6, ¶ 394.

202. *Id.* ¶¶ 396–400.

203. *Id.* ¶ 400.

204. *Id.* ¶¶ 403–4. For contrary views, *see* Pierre-Marie Dupuy, *A Crime without Punishment*, 14 J. Int'l Crim. Just. 879, 889 (2016); Jorritsma, *supra* note 9.

205. *Bosnian Genocide*, *supra* note 6, ¶ 405.

This "stretches too far, almost to breaking point, the connection which must exist between the conduct of a State's organs and its international responsibility."[206]

Having reaffirmed the effective control test, the ICJ applied it to the Bosnian Serbs' conduct relating to the genocide in Srebrenica. The Court found that the FRY was "making its considerable military and financial support available to the Republika Srpska"[207] and that had the FRY withdrawn its support, "this would have greatly constrained the options that were available to the Republika Srpska authorities."[208] However, despite the FRY's "undeniable influence" over the Bosnian Serbs,[209] the genocide was not attributable to the FRY. According to the ICJ, insufficient proof was provided that "instructions were issued" by the FRY regarding the commission of the massacre.[210] Instead, the evidence indicated that the decision to kill the adult male population of the Muslim community in Srebrenica was taken by members of the Bosnian Serb forces, "without instructions from or effective control by the FRY."[211]

Judge Al-Khasawneh dissented, describing the majority's conclusions on the issue of control as "unconvincing."[212] He considered there to be "massive and compelling evidence" of the FRY's involvement in the genocide,[213] opining that the court could have found the FRY responsible had it followed a different methodology.[214] Regarding the requisite level of control, Judge Al-Khasawneh asserted that this is varied in nature: "[D]ifferent types of activities, particularly in the ever-evolving nature of armed conflict, may call for subtle variations in the rules of attribution."[215] He referred to the factual background of the *Nicaragua* judgment, highlighting the shared objectives of the United States and the *contras* to overthrow the Nicaraguan government, but noting that these could have been achieved without committing IHL violations. He contrasted that situation with one in which the shared objective is the commission of international crimes, declaring that

> to require both control over the non-State actors and the specific operations in the context of which international crimes were committed is too high a threshold. The inherent danger in such an approach is that it gives States the opportunity

206. *Id.* ¶ 406.

207. *Id.* ¶ 241. Regarding the support provided, *see supra* ch. 4, sec. 4.4.1.2.

208. *Bosnian Genocide*, *supra* note 6, ¶ 241.

209. *Id.* ¶ 438.

210. *Id.* ¶ 413.

211. *Id.*

212. *Id.* dissenting opinion of Vice President Al-Khasawneh, ¶ 39.

213. *Id.* ¶ 3.

214. *Id.* ¶ 34.

215. *Id.* ¶ 39.

to carry out criminal policies through non-State actors or surrogates without incurring direct responsibility therefore.[216]

Judge Mahiou dissented on similar grounds, concluding that in view of the close links between the respective forces of the FRY and the Bosnian Serbs, "instructions and directions were in a way practically automatic as regards both the planning and implementation of the military operations carried out by the [Bosnian Serbs]."[217] Judge Mahiou distinguished the facts of the *Nicaragua* case from those at issue in *Bosnian Genocide* on the basis that in the latter, "there was a perfect similarity of views between the Respondent and the Republika Srpska on the Greater Serbia project bringing together all the Serbs under the authority of the two entities."[218] In such cases, in Judge Mahiou's view, there is no requirement to prove precise State control over each operation; instead the looser standard of overall control should suffice.[219]

Certain commentators echo and expand upon the objections raised by Judges Al-Khasawneh and Mahiou.[220] Antonio Cassese, one of the ICTY Appeals Chamber judges in *Tadić*, points to the lack of reasoned argument on the part of the ICJ to support its rejection of the overall control test.[221] Whereas the ICTY carried out a detailed review of previous authorities to support its argument, the ICJ looked only to its previous judgment in *Nicaragua*, together with the work of the ILC. Moreover, in Cassese's view, the test formulated by the ICJ is inconsistent with the basic principles of State responsibility, according to which a State cannot evade responsibility toward other States by acting through NSAs.[222] Some commentators also condemn the court's failure to consider degrees of State involvement in a wrongful act by setting an "either or" test under which a State is either fully responsible or not responsible at all.[223]

Other scholars, in contrast, welcomed the ICJ's judgment.[224] In Crawford's words, the determination in the *Bosnian Genocide* case "effectively ends the debate

216. *Id.*

217. *Id.* dissenting opinion of Judge ad hoc Mahiou, ¶ 112.

218. *Id.* ¶ 117.

219. *Id.*

220. *See, e.g.*, Cassese, *supra* note 9; Spinedi, *supra* note 9; Mark Gibney, *Genocide and State Responsibility*, 7 Hum. Rts. L. Rev. 760 (2007); Jörn Griebel & Milan Plücken, *New Developments Regarding the Rules of Attribution? The International Court of Justice's Decision in Bosnia v Serbia*, 21 Leiden J. Int'l L. 601 (2008).

221. Cassese, *supra* note 9, at 651, 653.

222. *Id.* at 654.

223. *See, e.g.*, Gibney, *supra* note 220, at 771; Oona A. Hathaway et al., *Ensuring Responsibility: Common Article 1 and State Responsibility for Non-State Actors*, 95 Tex. L. Rev. 539, 545 (2017).

224. *See, e.g.*, Marko Milanović, *State Responsibility for Genocide: A Follow-Up*, 18 Eur. J. Int'l L. 669 (2007); Akande, *supra* note 166, at 59–60; Crawford, *supra* note 9, at 156.

as to the correct standard of control to be applied under Article 8. Moreover, it does so in a manner that reflects the ILC's thinking on the subject from the time the term 'control' was introduced into then-Draft Article 8."[225]

6.4.2 ICRC Commentary to Common Article 2

While the debate, in Crawford's view, may be at an end, the International Committee of the Red Cross (ICRC) has advocated for a different stance in its revised commentaries to the Geneva Conventions.[226] In its commentary to common Article 2, relating to the application of the Conventions, the ICRC considered the circumstances in which State control over an NSA internationalizes a conflict. In the absence of a specific test within IHL to determine whether an armed group "belongs" to a supporting State, the ICRC echoed the approach taken by the ICTY in *Tadić*.[227]

The ICRC referred to the law of State responsibility and the debate surrounding the requisite level of control, as well as the relevant judgments of the ICJ, ICTY, and ICC.[228] In the ICRC's view, overall control is the appropriate test

> because the notion of overall control better reflects the real relationship between the armed group and the third State, including for the purpose of attribution. It implies that the armed group may be subordinate to the State even if there are no specific instructions given for every act of belligerency. Additionally, recourse to the overall control test enables the assessment of the level of control over the *de facto* entity or non-State armed group as a whole, and thus allows for the attribution of several actions to the third State.[229]

Thus, for the ICRC, the test used to identify the relationship between a group of individuals and a State should be the same for the purposes of both conflict

225. Crawford, *supra* note 9, at 156.

226. Int'l Comm. of the Red Cross, Commentary on the First Geneva Convention: Convention (I) for the Amelioration of the Condition of the Wounded and Sick in the Armed Forces in the Field ¶¶ 265–73 (2016) [hereinafter 2016 Cmt. to GC I]; Int'l Comm. of the Red Cross, Commentary on the Second Geneva Convention: Convention (II) for the Amelioration of the Condition of the Wounded, Sick and Shipwrecked Members of Armed Forces at Sea ¶¶ 287–95 (2017) [hereinafter 2017 Cmt. to GC II]; Int'l Comm. of the Red Cross, Commentary on the Third Geneva Convention: Convention (III) Relative to the Treatment of Prisoners of War ¶¶ 298–306 (2020) [hereinafter 2020 Cmt. to GC III].

227. 2016 Cmt. to GC I, *supra* note 226, ¶ 267; 2017 Cmt. to GCII, *supra* note 226, ¶ 289; 2020 Cmt. to GC III, *supra* note 226, ¶ 300. For comment in relation to the ICRC's approach, *see* Milanović, *Special Rules of Attribution*, *supra* note 191, at 321–23.

228. 2016 Cmt. to GC I, *supra* note 226, ¶¶ 269–70; 2017 Cmt. to GC II, *supra* note 226, ¶¶ 291–92; 2020 Cmt. to GC III, *supra* note 226, ¶¶ 303–4.

229. 2016 Cmt. to GC I, *supra* note 226, ¶ 271; 2017 Cmt. to GC II, *supra* note 226, ¶ 293; 2020 Cmt. to GC III, *supra* note 226, ¶ 304.

classification and attribution under the law of State responsibility.[230] This approach diverges from that of the ILC[231] and also the jurisprudence of the ICJ, according to which "logic does not require the same test to be adopted in resolving the two issues, which are very different in nature."[232] Indeed, it is unsurprising that different tests have arisen, given that the issue of conflict classification is governed by the primary norms of IHL, whereas the rules of State responsibility are secondary in nature.[233]

In asserting that the two tests should be identical, the ICRC's focus is not on the origin of the relevant rules but rather on their purpose. The ICRC argues that the question of attribution plays a significant role in defining an armed conflict as international since, by virtue of such attribution, the actions of the armed group can be considered those of the intervening State.[234] This view is supported by other commentators, who note that the issue of conflict classification turns upon whether or not an armed conflict exists between States, "which cannot mean anything other than that the armed forces involved form part of the "formal" or "effective" organization of the States which are party to the conflict."[235] In other words, both tests are applied to achieve the same end result, namely, to impute the acts of an NSA to the State, albeit in different factual contexts.[236]

If the overall control test applies for the purposes of conflict classification while the stricter test of effective control determines the issue of attribution, the ICRC

230. 2016 Cmt. to GC I, *supra* note 226, ¶ 271; 2017 Cmt. to GC II, *supra* note 226, ¶ 293; 2020 Cmt. to GC III, *supra* note 226, ¶ 304.

231. ARSIWA, *supra* note 1, art. 8, cmt. ¶ 5.

232. *Bosnian Genocide*, *supra* note 6, ¶ 405.

233. Milanović, *State Responsibility for Genocide*, *supra* note 9, at 587.

234. 2016 Cmt. to GC I, *supra* note 226, ¶ 268; 2017 Cmt. to GC II, *supra* note 226, ¶ 290; 2020 Cmt. to GC III, *supra* note 226, ¶ 301. *See also* Tristan Ferraro, *The ICRC's Legal Position on the Notion of Armed Conflict Involving Foreign Intervention and on Determining the IHL Applicable to this Type of Conflict*, 97 Int'l Rev. Red Cross 1227, 1235–36 (2015).

235. Condorelli & Kress, *supra* note 165, at 234. *See also* Spinedi, *supra* note 9, at 832–33; Jorritsma, *supra* note 9, at 419–21. The Mission of Experts established Under the Organization for Security and Cooperation in Europe (OSCE) Moscow Mechanism similarly supports the application of the overall control test for the purposes of attribution. *See* Wolfgang Benedek et al., OSCE, Report on Violations of International Humanitarian and Human Rights Law, War Crimes and Crimes Against Humanity Committed in Ukraine Since 24 February 2022, at 5 (Apr. 13, 2022), https://www.osce.org/odihr/515868; Moscow Mechanism Mission of Experts, OSCE, Report on Violations of International Humanitarian and Human Rights Law, War Crimes and Crimes Against Humanity Committed in Ukraine (April 1–June 25, 2022) 76–77 (July 14, 2022), https://www.osce.org/odihr/522616.

236. Manuel J. Ventura, *Two Controversies in the Lubanga Trial Judgment of the ICC: The Nature of Co-Perpetration's Common Plan and the Classification of the Armed Conflict*, *in* The War Report 2012 (Stuart Casey-Maslen ed., 2013). *But see* Carron, *supra* note 166, at 1026–28.

commentary highlights a potential gap in accountability.[237] The State could become a party to the conflict, with the full panoply of rights and obligations under IHL coming into play, without also bearing responsibility for any IHL violations committed by the NSA it supports.[238] The only recourse in such a situation would be against the NSA itself on the basis of its members' individual criminal responsibility[239] or against the State for its failure to comply with its positive duties to respect and ensure respect for IHL.[240]

There is thus a good deal of logic to the ICRC's reasoning. It makes little practical sense for a more lenient test to apply for the purpose of conflict classification than for the attribution of an NSA's conduct to the State. But the converse is not true; if a stricter test applied to determine when a conflict is internationalized, all acts governed by the law of international armed conflict would then be attributable to a State.[241] That the ICRC did not suggest a more stringent test is unsurprising. The whole tone of its commentary relating to common Article 2 is aimed at expanding, rather than limiting, the circumstances in which the full range of rights and obligations under IHL come into effect.

In sum, the ICRC's approach suffers from the same flaws as those highlighted in the context of the appeals judgment in *Tadić*.[242] For the purposes of determining a State's responsibility, the test of overall control is not supported by the jurisprudence of the ICJ, the work of the ILC, by many legal commentators,[243] or by those States that have opined on the issue.[244] For the time being, therefore, the

237. 2016 Cmt. to GC I, *supra* note 226, ¶ 273; 2017 Cmt. to GC II, *supra* note 226, ¶ 295; 2020 Cmt. to GC III, *supra* note 226, ¶ 306.

238. Spinedi, *supra* note 9, at 836; Gal, *supra* note 165, at 63.

239. For example, the ICC has also prosecuted members of NSAs for war crimes. *See, e.g.*, Prosecutor v. Thomas Lubanga Dyilo, Case No. ICC-01/04-01/06-2842, Judgment (Mar. 14, 2012).

240. *See* Convention (I) for the Amelioration of the Condition of the Wounded and Sick in the Armed Forces in the Field art. 1, Aug. 12, 1949, 6 U.S.T. 3114, 75 U.N.T.S. 31; Convention (II) for the Amelioration of the Condition of the Wounded, Sick, and Shipwrecked Members of Armed Forces at Sea art. 1, Aug. 12, 1949, 6 U.S.T. 3217, 75 U.N.T.S. 85; Convention (III) Relative to the Treatment of Prisoners of War art. 1, Aug. 12, 1949, 6 U.S.T. 3316, 75 U.N.T.S. 135; GC IV, *supra* note 143, art. 1; AP I, *supra* note 105, art. 1(1). For further discussion regarding the importance of common Article 1 in holding States to account for their support to NSAs, *see infra* ch. 7, sec. 7.3.3.

241. *See* Carron, *supra* note 166, at 1028–37; Jorritsma, *supra* note 9, at 425–26.

242. *See supra* sec. 6.4.1.2.

243. *See supra* note 166.

244. Those States that referred to the appropriate control test for the purposes of Article 8 in their national statements relating to the application of international law in the cyber domain expressed support for the effective control test. *See* Official Compendium, *supra* note 6, at 21, 61, 71 (the positions of Brazil, the Netherlands, and Norway). Tribunals dealing with investment disputes have also applied the effective control test to determine the issue of attribution.

effective control test remains *lex lata*. But ambiguity persists regarding the practical meaning of this threshold and its implications for those states that choose to act via NSAs.

6.4.3 The Meaning of Control

The overall and effective control tests differ not in their nature but rather in the extent of control that is required for private conduct to be attributed to a State. Both tests require evidence of an ongoing, agency-type relationship between the entity and the State that extends beyond mere State financing or the provision of equipment or training.[245] Before examining the precise meaning of effective control, it is first pertinent to consider in more detail the requirements of the overall control test, in order to better assess the practical differences between the respective thresholds.

6.4.3.1 Overall Control

The ICTY's test is satisfied if a State "wields overall control" over a hierarchically organized group not only by equipping and financing the group but also by coordinating or assisting in the planning of its military activity.[246] The assessment of these factors is made in respect of the entire relationship between the entity and the State, rather than focusing on the specific operations in which the relevant violations occurred. Importantly, there is no requirement for the State to plan or direct the specific private conduct that violates its international legal obligations; it is sufficient if those acts form part of broader activity on the part of the NSA over which the State exerts control.[247] The threshold might therefore be met if an NSA is not strictly subordinated to the State's authority but, instead, has "autonomous choices of means or tactics" in the conduct of its operations.[248]

See, e.g., White Industries Australia Limited v. Republic of India, Final Award, ¶¶ 8.1.1–8.1.21 (U.N. Comm'n on Int'l Trade Law Arb., Nov. 30, 2011); Teinver S.A. Transportes de Cercanías S.A. & Autobuses Urbanos del Sur S.A. v. Argentine Republic, Case No. ARB/09/1, ¶¶ 721–24 (Int'l Ctr. for Settlement of Inv. Disp., July 21, 2017); Georg Gavrilović & Gavrilović DOO v. Republic of Croatia, Case No. ARB/12/39, ¶¶ 828–31 (Int'l Ctr. for Settlement of Inv. Disp., July 26, 2018) [hereinafter *Gavrilović*]. *See also* Simon Olleson, *Attribution in Investment Treaty Arbitration*, 31 I.C.S.I.D. Rev. 457, 473 (2016).

245. Tal Becker, Terrorism and the State: Rethinking the Rules of State Responsibility 70–71 (2006).

246. *Tadić Appeals Chamber*, *supra* note 10, ¶¶ 131, 137.

247. Kress, *supra* note 25, at 127–28; Ferraro, *supra* note 234, at 1237; Renz, *supra* note 55, at 142.

248. *Delalić Appeals Chamber*, *supra* note 190, ¶ 47. *See also Aleksovski Appeals Chamber*, *supra* note 190, ¶ 143; Kress, *supra* note 25, at 128–31, 138; Gal, *supra* note 165, at 66–67.

In practice, the ICTY has considered a broader range of circumstances when assessing a State's potential exercise of overall control than the two key criteria articulated in *Tadić*. These include the transfer of officials from the State's armed forces to the NSA,[249] the sharing of forces,[250] the payment of fighters' wages by the State,[251] and shared military objectives and strategies between the entity and the State.[252]

Some of these factors are evident in Moscow's relationship with the rebels operating in eastern Ukraine prior to Russia's February 2022 invasion. Thus, the ICC Office of the Prosecutor indicated that it possessed evidence pointing to Russia's exercise of overall control in this context.[253] Meanwhile, legal commentators reached varying conclusions on the issue. While some asserted that Russia's relationship with the rebels did amount to overall control,[254] others assessed that there was insufficient information to reach a definitive view.[255]

The only judicial body to have ruled on the matter is a Dutch court, which addressed individual criminal responsibility for the downing of Malaysia Airlines Flight MH17.[256] Concluding that the overall control threshold was satisfied from

249. *Tadić Appeals Chamber*, *supra* note 10, ¶ 150; *Kordić Appeals Chamber*, *supra* note 160, ¶¶ 362-69.

250. *Blaškić Trial Chamber*, *supra* note 190, ¶ 114.

251. *Tadić Appeals Chamber*, *supra* note 10, ¶ 150; *Kordić Appeals Chamber*, *supra* note 160, ¶ 366.

252. *Tadić Appeals Chamber*, *supra* note 10, ¶ 151; *Blaškić Trial Chamber*, *supra* note 190, ¶ 108. *See also* SIVAKUMARAN, *supra* note 167, at 227.

253. Int'l Crim. Ct. Off. of the Prosecutor, REPORT ON PRELIMINARY EXAMINATION ACTIVITIES 2018, 21–22, ¶¶ 72–73 (Dec. 5, 2018), www.icc-cpi.int/itemsDocuments/181205-rep-otp-PE-ENG.pdf.

254. *See, e.g.*, Heinsch, *supra* note 165, at 360; Patycja Grzebyk, *Classification of the Conflict Between Ukraine and Russia in International Law (Ius ad Bellum and Ius in Bello)*, 34 POLISH Y.B. INT'L L. 39, 56 (2015). For analysis of the overall control test in the context of the Syrian conflict, *see* Mohamad Ghazi Janaby, *The Legal Status of Hezbollah in the Syrian Conflict: An International Humanitarian Perspective*, 33 ARIZ. J. INT'L & COMP. L. 383, 414–18 (2016).

255. *See, e.g.*, Shane R. Reeves & David Wallace, *The Combatant Status of the "Little Green Men" and Other Participants in the Ukraine Conflict*, 91 INT'L L. STUD. 361, 382 (2015); Noelle Quenivet, *Trying to Classify the Conflict in Eastern Ukraine*, INTLAWGRRLS (Aug. 28, 2014), https://ilg2.org/2014/08/28/trying-to-classify-the-conflict-in-eastern-ukraine/.

256. For commentary on the judgment, *see* Lachezar Yanev, *The MH17 Judgment: An Interesting Take on the Nature of the Armed Conflict in Eastern Ukraine*, EJIL:TALK! (Dec. 7, 2022), https://www.ejiltalk.org/the-mh17-judgment-an-interesting-take-on-the-nature-of-the-armed-conflict-in-eastern-ukraine/; Joëlle Trampert, *Possible Implications of the Dutch MH17 Judgment for the Netherlands' Inter-State Case Before the ECtHR*, EJIL:TALK! (Dec. 12, 2022), https://www.ejiltalk.org/possible-implications-of-the-dutch-mh17-judgment-for-the-netherlands-inter-state-case-before-the-ecthr/; Marieke de Hoon, *Dutch Court, in Life Sentences: Russia Had "Overall Control" of Forces in Eastern Ukraine Downing of Flight MH 17*, JUST SEC. (Dec. 19, 2022), https://www.justsecurity.org/84456/dutch-court-in-life-sentences-russia-had-overall-control-of-forces-in-eastern-ukraine-downing-of-flight-mh17/.

mid-May 2014, the court relied on evidence demonstrating the considerable links between Moscow and the rebel forces. This included Russia's supply of weapons, money, and military training to the rebels; recorded telephone conversations between rebel leaders and the Kremlin indicating that the former requested support from Russia and acted on Moscow's direct instructions; State involvement in coordinating and implementing the rebels' military activities; and Russia's decisive influence over the leadership of the rebel administrations.[257]

Other factors also support this conclusion. For instance, the integration of the rebel movement into Russia's military structure, the presence of Russian officers in command roles, and the rebel administrations' high degree of dependence on Russia all indicate an elevated level of State control.[258] In addition, the location of the Donbas next to the Russian border, together with the shared military objectives between Russia and the NSAs, suggests an enhanced ability on Russia's part to produce effects outside its own territory.[259] The available evidence, therefore, indicates that the non-international armed conflict between Ukraine and the rebels was internationalized through Russia's exercise of overall control.[260]

If that is correct, it is pertinent to consider the impact this would have from a State responsibility perspective, if the overall control test was applied to determine issues of both attribution and conflict classification. First, it is important to recall the ICTY's distinction between different categories of NSA.[261] As the rebels in Ukraine constituted an organized and hierarchically structured group, the overall control test assumes that they acted under the State's authority, even in the absence of evidence that their acts in potential violation of international law were conducted under the State's supervision.[262] Therefore, Russia's exercise of overall control would mean that the State bears responsibility for all the rebels' conduct in breach of its international legal obligations, unless such behavior is *ultra vires*.[263] For instance, Russia would bear international responsibility for rebel

257. Yanev, *supra* note 256; Trampert, *supra* note 256; de Hoon, *supra* note 256.

258. For detailed analysis of the relationship between Russia and the rebels, *see* Ukraine and the Netherlands v. Russia, App. No. 8019/16, 43800/14 and 28525/20, ¶¶ 576–696 (2022) (ECtHR).

259. *Tadić Appeals Chamber*, *supra* note 10, ¶¶ 138–40. *See also Bosnian Genocide*, *supra* note 6 dissenting opinion of Judge ad hoc Mahiou, ¶ 117.

260. For a similar analysis regarding Russia's relationship with the Wagner Group, *see* Jennifer Maddocks, *Does Russia Exercise Overall Control over the Wagner Group? Expert Q&A from Stockton Center's Russia-Ukraine Conference*, Just Sec. (Apr. 5, 2023), https://www.justsecurity.org/85819/does-russia-exercise-overall-control-over-the-wagner-group-expert-qa-from-stockton-centers-russia-ukraine-conference/.

261. *Tadić Appeals Chamber*, *supra* note 10, ¶ 120.

262. *Id.* ¶¶ 121–22.

263. ARSIWA, *supra* note 1, art. 8, cmt. ¶ 8.

forces' mistreatment of Ukrainian service personnel,[264] even if it had no involvement in, influence over, or knowledge of, the particular operations during which such abuses occurred. It is likely that Russia would only avoid such responsibility if the rebels acted contrary to specific State instructions.[265]

6.4.3.2 Effective Control

The ICJ's effective control test is more stringent in nature. This requires a hierarchical relationship between the entity and the State, enabling the latter to compel the NSA to follow a particular course of action. Such a relationship will normally arise due to the NSA's dependence on the State, which provides the State with authority and influence over the way in which the NSA behaves.[266] Russia, for instance, reportedly maintained control over the ceasefire agreed at Minsk by punishing or withholding military supplies from those fighters that acted in its breach.[267]

NSAs do not act under a State's effective control, therefore, when they support a State of their own free will. The actions of patriotic hackers, for instance, are unlikely to be attributable to a State because the State lacks the leverage to compel them to follow a particular course of action. To act under a State's effective control, an NSA must know that consequences will ensue, such as the withdrawal of financial support, if it fails to act in accordance with the State's wishes. While the NSA's reliance on the State need not be "complete," as discussed in Chapter 4,[268] it must be sufficient to establish a potential for control that the State then exercises.[269]

An additional requirement is that the State exerts its control "over the operations in the course of which the alleged violations were committed."[270] The ICJ's wording implies that a State's broad control over an operation suffices, rather than requiring the exercise of control over the individual elements of the operation that violate the State's international legal obligations. The *Tallinn Manual 2.0* thus construes effective control as including "both the ability to cause constituent activities of the operation to occur, as well as the ability to order the cessation of

264. *See, e.g.*, Rep. on the Human Rights Situation in Ukraine 12–13, ¶¶ 50–52 (Nov. 15, 2014), https://www.ohchr.org/sites/default/files/Documents/Countries/UA/OHCHR_sixth_report_on_Ukraine.pdf; Human Rights Violations and Abuses and International Humanitarian Law Violations Committed in the Context of the Ilovaisk Events in August 2014, 19–20, ¶¶ 84–87 (Aug. 9, 2018), www.ohchr.org/Documents/Countries/UA/ReportOnIlovaisk_EN.pdf.

265. ARSIWA, *supra* note 1, art. 8, cmt. ¶ 8. *See also supra* sec. 6.3.

266. Talmon, *supra* note 9, at 502.

267. Int'l Crisis Group, Russian and the Separatists in Eastern Ukraine 6, 9 (Feb. 5, 2016), https://www.crisisgroup.org/europe-central-asia/eastern-europe/ukraine/russia-and-separatists-eastern-ukraine.

268. *See supra* ch. 4, sec. 4.4.

269. Crawford's First Rep. on State Responsibility, *supra* note 16, at 56.

270. *Nicaragua*, *supra* note 10, ¶ 115.

those that are underway."[271] Support for this interpretation can be found in the jurisprudence of the Iran–U.S. Claims Tribunal[272] as well as in the *opinio juris* of Germany.[273] In the context of attribution in the cyber domain, the German government expressed the view that although a sufficient degree of control is necessary, "the State is not required to have detailed insight into or influence over all particulars, especially those of a technical nature, of the cyber operation."[274]

On this construction of the test, the State's capacity to exercise control over the individual elements of an operation is more important than the State's actual influence over the relevant violations. To illustrate, in June 2017, the U.S. Mission to the Organization for Security and Cooperation in Europe (OSCE) called upon Russia to "direct its separatist proxies to immediately stop this behavior that puts OSCE personnel at risk."[275] This language reveals a belief that Russia had the ability, at that time, to prevent the rebels in eastern Ukraine from firing warning shots that endangered OSCE personnel. If Russia had such a capacity, further to its exercise of control over the wider operation during which the shots were fired, then, on the *Tallinn Manual*'s reading of the effective control test, Russia bears responsibility for the rebels' potential breach of the IHL principle of distinction.[276] Moreover, that is the case even if Russian officials did not exercise control over the rebels' specific conduct in firing the shots complained of.

A close reading of the ICJ's jurisprudence, however, raises doubts regarding this interpretation. In the *Nicaragua* case, the court stipulated that evidence is required demonstrating that the State "directed or enforced the perpetration of the acts contrary to human rights and humanitarian law alleged by the [injured] State."[277] It is not clear from the judgment whether the ICJ viewed this requirement as a constituent element of effective control or a separate basis of attribution.[278] But if the former interpretation is correct, a mere ability by the State to

271. Tallinn Manual 2.0, *supra* note 48, r. 17, cmt. ¶ 6. *See also* Talmon, *supra* note 9, at 503; Michael N. Schmitt & Sean Watts, *Beyond State-Centrism: International Law and Non-State Actors in Cyberspace*, 21 J. Conflict & Sec. L. 595, 604 (2016); Schmitt, *"Virtual" Disenfranchisement*, *supra* note 63, at 62.

272. Kenneth P. Yeager v. Islamic Republic of Iran, Award No. 324-10199-1, ¶ 45 (Iran–U.S. Claims Trib., 1987). *See also* Kress *supra* note 25, at 111–12.

273. Official Compendium, *supra* note 6, at 39–40.

274. *Id.*

275. U.S. Mission to the OSCE, Ongoing Violations of International Law and Defiance of OSCE Principles by Russia in Ukraine, Delivered by Chargé d'Affaires Kate M. Byrnes to the Permanent Council (June 8, 2017), https://osce.usmission.gov/ongoing-violations-international-law-defiance-osce-principles-russia-ukraine-3/.

276. *See* Customary IHL, *supra* note 6, r. 1.

277. *Nicaragua*, *supra* note 10, ¶ 115.

278. Kress, *supra* note 25, at 105.

control an NSA's conduct during the operation in which a violation occurs is not, by itself, sufficient to lead to attribution.

Some clarity on this issue can be gained from Special Rapporteur Crawford's first report on State responsibility. In Crawford's view, "it is only if the State directed and controlled the specific operation and the conduct complained of was a necessary, integral or intended part of that operation, that the conduct should be attributable to the State."[279] He added, "The principle should not extend to conduct which was only incidentally or peripherally associated with an operation, or which escaped from the State's direction and control."[280] For Crawford, therefore, provided the State controlled the operation in which the relevant conduct took place, there is no requirement that the State's influence extended to the particular act at issue, for example by giving orders regarding its commission. It is necessary only that the relevant conduct formed an integral part of the operation conducted under the State's control.

The ILC Drafting Committee, however, adopted a stricter approach.[281] While the commentary to Article 8 initially replicates Crawford's language,[282] it later declares that the State's control "must relate to the conduct which is said to have amounted to an internationally wrongful act."[283] This latter wording indicates the ILC's intent that attribution should arise only if the State controls the particular acts that potentially violate international law.[284] Certain arbitral tribunals[285] and legal scholars[286] also interpret the ICJ's judgment in this way. Cassese, for instance, concluded that the ICJ intended effective control to mean either the ordering of such actions by the State or "forcefully making the rebels carry out those specific operations."[287] Or as Hessbruegge observed, the State's responsibility is engaged only if it "micromanages the conduct of the individual agents."[288]

279. Crawford's First Rep. on State Responsibility, *supra* note 16, at 43, ¶ 213.

280. *Id.*

281. ILC Y.B. 1998 vol. I, *supra* note 24, at 289, ¶ 79.

282. ARSIWA, *supra* note 1, art. 8, cmt. ¶ 3.

283. *Id.* cmt. ¶ 7.

284. *See* ILC Y.B. 1998 vol. I, *supra* note 24, at 289, ¶ 79.

285. *See, e.g.*, Jan de Nul N.V. & Dredging International N.V. v. Arab Republic of Egypt, Case No. ARB/04/13, ¶ 173 (Int'l Ctr. for Settlement of Inv. Disp., Nov. 6, 2008); *Gavrilović*, *supra* note 244, ¶ 829; Marfin Investment Group Holdings S.A., Alexandros Bakatselos & Others v. Republic of Cyprus, Case No. ARB/13/27, ¶ 679 (Int'l Ctr. for Settlement of Inv. Disp., July 26, 2018).

286. *See, e.g.*, Kaufman, *supra* note 53, at 2619; Eatwell, *supra* note 183, at 24–27; Tsagourias & Farrell, *supra* note 74, at 954.

287. Cassese, *supra* note 9, at 653. *See also Tadić Appeals Chamber*, *supra* note 10, ¶ 114.

288. Jan Arno Hessbruegge, *The Historical Development of the Doctrines of Attribution and Due Diligence in International Law*, 36 N.Y.U. J. INT'L L. & POL. 265, 273 (2004). *See also* Jan Arno Hessbruegge, *Human Rights Violations Arising from Conduct of Non-State Actors*, 11 BUFF. HUM. RTS. L. REV. 21, 53–55 (2005).

This strict interpretation of the test is further supported by the ICJ's judgment in *Bosnian Genocide*.[289] Here, the Court rejected the Applicant's contention that the State's exercise of effective control should be assessed "in relation to the whole body of operations carried out by the direct perpetrators of the genocide," confirming instead that when a breach consists of a number of separate acts, the State must exercise control over all constituent elements of the violation.[290] In the ICJ's view, the State must have "been the cause of the commission of acts in breach of its international obligations."[291]

In military parlance, this detailed level of oversight bears a greater resemblance to tactical, than operational, control.[292] Therefore, for the ICJ and the ILC, conduct is attributable to a State only if its officials exert tactical control over the specific acts at issue at the time of their commission. In practice, this seems to mean that State officials must be aware of, and actively enforce or condone, the NSA's acts in potential violation of international law.[293]

To illustrate, consider the attacks on Bunagana and surrounding towns conducted by M23 fighters in July 2012, during which a UN peacekeeper was killed.[294] If members of the Rwandan armed forces exerted tactical control over the M23 fighters throughout those attacks, the NSAs' conduct, including their potentially unlawful use of force against the UN peacekeeper, is attributable to the State.[295] But if Rwandan armed forces' involvement was limited to a broader level of oversight over the fighters' use of force, or they did not exert tactical control over the particular attack during which the peacekeeper was killed, the effective control threshold may not be satisfied. That is the case even if Rwandan officers played a significant role in the planning of the operation, they knew that the rebels might act in a manner that violated IHL, and they had the authority to intervene and stop such violations but failed to do so.

289. *Bosnian Genocide*, *supra* note 6, ¶ 401.

290. *Id. See also* Talmon, *supra* note 9, at 503.

291. *Bosnian Genocide*, *supra* note 6, ¶ 397.

292. Military doctrine distinguishes three levels of command and control, which range from the general to the specific: strategic, operational, and tactical. NATO defines tactical control as "the detailed and, usually, local direction and control of movements or manoeuvres necessary to accomplish missions or tasks assigned." *See* NATO, *supra* note 83, at 1.39–1.41.

293. Kress, *supra* note 25, at 141. This conclusion is supported by former Special Rapporteur Crawford's remarks before the ICJ, in which he referred in this context to "Control, in detail, not some umbrella control." *See* Application of the Convention on the Prevention and Punishment of the Crime of Genocide (Croatia v. Serbia), Verbatim Record, Mar. 6, 2014, C.R. 2014/10, Crawford (Croatia) 48, ¶ 37.

294. U.N.S.C., Final Rep. of the Group of Experts on the Democratic Republic of the Congo 10, U.N. Doc. S/2012/843 (Nov. 15, 2012) [hereinafter U.N. Nov. 2012 Rep.].

295. Depending on the circumstances, the killing of the peacekeeper may have violated the IHL principle of distinction. *See* Customary IHL, *supra* note 6, r. 1.

On this interpretation, therefore, the effective control test resembles the ILC's original conception of attribution, which required the State to instigate the acts in potential violation of international law.[296] But the ARSIWA commentary appears to allow a small degree of flexibility in this respect. When an NSA acts under a State's effective control, "the condition for attribution will still be met even if particular instructions may have been ignored."[297] Moreover, the ICJ acknowledged that attribution may be appropriate if the relevant conduct is committed only "in part" under the State's effective control.[298] Thus, if a State exerts tactical control over an operation, the NSA's actions during that operation might still be attributable to the State if members of the NSA fail to comply with certain commands, or if the State's officials do not control every aspect of the NSA's conduct. It seems that this would only be the case, however, if the instruction that is ignored, or the aspect of the NSA's behavior that falls outside the State's control, is peripheral to the violation or relates to a relatively insignificant aspect of the relevant conduct.

Imagine, for instance, that State officials exercise tactical control over a militia's operation against fighters located in a village and during that operation, the NSA targets civilians. If members of the militia ignore certain subsidiary commands, such as regarding the timing of the attack or the equipment they should use, the NSA's conduct in violation of IHL is attributable to the State. In this scenario, the relevant acts are still conducted under the State's control and, presumably, endorsed by State officials. But if the militia contravenes a more significant direction, for example, that it should target only fighters, the NSA's action in doing so may be considered *ultra vires* and not attributable to the State.[299]

In these examples, the effective control test would most likely be satisfied if the State's officials are physically present with the NSA and act in a command role at the time of the attacks. That does not mean, however, that physical presence is a prerequisite for effective control. With the advent of new technologies, State organs might maintain regular contact with an NSA's fighters and thereby exert control over their behavior from afar. If, by using communications or surveillance equipment, a State effectively controls an NSA's conduct, that conduct should be attributable to the State irrespective of the manner by which the State exerts its control or the precise location of its personnel at the relevant time.[300]

The potential for a State to control an operation from afar raises questions regarding the nature of that control. If the State's organs are remotely located, the only way in which they can effectively influence the NSA's behavior might be by issuing verbal or written commands. More nuanced methods of guidance may, however, be available if State officials are co-located with the NSA. For example,

296. ILC Y.B. 1974 vol. II, *supra* note 11, at 284–85 (draft art. 8, cmt. ¶ 8). *See also supra* sec. 6.2.1.

297. ARSIWA, *supra* note 1, art. 8, cmt. ¶ 8.

298. *Bosnian Genocide*, *supra* note 6, ¶ 401.

299. *See* Kress, *supra* note 25, at 136.

300. Renz, *supra* note 55, at 145.

they might demonstrate or gesture how they intend the NSA to behave, or exact punishment on an individual who does not follow an agreed course of action.

Effective control may thus be exercised through ongoing State guidance, supervision, or oversight of an NSA's activities. But because this assessment relates to the specific operation in which the potential violations occur, it cannot be assumed that just because the State exerts control over one operation, it also exercises the same degree of control over another. Instead, the State's exercise of control is a question of fact, to be assessed on a case-by-case basis. A more general assessment may be possible, however, in some circumstances. For example, if a State exercises a detailed level of control over all the operations conducted by a PMSC by virtue of its contractual relationship with the entity, it might be possible to conclude that the State's effective control extends to all the NSA's operations.[301]

6.4.3.3 Distinguishing Between Instructions and Effective Control

It is apparent from the preceding analysis that effective control necessarily involves some form of guidance or instruction by the State to the NSA regarding how the NSA should act. The ICJ's judgment in the *Bosnian Genocide* case supports this conclusion,[302] as does the ARSIWA commentary.[303] But that does not mean that the rules of attribution based upon State instructions and effective control are the same. The distinction between these two rules manifests most clearly in temporal terms. While effective control necessitates the State's influence over the NSA's execution of the acts in potential violation of international law, State instructions to commit a particular act might be issued at a much earlier point in time. An NSA acting on a State's instructions, therefore, has greater freedom of choice regarding the means and methods it chooses to adopt in performing the operation concerned.[304]

The duration of the State's relationship with the NSA may also differ. Thus, instructions might be issued on a one-off basis, with no continuing relationship between the parties. Effective control, however, endures over a longer period in the form of a subordinate relationship between the entity and the State.[305] That relationship must entail at least some degree of dependence by the NSA on the

301. Michael N. Schmitt & Liis Vihul, *Proxy Wars in Cyberspace: The Evolving International Law of Attribution*, Fletcher Sec. Rev. 54, 63 (2014); A.B.A., Ctr. for Hum. Rts., & Rule of L. Initiative, The Legal Framework Regulating Proxy Warfare 16 (December 2019), www.americanbar.org/content/dam/aba/administrative/human_rights/chr-proxy-warfare-report-2019.pdf. Note that the PMSC's conduct might alternatively be attributable to the State based on the rule reflected in art. 5. *See* ARSIWA, *supra* note 1, art. 5.

302. *Bosnian Genocide*, *supra* note 6, ¶ 413. *See also* Hathaway et al., *supra* note 223, at 552 n. 46.

303. ARSIWA, *supra* note 1, art. 8, cmt. ¶ 8. *See also* Cassese, *supra* note 9, at 663; Kaufman, *supra* note 53, at 2642–45.

304. Eatwell, *supra* note 183, at 25.

305. Kress, *supra* note 25, at 125.

State, which enables the State to control the NSA's activities. In contrast, attribution based on State instructions might arise without such dependence; all that is required is some form of authority on the part of the State at the time the instructions are issued, leading the entity to act upon those commands.[306]

A further difference between the two grounds of attribution relates to the specificity of the directives issued. As discussed in Section 6.3, to lead to attribution, a State's instructions to an NSA must relate to the specific conduct that violates the State's international legal obligations. In contrast, because effective control arises during a continuing relationship between the entity and the State, it may be that the State issues numerous commands, orders, or looser guidance or instructions during that relationship. These, taken together, may suffice to reach the conclusion that the State exercises effective control over the entity at the relevant time. It is not necessary for any individual command, considered independently, to define the acts that the State expects the entity to perform.

6.4.4 The Exercise of Effective Control During Armed Conflict

A review of the relationships arising between States and NSAs during armed conflict highlights the stringency of the effective control test. For a State's responsibility to be engaged on this basis, evidence is required that the State exerted tactical control over the NSA's conduct in violation of international law. Regarding Rwanda's support to the rebel group M23, for example, factors that might point to an exercise of effective control include the harmonization of communications equipment between the State and the rebels and the presence of Rwandan commanders during M23's operations.[307] From facts such as these, it might be possible to infer that Rwandan State organs "directed or enforced" at least some of M23 fighters' acts in breach of IHL.[308]

In many conflicts, however, it may not be possible to draw such an inference. Consider, for instance, Hezbollah's role in the Syrian hostilities. The NSA became involved in the conflict at Iran's instigation and acted alongside Syrian troops.[309]

306. *Id.* at 127.

307. U.N. Nov. 2012 Rep., *supra* note 294, at 8–10; Michelle Nichols, *Exclusive: Rwanda Exercises Command and Control Over M23 Rebels, Say UN Experts*, Reuters (July 2, 2025), https://www.reuters.com/world/africa/rwanda-exercises-command-control-over-m23-rebels-say-un-experts-2025-07-02/.

308. *Nicaragua, supra* note 10, ¶ 115. Regarding potential IHL violations committed by M23, *see, e.g.*, Hum. Rts. Watch, M23 Rebels Kill, Rape Civilians (July 22, 2013), https://www.hrw.org/news/2013/07/22/dr-congo-m23-rebels-kill-rape-civilians; Amnesty Int'l, DR Congo: Rwandan-Backed M23 Rebels Perpetrating Summary Killings and Rapes (Feb. 17, 2023), https://www.amnesty.org/en/latest/news/2023/02/dr-congo-rwandan-backed-m23-rebels-perpetrating-summary-killings-and-rapes/.

309. *See supra* ch. 2, sec. 2.4.1.2.

Reporting indicates, however, that the group did not operate under the effective control of either State.[310] Although the Islamic Revolutionary Guard Corps (IRGC) and the Syrian authorities reportedly coordinated the NSA's wider operations, Hezbollah fighters exercised a high degree of autonomy at the tactical level, to the extent that they even commanded Syrian government forces.[311] Assuming this was the case in all Hezbollah's operations in Syria, it means that neither Syria nor Iran bears responsibility for the NSA's acts in potential violation of IHL, such as its conduct in preventing the provision of food and water to civilians in towns under siege.[312]

A similar conclusion is likely regarding the numerous abuses committed by Syrian militias during Turkey's operations to take control of territory held by the SDF in northeast Syria.[313] Despite Turkey's reported "control over all strategic decision-making" and its oversight over the militias' broader operations,[314] its level of authority over fighters' actions in violation of IHL appears insufficient to satisfy the effective control threshold. Reporting indicates, for instance, that the militias' discipline was so poor that Turkish officials were incapable of preventing fighters from looting civilian properties.[315] As such, these and other acts by the militias that potentially violate Turkey's IHL obligations are unlikely to be attributable to the State.[316]

The position is more nuanced in the context of Russia's involvement in the conflict in eastern Ukraine. Notwithstanding the rebels' clear subordination to Russia, the effective control test requires evidence of Russian influence over the

310. Nadav Pollak, The Transformation of Hezbollah by its Involvement in Syria 5 (Aug. 4, 2016), www.washingtoninstitute.org/policy-analysis/transformation-hezbollah-its-involvement-syria.

311. Nicholas Blanford, *The Battle for Qusayr: How the Syrian Regime and Hizb Allah Tipped the Balance*, 6 CTC Sentinel 19–20 (Aug. 2013), https://ctc.westpoint.edu/the-battle-for-qusayr-how-the-syrian-regime-and-hizb-allah-tipped-the-balance/; Samia Nakhoul, *Special Report: Hezbollah Gambles All in Syria*, Reuters (Sept. 26, 2013), www.reuters.com/article/us-syria-hezbollah-special-report/special-report-hezbollah-gambles-all-in-syria-idUSBRE98P0AI20130926; Isabel Nassief, Inst. for the Study of War, The Campaign for Homs and Aleppo: The Assad Regime's Strategy in 2013 at 17, 25 (Jan. 2014), www.understandingwar.org/sites/default/files/Nassief-BattleforHomsAleppo-web.pdf; Ali Alfoneh, *Tehran's Shia Foreign Legions*, Carnegie Endowment for Int'l Peace (Jan. 30, 2018), https://carnegieendowment.org/research/2018/01/tehrans-shia-foreign-legions?lang=en; Pollak, *supra* note 310, at 3.

312. Rep. of the Indep. Int'l Comm'n of Inquiry on the Syrian Arab Republic, annex III, ¶¶ 6, 11, U.N. Doc. A/HRC/24/46 (Aug. 16, 2013).

313. *See supra* ch. 2, sec. 2.4.1.4.

314. Chulov, *supra* note 86.

315. Tsurkov, *supra* note 85. *See also* Rep. of the Indep. Int'l Comm'n of Inquiry on the Syrian Arab Republic 7, ¶ 28, U.N. Doc. A/HRC/39/65 (Aug. 9, 2018).

316. Note that alternatively, such acts could be deemed *ultra vires*. *See, e.g.*, Eatwell, *supra* note 183, at 28–32.

specific rebel acts that potentially violate international law. It is only if Russian military officers or other officials exercised a detailed level of oversight over the rebels' actions when shelling residential areas during the Debaltseve offensive,[317] for instance, that such conduct is attributable to the State pursuant to its exercise of effective control. Russian State organs must, effectively, have directed the rebels to conduct the battle by pursuing that specific tactic. But if Russian officers' involvement was confined to a strategic or operational level of control, for example, by giving orders to take control of the city but without stipulating or supervising the way this should be done, the effective control threshold is not met, and the indiscriminate attacks are not attributable to the State on this basis.

Thus, even if Russian officers commanded the rebel forces, Ukraine might still have difficulty proving Russia's exercise of effective control. Often, evidence that State officials sanctioned the specific conduct that violates the State's international legal obligations is simply not available. Such difficulties are further compounded in the cyber domain.[318] For example, if NSAs conducted some of the many hostile cyber operations directed against Ukraine,[319] the same evidential standards must be satisfied for their activities to be attributed to a State on this basis. In the event that technical attribution is possible—meaning that Ukraine is able and willing to identify the cyber operators responsible for a harmful operation—demonstrating the requisite links between those individuals and a State to satisfy the effective control test may be particularly challenging.[320]

Even in conventional operations, the covert nature of States' interactions with NSAs compounds the evidential difficulties posed to injured States.[321] Reporting indicates, for example, that the irregular forces, groups, and individuals acting in

317. Amnesty Int'l, Civilian Bloodshed, *supra* note 102; Mariner, *supra* note 102; Ukraine Rep. 2015, *supra* note 102, at 18, ¶ 83.

318. *See, e.g.*, Peter Margulies, *Sovereignty and Cyber Attacks: Technology's Challenge to the Law of State Responsibility*, 14 Melbourne J. Int'l L. 496 (2013); Thomas Rid & Ben Buchanan, *Attributing Cyber Attacks*, 38 J. Strategic Stud. 4 (2015); Herbert Lin, *Attribution of Malicious Cyber Incidents: From Soup to Nuts*, Hoover Inst. (Sept. 19, 2016), www.hoover.org/research/attribution-malicious-cyber-incidents-soup-nuts-0; William Banks, *State Responsibility and Attribution of Cyber Intrusions After Tallinn 2.0*, 95 Tex. L. Rev. 1487 (2017); Luke Chircop, *A Due Diligence Standard of Attribution in Cyberspace*, 67 Int'l & Comp. L.Q. 643, 645–48 (2018); Mačák, *Decoding Article 8*, *supra* note 9; Tsagourias & Farrell, *supra* note 74; William Banks, *Cyber Attribution and State Responsibility*, 97 Int'l L. Stud. 1039 (2021).

319. *See infra* ch. 2, sec. 2.4.2.2.

320. This has led some legal commentators to argue that a looser attribution standard should apply in the cyber domain. *See, e.g.*, Margulies, *supra* note 318, at 512–19; Shackelford & Andres, *supra* note 165, at 987–91; Chircop, *supra* note 318; Rebecca Crootof, *International Cybertorts: Expanding State Accountability in Cyberspace*, 103 Cornell L. Rev. 565 (2018); Tsagourias & Farrell, *supra* note 74, at 961–65.

321. Becker, *supra* note 245, at 71. *See also* Dieter Fleck, *Individual and State Responsibility for Intelligence Gathering*, 28 Mich. J. Int'l L. 687, 696 (2007).

support of U.S. special forces' counterterrorism operations might operate under the United States' effective control.[322] But given the highly classified nature of such activities, the necessary evidence to prove the State's exercise of control is unlikely to be readily available.

6.4.5 The Sufficiency of the Effective Control Test

The effective control test formulated by the ICJ ignores States' authority over NSAs' conduct at all levels except for the exercise of tactical control over the specific acts that violate international law.[323] This is problematic. Often, members of an NSA might act in a manner that violates international law without acting on specific orders from State officials.[324] If a fighter acts on the direction of one of the NSA's commanders, for instance, it may be that that order could be countermanded by a State representative, who exercises command and control over the operation as a whole.[325] In such circumstances, notwithstanding the State's exercise of control over the operation in which the conduct in violation of international law occurs, the ICJ's stringent effective control threshold would not be satisfied.[326]

To illustrate, consider Iran's relationship with Shi'a militia groups operating in Syria. If it is correct that IRGC officers led the militias in combat,[327] it may be that Iran exercised sufficiently detailed control over the militias' conduct in potential violation of IHL for these acts to be attributable to Iran.[328] But reporting indicates

322. Wesley Morgan, *Behind the Secret U.S. War in Africa*, Politico (July 2, 2018), www.politico.com/story/2018/07/02/secret-war-africa-pentagon-664005; Daniel R. Mahanty & Elias Youssef, Ctr. for Civilians in Conflict, Exception(s) to the Rule(s): Civilian Harm, Oversight, and Accountability in the Shadow Wars 13–14 (Nov. 2020), www.stimson.org/wp-content/uploads/2020/11/CIVIC_US_Report_ETR-FINAL1.pdf. For analysis regarding U.S. Special Forces' control over partners for the purposes of command responsibility, *see* Gregory Raymond Bart, *Special Operations Forces and Responsibility for Surrogates' War Crimes*, 5 Harv. Nat'l Sec. J. 513, 522–24 (2014).

323. Tom Dannenbaum, *Translating the Standard of Effective Control into a System of Effective Accountability: How Liability Should be Apportioned for Violations of Human Rights by Member State Troop Contingents Serving as United Nations Peacekeepers*, 51 Harv. Int'l L. J. 113, 156–57 (2010).

324. *Id.*

325. *Id.*

326. *See supra* sec. 6.4.3.2.

327. Paul Bucala & Frederick W. Kagan, Critical Threats, Iran's Evolving Way of War: How the IRGC Fights in Syria (Mar. 2016), www.criticalthreats.org/wp-content/uploads/2016/07/imce-imagesIrans_Evolving_Way_of_War_IRGC_in_Syria_FINAL-1.pdf.

328. *See supra* sec. 6.4.3.2.

that Hezbollah fighters commonly exercised command at the tactical level.[329] If this is accurate, doubts arise whether Iranian officials exerted the requisite quality of control over the militias' activities for their conduct during the hostilities to be attributable to the State. Even if IRGC officers commanded the operation in which the abuses occurred, if they did not exert tactical control over the violations themselves, the effective control threshold might not be satisfied.[330] This outcome leaves victims of IHL violations at the hands of the NSAs with limited means of recourse and fails to reflect the reality of Iran's considerable influence over their behavior.[331]

This reality is unsatisfactory, and it is compounded by the evidential hurdles facing injured States. The burden of proving that a State exercised effective control over an NSA's conduct in potential violation of international law falls to the injured State, to a standard of "reasonable certainty."[332] But even if a State closely supervised an NSA's conduct in breach of international law, that State might evade responsibility in the absence of "clear evidence"[333] or "adequate direct proof"[334] that it exercised the requisite control over the acts concerned.

The barriers injured States face in proving this elevated level of control are raised further by the covert nature of States' relationships with NSAs, which are often conducted via their intelligence services or their special forces.[335] This is a particular issue in the cyber domain. While a sophisticated commander might direct such operations with ease, obtaining evidence of the requisite levels of State control to prove attribution poses a potentially insurmountable challenge.[336] This reality creates a "normative safe zone" in which

329. Ben Hubbard, *Iran Out to Remake Mideast with Arab Enforcer: Hezbollah*, N.Y. Times (Aug. 27, 2017), https://www.nytimes.com/2017/08/27/world/middleeast/hezbollah-iran-syria-israel-lebanon.html.

330. *See supra* sec. 6.4.3.2.

331. *See generally* Ariane M. Tabatabai et al., RAND, The Iran Threat Network: Four Models of Iran's Nonstate Client Partnerships 19 (2021), www.rand.org/pubs/research_reports/RR4231.html.

332. ARSIWA, *supra* note 1, cmt. to ch. V, ¶ 8; *id.* chapeau to ch. II, ¶ 9. *See also* Schmitt & Vihul, *supra* note 301, at 65–66.

333. *Nicaragua*, *supra* note 10, ¶ 109.

334. *Id.* ¶ 111. *See also id.* Separate Opinion of Judge Ago ¶ 16; *Bosnian Genocide*, *supra* note 6, ¶ 209. Note, however, that the ECtHR has taken a more flexible approach to evidence in this context, drawing adverse inferences and reversing the burden of proof. *See* Carter v. Russia, App. No. 20914/07, ¶¶ 166–69 (2021) (ECtHR).

335. Geraint Hughes, My Enemy's Enemy: Proxy Warfare in International Politics 15–18 (2012); Becker, *supra* note 245, at 71, 241.

336. Margulies, *supra* note 318, at 500.

States can freely operate.[337] Moreover, it provides an incentive for States to use NSAs to commit acts that they could not legally perform directly, via their own organs.[338]

The ICJ thus formulated a rule of attribution that is of little practical relevance. This outcome may derive, at least in part, from the political pressures to which the Court was subject at the time of the *Nicaragua* judgment.[339] But due to the stringency of the test, no court or tribunal, to date, has found sufficient evidence of effective control to trigger State responsibility. As Kalshoven remarked, "one wonders how a State could ever achieve the required high level of control over a body of men operating in another country without actually incorporating it in its armed forces."[340]

The ICTY Appeals Chamber highlighted the effective control test's lack of consonance with the aims of the law of State responsibility.[341] This body of law should enhance the enforcement of, and compliance with, States' international legal obligations and thereby hold States to account for the conduct of NSAs that act on their behalf. But the effective control test, as interpreted by the ICJ and the ILC, is too inflexible to achieve that aim.

It is not surprising, therefore, that some jurists[342] and commentators[343] welcomed the ICTY's overall control test as offering a less rigid standard of attribution. The Netherlands similarly viewed the ARSIWA commentary's "inbuilt ambiguity" as to the applicable standard of control in a positive light, as offering flexibility and "scope for the progressive development of the legal rules on State

337. Schmitt & Vihul, *supra* note 301, at 71. *See also* Cassese, *supra* note 9; Vladislav Lanovoy, *The Use of Force by Non-State Actors and the Limits of Attribution of Conduct*, 28 Eur. J. Int'l L. 563, 578 (2017).

338. Christenson, *supra* note 33, at 337; Becker, *supra* note 245, at 71–72; Graham Cronogue, *Rebels, Negligent Support, and State Accountability: Holding States Accountable for the Human Rights Violations of Non-State Actors*, 23 Duke J. Comp. & Int'l L. 365, 384 (2013); Hathaway et al., *supra* note 223, at 562–65.

339. Francis A. Boyle, *Determining U.S. Responsibility for Contra Operations under International Law*, 81 Am. J. Int'l L. 86 (1987); Michael N. Schmitt, *Counter-Terrorism and the Use of Force in International Law*, 79 Int'l L. Stud. 7, 60 (2003); Hathaway et al., *supra* note 223, at 549.

340. Frits Kalshoven, *State Responsibility for Warlike Acts of the Armed Forces: From Article 3 of Hague Convention IV of 1907 to Article 91 of Additional Protocol I of 1977 and Beyond*, 40 Int'l & Comp. L.Q. 827, 855 (1991).

341. *Tadić Appeals Chamber*, *supra* note 10, ¶¶ 117, 123.

342. *Bosnian Genocide*, *supra* note 6, dissenting opinion of Vice President Al-Khasawneh; *id.* dissenting opinion of Judge ad hoc Mahiou.

343. *See, e.g.*, Cassese, *supra* note 9; Spinedi, *supra* note 9; Trapp, *supra* note 165, at 40–45; Heinsch, *supra* note 165; Jorritsma, *supra* note 9.

responsibility."[344] Yet the overall control test presents its own difficulties if utilized as a rule of attribution.

6.4.6 Overall Control as an Alternative to Effective Control

The stringency of the effective control test has led many commentators, as well as the ICRC, to argue that the looser standard of overall control should apply for the purposes of attribution, as well as conflict classification.[345] The overall control test focuses on the entire relationship between the entity and the State, rather than the State's control over the particular operation in which the alleged international law violation occurs.[346]

If the test applies to determine attribution and a State exercises overall control over an entity's wider operations, all the NSA's conduct in potential violation of international law is attributable to the State, with the exception of any acts that are *ultra vires*.[347] But while the application of this test would broaden the categories of NSA conduct that is attributable to a State, there is some merit to the concerns expressed by the ICJ in the *Bosnian Genocide* case.[348] The use of the overall control test as a rule of attribution potentially stretches the links that must exist between the State and the NSA too far.[349]

Consider, for example, U.S. support for the SDF in the fight against ISIS.[350] Given that the overall control test may be met if a State equips and finances an NSA and also plays a role in the planning of its military activity,[351] it is possible that the U.S. relationship with the SDF reached the threshold of overall control. If that is the case, and the overall control test applies for the purposes of attribution, all the SDF's conduct falling within the scope of U.S. control is attributable to the State. This means that the United States could bear responsibility for the SDF's conduct in recruiting children for military service even if it had no knowledge of, or involvement in, the NSA's recruitment practices.[352] Although such conduct

344. Int'l Law Comm'n, Comments and Observations Received from Governments 49, U.N. Doc. A/CN.4/515 and Add.1–3 (2001).

345. *See supra* sec. 6.4.3.

346. *Id.*

347. ARSIWA, *supra* note 1, art. 7; *id.* art. 8, cmt ¶ 8.

348. *Bosnian Genocide, supra* note 6, ¶ 406.

349. *Id. See also* Akande, *supra* note 166, at 60; Milanović, *From Compromise to Principle, supra* note 182, at 440.

350. *See supra* ch. 2, sec. 2.4.1.3.

351. *Tadić Appeals Chamber, supra* note 10, ¶¶ 131, 137. *See also supra* secs. 6.4.1.2, 6.4.3.1.

352. Rep. of the Indep. Int'l Comm'n of Inquiry on the Syrian Arab Republic 10, ¶ 42, U.N. Doc. A/HRC/37/72 (Feb. 1, 2018).

could be considered *ultra vires*, falling outside the scope of the State's control, this conclusion is by no means certain given the close links between the SDF's wider operations and its recruitment of personnel.[353]

The attribution of conduct in such circumstances, in the absence of any clear connection between the NSA's actions in potential breach of international law and those of the supporting State, overly expands the scope of the rule reflected in Article 8 and potentially holds States to account in respect of acts that cannot properly be characterized as their own.[354] In some circumstances, however, the overall control test may equally be underinclusive, in that it fails to attribute conduct to a State that is performed under that State's control. For instance, a State might maintain links with an NSA that do not rise to the level of overall control and make use of that group on an ad hoc basis to perform specific operations on its behalf. If the State exercises control over the group during an operation in which international law violations occur, the rule reflected in Article 8 should attribute the group's conduct to the State. But if the overall control standard applies for the purpose of determining attribution, and this test is not met in respect of the wider relationship between the State and the NSA, attribution will not arise.[355]

Consider, in this respect, Rwanda's involvement in the conflict in eastern DRC.[356] During the hostilities, Rwanda maintained connections with various NSAs and, on occasion, tasked these with specific missions, such as targeted killings.[357] Given Rwanda's diverse relationships with these groups, it may be that when considered as a whole, the State's involvement in their activities did not rise to the level of overall control. For instance, such groups might have obtained finance and equipment from sources other than the State, and Rwanda might not have assisted in "the general planning of [the groups'] military activity"[358] but only in the planning of specific operations.

Thus, Rwanda might not have exercised overall control over the wider activities of the group Nduma Defense of Congo at the time State officials entrusted the commander of that group with the task of killing the leader of a rival militia.[359] In that situation, if the overall control standard applied for the purposes of attribution, the killing would be attributable to Rwanda only if sufficient evidence was available to indicate that Rwanda instructed the commander to complete the

353. ARSIWA, *supra* note 1, art. 7; *id.* art. 8, cmt. ¶ 8.

354. Akande, *supra* note 166, at 60.

355. Ryan Goodman, *Legal Limits on Military Assistance to Proxy Forces: Pathway for State and Official Responsibility*, Just Sec. (May 14, 2018), www.justsecurity.org/56272/legal-limits-military-assistance-proxy-forces-pathways-state-official-responsibility/.

356. *See supra* ch. 2, sec. 2.4.3.1.

357. U.N. June 2012 Rep., *supra* note 113, at 17–23.

358. *Tadić Appeals Chamber*, *supra* note 10, ¶ 131.

359. U.N. June 2012 Rep., *supra* note 113, at 18, ¶ 36.

task.[360] In the absence of evidence of State instructions, however, Rwanda would avoid responsibility, even if State officials exercised a detailed level of oversight over the operation in which the killing occurred.

Determining the appropriate control standard for the purposes of Article 8 ARSIWA thus presents a paradox. The application of the effective control threshold leads to an accountability gap due to its very stringent nature and the ensuing evidential difficulties posed to an injured State.[361] Yet, the use of the overall control test creates problems of its own. On the one hand, this is overinclusive and might lead to State responsibility for conduct over which the State had minimal influence or oversight.[362] But on the other hand, the overall control test might fail to hold States to account for conduct over which they exercise a detailed level of oversight.[363]

The difficulties with the overall control standard derive from the test's emphasis on the broader relationship between the State and the NSA. While this focus is appropriate when determining de facto State organ status for the purposes of Article 4 ASRIWA, due to the very close links that must exist between an entity and the State in all the NSA's fields of activity,[364] it is not well suited to the rule of attribution reflected in Article 8. This rule aims to attribute to a State the conduct of persons or groups that, in fact, act on the State's behalf at the time the acts in potential violation of international law are committed. This is a question that can be answered most effectively by examining the State's exercise of control over the operation in which the violation occurs rather than the State's overall relationship with the NSA.[365]

6.4.7 An Alternative Test of Control

The preceding analysis reveals that to satisfy its object and purpose, the rule reflected in Article 8 ARSIWA should utilize a control test that sits in the middle ground between effective and overall control. While the effective control test correctly applies to the operation in which the alleged breach of a State's international legal obligation arises, the requirement for evidence of detailed State control over the NSA's conduct in violation of international law is overly stringent and impractical.[366] Instead, if a State is in a position of authority over an NSA such that

360. *See supra* secs. 6.4.1.2, 6.4.3.1.

361. *See supra* sec. 6.4.3.2.

362. *Bosnian Genocide*, *supra* note 6, ¶ 406; Akande, *supra* note 166, at 60.

363. Goodman, *supra* note 355.

364. *See supra* ch. 4, sec. 4.4.

365. *See* Talmon, *supra* note 9, at 5013; Marko Milanović, *State Responsibility for Acts of Non-State Actors: A Comment on Griebel and Plücken*, 22 Leiden J. Int'l L. 307, 316 (2009); Carron, *supra* note 166, at 1025.

366. *See supra* secs. 6.4.3.2, 6.4.4.

it can control the constituent acts performed in the course of an operation, or to order their cessation, this should be sufficient to attribute the NSA's conduct to the State.[367]

The position is analogous to the control exercised by commanders over their troops. Commanders have the power and authority to order their subordinates to act, or not to act, in a particular way but will not normally exert that control over every constituent element of an operation. By virtue of the principle of command responsibility, however, commanders may be criminally responsible if their troops violate IHL in the course of an operation.[368] Such responsibility arises not only in respect of acts performed under the commander's specific orders, but also pursuant to acts of which the commander was aware, or should have been aware, and did not take appropriate measures to prevent.[369] Similarly, a State should bear responsibility for an NSA's conduct if the relevant act was performed in the course of an operation over which the State had the capacity to exert its control and the State's organs knew or should have known of the potential legal violation.

This more flexible interpretation of the control threshold would hold States more effectively to account when they act through NSAs. Consider, for instance, the alleged torture of detainees by militia groups operating with Turkey's assistance in northern Syria.[370] According to the UN Commission of Inquiry, Turkish forces were regularly present in detention facilities where ill treatment of detainees was rampant, and Turkish officials attended some interrogation sessions when torture took place.[371] If this reporting is correct, it appears that Turkey had the capacity to stop the mistreatment, not only due to its officials' presence at the facilities but also because of the militias' dependence on the State for salaries and training,[372] which offered Turkey considerable leverage over their behavior. The militias' acts of mistreatment should therefore be attributable to Turkey, even if the State's organs did not "direct or enforce" the actual abuses perpetrated by the NSAs.[373]

367. TALLINN MANUAL 2.0, *supra* note 48, r. 17, cmt. ¶ 6. *See also* Talmon, *supra* note 9, at 503.

368. Rome Statute of the International Criminal Court art. 28, July 17, 1998, 2187 U.N.T.S. 90 [hereinafter Rome Statute]; AP I, *supra* note 105, art. 87; CUSTOMARY IHL, *supra* note 6, r. 153. *See also* Jenny S. Martinez, *Understanding Mens Rea in Command Responsibility: From Yamashita to* Blaškić *and Beyond*, 5 J. INT'L CRIM. JUST. 638 (2007); Geoffrey S. Corn, *Contemplating the True Nature of the Notion of "Responsibility" in Responsible Command*, 96 INT'L REV. RED CROSS 901 (2015); Elies van Sliedregt, *Command Responsibility and Cyberattacks*, 21 J. CONFLICT & SEC. L. 505 (2016).

369. Rome Statute, *supra* note 368, arts. 25(3)(b), 28; CUSTOMARY IHL, *supra* note 6, r. 153.

370. Rep. of the Indep. Int'l Comm'n of Inquiry on the Syrian Arab Republic 13–14, ¶¶ 37–46, U.N. Doc. A/HRC/46/55 (Mar. 2, 2021).

371. *Id.* at 15, ¶ 45.

372. Tsurkov, *supra* note 85.

373. *See Nicaragua*, *supra* note 10, ¶ 115.

The more remote the State organs' involvement in the relevant violation, however, the less appropriate attribution becomes. The rule reflected in Article 8 should attribute an NSA's conduct to a State only if the State exerts its authority over the operation concerned, meaning that its officials know or should know of the NSA's harmful conduct during that operation, and they have the capacity to exert control over the NSA's behavior at the time the relevant abuses occur. To illustrate, imagine that the SDF mistreats an ISIS detainee during a detention operation that the United States supports. On the predominant interpretation of effective control, the SDF's conduct in mistreating the detainee is only attributable to the United States if U.S. forces are in command of the SDF, and they actively enforce or condone the mistreatment.[374]

If a more flexible control test applied, however, attribution would also be appropriate if the State's armed forces were aware, or should have been aware, of the abuse and they had the requisite authority over the NSA's conduct of the operation to intervene to stop its occurrence. Such a scenario would normally arise if the State's armed forces were physically present during the operation. But if communications and surveillance technologies allowed State officials to exercise control over the NSA's conduct remotely, any acts committed in violation of international law should be attributed to the State.

Similarly, in the cyber domain, if a State's involvement in, or authority over, an operation is such that the NSA would act or cease to act on the State's command, the rule reflected in Article 8 should attribute to the State any private conduct during the operation that violates the State's international legal obligations.[375] This approach accords with the *opinio juris* of Germany, according to which attribution is appropriate even if the State does not have a detailed insight into or influence over all particulars of the relevant cyber operation.[376] In this regard, an observation made by the ICTY in the context of command responsibility is pertinent: "the power to give orders and have them executed can serve as an indicium of effective control."[377]

There is a fine line, however, between situations in which it is appropriate to attribute NSA conduct to a State and circumstances when it is not. It will be a question of fact in each case which side of that line any violations involving an NSA should fall. When a State's involvement in an operation involving potential breaches of international law is more peripheral—for instance, if it is limited to the provision of intelligence or malware—attribution would be a step too far. It is questionable, in such circumstances, whether the acts at issue can properly be characterized as the State's own conduct, performed on its behalf.[378] But consideration of a State's

374. *See supra* sec. 6.4.3.2.

375. TALLINN MANUAL 2.0, *supra* note 48, r. 17, cmt. ¶ 6.

376. Official Compendium, *supra* note 6, at 39–40.

377. Prosecutor v. Hadžihasanović and Kubura, Case No. IT-01-47-A, Appeals Chamber Judgment, ¶ 199 (Int'l Crim. Trib. for the former Yugoslavia, Apr. 22, 2008).

378. *See Bosnian Genocide*, *supra* note 6, ¶ 406.

knowledge of the breach and its capacity to ensure the NSA's compliance with international law would allow the full facts and circumstances to be considered when addressing the issue of attribution.

The effective control test formulated by the ICJ focuses solely on the State's level of control over the specific private conduct at issue, to the exclusion of other factors that might be pertinent to an assessment of the State's responsibility. But if attribution arises further to a State's ability to determine the course of a particular operation, many other facts become relevant. These include:

1. The nature and duration of the relationship between the entity and the State;
2. The financial or other support the State provides to the NSA;
3. The importance of such support to the NSA in the continued performance of its activities;
4. State organs' involvement in the planning of the operation concerned;
5. State organs' exercise of strategic, operational, or tactical control over that operation;
6. The content and timing of any instructions or guidance issued by the State;
7. The NSA's involvement in any previous violations of international law; and
8. State organs' knowledge of the particular violation(s) at issue.

An assessment of a State's capacity to exercise control in relation to a particular operation would thus allow a wider focus than just the circumstances of the operation itself. This would permit an examination of the broad relationship between the State and the NSA to the extent that it is pertinent to the State's ability to exert control over the operation concerned. A more flexible control test should therefore hold States more effectively to account when they act through NSAs, without going so far as to attribute private conduct to States that cannot properly be characterized as their own.

6.4.8 Direction as a Stand-Alone Basis of Attribution

Direction and control are commonly considered together and the differences between them, if any, are unclear. The ARSIWA commentary obfuscates the position by referring first to direction and control as a single attribution standard,[379] then later indicating that the terms are disjunctive, meaning that it is sufficient to establish either one of them.[380] Article 8's drafting history perhaps explains this anomaly.[381] But despite the ILC's stated intent that there should be no cumulative

379. ARSIWA, *supra* note 1, art. 8, cmt. ¶ 1.

380. *Id.* cmt. ¶ 7.

381. *See supra* sec. 6.2.1.

requirement for the establishment of both direction and control,[382] the commentary does not address direction as an independent rule of attribution. Further confusion arises due to the close relationship between the ordinary meanings of instructions and direction.[383] Both imply the issuing of some form of order by the State to the NSA and have been used interchangeably in the context of State responsibility.[384]

Because the concept of direction is rarely considered alone, minimal guidance is available to determine exactly what this entails. The ICJ indicated only that the State must have "provided the direction pursuant to which the perpetrators of the wrongful act acted."[385] Legal commentators suggest that "as distinct from merely giving instructions, in the case of 'direction' it is necessary that the state leads the steps to be taken in the commission of the unlawful conduct; it must show how the operation is to be conducted."[386] Alternatively, direction is assessed to mean "guidance over the entity that commits the wrongful act in the sense of the state taking the lead."[387] Yet, there is little to distinguish such interpretations from a State's exercise of effective control.

Crawford in his writings reinforced the tendency to consider direction and control together.[388] Nonetheless, in a footnote, he expressed the view that the independent concept of direction "implies a continuing period of instruction, or a relationship between the State and a non-State entity such that suggestion or innuendo may give rise to responsibility."[389] This explanation of direction is important because it potentially fills a lacuna that emerges between the predominant interpretations of instructions and effective control.

To illustrate, consider an enduring relationship between a State and an NSA in which the State provides the NSA with continuing support and the NSA regularly performs tasks on the State's behalf. In such circumstances, the NSA might act for the State based on its instinctive knowledge of the State's wishes, gained through prior training and guidance, rather than pursuant to instructions regarding each specific task. But if the State does not positively assign a task to the NSA, or exert

382. ARSIWA, *supra* note 1, art. 8, cmt. ¶ 7.

383. Cassese, *supra* note 9, at 663.

384. *See, e.g.*, Int'l Law Comm'n, Documents of the Fiftieth Session (1998), *in* [1998] 2 Y.B. INT'L L. COMM'N 40, ¶ 197, U.N. Doc. A/CN.4/SER.A/1998/Add.1 (Part 1); *Bosnian Genocide*, *supra* note 6, ¶ 406.

385. *Bosnian Genocide*, *supra* note 6, ¶ 406. *See also* Mačák, *Decoding Article 8*, *supra* note 9, at 417–18.

386. CAMERON & CHETAIL, *supra* note 9, at 209.

387. Tsagourias & Farrell, *supra* note 74, at 954.

388. CRAWFORD, *supra* note 9, at 146–56.

389. *Id.* at 146 n. 28.

control over its execution, the respective thresholds for attribution based on State instructions and effective control are unlikely to be satisfied.[390]

A "less rigorous" interpretation of direction[391] that encompasses a State's "suggestion or innuendo"[392] toward an NSA with which it maintains a continuing association could therefore play an important role in holding States to account. Attribution on this basis would be appropriate, however, only in the context of an enduring relationship. In other circumstances, vague and imprecise forms of guidance by the State are insufficient to lead to attribution.[393] But if a State fosters a hierarchical association with an NSA during which it habitually guides that NSA's conduct, the State should bear responsibility for acts on the part of the NSA that breach its international legal obligations, even in the absence of express instructions to commit those acts or detailed control over their execution.[394]

If this understanding of direction is applied to armed conflict, it is potentially pertinent to Iran's dealings with the Shi'a militia groups operating across the Middle East.[395] While uncertainty surrounds Iranian officials' precise influence over these groups' behavior, they all demonstrate considerable loyalty to Iran and benefit from the provision arms, finance, and training.[396] It is arguable, therefore, that the militias' conduct in violation of IHL, such as their indiscriminate attacks during the assault on Aleppo in Syria,[397] should be attributable to Iran based upon the State's direction of the group's activities, even if Iranian officials did not instruct the militias to conduct the attacks in this manner or exercise tactical control over the NSAs' conduct at the relevant time.

It is important to recall, however, that there is no State practice, *opinio juris*, or jurisprudence to support this suggested interpretation. Clear references to direction as a separate basis of attribution are lacking from the judgments of the ICJ and from most legal scholarship. The ILC, in its extensive deliberations on the issue, did not treat direction as a distinct basis of attribution until the Drafting Committee amended Special Rapporteur Crawford's proposed wording for Article 8 to refer to "direction or control" rather than using the conjunctive "and."[398] It

390. *See supra* secs. 6.3, 6.4.

391. *See Bosnian Genocide*, *supra* note 6, Verbatim Record 2006/8 ¶ 62 (Pellet), https://www.icj-cij.org/sites/default/files/case-related/91/091-20060303-ORA-01-00-BI.pdf.

392. Crawford, *supra* note 9, at 146 n. 28.

393. *See supra* sec. 6.3.1.

394. Mačák, *Decoding Article 8*, *supra* note 9, at 418.

395. *See, e.g.*, Liz Sly et al., *Iran Showcases Its Reach with Militia Attacks Across Middle East*, Wash. Post (Jan. 1, 2024), https://www.washingtonpost.com/world/2024/01/01/iran-militias-gaza-israel/.

396. *Id.*

397. *See, e.g.*, Rep. of the Indep. Int'l Comm'n of Inquiry on the Syrian Arab Republic 7–11, ¶¶ 25–50, U.N. Doc. A/HRC/34/64 (Feb. 2, 2017).

398. ILC Y.B. 1998 vol. I, *supra* note 24, at 289 ¶ 79; ILC Y.B. 2000 vol. II, *supra* note 26, at 65.

seems, therefore, that Crawford's original formulation better represents the underlying customary international law upon which Article 8 is based. Accordingly, until such time as the law may develop, direction refers to the need for the State to direct the manner in which the NSA acts, as an inherent part of its exercise of effective control.

6.5 CONCLUSION

The three grounds of attribution encompassed within Article 8 ARSIWA are frequently conflated. Indistinct lines separate the concepts of instructions, direction, and control, and there is a considerable overlap between them. In simple terms, however, the principal distinction between "instructions" and "direction or control" is temporal, depending on whether the State influences the NSA's decision to act or the act itself. In addition, direction and control require evidence of a continuing, hierarchical relationship between an NSA and a State, whereas instructions may be issued on an isolated basis. There is no reason, however, why attribution based on State instructions cannot also arise during an ongoing relationship between an entity and a State, provided sufficient evidence exists regarding the instructions issued and their nexus to the potential internationally wrongful act.

Considerable debate has arisen regarding the notion of control and how broadly this should be construed. In the context of armed conflict, this concept brings into stark relief the tensions between accountability concerns, which call for less stringent rules of attribution, and the principle that States should bear responsibility only for conduct that can be truly categorized as their own. The delicate balance between these competing interests, however, is not achieved by either the ICTY's overall control test or the ICJ's test of effective control. The former is overinclusive in the scope of conduct it attributes to a State, while the latter is overly stringent in its requirements and of little practical relevance. Accordingly, this chapter suggests an alternative control test that falls in the middle ground between effective and overall control.[399] If adopted, this would help narrow the accountability gap that allows States to act through NSAs in ways they could not lawfully act via their own organs.

Even if the law of State responsibility embraced a more flexible control test, however, concerns regarding an accountability gap would remain. Chapter 7 draws together the analysis of Articles 4, 5, and 8 ARSIWA to explore this legal lacuna, outlining potential developments to the law that might help to ensure the accountability of States that choose to achieve their aims during armed conflict via NSAs.

399. *See supra* sec. 6.4.7.

7

Conclusion to Part Three

State Organs and Agents

7.1 INTRODUCTION

The three rules of attribution discussed in the preceding chapters address States' use of non-State actors (NSA) to achieve their national security goals.[1] In each case, attribution is deemed appropriate because of the factual or legal relationship between the State and the NSA at the time the NSA acts in potential violation of international law. In other words, attribution pursuant to the rules reflected in Articles 4, 5, and 8 of the Draft Articles on Responsibility of States for Internationally Wrongful Acts (ARSIWA)[2] results from some form of action, taken by a State organ prior to or during the conduct in potential violation of international law, to empower, instruct, or enable the NSA to act on the State's behalf.[3] This feature distinguishes the rules reflected in Articles 4, 5, and 8 from the remaining rules of attribution, which are the focus of Part Four.

The detailed analysis of these rules in Chapters 4 to 6 reveals that they do not attribute to a State all the NSA conduct performed on its behalf. An examination of Russia's relationship with the Wagner Group, for instance, exposes the difficulties that arise when applying each of these rules to conduct that was clearly performed for the State and aimed to promote its foreign policy goals.[4] It is not the rules themselves that are at fault but rather their prevailing interpretation. Thus, the way in which the International Law Commission (ILC) and the International

1. *See supra* chs. 4–6.

2. Draft Articles on Responsibility of States for Internationally Wrongful Acts, with commentaries, arts. 4, 5, 8, *in* Int'l Law Comm'n, Rep. on the Work of its Fifty-Third Session, U.N. Doc. A/56/10 (2001), *reprinted in* [2001] 2 Y.B. INT'L L. COMM'N 31, 40–43, 47–49, U.N. Doc. A/CN.4/SER.A/2001/Add.1 (Part 2) [hereinafter ARSIWA].

3. JAMES CRAWFORD, STATE RESPONSIBILITY: THE GENERAL PART 116 (2013).

4. *See* Jennifer Maddocks, *Russia, The Wagner Group, and the Issue of Attribution*, ARTICLES OF WAR (Apr. 28, 2021), https://lieber.westpoint.edu/russia-wagner-group-attribution/.

Attribution of Non-State Actor Conduct During Armed Conflict. Jennifer Maddocks, Oxford University Press.
 DOI: 10.1093/oso/9780197842652.003.0007

Court of Justice (ICJ) have construed certain elements of the three rules severely limits their practical relevance and places a considerable evidential burden upon injured States.

This chapter draws together the analysis of Articles 4, 5, and 8 ARSIWA to consider the wider attribution regime that these articles represent. It examines the effectiveness of the rules expressed in Articles 4, 5, and 8 in holding States to account for conduct performed on their behalf, concluding that all three rules would better meet their object and purpose if interpreted less strictly. Even with a looser interpretation of these provisions, however, an accountability gap would remain.[5] The chapter explores the parameters of this lacuna before, in its final section, assessing potential developments to international law that might help to narrow the gap in accountability.[6] These include the evolution of the complicity rule reflected in Article 16 ARSIWA[7] to encompass States' aid or assistance to NSAs.[8]

7.2 THE EFFECTIVENESS OF THE ATTRIBUTION REGIME

The analysis in Chapters 4 to 6 demonstrates that when States support NSAs engaged in conflict, they can act with a high degree of confidence that if those NSAs engage in conduct that would violate the State's international legal obligations, the State will not bear international responsibility for the breach. Before assessing why this is the case, it helps to review the attribution regime that the rules expressed in Articles 4, 5, and 8 ARSIWA represent.

7.2.1 An Overview of the Rules Reflected in Articles 4, 5, and 8 ARSIWA

The purpose of the rules of attribution reflected in ARSIWA is to determine when conduct in potential violation of international law should be elevated to the public domain and thereby engage a State's responsibility. As noted previously, this involves a delicate balance.[9] On the one hand, States should bear responsibility

5. For academic discussion regarding this accountability gap, *see, e.g.*, Tal Becker, Terrorism and the State: Rethinking the Rules of State Responsibility 239–82 (2006); Monika Hakimi, *State Bystander Responsibility*, 21 Eur. J. Int'l L. 341 (2010); Vladyslav Lanovoy, Complicity and Its Limits in the Law of International Responsibility 319–28 (2016); Oona A. Hathaway et al., *Ensuring Responsibility: Common Article 1 and State Responsibility for Non-State Actors*, 95 Tex. L. Rev. 539 (2017).

6. *See infra* secs. 7.2.3, 7.3.

7. ARSIWA, *supra* note 2, art. 16.

8. *See infra* sec. 7.3.1.

9. *See supra* ch. 3, sec. 3.4.

only for conduct that can be truly categorized as their own.[10] This consideration is important in armed conflict, when NSAs often act with considerable autonomy and with varying levels of State support.[11] But in conflict situations, accountability is also key. To ensure maximum compliance with international humanitarian law (IHL), it is essential that States bear international responsibility when the NSAs that act on their behalf violate IHL.

The rules reflected in Articles 4, 5, and 8 ARSIWA regulate this balance in respect of private conduct performed by NSAs with which a State has chosen to engage.[12] Taken together, to meet their object and purpose, the rules should attribute to a State all the conduct that is performed on the State's behalf. Equally, they should exclude any conduct that cannot properly be classified as the State's own. When performing this difficult task, the three rules of attribution operate together, with each serving a different function. The rules' collective aim is to ensure that States bear international responsibility whenever persons or entities acting on their behalf violate international law.

Of course, States make international law, and it could be argued that States want to be free from international responsibility except in the clearest of cases, when the NSA concerned is plainly acting as an organ or agent of the State. Put differently, States want the liberty to engage with NSAs and to benefit from the plausible deniability and other advantages they gain from proxy relationships, as highlighted in Chapter 2.[13] It is important to recall, however, that if the law of State responsibility allows States to act freely via NSAs, while bearing a low risk of international responsibility if those NSAs violate international law, this limits States' ability to call out other States for acting via proxies that disregard IHL. States not only make use of NSAs during armed conflict; they might also be the victim of IHL violations perpetrated by NSAs acting for another State. It is therefore in States' interests for the law of State responsibility to include effective rules of attribution that properly attribute conduct performed on a State's behalf to the responsible State.

The starting point for any attribution analysis is Article 4 ARSIWA.[14] If a person or entity is designated as an organ of State by the State's internal law, all its conduct performed in its official capacity is attributable to the State.[15] Even if the State does not designate the relevant person or entity as a State organ, it could nevertheless qualify as such due to its factual relationship with the State.[16] De facto State organs

10. *See* Application of the Convention on the Prevention and Punishment of the Crime of Genocide (Bosn. & Herz. v. Serb. & Montenegro), Judgment, 2007 I.C.J. Rep. 43, ¶ 406 (Feb. 26) [hereinafter *Bosnian Genocide*].

11. *See supra* ch. 2, sec. 2.2.

12. ARSIWA, *supra* note 2, arts. 4, 5, 8.

13. *See supra* ch. 2, sec. 2.2.

14. ARSIWA, *supra* note 2, art. 4.

15. *Id. See also supra* ch. 4.

16. *See supra* ch. 4, sec. 4.4.

are those persons or entities that act, in all respects other than their legal status, as an organ of the State.[17]

Article 4 is therefore the most appropriate basis of attribution for those persons or entities that act exclusively for the State. In conflict situations, a State's organs, such as its armed forces and security services, might fight on the State's behalf or otherwise support the State's military operations, such as by collecting intelligence. Persons who qualify as State organs clearly have a private life and perform some conduct in their private capacity.[18] Outside this private realm, however, they act on behalf of the State and all their conduct is attributable to it, based on the rule reflected in Article 4.

If the person or entity concerned does not qualify as either a de jure or de facto State organ, the second potential basis of attribution is the rule reflected in Article 5 ASRIWA.[19] This rule is particularly pertinent when considering the conduct of private military and security companies (PMSC).[20] Its application involves an assessment of whether the State empowered the NSA to exercise public functions on its behalf.[21] If the State authorized the NSA to perform governmental tasks in a manner that accorded with its internal law and the NSA was acting in its public capacity at the time it breached the State's international legal obligations, the relevant violations are attributable to the State.[22]

One key difference between Articles 4 and 5 ARSIWA relates to the consequences of attribution. If attribution based on the rule reflected in Article 4 is appropriate, all the State organ's conduct is attributable to the State, unless it is performed in a private capacity.[23] As noted previously, this makes sense because the person or entity concerned acts exclusively for the State.

In contrast, the conduct to which Article 5 applies may be performed by persons or entities that carry out a range of tasks, in addition to the governmental functions they perform for the State. For example, a PMSC might act for a State when guarding a military base in a conflict zone but also work for a private company in the same locality, protecting its mining business. Thus, when Article 5 applies, it does not attribute all the entity's conduct to the State; it applies only to the governmental tasks the NSA performs on the State's behalf.[24] Accordingly, Article 5 represents a narrower basis of attribution than Article 4.

17. *Id.*

18. *Id.* sec. 4.5.

19. ARSIWA, *supra* note 2, art. 5.

20. *See supra* ch. 2, sec. 2.2.2; ch. 5.

21. ARSIWA, *supra* note 2, art. 5. *See also supra* ch. 5, sec. 5.4.

22. *See supra* ch. 5.

23. *See supra* ch. 4, sec. 4.2.2.

24. *See supra* ch. 5, sec. 5.2.2.

A further difference between the two rules relates to the types of conduct they can attribute to a State. While Article 5 includes a specific requirement for the acts concerned to be governmental in nature, Article 4 does not.[25] Thus, although the majority of functions State organs perform are public in character, the rule reflected in Article 4 can also attribute commercial or other nongovernmental acts to the State.[26]

The rules reflected in Articles 4 and 5 share the common feature of attributing to the State conduct that is *ultra vires*.[27] In other words, if a State organ or an entity empowered to perform governmental functions acts contrary to the State's instructions, or outside the scope of the authority the State has granted, that conduct is still attributable to the State. This principle is reflected in Article 7 ARSIWA.[28] Its purpose is to ensure that when persons or entities violate international law while acting in their official capacity, on behalf of a State, the State cannot avoid responsibility by claiming that the actor concerned was acting *ultra vires*.[29]

To complete the attribution regime, the final rule that may apply when a State exerts some form of influence over the NSA's conduct in potential violation of international law is reflected in Article 8.[30] This is a residual rule, meaning that it only applies if an assessment has first been made that the person or entity concerned is not a State organ for the purposes of Article 4, and it is not empowered to exercise elements of governmental authority within the meaning of Article 5. As such, it should attribute to a State the conduct of persons or entities that do not have a formal relationship with the State but that nevertheless act on its behalf.

The rule reflected in Article 8 is much more specific in its focus than those expressed in Articles 4 and 5.[31] While the latter rules attribute to a State all the conduct performed in the person or entity's public capacity,[32] the NSAs to which Article 8 applies do not normally have such an official role. Thus, rather than focusing on the wider conduct performed on behalf of the State, the rule centers on the specific conduct in violation of international law that was performed under the State's instructions, direction, or control.[33]

This focus on specific violations applies when determining both whether the rule applies and the consequences of attribution. Thus, if the acts that violate

25. ARSIWA, *supra* note 2, arts. 4, 5.

26. *Id.* art. 4, cmt. ¶ 6.

27. *Id.* art. 7.

28. *Id.*

29. *Id.* cmt. ¶¶ 2, 3.

30. ARSIWA, *supra* note 2, art. 8.

31. *See supra* ch. 6, sec. 6.2.2.

32. ARSIWA, *supra* note 2, art. 7. *See also supra* ch. 4, sec. 4.5; ch. 5, sec. 5.5.

33. ARSIWA, *supra* note 2, art. 8, cmt. ¶ 7.

international law were performed under the State's instructions, direction, or control, the rule operates to attribute those acts, and those acts alone, to the State.[34] A separate attribution assessment is required to ascertain whether any other conduct on the part of the NSA is attributable to the State.

One further difference between the rule reflected in Article 8 and those expressed in Articles 4 and 5 is the rule's treatment of *ultra vires* acts. Due to Article 8's narrow focus on the specific acts that violate international law, any conduct that is performed outside the State's authority, or in contravention of its instructions, is not attributable to the State.[35] Also, for the purposes of Article 8 there is no requirement for the conduct to be public in character. The rule encompasses any form of conduct performed on the State's behalf if this violates an international legal obligation that is binding on the State.[36]

Each of the three rules, therefore, has a different focus. Article 4 relates to the conduct of State organs, which act exclusively for the State.[37] Article 5 applies to the conduct of persons or entities that perform governmental functions on the State's behalf, but which might also perform tasks for entities other than the State.[38] Article 8, meanwhile, applies to any form of conduct, performed by any NSA. However, it has a narrower focus than the other rules, attributing to the State only those acts that were performed under the State's instructions, direction, or control.[39]

The rules may overlap, in the sense that more than one rule might apply to the same international law violations. For example, an NSA tasked to perform a mission for a State could be empowered to exercise governmental functions for the purposes of Article 5 and also act under the State's instructions for the purposes of Article 8. In such a situation, however, it is Article 5 that would apply. To determine the issue of attribution, the rules should be considered in order: first Article 4, then Article 5, and finally Article 8. This ensures that all the conduct performed on a State's behalf is attributed to it. Thus, if Article 5 applies, all the entity's public conduct is attributable to the State, including any *ultra vires* acts. Article 8, in contrast, would attribute only those acts to the State that were performed under its instructions, direction, or control.

In summary, therefore, the three rules operate together to ensure that States bear responsibility for all the international law violations committed by their organs and agents. Focusing on the rules themselves, there is no reason in principle why they should not achieve this goal. But it is apparent from the analysis in Chapters 4 to 6 that the three rules do not perform their respective functions

34. *Id. See also supra* ch. 6, sec. 6.2.2.

35. ARSIWA, *supra* note 2, art. 7, cmt. ¶ 9; *id.* art. 8, cmt. ¶ 8.

36. *Id.* art. 8, cmt. ¶ 2.

37. *See supra* ch. 4.

38. *See supra* ch. 5.

39. *See supra* ch. 6.

effectively.[40] Their predominant interpretations allow States to act via NSAs in a manner that they cannot lawfully act via their own organs.

7.2.2 Interpretive Concerns

The underlying basis of attribution for the three rules reflected in Articles 4, 5, and 8 ARSIWA is the proximity of the relationship between the act in potential violation of international law and the State.[41] While in the case of Articles 4 and 5, this relationship is established principally via the State's domestic law,[42] it is the factual relationship between the State and the NSA that is pertinent to the rule reflected in Article 8. Attribution on this basis, as well as de facto State organ status for the purposes of Article 4, is founded upon the existence of a principal–agent relationship, in which the NSA is subordinate to the State and does its bidding.[43]

7.2.2.1 Attribution Based on Law

Attribution pursuant to the rule reflected in Article 4 ARSIWA is determined primarily via the State's own domestic law.[44] If the State's internal law characterizes an entity as a State organ, all the entity's conduct performed in that public capacity is attributable to the State.[45] Domestic law is also critical to attribution under the rule reflected in Article 5. According to the ILC, the conduct of an NSA performing delegated public functions is only attributable to the State if the NSA was "empowered by law" to perform those functions.[46]

There is one key difference in the respective functions of the State's domestic law, however, that is pertinent to the gap in accountability. In the case of Article 4, a State should not be able to avoid responsibility simply by choosing to act via an NSA that it does not designate as one of its organs. If an NSA, in fact, acts as an organ of State, it should qualify as a de facto State organ, meaning that its conduct is attributable to the State even if it is not categorized as such by the State's internal law.[47] But there is no equivalent de facto status within Article 5. Under the rule's prevailing interpretation, if an NSA is not "empowered by law" to act, Article 5 does not attribute its conduct to the State, even if the State clearly authorized the NSA to exercise elements of its governmental

40. *See supra* chs. 4–6.

41. *Id.*

42. *See supra* ch. 4, sec. 4.3; ch. 5, sec. 5.4.

43. *See supra* ch. 4, sec. 4.4; ch. 6.

44. ARSIWA, *supra* note 2, art. 4. *See also supra* ch. 4, sec. 4.3.

45. *See supra* ch. 4, secs. 4.2.2, 4.3.

46. ARSIWA, *supra* note 2, art. 5. *See also supra* ch. 5, sec. 5.4.

47. ARSIWA, *supra* note 2, art. 4, cmt. ¶ 11. *See also supra* ch. 4, sec. 4.4.

authority.[48] Thus, the rule does not attribute the Wagner Group's harmful conduct to Russia, because Russian law did not properly empower the group to perform combat functions on the State's behalf.[49]

To address this deficiency, Chapter 5 proposes a more relaxed interpretation of the "empowerment" element of Article 5.[50] This would consider all relevant facts when assessing whether a State has empowered an NSA to perform governmental functions on its behalf, rather than focusing solely on the position under the State's domestic law. If the rule reflected in Article 5 were interpreted in this manner, it would more effectively hold States like Russia to account when they choose to delegate combat and other public functions to NSAs such as the Wagner Group. It is also more likely that the rule would fulfill its intended function within the wider attribution regime.[51]

7.2.2.2 Attribution Based on Fact

The rule reflected in Article 8 ARSIWA, as well as de facto State organ status for the purposes of Article 4, relies on an assessment of the factual relationship between the State and the NSA.[52] The most important factual circumstance in such an assessment is the State's exercise of control over the NSA's conduct. From an evidential perspective, however, control is often very difficult for an injured State to prove.

Even if evidence of State control is available, this is frequently insufficient to lead to attribution.[53] This is due to the rigidity of the tests the ICJ formulated to determine attribution for the purposes of Articles 4 and 8. These allow little room for nuance or an assessment of all relevant facts and circumstances.[54] Both tests are so focused on the presence or absence of State control that they ignore pertinent aspects of the broader circumstances, including the wider relationship between the State and the NSA.

Considering, first, the rule reflected in Article 4, it is right that de facto State organ status should arise only in exceptional circumstances, given that all the conduct of an entity with that status is attributable to the State. An application of the ICJ's test of complete dependence and control to situations of armed conflict, however, reveals its impracticality.[55] The dual requirements for the NSA to exhibit complete dependence on the State, and for the State to exercise strict control over

48. *See supra* ch. 5, sec. 5.4.

49. *Id.* sec. 5.4.3. *See also* Maddocks, *supra* note 4.

50. *See supra* ch. 5, sec. 5.4.4.

51. *Id.*

52. *See supra* ch. 4, sec. 4.4; ch. 6.

53. *See supra* ch. 4, sec. 4.4.2; ch. 6, sec. 6.4.4.

54. *See supra* ch. 4, sec. 4.4; ch. 6, sec. 6.4.

55. *See supra* ch. 4, sec. 4.4.2.

the NSA's conduct, exclude relationships in which the NSA acts with any degree of autonomy or it obtains funding or other resources from a source other than the State.[56]

The principal issue in the context of Article 8 is the requirement for the State to exercise a high level of control over the specific conduct on the part of an NSA that potentially violates international law.[57] Evidence of this elevated degree of control is lacking in many conflict scenarios.[58] Moreover, the test formulated by the ICJ ignores States' authority over NSAs' conduct at all levels other than the exercise of tactical control over the specific acts that violate international law.[59] It means, for example, that a State's exercise of control over the wider operation in which the NSA's harmful conduct occurs is insufficient to lead to attribution. This is unsatisfactory and acts as an incentive to States to achieve their conflict aims via NSAs, rather than directly via their own organs.

To address these concerns, Chapters 4 and 6 propose more flexible interpretations of the rules reflected in Articles 4 and 8 ARSIWA.[60] These would take into account all the relevant facts and circumstances of the relationship between a State and an NSA when assessing the issue of attribution. If adopted, these more relaxed tests would increase the range of circumstances in which conduct performed on a State's behalf is deemed to be attributable to it. They would help to ensure that the rules expressed in Articles 4 and 8 properly fulfill their respective roles within the broader attribution regime.

7.2.2.3 A More Relaxed Interpretation of All Three Rules

The analysis in Chapters 4 to 6 reveals that a more relaxed interpretation of the rules of attribution reflected in Articles 4, 5, and 8 ARSIWA would assist in narrowing the gap in accountability and allow all three rules to better meet their object and purpose.[61] A loosening of just one threshold, such as the effective control test for the purposes of Article 8, would help to close the accountability gap only in the specific circumstances that that particular rule of attribution is designed to address, namely, when an NSA acts on a State's behalf as its agent.[62] It would not address a situation in which a State delegates public functions to an NSA, when the exercise of control is not relevant to the issue of attribution,[63] or when a person or entity is integrated into a State's apparatus to such an extent that

56. *Id.*

57. *See supra* ch. 6, sec. 6.4.

58. *Id.* sec. 6.4.4.

59. *Id.*

60. *See supra* ch. 4, sec. 4.4.3; ch. 6, sec. 6.4.7.

61. *See supra* ch. 4, sec. 4.4.3, ch. 5, sec. 5.4.4; ch. 6, sec. 6.4.7.

62. ARSIWA, *supra* note 2, art. 8. *See also supra* ch. 6.

63. ARSIWA, *supra* note 2, art. 5. *See also supra* ch. 5.

all its official conduct should be attributed to the State.[64] Although their respective spheres of application overlap, the rules reflected in Articles 4, 5, and 8 serve different functions. Therefore, they each need to operate effectively in light of the realities of States' contemporary interactions with NSAs.

It is questionable, however, whether a looser interpretation of the rules reflected in Articles 4, 5, and 8 would hold States effectively to account. Attribution should occur only when the conduct concerned can properly be classified as an act of State. If the State plays a lesser role in the harmful conduct at issue, attribution is unlikely to be appropriate, even with a more flexible interpretation of the relevant rules. Consider, for instance, Iran's varied relationships with NSAs across the Middle East.[65] Reporting indicates that many of these groups operate with such a degree of autonomy that attribution of their conduct to Iran is not appropriate.[66] Yet, Iran nevertheless provides substantial support to these NSAs, which contributes significantly to their ability to commit violent acts in contravention of international law.

A more relaxed interpretation of the rules reflected in Article 4, 5, and 8 ARSIWA, therefore, would not close the accountability gap entirely. States would still be able to provide support to NSAs, such as intelligence, funding, arms and ammunition, without bearing responsibility for their contributions to the harms that may result. The following section explores the parameters of this lacuna and outlines why international law, including the attribution regime reflected in ARSIWA, allows it to persist.

7.2.3 The Remaining Gap in Accountability

The attribution regime reflected in ARSIWA cannot address States' involvement in all categories of private conduct. Armed conflicts involve a wide variety of actors, which act with varying degrees of State support.[67] When an NSA's acts can properly be characterized as the State's own conduct, one of the rules of attribution

64. ARSIWA, *supra* note 2, art. 4. *See also supra* ch. 4, sec. 4.4.

65. Int'l Inst. of Strategic Stud., Iran's Networks of Influence in the Middle East (Nov. 2019), https://www.iiss.org/publications/strategic-dossiers/iran-dossier/iran-19-02-introduction; Ariane M. Tabatabai et al., RAND, The Iran Threat Network: Four Models of Iran's Nonstate Client Partnerships 19 (2021), www.rand.org/pubs/research_reports/RR4231.html; Diane M. Zorri et al., Joint Special Operations University Report 20–5, Iranian Proxy Groups in Iraq, Syria, and Yemen: A Principal-Agent Comparative Analysis 4–5 (Dec. 2020), https://apps.dtic.mil/sti/pdfs/AD1146327.pdf.

66. *See, e.g.*, Erin Banco, *U.S. Intelligence Officials Estimate Tehran Does Not Have Full Control of Its Proxy Groups*, Politico (Feb. 1, 2024), https://www.politico.com/news/2024/02/01/iran-proxies-intel-houthis-00139099.

67. *See supra* ch. 2, sec. 2.2.

reflected in ARSIWA should apply. But in other situations, the State's involvement in the NSA's harmful acts might be more limited.

When a State facilitates an NSA's conduct in potential violation of international law, it does not necessarily follow that the NSA is acting on the State's behalf. The NSA might continue to act on its own account, with a high degree of autonomy. The conduct of the Houthis in Yemen, which act with the support of Iran, provides a pertinent example.[68] In situations such as this, attribution is unlikely to be appropriate. The NSA is not acting on the State's behalf but rather in pursuance of its own interests. Thus, an accountability gap would persist, even with a more effective attribution regime. This is due to several factors, including the public–private divide that the law of State responsibility creates.

7.2.3.1 The Public–Private Divide

As discussed in Chapter 3, the law of State responsibility is based upon a clear separation between the individual and the State. Conduct is either public in character, in which case it is attributable to a State and can constitute an internationally wrongful act, or it is private and cannot lead to State responsibility.[69] A clear delineation between the public and private domains is, however, a fiction.[70] If a bright line can be drawn at all between public and private activity, it varies from State to State.[71]

In authoritarian regimes such as China and Iran, for instance, the divide between public and private conduct is often indistinct, with considerable State involvement in ostensibly private activity.[72] Even in liberal democracies, the distinction between the public and private sectors is increasingly blurred due to the prevalence of outsourcing and the involvement of private companies in activities that implicate the public functions of the state.[73] And in States embroiled in

68. Michael Knights, *The Houthi War Machine: From Guerrilla War to State Capture*, CTC Sentinel (Sept. 2018), https://ctc.usma.edu/houthi-war-machine-guerrilla-war-state-capture/.

69. ARSIWA, *supra* note 2, art. 2.

70. *See generally* Robert H. Mnookin, *The Public/Private Dichotomy: Political Disagreement and Academic Repudiation*, 130 U. Pa. L. Rev. 1429 (1982); Christine Chinkin, *A Critique of the Public/Private Dimension*, 10 Eur. J. Int'l L. 387 (1999); Gurpreet Mahajan, *Reconsidering the Private-Public Distinction*, 12 Critical Rev. Int'l Soc. & Pol. Phil. 133 (2009); Constantijn van Aartsen, *The End of the Public-Private Divide*, Maastricht U. (Sept. 14, 2016), www.maastrichtuniversity.nl/blog/2016/09/end-public-private-divide.

71. Special Rapporteur Crawford acknowledged this during the ILC's work on State responsibility. *See* James Crawford (Special Rapporteur), First Rep. on State Responsibility 33–34, ¶ 154, U.N. Doc. A/CN.4/490 and Add.1–7 (1998), https://legal.un.org/ilc/documentation/english/a_cn4_490.pdf. *See also* Chinkin *supra* note 70, at 390; Becker *supra* note 5, at 273–74.

72. *See, e.g.*, Xingzhong Yu, *State Legalism and the Public/Private Divide in Chinese Legal Development*, 15 Theoretical Inquiries in L. 27 (2014); Mahrangiz Kar, *The Invasion of the Private Sphere in Iran*, 70 Soc. Res. 829 (2003). *See also* Mnookin, *supra* note 70, at 1440.

73. Becker, *supra* note 5, at 273–74; Kristen E. Eichensehr, *Public-Private Cybersecurity*, 95 Tex. L. Rev. 467, 475 (2017).

conflict, it may often be difficult to distinguish State actors from irregular or non-State groups operating within the same territory.[74]

Chapter 5 examines this issue in the context of Article 5 ARSIWA and the identification of functions that constitute an exercise of elements of governmental authority.[75] Despite the seemingly straightforward guidance in the ARSIWA commentary that these encompass "functions of a public character normally exercised by State organs,"[76] the chapter highlights the inherent difficulty in categorizing conduct as either public or private.[77] This is particularly apparent in contemporary armed conflict, where NSAs exert increasing levels of power and autonomy and, in some instances, act in a State-like manner through their control over territory.[78]

When an NSA acts with the benefit of State support, the NSA's conduct falls at the intersection of the public–private divide. It is not entirely private in nature, in view of the State assistance that enables its commission, but neither is it entirely public, given the private character of the actor concerned. During armed conflict, activities involving elements of both the public and the private abound. These range from the indiscriminate attacks perpetrated by the Houthis in Yemen using weapons supplied by Iran[79] to harmful cyber operations conducted by private hackers with the benefit of State support.[80]

In some of these scenarios, attribution will be appropriate because the NSA is acting for the State. In other situations, when the State's involvement in the relevant conduct is more limited, it would be inaccurate to classify the acts at issue as those of the State. A review of armed conflicts in recent decades reveals the wide variation in States' relationships with NSAs.[81] It can no longer be assumed that States are the only dominant actors on the world stage and that any NSAs with which they interact are necessarily subordinate to the State and do its bidding.

7.2.3.2 The Autonomy of Non-State Actors Engaged in Conflict

NSAs engaged in conflict frequently act with considerable sophistication and independence and their associations with States may be more akin to partnerships, in which the State and NSA pursue mutually beneficial goals, rather than hierarchical affiliations. States' connections with NSAs are wide-ranging and include

74. *See, e.g.*, Tim Eaton, *The Libyan Arab Armed Forces: A Hybrid Armed Actor?* War on the Rocks, (Jan. 27, 2021), https://warontherocks.com/2021/01/the-libyan-arab-armed-forces-a-hybrid-armed-actor/.

75. *See supra* ch. 5, sec. 5.3.

76. ARSIWA, *supra* note 2, art. 5, cmt. ¶ 2.

77. *See supra* ch. 5, sec. 5.3.

78. *See supra* ch. 2, sec. 2.2.

79. Knights, *supra* note 68.

80. *See generally* Tim Maurer, Cyber Mercenaries: The State, Hackers, and Power (2018).

81. *See supra* ch. 2, sec. 2.2.4.

alliances whereby the State provides material support to an NSA without also instructing or controlling its activities.[82] Thus, a high degree of State influence or control is often lacking from States' contemporary relationships with NSAs.

Conduct performed by a person or entity that does not qualify as a State organ for the purposes of Article 4 ARSIWA[83] should be attributed to a State only when the NSA is acting for the State, as its agent, at the relevant time.[84] But frequently, NSAs act with too much autonomy to be considered mere agents of a State. It is common for States to develop horizontal relationships with NSAs, whereby they assist them to act against a common enemy without also exercising a controlling influence over the NSA's activities.[85]

Hezbollah provides a stark example. The group participated in the Syrian conflict at Iran's instigation, commanding Shi'a militia groups and devising the battlefield tactics for military campaigns such as the assault on Aleppo.[86] Iran's relationship with Hezbollah demonstrates States' capacity to participate indirectly in armed conflict through powerful, autonomous entities, while bearing little risk of responsibility when those NSAs violate international law.[87] Tehran has replicated this model across the Middle East, from the Badr Brigades in Iraq to militia groups in Bahrain.[88] Although few of these NSAs exhibit equivalent levels of autonomy to Hezbollah, many act with a degree of independence that precludes the attribution of their conduct to Iran.[89]

Other NSAs, such as the Kurdish-led administration linked to the Syrian Democratic Forces (SDF), act in a State-like manner through their exercise of authority over territory and local populations.[90] NSAs' exercise of territorial control, however, is frequently contingent on external State support. When U.S. forces withdrew from some of their bases in Syria following the Turkish

82. *See supra* ch. 2, sec. 2.2.

83. ARSIWA, *supra* note 2. art. 4. For analysis of this rule of attribution, *see supra* ch. 4.

84. ARSIWA, *supra* note 2, art. 2, cmt. ¶ 5; *id.* general cmt. to ch. II, ¶ 2.

85. Int'l Inst. of Strategic Stud., *supra* note 65; Tabatabai et al., *supra* note 65.

86. Marisa Sullivan, Inst. for the Study of War, Hezbollah in Syria 4 (Apr. 2014), http://www.understandingwar.org/sites/default/files/Hezbollah_Sullivan_FINAL.pdf; Maria Abi-Habib, *Syria's Civil War Produces a Clear Winner: Hezbollah*, Wall St. J. (Apr. 3, 2017), www.wsj.com/articles/syrias-civil-war-produces-a-clear-winner-hezbollah-1491173790.

87. *See supra* ch. 4, sec. 4.4; ch. 5, sec. 5.4; ch. 6, sec. 6.4.4.

88. Borzou Daragahi, *Badr Brigade: Among the Most Consequential Outcomes of the Iran-Iraq War*, Atlantic Council (Aug. 16, 2018), www.atlanticcouncil.org/blogs/iransource/badr-brigade-among-most-consequential-outcomes-of-the-iran-iraq-war-2/; Norman Roule, *What a New Terrorist Designation Says About Iranian Action in Bahrain*, Just Sec. (Sept. 21, 2018), www.justsecurity.org/60818/terrorist-designation-iranian-action-bahrain/. *See also* Tabatabai et al., *supra* note 65.

89. *See supra* ch. 6, sec. 6.4.

90. *See supra* ch. 2, sec. 2.4.1.3.

incursion in October 2019, the administration linked to the SDF had little choice but to respond by ceding control over a proportion of its territory.[91] The Donetsk and Luhansk People's Republics in eastern Ukraine similarly relied for their continued survival on significant assistance from neighboring Russia.[92] Moscow installed the administrations' leadership, ran their military and financial affairs, and represented the region in conflict-resolution negotiations.[93]

Yet, despite the key role States play in bolstering de facto administrations, States are rarely held to account when those NSAs violate international law. For instance, the U.S. involvement in the SDF's mistreatment of ISIS detainees in northeast Syria[94] was likely too weak to lead to attribution; the SDF acted with U.S. assistance but not under U.S. authority or control. The same is true of other potential international law violations involving the SDF, such as its practice of recruiting children for military service.[95]

ARSIWA does not address the myriad ways in which States facilitate NSAs' harmful conduct without also exercising control over their behavior. In its early deliberations regarding "indirect" forms of responsibility, the ILC discounted States' complicity in the conduct of NSAs as a potential foundation of responsibility on the basis that "those persons cannot be regarded as separate subjects of international law."[96] While all States have international legal personality, which bestows a public character on their conduct, States bear responsibility for private

91. Int'l Crisis Group, *Steadying the New Status Quo in Syria's North East* (Nov. 27, 2019), www.crisisgroup.org/middle-east-north-africa/eastern-mediterranean/syria/b72-steadying-new-status-quo-syrias-north-east.

92. *See supra* ch. 2, sec. 2.4.2.

93. Thomas de Waal, Carnegie Europe, Uncertain Ground: Engaging with Europe's de facto States and Breakaway Territories 61, 64 (Dec. 3, 2018), https://carnegieeurope.eu/2018/12/03/uncertain-ground-engaging-with-europe-s-de-facto-states-and-breakaway-territories-pub-77823.

94. *See, e.g.*, Amnesty Int'l, Syria: Aftermath: Injustice, Torture and Death in Detention in North-East Syria (Apr. 17, 2024), https://www.amnesty.org/en/documents/mde24/7752/2024/en/.

95. *See, e.g.*, Rep. of the Indep. Int'l Comm'n of Inquiry on the Syrian Arab Republic 10, ¶ 42, U.N. Doc. A/HRC/37/72 (Feb. 1, 2018).

96. Int'l Law Comm'n, Documents of the Twenty-Seventh Session Including the Rep. of the Comm'n to the General Assembly (draft art. 11, cmt. ¶ 11) (1975), *in* [1975] 2 Y.B. Int'l L. Comm'n 73, U.N. Doc. A/CN.4/SER.A/1975/Add.1 73. *See also* Roberto Ago (Special Rapporteur), Fourth Rep. on State Responsibility, by Mr. Roberto Ago, Special Rapporteur—The Internationally Wrongful Act of the State, Source of International Responsibility (1972) *in* [1972] 2 Y.B. Int'l L. Comm'n 100, ¶ 72, U.N. Doc. A/CN.4/SER.A/1972/Add.1 (Part One); Roberto Ago (Special Rapporteur), Eighth Rep. on State Responsibility—the Internationally Wrongful Act of the State, Source of International Responsibility 4–5, ¶ 3, U.N. Doc. A/CN.4/318 and Add.1–4 (1979).

conduct only if the person or entity that performed the relevant acts is so closely linked to the State that attribution is appropriate, thereby elevating the conduct to the public domain.[97] In the absence of attribution, the conduct remains private and cannot amount to an internationally wrongful act.[98]

This reality is unsatisfactory. States' relationships with NSAs during armed conflict demonstrate their ability to achieve their conflict aims via proxy in a manner that they could not lawfully act via their own organs. To ensure respect for the international legal order, international law should hold States to account not only through the process of attribution, when an NSA acts on their behalf, but also when States knowingly facilitate legal violations by NSAs. The following section considers, in brief, potential developments in the law that could enhance States' accountability in this respect.

7.3 ADDRESSING THE GAP IN ACCOUNTABILITY

Through the support they provide to NSAs engaged in conflict, States often enable undisciplined individuals and groups, which lack the training and military command structures of the State's own armed forces, to cause great harm.[99] As discussed in the preceding analysis, a mechanism is therefore required, outside the attribution regime, to hold States to account when they knowingly facilitate acts by an NSA that violate international law.

7.3.1 A Non-State Actor Equivalent to Article 16 ARSIWA

One possible way to address the gap in accountability is to extend the scope of the assistance provisions within the law of State responsibility to encompass States' support to NSAs.[100] This legal development finds some support in the jurisprudence of the ICJ; the Court indicated in the *Bosnian Genocide* case that the rule reflected in Article 16 ARSIWA may apply by analogy when States provide aid or assistance to an NSA.[101]

97. Derek Jinks, *State Responsibility for the Acts of Private Armed Groups*, 4 CHI. J. INT'L L. 83, 90 (2003).

98. ARSIWA, *supra* note 2, art. 2.

99. *See supra* ch. 2, sec. 2.3.

100. For more detailed discussion of this possibility, *see* Jennifer Maddocks, *State Responsibility for International Law Violations Involving Non-State Actors in Armed Conflict* (Ph.D. dissertation, University of Reading) ch. 8 (Nov. 2021), https://centaur.reading.ac.uk/107450/1/28834464_MADDOCKS_Thesis.pdf [hereinafter Maddocks Dissertation].

101. *Bosnian Genocide*, *supra* note 10, ¶¶ 419–20.

Article 16 prohibits States from providing aid or assistance toward the commission of any internationally wrongful act on the part of the recipient State. The article provides:

> A State which aids or assists another State in the commission of an internationally wrongful act by the latter is internationally responsible for doing so if:
> (a) that State does so with knowledge of the circumstances of the internationally wrongful act; and
> (b) the act would be internationally wrongful if committed by that State.[102]

In its commentary, the ILC affirms that "the assisting State will only be responsible to the extent that its own conduct has caused or contributed to the internationally wrongful act."[103] Thus, the assisting State is not responsible for the principal wrong committed by the beneficiary State but rather for its own act of assistance, which constitutes an independent internationally wrongful act.[104]

The law of State responsibility could build upon the foundations the ICJ laid in the *Bosnian Genocide* case to include an NSA equivalent to Article 16. This could take the form of an interpretive extension of the customary norm that underlies Article 16, so that the rule applies equally to States' assistance to NSAs. Alternatively, it could constitute a new rule of international law, separate from the norm reflected in Article 16.

If agreed by States, either development would be a positive step forward in holding States to account for their complicity in NSAs' harmful conduct. However, applying the norm to States' assistance to NSAs is not straightforward. Responsibility under Article 16 is derivative in nature, in that it arises from the principal internationally wrongful act that the State's assistance facilitates. When the assisted conduct is private in character there is no primary wrong for the State to be complicit in.[105]

7.3.1.1 The Derivative Character of Article 16

A State's responsibility under the rule expressed in Article 16 derives from its assistance to another State in the commission of an internationally wrongful act. To

102. ARSIWA, *supra* note 2, art. 16.

103. *Id.* cmt. ¶ 1.

104. *Id.* cmt. ¶¶ 1, 9. *See also* Int'l Law Comm'n, Rep. of the Comm'n to the General Assembly on the Work of its Thirtieth Session (draft art. 27, cmt. ¶ 16) (1978), *in* [1978] 2 Y.B. Int'l L. Comm'n 103–4, U.N. Doc. A/CN.4/SER.A/1978/Add.1 (Part 2); Bernhard Graefrath, *Complicity in the Law of International Responsibility*, 29 Revue Belge de Droit Int'l 370, 371 (1996); Crawford, *supra* note 3, at 399; Lanovoy, *supra* note 5, at 4–5 (2016).

105. ARSIWA, *supra* note 2, art. 16, cmt. ¶ 11. *See also* Olivier de Frouville, *Attribution of Conduct to the State: Private Individuals*, *in* The Law of International Responsibility 257, 276 (James Crawford et al. eds., 2010); Miles Jackson, Complicity in International Law 5, 176 (2015).

illustrate, consider the detention of ISIS fighters by the SDF in northeast Syria.[106] If this conduct is attributable to the United States due to U.S. officials' exercise of effective control over the SDF's detention activities[107] and it violates the State's IHL obligations, it constitutes an internationally wrongful act.[108] Other members of the anti-ISIS coalition could then bear responsibility for their contributions toward such abuses under the rule reflected in Article 16.[109] But if, as is more likely, those abuses are not attributable to the United States or to any other State, there is no internationally wrongful act for the members of the coalition to assist. Therefore, unless their support for the SDF violates a primary norm that is binding on the assisting States,[110] their international responsibility is not engaged.

The same is true even if the NSA concerned violates an international legal obligation that binds the group itself. Organized armed groups are directly bound by IHL under common Article 3[111] and Additional Protocol II[112] to the Geneva Conventions. Legal scholars additionally argue that certain NSAs are subject to international human rights law (IHRL) obligations.[113] But even if the same norm of international law binds a State and an NSA, difficulties arise when seeking to hold the State accountable for complicity in its breach. This is because ARSIWA's foundational articles specifically link an internationally wrongful act to a State, meaning that when referring to an NSA's

106. *See, e.g.*, Human Rights Watch, Northeast Syria: Boys, Men Held in Inhumane Conditions (Oct. 8, 2019), www.hrw.org/news/2019/10/08/northeast-syria-boys-men-held-inhumane-conditions; Amnesty Int'l, *supra* note 94.

107. ARSIWA, *supra* note 2, art. 8. *See also supra* ch. 6, sec. 6.4.

108. ARSIWA, *supra* note 2, art. 2.

109. *See, e.g.*, Katie Bo Williams, *Coalition Plans to Expand Giant ISIS Prison in Syria*, Def. One (Feb. 24, 2021), www.defenseone.com/policy/2021/02/coalition-plans-expand-giant-isis-prison-syria/172270/.

110. For example, the State might violate the prohibition on the use of force or the principle of intervention. For further discussion of primary norms and their role in holding States to account when they act through NSAs, *see infra* sec. 7.3.2.

111. Convention (I) for the Amelioration of the Condition of the Wounded and Sick in the Armed Forces in the Field art. 3, Aug. 12, 1949, 6 U.S.T. 3114, 75 U.N.T.S. 31 [hereinafter GC I]. *See also* Int'l Committee of the Red Cross (ICRC), Commentary on the First Geneva Convention: Convention (I) for the Amelioration of the Condition of the Wounded and Sick in the Armed Forces in the Field art. 3, ¶¶ 505–8 (2016) [hereinafter 2016 Cmt. to GC I].

112. Protocol Additional to the Geneva Conventions of 12 August 1949, and relating to the Protection of Victims of Non-International Armed Conflicts (Protocol II), June 8, 1977, 1125 U.N.T.S. 609.

113. *See, e.g.*, Andrew Clapham, *Human Rights Obligations of Non-State Actors in Conflict Situations*, 88 Int'l Rev. Red Cross 491 (2006); Katharine Fortin, The Accountability of Armed Groups under Human Rights Law (2017).

conduct, there is no internationally wrongful act for a State to be complicit in.[114]

Of course, the law of international responsibility could develop to recognize armed groups' legal violations as internationally wrongful acts. But even if it did, the impact in narrowing the gap in accountability might not be significant. These violations represent only a fraction of the wrongs perpetrated by NSAs during armed conflict. States assist a wide variety of NSAs to act in a manner that potentially violates IHL, including in scenarios when the relevant IHL obligation does not directly bind the NSA concerned.[115]

For example, a State might train a group of individuals who are not party to the armed conflict to perform acts of sabotage against a common adversary. If those acts constitute attacks[116] and they are conducted in an indiscriminate manner, the NSA's conduct might breach the assisting State's IHL obligations.[117] But if the NSA is not a party to the conflict, it is not bound directly by IHL; therefore, there is no primary breach of international law that the State can be complicit in. The position would only be different if the individual members of the group violate international criminal law, and the law develops to recognize those violations as internationally wrongful acts that a State can be complicit in.[118]

Even regarding armed opposition groups, which are directly bound by IHL, ambiguity can prevail as to whether IHL applies to their conduct. It might not be clear, for instance, whether the intensity threshold for a non-international armed conflict (NIAC) has been reached,[119] particularly as governments often prefer to portray internal hostilities as a fight against criminals or terrorists.[120] Alternatively, the NSA in receipt of the State's assistance might be insufficiently organized to become a party to a NIAC. In this situation, although the individual members of the

114. ARSIWA, *supra* note 2, arts. 1, 2.

115. *See* Jean d'Aspremont et al., *Sharing Responsibility Between Non-State Actors and States in International Law: Introduction*, 62 Netherlands Int'l L. Rev. 49, 53 (2015).

116. *See* Protocol Additional to the Geneva Conventions of 12 August 1949, and Relating to the Protection of Victims of International Armed Conflicts, art. 49(1), June 8, 1977, 1125 U.N.T.S. 3.

117. *See* 1 Customary International Humanitarian Law rr. 11, 12 (Jean-Marie Henckaerts & Louise Doswald-Beck eds., 2005).

118. The ICJ seemed to indicate this might be possible when addressing the Federal Republic of Yugoslavia's potential complicity in the crime of genocide. *See Bosnian Genocide*, *supra* note 10, ¶¶ 171–74, 419–21.

119. *See* Prosecutor v. Tadić, Case No. IT-94-1-AR-72, Decision on the Defence Motion for Interlocutory Appeal on Jurisdiction, ¶ 70, (Int'l Crim. Trib. for the former Yugoslavia Oct. 2, 1995). *See also* Sandesh Sivakumaran, The Law of Non-International Armed Conflict 155–211 (2012); 2016 Cmt. to GC I, *supra* note 111, art. 3, ¶¶ 422–37.

120. The Ukrainian government, for example, referred to the deployment of its forces to the east of the country in 2014 as an "anti-terror" operation. *See, e.g.*, *Ukraine Says Donetsk "Anti-Terror Operation" Under Way*, BBC News (Apr. 16, 2014), www.bbc.com/news/world-europe-27035196.

NSA might be bound by international criminal law, the group itself would bear no obligations under IHL.[121]

A more effective rule, therefore, would be one that does not rely on the commission of an underlying international law violation by the NSA but holds States to account for their facilitation of conduct in breach of their own international legal obligations. Such a rule would better meet the object and purpose of the law of State responsibility and mean that a State truly "cannot do by another what it cannot do by itself."[122] The ICJ's judgment in *Bosnian Genocide* provides some support for this approach, given that the Court referred to Article 16 by analogy in the context of a State's potential complicity in the international crime of genocide, committed by an NSA's members, rather than the breach of an obligation that was binding on the NSA itself.[123]

This, however, would require a broadening of ARSIWA's foundational articles to allow for States to bear international responsibility for their complicity in conduct that does not constitute an internationally wrongful act.[124] While this would be a positive development in the law, questions nevertheless arise regarding Article 16's effectiveness as a model to hold States to account when they facilitate harmful conduct by NSAs. This is due to the constituent elements of Article 16, which regulate its scope of application.

7.3.1.2 The Objective and Subjective Elements of Article 16

The objective element of Article 16 relates to the assistance a State provides to the recipient and the nexus between that assistance and any subsequent wrongful conduct. While the rule applies to all forms of State assistance, some ambiguity remains regarding the nexus requirement. The commentary provides first that the assistance must be "clearly linked to the subsequent wrongful conduct" and contribute "significantly" to it.[125] Later, however, it states that "the assistance may have been only an incidental factor in the commission of the primary act, and may have contributed only to a minor degree, if at all, to the injury suffered."[126] This inconsistency is unhelpful. In practice, it means that the links between the State's support and the subsequent harmful conduct remain a question of fact, to be assessed on a case-by-case basis.

There is a similar lack of clarity in the wording of Article 16 and its commentary regarding the subjective element of the norm, namely, the requisite knowledge

121. 2016 Cmt. to GC I, *supra* note 111, art. 3, ¶¶ 429–30.

122. ARSIWA, *supra* note 2, art. 16, cmt. ¶ 6.

123. *Bosnian Genocide*, *supra* note 10, ¶¶ 171–74, 419–21.

124. Special Rapporteur Ago suggested this in the early stages of the ILC's deliberations. *See* Roberto Ago (Special Rapporteur), Second Rep. on State Responsibility—the Origin of International Responsibility 186–87, ¶ 29, U.N. Doc. A/CN.4/233 (1970).

125. ARSIWA, *supra* note 2, art. 16, cmt. ¶ 5.

126. *Id.* ¶ 10.

or intent on the part of the assisting State.[127] While Article 16 itself stipulates a requirement only for "knowledge of the circumstances of the internationally wrongful act,"[128] the commentary states that "the aid or assistance must be given with a view to facilitating the commission of that act . . . "[129] thereby indicating an additional requirement for intent.

This requirement for intent clearly limits Article 16's scope of application.[130] As former Special Rapporteur Crawford opined regarding States' obligations in respect of Israeli settlements in the occupied Palestinian territories, "it is not sufficient that the US supplies Israel with bulldozers which are subsequently utilized in the unlawful destruction of private property during construction of the Wall – the US must know and intend that those bulldozers are to be used in such a way."[131]

It is unclear precisely how this intent requirement would apply to an NSA-analogue to Article 16. For example, must the assisting State know and intend that its aid will facilitate an armed group's breach of its own IHL obligations, such as those arising under common Article 3 to the Geneva Conventions?[132] Or should the State's intent relate to conduct on the part of the NSA that would violate the State's international legal obligations, if the acts were attributable to it? In either case, a literal interpretation of the intent requirement would place a heavy burden on an injured State wishing to invoke the assisting State's responsibility. States' motivations for assisting NSAs are wide-ranging and typically relate primarily to the advancement of their own interests rather than a desire to cause harm.[133]

127. *See generally* Georg Nolte & Helmut Aust, *Equivocal Helpers—Complicit States, Mixed Messages and International Law*, 58 Int'l & Comp. L.Q. 1, 13–15 (2009); Christian Dominicé, *Attribution of Conduct to Multiple States and the Implication of a State in the Act of Another State*, *in* The Law of International Responsibility 281, 286 (James Crawford et al. eds., 2010); Helmut Philipp Aust, Complicity and the Law of State Responsibility 230–49 (2011); Crawford, *supra* note 3, at 405–8; Jackson, *supra* note 105, at 159–62; Lanovoy, *supra* note 5, at 99–101, 218–40; Harriet Moynihan, *Aiding and Assisting: The Mental Element under Article 16 of the International Law Commission's Articles on State Responsibility*, 67 Int'l & Comp. L.Q. 455 (2018); Marko Milanović, *Intelligence Sharing in Multinational Military Operations and Complicity under International Law*, 97 Int'l L. Stud. 1269 (2021).

128. ARSIWA, *supra* note 2, art. 16(a). *See also id.* cmt. ¶ 4.

129. *Id.* cmt. ¶ 3. *See also id.* cmt. ¶ 5.

130. Graefrath, *supra* note 104, at 375.

131. James Crawford, Opinion: Third Party Obligations with respect to Israeli Settlements in the Occupied Palestinian Territories ¶ 77 (Jan. 24, 2012), www.tuc.org.uk/sites/default/files/tucfiles/LegalOpinionIsraeliSettlements.pdf.

132. GC I, *supra* note 111, art. 3.

133. *See* Mark Gibney et al., *Transnational State Responsibility for Violations of Human Rights* 12 Harv. Hum. Rts. J. 267, 294 (1999); Alexandra Boivin, *Complicity and Beyond: International Law and the Transfer of Small Arms and Light Weapons*, 87 Int'l Rev. Red Cross 467, 471–72 (2005); Lanovoy, *supra* note 5, at 101–2. *See also* ICRC, Allies, Partners and Proxies: Managing Support Relationships in Armed Conflict to Reduce the Human Cost of War 23

It may be possible, however, to view the intent requirement more leniently. A State's intent could be inferred from its wider conduct if State officials clearly know of the risk of abuses but nevertheless provide the relevant assistance.[134] Inferences of a State's intent could be drawn from a range of factors, including the existence of shared goals between the State and the NSA, indications of knowledge on the part of State officials, or the previous conduct of the NSA concerned.[135] This would clearly broaden the circumstances in which an NSA-equivalent to Article 16 would apply.

Even with this looser interpretation of Article 16's subjective element, however, an NSA analogue to the rule would not fully regulate States' assistance to NSAs engaged in conflict. For example, States might choose to assist an NSA without inquiring into the NSA's prior conduct. In such cases, the State would not have knowledge of the NSA's previous acts in potential violation of international law, meaning that it is not possible to infer an intent to facilitate any subsequent harms. A more effective rule, therefore, would require States to undertake some form of prior investigation or risk assessment before they provide an NSA with aid, and to take feasible steps to mitigate the risks of harm. This type of rule would place positive obligations on States and is therefore not appropriate within the law of State responsibility.[136] A positive duty of this type is better imposed via primary norms of international law.

7.3.2 The Role of Primary Norms

Primary rules of international law can play an important role in holding States to account for their support to NSAs engaged in conflict. In contrast with the secondary law of State responsibility, these norms regulate State behavior and impose obligations upon them.[137] If private conduct is not attributable to a State, the State's act of assistance to an NSA might nevertheless violate a primary norm that is binding upon it. Relevant primary norms include the prohibition on the use of force and States' obligations under IHRL.[138]

(Mar. 2021), www.icrc.org/en/publication/4498-allies-partners-and-proxies-managing-support-relationships-armed-conflict-reduce.

134. *See, e.g.*, Crawford, *supra* note 3, at 408; Jackson, *supra* note 105, at 159–60; Lanovoy, *supra* note 5, at 228; Moynihan, *supra* note 127, at 467–70; Milanović, *supra* note 127, at 1308–16.

135. Lanovoy, *supra* note 5, at 238–39; Boivin, *supra* note 133, at 471.

136. This is because of the secondary character of the law of State responsibility, which does not place obligations on States. *See supra* ch. 3, sec. 3.2.

137. *See id.*

138. For further discussion regarding the role of relevant primary norms in holding States to account for their assistance to NSAs, *see* Maddocks Dissertation, *supra* note 104, ch. 6.

To illustrate, consider Iran's support to Hamas in connection with the group's attacks on Israel on October 7, 2023.[139] While it is unlikely that Iran's involvement in these attacks was sufficient to lead to attribution, Iran might nevertheless have violated the prohibition on the use of force through its provision of arms and other assistance to Hamas.[140] This norm prohibits not only a State's direct use of force, for example, via its own armed forces, but also its participation in forcible acts committed by NSAs.[141] In the latter situation, it is the State's own organs' conduct in assisting the NSA that amounts to a use of force that is attributable to the State based on the rule reflected in Article 4 ARSIWA.[142]

If Iran's support to Hamas violated the prohibition on the use of force, it constitutes an internationally wrongful act[143] involving legal consequences.[144] These include an obligation on Iran to make reparation in respect of any injury caused and Israel's right to take countermeasures.[145] Iran's violation of a primary norm thus gives rise to an autonomous claim of responsibility, which is independent from any claim arising directly from the Hamas attacks.

When assessing the attribution regime reflected in ARSIWA and its effectiveness in holding States to account, it is important to keep in mind the role of primary norms. In its jurisprudence, the ICJ has demonstrated a greater willingness to find that States violated primary norms of international law through their support to NSAs than to attribute private conduct to a State.[146] Thus, in the *Nicaragua* and *Bosnian Genocide* cases, the ICJ concluded that although attribution was not appropriate, the respective States had violated primary norms such as the prohibition on the use of force, the principle of non-intervention, and the duty to prevent acts of genocide.[147]

There are many primary norms that States might breach when they assist NSAs engaged in conflict. The aim here is not to enumerate them or to assess their respective roles in holding States to account for their assistance to NSAs. Rather, the purpose is to highlight not only the importance of primary norms in narrowing

139. *See* Jennifer Maddocks, *Iran's Responsibility for the Attack on Israel*, ARTICLES OF WAR (Oct. 20, 2023), https://lieber.westpoint.edu/irans-responsibility-attack-israel/.

140. *Id.*

141. Military and Paramilitary Activities in and Against Nicaragua (Nicar. v. U.S.), Judgment, 1986 I.C.J. Rep. 14, ¶¶ 205, 228 (June 27) [hereinafter *Nicaragua*].

142. ARSIWA, *supra* note 2, art. 4.

143. *Id.* art. 2.

144. *Id.* arts. 28–31.

145. ARSIWA, *supra* note 2, arts. 28–39.

146. *See Nicaragua*, *supra* note 141, ¶¶ 220, 227–28, 248–50, 255; *Bosnian Genocide*, *supra* note 10, ¶ 438.

147. *Nicaragua*, *supra* note 141, ¶¶ 220, 227–28, 248–50, 255; *Bosnian Genocide*, *supra* note 10, ¶ 438.

the gap in accountability but also their limitations, as well as ways they could develop to better hold States to account. Each primary norm has its own scope of application, meaning that its relevance to any instance of State support to an NSA depends on the particular facts and circumstances.

Consider, for example, Iran's support for Shi'a militia groups operating in Syria.[148] Iran provided these NSAs with significant assistance including training, funding, and military equipment.[149] This support likely facilitated the NSAs' conduct in potential violation of IHL, such as indiscriminate attacks.[150] However, Iran did not violate the prohibition on the use of force or the principle of non-intervention through its provision of aid to these NSAs because they fought in Syria alongside the Assad regime with governmental consent; this precludes the wrongfulness of Iran's conduct.[151] It may also be difficult to prove that Iran violated any other norms of international law. For instance, neither the due diligence principle nor IHRL may be engaged due to Iran's lack of territorial control over the areas of Syria in which the militias operated.[152] In the absence of attribution under the law of State responsibility, therefore, States that suffer injury through international law violations involving such groups may be left with little international legal remedy.

One primary norm that could fill this gap in accountability is the duty to respect and ensure respect for IHL, enshrined in common Article 1 to the Geneva Conventions.[153] For legal scholars who support the broad interpretation of the norm promoted by the International Committee of the Red Cross (ICRC),[154] common Article 1 "provides a source of state responsibility for the actions of [NSAs] that cures many of the deficiencies of [the] state attribution doctrine viewed on its own."[155] According to this expansive reading of the norm, the

148. *See supra* ch. 2, sec. 2.4.1.2.

149. *See, e.g.*, Michael Knights, *Iran's Foreign Legion: The Role of Iraqi Shiite Militias in Syria*, WASH. INST. (June 27, 2013) www.washingtoninstitute.org/policy-analysis/irans-foreign-legion-role-iraqi-shiite-militias-syria.

150. *See, e.g.*, Rep. of the Indep. Int'l Comm'n of Inquiry on the Syrian Arab Republic 7–11, ¶¶ 25–50, U.N. Doc. A/HRC/34/64 (Feb. 2, 2017).

151. ARSIWA, *supra* note 2, art. 20.

152. *See, e.g.*, Riccardo Pisillo-Mazzeschi, *The Due Diligence Rule and the Nature of the International Responsibility of States*, 35 GERMAN Y.B. INT'L L. 9 (1992); MARKO MILANOVIĆ, EXTRATERRITORIAL APPLICATION OF HUMAN RIGHTS TREATIES: LAW, PRINCIPLES, AND POLICY (2011). Both norms may, however, be implicated in respect of Iran's provision of training and other support to Shi'a militia groups from its own territory.

153. GC I, *supra* note 111, art. 1. For discussion regarding the development of common Article 1 to address this concern, *see* Kilian Roithmaier, *Holding States Responsible for Violations of International Humanitarian Law in Proxy Warfare: The Concept of State Complicity in Acts of Non-State Armed Groups*, 14 EUR. J. LEGAL STUD. 140 (2023).

154. *See* 2016 Cmt. to GC I, *supra* note 111, ¶¶ 118–91.

155. Hathaway et al., *supra* note 5, at 565.

provision imposes both negative and positive obligations on States to ensure that other actors engaged in conflict respect IHL, even if the former have no involvement in the hostilities.[156]

Many States and legal scholars, however, do not agree with this wide interpretation of the norm.[157] They highlight the norm's drafting history and subsequent State practice, which does not support the ICRC's assertion that all States are bound by an obligation to bring other States and NSAs into compliance with IHL. In addition, they maintain that common Article 1 does not apply to NIACs. Yet, in the specific context of States' support to NSAs engaged in conflict, there are strong arguments in favor of the norm's application.

Notwithstanding the continued debate regarding common Article 1's application, the ICJ ruled in the *Nicaragua* case that the parallel provisions of customary international law impose obligations on States not to encourage NSAs engaged in a NIAC to act in violation of common Article 3.[158] Ambiguity remains, however, regarding the types of State behavior that amount to "encouragement" for the purposes of the customary norm. It is unclear, for example, whether a State's continued provision of arms or funding to an NSA following the latter's alleged IHL violations could constitute encouragement for these purposes, particularly given the ICJ's failure to condemn U.S. material support to the *contras* on this basis.[159] But there is a compelling humanitarian logic for extending the ICJ's ruling to encompass States' material aid to NSAs. It makes little sense to prohibit States' encouragement of violations but not the material forms of aid and assistance that facilitate their commission.[160]

156. 2016 Cmt. to GC I, *supra* note 111, ¶¶ 164–73.

157. *See, e.g.*, Brian Egan, Keynote Address to the American Society of International Law (Apr. 2016), www.lawfareblog.com/state-department-legal-adviser-brian-egans-speech-asil; John Reid, *Ensuring Respect: The Role of State Practice in Interpreting the Geneva Conventions*, Int'l Law Ass'n Reporter (Nov. 9, 2016) https://ilareporter.org.au/2016/11/ensuring-respect-the-role-of-state-practice-in-interpreting-the-geneva-conventions-john-reid/; Paul Ney, *Remarks by Defense Dept. General Counsel Paul C. Ney Jr. on the Law of War*, Just Sec. (May 28, 2019), www.justsecurity.org/64313/remarks-by-defense-dept-general-counsel-paul-c-ney-jr-on-the-law-of-war/; Michael N. Schmitt & Sean Watts, *Common Article 1 and the Duty to "Ensure Respect,"* 96 Int'l L. Stud. 674 (2021).

158. *Nicaragua*, *supra* note 141, ¶¶ 220, 255.

159. In this context, the ICJ focused on U.S. violation of the prohibition on the use of force and the principle of non-intervention. *See Nicaragua*, *supra* note 141, ¶¶ 220, 227–28, 248–50, 255 *See also* Olivier Corten & Vaios Koutroulis, *The Illegality of Military Support to Rebels in the Libyan War: Aspects of the jus contra bellum and jus in bello*, 18 J. Conflict & Sec. L. 59, 84–87 (2013); Tom Ruys, *Of Arms, Funding and "Non-Lethal Assistance" – Issues Surrounding Third-State Intervention in the Syrian Civil War*, 13 Chinese J. Int'l L. 13, 26–31 (2014).

160. *See* Marko Milanović, *Common Article 1 Does Prohibit Complicity in IHL Violations, Through Arms Transfers or Otherwise*, EJIL:Talk! (Apr. 15, 2024), https://www.ejiltalk.org/common-article-1-does-prohibit-complicity-in-ihl-violations-through-arms-transfers-or-otherwise/.

When State officials assist an NSA, they gain an enhanced ability to influence its conduct. These relationships of influence are key to enhancing NSAs' compliance with international law.[161] If a State develops or sustains a relationship with an NSA engaged in conflict, thus furthering its own interests in the hostilities, the State's obligation to respect and ensure respect for IHL should clearly extend not only to its own armed forces, its population, and to other individuals or groups acting on its behalf, but also to any NSAs it supports and leverages to achieve its own conflict-related objectives. If it is internationally wrongful for States to encourage IHL violations on the part of an NSA, it must be similarly unlawful for them to provide material or other assistance to an NSA that facilitates such violations.[162]

While this interpretation of common Article 1 may not have been contemplated by the parties to the Geneva Conventions at the time these were agreed, negative obligations of this nature follow naturally from the ICJ's judgment in the *Nicaragua* case and are necessary to ensure the norm's effective operation. Moreover, in cases where such a support relationship exists, giving rise to an ability on the part of the State to influence the NSA's behavior, it is arguable that common Article 1 or its customary equivalent imposes positive as well as negative obligations on the supporting State.

The scope of States' positive duties under common Article 1 is particularly contentious. The ICRC and some scholars take an expansive view of such obligations[163] while certain States and other commentators deny that the norm imposes any positive duties on States to ensure external actors' compliance with IHL.[164] Drawing upon the ICJ's judgment in *Bosnian Genocide*, however, there is a sensible middle group between these opposing positions. While the ICRC's assertion that States are subject to a duty to ensure the IHL compliance of all conflict parties is overly broad and somewhat unrealistic,[165] the same is not true if the duty is restricted to situations where a relationship of influence exists.

To follow the ICJ's judgment in *Bosnian Genocide*, a State's "capacity to influence effectively" is key to the imposition of such positive obligations.[166] Thus, the extent of the duty might differ according to the strength of the State's relationship with the NSA. When a State has particularly strong links to an NSA, the steps it is expected to take might be greater than if its capacity to influence the

161. The ICJ recognized the importance of such relationships in the *Bosnian Genocide* case. *See Bosnian Genocide*, *supra* note 10, ¶ 434.

162. For discussion of this proposed interpretation of common article 1 in the context of States' support to SDF detentions in Syria, *see* Jennifer Maddocks, *ISIS Detentions in Syria and the Responsibility of Supporting States*, Articles of War (Aug. 16, 2024), https://lieber.westpoint.edu/isis-detentions-syria-responsibility-supporting-states/.

163. *See, e.g.*, 2016 Cmt. to GC I, *supra* note 111, art. 3, ¶¶ 164–73; Hathaway et al., *supra* note 5.

164. *See, e.g.*, Egan, *supra* note 157; Reid, *supra* note 157; Schmitt & Watts, *supra* note 157.

165. 2016 Cmt. to GC I, *supra* note 111, ¶ 153.

166. *Bosnian Genocide*, *supra* note 10, ¶ 430.

NSA's conduct is relatively weak. Other factors of relevance include the severity of the IHL violation and the means available to the State. These elements, together with the State's ability to influence the NSA's conduct, impact the steps a State can feasibly take to ensure the recipient of its assistance uses the aid provided in a manner that respects IHL.

This proposed interpretation of common Article 1 would heighten States' accountability in respect to their assistance to NSAs. If adopted by States, this could ultimately lead to its acceptance as the agreed construction of the norm. This would represent a clear step forward in the quest to hold States properly to account when they facilitate harms by NSAs. Moreover, it would enhance States' ability to call out other States like Iran that make extensive use of proxies, which frequently act with complete disregard for IHL.

7.4 CONCLUSION

International law has not kept pace with States' persistent use of proxies or the evolving nature of the NSAs themselves. In armed conflict, NSAs proliferate, and their conduct frequently straddles the public–private divide upon which the law of State responsibility is founded.[167] This is due, in part, to the fact that modern-day associations between states and NSAs do not fit neatly within the hierarchical model envisaged by the law of State responsibility reflected in ARSIWA. The rules of attribution are difficult to apply, and their strict interpretation means that they are of little practical relevance in holding States to account for the often-significant role they play in the harmful conduct perpetrated by NSAs.[168]

A more relaxed interpretation of the attribution standards reflected in Articles 4, 5, and 8 ARSIWA would undoubtedly assist in addressing this concern.[169] A move away from the stringent, inflexible rules formulated by the ICJ and the ILC would allow the full circumstances to be considered when assessing the issue of attribution and thereby hold States more effectively to account. But even with these changes, an accountability gap would remain.

Under the law of State responsibility, as interpreted by the ILC, a State may facilitate an NSA's conduct in breach of the State's international legal obligations without engaging its international responsibility.[170] Even if a State's support is critical to an NSA's conduct in potential violation of international law, ARSIWA includes no mechanism through which a State can be held to account for its own contribution to that wrong. This situation is unsatisfactory and can engender irresponsible State behavior and a lack of respect for the international legal order.

167. *See supra* sec. 7.2.3.

168. *See supra* chs. 4–6.

169. *See supra* ch. 4, sec. 4.4.3, ch. 5, sec. 5.4.4; ch. 6, sec. 6.4.7.

170. *See supra* sec. 7.2.3.

To operate effectively, international law should hold States to account when they knowingly facilitate harmful conduct by NSAs.

That aim could be achieved, in part, through extending the current complicity provisions in Article 16 ARSIWA to encompass States' assistance to NSAs.[171] While the ICJ's judgment in the *Bosnian Genocide* case provides a clear foundation for this development,[172] difficulties arise in conceptualizing how the provisions would operate in the absence of an internationally wrongful act from which responsibility can derive.[173] Moreover, it is evident that primary norms rather than the secondary rules of State responsibility are better suited to regulate States' assistance to NSAs in situations of conflict. It is only primary norms that can impose positive obligations on States, such as a duty to conduct risk assessments regarding the harms that a State's assistance could cause. Primary norms must therefore develop in tandem with the secondary law of State responsibility to properly hold States to account for the assistance they provide to NSAs engaged in conflict.[174]

One primary norm that is of particular relevance to States' support to NSAs engaged in conflict is common Article 1 to the Geneva Conventions.[175] When States build relationships of influence with NSAs engaged in conflict, whereby they assist those groups and develop the capacity to guide their behavior, there are compelling humanitarian reasons to interpret the norm as prohibiting States from facilitating IHL breaches on the part of those NSAs. This interpretation is both logical and necessary to ensure the effective operation of the duty to respect and ensure respect for IHL. When States choose to achieve their national security goals through the intermediary of an NSA, they should additionally be subject to a positive obligation to take feasible steps to ensure the recipient of that support uses the assistance provided in compliance with IHL. Interpreted in this manner, common Article 1 would play an important role in narrowing the gap in accountability.

171. *See supra* sec. 7.3.1.

172. *Bosnian Genocide*, *supra* note 10, ¶¶ 171–74, 419–21.

173. *See supra* sec. 7.3.1.1.

174. *See supra* sec. 7.3.2.

175. GC I, *supra* note 111, art. 1.

PART FOUR

Exceptional Rules of Attribution

8

Conduct Performed in the Absence or Default of the Official Authorities

8.1 INTRODUCTION

The chapters in Part Three of this book examined the attribution of private conduct to a State based upon that State's factual or legal relationship with the non-State actor (NSA) concerned. The Draft Articles on Responsibility of States for Internationally Wrongful Acts (ARSIWA) also envision attribution in other circumstances, when there might be no links whatsoever between the relevant State and the NSA at the time the latter acts in potential violation of international law. These exceptional rules of attribution have weaker foundations in customary international law and are invoked less frequently by States, international courts and tribunals, and humanitarian bodies.

One such rule relates to situations in which States cede control over parts of their territory or lose the ability to fulfill all the governmental functions that they would normally perform. In extreme cases, States might fail or collapse due to internal violence, leaving them unable to provide public services to their citizens.[1] Alternatively, a State's loss of authority might be less complete. This scenario can arise if armed opposition groups usurp the State's authority over certain regions, as occurred in Syria from 2011.[2] There can also be a vacuum of authority when States compete to control territory, as during Russia's 2022 invasion of Ukraine.[3]

1. Robert Rotberg, *Failed States, Collapsed States, and Weak States: Causes and Indicators*, Wilson Ctr. (July 7, 2011), www.wilsoncenter.org/publication/failed-states-collapsed-states-and-weak-states-causes-and-indicators.

2. For discussion of the conflict in Syria, *see supra* ch. 2, sec. 2.4.1.

3. For discussion of the conflict in Ukraine, *see supra* ch. 2, sec. 2.4.2.

Attribution of Non-State Actor Conduct During Armed Conflict. Jennifer Maddocks, Oxford University Press.
 DOI: 10.1093/oso/9780197842652.003.0008

Or an incident such as a malicious cyberattack might cause the State to lose the ability to fulfill one or more specific public functions.[4]

When a governance vacuum emerges, NSAs sometimes step in to perform public tasks that State officials can no longer fulfil. Following Russia's full-scale invasion of Ukraine, for example, local citizens grouped together to fight the enemy and to maintain law and order in areas where the Ukrainian authorities had ceded control.[5] It is possible that when performing tasks such as these, the NSAs concerned could violate one or more of the territorial State's international legal obligations. Local citizens enforcing law and order, for instance, might mistreat detainees in their custody, in breach of the State's duties under international humanitarian law (IHL).[6] The rule reflected in Article 9 ARSIWA addresses the potential attribution of such conduct to the territorial State.

Article 9 provides:

The conduct of a person or group of persons shall be considered an act of a State under international law if the person or group of persons is in fact exercising elements of the governmental authority in the absence or default of the official authorities and in circumstances such as to call for the exercise of those elements of authority.[7]

The rule's text and commentary make clear that three conditions must be satisfied for Article 9 to apply. First, the activities concerned must "effectively relate to the exercise of elements of the governmental authority."[8] Second, the conduct must "have been carried out in the absence or default of the official authorities."[9] And third, "the circumstances must have been such as to call for the exercise of those elements of authority."[10] The principal goal

4. An example is the situation in Estonia in 2007. *See* Eneken Tikk et al., International Cyber Incidents: Legal Considerations 14–34 (2010), https://ccdcoe.org/uploads/2018/10/legalconsiderations_0.pdf.

5. *See, e.g.*, Sam Mednick, *Russia-Ukraine: The Civilians Fighting on Kyiv's Front Lines*, Al Jazeera (Mar. 23, 2022), www.aljazeera.com/features/2022/3/23/the-civilian-fighters-taking-up-arms-on-ukraines-front-lines; Jeffrey Gettleman, *He Returned a Dazed Soldier to the Russians. Ukraine Calls It Treason*, N.Y. Times (Dec. 3, 2022), https://www.nytimes.com/2022/12/03/world/europe/ukraine-kherson-treason.html [hereinafter Gettleman, *Dazed Soldier*].

6. *See, e.g.*, Convention (III) Relative to the Treatment of Prisoners of War arts. 3, 13, Aug. 12, 1949, 6 U.S.T. 3316, 75 U.N.T.S. 135 [hereinafter GC III]; 1 Customary International Humanitarian Law r. 87 (Jean-Marie Henckaerts & Louise Doswald-Beck eds., 2005) [hereinafter Customary IHL].

7. Draft Articles on Responsibility of States for Internationally Wrongful Acts, with commentaries, art. 9, *in* Int'l Law Comm'n, Rep. on the Work of its Fifty-Third Session, U.N. Doc. A/56/10 (2001), *reprinted in* [2001] 2 Y.B. Int'l L. Comm'n 31, 49, U.N. Doc. A/CN.4/SER.A/2001/Add.1 (Part 2) [hereinafter ARSIWA].

8. *Id.* cmt. ¶ 3.

9. *Id.*

10. *Id.*

of this chapter is to add clarity regarding the meaning of all three of these requirements.[11]

First, however, the chapter addresses the historical background to Article 9.[12] It is evident from a review of the drafting history and relevant jurisprudence that the customary status of the rule is far from certain. Nevertheless, for the purposes of analysis, the chapter proceeds on the basis that Article 9 reflects a rule of customary international law. Even if that is the case, however, the rule remains "truly exceptional" in character[13] and applies only in very narrow circumstances. It is, therefore, of limited import when seeking to hold States to account for the harmful conduct of NSAs.

8.2 ATTRIBUTION PURSUANT TO ARTICLE 9

8.2.1 Drafting History

The principle now reflected in Article 9 ARSIWA has relatively recent origins. It did not appear in the preparatory work for the 1930 Hague Conference for the Codification of International Law, or the 1929 or 1961 Harvard Draft Conventions on State responsibility.[14] Instead, Special Rapporteur Roberto Ago first raised this as a potential basis of attribution in 1971, observing that private persons might assume governmental functions to ensure the continuation of essential services in the absence of the regular administrative authorities.[15] In World War II, for example, "private persons provisionally took charge of public affairs, issued

11. *See infra* secs. 8.3–8.5.

12. *See infra* sec. 8.2.

13. James Crawford, State Responsibility: The General Part 167 (2013). *See also* ARSIWA, *supra* note 7, art. 9, cmt. ¶ 1.

14. Bases of Discussion Drawn up in 1929 by the Preparatory Committee of the Conference for the Codification of International Law (The Hague, 1930), *reprinted in* Int'l Law Comm'n, Documents of the Eighth Session Including the Rep. of the Comm'n to the General Assembly (1956), *in* [1956] 2 Y.B. Int'l L. Comm'n 223, U.N. Doc, A/CN.4/SER.A/1956/Add.1; Harvard Draft Convention on Responsibility of States for Damage Done in Their Territory to the Person or Property of Foreigners (1929), *reprinted in* Int'l Law Comm'n, Documents of the Eighth Session Including the Rep. of the Comm'n to the General Assembly (1956), *in* [1956] 2 Y.B. Int'l L. Comm'n 229, U.N. Doc, A/CN.4/SER.A/1956/Add.1; Harvard Draft Convention on the International Responsibility of States for Injuries to Aliens (1961), *reprinted in* Int'l Law Comm'n, Documents of the Twenty-First Session Including the Rep. of the Comm'n to the General Assembly (1969), in [1969] 2 Y.B. Int'l L. Comm'n 142, 145-146, U.N. Doc A/CN.4/SER.A/1969/Add.1.

15. Roberto Ago (Special Rapporteur), Third Rep. on State Responsibility—the Internationally Wrongful Act of the State, Source of International Responsibility, U.N. Doc A/CN.4/246 and Add.1–3 (1971), *in* [1971] 2 Y.B. Int'l L. Comm'n 199, 262–64, U.N. Doc. A/CN.4/SER.A/1971/Add.1 (Part 1) [hereinafter Ago's Third Rep. on State Responsibility].

ordinances, performed legal acts, administered property, pronounced judgments, etc." after the local administrations disappeared.[16] Ago additionally referred to military functions performed by NSAs in the absence of the State's armed forces, "when the civilian population of a threatened city takes up arms and organizes its defense" as a *levée en masse*.[17]

In circumstances such as these, Ago considered that "[t]he State, as a subject of international law, should . . . bear responsibility for the acts of these various classes of person where they relate to one of the functions, tasks or missions mentioned above and have resulted in a breach of an international obligation of the State."[18] In Ago's view, the critical factor when assessing the issue of attribution is "the public character of the function or mission . . . rather than the formal link between the State organization and the person whose conduct is in question."[19] This focus is evident in the draft article that Ago formulated to express the principle.[20]

In its subsequent review of Ago's draft article, the International Law Commission (ILC) Drafting Committee clarified the circumstances in which the rule now reflected in Article 9 would apply. Rather than referring solely to the public character of the tasks, the amended draft article made clear that attribution is appropriate only if such functions are performed in the absence of the official authorities, in circumstances justifying the exercise of those elements of governmental authority.[21]

In essence, the rule aimed to capture situations in which individuals perform public functions of their own initiative to maintain the provision of services that are essential to the community.[22] As one ILC member put it in 1974, "The functions in question were functions which should normally have been performed by the State, but which the State had failed to perform. An individual then found himself performing them as a matter of necessity—rightly or wrongly."[23]

When Special Rapporteur Crawford reviewed the draft article in 1998, he noted the rule's exceptional character and the ILC's intent that this should apply only when the regular authorities cannot operate, for example, due to a situation of

16. *Id. See also* Int'l Law Comm'n, Rep. of the Comm'n to the General Assembly, draft art. 8, cmt. ¶ 10 (1974), *in* [1974] 2 Y.B. INT'L L. COMM'N 157, 285, U.N. Doc. A/CN.4/SER.A/1974/Add.1 (Part One) [hereinafter ILC Y.B. 1974 vol. II].

17. *Id. See also* Int'l Law Comm'n, Summary Records of the Twenty-Sixth Session (1974), *in* 1 Y.B. INT'L L. COMM'N 32, ¶ 5, U.N. Doc. A/CN.4/SER.A/1974 [hereinafter ILC Y.B. 1974 vol. I].

18. Ago's Third Rep. on State Responsibility, *supra* note 15, at 264, ¶ 191.

19. *Id.*

20. *Id.* at 267 (draft art. 8).

21. ILC Y.B. 1974 vol. I, *supra* note 17, at 152–53; ILC Y.B. 1974 vol. II, *supra* note 16, at 283.

22. ILC Y.B. 1974 vol. II, *supra* note 16, at 285 (draft art. 8, cmt. ¶ 9). *See also* ARSIWA, *supra* note 7, art. 9, cmt. ¶ 2.

23. ILC Y.B. 1974 vol. I, *supra* note 17, at 35, ¶ 30 (comments of Mr. Hambro).

revolution or armed conflict.[24] Regarding its grounding in customary international law, Crawford noted that there is "some authority in favour of the principle" but referred in its support only to "the old idea of the *levée en masse*" in IHL, together with the decision of the Iran–U.S. Claims Tribunal in the *Yeager* case.[25] This case concerned Iran's responsibility for the actions of the Revolutionary Guards during the 1979 Iranian revolution and is discussed in section 7.2.2.

Moving to address the draft article's wording, Crawford expressed concern that its formulation implied that harmful conduct leading to State responsibility could nevertheless be "justified."[26] He observed, "[I]f the conduct was wrongful it cannot have been 'justified.'"[27] In other words, the fact that there is a necessity to act does not automatically render the actions taken to meet that requirement either justified or lawful.[28] Crawford recommended that the draft article should be amended to make clear that "some exercise of governmental functions was called for, but not necessarily the conduct in question."[29]

The version of Article 9 adopted in 2001 reflects this recommendation. The only other substantive change made was to widen the circumstances in which the rule applies, to encompass not only situations of total State collapse but also cases where the official authorities are not exercising their functions, such as when there is a partial breakdown of the State.[30] To address this concern, the final text of Article 9 stipulates that the rule applies "in the absence *or default* of the official authorities," rather than solely in situations when State organs are entirely absent.[31]

24. James Crawford (Special Rapporteur), First Rep. on State Responsibility 43, ¶ 214, U.N. Doc. A/CN.4/490 and Add.1–7 (1998), https://legal.un.org/ilc/documentation/english/a_cn4_490.pdf [hereinafter Crawford's First Rep. on State Responsibility]. *See also* ARSIWA, *supra* note 7, art. 9, cmt. ¶ 1.

25. Crawford's First Rep. on State Responsibility, *supra* note 24, at 43–44, ¶ 216. For discussion of the *Yeager* case, *see infra* sec. 8.2.2.1.

26. Crawford's First Rep. on State Responsibility, *supra* note 24, at 44, ¶ 217.

27. *Id.* at 44, ¶ 217. *See also* Int'l Law Comm'n, Summary Records of the Fiftieth Session (1998), *in* [1998] 1 Y.B. Int'l L. Comm'n 230, ¶ 9, U.N. Doc. A/CN.4/SER.A/1998 [hereinafter ILC Y.B. 1998 vol. I]; Int'l Law Comm'n, Summary Records of the Fifty-Third Session (2001), *in* [2001] 1 Y.B. Int'l L. Comm'n 93-94, ¶ 30, U.N. Doc. A/CN.4/SER.A/2001 [hereinafter ILC Y.B. 2001 vol. I].

28. Olivier de Frouville, *Attribution of Conduct to the State: Private Individuals*, *in* The Law of International Responsibility 257, 272 (James Crawford et al. eds., 2010).

29. Crawford's First Rep. on State Responsibility, *supra* note 24, at 44, ¶ 218. *See also* ILC Y.B. 1998 vol. I, *supra* note 27, at 290, ¶ 82; ARSIWA, *supra* note 7, art. 9, cmt. ¶ 6; Crawford, *supra* note 13, at 169–70.

30. ILC Y.B. 1998 vol. I, *supra* note 27, at 289, ¶ 80.

31. ARSIWA, *supra* note 7, art. 9 (emphasis added). For discussion regarding this requirement, *see infra* sec. 8.4.

Given the ILC's acknowledgment that the rule expressed in Article 9 is "exceptional" in character,[32] it is perhaps unsurprising that this basis of attribution generated little attention from States. Prior to ARSIWA's adoption, Crawford reviewed the governmental comments received, noting that only Canada had reserved its position regarding the draft article on the ground that a more restrictive formulation might be desirable.[33] No other States had commented.[34]

The exceptional character of the rule may additionally explain why the ILC included so few examples of State practice or international jurisprudence within Article 9's commentary. When viewed alongside the commentaries relating to the other rules of attribution within ARSIWA, the ILC's commentary to Article 9 is notable both for its brevity and for the very limited international practice cited in its support.[35]

8.2.2 Guidance Provided by International Courts and Tribunals

During the ILC's discussions regarding the rule later enshrined in Article 9 ARSIWA, Special Rapporteur Ago expressed the view that there was "no doubt" that acts committed in the circumstances envisaged by the rule engaged the State's responsibility.[36] However, he did not cite any decisions of international courts or tribunals to justify this assertion[37] and the ILC acknowledged the scarcity of relevant international practice.[38]

Since ARSIWA's adoption in 2001, there has been little, if any, State practice or judicial consideration of the rule.[39] This absence of relevant international practice raises considerable doubts as to the rule's status in customary international law. It is noteworthy that the commentary to Article 9 refers to just one case in which an international tribunal mentioned the rule as a basis of attribution.[40] This

32. ARSIWA, *supra* note 7, art. 9, cmt. ¶ 1.

33. Crawford's First Rep. on State Responsibility, *supra* note 24, at 43, ¶ 215.

34. *Id.*

35. The commentary to Article 9 includes only six paragraphs and is thus considerably shorter than the commentaries to most other rules of attribution. *See* ARSIWA, *supra* note 7, cmt. to arts. 4–5, 8–11.

36. *See, e.g.*, ILC Y.B. 1974 vol. I, *supra* note 17, at 32, ¶ 4 (comments of Mr. Ago).

37. *Id.*; Ago's Third Rep. on State Responsibility, *supra* note 15, at 263–64, ¶¶ 189, 191.

38. ILC Y.B. 1974 vol. II, *supra* note 16, at 285 (draft art. 8, cmt. ¶ 11).

39. CRAWFORD, *supra* note 13, at 168; SIMON OLLESON, BRIT. INST. INT'L & COMP. L., THE IMPACT OF THE ILC'S ARTICLES ON RESPONSIBILITY OF STATES FOR INTERNATIONALLY WRONGFUL ACTS 94 (Oct. 10, 2007), www.biicl.org/files/3107_impactofthearticlesonstate_responsibilitypreliminarydraftfinal.pdf.

40. ARSIWA, *supra* note 7, art. 9, cmt. ¶ 2.

is the *Yeager* case, decided by the Iran–U.S. Claims Tribunal, relating to events during the 1979 Iranian Revolution.[41] However, as the following analysis reveals, the tribunal's decision includes a degree of ambiguity that considerably weakens its authority as support for the principle now expressed in Article 9.

8.2.2.1 The *Yeager* Case

Mr. Yeager was an American citizen who worked for a U.S. company in Iran until February 1979.[42] He departed due to the arrival of armed Revolutionary Guards at his apartment, who ultimately forced him to leave the country.[43] The Guards performed "immigration, customs and similar functions at Tehran airport"[44] and seized money from Yeager and his wife.[45] Yeager sought compensation for his wrongful expulsion from Iran, claiming that the actions of the Revolutionary Guards were attributable to the Iranian State.[46]

In its response to the claim, Iran admitted that Revolutionary Guards were engaged in the maintenance of law and order from January 1979, "as government police forces rapidly lost control over the situation."[47] However, Iran asserted that anti-American activity was not attributable to the State, partly on the basis that numerous revolutionary groups operated outside of the government's control at the time.[48]

The Iran–U.S. Claims Tribunal noted the inherent difficulty in identifying the individuals involved in Mr. Yeager's expulsion given the "revolutionary turmoil" within the country and the ongoing power struggles among different groups.[49] Nonetheless, it observed that many of Ayatollah Khomeini's supporters were organized into local revolutionary committees, or "Komitehs," which served as "local security forces in the immediate aftermath of the revolution."[50] Such groups reportedly "made arrests, confiscated property, and took people to prisons."[51] The tribunal concluded that the individuals involved in Yeager's expulsion belonged to this group.[52]

41. Kenneth P. Yeager v. Islamic Republic of Iran, Award No. 324-10199-1 (Iran-U.S. Claims Trib., 1987) [hereinafter *Yeager*].

42. *Yeager*, *supra* note 41, ¶¶ 12–14.

43. *Id.*

44. ARSIWA, *supra* note 7, art. 9, cmt. ¶ 2; *Yeager*, *supra* note 41, ¶¶ 13–14, 61.

45. *Yeager*, *supra* note 41, ¶ 14.

46. *Id.* ¶¶ 17, 33.

47. *Id.* ¶ 23.

48. *Id.* ¶¶ 22–23. Iran also resisted the claim on a number of other grounds. *See id.* ¶¶ 19–23.

49. *Id.* ¶ 38.

50. *Id.* ¶ 39.

51. *Id.*

52. *Id.* ¶ 41.

Addressing the issue of attribution, the tribunal referred to the ILC's ongoing work on State responsibility and in particular, draft article 8.[53] At that time, the draft article encompassed two separate attribution standards: the rule now reflected in Article 9 ARSIWA and the principle enshrined in Article 8.[54] The tribunal concluded that there was

> sufficient evidence in the record to establish a presumption that revolutionary "Komitehs" or "Guards" after 11 February 1979 were acting in fact on behalf of the new government, or at least exercised elements of governmental authority in the absence of official authorities, in operations of which the new Government must have had knowledge and to which it did not specifically object. Under those circumstances, and for the kind of measures involved here, the Respondent has the burden of coming forward with evidence showing that members of "Komitehs" or "Guards" were in fact not acting on its behalf, or were not exercising elements of government authority, or that it could not control them.[55]

The above passage reveals several possible grounds for attributing the Revolutionary Guards' conduct to Iran. First, the tribunal noted that the Guards were acting "in fact on behalf of the new government," indicating the potential attribution of their conduct to the State based on the rule now reflected in Article 8 ARSIWA. Second, the Guards' conduct was alternatively attributable to Iran on the grounds that they performed public functions in the absence of the official authorities, as envisaged by Article 9.[56] Third, the tribunal pointed to the fact that the new government must have known about the Guards' conduct and did not object to it, thereby suggesting a further potential basis of attribution, not reflected in ARSIWA.

The tribunal treated these factors as a basis on which to shift the burden of proof. As Iran failed to satisfy that burden by providing evidence that the Guards were not acting on behalf of the government, they did not exercise elements of governmental authority, or the Iranian government could not control them, the tribunal concluded that their conduct was attributable to the State.[57] Given this reasoning, the ARSIWA commentary is not entirely accurate in its assertion that the judgment in the *Yeager* case treated the Revolutionary Guards "as covered by the principle expressed in article 9."[58] The tribunal certainly mentioned the rule

53. *Id.* ¶ 42.

54. ILC Y.B. 1974 vol. II, *supra* note 16, at 283 (draft art. 8). *See supra* ch. 6 for further discussion regarding Article 8 ARSIWA.

55. *Yeager*, *supra* note 41, ¶ 43 (citations omitted).

56. *See* de Frouville, *supra* note 28, at 273; Jörn Griebel, Die Zurechnungskategorie der de-facto Organe im Recht der Staatenverantwortlichkeit 111 (2004).

57. *Yeager*, *supra* note 41, ¶¶ 44–45.

58. ARSIWA, *supra* note 7, art. 9, cmt. ¶ 2. Some commentators similarly interpret the judgment in *Yeager* as an example of Article 9's application. *See, e.g.*, Jann Arno Hessbruegge, *The Historical Development of the Doctrines of Attribution and Due Diligence in International Law*, 36 N.Y.U. J. Int'l L. & Pol. 265, 274 (2004); Danwood M. Chirwa, *The Doctrine of State*

now reflected in Article 9, but did so alongside other grounds of attribution and did not clearly attribute the Guards' conduct to Iran on this basis.[59]

Furthermore, the tribunal's conclusions do not align with the three conditions relevant to Article 9's application.[60] The first criterion is satisfied: The Revolutionary Guards were engaged in maintaining law and order; therefore, they were clearly performing governmental functions.[61] However, the same is not true regarding the second and third elements. The tribunal's finding that Iran had not "established that it could not control the revolutionary 'Komitehs' or 'Guards' in this operation"[62] suggests that the official authorities were present at the relevant time and could have asserted their authority.[63] Accordingly, they were not absent or in default.[64] The tribunal failed to even consider the third condition, namely, whether the Guards' conduct was "called for" in the circumstances.[65] Thus, although the *Yeager* case is illustrative of the types of revolutionary circumstances that Article 9 ARSIWA is designed to address, the decision fails to clearly apply this rule of attribution to the Revolutionary Guards' conduct.

8.2.2.2 Decisions of the 1923 General Claims Commission

The *Yeager* case involved the conduct of NSAs whose interests aligned with those of the Iranian State. However, Article 9 and its commentary do not specifically limit the rule's application to this category of private acts. This chapter examines later whether the rule could apply to the conduct of rebels who act against the interests of the State's de jure government.[66] A line of cases decided by the General

Responsibility as a Potential Means of Holding Private Actors Accountable for Human Rights, 5 Melbourne J. Int'l L. 1, 8 (2004).

59. For further discussion regarding the tribunal's judgment, *see* Gregory Townsend, *State Responsibility for Acts of De Facto Agents*, 14 Ariz. J. Int'l & Comp. L. 635, 650 (1997); de Frouville, *supra* note 28, at 273; David D. Caron, *The Basis of Responsibility: Attribution and Other Trans-Substantive Rules of State Responsibility*, *in* The Iran-United States Claims Tribunal: Its Contribution to the Law of State Responsibility 110, 141–43 (Richard B. Lillich & Daniel B. Magraw eds., 1998); Claus Kress, *L'Organe de facto en Droit International Public: Réflexions sur l'Imputation a l'État de l'Acte d'un Particulier à la Lumière des Développements Récents*, 105 Revue Générale de Droit International Public 93 (2001).

60. ARSIWA, *supra* note 7, art. 9, cmt. ¶ 3.

61. *See infra* sec. 8.3.2.

62. *Yeager*, *supra* note 41, ¶ 45. *See also id.* ¶ 61.

63. Kress, *supra* note 59, at 111 n. 74. *See also* Caron, *supra* note 59, at 142–43.

64. *See infra* sec. 8.4.

65. Kress, *supra* note 59, at 111 n. 74. Special Rapporteur Crawford noted that in the *Yeager* case, the tribunal did not use the actual formulation of the draft article put forward by the ILC and suggested that this may be due to the use of the word "justified" within the draft article. *See* Crawford's First Rep. on State Responsibility, *supra* note 24, at 44, ¶ 217. For further discussion regarding the "called for" element of the rule, *see infra* sec. 8.5.

66. *See infra* secs. 8.3.1 and 8.5.2.

Claims Commission of 1923 between the United States and Mexico assists in this analysis.[67]

These decisions are of interest due to their treatment of the different types of acts committed by insurgent groups operating in Mexico.[68] In each case, the Commission considered whether Mexico was bound by contracts signed by the revolutionary Huerta government.[69] This administration controlled large swathes of Mexico for about a year from early 1913.[70] The decisions did not address the attribution of the revolutionaries' conduct to Mexico. Nevertheless, in her analysis of Article 9, Fortin draws a parallel between these cases and the principle the rule enshrines, using the decisions as guidance to determine when the rule reflected in Article 9 might apply to the conduct of rebel groups.[71]

The General Claims Commission drew a distinction between routine governmental acts that must continue irrespective of the administration performing them, and "personal acts" aimed at promoting the rebels' own interests.[72] It noted that routine acts normally continue notwithstanding the insurgents' assumption of power, and that these were performed "in the service of the people . . . and in the name of Mexico."[73] In contrast, acts of a political or personal character aimed to advance the rebels' own aims and objectives.[74] These were intrinsically linked to the revolutionary regime and its goal of seizing and maintaining power.[75]

In the Commission's view, "routine" acts of government were binding on the State while any "personal" acts were invalid and void.[76] Regarding the latter, these would include the purchase of items to promote the entity's cause, such as arms

67. The ILC cites mixed claims commission decisions in relation to other rules of attribution but not regarding the rule reflected in art. 9. *See, e.g.*, ARSIWA, *supra* note 7, art. 10, cmt. ¶ 3.

68. For a wider review of mixed claims commissions' jurisprudence and its relevance to the law of state responsibility, *see* KATHRYN GREENMAN, STATE RESPONSIBILITY AND REBELS: THE HISTORY AND LEGACY OF PROTECTING INVESTMENT AGAINST REVOLUTION (2021).

69. George W. Hopkins (USA) v. United Mexica States, 4 R.I.A.A. 41, ¶ 4 (Gen. Claims Comm'n, 1926) [hereinafter *Hopkins*]. *See also* Haig Silvanie, *Responsibility of States for Acts of Insurgent Governments*, 33 AM. J. INT'L L. 78 (1939); KATHARINE FORTIN, THE ACCOUNTABILITY OF ARMED GROUPS UNDER HUMAN RIGHTS LAW 254–55 (2017).

70. GREENMAN, *supra* note 68, at 62–63.

71. FORTIN, *supra* note 69, at 254–58.

72. *Hopkins*, *supra* note 69, ¶ 4. *See also* Silvanie, *supra* note 69, at 95–103; FORTIN, *supra* note 69, at 254–58. The U.S. Supreme Court made a similar distinction in cases concerning U.S. responsibility for the acts of Confederates. *See* HAIG SILVANIE, RESPONSIBILITY OF STATES FOR ACTS OF UNSUCCESSFUL INSURGENT GOVERNMENTS 98–103 (1939); FORTIN, *supra* note 69, at 258–60.

73. *Hopkins*, *supra* note 69, ¶ 11.

74. *Id.* ¶ 5. *See also* Silvanie, *supra* note 69, at 96–97.

75. FORTIN, *supra* note 69, at 257.

76. *Hopkins*, *supra* note 69, ¶¶ 9–10.

and ammunition, and the forcible taking of property for use by the revolutionary movement.[77] The key issue is for whose benefit the NSA acts at the relevant time. The Commission expressed the view that even if the transactions were "of an unusual nature" rather than routine, Mexico would remain bound if it "received benefits" from the relevant acts.[78]

The British–Mexican Claims Commission adopted a similar approach when addressing Mexico's liability for the cost of cattle belonging to a British company. These were forcibly requisitioned by revolutionary troops following the end of the Huerta administration, when there was no established federal government in Mexico.[79] The Commission found that the cattle were "to a large extent confiscated in order to supply the population of the town of Muzquiz with meat."[80] Therefore, because the requisition was carried out in the public interest, the Commission concluded that Mexico was responsible for the loss.[81]

In summary, these decisions establish the principle that States should be bound by the acts of insurgents that benefit the State or its population, but not bound by other acts performed in the insurgents' own interests.[82] In section 7.5, this chapter assesses the cases' potential relevance to the "called for" element of the rule reflected in Article 9.

8.2.3 The Rule's Object and Purpose

In contrast with the rules of attribution considered in Part Three of this book,[83] the object and purpose of the rule reflected in Article 9 ARSIWA is not immediately apparent. Why should private conduct be attributable to a State if State officials have no knowledge of, or links to, the NSA responsible for the acts' commission? The rule seems particularly illogical when considering the consequences that flow from a State's international responsibility.[84] For instance, how can a State comply with its duty to cease an internationally wrongful act[85] if its officials were

77. *Id.*

78. *Hopkins*, *supra* note 69, ¶ 11. *See also* Silvanie, *supra* note 69, at 100–101.

79. The British Shareholders of the Mariposa Company (Great Britain) v. United Mexican States, 5 R.I.A.A 272 (Brit.-Mex. Claims Comm'n, 1931) [hereinafter *Mariposa Company*]. *See also* Silvanie, *supra* note 69, at 101–2.

80. *Mariposa Company*, *supra* note 79, ¶ 3.

81. *Id.*

82. Silvanie, *supra* note 69, at 103; FORTIN, *supra* note 69, at 254–58.

83. *See* ARSIWA, *supra* note 7, arts. 4, 5, 8.

84. *Id.* arts. 28–39.

85. *Id.* art. 30.

not involved in the acts that violate its international legal obligations, and they have no influence over the NSA concerned?[86]

The ILC's commentary to Article 9 provides minimal assistance in this regard. It simply makes reference to the notion of "agency of necessity" and "the idea that some exercise of governmental functions was called for" in the circumstances.[87] Further guidance can be gleaned, however, from Special Rapporteur Ago's more detailed consideration of this basis of attribution in 1971.[88] Here, Ago referred to persons taking on certain public functions "in order to render a service to the community" or to "carry on services which cannot be interrupted" in the absence of the regular administrative authorities.[89]

Ago observed, "At the internal level, the State often assumes responsibility for offenses committed by private persons exceptionally performing public functions in the place of *de jure* officials who omit to perform them or are unable to do so."[90] He went on to note that "[t]he State, as a subject of international law, should, *a fortiori* it seems, bear responsibility for the acts of these various classes of person" where the acts performed are public in character and result in a breach of the State's international legal obligations.[91] He concluded, "[I]t is logical that the act of a private person who, in one way or another, is performing a function or task of an obviously public character should be considered as an act attributable to the community and should engage the responsibility of the State at the international level."[92]

From Ago's perspective, therefore, attribution is appropriate only if the conduct concerns public functions performed in the interests of the community.[93] In the event that the State is unable to perform such functions due to a situation of armed conflict, for example, there continues to be a need for certain essential public tasks to be fulfilled. If private individuals step in to complete these tasks, they are performing a public service that benefits the population. The State should bear responsibility for those public acts, even if during their performance the NSA violates an international obligation to which the State is subject.[94]

86. Nicholas Tsagourias, *Non-State Actors, Ungoverned Spaces and International Responsibility for Cyber Acts*, 21 J. Conflict & Sec. L. 455, 461 (2016).

87. ARSIWA, *supra* note 7, art. 9, cmt. ¶¶ 2, 6.

88. Ago's Third Rep. on State Responsibility, *supra* note 15, at 262–67.

89. *Id.* at 263, ¶ 189.

90. *Id.* at 264, ¶ 191.

91. *Id.*

92. *Id. See also* ILC Y.B. 1974 vol. II, *supra* note 16, at 285 (draft art. 8, cmt. ¶ 11).

93. This view was echoed by other members of the ILC. *See, e.g.*, ILC Y.B. 1974 vol. I, *supra* note 17, at 37, ¶ 8 (comments of Mr. Ramangasoavina); *id.* at 38, ¶ 14 (comments of Mr. Pinto).

94. Although it will be rare for acts performed in the public interest to violate international law it is nevertheless possible, as later examples demonstrate. *See infra* sec. 8.5.

There are similarities between Ago's rationale for attribution and the conclusions reached by the General Claims Commission regarding Mexico's responsibility for the contractual obligations of the insurgent Huerta administration.[95] Just as States should be bound by contracts signed by NSAs that are performed for the benefit of the State or its people, they should also bear international responsibility for this category of conduct if it violates an international obligation that binds the State. However, personal conduct that advances the objectives of the NSA concerned rather than the interests of the wider community should remain private in character and not lead to State responsibility.[96]

Consideration of these cases, together with the work of the ILC, points to a narrow conception of the rule of attribution, relating solely to conduct that provides a clear public benefit. This interpretation accords with the ILC's commentary to Article 9, which repeatedly stresses the "exceptional" nature of the rule.[97] The criteria that govern the rule's application thus operate as limiting factors, both in terms of the factual situations to which the rule applies (in the absence or default of the official authorities) and the nature of the acts performed (which must be governmental in character and "called for" in the circumstances).

Thus, it is only on the rare occasions when all three conditions can be satisfied that the rule of attribution applies. Given this limited scope of application, the rule reflected in Article 9 seeks to strike a balance between the interests of the territorial State on the one hand and those of victims of international law violations on the other. While private conduct committed without the knowledge or involvement of State officials will not normally lead to State responsibility, the ILC considered an exception appropriate when the NSA's performance of governmental tasks is essential in the circumstances, to fulfill a public need that the State's own officials are unable to meet.

8.3 THE SCOPE OF THE RULE

Before examining the "called for" and "absence or default" elements of the rule, it is pertinent to consider Article 9's scope of application in more general terms. This analysis focuses principally on the types of conduct the rule attributes to a State, as well as the character of the NSA that performs the acts that potentially violate international law.

95. *See supra* sec. 8.2.2.2.

96. This reasoning is also evident in certain decisions of the U.S. Supreme Court relating to the American Civil War. *See* SILVANIE, *supra* note 72, at 98–103; FORTIN, *supra* note 69, at 258–60.

97. ARSIWA, *supra* note 7, art. 9, cmt. ¶ 1. *See also* ILC Y.B. 1974 vol. II, *supra* note 16, at 285 (draft art. 8, cmt. ¶ 8).

8.3.1 The Character of the Non-State Actor

The preceding conclusions regarding the object and purpose of the rule indicate that the type of conduct the NSA performs is key to Article 9's application. The critical issue is whether there is a pressing public need for those tasks to be fulfilled. Thus, the identity of the NSA performing those tasks should not preclude the rule's application. Article 9's text supports this approach due to its reference to the conduct of "a person or group of persons."[98] The same wording appears in Article 8 ARSIWA and applies in that case to all NSAs, regardless of their character.[99]

The position regarding Article 9, however, is more complex. Whereas Article 8 addresses the conduct of NSAs acting on the State's behalf,[100] Article 9 could apply to the conduct of NSAs that act against the State and seek to usurp the government's authority. In his subsequent work on State responsibility, former Special Rapporteur Crawford expressed the view that public functions exercised by an insurrectionist movement should not attach to the State unless the NSA succeeded in establishing a new government, as envisaged by the rule expressed in Article 10.[101]

Crawford's view, however, conflicts with the ILC's commentary on other rules of attribution. In its commentary to Article 10, the ILC noted that the principle enshrined in Article 9 might attribute the conduct of an unsuccessful insurrectional movement to a State if the "special circumstances" envisaged by the rule are satisfied.[102] Meanwhile, the commentary to Article 5 refers to Article 9's potential application "where an entity or group *seizes power* in the absence of State organs but in situations where the exercise of governmental authority is called for."[103] These references indicate that the categorization of a particular NSA as an armed group or an insurrectional movement does not exclude Article 9's

98. ARSIWA, *supra* note 7, art. 9.

99. *Id.* art. 8.

100. *Id. See also supra* ch. 6.

101. CRAWFORD, *supra* note 13, at 168. Special Rapporteur Ago similarly shared this view. *See* Int'l Law Comm'n, Documents of the Twenty-Seventh Session, *in* [1975] 2 Y.B. INT'L L. COMM'N 91–92 n. 205, U.N. Doc. A/CN.4/SER.A/1975/Add.1 [hereinafter ILC Y.B. 1975 vol. II]. For discussion regarding Article 10 ARSIWA, *see infra* ch. 9.

102. ARSIWA, *supra* note 7, art. 10, cmt. ¶ 2. A member of the ILC raised this possibility in 1974. *See* ILC Y.B. 1974 vol. I, *supra* note 17, at 37, ¶ 8 (comments of Mr. Ramangasoavina). *See also* Katharine Fortin, *The Relevance of Article 9 of the Articles on State Responsibility for the Internationally Wrongful Acts of Armed Groups*, in NON-STATE ACTORS AND INTERNATIONAL OBLIGATIONS 371, 371–76 (James Summers & Alex Gough eds., 2018) [hereinafter Fortin, *The Relevance of Article 9*].

103. ARSIWA, *supra* note 7, art. 5, cmt. ¶ 7 (emphasis added).

potential application.[104] Instead, the issue rests upon the satisfaction of the three criteria outlined in the rule.

An approach that focuses on the rule's three elements rather than the identity of the actor not only accords with the ARSIWA commentary; it also makes practical sense. To draw distinctions based on the NSA's role in overthrowing the government or its status as an insurrectional movement adds confusion rather than clarity to the rule's application. Non-international armed conflicts (NIAC) are often complex, involving numerous armed groups, and it might not be clear why the official authorities are absent or in default, whether this resulted from the actions of one NSA rather than another, or whether the NSA concerned is acting for or against the government.[105] Rather than inquiring into an armed group's influence in causing the government's absence or default, therefore, it is better to consider the rule's application through the lens of Article 9's three requisite elements.

The commentary to Article 9 nevertheless includes one express limitation regarding the NSAs to which the rule applies:

It must be stressed that the private persons covered by article 9 are not equivalent to a general *de facto* Government. The cases envisaged by article 9 presuppose the existence of a Government in office and of State machinery whose place is taken by irregulars or whose action is supplemented in certain cases. This may happen on part of the territory of a State which is for the time being out of control, or in other specific circumstances. A general *de facto* Government, on the other hand, is itself an apparatus of the State, replacing that which existed previously. The conduct of the organs of such a Government is covered by article 4 rather than article 9.[106]

This passage raises the question of what the ILC meant by its references to "a general *de facto* Government."[107] The ILC did not define the term within the ARSIWA commentary,[108] but its earlier work provides some clarification. This refers to "a government which, though not invested with power in accordance with the previously established constitutional forms, has fully and finally taken power, the previous government having disappeared."[109] Such circumstances might arise, for example, as the result of an armed group's military success or a coup d'état.[110]

104. Sten I. Verhoeven, *International Responsibility of Armed Opposition Groups, in* Responsibilities of the Non-State Actor in Armed Conflict and the Market Place: Theoretical Considerations and Empirical Findings 285, 295 (Noemi Gal-Or et al. eds., 2015).

105. Fortin, *The Relevance of Article 9*, *supra* note 102, at 379.

106. ARSIWA, *supra* note 7, art. 9 cmt. ¶ 4. *See also* ILC Y.B. 1974 vol. II, *supra* note 16, at 286 (draft art. 8, cmt. ¶ 12).

107. This term has several potential meanings. *See* Stefan Talmon, Recognition of Governments in International Law 60 (1998).

108. ARSIWA, *supra* note 7, art. 9, cmt. ¶ 4.

109. ILC Y.B. 1974 vol. II, *supra* note 16, at 286 (draft art. 8, cmt. ¶ 12). *See also* Ago's Third Rep. on State Responsibility, *supra* note 15, at 266, ¶ 196.

110. Fortin, *supra* note 69, at 252.

Thus, a general de facto government is one that controls the whole or the vast majority of the State's territory, even if it does not have de jure recognition as the sovereign authority of the State.[111] The Taliban government in Afghanistan, since August 2021, provides a pertinent example.[112]

If a de facto government exerts control over all the State's territory, thereby replacing the de jure government that existed previously, its acts are attributable to the State based on the rule reflected in Article 4 ARSIWA.[113] It follows that to determine Article 9's potential application to the acts of a de facto administration, it is necessary to assess whether the entity exerts its control over all or the majority of the State's territory and people, or only a portion of it. In the former case, illustrated by the situation in Afghanistan, as well as in Syria after Hay'at Tahrir al-Sham (HTS) took control over the government in late 2024,[114] the entity's acts are attributable to the State pursuant to the rule reflected in Article 4 ARSIWA.[115] But if a local administration governs only part of the State's territory, the rule expressed in Article 9 could apply to its conduct provided the rule's three elements are satisfied.[116] The first of these relates to the public character of the relevant acts.

8.3.2 The Conduct to Which the Rule Applies

The rule reflected in Article 9 attributes private conduct to the State only if the acts concerned amount to an exercise of "elements of the governmental authority."[117] This wording mirrors that employed in Article 5 ARSIWA.[118] Although the rules apply to different factual circumstances, attribution in each case is contingent upon the public character of the functions performed.

Chapter 5 includes a detailed analysis of the meaning of "elements of the governmental authority" for the purposes of Article 5, highlighting the difficulty in

111. Talmon, *supra* note 107, at 65–76; Crawford, *supra* note 13, at 168.

112. *See, e.g.*, Lindsay Maizland, *The Taliban in Afghanistan*, Council on Foreign Rel. (Aug. 17, 2022), www.cfr.org/backgrounder/taliban-afghanistan.

113. ARSIWA, *supra* note 7, art. 9, cmt. ¶ 4. *See also id.* art. 4.

114. William Christou, *Syrian Rebels Reveal Year-Long Plot That Brought Down Assad Regime*, The Guardian (Dec. 13, 2024), https://www.theguardian.com/world/2024/dec/13/syrian-rebels-reveal-year-long-plot-that-brought-down-assad-regime.

115. The rule reflected in Article 10 ARSIWA may also apply to retrospectively attribute the Taliban's acts, before it regained power, to the State. *See* ARSIWA, *supra* note 7, art. 10.

116. ARSIWA, *supra* note 7, art. 9, cmt. ¶ 4.

117. *Id.* art. 9.

118. *Id.* art. 5.

identifying the precise functions that qualify as governmental.[119] This section uses the analytical framework proposed in Chapter 5 to assess the activities that fall within the notion of governmental authority.[120] It does not repeat that analysis but rather focuses on the types of conduct that might amount to an exercise of public functions for the purposes of Article 9.

When considering each of the factors under this framework, it is important to recall that the assessment whether an NSA's conduct is a public or private must be examined in relation to each distinct act the NSA performs rather than its conduct as a whole.[121] NSAs acting in conflict situations often perform a range of tasks, some of which may be private in character, while others qualify as governmental.

8.3.2.1 Quintessentially Governmental Functions

A first consideration when assessing the public or private character of an NSA's acts in potential violation of international law is whether the conduct concerned is quintessentially governmental, in that it is ordinarily performed by the State and is central to the notion of government.[122] For example, the policing, immigration, and customs services performed by the Revolutionary Guards in the *Yeager* case were a clear exercise of governmental authority.[123] Certain tasks carried out by NSAs in more recent conflicts may also qualify as inherently governmental, such as the functions performed by the Free Syria Police in areas of Syria liberated from ISIS control.[124] The same is true of similar functions performed in the cyber domain, such as collecting taxes via cyber means.[125]

Military activities with direct operational effect form another important category of quintessentially governmental functions.[126] In the context of Article 9, the ARSIWA commentary highlights "the old idea of the *levée en masse*, the self-defense of the citizenry in the absence of regular forces" as a concept that underlies the attribution standard.[127] When civilians take up arms in this manner, to defend territory in the absence of the State's regular forces, they are

119. *See supra* ch. 5, sec. 5.3.

120. *Id.*

121. *See* Fortin, *supra* note 69, at 254.

122. *See supra* ch. 5, sec. 5.3.2 for further discussion regarding "quintessentially" governmental functions.

123. *Yeager*, *supra* note 41, ¶¶ 13–14, 61. *See also supra* sec. 8.2.2.1.

124. Chris Vallance, Free Syrian Police Go Unarmed to Help Their Community, BBC News (Apr. 3, 2017), https://www.bbc.com/news/world-middle-east-39458062.

125. Tsagourias, *supra* note 86, at 464.

126. *See supra* ch. 5, sec. 5.3.2.

127. ARSIWA, *supra* note 7, art. 9, cmt. ¶ 2. *See also* Ago's Third Rep. on State Responsibility, *supra* note 15, at 263, ¶ 189; ILC Y.B. 1974 vol. II, *supra* note 16, at 285 (draft art. 8, cmt. ¶ 9).

performing a public function, and the rule reflected in Article 9 might operate to attribute their conduct to the State under attack.[128]

Although an "old idea,"[129] the *levée en masse* gained renewed prominence during Russia's 2022 invasion of Ukraine. News reports indicate that thousands of Ukrainian civilians left their normal employment to take up arms.[130] Irrespective of whether these individuals constituted a *levée en masse* for the purposes of IHL,[131] they were clearly fighting for the State at the relevant time, performing quintessentially governmental functions. Therefore, in the event their actions were "called for" in the circumstances, in the absence or default of the official authorities, Article 9 would apply to attribute any of their conduct that violated international law to Ukraine.[132]

The same is true of the conduct of other NSAs performing military functions, such as the rebels operating in the east of Ukraine.[133] These groups committed more obvious violations of IHL in their battle against Ukrainian forces.[134] While it is highly questionable whether their conduct was "called for" in the circumstances,[135] it was undoubtedly public in character and therefore satisfies this element of the rule. In other situations, however, the public or private character of an NSA's conduct might be less apparent.

For instance, consider the actions of Ukraine's "IT Army" following Russia's invasion in February 2022. According to news reports, thousands of Ukrainian technology workers launched cyber operations targeting Russia's government, media,

128. de Frouville, *supra* note 28, at 273; Marco Sassòli, *State Responsibility for Violations of International Humanitarian Law*, 84 Int'l Rev. Red Cross 401, 409 (2002).

129. ARSIWA, *supra* note 7, art. 9, cmt. ¶ 2.

130. Mednick, *supra* note 5; Andrew E. Kramer, "*Everybody in Our Country Needs to Defend,*" N.Y. Times (Feb. 26, 2022), www.nytimes.com/2022/02/26/world/europe/ukraine-russia-civilian-military.html.

131. Regulations Respecting the Laws and Customs of War on Land, annexed to Convention No. IV Respecting the Laws and Customs of War on Land art. 2, Oct. 18, 1907, 36 Stat. 2277, T.S. No. 539 [hereinafter Hague Regulations]; GC III, *supra* note 6, art. 4A(6). *See also* David Wallace & Shane Reeves, *Levée en Masse in Ukraine: Applications, Implications, and Open Questions*, Articles of War (Mar. 11, 2022), https://lieber.westpoint.edu/levee-en-masse-ukraine-applications-implications-open-questions/.

132. Note that the rule reflected in Article 4 ARSIWA might attribute the conduct of some of these individuals to Ukraine, for example if they were members of Ukraine's Territorial Defense Force. *See* ARSIWA, *supra* note 7, art. 4; *see supra* ch. 4, sec. 4.3.

133. *See supra* ch. 2, sec. 2.4.2.

134. *See, e.g.*, Human Rights Violations and Abuses and International Humanitarian Law Violations Committed in the Context of the Ilovaisk Events in August 2014, at 19–20, ¶¶ 84–87 (Aug. 1, 2018), https://www.ohchr.org/sites/default/files/Documents/Countries/UA/ReportOnIlovaisk_EN.pdf.

135. *See infra* sec. 8.5.

and financial institutions.[136] These cyber operators not only took down websites or defaced them with antiwar messaging but also reportedly furnished direct support to the Ukrainian government by providing intelligence and attacking military systems.[137]

Given the diversity of these activities, it is necessary to disaggregate them and address the issue of attribution separately in each case. Some of the actions performed by Ukraine's IT Army may qualify as quintessentially governmental. For example, if individuals provided intelligence to Ukrainian forces regarding Russian troop locations or launched cyber operations against Russian military targets, such activities are military in character due to their close nexus to Ukraine's combat operations. But the status of other activities is less clear. These include the NSAs' participation in distributed denial of service attacks against Russian websites,[138] cyber operations causing disruption to rail services in Belarus,[139] and the publication of significant quantities of data linked to Russia.[140]

When considering activities such as these, it can assist to ask "whether, under ordinary circumstances, the government would reserve the actions or functions in question to itself."[141] In other words, can a private individual normally perform the task concerned without government authorization? If an NSA cannot lawfully perform the activity in the absence of an official mandate, it is likely to be governmental in character.[142] Applied to the conduct of the Ukraine's IT Army, in the absence of an official mandate, many of the group's activities would likely violate the domestic laws of those States with jurisdiction over the persons and activities

136. Sam Schechner, *Ukraine's "IT Army" Has Hundreds of Thousands of Hackers, Kyiv Says*, Wall St. J. (Mar. 4, 2022), www.wsj.com/livecoverage/russia-ukraine-latest-news-2022-03-04/card/ukraine-s-it-army-has-hundreds-of-thousands-of-hackers-kyiv-says-RfpGa5zmLtavrot27OWX; Kate Conger & Adam Satariano, *Volunteer Hackers Converge on Ukraine Conflict with No One in Charge*, N.Y. Times (Mar. 4, 2022), www.nytimes.com/2022/03/04/technology/ukraine-russia-hackers.html; Laurens Cerulus, *Kyiv's Hackers Seize Their Wartime Moment*, Politico (Mar. 10, 2022), www.politico.eu/article/kyiv-cyber-firm-state-backed-hacking-group/.

137. David Uberti, *Hackers Target Key Russian Websites*, Wall St. J. (Feb. 28, 2022), www.wsj.com/articles/volunteer-hackers-join-ukraines-fight-against-russia-11646082782; Frank Bajak, *Ukraine Digital Army Brews Cyberattacks, Intel and Infowar*, ABC News (Mar. 5, 2022), https://abcnews.go.com/Politics/wireStory/ukraine-digital-army-brews-cyberattacks-intel-infowar-83265880; Lukasz Olejnik, *Smartphones Blur the Line Between Civilian and Combatant*, Wired, (June 6, 2022), www.wired.com/story/smartphones-ukraine-civilian-combatant/.

138. Bajak, *supra* note 137.

139. *Id.*; James Pearson, *Ukraine's "IT Army" Targets Belarus Railway Network, Russian GPS*, Reuters (Mar. 3, 2022), www.reuters.com/article/ukraine-crisis-cyber-defense-idCAKCN2L01RM.

140. Matt Burgess, *Russia Is Leaking Data Like a Sieve*, Wired (Apr. 13, 2022), www.wired.com/story/russia-ukraine-data/?utm_source=pocket_mylist.

141. Crawford, *supra* note 13, at 169.

142. *Id.*

concerned.[143] Although highly fact-dependent, these cyber operations might, therefore, qualify as an exercise of governmental functions for the purposes of Article 9 ARSIWA.

The same is not necessarily true, however, of all the functions performed by the IT Army. For instance, some cyber operators reportedly sent information to Russian citizens regarding the atrocities committed in Ukraine.[144] Information regarding the conduct of hostilities and the perpetration of war crimes is commonly disseminated by private actors, such as journalists and humanitarian organizations. As such, these activities can lawfully be performed pursuant to a relationship between two private entities. Therefore, subject to further analysis regarding the overall context in which the activities were performed, they remain private in character and the rule reflected in Article 9 would not attribute them to Ukraine.

8.3.2.2 The Overall Context

Actions that are not by their nature inherently governmental, but which are conducted in the service of the State, may still be categorized as public rather than private. Particularly pertinent in this respect is the overall context in which the function is performed.[145] Consider, for example, the actions taken by NSAs in response to the significant cyber operations directed against Estonian government institutions and commercial entities in 2007.[146] To protect public and private computer networks against the intrusions, system administrators and experts from both within and outside Estonia stepped in to assist the government.[147] If any of the NSAs' conduct violated international law, a first issue to determine when assessing the potential attribution of such conduct to Estonia is whether the tasks they performed were governmental in character.

The NSAs' actions were not quintessentially governmental, given that they are commonly performed by private entities. However, the wider context in which the activity was undertaken is highly relevant. In this case, if the experts were working to defend Estonian government computer networks, the relevant conduct can be classified as public rather than private due to its close nexus to the aims and activities of the State.[148] If, conversely, the NSAs were acting to defend private networks, their conduct would remain private in character.

A review of the overall context also assists when characterizing the actions of cyber operators acting in support of Russia or Ukraine against the backdrop of the ongoing hostilities. Many of the activities carried out by these NSAs are clearly

143. *See* Tallinn Manual 2.0 on the International Law Applicable to Cyber Operations r. 4, cmt. ¶ 2 (Michael N. Schmitt ed., 2017) [hereinafter Tallinn Manual 2.0].

144. Bajak, *supra* note 137.

145. *See supra* ch. 5, sec. 5.3.3.

146. Tikk et al, *supra* note 4, at 16–23.

147. *Id.* at 24, 34.

148. *See infra* ch. 5 sec. 5.3.3.

private and criminal in nature, such as the ransomware attacks launched by pro-Kremlin groups against States bolstering Ukraine's war effort.[149] But if such operations were integral to the belligerent States' conduct of hostilities, it may be appropriate to characterize them as governmental. For example, the hostile cyber operations conducted by hackers linked to Moscow against the satellite company, Viasat, were timed to coincide with and support Russia's military invasion.[150] These were therefore public, not private, in character.

8.3.3 Conduct Instigated by the State

One unusual aspect of the rule of attribution reflected in Article 9 is its application to an NSA's conduct when that NSA acts spontaneously, without any State influence or encouragement. The question arises, however, whether the rule can apply if the NSA responds to a call for action by the State or acts in tandem with State officials. For instance, if the cyber operations launched against the satellite company Viasat were conducted by private individuals, Russia must have had some influence over their conduct to ensure that the operations were timed to coincide with the invasion of Ukraine.[151] If the individuals responsible were not State organs, it may be that they were acting under Russia's instructions at the relevant time, meaning that their conduct is attributable to the State pursuant to the rule reflected in Article 8.[152] But as discussed in Chapter 6, a State's call for action might be too vague and imprecise to satisfy this rule of attribution.[153]

It is therefore pertinent to consider whether the rule expressed in Article 9 could attribute conduct performed in response to a government call for action to the territorial State. Consider, for instance, the encouragement the Ukrainian government issued to its citizens to defend the nation against Russia's invasion,[154] including by manufacturing and using Molotov cocktails.[155] A similar inquiry is relevant when NSAs voluntarily fulfill public functions in coordination with State

149. Schechner, *supra* note 136; Bajak, *supra* note 137; Uberti, *supra* note 137.

150. Sam Cohen, *Acid Rain Malware and Viasat Network Downtime in Ukraine: Assessing the Cyber War Threat*, Just Sec. (Sept. 12, 2022), www.justsecurity.org/83021/acidrain-malware-and-viasat-network-downtime-in-ukraine-assessing-the-cyber-war-threat/.

151. *Id.*

152. ARSIWA, *supra* note 7, art. 8.

153. *Id.* sec. 6.3.

154. *Ukraine's Leader Urges Civilians to Fight, Promises to Arm All*, Al Jazeera (Feb. 24, 2022), www.aljazeera.com/news/2022/2/24/ukraines-leader-urges-civilians-to-fight-promises-to-arm-all.

155. Lexi Lonas, *Ukraine Defense Ministry Tells Residents to Use Molotov Cocktails in Kyiv*, The Hill (Feb. 25, 2022), https://thehill.com/policy/international/595802-ukraine-defense-ministry-tells-residents-to-make-molotov-cocktails-in/.

officials. In northern Nigeria, for example, community militias worked alongside State security forces to protect their communities against threats posed by Islamist militants.[156]

Article 9's commentary refers to NSAs acting "on their own initiative" and "without any actual authority to do so," thereby indicating the ILC's intent that the rule should apply to private conduct performed without any State approval or involvement.[157] Crawford confirms this understanding, writing that the NSAs in question "must be utilizing government functions on their own initiative."[158] In a footnote, Crawford remarks that if the NSAs were performing such tasks at the behest of the government, the rule reflected in Article 5 ARSIWA would attribute their conduct to the State.[159]

As discussed in Chapter 5, the rule reflected in Article 5 applies when a State legally empowers an NSA to perform public functions on its behalf.[160] But there are many situations during armed conflict when the "empowered by law" element of the rule is not satisfied.[161] If Article 5 does not apply and the conduct at issue satisfies the three criteria outlined in Article 9, the relevant acts are attributable to the State on this latter basis. In such circumstances, the grounds for attribution are more compelling than if State officials were not involved in the relevant conduct, due to the State encouragement that led to the acts' commission.[162] For the rule reflected in Article 9 to apply in such circumstances, it is necessary to establish not only that the performance of the public functions was "called for"[163] but also that the official authorities were "absent or in default" for the purposes of the rule.

8.4 THE ABSENCE OR DEFAULT OF THE OFFICIAL AUTHORITIES

The rule reflected in Article 9 ARSIWA applies only if the NSA concerned performs the relevant public tasks in the absence or default of the official authorities.[164] The ILC commentary indicates that such circumstances may arise "during revolution,

156. CTR. for Civilians in Conflict, NIGERIAN COMMUNITY MILITIAS: TOWARD A SOLUTION (Nov. 2019), https://civiliansinconflict.org/wp-content/uploads/2019/11/Issue-Brief_Africa_Final_Web.pdf.

157. ARSIWA, *supra* note 7, art. 9, cmt. ¶¶ 1, 4.

158. CRAWFORD, *supra* note 13, at 169.

159. *Id.* n. 13.

160. *See supra* ch. 5.

161. *Id.* sec. 5.4.

162. For discussion of the rule's object and purpose, *see supra* sec. 8.2.3.

163. *See infra* sec. 8.5.

164. ARSIWA, *supra* note 7, art. 9, cmt. ¶¶ 3, 5.

armed conflict or foreign occupation, where the regular authorities dissolve, are disintegrating, have been suppressed or are for the time being inoperative."[165] In addition, the commentary highlights that the rule of attribution might apply to cases where the lawful authority is gradually being restored, such as after a foreign occupation.[166]

During its early deliberations, the ILC illustrated the rule's scope of application with examples from World War II.[167] During that conflict, private citizens took on public functions in the absence of the local administrations, which had fled before the invaders or before the subsequent armies of liberation.[168] The ILC additionally observed that the rule of attribution might apply when "the organs of administration are unfortunately lacking as a result of natural events such as an earthquake, a flood or some other major disaster."[169]

The predecessor to Article 9 provided for its application only "in the absence of the official authorities . . . ."[170] When the ILC reviewed the draft article in 1998, it concluded that this wording was overly narrow, as it implied that attribution was appropriate only upon the complete disintegration of the State.[171] The provision was therefore amended to provide for its application "in the absence *or default of* the official authorities."[172] The commentary clarifies that this wording "is intended to cover both the situation of a total collapse of the State apparatus as well as cases where the official authorities are not exercising their functions in some specific respect, for instance, in the case of a partial collapse of the State or its loss of control over a certain locality."[173] Whether or not such circumstances exist is a question of fact in each case.[174]

These circumstances might become apparent in two distinct scenarios. First, it is clear from the ILC's reference to a State's "loss of control over a certain locality"[175] that a State's absence or default can be geographical in character. At one

165. *Id.* cmt. ¶ 1.

166. *Id.*

167. Ago's Third Rep. on State Responsibility, *supra* note 15, at 263, ¶ 189; ILC Y.B. 1974 vol. II, *supra* note 16, at 285 (draft art. 8, cmt. ¶ 9). *See also* ILC Y.B. 1974 vol. I, *supra* note 17, at 44, ¶ 15 (comments of Mr. Ustor).

168. Ago's Third Rep. on State Responsibility, *supra* note 15, at 263, ¶ 189.

169. *Id. See also* ILC Y.B. 1974 vol. I, *supra* note 17, at 32, ¶ 5 (comments of Special Rapporteur Ago).

170. ILC Y.B. 1974 vol. II, *supra* note 16, at 283 (draft art. 8(b)).

171. ILC Y.B. 1998 vol. I, *supra* note 27, at 289, ¶ 80.

172. *Id.*; ARSIWA, *supra* note 7, art. 9 (emphasis added).

173. ARSIWA, *supra* note 7, art. 9, cmt. ¶ 5. *See also* ILC Y.B. 1998 vol. I, *supra* note 27, at 289, ¶ 80; ILC Y.B. 2001 vol. I, *supra* note 27, at 93, ¶ 29.

174. Crawford, *supra* note 13, at 169.

175. ARSIWA, *supra* note 7, art. 9, cmt. ¶ 5.

extreme are "failed States," in which the machinery of State collapses almost entirely and the State is effectively absent from most of its territory.[176] Alternatively, the State might lose control over some territory but maintain its authority over other regions. This situation arose in Syria and Ukraine, where the respective governments retained control over parts of their territory, including Damascus and Kyiv, but lost control of other regions to rebel groups or an external State.[177]

Second, the official authorities' absence or default could be functional in character. In other words, although the official authorities are physically present in the region where the NSAs undertake the relevant public tasks, they are unable to perform one or more governmental functions. This situation might arise in a time of emergency or crisis, to which the government lacks the capacity or the expertise to respond effectively. Estonia in 2007 provides an apt illustration, when State authorities lacked the requisite expertise and capability to counter the multiple cyber operations directed against the State but otherwise continued to function normally.[178]

For the purposes of this analysis, "absence" has a geographical meaning, denoting the official authorities' lack of physical presence in the location where the NSAs undertake the relevant public tasks. "Default," meanwhile, refers to the official authorities' inability to perform a particular public function, although they might retain a presence in the locality concerned. Before examining each of these categories, it is first pertinent to clarify what the ILC meant by its reference to "the official authorities."

8.4.1 The Official Authorities

Article 9 requires that the NSA concerned exercises governmental functions "in the absence or default of the official authorities." However, the term "official authorities" is not defined within Article 9's commentary, and it does not appear anywhere else within ARSIWA.[179] It seems surprising that the ILC did not refer instead to State organs, which the commentary to Article 4 defines as "all the individual or collective entities which make up the organization of the State and act on its behalf."[180]

A review of the ILC's discussions in 1998 provides some clarity. Here, the ILC explained that the expression "official authorities" covers both organs of State within the meaning of Article 4 and entities exercising elements of governmental

176. Rotberg, *supra* note 1, at 9–10; Tsagourias, *supra* note 86, at 457.

177. *See supra* ch. 2, secs. 2.4.1, 2.4.2.

178. Tikk et al, *supra* note 4, at 16–23.

179. ARSIWA, *supra* note 7.

180. *Id.* art. 4, cmt. ¶ 1. For discussion regarding Article 4 ARSIWA, *see supra* ch. 4.

authority within the meaning of Article 5.[181] Thus, the rule reflected in Article 9 can apply even if the government normally outsources the public tasks in question, provided that the entity that ordinarily performs those tasks is absent or in default at the relevant time.

The ILC also considered that the term "official authorities" is broad enough to encompass the organs of a group that has gained de facto control over the entirety of a State's territory.[182] Thus, the rule reflected in Article 9 would not apply "as long as there was some 'official authority', even if said 'authority' was not competent to exercise the particular functions under domestic law."[183] This statement links to the section of the ILC commentary that addresses general de facto governments, meaning an entity that exerts its authority over the whole of the State's territory and population, even if other States do not recognize it as the legitimate government.[184] In this situation, the rebel group becomes the official authorities, replacing those that exercised power previously. For instance, notwithstanding the Taliban's lack of international recognition,[185] as long as the group retains de facto authority over the people and the territory of Afghanistan, its representatives are the official authorities of the State for the purposes of ARSIWA.[186]

This broad interpretation of the term "official authorities" within Article 9 indicates the rule's potential application to any governance vacuum. It does not matter whether it is officials of the de jure government who are absent, private contractors who would normally fulfill the relevant tasks on the government's behalf, or members of an armed group that exerts de facto control over the entirety of the State. If any such authorities are absent or in default, and NSAs step in to perform essential public tasks, the rule reflected in Article 9 may apply.

8.4.2 Absence of the Official Authorities: A Geographical Perspective

There are numerous examples during armed conflict of State authorities losing control over parts of their territory. In Syria, for example, the Assad regime was estimated to govern less than 20 percent of Syrian territory in 2017, with much of the remainder controlled by NSAs including ISIS, the Syrian Democratic Forces

181. ILC Y.B. 1998 vol. I, *supra* note 27, at 289–90, ¶ 81. *See also* ILC Y.B. 1974 vol. II, *supra* note 16, at 285 (draft art. 8, cmt. ¶ 11). For discussion regarding Article 5 ARSIWA, *see supra* ch. 5.

182. ILC Y.B. 1998 vol. I, *supra* note 27, at 289–90, ¶ 81. *See also* ARSIWA, *supra* note 7, art. 9, cmt. ¶ 4.

183. ILC Y.B. 1998 vol. I, *supra* note 27, at 289–90, ¶ 81.

184. ARSIWA, *supra* note 7, art. 9, cmt. ¶ 4. *See also* Talmon, *supra* note 107, at 65–76; Crawford, *supra* note 13, at 168. For discussion regarding *de facto* governments, *see supra* sec. 8.3.1.

185. *See* Maizland, *supra* note 112.

186. ARSIWA, *supra* note 7, art. 9, cmt. ¶ 4.

(SDF), and various rebel and Islamic factions.[187] In Ukraine, the government lost control over both the Crimean Peninsula and territory in the Donbas in 2014. Then, with the 2022 invasion, Russia occupied additional areas of Ukrainian territory, some of which were subsequently retaken by Ukraine's armed forces.[188]

If there is a complete vacuum of authority in the location where the NSA undertakes the relevant public functions, the official authorities are clearly absent for the purposes of the rule reflected in Article 9. However, in some armed conflict scenarios the assessment may be more complex. For instance, are the official authorities absent when an NSA controls part of the State's territory and performs public functions as part of its day-to-day governance of the area? Is the position any different when the relevant area is controlled by an external State rather than by an NSA? This section addresses each of these scenarios in turn before turning to consider when the official authorities may be "in default" from a functional perspective.

8.4.2.1 Territory Controlled by a Local De Facto Administration

Armed groups in locations across the globe exercise some form of control over territory. These range from de facto authorities that develop sophisticated State-like bureaucracies to local networks embedded in communities that emerge in political and security vacuums.[189] In 2024, the International Committee of the Red Cross (ICRC) estimated that 210 million people lived in areas controlled by armed groups; some exercised full control over territory while others contested or fluidly controlled the relevant areas.[190]

Given this reality, it is pertinent to assess whether the rule reflected in Article 9 could attribute the public conduct of such local de facto administrations to the territorial State. Could Syria, for instance, bear international responsibility for the potential breaches of its humane treatment obligations associated with detentions conducted by the SDF in northeast Syria?[191] Section 7.5 considers whether such conduct could be "called for" for the purposes of Article 9.[192] However, it is also

187. *A Year on Astana Agreement, the Winners Are Iranians, Russians, Turks, the Regime, and the Biggest Losers Are the Opposition Factions, Tahrir al-Sham and ISIS*, Syrian Observatory for Hum. Rts. (May 4, 2018), www.syriahr.com/en/91151/.

188. *Ukraine in Maps: Tracking the War with Russia*, BBC News (Nov. 19, 2024), https://www.bbc.com/news/world-europe-60506682 [hereinafter *Ukraine in Maps*].

189. Irénée Herbet & Jérôme Drevon, *Engaging Armed Groups at the International Committee of the Red Cross: Challenges, Opportunities and COVID-19*, 102 Int'l Rev. Red Cross 1021, 1022–23 (2020).

190. Matthew Bamber-Zryd, *ICRC Engagement with Armed Groups in 2024*, ICRC (Oct. 31, 2024), https://blogs.icrc.org/law-and-policy/2024/10/31/icrc-engagement-with-armed-groups-in-2024/.

191. *See, e.g.*, Amnesty Int'l, Syria: Aftermath: Injustice, Torture and Death in Detention in North-East Syria (Apr. 17, 2024), https://www.amnesty.org/en/documents/mde24/7752/2024/en/.

192. *See infra* sec. 8.5.

necessary to assess whether the official authorities are "absent or in default" in such circumstances.

It is apparent from Article 9's commentary that although the rule does not apply to the conduct of a general de facto government that exerts control over the whole or the majority of a State's territory, the same is not true of a local administration, which controls only part.[193] Thus, while Article 9 does not apply to the conduct of HTS after the group ousted President Assad and took control over the Syrian government in late 2024,[194] the rule could apply to the acts of an NSA that controls part of a State's territory, such as those of the Kurdish administration in northeast Syria.[195] In such circumstances, the "official authorities" are the representatives of the State's de jure or de facto government.[196] If they are not physically present in the region where the NSA exerts its control, the official authorities are absent for the purposes of Article 9.

This means that the "absence or default" element of the rule is likely to be satisfied when a local administration performs governance functions in one region of a State's territory. The requirement is similarly satisfied when an NSA undertakes public tasks in an area over which it exercises only temporary control. Provided that government representatives are not physically present in the region at the time the relevant functions are performed, leading to a vacuum of authority, the official authorities are absent for the purposes of Article 9.

8.4.2.2 Occupied Territory

Since the commencement of the conflict in Ukraine, actors other than the State's own authorities have exerted control over parts of Ukraine's sovereign territory. These areas include the Crimean Peninsula, occupied by Russia since 2014, as well as territory in the south and the east of the country that Russia occupied in 2022.[197] The question therefore arises whether, in occupied territory, the official authorities are absent for the purposes of Article 9. In other words, do Russian armed forces or other representatives of the Kremlin constitute the "official authorities" for the purposes of Article 9?

To illustrate, consider the city of Kherson that fell to Russian forces in February 2022. The invasion reportedly caused Ukrainian officials to flee from the city,

193. ARSIWA, *supra* note 7, art. 9, cmt. ¶ 4 ("The cases envisaged by article 9 presuppose the existence of a Government in office and of State machinery whose place is taken by irregulars or whose action is supplemented in certain cases. This may happen on part of the territory of a State which is for the time being out of control."). *See also* ILC Y.B. 1998 vol. I, *supra* note 27, at 289–90, ¶ 81. For discussion regarding general de facto administrations, *see supra* sec. 8.3.1.

194. Christou, *supra* note 114.

195. *See, e.g.*, Rana Khalaf, Chatham House, Governing Rojava: Layers of Legitimacy in Syria (Dec. 2016), https://www.chathamhouse.org/sites/default/files/publications/research/2016-12-08-governing-rojava-khalaf.pdf.

196. *See supra* sec. 8.4.1.

197. *Ukraine in Maps*, *supra* note 188.

the army to disappear, and police officers to vanish from the streets.[198] Russian troops were physically present in the city but initially had no interest in taking on administrative tasks.[199] To prevent extensive looting, therefore, local civilians organized neighborhood patrols to police the city.[200] This scenario raises the question whether the local civilians' conduct in undertaking public functions in the absence of the Ukrainian authorities could be attributed to Ukraine. Does the presence of Russian armed forces, which could have performed these policing functions, preclude attribution?

This question is of potential significance given the resistance activities undertaken by Ukrainian citizens within Russian-occupied territory.[201] The conduct of some individuals, such as those who operated within "small attack teams that picked off Russian soldiers at night"[202] might have violated IHL, for example, if members of the team attacked soldiers who were *hors de combat* due to wounds.[203] It is therefore pertinent to consider whether the rule reflected in Article 9 could attribute such conduct to Ukraine.

Looking first to Article 9's commentary, it indicates that the rule of attribution can apply during foreign occupation, as well as in situations where the lawful authority is being gradually restored.[204] The commentary additionally states that attribution is appropriate "where the regular authorities dissolve, are disintegrating, have been suppressed or are for the time being inoperative."[205] This latter wording suggests that the absence or default criterion requires some form of vacuum of authority, such as before an occupying power has established its control. It follows that there would be no such absence or default when an occupying power is in full control of the territory and able to ensure the performance of all necessary public functions.

Limiting the rule's application to periods when there is a vacuum of authority in the relevant locality accords with the rule's object and purpose.[206] In occupied

198. Gettleman, *Dazed Soldier*, *supra* note 5. *See also* Sarah Rainsford, *Ukraine's Shadow Army Resisting Russian Occupation*, BBC News (July 29, 2022), www.bbc.com/news/world-europe-62333795.

199. Gettleman, *Dazed Soldier*, *supra* note 5.

200. *Id.*

201. Jeffrey Gettleman, *How Citizen Spies Foiled Putin's Grand Plan for One Ukrainian City*, N.Y. Times (Dec. 25, 2022), https://www.nytimes.com/2022/12/25/world/europe/ukraine-kherson-defiance-russia.html [hereinafter Gettleman, *Citizen Spies*].

202. *Id.*

203. Customary IHL, *supra* note 6, r. 47.

204. ARSIWA, *supra* note 7, art. 9, cmt. ¶ 1.

205. *Id.*

206. *See supra* sec. 8.2.3. *See also* ARSIWA, *supra* note 7, art. 9, cmt. ¶ 2; ILC Y.B. 1974 vol. II, *supra* note 16, at 285 (draft art. 8, cmt. ¶ 11).

territory, once the occupying power has established its control, there is no such vacuum.[207] Instead, there is some "official authority" that is competent to ensure the performance of essential public functions, even if it is not the de jure authority of the State.[208]

To assess the potential relevance of the rule reflected in Article 9 to situations of occupation, therefore, it is pertinent to consider when and where the relevant conduct took place and whether any power exercised authority over that location at the relevant time. In Kherson, for instance, reporting indicates that resistance activities took place both before and after Russia gained control over the city.[209] With regard to the latter activities, once Russian forces had established control, there was no vacuum of authority; Russian officials were in control and able to govern. Regarding the policing and other activities that local citizens commenced soon after the departure of Ukrainian officials, however, the position might be different. If those individuals committed an act that violated Ukraine's international legal obligations before Russia established its authority over the city, the "absence or default" element of Article 9 is likely to be satisfied.

8.4.3 Default of the Official Authorities: A Functional Perspective

It is apparent from the preceding analysis that an assessment whether the official authorities were absent from a particular location for the purposes of Article 9 is straightforward. This can be assessed by examining whether State officials were physically present at the time and in the place where the NSAs acted. The "absence or default" analysis may be more complex, however, if government representatives are still operating in the areas where the relevant NSA is located. In this situation, the official authorities are not absent, but they may nevertheless be "in default" from a functional perspective meaning that they lack the capacity to fulfil all necessary governmental tasks.

In its discussions related to the rule reflected in Article 9, the ILC indicated that this may be the case when the official authorities are "not exercising their functions"[210] or when they are "incapable of taking any action."[211] However, the

207. *See* Hague Regulations, *supra* note 131, art. 42.

208. The ILC noted in 1998 that "the article did not apply as long as there was some 'official authority,' even if said 'authority' was not competent to exercise the particular functions under domestic law." While this remark related to general de facto administrations, it could apply equally to situations of occupation. *See* ILC Y.B. 1998 vol. I, *supra* note 27, at 289–90, ¶ 81.

209. Rainsford, *supra* note 198; Gettleman, *Dazed Soldier*, *supra* note 5; Gettleman, *Citizen Spies*, *supra* note 201.

210. ILC Y.B. 1998 vol. I, *supra* note 27, at 289, ¶ 80.

211. ILC Y.B. 2001 vol. I, *supra* note 27, at 93, ¶ 29.

commentary to Article 9 provides little guidance regarding the notion of "default" or how far this should extend. For example, if State organs are present in the relevant locality but they lack the capacity or have received inadequate training to deal with a particular situation, could the rule apply to the actions of private citizens who step in to assist?[212]

Ruys addressed this issue in the context of Hezbollah's activities in southern Lebanon in 2006.[213] At that time, the official authorities were present throughout the country, including in the south, albeit that the Lebanese police and military forces kept a low profile in that area.[214] The official Lebanese authorities also continued to collect taxes and to organize immigration, customs, and the judiciary in all areas of Lebanese territory. There was, accordingly, no absence of the official authorities from a geographic perspective.

In regions with a large Shi'a majority, however, Hezbollah performed a range of governmental functions.[215] For instance, the UN reported that Hezbollah maintained and reinforced a visible presence in the vicinity of the Blue Line that divides Lebanon from Israel and the Golan Heights, with permanent observation posts, temporary checkpoints, and patrols.[216] Given the Lebanese authorities' inability to police these areas directly, it seems reasonable to conclude that Hezbollah was performing public tasks in the default of the official authorities for the purposes of Article 9.[217]

The same conclusion is likely regarding other NSAs that perform public functions alongside State authorities. In areas controlled by the Tamil Tigers in Sri Lanka, for example, the rebel-led administration secured the territory, exercising exclusive control over the police and judiciary, but worked alongside de jure government institutions to provide other services to the civilian population.[218] Therefore, although government officials were present, they were "in default" with regard to the security tasks the rebels performed.[219]

The *Tallinn Manual 2.0* addresses a similar issue in the cyber context. Here, the *Manual* gives the example of a rootkit attack on a State's civil defense computers during a NIAC, the effects of which make it impossible for the State to issue

212. Griebel, *supra* note 56, at 62.

213. Tom Ruys, *Crossing the Thin Blue Line: An Inquiry into Israel's Recourse to Self-Defense Against Hezbollah*, 43 Stan. J. Int'l L. 265, 287–89 (2007).

214. *Id.* at 288.

215. *Id.*

216. *Id.*, *citing* U.N. Security Council, Rep. of the Secretary-General on the United Nations Interim Force in Lebanon ¶¶ 27–28, U.N. Doc. S/2006/560 (July 21, 2006).

217. Ruys, *supra* note 213, at 289.

218. Zachariah Cherian Mampilly, Rebel Rulers: Insurgent Governance and Civilian Life During War 94, 112 (2011).

219. For discussion whether these security tasks were "called for," *see infra* sec. 8.5.3.3.

warnings by cyber means.[220] If the State then disconnects its host from the network, with the result that it is unable to transmit the necessary warnings, the *Tallinn Manual* experts concluded that the official authorities would be "in default" in respect of the narrow exercise of that particular public function.[221] Therefore, if an NSA stepped in to carry out the task from an uninfected host until the government could again transmit the warnings directly, the rule reflected in Article 9 might attribute that conduct to the State.[222]

Several conclusions regarding the "in default" criterion can be drawn from the preceding examples and from the ILC's work. First, the official authorities' default must result from some form of emergency. This is apparent from the commentary to Article 9, which emphasizes the "exceptional" character of the rule.[223] Thus, it would not apply to the conduct of private companies that work with States to fill capability gaps in the cyber domain, for example, by securing the State's computer networks and responding to day-to-day cyber threats.[224] Such operations occur on a routine basis and with State authorization. Therefore, the appropriate basis of attribution is Article 5 ARSIWA, not Article 9.

Second, provided the default results from some form of emergency, it should not matter why the official authorities fail to fulfill the relevant public tasks.[225] For instance, there might be an insufficient number of officials available to address the situation, a lack of staff with the requisite expertise or training, or even failings due to the incompetence or corruption of those officials tasked to act. Article 9's commentary requires only that "the regular authorities dissolve, are disintegrating, have been suppressed or are for the time being inoperative."[226] There is no stipulation as to the reasons behind those authorities' absence or default.

Third, the NSAs' performance of governmental tasks must pertain solely to the functions in relation to which the official authorities are in default. To illustrate, consider the situation in Estonia in 2007. If the experts took it upon themselves

220. Tallinn Manual 2.0, *supra* note 143, r. 15, cmt. ¶ 17.

221. *Id.*

222. *Id.*

223. ARSIWA, *supra* note 7, art. 9, cmt. ¶ 1.

224. Few states have the requisite cyber expertise to respond promptly and adequately to threats without support from the private sector. *See* Tim Maurer, Cyber Mercenaries: The State, Hackers, and Power 38–39 (2018); Kristen E. Eichensehr, *Public-Private Cybersecurity*, 95 Tex. L. Rev. 467, 479–82 (2017).

225. Special Rapporteur Ago referred to the rule's application when the official authorities simply "omit to perform" essential public functions, as well as when they are unable to do so. *See* Ago's Third Rep. on State Responsibility, *supra* note 15, at 264, ¶ 191.

226. ARSIWA, *supra* note 7, art. 9, cmt. ¶ 1. Note, however, that the *Tallinn Manual* suggests a narrower construction of the rule, cautioning that attribution is appropriate only when "the State is *powerless* to perform its governmental functions." *See* Tallinn Manual 2.0, *supra* note 143, r. 15, cmt. ¶ 17 (emphasis added).

not only to combat the malicious cyber operations but also to perform other governmental tasks during this period, such as by seeking to identify and take action against the perpetrators of the harm, the rule reflected in Article 9 would not attribute those acts to the State as the official authorities responsible for exercising such powers were still active at the relevant time.

Finally, the official authorities' default continues only for as long as they fail to fulfill the public task in question. Once the emergency has passed, or the official authorities regain the capacity to act, there is no longer any necessity for NSAs to perform the function concerned. Therefore, the rule reflected in Article 9 will not attribute any private conduct to the State that is performed once the official authorities are no longer "in default."

Determining whether the "absence or default" requirement is satisfied thus necessitates a factual assessment, considering all the relevant circumstances at the time the NSAs perform the public acts in question. As such, this element of Article 9 may be straightforward to evaluate. The more difficult and often the determinative question is whether the NSAs' performance of those tasks was "called for" in the circumstances.

8.5 CIRCUMSTANCES SUCH AS TO CALL FOR THE EXERCISE OF GOVERNMENTAL AUTHORITY

If the first two elements of the rule reflected in Article 9 can be satisfied, namely, that the NSA exercised public functions in the absence or default of the official authorities, the attribution analysis then turns to assess whether the NSA's conduct was "called for" in the circumstances. This is the key "normative element" governing the rule's application[227] and the most ambiguous of the three criteria.[228]

8.5.1 Guidance Provided by the ILC

The ILC only formulated the "called for" language shortly prior to ARSIWA's adoption in 2001.[229] It had referred previously to NSAs acting "in circumstances which *justified* the exercise of those elements of authority."[230] As outlined in section 7.2.1, the reason for the change was a concern that wrongful conduct, in violation of international law, cannot have been

227. ARSIWA, *supra* note 7, art. 9, cmt. ¶ 6.

228. Ruys, *supra* note 213, at 289.

229. Crawford's First Rep. on State Responsibility, *supra* note 24, at 44, ¶ 217–18. *See also supra* sec. 8.2.1.

230. ILC Y.B. 1974 vol. II, *supra* note 16, at 283 (draft art. 8) (emphasis added).

"justified."[231] In other words, the fact that there is a necessity to act does not automatically mean that the actions taken in response are either justified or lawful.[232]

In its discussions regarding this criterion, the ILC provided some limited illustrations of the types of conduct that might be "called for" for the purposes of the rule. Special Rapporteur Ago referred in this context to private persons who assume public functions "in order to carry on services which cannot be interrupted, or which must be provided precisely because of the exceptional situation."[233] He added that such action would have to be justified "by a genuine failure of the authorities to act."[234] More recently, the ILC illustrated the "called for" requirement by referring to a group of private individuals that takes over the running of an airport and assumes responsibility for immigration during or in the immediate aftermath of a revolution.[235]

These examples confirm the rationale for attribution as "a form of agency of necessity."[236] Thus, due to the specific factual circumstances, there is "the actual need for *someone* to fulfil the internal functions of the absent State."[237] There is, however, a dearth of scholarship, State practice, or jurisprudence to clarify the precise parameters of the requirement. Although the airport example given by the ILC bears a resemblance to the facts of the *Yeager* case, the Iran–U.S. Claims Tribunal failed to even contemplate the issue of whether the Revolutionary Guards' actions were "called for" in the circumstances.[238]

Certain conclusions can nonetheless be drawn from the ARSIWA commentary and the ILC's discussions. The first and most important of these is that the NSA's actions must be necessary to ensure the proper functioning of the State or to satisfy the essential needs of the community.[239] It may be that State officials were previously performing the functions concerned but can do so no longer, meaning

231. Crawford's First Rep. on State Responsibility, *supra* note 24, at 44, ¶ 217. *See also* ILC Y.B. 1998 vol. I, *supra* note 27, at 230, ¶ 9; ILC Y.B. 2001 vol. I, *supra* note 27, at 93–94, ¶ 30.

232. de Frouville, *supra* note 28, at 272.

233. Ago's Third Rep. on State Responsibility, *supra* note 15, at 263, ¶ 189. *See also* ILC Y.B. 1974 vol. II, *supra* note 16, at 285 (draft art. 8, cmt. ¶ 9).

234. ILC Y.B. 1974 vol. I, *supra* note 17, at 46, ¶ 26 (comments of Special Rapporteur Ago). *See also* Tal Becker, Terrorism and the State: Rethinking the Rules of State Responsibility 75–76 (2006); Griebel, *supra* note 56, at 62.

235. ILC Y.B. 2001 vol. I, *supra* note 27, at 93–94, ¶ 30.

236. ARSIWA, *supra* note 7, art. 9, cmt. ¶ 2. *See also* Crawford, *supra* note 13, at 169; de Frouville, *supra* note 28, at 272; Hessbruegge, *supra* note 58, at 274; Kress, *supra* note 59, at 121.

237. Crawford, *supra* note 13, at 169 (emphasis in original). *See also* ILC Y.B. 1974 vol. II, *supra* note 16, at 285 (draft art. 8, cmt. ¶ 11); Griebel, *supra* note 56, at 111.

238. *Yeager*, *supra* note 41. Crawford suggested that the Iran–U.S. Claims Tribunal did not refer in its judgment to the actual formulation of the draft article because of the problem caused by the word "justified." *See* Crawford's First Rep. on State Responsibility, *supra* note 24, at 44, ¶ 217.

239. ARSIWA, *supra* note 7, art. 9, cmt. ¶ 6.

that it is necessary for NSAs to step in to ensure their continuance.[240] For instance, when Kherson in Ukraine initially fell to Russian forces, there was a vacuum of authority that local citizens sought to fill by establishing neighborhood patrols.[241] Alternatively, the performance of the public functions might become necessary because of the crisis that has arisen.[242] In northern Nigeria, for example, civilians formed community militias to counter Islamist extremists who were threatening their neighborhoods and thereby fill existing security gaps left by the State's military and police forces.[243]

The *levée en masse* example within the ILC's commentary demonstrates a further scenario when the exercise of public functions becomes necessary due to the exceptional circumstances arising: an invasion by an aggressor.[244] For instance, as Russian troops advanced into and later retreated from regions of Ukrainian territory in 2022, Ukrainian civilians undertook various public tasks, ranging from active participation in hostilities[245] to using applications on their phones to report the locations of incoming missiles.[246] While it is unclear whether any Ukrainian civilians formed a *levée en masse* within the meaning of IHL,[247] their conduct following Russia's invasion echoes the general idea expressed in Article 9's commentary of citizens acting to defend their homeland, in the absence of the regular armed forces.[248]

It is arguable that the NSA's conduct in all these examples benefits the territorial State and its population. Yet, it could nevertheless involve violations of international law. For instance, Ukrainian citizens might have thrown Molotov cocktails at Russian forces in a manner that violated IHL, for example, by aiming the weapons at a Russian tank located among civilians.[249] In Nigeria, although the local militias protected their communities against Islamist threats, they also engaged in behavior that might violate Nigeria's international legal obligations such as by engaging in sexual violence.[250]

240. Ago's Third Rep. on State Responsibility, *supra* note 15, at 263, ¶ 189.

241. Gettleman, *Dazed Soldier*, *supra* note 5.

242. Ago's Third Rep. on State Responsibility, *supra* note 15, at 263, ¶ 189.

243. Ctr. for Civilians in Conflict, *supra* note 156.

244. ARSIWA, *supra* note 7, art. 9, cmt. ¶ 2. *See also* Hague Regulations, *supra* note 131, art. 2.

245. Mednick, *supra* note 5.

246. Dan Sabbagh, *Ukrainians Use Phone App to Spot Deadly Russian Drone Attacks*, The Guardian (Oct. 29, 2022), www.theguardian.com/world/2022/oct/29/ukraine-phone-app-russia-drone-attacks-eppo.

247. Wallace & Reeves, *supra* note 131.

248. ARSIWA, *supra* note 7, art. 9, cmt. ¶ 2.

249. Sean Watts, *Are Molotov Cocktails Lawful Weapons?* Articles of War (Mar. 2, 2022), https://lieber.westpoint.edu/are-molotov-cocktails-lawful-weapons/.

250. Ctr. for Civilians in Conflict, *supra* note 156, at 4.

When assessing whether such conduct in violation of international law could be "called for" for the purposes of Article 9, it is first necessary to clarify the focus of this analysis. Regarding the Nigerian militias, for example, should the "called for" assessment consider solely their conduct in violation of international law or rather their wider conduct in defending local populations from Islamist extremists? The ARSIWA commentary indicates that a broader focus is appropriate: "The term 'call for' conveys the idea that some exercise of governmental functions was called for, though not necessarily the conduct in question."[251]

The commentary goes on to state that the circumstances surrounding the NSA's exercise of public functions "must have justified the attempt to exercise police or other functions in the absence of the constituted authority."[252] Thus, the wider attempt to perform the relevant public functions must be "called for" in the circumstances, not the specific acts that violate international law. This broader focus makes sense and accords with the rule's object and purpose.[253] If the "called for" analysis concentrated solely upon the specific acts that breach the territorial State's international legal obligations, it is doubtful that any private conduct could satisfy this element of the rule. To determine whether conduct was "called for," it is therefore pertinent to consider all the surrounding circumstances, including the wider course of conduct in which the acts in potential violation of international law were performed.

A consideration of the broader context necessarily encompasses the identity of the NSA and its relationship with the territorial State. It is evident that the ILC principally intended the rule of attribution reflected in Article 9 to apply to the conduct of NSAs that act in the interests of the State and its government.[254] This also makes sense from a practical perspective. When an NSA acts for the State, it is more realistic to expect the State to comply with its duties under the law of State responsibility, including its obligation to ensure that the NSA concerned ceases the internationally wrongful conduct.[255]

Yet as discussed previously, NSAs that act against the interests of the State are not excluded from the rule's scope.[256] Indeed, the ASRIWA commentary indicates that Article 9 can apply to the conduct of rebel groups provided the "special circumstances" envisaged by the rule can be satisfied.[257] One of these "special circumstances" is that the conduct in question is "called for" in the circumstances.

251. ARSIWA, *supra* note 7, art. 9, cmt. ¶ 6.

252. *Id.*

253. *See supra* sec. 8.2.3.

254. *See supra* sec. 8.2.1.

255. ARSIWA, *supra* note 7, art. 30. *See also* Tsagourias, *supra* note 86, at 461.

256. *See supra* sec. 8.3.1.

257. ARSIWA, *supra* note 7, art. 10, cmt. ¶ 2. *See also id.* art. 5, cmt. ¶ 7.

The following section assesses whether this can ever be the case when considering the conduct of rebel groups.

8.5.2 Can a Rebel Group's Conduct Ever Be "Called For"?

The commentary to Article 9 is silent regarding the rule's application to the conduct of rebel groups,[258] and legal scholars take divergent views on the issue. Some are clear that the rule should not apply to the conduct of NSAs that act in opposition to the State.[259] Others acknowledge that the rule reflected in Article 9 could apply, at least theoretically, to the conduct of a rebel movement.[260]

Instinctively, it seems wholly inappropriate for a State to bear international responsibility for the acts of an NSA that seeks to usurp the government's authority, especially when the NSA commits atrocities in the process. This view accords with the ILC's discussions during the drafting process,[261] as well as its broader conclusions on attribution. The ILC's earlier work included two draft articles that specifically articulated the principle that the conduct of NSAs acting against the State is not considered an act of State under international law.[262] These draft articles and their commentaries were not included in ARSIWA because they represented negative rules of attribution and were therefore deemed unnecessary.[263] Nevertheless, the principle they articulate remains valid.

That principle appears in ARSIWA in the commentary to Article 10.[264] As discussed further in Chapter 9, it is only if rebel groups meet with success in becoming the new government or in creating a new State that their conduct is attributable to the State.[265] Yet despite the "well-established principle of international

258. *Id.* art. 9, cmt. ¶¶ 1–6.

259. *See, e.g.*, Crawford, *supra* note 13, at 168–69; Tilman Rodenhäuser, Organizing Rebellion: Non-State Armed Groups Under International Humanitarian Law, Human Rights Law, and International Criminal Law, 138–39 (2018); Tsagourias, *supra* note 86, at 464; Tatyana Jane Eatwell, State Responsibility for the Unlawful Conduct of Armed Groups (Ph.D. dissertation, University of Cambridge) 116–66 (2019), www.repository.cam.ac.uk/bitstream/handle/1810/302004/Eatwell%20Thesis%20May%202020%20updated%20Electronic%20Final.pdf?sequence=8&isAllowed=y.

260. *See, e.g.*, Gérard Cahin, *The Responsibility of Other Entities: Armed Bands and Criminal Groups*, *in* The Law of International Responsibility 331, 335 (James Crawford et al. eds., 2010); Ruys, *supra* note 213; Verhoeven, *supra* note 104, at 295–96; Fortin, *The Relevance of Article 9*, *supra* note 102.

261. *See supra* sec. 8.2.1.

262. ILC Y.B. 1975 vol. II, *supra* note 101, at 70, 91 (draft arts. 11, 14).

263. Crawford's First Rep. on State Responsibility, *supra* note 24, at 48–49, 53–54.

264. ARSIWA, *supra* note 7, art. 10, cmt. ¶¶ 2–3.

265. *See infra* ch. 9.

law" that no State should bear responsibility for the acts of rebel groups committed in violation of its authority,[266] the commentary to Article 10 indicates that the rule reflected in Article 9 could nevertheless apply to such conduct.[267]

This guidance makes more sense when considering rebel groups' acts of governance, rather than their hostile acts against the territorial State. According to ICRC research, over half of all armed groups that control territory enforce security, while a smaller proportion levy a form of taxation and provide social support to civilians.[268] Meanwhile, NSAs that maintain long-standing control over territory, such as the Kurdish administration in northeast Syria, often establish sophisticated governance mechanisms and offer comprehensive services to local communities.[269]

The attribution of this type of conduct, performed for the benefit of local populations, accords more readily with Article 9's object and purpose.[270] Armed groups often perform essential governance functions in the territory they control to fill gaps left by government officials.[271] Fortin argues, therefore, that fulfillment of Article 9's "called for" criterion should turn upon the question "whether the functions of government were 'necessary' in the circumstances ruling at the time; a condition that could be fulfilled by the absence of the *de jure* government in the territory in question" and based on the public good that those functions served.[272] This approach focuses on the character of the act and whether it was objectively necessary to perform it.[273] The analysis that follows refers to this as an act-based approach.

Other commentators focus instead on the actor responsible for the relevant conduct, including the circumstances that led to the NSA's control over territory and its relationship with the State.[274] The ensuing analysis refers to this as an actor-based approach. Eatwell, for example, argues that if an NSA caused the official authorities' absence or default, its conduct should be excluded from Article 9's scope.[275] Eatwell maintains that the rule reflected in Article 9 should only attribute

266. ARSIWA, *supra* note 7, art. 10, cmt. ¶ 3, *citing* Home Frontier and Foreign Missionary Society of the United Brethren in Christ (United States) v. Great Britain, 6 R.I.A.A. 42, 44 (Arb. Trib., 1920).

267. ARSIWA, *supra* note 7, art. 10, cmt. ¶ 2.

268. Bamber-Zryd, *supra* note 190.

269. *Id.*; MAMPILLY, *supra* note 218, at 3. *See also* KHALAF, *supra* note 195.

270. *See supra* sec. 8.2.3.

271. FORTIN, *supra* note 69, at 273.

272. Fortin, *The Relevance of Article 9*, *supra* note 102, at 385.

273. *Id.*

274. Eatwell, *supra* note 259, at 129–44.

275. *Id.* at 129–44. *See also* Veronika Bílková, *Establishing Direct Responsibility of Armed Opposition Groups for Violations of International Humanitarian Law?*, *in* RESPONSIBILITIES OF

an NSA's conduct to the State if "it can be shown that by an express act the State acquiesces in the exercise of governmental functions by an armed opposition group or, as in *Yeager*, the State must have known and did not specifically object to the exercise of the governmental function by the armed group . . . ."[276]

Neither approach is ideally suited to determine whether private conduct was "called for" for the purposes of Article 9. Considering first the act-based approach, this employs the distinction made by the General Claims Commission between "routine" acts of government that serve the public interest and "personal" acts that benefit the group concerned.[277] Applied to the conduct of the Kurdish administration in northeast Syria, it could lead to the attribution of the NSA's routine governmental acts to Syria. For instance, if while maintaining regional security the group treats criminal detainees in a way that violates Syria's international legal obligations, that violation could be attributable to Syria.[278]

States would surely reject any suggestion that they should bear international responsibility for conduct such as this, performed by groups that usurped the government's authority. Concerns in this regard lead to an actor-based approach that focuses on the identity of the NSA and its relationship to the State. This, however, also has weaknesses. First, it appears inconsistent with the ARSIWA commentary.[279] Second, and more importantly, excluding consideration of the act itself from the "called for" determination goes too far. The character of the act is highly relevant to any assessment of whether the NSA's performance of public functions was objectively necessary in the circumstances.[280]

The actor-based approach focuses solely upon the character of the NSA, its role in causing the official authorities' absence or default, and its relationship with the State. All such factors may be relevant to determining whether the relevant conduct was "called for" in the circumstances. However, focusing on these issues to the exclusion of the act itself seems not to accord with the ILC's intent. According to Article 9's commentary, "the nature of the activity performed is given more weight than the existence of a formal link between the actors and the organization of the State."[281]

THE NON-STATE ACTOR IN ARMED CONFLICT AND THE MARKET PLACE 263, 269 (Noemi Gal-Or et al. eds., 2015).

276. Eatwell, *supra* note 259, at 167.

277. Fortin, *The Relevance of Article 9*, *supra* note 102. *See also supra* sec. 8.2.2.2.

278. Regarding the legal framework that governs detentions by armed groups, *see* Katharine Fortin, *Which Legal Framework Applies to Deprivation of Liberty by Non-State Armed Groups and Do They Address the Particular Challenges When Detention Is Conducted by Non-State Armed Groups?*, *in* DEPRIVATION OF LIBERTY AND ARMED CONFLICTS: EXPLORING REALITIES AND REMEDIES 200 (Giorgio Battisti ed., 2018).

279. ARSIWA, *supra* note 7, art. 5, cmt. ¶ 7; *id.* art. 10, cmt. ¶ 2.

280. *Id.* art. 9, cmt. ¶ 6.

281. *Id.* art. 9, cmt. ¶ 4.

An actor-based approach could additionally raise practical difficulties. Scholars who support this view argue that the rule reflected in Article 9 should not apply to insurrectional movements that caused the State's absence or default.[282] While, at first glance, this assertion appears sensible, it does not reflect the realities of contemporary armed conflict. In a complex NIAC, it may be unclear which party was to blame for the absence of the official authorities.[283] In Syria, for instance, the forces opposing the Assad regime comprised a vast array of rebel groups that would frequently amalgamate and divide.[284] Thus, in any given situation, it might not be possible to determine which NSA was responsible for the Syrian authorities' absence or default at the particular time and place concerned.

It may be equally difficult to ascertain whether the State acquiesced in the NSA's exercise of governmental functions. For example, did the Assad regime acquiesce in the Kurds' assumption of governance functions over northeast Syria? One author describes the relationship between the State and the administration as "a marriage of convenience," thereby suggesting that the Assad regime was not wholly opposed to the Kurds' exercise of control over the territory.[285]

In other conflicts, the links between the State and rebels controlling territory may be even closer. In Sri Lanka prior to 2009, for instance, the rebel-led administration worked alongside government institutions in areas under rebel control.[286] While the insurgents took charge of security in the region, including the police and judiciary, they worked in tandem with government officials to provide other essential services to the local population.[287] Facts such as this are clearly significant to any "called for" assessment. However, other factors relating to the acts themselves may be equally relevant.

Rather than focusing solely on the act performed or on the NSA and its relationship to the State, a multifaceted approach to the "called for" criterion is appropriate. The text of Article 9 supports this broader stance, with its reference to "circumstances such as to call for" the exercise of governmental functions.[288] It is all the surrounding circumstances that are relevant to Article 9's application, not only those that relate to either the act or the actor concerned.

282. Bílková, *supra* note 275, at 269; Eatwell, *supra* note 259, at 129–44.

283. Fortin, *The Relevance of Article 9*, *supra* note 102, at 379.

284. *See, e.g.*, Brian M. Jenkins, RAND, The Dynamics of Syria's Civil War 8 (2014), www.rand.org/pubs/perspectives/PE115.html.

285. Robert Lowe, LSE Middle East Centre, Rojava at 4: Examining the Experiment in Western Kurdistan 8 (Aug. 2016), https://eprints.lse.ac.uk/67515/1/Rojavaat4.pdf.

286. Mampilly, *supra* note 218, at 94.

287. *Id.* at 112.

288. ARSIWA, *supra* note 7, art. 9.

While it will be rare for the rule reflected in Article 9 to attribute rebels' conduct to a territorial State, it is not appropriate to entirely exclude the actions of NSAs that act against the interests of the State's de jure or de facto government from the rule's scope. When considering whether the "called for" requirement is satisfied, all the circumstances should be considered. The following section examines factors that might be relevant to this assessment for different categories of private conduct.

8.5.3 Application of the "Called For" Requirement to Different Categories of Conduct

8.5.3.1 Conduct Performed in the Interests of the Territorial State

The rule reflected in Article 9 is most likely to apply if the conduct at issue was performed in the interests of the territorial State and its people. It is this scenario that the ILC focused on when formulating the rule,[289] and the one most likely to be acceptable to States. Moreover, in such circumstances, the State can more readily comply with its duties under the law of State responsibility, including the obligation to ensure the cessation of the internationally wrongful conduct.[290]

To determine whether such conduct was "called for" for the purposes of Article 9, it is first necessary to consider the acts concerned and assess whether these were objectively necessary in all the circumstances.[291] As noted in section 8.5.1, it is the broader course of conduct that is relevant to this assessment rather than the specific acts on the part of the NSA that violate the State's international legal obligations.

To illustrate, consider the actions of local citizens in Kherson, Ukraine, who established neighborhood patrols to prevent looting and chaos following the fall of the city to Russian forces.[292] Likely, most of the policing functions they performed did not violate Ukraine's international legal obligations. However, one report refers to the NSA's capture of a Russian pilot, whom they subsequently returned to the Russians.[293] Had they instead mistreated or killed the pilot, in potential violation of IHL,[294] it is pertinent to consider whether their conduct could have been "called for" and therefore attributable to Ukraine.

It seems likely that the wider policing functions were necessary in the interests of the local population to fill the vacuum of authority that resulted from Russia's

289. *See supra* sec. 8.2.1.

290. ARSIWA, *supra* note 7, art. 30. *See also* Tsagourias, *supra* note 86, at 461.

291. ARSIWA, *supra* note 7, art. 9, cmt. ¶ 6.

292. Gettleman, *Dazed Soldier*, *supra* note 5.

293. *Id.*

294. Customary IHL, *supra* note 6, r. 87.

invasion. If that is the case, the attribution to Ukraine of the specific conduct that violated IHL turns upon the nexus between those acts and the broader policing functions the NSAs performed. If the international law violations were closely linked to and formed part of the NSA's performance of the wider beneficial functions, it seems reasonable to conclude that this conduct was "called for" and therefore attributable to Ukraine. However, the conclusion might be different if the acts in question had only a weak nexus to the functions the NSAs performed in the interests of the State.

An additional relevant factor is the State's attitude toward the conduct. It may be that State organs are unaware of the conduct, in which case they cannot react to it. But in other circumstances, State organs might support, tolerate, or disapprove the conduct concerned. The State's response might be highly relevant when determining whether the conduct at issue was "called for" in the circumstances.

In some cases, the State might demonstrate its approval through its officials' words or actions. For instance, State security forces in northern Nigeria acted alongside the community militias, thereby exhibiting the State's support for the NSA's conduct.[295] In other situations, the State might even encourage the relevant acts. Section 8.3.3 addresses this possibility, concluding that conduct instigated by the State should not be excluded from Article 9's scope. Indeed, the rationale for attribution is stronger when State officials motivate acts that violate the State's international legal obligations.

For example, if members of Ukraine's IT Army breached any international legal obligations to which the State was bound, it is relevant to Article 9's potential application that a government minister made a public appeal for Ukraine's technology workers to launch harmful cyber operations against Russian websites.[296] This fact supports the conclusion that the conduct in question may have been "called for," even if it violated international law. However, State officials' clear disapproval of the conduct concerned might point to the opposite conclusion. This is likely to be the case regarding conduct performed against the interests of the territorial State.

8.5.3.2 Conduct Performed Against the Interests of the Territorial State

It is evident from the ARSIWA commentary that Article 9 potentially applies to the conduct of groups that act against the interests of the territorial State and its government.[297] It is important to emphasize, however, that the rule's application in these circumstances will be extremely rare. In this context, it may assist to distinguish the governance activities rebels perform pursuant to their exercise of territorial control from acts that more directly challenge the State's authority.

295. Ctr. for Civilians in Conflict, *supra* note 156.

296. Schechner, *supra* note 136; Bajak, *supra* note 137.

297. ARSIWA, *supra* note 7, art. 5, cmt. ¶ 7; art. 10, cmt. ¶ 2. *See also supra* sec. 8.3.1.

Regarding the latter category of conduct, it is difficult to envisage any circumstances in which the attribution of a rebel group's conduct to the State against which it fights would accord with the rule's object and purpose. Article 9's "called for" element implies that the acts concerned must be necessary in the interests of the State or its population. Thus, the rule's object and purpose would be defeated if it attributed harmful conduct to States that, viewed objectively, serves solely to promote the NSA's own interests rather than those of the State or the local community.[298]

Of course, a rebel group might argue that it is acting in the interests of the State and its population, for example, to defeat a de jure government that committed human rights abuses against its own people. The Free Syrian Army, which formed in 2011 to fight the Assad regime, provides a pertinent example.[299] However, during armed conflict, there will always be contradictory views regarding which party is acting in the interests of the State and its population. Irrespective of the clear harm the Assad regime caused to Syria's people, it seems wholly inappropriate for the Syrian State to bear international responsibility for the alleged abuses committed by the Free Syrian Army, including torture, executions, and hostage-taking.[300] It is clear from the rule's drafting history that this was not the ILC's intent.[301] This outcome would also be politically unacceptable, as it would hold a State responsible for the acts of an entity against which it fights.[302]

Thus, the rule reflected in Article 9 is not an appropriate basis on which to attribute any private conduct to a State that is committed in violation of the government's authority during the perpetrator's fight against that State. The position may be different, however, for legal violations relating to a rebel group's governance of territory. In such circumstances, whatever the NSA's allegiances, its conduct is likely to include routine governmental acts that are performed in the interests of the community that it governs.

8.5.3.3 Conduct by Non-State Actors that Control Territory

As discussed in section 8.5.2, a rebel group's conduct in violation of international law could potentially be "called for" for the purposes of Article 9 if it relates to the NSA's performance of governance functions that benefit the local population. While such routine conduct might rarely violate the territorial State's international legal obligations, this is nevertheless possible. For example, the judicial system the administration in northeast Syria established might include insufficient fair

298. *See supra* sec. 8.2.3.

299. *See supra* ch. 2, sec. 2.4.1.

300. *See, e.g.*, Rep. of the Indep. Int'l Comm'n of Inquiry on the Syrian Arab Republic 20–21, ¶¶ 110–120, U.N. Doc. A/HRC/19/69 (Feb. 22, 2012).

301. *See supra* sec. 8.2.1. *See also* Crawford, *supra* note 13, at 168.

302. Fortin, *supra* note 69, at 277.

trial guarantees and thereby violate Syria's obligations under international human rights law.[303]

When assessing whether such conduct could satisfy the "called for" element of the rule, it is helpful to recap the conclusions reached in the preceding analysis. First, this assessment should focus not only on the identity of the actor and its relationship with the territorial State's government but also on the character of the act itself.[304] Second, the analysis of the act should consider the wider conduct during which the act in potential violation of international law was committed, rather than focusing solely on the violation itself.[305] In other words, it is pertinent to ask what gap the NSA sought to fill through its wider actions and whether this was a lacuna that needed to be filled, given the absence or default of the official authorities.[306]

This assessment should not depend on the NSA's own motivations, which are often mixed or hard to ascertain.[307] Instead, it should focus on the acts themselves and the circumstances surrounding their performance, viewed objectively. It may help to consider whether those acts primarily served the public interest or promoted the personal objectives of the NSA concerned, in accordance with the approach adopted by the General Claims Commission.[308]

To illustrate, consider the detention of ISIS fighters by the SDF in Syria. The detentions served a clear public interest as they kept militants off the battlefield and prevented ISIS from reestablishing control over Syrian territory.[309] Yet they also benefited the local de facto administration by minimizing the threat posed by ISIS and enhancing the administration's legitimacy on the international stage, thereby reinforcing its authority over the territory concerned. Thus, the detentions were not "routine" acts of government; they have closer links to the NSA's conduct of hostilities than to its governance over territory.[310] But they are not entirely "personal" acts either, given their wider public benefit. Given this ambiguity, it is pertinent to consider other relevant circumstances, including the NSA's relationship with the State.

303. For information regarding the justice system in northeast Syria, *see, e.g.*, *Ten Years of the Rojava Revolution: The Legal System of North and East Syria*, Civil Diplomacy Ctr., https://nescivildiplomacy.com/?p=2554. Syria is a party to the International Covenant on Civil and Political Rights, which includes fair trial guarantees. *See* International Covenant on Civil and Political Rights art. 9, Dec. 16, 1966, 999 U.N.T.S. 171.

304. *See supra* sec. 8.5.2.

305. *See supra* sec. 8.5.1.

306. Fortin, *The Relevance of Article 9*, *supra* note 102, at 384–85.

307. *Id.* at 384.

308. *See supra* sec. 8.2.2.2.

309. *See* ch. 2, sec. 2.4.1.3.

310. *See supra* secs. 8.2.2.2, 8.5.1.

As noted previously,[311] the relationship between the de facto administration in northeast Syria and the Assad regime was complex.[312] While it is arguable that the Assad regime tacitly accepted the administration's control over territory, it is doubtful that it acquiesced in the specific conduct at issue, namely, the SDF's detention of ISIS fighters. Syria likely viewed the Kurds' conduct in this respect as an encroachment upon its own territorial sovereignty. On balance, therefore, it seems a step too far for Syria to bear international responsibility for any international law violations related to the detentions.[313] A better conclusion, taking all relevant circumstances into account, is that the SDF's conduct was not "called for" for the purposes of Article 9.

This example demonstrates that there will often be compelling facts that point away from the rule's application. An assessment that a rebel group's conduct was "called for" is likely to be appropriate only if the NSA's performance of the functions concerned was essential to satisfy the needs of the local population. Any benefit accruing to the NSA itself must be ancillary to that clear purpose. In addition, the government's stance toward the NSA's assumption of the public tasks is key. If the government objects to the NSA's conduct, this may be a strong indicator that the acts were not "called for." But if the government tolerates or acquiesces in the rebels' performance of public tasks, as occurred in Sri Lanka,[314] it may be apt to conclude that the "called for" requirement is satisfied.

8.5.3.4 Conduct Performed Against an External State

Some legal scholars have argued that the rule reflected in Article 9 could potentially apply when an NSA attacks an external State. For instance, certain commentators claim that Hamas's attacks against Israel on October 7, 2023, could be attributable to Palestine on the basis that the NSA's actions were "called for" in the absence or default of the Palestinian authorities.[315] Other scholars contend that the rule could attribute Hezbollah's attacks on Israel to Lebanon,[316] or Al Qaeda's commission of the 9/11 terrorist attacks to Afghanistan.[317]

311. *See supra* sec. 8.5.2.

312. Lowe, *supra* note 285, at 8.

313. *See, e.g.*, Amnesty Int'l, *supra* note 191.

314. Mampilly, *supra* note 218, at 94. For discussion regarding the potential application of art. 9 to rebels' conduct in Sri Lanka, *see* Eatwell, *supra* note 259, at 163–64.

315. David J. Scheffer, *Holding Hamas Accountable at the ICJ Through Palestine*, Lawfare (June 26, 2024), https://www.lawfaremedia.org/article/holding-hamas-accountable-at-the-icj-through-palestine. *See also* Marko Milanovic, *Does Israel Have the Right to Defend Itself?* EJIL: Talk! (Nov. 14, 2023), https://www.ejiltalk.org/does-israel-have-the-right-to-defend-itself/; Chile Eboe-Osuji, *International Courts as the Last Hope for Humanity*, Just Sec. (Jan. 24, 2024), https://www.justsecurity.org/91448/international-courts-as-the-last-hope-for-humanity/.

316. Ruys, *supra* note 213, at 289–90.

317. Sean D. Murphy, *Terrorism and the Concept of "Armed Attack" in Article 51 of the U.N. Charter*, 43 Harv. Int'l L.J. 41, 50 (2002). For a critique of this view, *see* Rüdiger Wolfrum &

These interpretations of Article 9 do not accord with the rule's object and purpose.[318] The ILC's intent was that the rule should attribute conduct to a State only when this fulfills a clear public need that the State's officials are unable to meet.[319] In the case of the attacks perpetrated by Hamas, Hezbollah, or other armed groups, it seems that these could satisfy the "called for" requirement only if it is possible to conclude that the respective groups' conduct was objectively necessary in the circumstances to protect the interests of the States from which they operate or their local populations.

It could be argued, for instance, that the attacks perpetrated by groups such as Hamas and Hezbollah were "called for" in a similar manner to the acts of citizens who use force to defend their homeland against an aggressor. Yet there is a clear difference between private individuals acting defensively to protect their State against a foreign invasion and the conduct of armed groups that instigate attacks against an external State. In the case of the *levée en masse*, it is far more evident that the participants are acting in the interests of the State to defend it against an aggressor. It is much harder to reach this conclusion regarding the actions of groups such as Hamas and Hezbollah. In each case, it seems that the groups' attacks promoted their own aims and objectives rather than the interests of the respective States from which they operated.[320] Applying the rule reflected in Article 9 to such attacks would not only defeat the rule's object and purpose. It would also be wholly unacceptable to States.

8.6 CONCLUSION

Former Special Rapporteur Crawford described the principle reflected in Article 9 ARSIWA as "truly exceptional."[321] The unusual character of the rule of attribution and the considerable ambiguity regarding its application are apparent throughout this chapter. There is limited State practice or jurisprudence to rely upon when seeking to interpret the rule, and it is highly questionable whether it has attained customary status.[322]

Christiane E. Philipp. *The Status of the Taliban: Their Obligations and Rights Under International Law*, 6 Max Planck Y.B. U.N. Law 559, 594–95 (2002); Michal Kowalski, *Armed Attack, Non-State Actors and a Quest for the Attribution Standard*, 30 Polish Y.B. Int'l L. 101, 117–118 (2010).

318. *See supra* sec. 8.2.3. *See also* Becker, *supra* note 234, at 222–23; Eatwell, *supra* note 259, at 154.

319. *See supra* sec. 8.2.3.

320. For discussion regarding the distinction between acts performed in the interests of the State or its population and those that promote the personal interests of the NSA, *see supra* secs. 8.2.2.2, 8.5.2.

321. Crawford, *supra* note 13, at 167.

322. In the *Bosnian Genocide* case, the ICJ declined to opine upon whether the rule enshrined in Article 9 reflects customary international law. *See* Application of the Convention on the

Nevertheless, if the rule does reflect customary international law, it has some practical relevance in conflict situations. This is particularly apparent in Ukraine, where private citizens performed a range of public functions in the face of Russia's aggression. The conflict demonstrates that in certain situations, NSAs do step in to perform governmental tasks in the absence or default of the official authorities, such as the citizens who formed neighborhood patrols to fill the security vacuum when Ukrainian territory fell to Russian forces.[323] Moreover, the "total defense" policies of other States demonstrate that such scenarios are not unique to Ukraine.[324] Future conflict may also involve NSAs performing governmental functions to support the defense of their nations.

In situations such as these, the rule reflected in Article 9 might attribute the NSA's conduct in violation of international law to the territorial State. This is appropriate, however, only in very limited cases, when the NSA's performance of the public functions is objectively necessary considering all the surrounding circumstances.

Regarding Article 9's place within the wider attribution regime, the rule does not play a significant role in holding States to account or in regulating their conduct toward NSAs. Instead, it may provide injured States with an enhanced possibility to obtain reparations if they are harmed by NSAs' activities, performed in the absence or default of the official authorities. Yet the rule's narrow scope, together with continued ambiguity regarding its application, limits its importance. The rule has been rarely invoked since ARSIWA's adoption,[325] and this seems unlikely to change in the foreseeable future.

Prevention and Punishment of the Crime of Genocide (Bosn. & Herz. v. Serb. & Montenegro), Judgment, 2007 I.C.J. Rep. 43, ¶ 414 (Feb. 26).

323. Gettleman, *Dazed Soldier*, *supra* note 5.

324. *See, e.g.*, James Kenneth Wither, *Back to the Future? Nordic Total Defence Concepts*, 20 Def. Stud. 61 (2020); Jeremiah Lumbaca, *Every Taiwan Citizen a Resistance Member: Preparing for a Chinese Occupation*, Modern War Inst. (Sept. 14, 2023), https://mwi.westpoint.edu/every-taiwan-citizen-a-resistance-member-preparing-for-a-chinese-occupation/; Singapore Ministry of Defence, Total Defence, https://www.mindef.gov.sg/defence-matters/defence-topics/total-defence/.

325. *See* Crawford, *supra* note 13, at 168; Olleson, *supra* note 39, at 94.

9

The Conduct of a Successful Insurrectional Movement

9.1 INTRODUCTION

When a government loses control over all or part of its territory, complex issues of State responsibility may arise. As discussed in the preceding chapter, private citizens might step in to perform governmental functions in the absence or default of the official authorities. Alternatively, the rebel movement challenging the government's authority might succeed in taking power in all or part of the territory concerned. This chapter addresses the attribution of conduct to a State in the latter situation, examining a State's responsibility for the acts of a specific subcategory of non-State actor (NSA), namely, a successful insurrectional movement.

The relevant rule of attribution is reflected in Article 10 of the Draft Articles on Responsibility of States for Internationally Wrongful Acts (ARSIWA). This provides:

> 1. The conduct of an insurrectional movement which becomes the new Government of a State shall be considered an act of that State under international law.
> 2. The conduct of a movement, insurrectional or other, which succeeds in establishing a new State in part of the territory of a pre-existing State or in a territory under its administration shall be considered an act of the new State under international law.
> 3. This article is without prejudice to the attribution to a State of any conduct, however related to that of the movement concerned, which is to be considered an act of that State by virtue of articles 4 to 9.[1]

1. Draft Articles on Responsibility of States for Internationally Wrongful Acts, with commentaries, art. 10, *in* Int'l law Comm'n, Rep. on the Work of Its Fifty-Third Session, U.N. Doc. A/56/10 (2001), *reprinted in* [2001] 2 Y.B. Int'l L. Comm'n 31, 50, U.N. Doc. A/CN.4/SER.A/2001/Add.1 (Part 2) [hereinafter ARSIWA].

Attribution of Non-State Actor Conduct During Armed Conflict. Jennifer Maddocks, Oxford University Press.
 DOI: 10.1093/oso/9780197842652.003.0009

Put simply, when an insurrectional movement succeeds in its struggle for power and becomes either the new government in the conflict territory or establishes a new State in part of that territory, the movement's prior conduct is regarded as the conduct of the State it comes to govern.[2] The rule reflected in Article 10 therefore operates retrospectively; it attributes private conduct to a State based on the actor's subsequent change of status. At the time the relevant acts are committed, these are entirely private in character and not attributable to the territorial State. This position only changes if, at a later point in time, the rebels responsible for the harmful acts take power and become organs of State.[3]

The rule envisages two possible scenarios. First, the insurrectional movement succeeds in becoming the new government in the entirety of the preexisting State's territory.[4] In this situation, the State remains the same; only its government changes. Second, the insurrectional movement successfully establishes a new State within part of the preexisting State's territory.[5] In this scenario, the State that bears responsibility for the rebels' acts comes into existence after the date on which those acts were committed. If the movement's efforts fail, the State bears no responsibility for the movement's conduct. But if the movement succeeds, as reflected in the first two hypotheses, the rule expressed in Article 10 operates to retroactively attribute the movement's conduct to the State.[6]

Article 10 thus reflects an unusual rule of attribution.[7] In contrast to the attribution standards discussed in Part Three, it does not address the conduct of NSAs

2. *Id.* cmt. ¶ 4.

3. For discussion regarding organs of State, *see supra* ch. 4.

4. ARSIWA, *supra* note 1, art. 10(1).

5. *Id.* art. 10(2).

6. *See* Roberto Ago (Special Rapporteur), Fourth Rep. on State Responsibility, by Mr. Roberto Ago, Special Rapporteur—The Internationally Wrongful Act of the State, Source of International Responsibility (1972), *in* [1972] 2 Y.B. INT'L L. COMM'N 71, 145, ¶ 197, U.N. Doc. A/CN.4/SER.A/1972/Add.1 (Part One) [hereinafter Ago's Fourth Rep. on State Responsibility].

7. The International Law Commission noted in its discussions that the rule's basis in international law was unclear, but that it was clearly established in international practice. *See* James Crawford (Special Rapporteur), First Rep. on State Responsibility 52, ¶ 264, U.N. Doc. A/CN.4/490 and Add.1–7 (1998) [hereinafter Crawford's First Rep. on State Responsibility]; Int'l Law Comm'n, Summary Records of the Fiftieth Session (1998), *in* [1998] 1 Y.B. INT'L L. COMM'N 248, ¶ 50, U.N. Doc. A/CN.4/SER.A/1998 [hereinafter ILC Y.B. 1998 vol. I]. For critiques of the rule of attribution, *see, e.g.*, Jann Arno Hessbruegge, *The Historical Development of the Doctrines of Attribution and Due Diligence in International Law*, 36 N.Y.U. J. INT'L L. & POL. 265, 273–74, 300 (2004); Eyassu Gayim, *Reflections on the Draft Articles of the International Law Commission on State Responsibility: Articles 14; 15; & 19, in the Context of the Contemporary International Law of Self-Determination*, 54 NORDIC J. INT'L L. 85, 96–98 (1985); Jean d'Aspremont, *Rebellion and State Responsibility: Wrongdoing by Democratically Elected Insurgents*, 58 INT'L & COMP. L.Q. 427, 427–33 (2009); Kathryn Greenman, *The Secret History of Successful Rebellions in the Law of State Responsibility*, 6 ESIL REFLECTIONS (2017), https://esil-sedi.eu/post_name-116/.

that act on behalf of a State. Rather, it ensures that when an insurrectional movement succeeds in taking power, the State that the movement comes to govern bears responsibility for any violations of the State's international legal obligations that the movement committed during its earlier struggle for power. Thus, the rule's application cannot be determined at the time the relevant conduct occurs. It is necessary for a State that is injured by the insurrectional movement's conduct to wait before invoking another State's responsibility, to establish whether the rebels succeed in either taking power over the entire State, or in establishing a new State.

Compared to the other attribution standards reflected in ARSIWA, the rule expressed in Article 10 has a limited scope. First, it applies only to the conduct of one specific type of NSA: an insurrectional movement.[8] Second, it applies only to one particular type of hostilities: a conflict between a rebel group and the territorial State, during which the former challenges the latter's authority over all or part of its territory.[9] Third, it relates only to the international responsibility of the territorial State; it does not address the potential responsibility of an external State, located outside the territory concerned.

This chapter begins by considering the historical background to the rule, assessing relevant arbitral jurisprudence, the drafting history within the International Law Commission (ILC), and the rule's object and purpose. It is evident from this analysis that the rule's customary status is uncertain. While numerous arbitral decisions support the first principle of attribution expressed in Article 10, when the insurrectional movement becomes the new government, there is minimal authority for attribution in the second scenario—when the rebels establish a new State. Moreover, there is very little recent State practice to support either aspect of the rule.

For the purposes of analysis, the chapter nevertheless proceeds on the basis that both elements of the rule reflect customary international law. It addresses the two attribution scenarios envisaged in Article 10 before examining some of the ambiguities arising from the rule. These include questions surrounding the concept of an "insurrectional movement," including the issue of how to determine when conduct is performed on behalf of that movement and how to identify the specific international obligations that the movement could violate. The chapter concludes that uncertainties such as these seriously diminish the rule's importance in attributing harmful NSA conduct to a State during armed conflict.

8. ARSIWA, *supra* note 1, art. 10. For discussion regarding the meaning of "insurrectional movement" for the purposes of rule, *see infra* sec. 9.5.

9. *See* Patrick Dumberry, Rebellions and Civil Wars 12 (2022) [hereinafter Dumberry, Rebellions]. Such a conflict will normally be non-international in character. However, the rule could also apply to an internationalized armed conflict if an external State exercises overall control over the conduct of the insurrectional movement. For discussion regarding overall control, *see supra* ch. 6, sec. 6.4.

9.2 ATTRIBUTION PURSUANT TO ARTICLE 10

Article 10 ARSIWA originated in the rules formulated in the late nineteenth and early twentieth centuries to address State responsibility for the injuries that rebel movements caused to foreign nationals.[10] The doctrine developed as Western governments sought to protect their expanding interests in foreign trade and investment if these were threatened by insurgent activity.[11] Early claims related to the territorial State's duty to satisfy aliens' contracts with or loans made to rebels, rather than the attribution to the State of the rebels' conduct in violation of international law.[12] The distinction between successful and unsuccessful rebel groups then evolved in a series of arbitrations involving the actions of rebels operating in Latin America and elsewhere.[13] As these predated the ILC's work on State responsibility, this section first addresses the relevant arbitral jurisprudence before considering the rule's drafting history within the ILC.

9.2.1 Relevant Jurisprudence

9.2.1.1 The Movement Fails

From the nineteenth century, arbitral tribunals applied the general rule that States are not responsible for injuries caused to foreign nationals by members of an armed insurrection that ultimately fails in its aim to take power.[14] In the *Sambiaggio* case, for instance, the Italian-Venezuelan Mixed Claims Commission found that Venezuela was not liable for "losses and damages suffered at the hands of revolutionists who failed" on the basis that the revolutionists were not the

10. *See generally* Kathryn Greenman, State Responsibility and Rebels: : The History and Legacy of Protecting Investment Against Revolution (2021); Hessbruegge, *supra* note 7, at 300; Andrew Clapham, *Human Rights Obligations of Non-State Actors in Conflict Situations*, 88 Int'l Rev. Red Cross 491, 509 (2006).

11. Greenman, *supra* note 7.

12. *Id.*

13. *Id.*

14. *See, e.g.*, Salvador Prats v. U.S.A., 29 R.I.A.A. 187 (Mex.-U.S.A. Mixed Claims Comm'n, 1868) [hereinafter *Salvador Prats*]; John H. Hanna v. United States of America, 29 R.I.A.A. 143 (Am.-Brit. Comm'n, 1873); Several British Subjects (Great Britain) v. United States (the Iloilo Claims), 6 R.I.A.A. 158 (U.S.-G.B. Claims Comm'n, 1925); British Claims in the Spanish Zone of Morocco (U.K./Spain), 2 R.I.A.A. 615, 642 (1925); G. L. Solis (U.S.A.) v. United Mexican States, 4 R.I.A.A. 358, 361 (Gen. Claims Comm'n, 1928). *See also* Int'l Law Comm'n, Rep. of the Comm'n to the General Assembly (1975), *in* 2 Y.B. Int'l L. Comm'n 94–95, ¶¶ 12–19, U.N. Doc. A/CN.4/SER.A/1975/Add.1 [hereinafter ILC Y.B. 1975 vol. II]. For further discussion of the case law supporting this aspect of the rule, *see* Dumberry, State Succession to International Responsibility 225–30 (2007) [hereinafter Dumberry, State Succession].

agents of government, their acts were committed to destroy the government, and they were beyond governmental control.[15]

The commentary to Article 10 notes that State practice in support of this principle is "remarkably consistent."[16] This is evident in the preparatory work for the 1930 Hague Conference on the Codification of International Law, in which governments indicated their substantial agreement that States should not bear responsibility for the conduct of persons involved in insurrections, riots, or mob violence.[17] The 1929 and 1961 Harvard Draft Conventions on State responsibility similarly reflect this understanding.[18]

The law of State responsibility accordingly treats unsuccessful insurrectional movements in the same manner as other NSAs.[19] Their conduct is private in character and unless another rule of attribution applies, the State does not bear responsibility for any conduct on the part of the insurgents that might breach its international legal obligations.[20] That remains the case both during the

15. *Sambiaggio* case, 10 R.I.A.A. 499, 512–13 (It.-Venez. Mixed Claims Comm'n, 1903) [hereinafter *Sambiaggio*]. For further discussion of the case, *see* GREENMAN, *supra* note 10, at 91–95. *See also* Ago's Fourth Rep. on State Responsibility, *supra* note 6, at 132–33, ¶ 161; ILC Y.B. 1975 vol. II, *supra* note 14, at 94, ¶ 14; Gregory Townsend, *State Responsibility for Acts of De Facto Agents*, 14 ARIZ. J. INT'L & COMP. L. 635, 648 (1997).

16. ARSIWA, *supra* note 1, art. 10, cmt. ¶ 3.

17. *Id.*, *citing* Bases of Discussion Drawn up in 1929 by the Preparatory Committee of the Conference for the Codification of International Law, Basis of Discussion No. 22 (The Hague, 1930), *reprinted in* Int'l Law Comm'n, Documents of the Eighth Session Including the Rep. of the Comm'n to the General Assembly (1956) *in* [1956] 2 Y.B. INT'L L. COMM'N 223, 224, U.N. Doc, A/CN.4/SER.A/1956/Add.1 [hereinafter Hague Conference Bases of Discussion]. *See also* Gérard Cahin, *Attribution of Conduct to the State: Insurrectional Movements*, *in* THE LAW OF INTERNATIONAL RESPONSIBILITY 247, 253 (James Crawford et al. eds., 2010).

18. Harvard Draft Convention on Responsibility of States for Damage Done in Their Territory to the Person or Property of Foreigners, art. 13(a) (1929), *reprinted in* Int'l Law Comm'n, Documents of the Eighth Session Including the Rep. of the Comm'n to the General Assembly (1956), *in* [1956] 2 Y.B. INT'L L. COMM'N 229, U.N. Doc, A/CN.4/SER.A/1956/Add.1 [hereinafter 1929 Harvard Draft Convention]; Harvard Draft Convention on the International Responsibility of States for Injuries to Aliens, art. 18(2) (1961), *reprinted in* Int'l Law Comm'n, Documents of the Twenty-First Session Including the Rep. of the Comm'n to the General Assembly (1969), in [1969] 2 Y.B. INT'L L. COMM'N 142, 146, U.N. Doc A/CN.4/SER.A/1969/Add.1 [hereinafter 1961 Harvard Draft Convention]. *See also* Patrick Dumberry, *New State Responsibility for Internationally Wrongful Acts by an Insurrectional Movement*, 17 EUR. J. INT'L L. 605, 606 (2006) [hereinafter Dumberry, *New State Responsibility*]; JAMES CRAWFORD, STATE RESPONSIBILITY: THE GENERAL PART 179 (2013); Cahin, *supra* note 17, at 252–53; YORAM DINSTEIN, NON-INTERNATIONAL ARMED CONFLICTS IN INTERNATIONAL LAW 123–24 (2014).

19. ARSIWA, *supra* note 1, art. 10, cmt. ¶ 2; ILC Y.B. 1975 vol. II, *supra* note 14, at 91–92 (draft art. 14, cmt. ¶ 3).

20. *See, e.g.*, *Sambiaggio*, *supra* note 15, at 513; *Salvador Prats*, *supra* note 14, at 192. *See also* Ago's Fourth Rep. on State Responsibility, *supra* note 6, at 130, ¶ 156; *id.* at 132, ¶ 160; DINSTEIN, *supra* note 18, at 124.

insurrectional movement's existence and following its defeat.[21] The position is different, however, if the movement succeeds in taking power.

9.2.1.2 The Movement Establishes a New Government

The positive rule of attribution enshrined in Article 10(1) has a similarly long history. This new government rule was recognized within the 1929 Harvard Draft Convention on State Responsibility,[22] as well as in the comments sent by governments to the Preparatory Committee of the 1930 Hague Conference. Based on these observations, the committee formulated the following basis for discussion: "A State is responsible for damage caused to foreigners by an insurrectionist party which has been successful and has become the Government to the same degree as it is responsible for damage caused by acts of the Government *de jure* or its officials or troops."[23]

These sources indicate a long-standing acceptance by States and legal commentators of the new government rule reflected in Article 10(1). A review of the arbitral decisions that underlie the rule reveals, however, that this emerged "more by accident than as a matter of logic or policy."[24] The leading authority the ILC cites is the 1903 *Bolivar Railway Company* case, in which the Mixed Claims Commission confirmed that "[t]he nation is responsible for the obligations of a successful revolution from its beginning."[25] However, the decision's authority as a basis for the new government rule is doubtful. First, it related to a lawful act by the insurgents rather than to an act that potentially violated international law.[26] Second, the Umpire in the case misinterpreted the only authority he cited in support of the principle, namely, the 1877 decision of the U.S. Supreme Court in *Williams v. Bruffy*.[27]

Williams v. Bruffy concerned the issue of responsibility for the Confederates' conduct during the American Civil War.[28] In its judgment, the Supreme Court distinguished between two situations: first, when the rebels succeed in establishing a new State, and second, when they establish a de facto government that replaces

21. ILC Y.B. 1975 vol. II, *supra* note 14, at 93 (draft art. 14, cmt. ¶ 12).

22. 1929 Harvard Draft Convention, *supra* note 18, art. 13(b). The rule is also reflected in the 1961 Harvard draft. *See* 1961 Harvard Draft Convention, *supra* note 18, art. 18(1).

23. Hague Conference Bases of Discussion, *supra* note 17, at 224 (basis of discussion no. 22(c)).

24. Greenman, *supra* note 10, at 86.

25. ARSIWA, *supra* note 1, art. 10, cmt. ¶ 12, *citing* Bolivar Railway Company, 9 R.I.A.A. 445, 453 (G.B.-Venez. Mixed Claims Comm'n, 1903) [hereinafter *Bolivar Railway*].

26. Ago's Fourth Rep. on State Responsibility, *supra* note 6, at 146, ¶ 201. *See also* Dumberry, Rebellions, *supra* note 9, at 93.

27. Greenman, *supra* note 10, at 87–88.

28. Williams v. Bruffy, 96 U.S. 176 (U.S. 1877) [hereinafter *Williams v. Bruffy*].

the authorities within the entirety of the State.[29] It was only in the first situation that the Supreme Court held that the rebels' acts "from the commencement of [the rebel movement's] existence" are attributable to the State.[30] In the second scenario, the court concluded that the continuity of government rule should apply, meaning that the State bears responsibility for the acts of all successive governments.[31] This differs from the new government rule reflected in Article 10(1) because it applies only to the acts of a de facto government while it is in power. Importantly, it does not retroactively attribute the prior conduct of the rebels, before they assume power, to the State.[32]

Later arbitral rulings, including *Bolivar Railway Company*, failed to reflect the distinction laid out in *Williams v. Bruffy*.[33] The *Dix* case, for example, involved the confiscation of cattle belonging to a U.S. national by the revolutionary army in Venezuela.[34] In light of the revolution's success, the American-Venezuelan Commission confirmed Venezuela's liability under a "well-established rule of international law," but omitted to give any further explanation regarding its reasoning.[35] The principle has since been reaffirmed by other arbitral tribunals,[36] and by the Iran-U.S. Claims Tribunal.[37]

Despite the absence of a firm legal foundation, the new government rule reflected in Article 10(1) has proven uncontroversial.[38] States historically demonstrated a broad agreement with the principle that the conduct of a successful insurrectional movement is attributable to the State it comes to govern.[39] For instance, Peru accepted responsibility for the ill treatment of a U.S. consular agent in 1885 on the basis that the revolutionary movement that caused the harm later took power and

29. Greenman, *supra* note 10, at 87.

30. *Id.*

31. *Id.*

32. *Id.* at 87–88. *See also* Dumberry, Rebellions, *supra* note 9, at 94–95.

33. *See* Greenman, *supra* note 7; Hessbruegge, *supra* note 7, at 301; Dumberry, Rebellions, *supra* note 9, at 95–100.

34. *Dix* case, 9 R.I.A.A. 119 (Am.-Venez. Comm'n, 1903).

35. *Id.* at 120. *See also* Greenman, *supra* note 7; Hessbruegge, *supra* note 7, at 301–2.

36. *See* ARSIWA, *supra* note 1, art. 10, cmt. ¶ 12; ILC Y.B. 1975 vol. II, *supra* note 14, at 102 (draft art. 15, cmt. ¶ 11); Dumberry, Rebellions, *supra* note 9, at 95–100.

37. *See, e.g.*, Alfred L. W. Short v. The Islamic Republic of Iran, Award No. 312-11135-3, ¶¶ 34–35 (Iran-U.S. Claims Trib., 1987) [hereinafter *Short*]; Arthur Young & Company v. The Islamic Republic of Iran & Others, Award No. 338-484-1, ¶ 33 (Iran-U.S. Claims Trib., 1987).

38. Greenman, *supra* note 10, at 88.

39. *See* ARSIWA, *supra* note 1, art. 10, cmt. ¶ 13. *See also* Ago's Fourth Rep. on State Responsibility, *supra* note 6, at 148, ¶ 207; ILC Y.B. 1975 vol. II, *supra* note 14, at 104 (draft art. 15, cmt. ¶ 16).

became the government.[40] There is, however, a notable absence of recent State practice to support the rule, as discussed further in section 9.3.[41]

9.2.1.3 The Movement Establishes a New State

The foundations of the new State rule, reflected in Article 10(2) ARSIWA, are even weaker than those relating to insurrectional movements that form a new government.[42] All the arbitral decisions and State practice the ILC refers to in its commentary to Article 10 relate to the new government rule, not to the creation of a new State.[43] Thus, many legal scholars have highlighted the absence of State practice or relevant jurisprudence to support this element of Article 10.[44]

Special Rapporteur Šturma made a similar observation in his second report on the succession of States in respect of State responsibility.[45] He nevertheless identified several authorities that support the new State rule reflected in Article 10(2). The first is the jurisprudence of the French municipal courts related to Algerian independence.[46] French courts consistently ruled that the new State of Algeria should bear responsibility for obligations arising from harmful acts committed by the insurrectional movement, the FLN, prior to its success in taking power.[47] It is notable, however, that Algeria was not a party to the proceedings. As such, these decisions did not formally hold Algeria to account but rather, found that France was not responsible for such acts.[48]

40. *See* ILC Y.B. 1975 vol. II, *supra* note 14, at 104 (draft art. 15, cmt. ¶ 17). For further discussion regarding this incident, *see* Michael Akehurst, *State Responsibility for the Wrongful Acts of Rebels—An Aspect of the Southern Rhodesian Problem*, 43 Brit. Y.B. Int'l L. 49, 60 (1968–1969).

41. *See also* d'Aspremont, *supra* note 7, at 432; Simon Olleson, Brit. Inst. Int'l & Comp. L., The Impact of the ILC's Articles on Responsibility of States for Internationally Wrongful Acts 95 (Oct. 10, 2007), www.biicl.org/files/3107_impactofthearticlesonstate_responsibilitypreliminarydraftfinal.pdf.

42. *See generally* Dumberry, Rebellions, *supra* note 9, at 324–29, 333–39.

43. ARSIWA, *supra* note 1, art. 10, cmt. ¶ 12.

44. *See, e.g.*, d'Aspremont, *supra* note 7, at 427, 431–32; Dumberry, State Succession, *supra* note 14, at 232–39; Dumberry, *New State Responsibility*, *supra* note 18, at 607, 613; Sten I. Verhoeven, *International Responsibility of Armed Opposition Groups*, *in* Responsibilities of the Non-State Actor in Armed Conflict and the Market Place 285, 288 (Noemi Gal-Or et al. eds., 2015); Dinstein, *supra* note 18, at 130.

45. Pavel Šturma (Special Rapporteur), Second Rep. on Succession of States in Respect of State Responsibility 31, ¶ 116, U.N. Doc. A/CN.4/719 (Apr. 6, 2018) [hereinafter Šturma's Second Rep. on State Succession]. *See also* Crawford, *supra* note 18, at 176.

46. Šturma's Second Rep. on State Succession, *supra* note 45, ¶¶ 116, 117.

47. *Id.* ¶ 117; Crawford, *supra* note 18, at 178.

48. Crawford, *supra* note 18, at 178.

In addition, Special Rapporteur Šturma referred to the U.S. Supreme Court decision in *Williams v. Bruffy*.[49] Here, the Court noted that where a movement aims to secede and establish a new State

> [t]he validity of its acts, both against the parent State and the citizens or subjects thereof, depends entirely upon its ultimate success; if it fail[s] to establish itself permanently, all such acts perish with it; if it succeed[s] and become recognized, its acts from the commencement of its existence are upheld as those of an independent nation.[50]

There is, however, some inconsistency in the Court's judgment. It later referred to the example of the U.S. separation from Great Britain and said that everything the American insurgents did from "their declaration of independence" was attributable to the new State.[51] This precedent, therefore, does not provide strong endorsement for the attribution of acts committed during the insurgency, prior to any declaration of independence, to the new State.[52]

The other authorities Šturma cites are also relatively weak. One is a legal opinion given by the Law Officers of the British Crown in 1863 regarding the American Civil War.[53] The opinion stated that if the rebels were to succeed in their efforts to secede from the United States, the new State would be held responsible for the Confederate authorities' acts committed prior to independence.[54] Another is an *obiter dictum* in the *Socony Vacuum Oil Company* case before the U.S. International Claims Commission.[55] While the case related to an unsuccessful insurrectional movement, the commission observed in passing that in the case of a successful secession, such as that of the United States from the British Crown in 1776, the new State bears responsibility for the rebels' acts.[56]

More recently, Croatia invoked the new State element of Article 10 in the *Application of the Genocide Convention (Croatia v. Serbia)* before the International Court of Justice (ICJ).[57] In its response, Serbia highlighted the absence of State

49. Šturma's Second Rep. on State Succession, *supra* note 45, ¶ 118.

50. *Williams v. Bruffy*, *supra* note 28, at 177.

51. *Id.* at 186.

52. Dumberry, Rebellions, *supra* note 9, at 334; Tatyana Jane Eatwell, State Responsibility for the Unlawful Conduct of Armed Groups (Ph.D. dissertation, University of Cambridge) 221–24 (2019), www.repository.cam.ac.uk/bitstream/handle/1810/302004/Eatwell%20Thesis%20May%202020%20updated%20Electronic%20Final.pdf?sequence=8&isAllowed=y [hereinafter Eatwell, *Armed Groups*].

53. Šturma's Second Rep. on State Succession, *supra* note 45, ¶ 116. *See also* Dumberry, Rebellions, *supra* note 9, at 333; Crawford, *supra* note 18, at 176–77.

54. Šturma's Second Rep. on State Succession, *supra* note 45, ¶ 116.

55. *Id.*

56. Dumberry, Rebellions, *supra* note 9, at 336–37; Crawford, *supra* note 18, at 177.

57. Application of the Convention on the Prevention and Punishment of the Crime of Genocide (Croatia v. Serbia), Judgment, 2015 I.C.J. Rep. 3 ¶¶ 102–5 (Feb. 3) [hereinafter *Croatia v. Serbia*].

practice to support the rule, arguing that this was not reflective of customary international law.[58] Croatia then acknowledged that "much of the practice relates to insurrectional governments rather than movements to create a new State" but claimed that there were "good reasons" to cover both situations, pointing to the uncontroversial nature of the rule.[59] In its judgment on the merits, the ICJ did not take an explicit position on the rule's customary nature or otherwise.[60] This may suggest a lack of conviction on the part of the ICJ majority regarding the rule's foundations in customary international law. The Serbian judge in the case, Judge Kreća, was more direct, dismissing the ILC's conclusions regarding the rule's basis in law as "wishful thinking rather than a respectable argument."[61]

Given the dearth of State practice or international jurisprudence to support the new State rule reflected in Article 10(2), Judge Kreća's characterization has some merit. Considerable doubts remain regarding the rule's status in customary international law. Nonetheless, the ILC concluded that the principle of retrospective attribution should apply not only when a rebel group becomes the new government but also when it establishes a new State.[62] The same view is reflected within the 1961 Harvard Draft Convention on State Responsibility[63] as well as in the ILC's more recent work on the succession of States in respect of State responsibility.[64]

9.2.2 Drafting History

Prior to Roberto Ago's appointment as Special Rapporteur, the ILC envisaged State responsibility for rebels' conduct arising in two situations: first, if the State failed to take measures to prevent or punish the acts in question; and second if the insurrection was successful.[65] When Special Rapporteur Ago separated primary norms of international law from the secondary rules of State responsibility[66] the

58. *Id.* Serbia Counter-Memorial, ¶¶ 284, 286, 289–93; *id.* Serbia rejoinder ¶¶ 161–66.

59. *Id.* Croatia reply, vol. I, Dec. 20, 2010, ¶¶ 7.54–7.57. *See also id.* Verbatim Record, Mar. 6, 2014, C.R. 2014/10, Crawford (Croatia), at 40–41, ¶ 20.

60. *Id.* Judgment on the Merits ¶ 105. *See also id.* Preliminary Objections, 2008 I.C.J. Rep. at 459, ¶¶ 126–27.

61. *Id.* Separate Opinion of Judge Kreća, ¶ 66.2.

62. ARSIWA, *supra* note 1, art. 10.

63. 1961 Harvard Draft Convention, *supra* note 18, art. 18(1).

64. Pavel Šturma, Fifth Rep. on Succession of States in Respect of State Responsibility 26–27 (draft art. 8), U.N. Doc. A/CN.4/751 (Apr. 1, 2022).

65. García Amador, International Responsibility: Second Rep. 121 (draft arts. 10, 12(2)), U.N. Doc. A/CN.4/106 (Feb. 15, 1957). *See also* GREENMAN, *supra* note 10, at 179.

66. For further discussion regarding the distinction between primary and secondary norms, *see supra* ch. 3, sec. 3.2.

concept of due diligence (represented in the first basis of responsibility) fell into the realm of primary norms.[67] Meanwhile, the principles now reflected in Article 10 were translated into rules of attribution within the law of State responsibility.[68]

On first reading, the rules enshrined in Article 10 ARSIWA were encompassed within two articles. Draft article 15 provided for the attribution of an insurrectional movement's prior conduct to the State in the event of its success,[69] while draft article 14 provided that there would be no attribution of conduct in cases where the movement was unsuccessful.[70] In his first report on State responsibility, Special Rapporteur Crawford noted the superfluity of draft article 14.[71] This was subsequently deleted, and the relevant principles restated within a single article.[72]

The version of Article 10 included in ARSIWA is simpler in its construction than its predecessors.[73] First, it refers to "[t]he conduct of an insurrectional movement" rather than referring to those movements' "organs."[74] Second, Article 10 omits any requirement that the movement was "established in opposition to a State or to its government."[75] These two changes broaden the rule's scope, so that it can apply to groups that are insufficiently structured to have "organs" as well as those initially established for a different purpose.[76] Third, Article 10 does not include any reference to the "retroactive attribution" of conduct to a State, which appeared in the 1972 version of the rule.[77] The removal of this wording, however, does not change the nature of attribution on this basis, which is necessarily retroactive in character.

When States had the opportunity to comment on the proposed rule of attribution prior to its adoption in ARSIWA, most declined to do so.[78] Of those States

67. ARSIWA specifically recognizes that a State may bear responsibility for its own organs' failure to exercise due diligence regarding the conduct of an insurrectional movement. *See* ARSIWA, *supra* note 1, art. 10(3); *id.* cmt. ¶ 15.

68. Ago's Fourth Rep. on State Responsibility, *supra* note 6, at 151–52 (draft art. 13). *See also* GREENMAN, *supra* note 10, at 179–80.

69. ILC Y.B. 1975 vol. II, *supra* note 14, at 47, 99–100.

70. *Id.* at 91.

71. Crawford's First Rep. on State Responsibility, *supra* note 7, at 53, ¶¶ 272–73. *See also* ILC Y.B. 1998 vol. I, *supra* note 7, at 269, ¶ 52.

72. *See* Crawford's First Rep. on State Responsibility, *supra* note 7, at 57.

73. *See generally* DUMBERRY, REBELLIONS, *supra* note 9, at 66–69.

74. Crawford's First Rep. on State Responsibility, *supra* note 7, at 57.

75. *Id.*

76. ILC Y.B. 1998 vol. I, *supra* note 7, at 290, ¶¶ 86, 87.

77. *See* Ago's Fourth Rep. on State Responsibility, *supra* note 6, at 151–52 (draft art. 13).

78. *See* Int'l Law Comm'n, Comments and Observations Received from Governments 110, 131, U.N. Doc. A/CN.4/488 and Add.1–3 (1998) [hereinafter 1998 Comments and Observations]; Int'l Law Comm'n, Comments and Observations Received from Governments 50, U.N. Doc. A/CN.4/515 and Add.1–3 (2001) [hereinafter 2001 Comments and Observations]. States raised

that did choose to comment, some, including the United Kingdom and Chile, expressed explicit support for the rule.[79] A small number of others articulated concerns.[80] The failure by the vast majority of States to comment on the principles now expressed in Article 10 could indicate their general acceptance of the rule, or alternatively, their lack of interest in it as a basis for State responsibility.

9.2.3 The Rule's Object and Purpose

It is clear from Article 10's commentary that for the ILC, the rationale for both elements of the rule "lies in the continuity between the movement and the eventual Government."[81] Where the insurrectional movement becomes the new government, such continuity between the structures of the movement and the government it ultimately establishes "leads naturally to the attribution to the State of conduct which the insurrectional movement may have committed during the struggle."[82] The same is true when the movement succeeds in creating a new State: "Effectively the same entity which previously had the characteristics of an insurrectional or other movement has become the Government of the State it was struggling to establish."[83]

Other theories to support the rule have nevertheless been advanced.[84] For example, regarding the new government element of Article 10, the Umpire in the *Bolivar Railway* case asserted that "[t]he nation is responsible for the obligations of a successful revolution from its beginning, because in theory, it represented ab

only minor comments regarding the draft rule of attribution on earlier occasions. *See* Int'l Law Comm'n, Documents of the Thirty-Second Session (1980), *in* [1980] 2 Y.B. INT'L L. COMM'N 88–106, U.N. Doc. A/CN.4/SER.A/1980/Add.1 (Part 1) [hereinafter ILC Y.B. 1980 vol. II]; Int'l Law Comm'n, Documents of the Thirty-Eighth Session (1986), *in* [1986] 2 Y.B. INT'L L. COMM'N 13, U.N. Doc. A/CN.4/SER.A/1986/Add.1 (Part 1). *But see infra* note 217 regarding States' comments on the rule in the context of national liberation movements.

79. ILC Y.B. 1980 vol. II, *supra* note 78, at 98, ¶ 19 (comments of Chile); 1998 Comments and Observations, *supra* note 78, at 131 (comments of the United Kingdom).

80. *See, e.g.*, 2001 Comments and Observations, *supra* note 78, at 50 (comments of the Netherlands); U.N.G.A., Responsibility of States for Internationally Wrongful Acts: Comments and Information Received from Governments 6, ¶ 4 (comments of Sudan), U.N. Doc. A/74/156 (July 12, 2019).

81. ARSIWA, *supra* note 1, art. 10, cmt. ¶ 4. *See also* Ago's Fourth Rep. on State Responsibility, *supra* note 6, at 144, ¶¶ 193–95; *id.* at 145, ¶ 199; ILC Y.B. 1975 vol. II, *supra* note 14, at 100 (draft art. 15, cmt. ¶ 3); Crawford's First Rep. on State Responsibility, *supra* note 7, at 51–52, ¶ 264. *But see* Gayim, *supra* note 7, at 85, 98 (opining that the principle of continuity was used as a pretext by the ILC and the attribution standard is, in reality, based upon past practice).

82. ARSIWA, *supra* note 1, art. 10, cmt. ¶ 5.

83. *Id.* ¶ 6.

84. *See generally* DUMBERRY, REBELLIONS, *supra* note 9, at 74–86, 312–21.

initio a changing national will, crystallizing in the finally successful result."[85] As the ILC noted in 1975, however, this rationale for the rule is open to question. It is highly debatable whether all insurrectional movements truly represent the "national will."[86]

Continuity between the organizational structures of the successful insurrectional movement and those of the State that it comes to govern provides a firmer basis for the rule reflected in Article 10. Two decisions of the Iran-U.S. Claims Tribunal support this view. In *Alfred L.W. Short v. Iran*, the tribunal referred to attribution on this basis "as a consequence of the continuity existing between the new organization of the State and the organization of the revolutionary movement."[87] Meanwhile, in the *Yeager* case, the tribunal focused on continuity of leadership. It noted that the conduct of a revolutionary movement may be attributed to a State when there is continuity in the person of the leader of the revolutionaries, who later becomes the leader of the new government.[88]

The importance of continuity becomes apparent when applying the rule to the situation in Syria. If it reflects customary international law, the new government rule expressed in Article 10(1) ensures that the rebel group Hay'at Tahrir al-Sham (HTS) cannot deny responsibility for its acts in violation of Syria's international legal obligations, such as its executions of detainees, committed before it took power in December 2024.[89] As former Special Rapporteur Crawford put it, "the State represented by the successful insurgents is precluded from denying the attribution to it of their conduct in the course of the insurgency."[90] Although the acts in question were not the State's own at the time of their commission, the continuity that exists between the rebel movement and the State means that in these limited circumstances, the interests of victims should take precedence.

This is key to ensuring accountability, given the practical impossibility of holding insurrectional movements directly to account for their conduct. Although some rebel groups, in principle, bear international responsibility for their own

85. *Bolivar Railway*, *supra* note 25, at 452–53. Other theories to justify the rule include the continuity of government, the legitimacy of the struggle, and the "resurrection" of State. *See* Dumberry, State Succession, *supra* note 14, at 239–46; Dumberry, *New State Responsibility*, *supra* note 18, at 609–12; Hessbruegge, *supra* note 7, at 265, 273–74.

86. ILC Y.B. 1975 vol. II, *supra* note 14, at 100 (draft art. 15, cmt. ¶ 2).

87. *Short*, *supra* note 37, ¶ 33.

88. Kenneth P. Yeager v. Islamic Republic of Iran, Award No. 324-10199-1, ¶ 35 (Iran-U.S. Claims Trib., 1987) [hereinafter *Yeager*]. *See also* Dumberry, Rebellions, *supra* note 9, at 86.

89. *See, e.g.*, Ravina Shamdasani, Spokesperson for the U.N. High Commissioner for Human Rights, Press Briefing Note on Syria–Idlib Violations and Abuses (Nov. 20, 2020), https://www.ohchr.org/en/press-briefing-notes/2020/11/press-briefing-note-syria-idlib-violations-and-abuses.

90. Crawford, *supra* note 18, at 171.

wrongful acts,[91] in practice it is extremely difficult for those harmed by an NSA's conduct to bring claims against it. Insurrectional movements exist only temporarily: They disintegrate, are defeated, or succeed and become the government. Any claim against the movement as an entity must be brought while it still exists. In practice, such claims are extremely rare and unlikely to succeed.[92] Therefore, the only realistic option for injured States is to wait until the end of the insurgency to assess whether the rebel group is successful, so that it can seek reparations from the State that the movement comes to govern.[93]

This objective is evident in the ARSIWA commentary. Regarding the new government element of Article 10, the commentary highlights that the State "is the only subject of international law to which responsibility can be attributed. The situation requires that acts committed during the struggle for power by the apparatus of the insurrectional movement should be attributable to the State"[94] With respect to the new State rule, the commentary notes that the predecessor State will not be responsible for the acts of the insurrectional movement: "The only possibility is that the new State be required to assume responsibility for conduct committed with a view to its own establishment."[95]

The rule of attribution expressed in Article 10, therefore, fulfills an important aim. If it reflects customary international law, it ensures that a State cannot deny responsibility for the prior conduct of an insurrectional movement whose structures have become integrated into the State's own government. This provides an avenue of accountability, alongside the rebels' potential individual criminal responsibility, where otherwise there might be none.[96] However, as the following analysis demonstrates, practical difficulties related to the rule's practical application minimize its significance in achieving this goal.

9.3 THE INSURRECTIONAL MOVEMENT BECOMES THE NEW GOVERNMENT

The first paragraph of Article 10 ARSIWA provides for the attribution of an insurrectional movement's conduct to a State when that movement's ruling

91. For instance, organized armed groups bear responsibility for violations of IHL. *See* ARSIWA, *supra* note 1, art. 10, cmt. ¶ 16. For discussion regarding an insurrectional movement's responsibility for its own wrongful acts, *see* Dumberry, Rebellions, *supra* note 9, at 196–209.

92. *See* Dumberry, Rebellions, *supra* note 9, at 204–9.

93. *Id.* at 147.

94. ARSIWA, *supra* note 1, art. 10, cmt. ¶ 5.

95. *Id.* ¶ 6.

96. d'Aspremont, *supra* note 7, at 432–33; Hessbruegge, *supra* note 7, at 274.

organization becomes the new government in the entirety of the State's territory.[97] As noted previously, in this situation, the identity of the State as a subject of international law does not change.[98] Therefore, following the movement's success, the State bears responsibility not only for the insurrectional movement's conduct during its fight for power, but also for the acts and omissions of the previous government in countering the insurrection.[99] For instance, following HTS's success in toppling President Assad from power in December 2024, Syria bears international responsibility both for HTS's prior conduct in violation of international humanitarian law (IHL)[100] and also for the many international law violations committed by the Assad regime.[101]

While at the time of writing it appears that HTS has achieved complete success and entirely replaced the previous government in Syria,[102] an insurrectional movement might alternatively become incorporated into the existing governmental structures via a peace deal. The analysis that follows addresses each of these scenarios in turn.

9.3.1 The Insurrectional Movement Replaces the Previous Government

When an insurrectional movement triumphs and its structures replace those of the previous government, there is a clear continuity between the movement and the new government of the State.[103] For instance, although HTS in Syria transitioned from an Islamist group to a functioning government, there are evident connections

97. ARSIWA, *supra* note 1, art. 10; *id.* art. 10, cmt. ¶¶ 5, 7; Ago's Fourth Rep. on State Responsibility, *supra* note 6, at 131, ¶ 157.

98. *Id.* art. 10, cmt. ¶ 5; Ago's Fourth Rep. on State Responsibility, *supra* note 6, at 131, ¶ 158; ILC Y.B. 1975 vol. II, *supra* note 14, at 100–101 (draft art. 15, cmt. ¶ 5).

99. ARSIWA, *supra* note 1, art. 10, cmt. ¶¶ 5; Ago's Fourth Rep. on State Responsibility, *supra* note 6, at 145, ¶ 197; CRAWFORD, *supra* note 18, at 175.

100. *See, e.g.*, Shamdasani, *supra* note 89. HTS's mistreatment of detainees potentially violates the fundamental guarantees that should be afforded to all civilians and persons *hors de combat*. *See* 1 CUSTOMARY INTERNATIONAL HUMANITARIAN LAW, RR. 87–90 (Jean-Marie Henckaerts & Louise Doswald-Beck eds., 2005) [hereinafter CUSTOMARY IHL].

101. *See, e.g.*, SYRIAN NETWORK FOR HUM. RTS., SUMMARY OF THE ASSAD REGIME'S CRIMES AGAINST THE SYRIAN PEOPLE OVER THE LAST 14 YEARS (Dec. 20, 2024), https://snhr.org/blog/2024/12/20/summary-of-the-assad-regimes-crimes-against-the-syrian-people-over-the-last-14-years/.

102. *See, e.g.*, Chrsitina Goldbaum, *Rebel Leader Who Overthrew al-Assad Is Declared Syria's President*, N.Y. TIMES (Jan. 29, 2025), https://www.nytimes.com/2025/01/29/world/middleeast/syria-leader-al-shara-government.html.

103. ARSIWA, *supra* note 1, art. 10, cmt. ¶ 5; CRAWFORD, *supra* note 18, at 175; Cahin, *supra* note 17, at 249.

between the movement's leadership and organizational structures before and after the group's assumption of power.[104] As such, assuming it reflects customary international law, the new government rule enshrined in Article 10(1) attributes HTS's conduct during its struggle for power to Syria.[105]

That is the case even if other States refuse to recognize HTS as Syria's legitimate government.[106] The new government rule applies once an insurrectional movement exercises *de facto* control over a State's territory and assumes the functions of government.[107] Accordingly, it is the factual situation on the ground that is relevant, not the recognition of the new government by other States. In the case of HTS, by mid-December 2024, the group controlled most Syrian territory and President Assad had fled the country.[108] Although certain regions of Syria were still controlled by other armed groups, from that date onwards the group's success was clear.[109] Therefore, the new government element of Article 10 applies.

Nevertheless, recognition by other States inevitably impacts the effectiveness of this rule of attribution. An injured State may be reluctant to pursue a claim based on the new government rule if it does not recognize the movement in power as the legitimate government. Consider, for instance, the Taliban's resumption of power in Afghanistan in August 2021.[110] A claim against Afghanistan in respect of the Taliban's conduct prior to that date could have the politically unacceptable consequence of conferring legitimacy on the Taliban government. Political

104. *What to Know About Syria's New Caretaker Government*, AL JAZEERA (Dec. 15, 2024), https://www.aljazeera.com/news/2024/12/15/what-to-know-about-syrias-new-caretaker-government.

105. *See* Philippa Westling, The Past Is a Foreign Country: An Examination of the Retrospective Attribution of Organized Armed Groups According to Article 10 ARSIWA (Bachelor's thesis, Swedish Defence University) (2022), https://fhs.diva-portal.org/smash/get/diva2:1636844/FULLTEXT01.pdf.

106. At the time of writing, it remains unclear what stance States will take towards the Syrian government led by HTS. For discussion regarding recognition, *see, e.g.*, Justin Cole & Oona A. Hathaway, *Should the Rebels Be Recognized as the New Government of Syria? How International Law Could Provide a Clearer Answer*, JUST SEC. (Jan. 6, 2025), https://www.justsecurity.org/106124/recognition-government-syria-international-law/.

107. Aguilar-Amory & Royal Bank of Canada Claims (Great Britain v. Costa Rica) 1 R.I.A.A. 369, 377-82 (1923); Legal Consequences for States of the Continued Presence of South Africa in Namibia, Advisory Opinion, 1971 I.C.J. Rep. ¶ 118 (June 21). *See also* Verhoeven, *supra* note 44, at 290; DUMBERRY, REBELLIONS, *supra* note 9, at 100-07.

108. William Christou, *Syrian Rebels Reveal Year-Long Plot That Brought Down Assad Regime*, THE GUARDIAN (Dec. 13, 2024), https://www.theguardian.com/world/2024/dec/13/syrian-rebels-reveal-year-long-plot-that-brought-down-assad-regime.

109. *Id.*

110. Lindsay Maizland, *The Taliban in Afghanistan*, COUNCIL ON FOREIGN REL. (Jan. 19, 2023), https://www.cfr.org/backgrounder/taliban-afghanistan.

considerations may thus diminish the practical impact of this element of Article 10 in holding successful revolutionary movements to account.

This reality may help to explain why the new government rule reflected in Article 10(1) is so seldom invoked by States, or in the decisions of international courts and tribunals. One rare exception is the case of *Cengiz v. Libya*, which related to attacks against the property of a Turkish investor during the Libyan conflict from 2011 and 2014.[111] The International Court of Arbitration noted that pursuant to the new government rule expressed in Article 10(1), Libya bears responsibility for acts and omissions committed "by all insurrectional groups and militias, which defended the [National Transitional Council (NTC)] Government and fought the Gaddafi regime, and which ultimately were successful."[112] Dumberry has rightly questioned Article 10's relevance to the facts given the court's conclusion that the NTC had already established itself as Libya's new government at the time the relevant attacks took place.[113] If that is correct, the attacks would be attributable to the State pursuant to the rule reflected in Article 4 ARSIWA.[114] But if the rebel groups fighting the Gaddafi regime had not yet taken power at the time of these attacks, as seems more likely on the facts, the new government rule expressed in Article 10 would attribute these to Libya.[115]

Prior to the *Cengiz* case, the UN High Commissioner for Human Rights invoked the new government element of Article 10 in the context of a transfer of power in the Central African Republic (CAR) in 2013.[116] The new government was formed by the Séléka coalition, a rebel group that toppled former President Bozizé and drove him into exile.[117] During the prior conflict, Séléka soldiers committed numerous acts that potentially violated international law, including summary executions, attacks on civilians, torture, and sexual violence.[118] The UN High Commissioner noted that "in accordance with Article 10 [ARSIWA], the Séléka, after it seized power, engaged the State responsibility of the Central African Republic for all violations committed by the Séléka members in the country during the armed conflict."[119]

111. Cengiz Construction, Industry & Trade Company v. Libya, Case No. 21537/ZF/AYZ, Final Award ¶¶ 423, 429-31 (Int'l Ct. Arb. of the Int'l Chamber of Commerce, 2018).

112. *Id.* ¶ 431.

113. Dumberry, Rebellions, *supra* note 9, at 158-68.

114. ARSIWA, *supra* note 1, art. 4. *See also supra* ch. 4.

115. Dumberry, Rebellions, *supra* note 9, at 165-68.

116. Navenethem Pillay (U.N. High Commissioner for Human Rights), Situation of Human Rights in the Central African Republic ¶ 25, U.N. Doc. A/HRC/24/59 (Sept. 12, 2013). *See also* Eatwell, *Armed Groups*, *supra* note 52, at 169-70; Dumberry, Rebellions, *supra* note 9, at 90-92.

117. Pillay, *supra* note 116, ¶¶ 8-10.

118. *Id.* ¶¶ 35–50.

119. *Id.* ¶ 25.

The new government in the CAR survived for only a short period of time.[120] Nevertheless, Article 10 continues to attribute the Séléka coalition's conduct to the CAR, notwithstanding the group's ultimate defeat.[121] Thus, if an insurrectional movement loses power, the State continues to bear responsibility for its prior conduct, despite the lack of ongoing continuity between that movement and the State.[122] In Dinstein's words, "As long as it lasted, the insurgent Government (and no other) was the Government of the State and the acts attributed remain acts of State."[123]

9.3.2 Governments of National Reconciliation

The ILC initially envisaged that the new government element of Article 10 should apply both when an insurrectional movement achieves a total victory and therefore replaces the government, and when it integrates into existing government structures following a power-sharing agreement.[124] The ILC's stance on the issue changed, however, later in ARSIWA's development. Special Rapporteur Crawford proclaimed that it would be "unwise and unrealistic" for the rule of attribution to apply in cases where a government of national reconciliation is formed.[125] He asserted that if the attribution standard did apply in such circumstances,

> existing Governments which had been neither overthrown nor replaced and had shown a spirit of conciliation by incorporating elements of insurrectional movements in the Government would be too heavily penalized: they would in fact pay for their policy of reconciliation by being required to shoulder the full responsibility for the acts committed by the insurrectional movements during the insurrection.[126]

Crawford's concerns in this respect are valid, given the desirability of encouraging national reconciliation as a means of ending conflict.[127] If by entering a

120. *See generally*, Lewis Mudge, *Decade After Central African Takeover, Justice Still Needed*, Hum. Rts. Watch (Mar. 27, 2023), https://www.hrw.org/news/2023/03/27/decade-after-central-african-takeover-justice-still-needed.

121. *See* Dinstein, *supra* note 18, at 129.

122. *Id.*

123. *Id.*

124. Ago's Fourth Rep. on State Responsibility, *supra* note 6, at 146, ¶ 199; Int'l Law Comm'n, Summary Records of the Twenty-Seventh Session (comments of Special Rapporteur Ago) (1975), *in* [1975] 1 Y.B. Int'l L. Comm'n 62, ¶ 4, U.N. Doc. A/CN.4/SER.A/1975 [hereinafter ILC Y.B. 1975 vol. I]; *id.* at 66, ¶ 38 (comments of Mr. Elias); ILC Y.B. 1975 vol. II, *supra* note 14, at 100-01 (draft art. 15, cmt. ¶ 5); *id.* at 104 (draft art. 15, cmt. ¶ 17).

125. ILC Y.B. 1998 vol. I, *supra* note 7, at 248-49, ¶ 55.

126. *Id.*

127. *See id.* at 251, ¶ 8 (comments of Special Rapporteur Crawford).

power-sharing agreement the State must automatically assume responsibility for earlier acts of the insurrectional movement, this could impede peace negotiations and thereby prolong the conflict.[128] However, as Eatwell observes, there are compelling counter-arguments that favor the attribution of the rebel movement's conduct to the State.[129] For instance, the exclusion of governments of national reconciliation from Article 10's scope could "entrench impunity and non-responsibility" and also lead to an unjustifiable inequality between the conduct of the pre-existing government (for which the State would bear international responsibility) and that of the former insurrectional movement (for which it would not).[130]

Considerations such as these may have factored into the ILC's nuanced stance on the issue, reflected in Article 10's commentary. Rather than entirely excluding the rule's application to governments of national reconciliation, the commentary provides that the new government rule reflected in Article 10(1) "should not be pressed too far" in this context.[131] It continues,

> [t]he State should not be made responsible for the conduct of a violent opposition movement merely because, in the interests of an overall peace settlement, elements of the opposition are drawn into a reconstructed Government. Thus, the criterion of application of paragraph 1 is that of a real and substantial continuity between the former insurrectional movement and the new Government it has succeeded in forming.[132]

This position has merit. It allows a factual determination of the insurrectional movement's level of representation in the new government and in particular, the degree of "real and substantial continuity" between the rebel organization and the government formed following the peace deal.[133] It also accords with the rule's object and purpose.[134] Moreover, if substantial continuity exists between a new government and the former insurrectional movement, the State's responsibility for the acts of that movement may offer the new government increased legitimacy in the eyes of both the local population and the international community.[135]

128. *Id.*; d'Aspremont, *supra* note 7, at 436.

129. Tatyana Eatwell, *State Responsibility, "Successful" Insurrectional Movements and Governments of National Reconciliation*, *in* NON-STATE ACTORS AND INTERNATIONAL OBLIGATIONS 388, 394–96 (James Summers & Alex Gough eds., 2018) [hereinafter Eatwell, *Successful Insurrectional Movements*].

130. *Id.*

131. ARSIWA, *supra* note 1, art. 10, cmt. ¶ 7.

132. *Id.*

133. *Id.* For further discussion regarding Article 10's application to situations of national reconciliation, *see* d'Aspremont, *supra* note 7, at 436–37; Eatwell, *Successful Insurrectional Movements*, *supra* note 129.

134. *See supra* sec. 9.2.3.

135. *See generally* Eatwell, *Successful Insurrectional Movements*, *supra* note 129.

The question remains, however, what degree of continuity should suffice for the rule to apply. This may vary widely, from the insurrectional movement's complete assumption of power at one end of the spectrum to a minimal role for a small number of its leaders at the other.[136] Between those two extremes, some organs of the preexisting State might disappear, replaced by structures of the insurrectional movement, while others remain in place.[137]

Akehurst highlights certain factors that may assist when considering Article 10's potential application in such circumstances. These include the seniority of the governmental roles assumed by members of the insurrectional movement, the retroactive confirmation of rebels in official positions they seized during the insurrection, and the levels of power and influence held by the group's representatives in government.[138] Added to these, the degree of authority the former insurrectional movement wields in the new government is highly relevant.[139] Thus, Article 10 should not apply when the movement's representatives perform a minority role in the government but only when the rebels achieve "a significant share of power."[140] It may help to consider whether elements of the movement retain their integrity within the structures of government, or whether the movement substantially loses its identity following implementation of the peace agreement.

These factors all link to the requirement for "real and substantial continuity" between the rebel movement and the new government.[141] When only a few rebel leaders have a role in the government, this criterion is not satisfied.[142] To illustrate, the 2016 Peace Accord in Colombia guaranteed the former rebel group, the FARC, just five seats in each house of Congress from 2018 to 2026.[143] This represents such a small proportion of the overall number of legislative seats that there is minimal continuity between the FARC and the new government, meaning that the rule of attribution would not apply.[144] In contrast, if the rule

136. *See, e.g.*, ILC Y.B. 1998 vol. I, *supra* note 7, at 290, ¶ 87.

137. ILC Y.B. 1975 vol. I, *supra* note 124, at 62, ¶ 4 (comments of Special Rapporteur Ago).

138. Akehurst, *supra* note 40, at 60–61.

139. Eatwell, *Successful Insurrectional Movements*, *supra* note 129, at 404.

140. *Id. See also* Eatwell, *Armed Groups*, *supra* note 52, at 184–86; Dumberry, Rebellions, *supra* note 9, at 131–33.

141. ARSIWA, *supra* note 1, art. 10, cmt. ¶ 7.

142. Dumberry, Rebellions, *supra* note 9, at 132–33.

143. Final Agreement Between the National Government of Colombia and the FARC-EP 72 (Nov. 24, 2016), https://www.peaceagreements.org/viewmasterdocument/1845. *See also* Miguel García-Sánchez & Ryan E. Carlin, *The FARC in the Public Eye: Negotiation, Integration, and Political Participation*, 12 J. of Pol. in Latin America 239, 241 (2020).

144. ARSIWA, *supra* note 1, art. 10, cmt. ¶ 7. There are 172 seats in the House of Representatives and 108 seats in the Senate. *See* International Foundation for Electoral Systems, Election Guide: Republic of Colombia (Mar. 13, 2022), https://www.electionguide.org/elections/id/3756/.

reflects customary international law, it would likely attribute the conduct of Maoist rebels to the State of Nepal following the 2006 peace deal.[145] This is on the basis that the Maoists had significant representation in the new government, gaining half the directly elected seats, with their leader elected as Prime Minister.[146]

Difficult questions regarding the rule's application may also arise when a peace deal grants an insurrectional movement the ability to govern part of the State's territory. This option was suggested as an early possibility for resolving the conflict in eastern Ukraine.[147] In such a scenario, there may be "real and substantial continuity"[148] between the ruling organization of the insurrectional movement and the governing structures within one part of the State. However, such continuity relates only to a fraction of the State's overall territory. Although the insurrectional movement becomes a State organ, it cannot be said to become the new government of the State.[149]

One answer might be, therefore, that the rule of attribution does not apply; it is pertinent only when there is clear continuity between the insurrectional movement and the State's central government. But this outcome ignores the significant continuity that might exist between the rebels and the entity responsible for governing a potentially large proportion of the State's territory. A better approach, therefore, is to assess the degree of continuity on a case-by-case basis. Relevant factors might include, but are not limited to, the size of the territory the former insurrectional movement governs, the region's importance within the State, and the degree of power that the movement exercises within that territory. If facts such as these demonstrate a real and substantial continuity between the rebel movement and the governance structures of the State, considered as a whole, the rule's object and purpose point to its application.[150]

145. Comprehensive Peace Agreement Between the Government of Nepal and the Communist Party of Nepal (Maoist) (Nov. 22, 2006), https://peacemaker.un.org/en/node/9215.

146. Jhalak Subedi, *Transformation of the Maoists*, 26 ACCORD 39 (Mar. 2017), https://www.c-r.org/accord/nepal/transformation-maoists. *See also* Eatwell, *Armed Groups*, *supra* note 52, at 170.

147. *See, e.g.*, Ilya Somin, *Russian Government Advocates "Federal System" for Ukraine*, WASH. POST (Mar. 31, 2014), https://www.washingtonpost.com/news/volokh-conspiracy/wp/2014/03/31/russian-government-advocates-federal-system-for-ukraine/?noredirect=on&utm_term=.c16941ae5cec.

148. *See* ARSIWA, *supra* note 1, art. 10, cmt. ¶ 7.

149. *Id.* art. 10(1).

150. *See supra* sec. 9.2.3.

9.4 THE INSURRECTIONAL MOVEMENT ESTABLISHES A NEW STATE

The second paragraph of Article 10 ARSIWA addresses the attribution of private conduct to a new State formed by a successful rebel movement.[151] When compared to the other rules of attribution enshrined in ARSIWA, this element of Article 10 is particularly unusual. All the other rules envisage attribution of conduct to a State that exists at the time the acts in potential violation of international law occur. The new State rule reflected in Article 10(2), however, attributes conduct to a State that has not yet come into being. It is therefore "quite exceptional."[152]

9.4.1 The Scope of the Rule

The new State rule applies "where the structures of the insurrectional or other revolutionary movement become those of a new State, constituted by secession or decolonization in part of the territory which was previously subject to the sovereignty or administration of the predecessor State."[153] The reference to secession envisages the emergence of a new State in part of the territory of a preexisting State, as occurred in South Sudan in 2011.[154] In this situation, the parent State continues to exist, albeit with reduced territory.

The second scenario to which the rule can apply is decolonization. Here, Article 10(2) refers to the establishment of a new State "in a territory under its administration."[155] This element of the rule relates to colonies that become newly independent States, where the colony was not considered to form part of the territory of the colonial State that administrated it.[156] Angola's fight for independence from Portugal provides a pertinent example.[157]

In both the factual situations to which the rule may apply, the new State has an international identity that is entirely independent from that of the preexisting State.[158] The parent or colonial State continues to exist and retains responsibility

151. ARSIWA, *supra* note 1, art. 10(2).

152. *Croatia v. Serbia, supra* note 57, Serbia Counter-Memorial ¶ 330 (Dec. 2009). *See also* Dumberry, Rebellions, *supra* note 9, at 308.

153. ARSIWA, *supra* note 1, art. 10, cmt. ¶ 8.

154. *Id.* art. 10(2). *See also* Dumberry, *New State Responsibility*, *supra* note 18, at 617; Jure Vidmar, *South Sudan and the International Legal Framework Governing the Emergence and Delimitation of New States*, 47 Tex. Int'l L.J. 541 (2012).

155. ARSIWA, *supra* note 1, art. 10(2).

156. *Id.* art. 10, cmt. ¶ 8. *See also* Dumberry, *New State Responsibility*, *supra* note 18, at 618.

157. *See generally* Christopher Paul et al., *Angolan Independence, 1961-1974*, *in* Paths to Victory: Detailed Insurgency Case Studies 226 (2013).

158. ILC Y.B. 1975 vol. II, *supra* note 14, at 101 (draft art. 15, cmt. ¶ 7).

for any violations of international law its organs or agents may have committed in opposing the movement's quest for independence.[159] The preexisting State does not, however, bear responsibility for the rebels' conduct.[160] Instead, assuming it reflects customary international law, the new State rule operates to retroactively attribute to the new State any acts or omissions on the part of the independence movement that violate the new State's international legal obligations.[161]

According to the ILC, the rule does not apply in other circumstances involving the creation of a new State. Thus, it does not apply to the dissolution of States, when a predecessor State disappears resulting in the creation of two or more new States on its former territory.[162] The commentary additionally specifies two further exclusions. First, the new State rule does not "cover the situation where an insurrectional movement within a territory succeeds in its agitation for union with another State."[163] The conflict in eastern Ukraine illustrates this scenario, where Russian-backed rebels exercised de facto control over territory in the Donbas before Russia's purported annexation of the region in September 2022.[164] Article 10's exclusion in such circumstances means that Russia does not bear responsibility on this basis for any violations of its international legal obligations committed by rebels in the Donbas prior to the annexation. This outcome makes sense given that no new State is created; therefore, the scenario falls outside the scope of the new State rule reflected in Article 10(2).[165]

The basis for the second exclusion is less clear. This relates to the creation of a new State "carried out within the framework of the predecessor State."[166] For

159. ARSIWA, *supra* note 1, art. 10(3). *See also* ILC Y.B. 1975 vol. II, *supra* note 14, at 105–6 (draft art. 15, cmt. ¶ 22); Šturma's Second Rep. on State Succession, *supra* note 45, at 13–14, ¶¶ 46–47; *id.* at 21 (draft art. 6(2)). For further discussion regarding the predecessor State's responsibility in respect of its own violations, *see* Dumberry, State Succession, *supra* note 14, at 222–24, 251–58.

160. ARSIWA, *supra* note 1, art. 10, cmt. ¶ 6.

161. *Id. See also* ILC Y.B. 1975 vol. II, *supra* note 14, at 101 (draft art. 15, cmt. ¶¶ 6–7); *id.* at 105–6 (draft art. 15, cmt. ¶ 22). *See infra* sec. 9.6.2 for a discussion regarding the international legal obligations that the rebel movement might violate.

162. For further discussion regarding the rule's potential application in other contexts, *see* Dumberry, State Succession, *supra* note 14, at 246; Dumberry, *New State Responsibility*, *supra* note 18, at 617; Verhoeven, *supra* note 44, at 292–93.

163. ARSIWA, *supra* note 1, art. 10, cmt. ¶ 10.

164. Laris Karklis & Erin Cunningham, *Three Maps That Explain Russia's Annexations and Losses in Ukraine*, Wash. Post (Sept. 30, 2022), https://www.washingtonpost.com/world/2022/09/30/map-ukraine-regions-annexation-russia/.

165. *See* Int'l Law Comm'n, Summary Records of the Fifty-Third Session (2001), *in* [2001] 1 Y.B. Int'l L. Comm'n 94, ¶ 33, U.N. Doc. A/CN.4/SER.A/2001 [hereinafter ILC Y.B. 2001 vol. I]. For a contrary view, *see* Dumberry, State Succession, *supra* note 14, at 249; Dumberry, *New State Responsibility*, *supra* note 18, at 619–20.

166. ARSIWA, *supra* note 1, art. 10, cmt. ¶ 10.

instance, if the rebels in eastern Ukraine had established their own State with the agreement of Ukraine's government and in accordance with Ukrainian law, their prior conduct that violated international law would not be attributable to the new State. Given that Article 10 rests upon the principle of continuity, this conclusion is problematic. While the ILC's approach could encourage insurgent movements to abide by the State's internal laws when seeking independence, if continuity exists between the structures of the insurrectional movement that commits the relevant violations and those of the new State, it seems anomalous for the new State to be absolved of responsibility.[167]

9.4.2 Practical Difficulties Related to the Rule's Application

Considerable difficulties surround the practical application of the new State rule reflected in Article 10(2). These derive principally from factual and legal uncertainties surrounding the creation of new States.[168] From a factual perspective, the activities of an insurrectional movement often lead to ambiguity and turmoil within the region concerned. As a conflict progresses, it may be unclear which entity, if any, exercises control over the relevant territory. Even if it is apparent that the insurrectional movement exercises de facto control over territory, this does not lead inevitably to the establishment of a new State under international law.[169]

If the insurrectional movement unilaterally declares its independence, the territorial State is unlikely to consent to the secession.[170] The legal status of the territory concerned may therefore remain opaque, particularly in view of the lack of consensus regarding the appropriate legal test for determining the existence of a new State.[171] For the purposes of this analysis, it suffices to outline the two competing theories and the impact this legal ambiguity has on the potential attribution of conduct pursuant to the new State rule.

167. For further discussion, *see* DUMBERRY, STATE SUCCESSION, *supra* note 14, at 259–62.

168. For discussion of the legal framework relevant to the emergence of new States in the context of South Sudan, *see* Vidmar, *supra* note 154.

169. Issues concerning the creation and succession of states are beyond the scope of this work. For discussion of the legal issues concerned, *see, e.g.*, JAMES CRAWFORD, THE CREATION OF STATES IN INTERNATIONAL LAW (2006) [hereinafter CRAWFORD, CREATION OF STATES].

170. Regarding the legality of unilateral declarations of independence, *see* Accordance with International Law of the Unilateral Declaration of Independence in respect of Kosovo, Advisory Opinion, 2010 I.C.J. Rep. 403, ¶ 81 (July 2010).

171. For discussion of these competing theories, *see, e.g.*, William T. Worster, *Law, Politics, and the Conception of the State in State Recognition Theory*, 27 B.U. INTL L.J. 115 (2009); Cedric Ryngaert & Sven Sobrie, *Recognition of States: International Law or Realpolitik? The Practice of Recognition in the Wake of Kosovo, South Ossetia, and Abkhazia*, 24 LEIDEN J. INT'L L. 467 (2011).

Traditionally, the establishment of a new State was determined by reference to the four factual criteria for statehood expressed in the Montevideo Convention, namely, a permanent population, defined territory, a government, and the capacity to enter into relations with other States.[172] Under this declaratory theory, recognition of the new State by other States merely confirms the preexisting fact that a new State has come into being. This remains the predominant theory in legal doctrine and jurisprudence.[173] The constitutive theory, however, holds that other States' recognition is an essential requirement for statehood.[174] This raises further questions, such as how many recognizing States are necessary before an entity can transform into a new State.[175]

Such uncertainties may be particularly apparent when the purported new State comes into being through the conduct of an insurrectional movement. States may be reluctant to recognize the independence of secessionist entities due to the perceived boost that this may give to separatist organizations within their own territory. For example, research indicates that Spain's decision not to recognize Kosovo as a State is linked to concerns regarding its own internal Catalonian and Basque independence movements.[176]

Alternatively, States' decisions to recognize new States may be influenced by political considerations, including the State's own interests and alliances.[177] Consider, for instance, the region of northeast Syria governed by the autonomous administration linked to the Syrian Democratic Forces.[178] This region had its own constitution and arguably satisfied all four Montevideo criteria.[179] However, even those States that provided significant support to the administration were unlikely to ever recognize the territory as a new State. This is due to key political

172. Montevideo Convention on the Rights and Duties of States art. 1, Dec. 26, 1933, 165 L.N.T.S. 19.

173. Crawford, Creation of States, *supra* note 169, at 19–26; Ryngaert & Sobrie, *supra* note 171, at 470.

174. Ryngaert & Sobrie, *supra* note 171, at 469.

175. *Id. See also* Christian Hillgruber, *The Admission of New States to the International Community*, 9 Eur. J. Int'l L. 491 (1998).

176. Pol Vila Sarriá & Agon Demjaha, *Kosovo-Spain Relations and the Dilemmas on the Problem of Non-Recognition*, 14 S.E. Eur. U. Rev. 69 (2019).

177. *Id.*

178. *See supra* ch. 2, sec. 2.4.1.3.

179. *See, e.g.*, Mohammed A. Salih, *Syria's Kurdish Northeast Ratifies a New Constitution*, New Lines Mag. (Jan. 31, 2024), https://newlinesmag.com/argument/syrias-kurdish-northeast-ratifies-a-new-constitution/. At the time of writing, the future of this region remains unclear. *See* Gregory Aftandilian, *Syrian Kurds Attempt to Maneuver amid New Realities*, Arab Ctr. Wash. D.C. (June 27, 2025), https://arabcenterdc.org/resource/syrian-kurds-attempt-to-maneuver-amid-new-realities/.

considerations such as those States' alliances with Turkey, which viewed the administration as a terrorist entity linked to the PKK.[180]

Thus, even if a territory is clearly under the de facto control of an insurrectional movement, it may not gain recognition as a State by the broader international community. This means that its status under international law remains ambiguous. Moreover, as noted in the context of the new government rule, a State that is injured by an insurrectional movement's conduct may be reluctant to claim reparations against the purported new State, as this may have the unwelcome effect of conferring legitimacy upon it. This reality diminishes the contemporary relevance of the new State rule reflected in Article 10(2). Although many regions throughout the world continue to seek their independence,[181] situations in a which a new State is successfully established are rare.

Further ambiguity arises when considering the NSAs to which the rule reflected in Article 10(2) applies. While the new government rule enshrined in Article 10(1) refers only to "an insurrectional movement," the new State rule expressed in Article 10(2) applies to the broader category of "insurrectional or other" movements.[182] This raises the question why the ILC used different terminology to describe the movements to which each element of the rule may apply.

9.5 INSURRECTIONAL MOVEMENTS

Article 10 is unique among the rules of attribution reflected in ARSIWA in that it relates only to the conduct of insurrectional movements.[183] This raises several inquiries. In particular, what characteristics must an NSA have to qualify as an insurrectional movement? What did the ILC mean by its reference to "insurrectional or other" movements in Article 10(2) relating to new States? When applying the rule of attribution, how can one determine whether conduct was performed on behalf of an insurrectional movement? And how does Article 10 apply when two or more rebel movements are involved in the struggle for power? This section considers each of these issues in turn.

180. Aron Lund, *Origins of the Syrian Democratic Forces: A Primer*, New Humanitarian (Jan. 22, 2016), https://deeply.thenewhumanitarian.org/syria/articles/2016/01/22/origins-of-the-syrian-democratic-forces-a-primer.

181. *See, e.g.*, Shane Savitsky & Shannon Vavra, *The Independence Movements Around the World*, Axios (Oct. 22, 2017), https://www.axios.com/2017/12/15/the-independence-movements-around-the-world-1513306345.

182. ARSIWA, *supra* note 1, art. 10.

183. *Id.*

9.5.1 The Character of an Insurrectional Movement

The notion of an "insurrectional movement" is central to Article 10 ARSIWA. The ILC did not define the term, however, noting instead that the movements to which the article applies may take a wide variety of forms.[184] These may range from groups involved in a limited armed opposition to the government in one area of the country, such as M23 in eastern Democratic Republic of the Congo (DRC),[185] to organizations controlling vast swathes of territory, like ISIS. Moreover, the size and character of these organizations often changes as a conflict progresses.[186] The Free Syrian Army, for example, fluctuated considerably during the early years of the Syrian conflict in terms of its composition, size, strength, and control over territory.[187]

Insurrectional movements, however, always have the same goal: to take power either by replacing the existing government or by creating a new State.[188] As such, they always operate in opposition to the territorial State. Moreover, these entities are, by their nature, temporary and transient.[189] While some may exist for decades, such as the FARC in Columbia, many survive for a much shorter duration.[190] If the movement succeeds, it integrates itself into the structures of the State or establishes a new State.[191] Alternatively, if the movement fails in its efforts to gain power, at some point in time, it will fragment or change in form.[192] For instance, although at the time of writing ISIS still exists as an entity, it is questionable whether it can still be described as an insurrectional movement, given that it no longer controls territory and its organizational structures no longer focus on governance but instead on terrorism and insurgency.[193]

184. *Id.* art. 10, cmt. ¶ 9.

185. *See supra* ch. 2, sec. 2.4.3.

186. Ago's Fourth Rep. on State Responsibility, *supra* note 6, at 129–30, ¶ 154.

187. *See infra* ch. 2 sec. 2.4.1.1.

188. Dumberry, Rebellions, *supra* note 9, at 22.

189. *See* Ago's Fourth Rep. on State Responsibility, *supra* note 6, at 129–30, ¶ 154.

190. *See* ILC Y.B. 1975 vol. I, *supra* note 124, at 49, ¶ 19 (comments of Mr. Bedjaoui); Verhoeven, *supra* note 44, at 296; Jann K. Kleffner, *The Collective Accountability of Organized Armed Groups for System Crimes*, *in* System Criminality in International Law 238, 265 (André Nollkaemper & Harmen Van Der Wilt eds., 2009).

191. Ago's Fourth Rep. on State Responsibility, *supra* note 6, at 129–30, ¶ 154.

192. *Id.* at 129, ¶ 152; ILC Y.B. 1975 vol. II, *supra* note 14, at 93 (draft art. 14, cmt. ¶ 8).

193. *See, e.g.*, Aaron Y. Zelin & Devorah Margolin, *The Islamic State's Shadow Governance in Eastern Syria Since the Fall of Baghuz*, Combating Terrorism Ctr. (Sept. 2023), https://ctc.westpoint.edu/the-islamic-states-shadow-governance-in-eastern-syria-since-the-fall-of-baghuz/; Kim Cragin, *Taking Stock of the Islamic State*, Lawfare (Dec. 15, 2024), https://www.lawfaremedia.org/article/taking-stock-of-the-islamic-state.

The example of ISIS highlights the question of whether territorial control and/or a certain degree of organization is required for an entity to qualify as an insurrectional movement. This enquiry is relevant not to determine whether Article 10 applies, as this can be decided only once the movement has assumed power. Rather, it is pertinent to establishing how much of the movement's prior conduct can be attributed to the State following its success.[194] In other words, when does an NSA become an insurrectional movement, meaning that Article 10 potentially applies to its conduct from that time on, in the event it ultimately gains power?

In this context, the commentary to Article 10 refers to Additional Protocol II to the Geneva Conventions (AP II) as a guide.[195] AP II applies to armed conflicts involving "dissident armed forces or other organized armed groups which, under responsible command, exercise such control over a part of [a State's] territory as to enable them to carry out sustained and concerted military operations and to implement this Protocol."[196]

This reference appears to limit Article 10's application to those insurrectional movements that are highly organized and exercise territorial control.[197] Crawford similarly highlights an insurrectional movement's control of territory, in a public or governmental capacity, as a factor that often distinguishes it from other NSAs.[198] However, a prerequisite of territorial control would mean that any potential international law violations an NSA commits prior to exercising such control could not be attributed to the State it comes to govern, even if there is clear continuity between the NSA's structures at that time and those of the State.[199] Such violations might include, for example, mistreatment of civilians or detainees in breach of common Article 3 to the Geneva Conventions.[200]

The ILC's early deliberations regarding the rule of attribution indicate that this was not its original intent. The commentary to draft article 15 emphasized that "no distinction is made between the acts of organs of the insurrectional movement

194. Ago's Fourth Rep. on State Responsibility, *supra* note 6, at 151, ¶ 213. *See also* DUMBERRY, REBELLIONS, *supra* note 9, at 112–15.

195. ARSIWA, *supra* note 1, art. 10, cmt. ¶ 9, *citing* Protocol Additional to the Geneva Conventions of August 12, 1949, and Relating to the Protection of Victims of Non-International Armed Conflicts, June 8, 1977, 1125 U.N.T.S. 609 (AP II). *See also* Crawford's First Rep. on State Responsibility, *supra* note 7, at 52, ¶ 270.

196. AP II, *supra* note 195, art. 1.

197. *See* Cahin, *supra* note 17, at 252.; d'Aspremont, *supra* note 7, at 433; Nicholas Tsagourias, *Non-State Actors, Ungoverned Spaces and International Responsibility for Cyber Acts*, 21 J. CONFLICT & SEC. L. 455, 464–65 (2016).

198. CRAWFORD, *supra* note 18, at 171.

199. *See* DINSTEIN, *supra* note 18, at 127; Eatwell, *Armed Groups*, *supra* note 52, at 178.

200. Convention (I) for the Amelioration of the Condition of the Wounded and Sick in the Armed Forces in the Field art. 3, Aug. 12, 1949, 6 U.S.T. 3114, 75 U.N.T.S. 31 [hereinafter GC I].

according to whether they preceded or followed the acquisition by the movement of effective power over a given region."[201] This position accords with the object and purpose of the rule, which rests upon the principle of continuity.[202] If there is clear continuity between the structures of a movement that acts in violation of international law and the government it later creates, the rule's object and purpose support the attribution of the relevant conduct to the State, irrespective of whether the group exercised territorial control at the time of the acts' commission.

The same principle extends to a situation in which a movement gains power or independence without first controlling territory. A very popular insurgent movement could take power without engaging in prolonged hostilities or exercising de facto control over territory, as occurred in revolutionary Iran.[203] This conclusion is supported by the commentary's indication that a group may qualify as an insurrectional movement even if it is located outside the borders of the State it opposes.[204] Thus, if it achieved success in establishing a new State, the rebel group M23 might qualify as an insurrectional movement even if it did not first establish territorial control within the DRC but continued to base itself out of neighboring Rwanda.[205]

If territorial control is not required for an NSA to qualify as an insurrectional movement, the question remains whether such a movement must exhibit a particular level of organization.[206] Returning to the principle of continuity, it seems clear that an NSA must have some degree of organization for the structures of the government it later establishes to bear a resemblance to those it had as an NSA. But the organizational assessment will vary from case to case.[207] Factors that may assist in this regard include the existence of a command structure, the leadership's capacity to enforce organizational decisions, and the level of disruption the group is able to cause.[208] There are accordingly parallels between this assessment and the intensity and organizational criteria that must be satisfied for hostilities to be

201. ILC Y.B. 1975 vol. II, *supra* note 14, at 100 (draft art. 15, cmt. ¶ 2). *See also* Ago's Fourth Rep. on State Responsibility, *supra* note 6, at 150, ¶ 210; ARSIWA, *supra* note 1, art. 10, cmt. ¶ 12, citing *Bolivar Railway*, *supra* note 25, at 453 (the tribunal referred to a nation bearing responsibility for the obligations of a successful revolution "from its beginning").

202. *See supra* sec. 9.2.3.

203. *Short*, *supra* note 37, ¶ 33; *id.* dissenting opinion of Judge Brower, ¶ 27.

204. ARSIWA, *supra* note 1, art. 10, cmt. ¶ 9. *See also* Cahin, *supra* note 17, at 251.

205. *See* ch. 2, sec. 2.4.3.

206. *See* Ago's Fourth Rep. on State Responsibility, *supra* note 6, at 129, ¶ 153; ILC Y.B. 1975 vol. II, *supra* note 14, at 98 (draft art. 14, cmt. ¶ 28).

207. Cahin, *supra* note 17, at 252.

208. Ago's Fourth Rep. on State Responsibility, *supra* note 6, at 129, ¶ 153; ILC Y.B. 1975 vol. II, *supra* note 14, at 92 (draft art. 14, cmt. ¶ 6); Crawford's First Rep. on State Responsibility, *supra* note 7, at 57 (draft art. 15, cmt. ¶ 3).

classified as a non-international armed conflict (NIAC).[209] If a movement is sufficiently organized for the hostilities to qualify in a NIAC, it is highly likely that the group constitutes an insurrectional movement for the purposes of Article 10.

However, the two tests are not identical. Although the ILC envisaged that rebel groups would normally succeed following an armed struggle,[210] this is not an express requirement for Article 10's application.[211] Successful rebels normally employ some degree of violence, but there is no requirement for this to reach a certain level of intensity before the NSA amounts to an insurrectional movement. For example, in Tunisia's Jasmine Revolution of 2011, protesters succeeded in toppling the government largely through nonviolent means, including a cyber operation to shut down government websites, the staging of a general strike, and the effective use of social media.[212] To accord with the rule's object and purpose, if there is clear continuity between the structures of the State and the former rebel movement, this suffices for Article 10 to apply even if the series of events leading up to the group's success does not constitute a NIAC.[213]

Of course, if the NIAC threshold is not satisfied, IHL would not apply to the movement's struggle for power and Article 10 would not attribute any IHL violations to the State. Attribution might nevertheless be appropriate in respect of other international law violations on the part of the movement, such as breaches of the State's international human rights law obligations. The conduct that might constitute an internationally wrongful act for these purposes is examined further in section 9.6.

9.5.2 "Insurrectional or Other" Movements

The new State rule expressed in Article 10(2) appears from its text to be broader in scope than the new government rule in Article 10(1), in that the former applies not only to insurrectional movements that establish a new State but also to "other" movements.[214] The ILC Drafting Committee added this wording in 1998 due to concerns that the concept of an insurrectional movement might be too restrictive in this context.[215] The commentary explains, "This terminology reflects the

209. Prosecutor v. Tadić, Case No. IT-94-1-AR-72, Decision on Defence Motion for Interlocutory Appeal on Jurisdiction, ¶ 70 (Int'l Crim. Trib. for the former Yugoslavia, Oct. 2, 1995).

210. *See* ARSIWA, *supra* note 1, art. 10, cmt. ¶ 9.

211. *Id.* art. 10. *See also* d'Aspremont, *supra* note 7, at 428. *But see* Verhoeven, *supra* note 44, at 298 (opining that the existence of a NIAC is a prerequisite to art. 10's application).

212. *See, e.g.*, Mohamed A. El-Khawas, *Tunisia's Jasmine Revolution: Causes and Impact*, 23 Mediterranean Q. 1, 10 (2012).

213. *See supra* sec. 9.2.3. *See also* Clapham, *supra* note 10, at 508–9.

214. ARSIWA, *supra* note 1, art. 10.

215. ILC Y.B. 1998 vol. I, *supra* note 7, at 290, ¶ 88.

existence of a greater variety of movements whose actions may result in the formation of a new State."[216]

The ILC's intent was to ensure that the rule encompassed the conduct of national liberation movements fighting against a colonial or racist power, in the event they established a new State in the context of decolonization. Some States had previously expressed concern that these should not be equated with insurrectional movements.[217] Nevertheless, Article 10 treats national liberation movements the same as any other movement fighting the government, declining to grant them any special status.[218] The commentary justifies this stance by asserting, "[I]t is unnecessary and undesirable to exonerate a new Government or a new State from responsibility for the conduct of its personnel by reference to considerations of legitimacy or illegitimacy of its origin."[219]

The ILC's approach in this respect has merit. It focuses not on subjective questions of legitimacy but on the more objective issue of the continuity between an insurrectional movement and the new government or State.[220] When such continuity exists, both elements of the rule expressed in Article 10 can apply to a movement's conduct, irrespective of its legitimacy or goals.[221] Indeed, shortly prior to ARSIWA's adoption, the Drafting Committee "decided that national liberation movements were included in the term 'insurrectional movement.'"[222] It is therefore questionable why the ILC included a reference to "other" movements at all.

216. ARSIWA, *supra* note 1, art. 10, cmt. ¶ 10.

217. *See, e.g.*, U.N. GAOR, 13th Sess., 1539th mtg., ¶ 3 (comments of the Ger. Dem. Rep.), U.N. Doc. A/C.6/SR.1539 (Oct. 15, 1975); U.N. GAOR, 13th Sess., 1542d mtg., ¶ 12 (comments of Tanz.), U.N. Doc. A/C.6/SR.1542 (Oct. 17, 1975); U.N.G.A., 13th Sess., 1546th mtg., ¶ 3 (comments of Czechoslovakia), U.N. Doc. A/C.6/SR.1546 (Oct. 22, 1975); *id.* ¶ 42 (comments of Oman); *id.* ¶ 54 (comments of Madag.); U.N. GAOR, 13th Sess., 1548th mtg., ¶ 54 (comments of Syria), U.N. Doc. A/C.6/SR.1548 (Oct. 24, 1975); U.N. GAOR, 13th Sess., 1549th mtg., ¶ 28 (comments of Swaz.), U.N. Doc. A/C.6/SR.1549 (Oct. 27, 1975); *id.* ¶ 42 (comments of Ghana); U.N. GAOR, 13th Sess., 1550th mtg., ¶ 3 (comments of Zam.), U.N. Doc. A/C.6/SR.1550 (Oct. 28, 1975). For commentary regarding the rule's application to national liberation movements, *see* Hazem Atlam, *National Liberation Movements and International Responsibility*, *in* United Nations Codification of State Responsibility (Marina Spinedi & Bruno Simma eds., 1987); Gayim, *supra* note 7, at 99–103; Crawford, *supra* note 18, at 173; Dumberry, State Succession, *supra* note 14, at 247–48.

218. ARSIWA, *supra* note 1, art. 10, cmt. ¶ 11. The ILC takes the same approach in its work on State succession. *See* Šturma's Second Rep. on State Succession, *supra* note 45, ¶ 108.

219. ARSIWA, *supra* note 1, art. 10, cmt. ¶ 11. *See also* ILC Y.B. 1975 vol. I, *supra* note 124, at 60, ¶ 43 (comments of Special Rapporteur Ago).

220. *See, e.g.*, ILC Y.B. 1998 vol. I, *supra* note 7, at 251, ¶ 10 (comments of Mr. Dugard).

221. *See* Verhoeven, *supra* note 44, at 298.

222. ILC Y.B. 2001 vol. I, *supra* note 165, at 94, ¶ 34.

9.5.3 The Conduct of the Movement

Article 10 ARSIWA addresses States' potential responsibility for "the conduct of an insurrectional movement."[223] Accordingly, before such conduct can be attributed to a State, it is necessary to determine whether the relevant acts or omissions were performed on the movement's behalf.[224] Given that there is no legal framework in international law for determining when an individual's conduct is attributable to a NSA, this is not a straightforward determination.[225]

A sensible starting point is the rules codified in ARSIWA that apply to determine when conduct is attributable to a State.[226] In its earlier drafts of the rule reflected in Article 10, the ILC referred to "the conduct of an organ of an insurrectional movement."[227] This wording raises clear parallels with Article 4 ARSIWA, which provides for the attribution to a State of the conduct of its organs.[228] Sophisticated NSAs often adopt State-like structures, which may bear a resemblance to the organs of a State.[229] This is particularly the case if the group exercises de facto control over territory and sets up its own institutions, such as police and military forces.[230]

However, while States promulgate laws to designate the entities that qualify as de jure organs of State, the same is not true of NSAs. A recognition that NSAs can create "laws" remains controversial, due to the perceived legitimacy that this may bestow upon the entity. An NSA's own internal rules and regulations nevertheless provide one means by which to identify the group's organs.[231] For example, the *Mouvement de Libération du Congo* designates four "organs" in its statute, including the group's military wing.[232]

223. ARSIWA, *supra* note 1, art. 10.

224. *See* Verhoeven, *supra* note 44, at 299.

225. For further discussion regarding the attribution of conduct to armed groups, *see* Kleffner, *supra* note 190, at 257; Verhoeven, *supra* note 44, at 299–303.

226. ARSIWA, *supra* note 1, arts. 4, 5, 8–11. *See also* Kleffner, *supra* note 190, at 260; David D. Caron, *The Basis of Responsibility: Attribution and Other Trans-Substantive Rules of State Responsibility*, *in* THE IRAN-UNITED STATES CLAIMS TRIBUNAL: ITS CONTRIBUTION TO THE LAW OF STATE RESPONSIBILITY 109, 147–49 (Richard B. Lillich & Daniel B. Magraw eds., 1998).

227. Crawford's First Rep. on State Responsibility, *supra* note 7, at 57 (draft art. 15); ILC Y.B. 1975 vol. II, *supra* note 14, at 151–52 (draft art. 13). *See also id.* at 91–92 (draft art. 14, cmt. ¶ 3).

228. ARSIWA, *supra* note 1, art. 4. *See also supra* ch. 4.

229. *See* Cahin, *supra* note 17, at 255.

230. *See* Kleffner, *supra* note 190, at 263–64.

231. Ezequiel Heffes & Brian E. Frenkel, *The International Responsibility of Non-State Armed Groups: In Search of the Applicable Rules*, 8 GÖTTINGEN J. INT'L L. 39, 61–64 (2017).

232. *Id.* at 62, *citing* Mouvement de Libération du Congo, Statuts du Mouvement de Libération du Congo, arts. 11–16 (1999).

An NSA's internal documentation may therefore assist in identifying its organs, but this does not provide a complete answer. Insurrectional movements are generally not as well-structured as States, and their level of organization may vary over time.[233] Less organized movements, or those not exercising territorial control, might not have detailed rules or regulations through which they can create organs. In these cases, a consideration of the de facto role of the persons or entities concerned is more helpful to ascertain whether they are manifesting the policy of the group.[234]

The characterization of an individual or group as a de facto organ of an insurrectional movement is necessarily a question of fact, to be determined on a case-by-case basis. To ascertain whether a person or entity qualifies as such, it is not appropriate to apply the test that the ICJ formulated for this purpose in the context of de facto State organs.[235] This very stringent test requires evidence that the person or entity acts in complete dependence on the State, and that the State exercises strict control over its activities.[236] In view of the more flexible structure of many NSAs, the units through which they act are likely to exercise a degree of autonomy in their operations that is inconsistent with a high degree of dependence or control.[237] Moreover, while States act only exceptionally through de facto organs, the opposite is true for insurrectional movements.[238] Accordingly, a demanding test of this nature would deprive the rule of attribution reflected in Article 10 of much of its effect.

A more flexible test is therefore required to identify the de facto organs of an insurrectional movement. In some cases, it may be clear from the role that a particular individual or group performs that it acts as an organ of the NSA. For instance, in the *Yeager* case, the Iran-U.S. Claims Tribunal concluded that the statements and acts of Ayatollah Khomeini were attributable to Iran "as it is beyond doubt that he was the leading organ of the revolutionary movement which became the new Government."[239] Thus, it may be evident from the key position an individual holds within an insurrectional movement that that person qualifies as one of its organs. There is no doubt, for instance, that HTS's leaders,

233. Verhoeven, *supra* note 44, at 299.

234. Cahin, *supra* note 17, at 255; Luigi Condorelli & Claus Kress, *The Rules of Attribution: General Considerations*, *in* THE LAW OF INTERNATIONAL RESPONSIBILITY 221, 231 (James Crawford et al. eds., 2010); Kleffner, *supra* note 190, at 245; Verhoeven, *supra* note 44, at 299.

235. Application of the Convention on the Prevention and Punishment of the Crime of Genocide (Bosn. & Herz. v. Serb. & Montenegro), Judgment, 2007 I.C.J. Rep. 43, ¶¶ 391–94 (Feb. 26).

236. For further discussion of this test, *see supra* ch. 4, sec. 4.4.

237. Verhoeven, *supra* note 44, at 300. *See also* Condorelli & Kress, *supra* note 234, at 231; Cahin, *supra* note 17, at 255; Kleffner, *supra* note 190, at 241–42.

238. Verhoeven, *supra* note 44, at 300.

239. *Yeager*, *supra* note 88, ¶ 35.

including Abu Mohammad al-Jolani, are organs of the insurrectional movement that succeeded in taking power in Syria.[240]

An additional factor of significance is the person or entity's place within the movement's organizational structure. In the *Yeager* case, the Tribunal noted the Ayatollah's support for the local revolutionary committees or "Komitehs" and their loyalty to him.[241] These groups acted to promote the aims of the movement, with the endorsement of its leadership. This reality points to their status as organs of the insurrectional movement.

The nature of the role the Komitehs performed, serving as "local security forces," making arrests, and confiscating property,[242] is also relevant. These functions are clearly governmental in the sense that they would typically be performed only by entities that act with the support of the governing authorities; otherwise, they would be criminal acts.[243] Similarly, it appears likely that the persons and entities that formed part of the Syrian Salvation Government, created by HTS to govern Idlib in northwest Syria, were organs of HTS.[244]

When assessing whether a person or entity is a de facto organ of an insurrectional movement, it may also be pertinent to consider whether its sole or principal function is to promote the movement's goals. In the case of organs of State, all the organ's conduct is attributable to the State unless it is performed in a private capacity.[245] The same is true of organs of an insurrectional movement, meaning that only those persons or entities that act exclusively or predominantly for the movement should qualify as its organs. Other individuals or groups may, however, act on behalf of the NSA on an ad hoc basis. For example, they might perform discrete tasks for the movement, or act on its behalf for only a short period of time.

To identify agents of the movement, who do not qualify as de facto organs of the NSA but perform some functions on its behalf, a first consideration is whether the individuals concerned were acting to promote the aims of the insurrectional movement or merely taking advantage of the revolutionary turmoil for personal gain.[246] According to Article 10's commentary, the reference to a movement's conduct "only concerns the conduct of the movement as such

240. Al Jazeera, *supra* note 104; Aaron Y. Zelin, *What to Know About the Man Who Toppled Assad*, Wash. Inst. (Dec. 11, 2024), https://www.washingtoninstitute.org/policy-analysis/what-know-about-man-who-toppled-assad.

241. *Yeager*, *supra* note 88, ¶ 39.

242. *Id.*

243. For further discussion regarding functions that can be characterized as governmental in character, *see supra* ch. 5, sec. 5.3; ch. 8, sec. 8.3.2.

244. Al Jazeera, *supra* note 104.

245. *See* ARSIWA, *supra* note 1, art. 7. For discussion regarding the distinction between *ultra vires* and private acts in the context of State organs' conduct, *see supra* ch. 4, sec. 4.5.

246. Dinstein, *supra* note 18, at 127.

and not the individual acts of members of the movement, acting in their own capacity."[247] Thus, the acts of mere supporters of the organization, over whom the movement has no means of control, do not qualify as conduct that the rule would potentially attribute to a State.[248] Instead, as with the attribution of private conduct to States, there must be evidence to indicate that the person or entity concerned was acting pursuant to some form of tasking or authority from the movement's organs or leadership.

Here, the rule reflected in Article 8 ARSIWA provides some assistance.[249] As with the attribution of conduct to States, the acts of individuals or groups acting on an insurrectional movement's instructions, or under its direction or control, are attributable to the NSA.[250] However, the precise meaning that is given to the terms "instructions, direction or control" is critical.[251] A very stringent control threshold, such as the effective control test formulated by the ICJ, would be unworkable in the context of NSAs.[252] As NSAs tend to be less organized than States, it is highly unlikely that evidence would be available to prove that organs of an insurrectional movement "directed or enforced" the relevant conduct in potential violation of international law.[253]

Rather than applying a strict rule of attribution, the sheer diversity of revolutionary movements calls for a more flexible approach, allowing for the assessment of claims on a case-by-case basis. This is particularly appropriate when considering conduct performed by individuals and entities that do not qualify as organs of the movement. Here, it may be beneficial to assess a wide range of factors to determine whether conduct was performed on the movement's behalf. These might include the identity of the actor, the context in which the act was performed, and any evidence of links between the perpetrators and the movement's leadership or organs. Nevertheless, this enduring uncertainty regarding the conduct to which the rule expressed in Article 10 may apply will naturally serve to limit the rule's practical relevance in situations of armed conflict.

247. ARSIWA, *supra* note 1, art. 10, cmt. ¶ 4. *See also Short*, *supra* note 37, ¶ 34.

248. Crawford's First Rep. on State Responsibility, *supra* note 7, at 57 (draft art. 15, cmt. ¶ 3). *See also* Eatwell, *Armed Groups*, *supra* note 52, at 179–83; Dumberry, Rebellions, *supra* note 9, at 115–17.

249. ARSIWA, *supra* note 1, art. 8. *See also* Eatwell, *Armed Groups*, *supra* note 52, at 183.

250. Kleffner, *supra* note 190, at 263–64.

251. *See supra* ch. 6.

252. For a discussion of the effective control test in the context of the attribution of conduct to States, *see supra* ch. 6, sec. 6.4.

253. Military and Paramilitary Activities in and against Nicaragua (Nicar. v. U.S.), Judgment, 1986 I.C.J. at 14 ¶ 115 (June 27). *See also supra* ch. 6, sec. 6.4.

9.5.4 The Involvement of Two or More Insurrectional Movements

The wording of Article 10 and its commentary indicates an assumption on the part of the ILC that only one insurrectional movement succeeds in either replacing the government or establishing a new State.[254] Yet, in some cases, several distinct opposition groups might be involved in the fight for power and have varying levels of representation in the new government that subsequently forms. For example, HTS was not the only NSA involved in the overthrow of President Assad; other rebel movements, including the Druse militia based in southwest Syria, also joined the fight against government forces.[255] Following the rebels' success, some of these factions reportedly agreed to dissolve and integrate into the new defense ministry.[256]

In such a situation, Article 10's application becomes yet more complex. Should the conduct of all the insurrectional movements involved in the struggle for power be attributed to the State? What should happen if one or more of those movements have no representation in the structures of the State? In Angola, for instance, three revolutionary movements fought to overthrow Portuguese rule, but only one consolidated power to the extent that it was able to form a government.[257] If the new governmental structures derive from just one of the insurrectional movements involved in the struggle for power, does that mean that the State should not bear responsibility for violations committed by the other movements, even if these acts significantly contributed to the movements' success?[258]

The principle of continuity assists in answering such questions. If an insurrectional movement has no representation within the new government, there is no continuity between its structures and those of the State.[259] As such, the main rationale supporting the rule of attribution reflected in Article 10 does not

254. ARSIWA, *supra* note 1, art. 10; *id.* cmt. ¶¶ 1–16 (art. 10 and its commentary refer throughout to "an insurrectional movement" in the singular).

255. Ephrat Livni, *How to Understand the Armed Factions Operating in Syria*, N.Y. Times (Dec. 10, 2024), https://www.nytimes.com/2024/12/10/world/middleeast/syria-rebels-government-assad.html.

256. Adam Rasgon & Ephrat Livni, *Syria's New Leaders Try to Unite Rebel Factions Under a Single Government*, N.Y. Times (Dec. 25, 2024), https://www.nytimes.com/2024/12/25/world/middleeast/syria-rebels-government-assad.html?searchResultPosition=24.

257. *See, e.g.*, Jeremiah Bvirindi, *Angolan Conflict Analysis: A Lesson for Africa's Emerging Leaders*, 3 Int'l J. Res. & Innovation in Soc. Sci. 2454 (July 2019).

258. Dumberry, *New State Responsibility*, *supra* note 18, at 611–12.

259. *See supra* sec. 9.2.3.

apply.[260] The same is true if a movement succeeds in toppling the government but then allows other political actors to step in and govern.[261]

But in cases involving insurrectional movements that have some degree of representation within a coalition government, the position may be different. Here, as in the case of governments of national reconciliation discussed in section 9.3.2, it is helpful to consider the requirement for "real and substantial continuity" between each rebel organization and the government that subsequently forms.[262] If such continuity exists, meaning that the movement has a genuine share of power, the rule reflected in Article 10 applies to attribute the movement's prior conduct to the State.

9.6 THE CONDUCT THAT CAN CONSTITUTE AN INTERNATIONALLY WRONGFUL ACT

To engage a State's responsibility, conduct must not only be attributable to a State, it must also constitute "a breach of an international obligation of the State."[263] When considering retrospective attribution, as envisaged by Article 10 ARSIWA, this raises an interesting question. Which primary norms of international law can a State violate through the prior conduct of an insurrectional movement? When the relevant conduct is performed, it does not breach any obligations binding on the State because at that time, the insurrectional movement is a private actor. But when those acts subsequently gain a public character due to the application of the rule reflected in Article 10, it is necessary to ascertain whether the conduct at issue violates an international obligation that binds the State and therefore constitutes an internationally wrongful act.

The approach to this question varies according to which provision of Article 10 applies. If the insurrectional movement establishes a new government, the State to which the movement's conduct is later attributed exists at the time the relevant acts are performed, and it bears identifiable obligations under treaties and customary international law. Conversely, when the rebel movement establishes a new State, that entity did not exist at the time the NSA performed the relevant harmful acts. Therefore, it is more difficult to ascertain which international legal obligations the rebels might breach.

260. CRAWFORD, *supra* note 18, at 179; DINSTEIN, *supra* note 18, at 130. For a contrary view, *see* Dumberry, *New State Responsibility*, *supra* note 18, at 612.

261. *See* Verhoeven, *supra* note 44, at 295.

262. ARSIWA, *supra* note 1, art. 10, cmt. ¶ 7.

263. *Id.* art. 2.

9.6.1 The Movement Becomes the New Government

Some legal scholars take the view that whichever element of Article 10 applies, the rule only attributes conduct to a State if it breached an international legal obligation that was binding on the insurrectional movement at the time it was committed.[264] For example, many insurrectional movements are organized armed groups bound by IHL.[265] In their struggle for power, they might breach the rules of IHL that apply in a NIAC, such as by conducting indiscriminate attacks in violation of the principle of distinction.[266] Once the movement achieves success, such violations by the NSA of its own IHL obligations would be attributed to the State it comes to govern. This approach finds support in the early work of the ILC.[267] However, neither the text of Article 10 nor the commentary addresses the point directly.[268]

Alternatively, the rule could apply to any rebel conduct that would have violated an obligation binding on the State, had that conduct been attributable to the State at the time it was committed. The Iran-U.S. Claims Tribunal followed this latter approach, concluding that the revolutionary movement could breach any primary norms that were binding on the State of Iran at the time the acts occurred.[269] The tribunal accordingly found that the revolutionaries could violate Iran's obligations arising not only under customary international law, but also the Treaty of Amity between Iran and the United States.[270] This bilateral treaty afforded certain rights to U.S. citizens in Iran that claimants before the tribunal alleged the revolutionary movement had breached.[271]

These opposing views impact the practical application of the new government rule. The latter interpretation would widen the scope of conduct to which Article 10 applies because States are subject to far more extensive international legal obligations than NSAs. For instance, although it is commonly accepted that armed groups are subject to IHL obligations, for example, under common Article 3 to the Geneva Conventions,[272] they are not subject to treaty obligations, including

264. *See, e.g.*, Robert Kolb, The International Law of State Responsibility 98 (2018).

265. Jann Kleffner, *The Applicability of International Humanitarian Law to Organized Armed Groups*, 93 Int'l Rev. Red Cross 443 (2011) [hereinafter Kleffner, *Armed Groups*].

266. *See* Customary IHL, *supra* note 100, rr. 11–12

267. ILC Y.B. 1975 vol. II, *supra* note 14, at 91–92 (cmt. to draft art. 14).

268. ARSIWA, *supra* note 1, art. 10; *id.* cmt. ¶¶ 1–16.

269. Caron, *supra* note 226, at 146, *citing* Short, *supra* note 37, dissenting opinion of Judge Brower ¶ 3, Jack Rankin v. The Islamic Republic of Iran, Award No. 326-10913-2, ¶¶ 22–24 (Iran-U.S. Claims Trib., 1987) [hereinafter *Rankin*].

270. Caron, *supra* note 226, at 146. *See* Treaty of Amity, Economic Relations, and Consular Rights, Aug. 15, 1955, 284 U.N.T.S. 93.

271. *See, e.g.*, *Rankin*, *supra* note 269, ¶¶ 22–25.

272. GC I, *supra* note 200, art. 3. *See also* Kleffner, *Armed Groups*, *supra* note 265.

those related to human rights.[273] But if the same primary norms are deemed to bind both the insurrectional movement and the State, and the movement's conduct violates human rights obligations owed by the State to individuals within its jurisdiction, that conduct could engage the State's responsibility once the insurrectional movement gains power.[274]

There are clear policy reasons for construing Article 10 more broadly to encompass breaches of the State's international legal obligations rather than solely those of the insurrectional movement.[275] This would enable human rights bodies to criticize a revolutionary movement on the basis that if it achieves its goal, "its atrocities would become human rights violations attributed to the state it comes to govern."[276] To illustrate, consider the Taliban's conduct in potential breach of Afghanistan's human rights obligations during its fight for power, such as its discriminatory practices against women.[277] The new government rule reflected in Article 10(1) would be more effective if this conduct can constitute an internationally wrongful act, in addition to the Taliban's violations of its own obligations under IHL.

This broader construction also accords with the general attribution regime reflected in ARSIWA. All the other rules relate to the attribution of private conduct to a State, not the attribution of responsibility for violations committed by another subject of international law.[278] The references to attribution of conduct within the commentary indicate that the same is true of Article 10.[279] The rule does not provide for the State to succeed to the obligations the insurrectional movement itself incurs, but rather for the group's conduct to be attributed to the State following its success.[280] There is, accordingly, no requirement for the acts in question to amount to international law violations at the time of their commission. Instead, the rule attributes the prior conduct of the insurrectional movement to the State, treating such conduct retrospectively as if it were performed on the State's behalf.

273. For further discussion regarding armed groups' human rights obligations, *see, e.g.*, Clapham, *supra* note 10; Katharine Fortin, The Accountability of Armed Groups Under Human Rights Law (2017).

274. *See* Hessbruegge, *supra* note 7, at 274; Gayim, *supra* note 7, at 100; Caron, *supra* note 226, at 146.

275. Hessbruegge, *supra* note 7, at 274.

276. *Id.*

277. *See generally* Sebghatullah Qazi Zada & Mohd Ziaolhaq Qazi Zaba, *The Taliban and Women's Human Rights in Afghanistan: The Way Forward*, Int'l J. Hum. Rts. 1687 (2024).

278. ARSIWA, *supra* note 1, arts. 5, 8, 9, 11.

279. *Id.* art. 10, cmt. ¶¶ 5, 7. Note, however, that one paragraph of the commentary refers to the attribution of responsibility to the State. *See id.* ¶ 5.

280. *See* Ago's Fourth Rep. on State Responsibility, *supra* note 6, at 145, ¶ 196; d'Aspremont, *supra* note 7, at 430.

Finally, this interpretation aligns with the conclusions reached in section 9.5 regarding the character of insurrectional movements. A rebel group might assume power without first engaging in violence of sufficient intensity to cross the NIAC threshold. In such situations, IHL does not apply, and the group has no international legal obligations of its own. If the rule reflected in Article 10 only attributed conduct to a State in the event it violated an international legal obligation that was binding on the insurrectional movement, this would limit the rule's application to breaches of IHL committed during a NIAC. This narrow construction of the rule does not accord with its object and purpose, which focuses instead on the principle of continuity.[281] Thus, if there is clear continuity between the structures of the State and the former rebel movement, the new government rule expressed in Article 10(1) should attribute to the State any of the group's conduct that violates the State's international legal obligations, such as breaches of the State's duties under international human rights law.

One outstanding question, however, remains. In the case of the new government rule reflected in Article 10(1), there is no change to the identity of the State; only its government changes. It may also be the case that the State's international legal obligations remain the same. But what happens if the State agrees to new treaty obligations that bind the State at the time the insurrectional movement takes power but are not in force at the time the movement acts in a manner that would breach those obligations? In other words, for a State to bear responsibility for violations of its international legal obligations committed by an insurrectional movement, must the State be bound by those obligations on the date the insurrectional movement acts in their potential breach? Similar questions arise when an insurrection movement creates a new State, which did not exist and thus had no legal obligations at the time of the insurrectional movement's harmful acts.

9.6.2 The Movement Creates a New State

The commentary to Article 2 ARSIWA, relating to the elements of an internationally wrongful act, states that "for responsibility to attach to the act of the State, the conduct must constitute a breach of an international legal obligation *in force for that State at that time*."[282] Similarly, Article 13 ARSIWA provides, "An act of a State does not constitute a breach of an international obligation unless *the State is bound by the obligation in question at the time the act occurs*."[283]

281. *See supra* sec. 9.2.3.

282. ARSIWA, *supra* note 1, art. 2, cmt. ¶ 1 (emphasis added).

283. *Id.* art. 13 (emphasis added).

These provisions appear to conflict with the new State rule reflected in Article 10(2). When members of an insurrectional movement act in potential violation of international law, the State to which their conduct may subsequently be attributed has not yet been created, and it does not bear any international legal obligations.

One way to reconcile these provisions is to interpret the new State element of Article 10 as applying only to those acts that violated the insurrectional movement's own international legal obligations.[284] In other words, the rule attributes to the new State the insurrectional movement's international responsibility for the conduct at issue.[285] But for the reasons outlined above in the context of the new government rule, this conclusion does not accord with either the wider attribution regime reflected in ARSIWA or the rule's object and purpose.[286] Instead, assuming that the new State element of Article 10 operates as a rule of attribution of conduct, it is pertinent to explore which primary norms of international law a newly established State could be deemed to violate through the prior conduct of the insurrectional movement responsible for its creation.

This requires an assessment of the treaty and customary international law obligations to which the new State becomes bound. Regarding treaties, the law of State succession is complex and subject to continuing debate.[287] While the 1978 Vienna Convention on Succession of States provides for a successor State to be bound by the treaty obligations of its predecessor,[288] the Convention has not received significant State support and does not reflect customary international law.[289] Accordingly, new States are considered to have a "clean slate" in respect of their international obligations.[290] A newly created State is therefore not bound by its predecessor's treaty obligations unless it agrees otherwise. Some commentators

284. *See* Eatwell, *Armed Groups*, *supra* note 52, at 229–30.

285. *Id.*

286. *See supra* sec. 9.6.1.

287. A detailed examination of this area of law is beyond the scope of this work. For further discussion on the issue as it relates to human rights treaties, *see, e.g.*, Menno T. Kamminga, *State Succession in Respect of Human Rights Treaties*, 7 Eur. J. Int'l L. 496 (1996); Akbar Rasulov, *Revisiting State Succession to Humanitarian Treaties: Is There a Case for Automaticity?* 14 Eur. J. Int'l L. 141 (2003).

288. Vienna Convention on Succession of States in Respect of Treaties art. 34(1)(a), Aug. 23, 1978, 1946 U.N.T.S. 3.

289. *See, e.g.*, Rasulov, *supra* note 287, at 149–50; Kamminga, *supra* note 287, at 471–72; Marko Milanović, *The Tricky Question of State Succession to International Responsibility*, EJIL: Talk! (Feb. 16, 2009), www.ejiltalk.org/the-tricky-question-of-state-succession-to-international-responsibility/.

290. Milanović, *supra* note 289.

and human rights bodies argue, nonetheless, that treaties offering humanitarian protections to individuals should apply automatically to the successor State, even without its consent.[291]

Whether or not this is correct, many of the provisions of humanitarian treaties reflect customary international law.[292] As customary duties apply to all States from the moment they are created, it is arguable that these should be treated differently from treaty obligations. This would mean that conduct on the part of an insurrectional movement that breaches a treaty obligation the new State assumes following its creation would not constitute an internationally wrongful act, whereas rebel conduct that violates the new State's customary international law obligations would engage the State's responsibility.

The ICJ addressed this distinction between treaty and customary obligations in *Croatia v. Serbia*.[293] The case concerned Croatia's claim against Serbia, formerly known as the Federal Republic of Yugoslavia (FRY), under the Genocide Convention. Although the FRY was not proclaimed as a State until April 1992, Croatia argued that the new State rule reflected in Article 10(2) attributed the acts of the "Greater Serbia" movement prior to that date to the FRY, including the movement's violations of the Genocide Convention.[294] In response, Serbia countered that even if Article 10 applied, it did not "make treaty obligations accepted by the new State after its emergence retroactively applicable to acts of the pre-State 'movement', even if it treats those acts as attributable to the new State."[295] Serbia argued instead that any movement that existed prior to April 1992 could only be bound by the customary international law prohibition of genocide.[296]

The ICJ agreed, finding that the new State rule enshrined in Article 10(2) "is concerned only with the attribution of acts to a new State; it does not create obligations binding upon either the new State or the movement that succeeded in establishing that new State."[297] Therefore, "even if the acts prior to 27 April 1992 . . . were attributable to a 'movement', within the meaning of Article 10(2) of the ILC Articles, and became attributable to the FRY by operation of the principle set out in that Article, they cannot have involved a violation of the provisions of

291. *See, e.g.*, Kamminga, *supra* note 287; Bijelić v. Montenegro & Serbia, App. No. 11890/05, ¶ 69 (Apr. 28, 2009) (ECtHR). For a contrary view, *see* Rasulov, *supra* note 287. *See also* Šturma's Second Rep. on State Succession, *supra* note 45, at 32–33, ¶¶ 120–21.

292. *See, e.g.*, Hurst Hannum, *The Status of the Universal Declaration of Human Rights in National and International Law*, 25 Ga. J. Int'l & Comp. L. 287 (1996).

293. *Croatia v. Serbia*, *supra* note 57. For commentary, *see, e.g.*, Dumberry, Rebellions, *supra* note 9, at 309–11.

294. *Croatia v. Serbia*, *supra* note 57, ¶ 102.

295. *Id.* ¶ 103.

296. *Id.*

297. *Id.* ¶ 104.

the Genocide Convention but, at most, only of the customary international law prohibition of genocide."[298]

When reaching this conclusion, the ICJ noted that the new State rule does not affect the principle stated in Article 13 ARSIWA.[299] The ILC made the same conclusion in its later work on State responsibility in the context of State succession, finding that there is no contradiction between Articles 10 and 13 due to their differing purposes, dealing respectively with attribution and breach.[300] The ILC interpreted the ICJ's judgment to mean that the new State rule expressed in Article 10(2) "will have its full effect in cases where the breached obligation continues to be binding on a new State."[301] This is the case with customary obligations, and "may also include obligations under treaty law to the extent that the principle of automatic succession applies."[302]

It follows that when an insurrectional movement succeeds in creating a new State, any conduct on the part of the movement that violates the new State's obligations under customary international law is attributable to that State and constitutes an internationally wrongful act. Regarding treaty obligations, the ICJ's jurisprudence indicates that an insurrectional movement's violations of any treaty provisions that bind the new State would not engage the State's responsibility. However, if the principle of automatic succession in respect of humanitarian treaties develops into a norm of customary international law,[303] a broader range of conduct on the part of an insurrectional movement might engage the international responsibility of the new State that the movement creates.

9.7 CONCLUSION

Article 10 ARSIWA expresses a highly unusual rule of attribution that is rarely invoked by States, international courts or tribunals, or by human rights monitoring bodies. Although the new government element of the rule has clear historical foundations, these have not been strengthened through recent State practice or jurisprudence, particularly in the postcolonial era.[304] Considerable doubts therefore

298. *Id.* ¶ 105.

299. *Id.* ¶ 104; ARSIWA, *supra* note 1, art. 13.

300. Šturma's Second Rep. on State Succession, *supra* note 45, at 32, ¶ 119.

301. *Id.*

302. *Id.* Regarding the principle of automatic succession, see the text accompanying note 291.

303. *See, e.g.*, Kamminga, *supra* note 287.

304. Olleson, for instance, noted in 2007 that "there appears to have been no international judicial reference to Article 10." *See* Olleson, *supra* note 41, at 95.

remain as to whether the rule reflects customary international law, particularly the element relating to the attribution of conduct to newly created States.[305]

Nonetheless, the success of HTS in Syria and the Taliban in Afghanistan demonstrates the rule's continued relevance. Both groups acted in a manner that potentially violated international law prior to taking power,[306] and continuity exists between the structures of the respective insurrectional movements and the new governments they created.[307] The rule reflected in Article 10 ensures that insurgents who commit acts that potentially violate international law during their struggle for power cannot later deny responsibility for those same abuses once they are in government. Moreover, it sidesteps the difficulties involved in invoking the responsibility of the movement itself.[308]

Yet as this chapter highlights, considerable impediments remain for those States injured by an insurrectional movement's conduct that wish to invoke the rule by holding the State that the movement later governs to account.[309] First, their prospects of making a claim are subject to significant uncertainty pending the outcome of the movement's struggle. Second, States may be reluctant to pursue a claim due to the perceived legitimacy it may confer on the successful government or State.[310] And third, claimants may face serious evidential difficulties, such as in proving that the conduct complained of is attributable to the insurgent group.[311] Uncertainties such as these seriously diminish Article 10's relevance to situations of armed conflict and also impede its crystallization into a norm of customary international law.

305. The ICJ did not find it necessary to rule on this issue. *See Croatia v. Serbia*, *supra* note 57, ¶ 104. *See also* Verhoeven, *supra* note 44, at 286; d'Aspremont, *supra* note 7, at 433. The International Group of Experts involved in *Tallinn Manual 2.0* expressed uncertainty as to whether Article 10 accurately reflects customary international law. *See* TALLINN MANUAL 2.0 ON THE INTERNATIONAL LAW APPLICABLE TO CYBER OPERATIONS 32, n. 46 (Michael N. Schmitt ed., 2017). *But see also* DINSTEIN, *supra* note 18, at 236 (describing the rule as "a snapshot of customary international law").

306. *See, e.g.*, Shamdasani, *supra* note 89; HUMAN RTS. WATCH, AFGHANISTAN WORLD REPORT 2020, https://www.hrw.org/world-report/2020/country-chapters/afghanistan#.

307. Al Jazeera, *supra* note 104; Maizland, *supra* note 110. Regarding the rule's object and purpose, *see also supra* sec. 9.2.3.

308. Verhoeven, *supra* note 44, at 294–95.

309. The ILC recognized such difficulties. *See, e.g.*, Ago's Fourth Rep. on State Responsibility, *supra* note 6, at 129–30, ¶ 154; ILC Y.B. 1975 vol. I, *supra* note 124, at 65, ¶ 28 (comments of Mr. Ramangasoavina). *See also* Cahin, *supra* note 17, at 248; Atlam, *supra* note 217, at 50.

310. *See supra* secs. 9.3.1, 9.4.2.

311. *See supra* sec. 9.5.3.

10

Conduct Acknowledged and Adopted by the State

10.1 INTRODUCTION

The preceding two chapters explore the exceptional rules of attribution expressed in Articles 9 and 10 of the Draft Articles on Responsibility of States for Internationally Wrongful Acts (ARSIWA).[1] These are rarely invoked by States, judicial bodies, or humanitarian organizations, and their interpretation, as well as their relevance, are subject to ongoing debate. The same can be said regarding the rule enshrined in Article 11 ARSIWA.[2] This envisages the retrospective attribution of private conduct to a State after the relevant acts in potential violation of international law have been committed. It provides, "Conduct which is not attributable to a State under the preceding articles shall nevertheless be considered an act of that State under international law if and to the extent that the State acknowledges and adopts the conduct in question as its own."[3]

Unlike the other rules of attribution discussed in this book, Article 11 can apply to the prior conduct of States as well as that of non-State actors (NSA).[4] This chapter, however, considers the rule's application solely to the conduct of NSAs. In that context, the rule attributes to a State conduct that was private in character at the time of its commission if the State subsequently acknowledges and adopts the relevant acts as its own.[5] Thus, it is the State's own ratification of the conduct

1. *See supra* chs. 8, 9.

2. Draft Articles on Responsibility of States for Internationally Wrongful Acts, with commentaries, art. 11, *in* Int'l Law Comm'n, Rep. on the Work of its Fifty-Third Session, U.N. Doc. A/56/10 (2001), *reprinted in* [2001] 2 Y.B. Int'l L. Comm'n 31, 52, U.N. Doc. A/CN.4/SER.A/2001/Add.1 (Part 2) [hereinafter ARSIWA].

3. *Id.*

4. *Id.*, cmt. ¶ 3. *See also* James Crawford, State Responsibility: The General Part 183 (2013).

5. ARSIWA, *supra* note 2, art. 11, cmt. ¶ 1.

Attribution of Non-State Actor Conduct During Armed Conflict. Jennifer Maddocks, Oxford University Press.
 DOI: 10.1093/oso/9780197842652.003.0010

rather than the relationship between the State and the NSA that provides the basis for attribution.[6]

The chapter begins by addressing Article 11's drafting history, relevant jurisprudence, and the rule's object and purpose. Thereafter, it explores the meaning of the acknowledgment and adoption requirements, using examples from armed conflict to illustrate the rule's potential application. Finally, the chapter examines the rule's place and importance within the wider attribution regime. It considers, first, whether the rule serves any real purpose given States' ability to voluntarily accept responsibility for prior conduct without the need for any rule of attribution. Second, it assesses the rule's status, concluding that the principle of retrospective attribution expressed in Article 11 does not reflect customary international law. Moreover, even if it did, the rule's scope of application is so narrow that it has little practical impact in holding States to account for the harmful conduct of NSAs in contemporary conflict.

10.2 ATTRIBUTION PURSUANT TO ARTICLE 11

10.2.1 Drafting History

Article 11 differs from the other rules of attribution reflected in ARSIWA in that the principle it enshrines did not feature in the draft articles adopted by the International Law Commission (ILC) on first reading.[7] Nonetheless, the principle has a far longer history. According to the eighteenth-century jurist Emer de Vattel, "If the nation, or its ruler, approve and ratify the act of the citizen, it takes upon itself the act, and may then be regarded by the injured party as the real author of the affront of which the citizen was perhaps the only instrument."[8]

Special Rapporteur Ago considered Vattel's work but did not specifically examine whether the principle Vattel expressed should be reflected in a rule of attribution.[9] In his review of case law raising the principle, Ago focused on other

6. *See* Tal Becker, Terrorism and the State: Rethinking the Rules of State Responsibility 75 (2006).

7. Draft Articles on State Responsibility with Commentaries thereto Adopted by the ILC on First Reading, pt. 1 ch. 2 (1996), *in* Int'l Law Comm'n, Rep. on the Work of its Forty-Eighth Session, U.N. Doc. A/51/10, *reprinted in* [1996] 2 Y.B. Int'l L. Comm'n 59, U.N. Doc. A/CN.4/SER.A/1996/Add.1 (Part 2) [hereinafter Draft Articles Adopted on First Reading].

8. Roberto Ago (Special Rapporteur), Fourth Rep. on State Responsibility, by Mr. Roberto Ago, Special Rapporteur—The Internationally Wrongful Act of the State, Source of International Responsibility (1972), *in* [1972] 2 Y.B. Int'l L. Comm'n 71, 121, U.N. Doc. A/CN.4/SER.A/1972/Add.1 (Part One) [hereinafter Ago's Fourth Rep. on State Responsibility], *citing* 2 Emer de Vattel, Le Droit des Gens, ou Principes de la Loi Naturelle 72 (1802). *See also* Crawford, *supra* note 4, at 181.

9. Ago's Fourth Rep. on State Responsibility, *supra* note 8, at 121.

aspects of the judgments, not the potential attribution of conduct to the State based on the State's subsequent approval or ratification.[10]

Attribution on this basis nevertheless featured, to a limited extent, in the ILC's discussions. For instance, in 1974, one ILC member indicated his belief that the rule now reflected in Article 8 ARSIWA should apply either when an individual acts with the authority of the State "or, where no such authority existed, the State subsequently approved, adopted or ratified the act, thereby becoming responsible for it."[11] However, no mention of this principle appears in the commentary to Draft Article 8, or in any of the other draft articles adopted on first reading.[12]

Special Rapporteur Crawford proposed the rule now reflected in Article 11 in his first report on State responsibility in 1998.[13] In the report, Crawford highlighted a potential lacuna in the standards of attribution formulated by Ago.[14] Citing certain case law in support,[15] Crawford recommended that "the draft articles should contain a provision stating that conduct not otherwise attributable to a State is so attributable if and to the extent that the conduct is subsequently adopted by that State."[16]

In their subsequent discussions, members of the ILC generally agreed to Crawford's proposal,[17] with one member describing this as "an indispensable provision."[18] When given the opportunity to comment on the draft article, governments largely remained silent.[19] Only the Netherlands saw fit to comment, raising just one minor issue regarding the wording.[20] The UN General Assembly

10. *Id.* at 101, ¶ 77. *See also* Olivier de Frouville, *Attribution of Conduct to the State: Private Individuals*, *in* THE LAW OF INTERNATIONAL RESPONSIBILITY 257, 273 (James Crawford et al. eds., 2010).

11. Int'l Law Comm'n, Summary Records of the Twenty-Sixth Session (1974), *in* [1974] 1 Y.B. INT'L L. COMM'N 36, ¶ 2 (comments of Sir Francis Vallat), U.N. Doc. A/CN.4/SER.A/1974. *See also id.* at 37, ¶ 4. For discussion regarding Article 8 ARSIWA, *see supra* ch. 6.

12. Draft Articles Adopted on First Reading, *supra* note 7, pt. 1 ch. 2.

13. James Crawford (Special Rapporteur), First Rep. on State Responsibility 54–55, 57–58, U.N. Doc. A/CN.4/490 and Add.1–7 (1998) [hereinafter Crawford's First Rep. on State Responsibility].

14. *Id.* at 54–55.

15. *Id. See also infra* sec. 10.2.3.

16. Crawford's First Rep. on State Responsibility, *supra* note 13, at 54, ¶ 281.

17. *See, e.g.*, Int'l Law Comm'n, Summary Records of the Fiftieth Session (1998), *in* [1998] 1 Y.B. INT'L L. COMM'N 250 ¶ 6, 254 ¶ 47, 255 ¶ 55 (comments of Mr. Hafner, Mr. Addo, Mr. Pellet), U.N. Doc. A/CN.4/SER.A/1998 [hereinafter ILC Y.B. 1998 vol. I].

18. *Id.* at 258, ¶ 48 (comments of Mr. Economides).

19. *Id.* at 254, ¶ 39 (comments of Special Rapporteur Crawford).

20. Int'l Law Comm'n, Comments and Observations Received from Governments 50, U.N. Doc. A/CN.4/515 and Add.1-3 (2001) [hereinafter 2001 Comments and Observations].

subsequently adopted Article 11 ARSIWA in substantially the same form as that originally proposed by Crawford.[21]

10.2.2 Guidance Within the Commentary

Notwithstanding the ILC's very limited discussions regarding this basis of attribution, the commentary to Article 11 provides some clarification regarding its intended scope of application. This begins by highlighting the rule's unusual nature, in that it "provides for the attribution to a State of conduct that was not or may not have been attributable to it at the time of commission."[22] Thus, the ILC makes clear from the outset that it intends the rule to have retrospective effect.

This means that the State might have no involvement whatsoever in the acts it subsequently adopts.[23] The State might even have condemned and sought to prevent the acts concerned.[24] For instance, to promote peace following the conclusion of a conflict, government officials might identify conduct on the part of rebels that violates the State's international legal obligations and express the clear intent to recognize these as acts of State and to compensate the victims.[25] Alternatively, the State's adoption of the conduct might recognize that the NSA was, in fact, acting for the State at the relevant time.[26]

In this latter scenario, it may be that the State's adoption simply provides proof that the earlier acts were attributable to it from the outset, perhaps based on the rule reflected in Article 8.[27] In this situation, there is no retrospective attribution and the rule expressed in Article 11 plays no role; the State's act of adoption simply provides evidence to support the attribution of the conduct to the State on another basis. Article 11 comes into play only if the State endorses conduct that is otherwise not attributable to it. For example, the State might adopt private acts

21. ARSIWA, *supra* note 2, art. 11. Regarding the article's evolution, *see* Crawford's First Rep. on State Responsibility, *supra* note 13, at 57; Int'l Law Comm'n, Rep. of the Comm'n to the General Assembly on the Work of its Fifty-Second Session (2000), *in* [2000] 2 Y.B. Int'l L. Comm'n 66, U.N. Doc. A/CN.4/SER.A/2000/Add.1 (Part 2)/Rev.1; Int'l Law Comm'n, Summary Records of the Fifty-Third Session (2001), *in* [2001] 1 Y.B. Int'l L. Comm'n 94, ¶ 36, U.N. Doc. A/CN.4/SER.A/2001 [hereinafter ILC Y.B. 2001 vol. I].

22. ARSIWA, *supra* note 2, art. 11, cmt. ¶ 1.

23. *See* ILC Y.B. 1998 vol. I, *supra* note 17, at 256, ¶ 62 (comments of Special Rapporteur Crawford).

24. ARSIWA, *supra* note 2, art. 11, cmt. ¶ 6. *See also* ILC Y.B. 1998 vol. I, *supra* note 17, at 291, ¶ 90.

25. *See* ILC Y.B. 1998 vol. I, *supra* note 17, at 249, ¶ 58 (comments of Special Rapporteur Crawford).

26. ARSIWA, *supra* note 2, art. 11, cmt. ¶ 5. *See also* ILC Y.B. 1998 vol. I, *supra* note 17, at 256, ¶ 62 (comments of Special Rapporteur Crawford).

27. *Id. See also* ILC Y.B. 1998 vol. I, *supra* note 17, at 256, ¶ 66 (comments of Mr. Bennouna).

committed with the benefit of weapons it provided, but where its involvement in that conduct was insufficient to amount to instructions, direction, or control.[28]

Regarding the wording "if and to the extent that," the commentary to Article 11 makes clear that States can elect the precise private conduct they wish to acknowledge and adopt.[29] This is not an "all or nothing" decision.[30] To illustrate, the *Tallinn Manual 2.0* gives the example of a hacker group that engages in a variety of operations against different targets.[31] In such a situation, "[t]he State might acknowledge and adopt operations by the group against another State's government agency, but not those that the group is directing against the families of State officials."[32]

Importantly, the commentary distinguishes a State's acknowledgment and adoption of conduct from mere support or endorsement.[33] According to the ILC, "conduct will not be attributable to a State under article 11 where a State merely acknowledges the factual existence of conduct or expresses its verbal approval of it."[34] Instead, the requirement for adoption "carries with it the idea that the conduct is acknowledged by the State as, in effect, its own conduct." In other words, "the State identifies the conduct in question and makes it its own."[35] This seems to set a high threshold. However, as discussed further in section 10.3, the commentary leaves considerable room for doubt about the precise types of State conduct that would satisfy the acknowledgment and adoption thresholds.[36] Some further clarity on the issue can be gained from the decisions of courts and tribunals that address this basis of attribution.

10.2.3 Relevant Jurisprudence

The ARSIWA commentary refers to certain cases that it views as supporting the rule of attribution reflected in Article 11.[37] The most important of these is the

28. *See* ARSIWA, *supra* note 2, art. 8.

29. ARSIWA, *supra* note 2, art. 11, cmt. ¶ 8. *See also* ILC Y.B. 2001 vol. I, *supra* note 21, at 94, ¶ 38; de Frouville, *supra* note 10, at 275; Crawford, *supra* note 4, at 187.

30. Crawford, *supra* note 4, at 187.

31. Tallinn Manual 2.0 on the International Law Applicable to Cyber Operations r. 17, cmt. ¶ 17 (Michael N. Schmitt ed., 2017) [hereinafter Tallinn Manual 2.0].

32. *Id.*

33. ARSIWA, *supra* note 2, art. 11, cmt. ¶ 6.

34. *Id.*

35. *Id.*

36. *See infra* sec. 10.3.

37. ARSIWA, *supra* note 2, art. 11, cmt. ¶¶ 3–5.

judgment of the International Court of Justice (ICJ) in *Tehran Hostages*,[38] which Crawford described as "the archetype of how Article 11 works."[39] This section considers, first, the authorities the ILC refers to in the commentary to Article 11 before turning to address other relevant jurisprudence that assists in clarifying the rule's scope and application. As the following analysis demonstrates, it is doubtful whether *Tehran Hostages* or any of the other cases provides clear authority for the retrospective attribution of private conduct to a State, as enshrined in Article 11.

10.2.3.1 *Tehran Hostages*

The *Tehran Hostages* case concerned the occupation of the U.S. Embassy in Tehran in the context of the 1979 Iranian Revolution. A group of several hundred people, described by the ICJ as "the militants," gained access to the compound by force and held diplomatic and consular staff hostage.[40] The ICJ considered the status of the militants at the time of the attack to assess whether their actions were potentially attributable to Iran. Despite the previous public declarations issued by the country's religious leader calling upon citizens "to expand with all their might their attacks against the United States," the Court concluded that the militants were not acting for the State at the time of the attack.[41] Instead, the evidence indicated that the militants devised and carried out the plan themselves.[42]

The Court then moved to consider the second phase of events, which occurred after completion of the Embassy's occupation.[43] At that time, numerous Iranian officials publicly expressed their approval for the militants' actions.[44] The foreign minister, for instance, announced that the students' conduct "enjoys the endorsement and support of the government, because America herself is responsible for this incident."[45] Religious, judicial, executive, police, and broadcasting authorities made additional statements to this effect, including the Ayatollah Khomeini himself, who "made crystal clear the endorsement by the State both of the takeover of the Embassy and Consulates and of the detention of the Embassy staff as hostages."[46]

38. United States Diplomatic and Consular Staff in Tehran (U.S. v. Iran), Judgment, 1980 I.C.J. Rep. 3 (May 24) [hereinafter *Tehran Hostages*].

39. Crawford, *supra* note 4, at 183.

40. *Tehran Hostages*, *supra* note 38, ¶ 17.

41. *Id.*, ¶¶ 58–59. See *supra* ch. 6, sec. 6.3.1 for discussion whether the militants were acting on the State's instructions for the purposes of the rule of attribution reflected in art. 8 ARSIWA.

42. *Tehran Hostages*, *supra* note 38, ¶ 59.

43. *Id.*, ¶ 69.

44. *Id.*, ¶¶ 70–71.

45. *Id.*, ¶ 70.

46. *Id.*, ¶ 71.

Fortified by this unambiguous State support, the militants proclaimed that the Embassy would remain under their occupation.[47] Some days later, the Ayatollah Khomeini gave a final "seal of official government approval" to their actions by issuing a decree.[48] This described the American Embassy as "a center of espionage and conspiracy" and expressly declared that the position of the Embassy and the hostages would not change until the United States returned the former Shah to Iran for trial.[49] With the exception of women and African Americans, the Ayatollah asserted that "[t]he noble Iranian nation will not give permission for the release of the rest of them. Therefore, the rest of them will be under arrest until the American Government acts according to the wish of the nation."[50]

Other Iranian authorities complied with and repeatedly endorsed the policy enshrined in the decree.[51] This led the ICJ to conclude:

> The result of that policy was fundamentally to transform the legal nature of the situation created by the occupation of the Embassy and the detention of its diplomatic and consular staff as hostages. The approval given to these facts by the Ayatollah Khomeini and other organs of the Iranian State, and the decision to perpetuate them, translated continuing occupation of the Embassy and detention of the hostages into acts of that State. The militants, authors of the invasion and jailers of the hostages, had now become agents of the Iranian State for whose acts the State itself was internationally responsible.[52]

It is apparent from this passage that the militants' actions, following the Ayatollah's decree, were attributable to the State. From this time on, the militants acted as agents of the State, executing Iran's clearly stated policy of maintaining the occupation as a means of coercing the United States.[53] However, it is not clear that the court also intended Iran to bear responsibility for the original attack on the Embassy conducted by the militants. The ICJ had already held Iran responsible regarding the early period of the occupation on a different legal basis, namely, its own organs' failure to take sufficient action to prevent the seizure of the Embassy or to bring it to an end, which violated Iran's positive obligations under the 1961 Vienna Convention on Diplomatic Relations.[54]

Nevertheless, some legal scholars interpret the ICJ's judgment in *Tehran Hostages* as authority for the principle of retrospective attribution enshrined in

47. *Id.*, ¶ 72.

48. *Id.*, ¶ 73.

49. *Id.*, ¶ 73.

50. *Id.*

51. *Id.*, ¶ 74.

52. *Id.*

53. *Id.*, ¶¶ 74, 87.

54. *Id.* ¶¶ 61, 66–67. *See also* ARSIWA, *supra* note 2, art. 11, cmt. ¶ 4.

Article 11.[55] Hessbruegge, for instance, concludes that although the occupation of the embassy and detention of its staff "were committed by militant private individuals," the ICJ held Iran responsible for this conduct "because Ayatollah Khomeini had endorsed the acts publicly as a matter of State policy and other Iranian authorities complied with his statements."[56] Other scholars and the ILC, however, have taken a more nuanced view of the judgment.

In his first report on State responsibility, Special Rapporteur Crawford noted that it was not clear from the judgment "whether the effect of the 'approval' of the conduct of the militants was merely prospective, or whether it made the State of the Islamic Republic of Iran responsible for the whole process of seizure of the embassy and detention of its personnel *ab initio*."[57] Observing that it made little difference in this case, due to Iran's responsibility for the conduct of its own organs in respect of the Embassy seizure, Crawford pointed out that there may be cases in which no such prior responsibility exists.[58] He stated, "If the adoption is unequivocal and unqualified (as was the statement of the Minister for Foreign Affairs of the Islamic Republic of Iran . . .), there is good reason to give it retroactive effect."[59]

Crawford therefore placed particular weight on the statement of the Iranian Minister of Foreign Affairs, who reportedly said in a television interview that the occupation of the U.S. Embassy had been "done by our nation."[60] In Crawford's view, this was a clear indication of the State's intent to assume responsibility for the militants' initial actions in occupying the Embassy.[61] However, the same interpretation is not evident from the ICJ's judgment. While the Court mentioned the Minister's statement, it did not highlight this as being any different from the other official pronouncements made, or of any particular importance in terms of the legal effect it had on Iran's international responsibility.[62]

Earlier in its judgment, moreover, the ICJ indicated unambiguously that the initial attack was not attributable to Iran. The Court stated, "[C]ongratulations after the event . . . and other subsequent statements of official approval, though highly significant in another context shortly to be considered, do not alter the initially independent and unofficial character of the militants' attack on the Embassy."[63]

55. *See, e.g.*, TALLINN MANUAL 2.0, *supra* note 31, r. 17, cmt. ¶¶ 15–18.

56. Jan Arno Hessbruegge, *The Historical Development of the Doctrines of Attribution and Due Diligence in International Law*, 36 N.Y.U. J. INT'L L. & POLITICS 265, 271 (2004).

57. Crawford's First Rep. on State Responsibility, *supra* note 13, at 54, ¶ 280.

58. *Id.*

59. *Id.*

60. *Tehran Hostages, supra* note 38, ¶ 74. The television interview reportedly took place on May 6, 1980, six months after the Embassy seizure on November 4, 1979.

61. Crawford's First Rep. on State Responsibility, *supra* note 13, at 54, ¶ 280.

62. *Tehran Hostages, supra* note 38, ¶ 74.

63. *Id.*, ¶ 59.

The ICJ's judgment on this issue accordingly seems clear. The Court ruled only that the militants' future actions, after the date of the Ayatollah's official decree, were attributable to the State.[64]

Crawford nonetheless interprets the ICJ's reference to the congratulations' significance "in another context" as meaning that these modified the legal position on attribution.[65] Although as a matter of fact the attacks remained independent, "the legal consequences which flowed from that fact were altered by the approval and adoption such that the attacks could now be attributed *a posteriori* to the Iranian State."[66] However, that conclusion does not necessarily follow from the Court's judgment. Given the ICJ's explicit assertion that subsequent official statements did not alter the independent and unofficial character of the militants' actions,[67] the Court was more likely referring to the effect that the State's congratulations had on the militants' legal status after such declarations were made.[68]

In view of the lack of support for retrospective attribution in the *Tehran Hostages* judgment, Condorelli and Kress argue that *post factum* recognition should be viewed "not as a legal basis for attribution, but as furnishing sufficient and conclusive proof of the fact that, at the moment at which the conduct in question took place, a legal basis for attribution was in fact present."[69] In other words, the State's acknowledgment and adoption of the private conduct simply provide evidence that the militants were acting on behalf of the State at the time they committed the acts that violated international law. One problem with this analysis, however, is that this was not the case in *Tehran Hostages*. The ICJ concluded that the militants devised and carried out the plan to occupy the Embassy themselves.[70] Moreover, if at the time the relevant conduct occurs, attribution is appropriate on another basis, retrospective attribution pursuant to Article 11 is unnecessary.

Thus, in *Tehran Hostages*, Iran's endorsement of the militants' actions did not provide proof of the State's involvement in the initial occupation of the Embassy.

64. Certain legal scholars agree with this conclusion. *See, e.g.*, Claus Kress, *L'organe de facto en droit international public: réflexions sur l'imputation à l'État de l'acte d'un particulier à la lumière des développements récents*, 105 Revue Générale de Droit International Public 93, 121 (2001); Luigi Condorelli & Claus Kress, *The Rules of Attribution: General Considerations*, *in* The Law of International Responsibility 221, 231–32 (James Crawford et al. eds., 2010); Olivier Corten & François Dubuisson, *Operation "Liberté Immuable": Une Extension Abusive de Concept de Légitime Defense*, 106 Revue General de Droit International Public 51, 68 (2002); Becker, *supra* note 6, at 63, 74; Tallinn Manual 2.0, *supra* note 31, r. 17, cmt. ¶ 18.

65. Crawford, *supra* note 4, at 185.

66. *Id.* (emphasis in original).

67. *Id.*

68. *See Tehran Hostages*, *supra* note 38, ¶ 74.

69. Condorelli & Kress, *supra* note 64, at 232.

70. *Tehran Hostages*, *supra* note 38, ¶ 59.

Instead, it changed the militants' status going forward, making them "agents of the Iranian State" from that point on.[71] This raises questions regarding the basis on which the militants' conduct, after the Ayatollah's decree, was attributable to Iran. In general terms, agency relationships are pertinent to the rule of attribution reflected in Article 8 ARSIWA.[72] However, the ILC does not mention the *Tehran Hostages* case in its commentary to Article 8.[73] Moreover, the ICJ, when addressing attribution based on the rule now reflected in Article 8 in the *Nicaragua* case, made no mention of its earlier judgment in *Tehran Hostages*.[74]

In his separate opinion in *Nicaragua*, Judge (and former Special Rapporteur) Ago expressed regret that the court did not refer to the precedent set by its decision in *Tehran Hostages*.[75] He stated, "The Court seems to me to have overlooked the fact that, at that time, it was faced with a situation in many ways similar to the present one."[76] In line with Ago's approach, the *Tehran Hostages* case may be better viewed as an example of attribution pursuant to Article 8, rather than as authority for retrospective attribution.[77] Although the ICJ did not refer to the militants acting under Iran's instructions, direction, or control after the date of the Ayatollah's decree, the militants were plainly acting on the State's behalf, executing its clearly stated policy.[78]

Alternatively, the State's endorsement of the militants' conduct could constitute legal empowerment, authorizing them to perform governmental functions on the State's behalf.[79] Notably, the Ayatollah Khomeini described those U.S. citizens held hostage as being "under arrest."[80] Powers to make arrests and detain individuals are quintessentially governmental in character.[81] Moreover, through the decree, the Ayatollah seemingly empowered the militants to act on Iran's behalf in a manner that accorded with the State's domestic laws. It is arguable,

71. *Id.*, ¶ 74.

72. *See, e.g.*, Crawford's First Rep. on State Responsibility, *supra* note 13, at 34, ¶ 158. For further discussion regarding Article 8 ARSIWA, *see supra* ch. 6.

73. *See* ARSIWA, *supra* note 2, art. 8, cmt. ¶¶ 1–9.

74. Military and Paramilitary Activities in and against Nicaragua (Nicar. v. U.S.), Judgment, 1986 I.C.J. Rep. 14, ¶¶ 93–116 (June 27).

75. *Id.* Separate Opinion of Judge Ago ¶ 18.

76. *Id.*

77. For further discussion regarding the rule of attribution reflected in Article 8 ARSIWA, *see supra* ch. 6.

78. Kress, *supra* note 64, at 131.

79. ARSIWA, *supra* note 2, art. 5.

80. *Tehran Hostages, supra* note 38, ¶ 73. *See also* Gregory Townsend, *State Responsibility for Acts of De Facto Agents*, 14 ARIZ. J. INT'L & COMP. L. 635, 647 (1997).

81. *See supra* ch. 5, sec. 5.3.2.

therefore, that from the date of the decree, the militants' conduct was attributable to Iran based on the rule reflected in Article 5 ARSIWA.[82]

10.2.3.2 *Lighthouses* Arbitration

The only other decision the ILC cites in its commentary to Article 11 is the *Lighthouses* arbitration, decided in 1956 by the French-Greek Arbitral Tribunal established under the rules of the Permanent Court of Arbitration.[83] This case relates not to the attribution of private conduct to a State but rather to State succession. It concerned concession rights that a French company obtained from the Ottoman Empire for maintaining lighthouses on the island of Crete. When Greece gained sovereignty over Crete in 1913, the French owner of the concession brought several claims against Greece.[84]

One of those claims was for damages resulting from the Cretan government's failure to charge a Greek shipping company lighthouse fees, which were payable under the terms of the concession.[85] The tribunal had to determine whether Greece, as the successor State, should bear responsibility for the acts of the Cretan government prior to 1913, when Crete was an autonomous territory of the Ottoman Empire.[86] In the context of State succession, it remains unclear whether a new State succeeds to State responsibility in respect of the acts of its predecessor.[87]

When deciding the claim, the tribunal considered Greece's conduct after 1913. It found that Greece was liable for Crete's breach of the concession agreement because the violation had been "endorsed by [Greece] as if it had been a regular transaction . . . and eventually continued by her, even after the acquisition of territorial sovereignty over the island."[88] The tribunal reached this conclusion because after 1913, Greece continued to exempt the shipping company from the fees that were owing and therefore continued the same breach.[89]

82. ARSIWA, *supra* note 2, art. 5. For further discussion regarding the rule reflected in Article 5, *see supra* ch. 5.

83. ARSIWA, *supra* note 2, art. 11, cmt. ¶¶ 3–4, *citing* Affaire Relative à la Concession des Phares de l'Empire Ottoman (Greece v. France) 12 R.I.A.A. 155 (Perm Ct. Arb., 1956) [hereinafter *Lighthouses Arbitration*]. For further discussion regarding the case, *see, e.g.*, Wladyslaw Czaplinski, *State Succession and State Responsibility*, 28 Canadian Y.B. Int'l L. 339, 344–46 (1990); Michael John Volkovitsch, *Righting Wrongs: Towards a New Theory of State Succession to Responsibility for International Delicts*, 92 Colum. L. Rev. 2162, 2187–90 (1992); Patrick Dumberry, *Turkey's International Responsibility for Internationally Wrongful Acts Committed by the Ottoman Empire*, 42 Revue Générale de Droit 561, 575–78 (2012); Crawford, *supra* note 4, at 443–45.

84. *Lighthouses Arbitration*, *supra* note 83.

85. *Id.* at 191. *See also* Czaplinski, *supra* note 83, at 345; Volkovitsch, *supra* note 83, at 2188–89.

86. *Lighthouses Arbitration*, *supra* note 83, at 192.

87. *See generally*, Crawford, *supra* note 4, at 435–56.

88. *Lighthouses Arbitration*, *supra* note 83, at 198. *See also* ARSIWA, *supra* note 2, art. 11, cmt. ¶ 3.

89. *Lighthouses Arbitration*, *supra* note 83, at 197.

After outlining the tribunal's decision, the ARSIWA commentary asserts that "if the successor State, faced with a continuing wrongful act on its territory, endorses and continues that situation, the inference may readily be drawn that it has assumed responsibility for it."[90] The ILC then applied the same principle by analogy to a State's endorsement of private acts.[91] Thus, the ILC used the decision in the *Lighthouses* arbitration to support its argument that a State's acknowledgment and adoption of an NSA's prior conduct leads to the retrospective attribution of that conduct to the State.[92]

Doubts remain, however, whether it is appropriate to apply a decision relating to State succession to the distinct context of private conduct and its potential attribution to a State.[93] It is quite different conceptually for a State to assume responsibility for the earlier actions of its predecessor, which exercised sovereign rights over the territory concerned, as opposed to the conduct of NSAs, whose actions are not generally regulated by international law.

If an analogy can be drawn between these two sets of circumstances, it seems that this should be quite limited. In the *Lighthouses* arbitration, Greece was responsible for the actions of the Cretan government because the State continued that same wrongful conduct after it assumed sovereignty over the territory.[94] Applied to the rule reflected in Article 11, it may be appropriate to conclude that if a State endorses and continues the acts that an NSA initiates, the entire course of conduct is attributable to the State, including the initially private element. Section 10.3.2 addresses this possibility in more detail, in the context of armed conflict.

10.2.3.3 Adolf Eichmann

Article 11's commentary additionally refers to the capture and subsequent trial in Israel of Adolf Eichmann, a principal perpetrator of the Holocaust.[95] A group of Israelis captured Eichmann in Argentina in 1960 and he was subsequently flown to Israel and tried by the Israeli government.[96] Argentina complained to the UN Security Council regarding the violation of its sovereignty, claiming that Israel was "responsible for the secret and unlawful transfer of Adolf Eichmann to the

90. ARSIWA, *supra* note 2, art. 11, cmt. ¶ 3. *See also* Crawford's First Rep. on State Responsibility, *supra* note 13, at 54, ¶ 279.

91. ARSIWA, *supra* note 2, art. 11, cmt. ¶ 4; Crawford, *supra* note 4, at 183.

92. ARSIWA, *supra* note 2, art. 11, cmt. ¶ 4.

93. *See* Kress, *supra* note 64, at 136–37 (opining that the *Lighthouses Arbitration* may be interpreted as a simple assumption of responsibility by the State).

94. *Lighthouses Arbitration*, *supra* note 83, at 197.

95. ARSIWA, *supra* note 2, art. 11, cmt. ¶ 5.

96. For legal commentary regarding Eichmann's capture and trial, *see, e.g.*, James E. S. Fawcett, *The Eichmann Case*, 38 Brit. Y.B. Int'l L. 181 (1962); William Schabas, *The Contribution of the Eichmann Trial to International Law*, 26 Leiden J. Int'l L. 667 (2013).

territory of Israel."[97] In response, Israel's Foreign Minister referred to the captors as a "volunteer group" and denied that "the illegal acts of individuals" amounted to a sovereignty violation.[98]

The following day, the UN Security Council passed a resolution in which it accepted that the abduction violated Argentina's sovereignty and requested the Israeli government "to make appropriate reparation in accordance with the Charter of the United Nations and the rules of international law."[99] In so doing, the Council seems to implicitly acknowledge that the abduction and the consequent violation of Argentina's sovereignty was attributable to Israel.

The precise basis of attribution, however, remains unclear. The ARSIWA commentary recognizes this ambiguity, accepting that the group's conduct may have been attributable to Israel based on the rule reflected in Article 8.[100] The commentary then goes on to state, "[W]here there are doubts about whether certain conduct falls within article 8, these may be resolved by the subsequent adoption of the conduct in question by the State."[101] But the commentary fails to clarify how exactly this resolves the issue. The ILC could have meant by this that Israel's conduct in accepting custody of Eichmann and placing him on trial should be treated as evidence of the State's involvement in the original abduction, in which case the basis of attribution remains the rule reflected in Article 8. Alternatively, the ILC's intent may have been that even if the "volunteers" were not acting on Israel's behalf at the relevant time, the State's conduct following Eichmann's capture led to the retroactive attribution of the abduction to Israel.

Some clarification can be gained from Crawford's later work, in which he stated,

> In the unlikely event that the group that captured Eichmann were non-state actors of whose plans Israel was genuinely unaware, its conduct in accepting custody of Eichmann, and in subsequently trying and executing him, may be taken as adoption of the abduction, giving rise to attribution under ARSIWA Article 11.[102]

Thus, Crawford clearly accepted the likelihood that the "volunteers" were, in fact, either Israeli State organs or private individuals tasked to undertake the abduction on Israel's behalf, meaning their conduct was attributable to Israel based on the rule reflected in either Article 4 or Article 8 ARSIWA.[103] Retrospective attribution

97. U.N. SCOR, 15th Sess., 865th mtg. ¶ 5 (June 22, 1960), https://documents-dds-ny.un.org/doc/UNDOC/GEN/N60/253/73/PDF/N6025373.pdf?OpenElement [hereinafter U.N. SCOR 865th mtg.].

98. U.N. SCOR, 15th Sess., 866th mtg. ¶¶ 18, 41 (June 22, 1960), https://documents-dds-ny.un.org/doc/UNDOC/GEN/NL6/000/01/PDF/NL600001.pdf?OpenElement [hereinafter U.N. SCOR 866th mtg.].

99. S.C. Res. 138 (1960) ¶¶ 1–2 (June 23).

100. ARSIWA, *supra* note 2, art. 11, cmt. ¶ 5.

101. *Id.*

102. Crawford, *supra* note 4, at 183.

103. *See supra* chs. 4, 6.

based on the rule now reflected in Article 11 is put forward as a mere possibility in the event that this was not the case. This accords with the ARSIWA commentary, which tentatively suggests that Eichmann's capture and subsequent trial "*may* provide an example of the subsequent adoption of private conduct by a State."[104]

However, the UN Security Council Resolution and the records of prior discussions on the issue reveal nothing to indicate States' acceptance of the principle expressed in Article 11 as a basis on which to attribute the abduction to Israel.[105] Moreover, even if the Eichmann case does support the notion of retrospective attribution, the ILC did not clearly explain why Israel's conduct should be characterized as adoption that satisfies the rule. While the State certainly benefited from the abduction, it does not necessarily follow that Israel's actions in prosecuting Eichmann amounted to Israel's acknowledgment of his abduction and the consequent violation of Argentina's sovereignty as its own conduct, as the ARSIWA commentary requires.[106] Indeed, the Israeli Foreign Minister's comments before the Security Council demonstrate the opposite.[107]

10.2.3.4 *Prosecutor v. Nikolić*

More than four decades after Eichmann's abduction, the International Criminal Tribunal for the former Yugoslavia (ICTY) considered the effects of a defendant's unlawful abduction on the tribunal's jurisdiction to hear the case.[108] Dragan Nikolić was kidnapped in Serbia then taken to Bosnia and Herzegovina, where the Stabilization Force (SFOR) arrested him and transferred him to the ICTY.[109] The parties agreed that the individuals responsible for the abduction had "no connection whatsoever with SFOR and/or the Tribunal."[110]

Nikolić challenged the ICTY's jurisdiction, arguing that by taking custody of him, the Prosecution and/or SFOR "acknowledged and adopted the alleged illegal conduct of those individuals."[111] His defense submitted that "by not only ignoring the illegality [of the abduction] but, by actively taking advantage of the situation and taking into custody the accused, SFOR's exercise of jurisdiction

104. ARSIWA, *supra* note 2, art. 11, cmt. ¶ 5 (emphasis added).

105. *See* S.C. Res. 138 (1960), *supra* note 99; U.N. SCOR 865th mtg., *supra* note 97; U.N. SCOR 866th mtg., *supra* note 98. For a contrary view, *see, e.g.*, Jan Arno Hessbruegge, *Human Rights Violations Arising from Conduct of Non-State Actors*, 11 Buff. Hum. Rts. L. Rev. 21, 51 (2005) [hereinafter Hessbruegge, *Human Rights Violations*].

106. ARSIWA, *supra* note 2, art. 11, cmt. ¶ 7.

107. U.N. SCOR 866th mtg., *supra* note 98, ¶¶ 2-49.

108. Prosecutor v. Dragan Nikolić, Case No. ICTY IT-94-2-PT, Decision on Defence Motion Challenging the Exercise of Jurisdiction by the Tribunal (Int'l Crim. Trib. for the former Yugoslavia Oct. 9, 2002) [hereinafter *Nikolić*].

109. *Id.*, ¶¶ 15, 57.

110. *Id.*, ¶ 57.

111. *Id.*, ¶ 29.

over Nikolic was an adoption of the illegality—of which they were aware—and thus, an extension of the unlawful detention."[112] The Prosecution contended in response that SFOR was merely "a fortuitous recipient of the Accused" and that any irregularities committed by individuals prior to the defendant's delivery to the ICTY should not divest the tribunal of jurisdiction over him.[113]

In its decision, the ICTY Trial Chamber referred to Article 11 ARSIWA "[p]urely as *general* legal guidance" to assist in determining the issue at hand.[114] The law of State responsibility did not apply directly because the tribunal was examining the attribution of conduct to SFOR and the Prosecution, neither of which is a State.[115] Nevertheless, the ICTY noted that the parties used similar criteria of "acknowledgment," "adoption," "recognition," "approval," and "ratification" to those employed by the ILC.[116] The tribunal went on to observe that when SFOR first came into contact with Nikolić, all it did was transfer him to the ICTY, as it was obliged to do under the terms of the tribunal's statute and rules.[117] Dismissing Nikolić's argument on the issue of jurisdiction, the ICTY concluded that "the alleged illegal conduct of unknown individuals cannot be attributed to SFOR, for lack of acknowledgment and ratification."[118]

Although lacking in detail, the ICTY's decision on attribution appears to accord with the commentary to Article 11 ARSIWA. There is nothing within the facts set out by the Trial Chamber to indicate that SFOR or the Prosecution endorsed Nikolić's abduction in the sense that they identified the conduct and indicated an intent to accept responsibility for it.[119] Applied in the context of State responsibility, therefore, the ICTY's decision indicates that if a State merely benefits from an NSA's prior conduct, that alone is insufficient to lead to attribution.[120]

112. *Id.*, ¶ 32.

113. *Id.*, ¶¶ 33, 59.

114. *Id.*, ¶ 61 (emphasis in original).

115. *Id.*, ¶ 60. *See also* Simon Olleson, Brit. Inst. of Int'l & Comp. L., The Impact of the ILC's Articles on Responsibility of States for Internationally Wrongful Acts 1, 96 (Oct. 10, 2007), www.biicl.org/files/3107_impactofthearticlesonstate_responsibilitypreliminarydraftfinal.pdf.

116. *Nikolić*, *supra* note 108, ¶ 64.

117. *Id.*, ¶ 67.

118. *Id.*, ¶ 68. On appeal, the ICTY Appeals Chamber sidestepped the issue of attribution, finding that even if the abduction was attributable to SFOR, there was no basis upon which it should not exercise jurisdiction. *See* Prosecutor v. Nikolić, Case No. ICTY-94-2-AR73, Decision on Interlocutory Appeal Concerning Legality of Arrest, ¶ 33 (Int'l Crim. Trib. for the former Yugoslavia, June 5, 2003).

119. *See* ARSIWA, *supra* note 2, art. 11, cmt. ¶ 6.

120. Richard Mackenzie-Gray Scott, State Responsibility for Non-State Actors: Past, Present and Prospects for the Future 129 (2022).

Something more is needed on the part of the State to indicate its intention to accept responsibility for the private conduct and make it its own.[121]

10.2.3.5 *Makuchyan and Minasyan v. Azerbaijan and Hungary*

In 2020, the European Court of Human Rights (ECtHR) noted the "very high threshold" that the ARSIWA commentary sets for attribution pursuant to Article 11.[122] The case concerned an Azerbaijani officer, referred to in the judgment as R.S., who attended a NATO-sponsored course in Budapest.[123] Two members of the Armenian military were also on the course; a significant fact due to the long-running conflict in Nagorno-Karabakh, in which Azerbaijan and Armenia were opposing parties. In February 2004, on the anniversary of the start of the Nagorno-Karabakh conflict, R.S. decapitated one of the Armenians with an axe while he was sleeping. He also attempted to attack the second Armenian but was prevented from doing so by the arrival of the police.[124]

R.S. was convicted of murder and attempted murder in Hungary and sentenced to life imprisonment.[125] He subsequently requested transfer to Azerbaijan and in 2012, the Hungarian authorities granted the request, having received assurances from the Azerbaijani government that R.S. would serve the remainder of his sentence there.[126] Immediately upon his return, R.S. was pardoned by Azerbaijan's President and given a hero's welcome. He was additionally promoted in military rank, paid salary arrears, and offered a State-funded apartment.[127]

Before the ECtHR, the surviving Armenian and a relative of the officer killed complained that Azerbaijan and Hungary, through their respective actions, had violated the right to life.[128] To decide the claim, one of the issues the ECtHR

121. ARSIWA, *supra* note 2, art. 11, cmt. ¶ 6.

122. Makuchyan & Minasyan v. Azerbaijan & Hungary, App. No. 17247/13, ¶ 112 (2020), (ECtHR) [hereinafter *Makuchyan & Minasyan*].

123. *Id.* ¶ 8. For commentary on the case, *see* Marko Milanović, *Attribution, Jurisdiction, Discrimination, Decapitation: A Comment on* Makuchyan and Minsyan v. Azerbaijan and Hungary, EJIL:Talk! (July 10, 2020), https://www.ejiltalk.org/attribution-jurisdiction-discrimination-decapitation-a-comment-on-makuchyan-and-minasyan-v-azerbaijan-and-hungary/; Marko Milanović & Tatjana Papić, Makuchyan and Minasyan v. Azerbaijan and Hungary, 115 Am. J. Int'l L. 294 (2021); Kushtrim Istrefi & Cedric Ryngaert, Makuchyan and Minasyan v Azerbaijan and Hungary: *Novel Questions of State Responsibility, Presidential Pardon, and Due Diligence of Sentencing Transfer Meet in a Rare Case of the Right to Life*, 3 ECHR L. Rev. 263 (2021).

124. *Makuchyan & Minasyan*, *supra* note 122, ¶¶ 9, 11.

125. *Id.* ¶ 15.

126. *Id.* ¶ 19.

127. *Id.* ¶¶ 20–21.

128. *Id.* ¶ 4. The applicants also claimed that Azerbaijan had violated the prohibition on discrimination. *See id.*

had to address was the potential attribution of R.S.'s actions to Azerbaijan. The Court first assessed whether the murder and attempted murder were attributable to Azerbaijan based on the rule reflected in Article 4 ARSIWA.[129] R.S. was a member of the military and therefore an organ of State at the time of the killing. However, the ECtHR concluded that he was not acting in his official capacity but rather acted further to his "private decision to kill, during the night and outside of training hours . . . ."[130] As such, Article 4 did not apply.[131]

The ECtHR then turned its focus to Article 11.[132] First, the court highlighted the stringent threshold provided for in the ARSIWA commentary, noting the ILC's differentiation between mere approval and endorsement of the act in question and a State's assumption of responsibility.[133] The court additionally noted the cumulative nature of the acknowledgment and adoption requirements, and the fact that these must be "clear and unequivocal."[134] Regarding R.S.'s conduct, the ECtHR concluded that for this to be attributable to Azerbaijan, there must be evidence of State authorities "directly and categorically assuming responsibility" for the killing and attempted killing of the two Armenians.[135]

Next, the court examined Azerbaijan's conduct toward R.S., including his release, pardoning, promotion, and the "glorifying statements" made about him by various Azerbaijani officials.[136] While each of these measures amounted to approval and endorsement of R.S.'s actions, the ECtHR declined to find that they constituted "clear and unequivocal" acknowledgment and adoption of R.S.'s conduct.[137] The court concluded that instead, these had "the purpose of publicly addressing, recognising and remedying R.S.'s adverse personal, professional and financial situation, which the authorities of Azerbaijan perceived, unjustifiably in the Court's view, as being the consequence of the allegedly flawed criminal proceedings in Hungary."[138] Therefore, R.S.'s conduct was not attributable to Azerbaijan based on the rule reflected in Article 11.

In his partly dissenting opinion, Judge Pinto de Albuquerque concluded that Azerbaijan's conduct went beyond mere approval or endorsement.[139] He did not

129. ARSIWA, *supra* note 2, art. 4. *See also supra* ch. 4.

130. *Makuchyan & Minasyan*, *supra* note 122, ¶ 111.

131. *Id. See also* ARSIWA, *supra* note 2, art. 7. For discussion of the case in this context, *see supra* ch. 4, sec. 4.5.1.

132. *Makuchyan & Minasyan*, *supra* note 122, ¶¶ 112–18.

133. *Id.* ¶ 112.

134. *Id.*

135. *Id.* ¶ 113.

136. *Id.* ¶¶ 115–16.

137. *Id.* ¶¶ 115–18.

138. *Id.* ¶ 118.

139. *Id.* Partly Dissenting Opinion of Judge Pinto de Albuquerque ¶ 4.

dispute the standard the court applied to determine attribution on this basis, but pointed to the very active steps taken by Azerbaijani officials to legitimize and glorify R.S.'s actions.[140] The Judge distinguished this behavior from the *Nikolić* case, in which SFOR were "mere beneficiaries" of the unlawful abduction.[141] He concluded, "Azerbaijan does not expressly claim to have acknowledged and adopted the acts of R.S. as its own, but it is clear from the facts that it behaved in a manner from which such acknowledgment and adoption can be inferred."[142]

This judgment is significant due to the court's detailed examination of Article 11 ARSIWA, which is more thorough than in any other case to date.[143] The ECtHR closely followed the guidance in the ARSIWA commentary, thereby accepting that attribution on this basis is appropriate only when a State clearly and unequivocally indicates its intent to accept responsibility for the conduct concerned.[144] Judge Pinto de Albuquerque's partial dissent, however, highlights the difficulty in determining the precise State conduct that satisfies the rule.[145] Section 10.3 considers this issue in further detail in the context of NSA conduct performed during armed conflict.

10.2.3.6 *Saint-Gobain Performance Plastics Europe v. Venezuela*

Since ARSIWA's adoption, there have been at least seven investment arbitral awards in which the tribunal referred to Article 11.[146] This basis of attribution, however, was not essential to any of the decisions. In each case, the tribunal found

140. *Id.* ¶¶ 4–8. *See also* Milanović, *supra* note 123.

141. *Makuchyan & Minasyan*, *supra* note 122, Partly Dissenting Opinion of Judge Pinto de Albuquerque, ¶¶ 9–10.

142. *Id.* ¶ 10.

143. *See* Milanović & Papić, *supra* note 123, at 299; Istrefi & Ryngaert, *supra* note 123, at 267.

144. *Makuchyan & Minasyan*, *supra* note 122, ¶¶ 112, 118. *See also* Milanović & Papić, *supra* note 123, at 299.

145. *Makuchyan & Minasyan*, *supra* note 122, Partly Dissenting Opinion of Judge Pinto de Albuquerque, ¶¶ 4–10. *See also* Istrefi & Ryngaert, *supra* note 123, at 270.

146. Mondev International Ltd. v. United States of America, Case No. ARB(AF)/99/2, ¶ 115 n. 47 (Int'l Ctr. for Settlement of Inv. Disp., Oct. 11, 2002) [hereinafter *Mondev International*]; Luigiterzo Bosca v. Republic of Lithuania, Case No. 2011-05, ¶¶ 127–28 (Perm. Ct. Arb., May 17, 2013) [hereinafter *Luigiterzo Bosca*]; Bernhard von Pezold & Others v. Republic of Zimbabwe, Case No. ARB/10/15, ¶¶ 447-49 (Int'l Ctr. for Settlement of Inv. Disp., July 28, 2015) [hereinafter *Bernhard von Pezold*]; Clayton and Bilcon of Delaware, Inc. v. Government of Canada, Case No. 2009-04, ¶¶ 321–24 (Perm. Ct. Arb., Mar. 17, 2015) [hereinafter *Clayton and Bilcon*]; Saint-Gobain Performance Plastics Europe v. Bolivarian Republic of Venezuela, Case. No. ARB/12/13, ¶¶ 456–66 (Int'l Ctr. for Settlement of Inv. Disp., Dec. 30, 2016) [hereinafter *Saint-Gobain*]; Ampal-American Israel Corp. & others v. Arab Republic of Egypt, Case No. ARB/12/11, ¶¶ 90–91, 140, 146 (Int'l Ctr. for Settlement of Inv. Disp., Feb. 21, 2017) [hereinafter *Ampal-American Israel Corp.*]; Unión Fenosa Gas, S.A. v. Arab Republic of Egypt, Case No. ARB/14/4, ¶¶ 9.120–9.121 (Int'l Ctr for Settlement of Inv. Disp., Aug. 31, 2018) [hereinafter *Unión Fenosa Gas*].

either that Article 11 did not apply,[147] or that the relevant conduct was also attributable to the State on another basis.[148] The decisions nevertheless clarify how judicial bodies view and interpret the rule reflected in Article 11 in situations not relating to conflict.

The cases of most interest are those in which the tribunal concluded that Article 11 applied, given the greater level of detail in the tribunal's analysis.[149] One such case was *Saint-Gobain Performance Plastics Europe v. Venezuela*. The claim concerned Venezuela's refusal to compensate Saint-Gobain for the expropriation of its investment in a subsidiary, Norpro Venezuela C.A.[150] The Venezuelan President made a televised speech on May 15, 2010, during which he expressed his support for a union proposal that Norpro Venezuela should be transferred to a State-owned company, PDVSA.[151] The same day, members of the union took over the proppants plant operated by Norpro Venezuela, and soon thereafter, PDVSA moved in and nationalized the plant.[152] One issue the tribunal had to consider was whether the expropriation of the plant was attributable to Venezuela.

The tribunal first noted that the plant takeover was carried out by union members and sympathizers who were not acting under the State's instructions, direction, or control at the relevant time.[153] Nevertheless, the tribunal concluded that PDVSA, which was empowered to exercise governmental authority on Venezuela's behalf,[154] "acknowledged and adopted the union's actions as its own" meaning that the expropriation was attributable to Venezuela.[155]

In reaching this conclusion, the tribunal observed that "[i]n a number of internal notes and reports, PDVSA made clear that the union's plant takeover was not only in line with [Venezuela's] intentions with regard to the expropriation of the plant, but was subsequently made an integral part of the process of nationalizing Norpro Venezuela."[156] Moreover, PDVSA "built upon the situation created by the union members in order to carry out the nationalization process,"

147. *Mondev International, supra* note 146, ¶ 115; *Bernhard von Pezold, supra* note 146, ¶¶ 447–49; *Unión Fenosa Gas, supra* note 146, ¶¶ 9.120–.21.

148. *Luigiterzo Bosca, supra* note 146, ¶¶ 127–28; *Clayton and Bilcon, supra* note 146, ¶¶ 319–24; *Saint-Gobain, supra* note 146, ¶¶ 456–66; *Ampal-American Israel Corp., supra* note 146, ¶ 146.

149. In the other cases, the tribunal addressed Article 11 ARSIWA very briefly. *See Mondev International, supra* note 146, ¶ 115; *Bernhard von Pezold, supra* note 146, ¶¶ 447–49; *Unión Fenosa Gas, supra* note 146, ¶¶ 9.120–.21.

150. *Saint-Gobain, supra* note 146, ¶ 5.

151. *Id.* ¶ 216.

152. *Id.* ¶ 217.

153. *Id.* ¶¶ 448–54. *See also* ARSIWA, *supra* note 2, art. 8.

154. *Saint-Gobain, supra* note 146, ¶¶ 457–60. *See also* ARSIWA, *supra* note 2, art. 5.

155. *Saint-Gobain, supra* note 146, ¶ 456.

156. *Id.* ¶ 462.

including by establishing a permanent presence at the plant.[157] Thus, although Venezuela did not anticipate or intend that the union's members would take over the plant, "PDVSA immediately availed itself of this situation for the purpose of carrying out the nationalization process, thereby acknowledging and adopting the union members' conduct as its own."[158]

This case bears similarities to *Tehran Hostages*.[159] In each case, a group of private individuals acted on their own initiative, further to encouragement from the State, and the State subsequently endorsed their conduct. The main difference between the cases concerns the identity of the persons who acted to continue the conduct at issue. In *Tehran Hostages*, it was the same militants who continued the occupation, although their status had changed due to the State's endorsement of their actions, meaning that for the remainder of the occupation they acted as State agents.[160] In *Saint-Gobain*, it was not the union members who continued the plant's take-over but rather a State-owned company that was empowered to perform governmental functions on the State's behalf.[161]

In this respect, *Saint-Gobain* is comparable to the *Lighthouses* arbitration. In both cases, following the initial conduct that was not attributable to the State, an entity acting on the State's behalf took active steps to continue the wrongful conduct. In *Saint-Gobain*, "PDVSA had *de facto* control of the plant on or shortly after 15 May 2010, with no prospect of giving it back to its owners, and used it to prepare and restart operation and production of proppants."[162] This case, therefore, supports the ILC's assertion that when a State endorses and continues an ongoing wrongful act, "the inference may readily be drawn that it has assumed responsibility for it."[163]

10.2.4 The Rule's Object and Purpose

Before exploring the conclusions regarding the acknowledgment and adoption criteria that can be drawn from the cases outlined above, it is pertinent to consider the object and purpose of the rule reflected in Article 11. Some guidance in this respect can be found within the ARSIWA commentary. After discussing *Tehran Hostages*, the commentary states:

157. *Id.* ¶ 464.

158. *Id.* ¶ 466.

159. *Tehran Hostages*, *supra* note 38. *See also supra* sec. 10.2.3.1.

160. *Tehran Hostages*, *supra* note 38, ¶ 74. *See also supra* sec. 10.2.3.1.

161. *Saint-Gobain*, *supra* note 146, ¶¶ 462–66.

162. *Id.* ¶ 474.

163. ARSIWA, *supra* note 2, art. 11, cmt. ¶ 3. For further discussion regarding the meaning of acknowledgment and adoption, *see infra* sec. 10.3.

Where the acknowledgment and adoption is unequivocal and unqualified there is good reason to give it retroactive effect, which is what the tribunal did in the *Lighthouses* arbitration. This is consistent with the position established by article 10 for insurrectional movements and avoids gaps in the extent of responsibility for what is, in effect, the same continuing act.[164]

One purpose of the rule, therefore, is to avoid gaps in responsibility when a continuing act that is initially private in character later becomes an act of the State. This is evident from the facts of the *Saint-Gobain* case.[165] Retrospective attribution provides better outcomes for the victims of the harmful conduct because it allows an injured State to seek reparations regarding the entire course of conduct, rather than only the later conduct performed on behalf of the responsible State.[166]

Regarding acts that have ceased at the time of the State's acknowledgment and adoption, the ARSIWA commentary sets out a further purpose of the rule. After discussing Israel's capture of Adolf Eichmann, it states, "[W]here there are doubts about whether certain conduct falls within article 8, these may be resolved by the subsequent adoption of the conduct in question by the State."[167] This rationale is again limited, as it applies only to instances where the State had some involvement in the acts at issue, but the evidence is insufficient to prove that those responsible were acting as organs or agents of the State. The State's subsequent acknowledgment and adoption of the conduct can resolve this ambiguity.

In this situation, however, the State's subsequent acknowledgment and adoption provides evidence of the State's involvement in the acts at the time they occurred. It does not provide a basis for retrospective attribution.[168] For example, in the *Rainbow Warrior* case, when France eventually admitted its responsibility for the destruction of the Greenpeace vessel in breach of New Zealand's sovereignty, the State's acknowledgment and adoption of the conduct provided proof that the violation was attributable to France based on Article 4 ARSIWA because the individuals involved were organs of State.[169] The question of attribution based on the rule reflected in Article 11 did not arise.

This rationale for Article 11's inclusion within ARSIWA, therefore, appears weak. However, legal scholars have offered further observations regarding the rule's object and purpose. Becker, for instance, argues that if a State unequivocally adopts private conduct as its own, it should not later be able to deny responsibility for the acts at issue.[170] Mackenzie-Gray Scott goes further, suggesting that

164. ARSIWA, *supra* note 2, art. 11, cmt. ¶ 4

165. *Saint-Gobain*, *supra* note 146.

166. Crawford's First Rep. on State Responsibility, *supra* note 13, at 54.

167. ARSIWA, *supra* note 2, art. 11, cmt. ¶ 5.

168. *See* ILC Y.B. 1998 vol. I, *supra* note 17, at 255, ¶ 57 (comments of Mr. Bennouna).

169. *See generally* J. Scott Davidson, *The Rainbow Warrior Arbitration Concerning the Treatment of the French Agents Mafart and Prieur*, 40 Int'l & Comp. L.Q. 446 (1991).

170. Becker, *supra* note 6, at 75.

the rule might contribute to a "slightly thicker form of justice."[171] He views Article 11 as "a moral ideal" whereby a State that considers itself completely or partially responsible for prior private conduct might consider itself "morally duty-bound" to accept responsibility for it.[172]

As attractive as this view of Article 11 may be, it does not reflect the reality of States' interactions with NSAs in contemporary conflict.[173] In practice, States that support NSAs rarely accept responsibility for an NSA's conduct in violation of international law, even if their assistance was instrumental to the breach.[174] In the context of armed conflict, there are few scenarios in which States would voluntarily assume responsibility for prior private conduct, except perhaps as a means to achieve peace or for political reasons, as demonstrated by the *Makuchyan and Minasyan* case.[175]

The ARSIWA commentary recognizes the rule's relevance to peace agreements, observing that Article 11 "may cover cases where a State has accepted responsibility for conduct of which it did not approve, which it had sought to prevent and which it deeply regretted."[176] Thus, to promote peace following an internal conflict, State officials might identify conduct on the part of rebels that violates the State's international legal obligations and express the intent to recognize these as acts of State and compensate the victims.[177] In this context, however, when States freely agree to accept responsibility for prior private conduct, it is questionable whether a rule of attribution is necessary at all. As discussed in section 10.4.1, States are free to assume responsibility for any conduct they wish; there is no need for a rule of attribution to allow them to do so.[178]

In the absence of an express agreement on the part of the State, the significance of the rule in situations of conflict turns upon the types of State behavior from which an inference could be drawn that the State has acknowledged and adopted an NSA's prior conduct. To illustrate, if the acknowledgment and adoption criteria are construed loosely, the rule reflected in Article 11 might attribute the September 11 attacks to Afghanistan due to the Taliban government's offer of sanctuary to Al Qaeda and its refusal to extradite the group's fighters.[179] Yet such an interpretation raises concerns that the rule would apply too broadly, for

171. Mackenzie Gray-Scott, *supra* note 120, at 135.

172. *Id.*

173. *See supra* ch. 2, sec. 2.2.

174. Veronika Bílková, *Establishing Direct Responsibility of Armed Opposition Groups for Violations of International Humanitarian Law?*, *in* Responsibilities of the Non-State Actor in Armed Conflict and the Market Place 263, 270 (Noemi Gal-Or et al. eds., 2015).

175. *Makuchyan & Minasyan*, *supra* note 122. *See also supra* sec. 10.2.3.5.

176. ARSIWA, *supra* note 2, art. 11, cmt. ¶ 6.

177. ILC Y.B. 1998 vol. I, *supra* note 17, at 249, ¶ 58 (comments of Special Rapporteur Crawford).

178. *See infra* sec. 10.4.1.

179. For legal commentary in support of such an interpretation, *see* Michael Byers, *Terrorism, the Use of Force and International Law After 11 September*, 51 Int'l & Comp. L.Q. 401, 408–9

example, when State officials merely express approval of private conduct or fail to condemn it.[180] The following section examines the acknowledgment and adoption criteria, using examples from conflict situations to add clarity to the rule's scope of application.

10.3 ACKNOWLEDGMENT AND ADOPTION

The rare cases in which courts and tribunals have applied the rule reflected in Article 11 leave open questions regarding the types of State conduct that could amount to acknowledgment and adoption. The ARSIWA commentary indicates that the threshold is high, but identifying the precise State conduct that leads to attribution remains a challenge. This section takes on that task, first considering what guidance can be gleaned from relevant jurisprudence, scholarship, and the ARSIWA commentary before amplifying the acknowledgment and adoption criteria using examples from armed conflict.

10.3.1 What It Means to "Acknowledge and Adopt"

The ARSIWA commentary stipulates that for the rule reflected in Article 11 to apply, States must "acknowledge and adopt" private conduct, rather than merely support or endorse it.[181] The criteria of acknowledgment and adoption are cumulative, meaning that the State, through its statements or its actions, must satisfy both conditions.[182] The ILC Drafting Committee considered a proposal to delete the reference to acknowledgment, on the basis that this is implied in the word "adoption."[183] However, the ILC opted to retain both words in Article 11, thus requiring the State to "identify the conduct and make it its own."[184]

Regarding the question of who can acknowledge and adopt conduct on the State's behalf, this can be done by an organ of State or by any other individual, group, or entity, whose actions are attributable to the State.[185] Thus, it does not have to be the State's leaders who demonstrate their intent to accept responsibility

(2002); Sean D. Murphy, *Terrorism and the Concept of "Armed Attack" in Article 51 of the U.N. Charter*, 43 Harv. J. Int'l L., 41, 50–51 (2002); Yoram Dinstein, War, Aggression and Self-Defence, 261 (5th ed., 2011).

180. Hessbruegge, *Human Rights Violations*, *supra* note 105, at 52; Milanović, *supra* note 123.

181. ARSIWA, *supra* note 2, art. 11, cmt. ¶ 6.

182. *Id.* cmt. ¶ 9. The ILC Drafting Committee rejected a proposal to use the disjunctive "or" between the words acknowledge and adopt. *See* ILC Y.B. 2001 vol. I, *supra* note 21, at 94, ¶ 37.

183. ILC Y.B. 2001 vol. I, *supra* note 21, at 94, ¶ 37.

184. *Id.*; ARSIWA, *supra* note 2, art. 11, cmt. ¶ 6.

185. Hessbruegge, *Human Rights Violations*, *supra* note 105, at 51.

for the conduct at issue. In *Saint-Gobain*, for instance, it was the actions of a State-owned company empowered to exercise governmental functions on the State's behalf that acknowledged and adopted the union members' conduct.[186] In most cases, however, the conduct of State organs is most relevant when considering the rule's potential application.

Turning to the types of State action that can amount to acknowledgment and adoption, the ARSIWA commentary indicates that this can take the form of words or conduct.[187] While the commentary fails to provide any concrete illustrations regarding the particular State pronouncements or actions that might satisfy the rule,[188] it is nevertheless possible to draw certain conclusions from the commentary to Article 11, as well as from relevant cases and scholarship.

First, it is clear that a State, through its organs or agents, might explicitly announce that it considers the prior conduct to be an act of State and accept responsibility for it.[189] An example of such behavior can be seen in the *Priebke* case, decided by the Military Tribunal of Rome in 1996, and cited by the International Committee of the Red Cross (ICRC) in support of the rule expressed in Article 11.[190] This concerned an attack that Italian partisans perpetrated against German soldiers in occupied Italy during World War II and Priebke's individual criminal responsibility for the Nazis' massacre of civilians in response.[191] One issue the tribunal had to consider was whether the partisans' conduct in attacking the German soldiers was attributable to Italy.[192] Concluding that the attack was so attributable, the tribunal referred to Italy's subsequent actions, particularly the State's confirmation that it considered the partisans who conducted military acts against the Nazis to be its own fighters and its grant to them of awards for military valor.[193]

A second conclusion that may be drawn regarding acknowledgment and adoption is that these criteria might be satisfied if the State takes steps to formally

186. *See supra* sec. 10.2.3.6.

187. ARSIWA, *supra* note 2, art. 11, cmt. ¶ 8.

188. de Frouville, *supra* note 10, at 274.

189. ARSIWA, *supra* note 2, art. 11, cmt. ¶ 6.

190. 1 Customary International Humanitarian Law r. 149 (Jean-Marie Henckaerts & Louise Doswald-Beck eds., 2005) [hereinafter Customary IHL: Rules], *citing* the Priebke case, Judgment in Trial of First Instance (Military Trib. Rome, 1996), https://www.asser.nl/upload/documents/DomCLIC/Docs/NLP/Italy/Priebke_TribunaleRoma_Sentenza_1-8-1996.pdf [hereinafter *Priebke*].

191. 2 Customary International Humanitarian Law 3511 (Jean-Marie Henckaerts & Louise Doswald-Beck eds., 2005) [hereinafter Customary IHL: Practice].

192. *Priebke*, *supra* note 190, sec. 6.

193. *Id.*

legalize or otherwise authorize private conduct that is ongoing.[194] In *Tehran Hostages*, the Ayatollah issued a decree asserting that Iran would not allow most of the hostages to leave the Embassy, thereby officially approving the students' conduct and authorizing them to continue to hold the Embassy staff hostage in the name of the State. While it is far from certain that the ICJ concluded that this should lead to the retrospective attribution of the initial attack to Iran, the ILC considered that such behavior satisfied the acknowledgment and adoption criteria.[195]

Third, a State might acknowledge or adopt prior private acts if it continues the same conduct via its own organs or agents. This is what happened in the *Lighthouses* arbitration. Greece, after assuming sovereignty over Crete, continued to violate the terms of the concession by exempting the shipping company from the fees owed.[196] Similar facts are evident in the *Saint-Gobain* investment arbitration. Here, a State-owned company, empowered to perform governmental functions on the State's behalf, continued the actions of union members who had taken control of a proppants plant, resulting in the State's expropriation of the plant.[197] Provided it is "unequivocal and unqualified," the ILC considered that such behavior amounts to acknowledgment and adoption for the purposes of the rule.[198]

A fourth example emerges not from the ARSIWA commentary but rather from legal scholarship. A State might acknowledge and adopt private conduct if, through its own acts or omissions, it knowingly and intentionally enables the NSA to continue the wrongful acts.[199] For instance, the group of experts involved in drafting the *Tallinn Manual 2.0* expressed the view that if a State "intentionally employ[s] its cyber capabilities to protect the non-State actor against counter-cyber operations so as to facilitate their continuance as acts of that State, the requirements for attribution have been met."[200] Section 10.3.2 explores this and other possible bases of attribution in the context of armed conflict.

Beyond these four scenarios, it is difficult to discern any further positive illustrations of conduct that might amount to acknowledgment and adoption in a conflict situation. The relevant jurisprudence, together with the ARSIWA commentary, nevertheless provides further guidance regarding the types of conduct that would not satisfy the rule. First, it is not sufficient for a State merely to benefit from the NSA's acts. This is clear from the commentary to Article 11, as well as the

194. Hessbruegge, *Human Rights Violations*, *supra* note 105, at 53.

195. ARSIWA, *supra* note 2, art. 11, cmt. ¶ 4. *See also supra* sec. 10.2.3.1.

196. *See supra* sec. 10.2.3.2.

197. *See supra* sec. 10.2.3.6.

198. ARSIWA, *supra* note 2, art. 11, cmt. ¶ 4.

199. Mackenzie-Gray Scott, *supra* note 120, at 129.

200. Tallinn Manual 2.0, *supra* note 31, r. 17, cmt. ¶ 17.

ICTY's judgment in *Nikolić*.[201] Instead, to constitute acknowledgment and adoption, the State's actions or statements relating to the NSA's conduct must involve an "assumption of responsibility."[202]

Second, as noted previously, it is not enough for a State to express its support or approval for the NSA's conduct or to take steps such as to pardon the offender or refuse to compensate victims.[203] Article 11's commentary, as well as the ECtHR judgment in *Makuchyan and Minasyan*, make clear that for attribution to arise, the State's response to an NSA's wrongful conduct must go beyond mere expressions of support or approval.[204] The State's organs or agents must identify the relevant private conduct as an act of State and demonstrate the State's intent to take responsibility for it.[205]

Thus, the acknowledgment and adoption thresholds are very high. This narrow interpretation makes sense, however, when considering the effects of the rule of attribution. Article 11 attributes conduct retrospectively to a State, meaning that the State can bear international responsibility for acts that it was not involved in at the time of their commission.[206] Moreover, although the rule applies only if the State demonstrates its intent to accept responsibility for the acts at issue, the ILC indicated that the State's intent can be inferred from its conduct.[207] As such, in some limited circumstances, the rule could attribute conduct to a State against the State's wishes. Considerations such as these explain the distinction the commentary makes between mere expressions of approval or endorsement and a State's assumption of responsibility.[208] As Milanović put it, "one can approve of many things without necessarily assuming responsibility for doing those things."[209]

Nonetheless, uncertainties remain regarding the precise State behavior that could amount to acknowledgment and adoption. Whether a State's actions or words satisfy the thresholds must be assessed on a case-by-case basis, taking into account the surrounding circumstances including any evidence regarding the State's intent. Further clarity in this regard can be gained by assessing examples of State behavior during armed conflict.

201. ARSIWA, *supra* note 2, art. 11, cmt. ¶ 6; *Nikolić*, *supra* note 108, ¶ 68. For a contrary view, *see* Hessbruegge, *Human Rights Violations*, *supra* note 105, at 53.

202. ARSIWA, *supra* note 2, art. 11, cmt. ¶ 6.

203. *Id. See also* ILC Y.B. 1998 vol. I, *supra* note 17, 249, ¶ 58 (comments of Special Rapporteur Crawford).

204. *See supra* sec. 10.2.3.5.

205. ARSIWA, *supra* note 2, art. 11, cmt. ¶ 6.

206. Hessbruegge, *Human Rights Violations*, *supra* note 105, at 52.

207. ARSIWA, *supra* note 2, art. 11, cmt. ¶ 9.

208. *Id.* cmt. ¶ 6.

209. Milanović, *supra* note 123. *See also* Istrefi & Ryngaert, *supra* note 123, at 272.

10.3.2 Acknowledgment and Adoption During Armed Conflict

It is worth noting at the outset that in conflict situations, there are few examples of States unequivocally acknowledging and adopting private conduct as their own. If they did, they would bear international responsibility for any breaches of international humanitarian law (IHL) and be liable to pay compensation for any loss or injury caused.[210] Thus, it is far more common for States to use proxies as a means to plausibly deny their involvement in potential breaches of international law, as the conflicts outlined in Chapter 2 demonstrate.[211]

It is nevertheless instructive to consider States' behavior during armed conflict to assess whether there are any cases in which the rule reflected in Article 11 might apply. As the act of acknowledgment and adoption can take the form of words or conduct,[212] this section first considers States' verbal or written statements before turning to examine conduct from which the State's acknowledgment and adoption of the relevant acts might be inferred.

10.3.2.1 Acknowledgment and Adoption via Verbal or Written Statements

States' announcements that merely praise or express approval for private conduct do not amount to acknowledgment and adoption for the purposes of the rule reflected in Article 11. For instance, statements made by the Taliban leader after the attacks of September 11, 2001, in which he refused to condemn the attacks or to expel Osama bin Laden,[213] are insufficient to attribute al Qaeda's actions in conducting the attacks to Afghanistan.[214] Similarly, the United States' official statements congratulating the Syrian Democratic Forces (SDF) for liberating territory from ISIS control[215] do not indicate any intent on the part

210. Hague Convention No. IV Respecting the Laws and Customs of War on Land art. 3, Oct. 18, 1907, 36 Stat. 2227, T.S. No. 539; Protocol Additional to the Geneva Conventions of 12 August 1949, and Relating to the Protection of Victims of International Armed Conflicts art. 92, June 8, 1977, 1125 U.N.T.S. 3; Customary IHL: Rules, *supra* note 190, r. 150. *See also* ARSIWA, *supra* note 2, arts. 28–33.

211. *See supra* ch. 2. *See also* Crawford, *supra* note 4, at 182.

212. ARSIWA, *supra* note 2, art. 11, cmt. ¶ 8.

213. *See, e.g.*, *Mullah Omar–In His Own Words*, The Guardian (Sept. 26, 2001), https://www.theguardian.com/world/2001/sep/26/afghanistan.features11.

214. Rüdiger Wolfrum & Christiane E. Philipp, *The Status of the Taliban: Their Obligations and Rights Under International Law*, 6 Max Planck Y.B. of U.N. L. 559, 594–95 (2002); Becker, *supra* note 6, at 226. For a contrary view, *see* Byers, *supra* note 179, at 409; Murphy, *supra* note 179, at 50–51; Dinstein, *supra* note 179, at 261.

215. *See, e.g.*, Statement by Secretary Tillerson, Raqqa's Liberation from ISIS (Oct. 20, 2017), https://2017-2021.state.gov/raqqas-liberation-from-isis-2/.

of the United States to accept responsibility for the SDF's conduct during those operations.[216]

Announcements indicating that a State shares the aims of an NSA are equally insufficient to lead to attribution. For example, the statements made by government officials of the Federal Republic of Yugoslavia indicating that the State shared the goals and the vision of a "Greater Serbia" with Bosnian Serb forces[217] did not constitute acknowledgment and adoption of the NSA's prior acts of ethnic cleansing.[218]

In addition, general announcements made by States regarding an NSA cannot constitute acknowledgment and adoption of their conduct. President Putin's admission that Russia fully funded the Wagner Group[219] is too imprecise to lead to the attribution of the group's prior conduct in violation of IHL to Russia. While the statement might indicate that the group's conduct is attributable to the State on another basis,[220] it does not meet the requirements of Article 11. Putin did not identify the acts on the part of the Wagner Group that potentially violate Russia's international legal obligations and make clear that he considered those acts to be Russia's own.[221]

The cases in which a State's verbal or written statements are sufficiently explicit to satisfy Article 11's requirements will be rare. One situation in which this might happen is when a State acknowledges and adopts private acts of resistance or sabotage against an occupying power.[222] The *Priebke* case provides an example in which Italy stated that it considered the partisans who conducted military acts against the Nazis to be its own fighters.[223] Ukraine

216. ARSIWA, *supra* note 2, art. 11, cmt. ¶ 6.

217. Application of the Convention on the Prevention and Punishment of the Crime of Genocide (Bosn. & Herz. v. Serb. & Montenegro), Judgment, 2007 I.C.J. Rep. 43, ¶ 237 (Feb. 26) [hereinafter *Bosnian Genocide*].

218. Hessbruegge, *Human Rights Violations*, *supra* note 105, at 52–53. For a contrary view, *see* John Quigley, *State Responsibility for Ethnic Cleansing*, 32 U. CALIFORNIA DAVIS L. REV. 341, 367 (1999).

219. Nicolas Camut, *Putin Admits Kremlin Gave Wagner Nearly $1 Billion in the Past Year*, POLITICO (June 27, 2023), https://www.politico.eu/article/vladimir-putin-yevgeny-prigozhin-russia-kremlin-gave-wagner-group-nearly-1-billion-in-the-past-year/.

220. For example, Putin's statement could indicate that the Wagner Group was completely dependent on Russia, leading to a conclusion that it had the status of a de facto State organ for the purposes of Article 4 ARSIWA. *See* Jennifer Maddocks, *Putin Admits to Funding the Wagner Group: Implications for Russia's State Responsibility*, ARTICLES OF WAR (June 30, 2023), https://lieber.westpoint.edu/putin-admits-funding-wagner-group-implications-russias-state-responsibility/.

221. ARSIWA, *supra* note 2, art. 11, cmt. ¶ 6.

222. Bílková, *supra* note 174, at 270.

223. *Priebke*, *supra* note 190.

might similarly acknowledge and adopt the conduct of private individuals acting against Russian occupiers, even if some of their acts violate Ukraine's IHL obligations.[224] For instance, Ukraine might announce that it considers the acts of partisans involved in the targeted killings of civilian collaborators as its own.[225] However, Ukraine's statements would satisfy Article 11 only if they identify the conduct at issue and make clear that Kyiv deems these to be acts of State for which it bears international responsibility.[226] As the *Makuchyan and Minasyan* case highlights, statements that serve a different purpose do not suffice.[227]

10.3.2.2 Acknowledgment and Adoption via State Conduct: Ongoing Acts

According to the ARSIWA commentary, a State's acknowledgment or adoption of prior private acts "might be inferred from the conduct of the State in question."[228] This indicates that the State's acts alone can demonstrate its intent to bear responsibility for the conduct at issue, even without accompanying verbal or written statements. Yet, in the absence of such statements, it is challenging to identify the types of conduct from which a State's intent to acknowledge and adopt private conduct might be inferred.

The review of jurisprudence relevant to Article 11 in section 10.2.3 indicates that the acknowledgment and adoption thresholds are most likely to be satisfied if the relevant private conduct is ongoing at the time the State acts. Thus, if the State legalizes or otherwise authorizes the continued conduct, it continues the harmful conduct via its own organs or agents, or it knowingly and intentionally facilitates the NSA's ongoing commission of the relevant acts, this conduct on the part of the State might satisfy the rule's requirements.[229]

To test the practical application of such forms of acknowledgment and adoption, consider the Wagner Group's operations in the Central African Republic (CAR). These commenced in 2018 and were ongoing as at the date of Yevgeny

224. *See, e.g.*, Jeffrey Gettleman, *How Citizen Spies Foiled Putin's Grand Plan for One Ukrainian City*, N.Y. Times (Dec. 25, 2022), https://www.nytimes.com/2022/12/25/world/europe/ukraine-kherson-defiance-russia.html.

225. David L. Stern, *Ukrainian Hit Squads Target Russian Occupiers and Collaborators*, Wash. Post (Sept. 8, 2023), https://www.washingtonpost.com/world/2022/09/08/ukraine-assassinations-occupied-territory-russia/. For legal analysis, *see, e.g.*, Shane Darcy, *Confronting the Collaborators*, Opinio Juris (Nov. 7, 2022), http://opiniojuris.org/2022/11/07/confronting-the-collaborators/.

226. ARSIWA, *supra* note 2, art. 11, cmt. ¶ 6.

227. *See supra* sec. 10.2.3.5.

228. ARSIWA, *supra* note 2, art. 11, cmt. ¶ 9.

229. *Id.*

Prigozhin's death in August 2023.[230] The Wagner Group supported the government in its fight against rebel forces, and the NSA's frequent violations of IHL throughout this period are well documented.[231] It is therefore pertinent to examine whether Russia's subsequent actions could constitute an acknowledgment and adoption of those IHL violations, leading to their attribution to the State.

Following Prigozhin's demise, Russia brought the Wagner Group's operations in CAR under State control as part of the Africa Corps.[232] From that time on, the group was integrated into the State and its activities in Africa fell directly under the command of Russia's military intelligence.[233] Notwithstanding this change, reporting indicates that Russian-linked fighters in CAR continued to act in a manner that violates IHL.[234] Any international law violations committed by members of the Wagner Group after the date on which they became organs of State are attributable to Russia pursuant to the rule reflected in Article 4 ARSIWA.[235]

This scenario raises the question whether the fighters' acts in violation of IHL, first as private entities and later as State organs, constitute a course of conduct that Russia continued. The answer is likely to turn on the facts, including the nature and frequency of the IHL violations and the degree of change (if any) to the fighters' behavior once they became State organs. The fighters' actions are most likely to constitute a continuing course of conduct if there was little discernible adjustment to their behavior once they became subject to Russia's command and control, meaning their acts in violation of IHL continued with a similar regularity and brutality. But even if that were the case, the situation does not precisely correspond to the facts of the *Lighthouses* arbitration or *Saint-Gobain*.[236] Those cases involved the State's continuation of one ongoing international law violation, respectively, the breach of a concession agreement and the expropriation of an

230. Sebastian Shukla et al., *What Wagner's Post-Prigozhin Future Looks Like on the Ground in the Central African Republic*, CNN (Sept. 18, 2023), https://www.cnn.com/2023/09/18/africa/central-african-republic-wagner-post-prigozhin-cmd-intl/index.html.

231. *See, e.g.*, HUM. RTS. WATCH, CENTRAL AFRICAN REPUBLIC: ABUSES BY RUSSIA-LINKED FORCES (May 3, 2022), https://www.hrw.org/news/2022/05/03/central-african-republic-abuses-russia-linked-forces.

232. *See, e.g.*, John A. Lechner, *Is Africa Corps a Rebranded Wagner Group?* FOREIGN POL'Y (Feb. 7, 2024), https://foreignpolicy.com/2024/02/07/africa-corps-wagner-group-russia-africa-burkina-faso/; Kimberly Marten, *Where's Wagner Now? One Year After the Mutiny*, PONARS EURASIA (June 21, 2024), https://www.ponarseurasia.org/wheres-wagner-now-one-year-after-the-mutiny/; Marcel Plichta et al., *The Wagner Group Lives on in Africa*, LAWFARE (July 21, 2024), https://www.lawfaremedia.org/article/the-wagner-group-lives-on-in-africa.

233. Lechner, *supra* note 232; Marten, *supra* note 232; Plichta et al., *supra* note 232.

234. *See, e.g.*, Philip Obaji Jr., *Putin's Private Army Accused of Massacring Dozens to Seize Gold Mine*, DAILY BEAST (Dec. 23, 2023), https://www.thedailybeast.com/putins-private-army-accused-of-massacring-dozens-to-seize-gold-mine.

235. ARSIWA, *supra* note 2, art. 4. *See also supra* ch. 4.

236. *See supra* secs. 10.2.3.2, 10.2.3.6.

investment. In contrast, the Wagner Group's conduct in CAR is characterized by numerous distinct IHL violations, albeit of a similar nature. This reality reduces the likelihood that the Wagner Group's conduct in CAR can be viewed as one continuing course of conduct.

If the fighters' actions do constitute a course of conduct, a second question is whether Russia, by continuing that conduct, clearly and unequivocally indicated its intention to bear responsibility for the fighters' earlier IHL violations.[237] This seems doubtful on the facts. Although it appears that Russia tolerates, or even encourages, the Wagner fighters' brutal conduct in CAR, it is difficult to infer from this an intent to accept responsibility for similar past behavior. In the words of Article 11's commentary, Russia has not "identifie[d] the conduct in question and ma[de] it its own."[238]

Had Wagner Group fighters retained their status as NSAs but continued to act with Russia's support, it would be even harder to infer an intent on Moscow's part to accept responsibility for the group's prior IHL breaches. Russia provided significant and wide-ranging assistance to the Wagner Group in its operations in Africa and elsewhere, and it is likely that the NSA could not have operated in such locations without the Kremlin's backing.[239] However, the links between that assistance and the group's conduct in violation of IHL are weak. Russia's support facilitated Wagner's wider military operations in CAR; any assistance related to the various IHL breaches its fighters committed seems purely incidental.

From the guidance in the ARSIWA commentary,[240] the conclusion can be drawn that a close nexus is required between the State's acts of facilitation and the specific conduct on the part of the NSA that violates international law. It is not enough for the State to facilitate the NSA's operations more broadly. The example given in *Tallinn Manual 2.0* of a State intentionally protecting an NSA with the intent to facilitate its continued conduct in violation of international law[241] illustrates one type of conduct that might satisfy the rule. In other words, the State's acts of facilitation must be directly targeted at enabling the NSA to continue its harmful conduct. In the case of the Wagner Group, Russia's facilitation had a broader aim, namely, to facilitate the NSA's overall operations in CAR. Therefore, Moscow's provision of support is insufficient to infer an intent to acknowledge and adopt Wagner's earlier acts in breach of IHL.[242]

237. ARSIWA, *supra* note 2, art. 11, cmt. ¶ 8.

238. *Id.* cmt. ¶ 6.

239. *See generally* Candace Rondeaux, *Decoding the Wagner Group: Analyzing the Role of Private Military Security Contractors in Russian Proxy Warfare*, New America (Nov. 7, 2019), https://www.newamerica.org/future-security/reports/decoding-wagner-group-analyzing-role-private-military-security-contractors-russian-proxy-warfare/.

240. ARSIWA, *supra* note 2, art. 11, cmt. ¶¶ 1–9.

241. Tallinn Manual 2.0, *supra* note 31, r. 17 cmt. ¶ 16.

242. For a contrasting analysis, *see* Mackenzie-Gray Scott, *supra* note 120, at 129.

10.3.2.3 Acknowledgment and Adoption via State Conduct: Acts That Have Ceased

The jurisprudence relating to Article 11 ARSIWA includes a few examples of cases in which States have acknowledged and adopted prior private conduct that has already ceased. The *Priebke* case demonstrates Italy's acknowledgment and adoption of acts of sabotage via statements made after the acts were committed.[243] However, it is difficult to conceive of a situation in which a State could unambiguously adopt prior conduct in violation of international law solely through its acts or omissions, rather than via express statements made by its officials. This scenario arose in *Nikolić* and in *Makuchyan and Minasyan*, but in each case, the ICTY and ECtHR concluded that the subsequent conduct was insufficient to constitute acknowledgment and adoption of the acts at issue.[244]

It is nevertheless worthwhile examining scenarios from armed conflict to assess how States might acknowledge and adopt prior private acts that violate international law, without making explicit statements to that effect. Some of the incidents that occurred during the conflict in the Democratic Republic of the Congo (DRC) provide pertinent examples.[245]

For instance, the UN Group of Experts tasked with examining the conflict in eastern DRC reported that in 2011, Rwandan officials were in direct contact with the commander of an armed group, Nduma Defense of Congo, and entrusted him with the task of killing the commander of a rival group.[246] It seems likely that the commander acted on Rwanda's instructions, meaning that the killing is attributable to the State under the rule reflected in Article 8 ARSIWA.[247] But if attribution on this basis cannot be proven, the question arises whether the subsequent actions of Rwanda's head of military intelligence, in arranging for the commander's evacuation to Rwanda following his surrender to DRC armed forces,[248] could satisfy the requirements of Article 11.

The actions of the head of military intelligence clearly indicate Rwanda's support for the commander who perpetrated the assassination. However, it is questionable whether this conduct alone also demonstrates Rwanda's intent to acknowledge and adopt the assassination as its own act.[249] Rwanda could have

243. *Priebke*, *supra* note 190.

244. *See supra* secs. 10.2.3.4, 10.2.3.5.

245. *See supra* ch. 2, sec. 2.4.3.

246. Add. to the Interim Rep. of the Group of Experts on the Democratic Republic of the Congo Concerning Violations of the Arms Embargo and Sanctions Regime by the Government of Rwanda 18, ¶ 36, U.N. Doc. S/2012/348/Add.1 (June 27, 2012) [hereinafter U.N. June 2012 Rep.].

247. For discussion regarding the potential attribution of such conduct to Rwanda further to the issuance of State instructions, *see supra* ch. 6, sec. 6.3.2.

248. U.N. June 2012 Rep., *supra* note 246, at 18, ¶ 36.

249. ARSIWA, *supra* note 2, art. 11; ILC Y.B. 1998 vol. I, *supra* note 17, at 291, ¶ 90.

arranged the commander's evacuation for another reason that did not relate directly to the killing he had committed.[250] Moreover, there is nothing in the UN reports to indicate that Rwandan officials expressly endorsed the killing or claimed responsibility for it.[251] Without further evidence, therefore, it seems that the rule reflected in Article 11 would not attribute the assassination to Rwanda.

There are numerous other examples within the UN reports of Rwanda offering shelter or other types of support to armed groups or individual fighters following their involvement in potential breaches of international law. For example, Rwandan officers frequently returned deserters to the armed group M23, including children recruited in violation of international law.[252] While Rwanda clearly bears responsibility for the actions of its own armed forces in this respect,[253] it is questionable whether the officers' conduct in returning the children to M23 also demonstrated Rwanda's assumption of responsibility for the original child recruitment carried out by the NSA. As with the assassination example considered previously, in the absence of statements indicating that Rwanda accepted the private conduct as its own,[254] attribution based on the rule reflected in Article 11 appears doubtful.

Some scholars have suggested a lower acknowledgment and adoption threshold, arguing, for example, that the Taliban's refusal to take any measures against Al Qaeda should lead to the attribution of the September 11 attacks to Afghanistan.[255] This loose interpretation, however, does not accord with the ARSIWA commentary or with relevant case law, such as the ECtHR's judgment in *Makuchyan and Minasyan*.[256] Moreover, it could lead to attribution in a very broad range of circumstances, such as when a State's actions demonstrate its mere approval or endorsement of the prior conduct. This is an outcome that States, as the principal architects of international law, are unlikely to accept.

250. The ECtHR in *Makuchyan & Minasyan* found that the State's acts had a purpose other than the acknowledgment and adoption of the conduct at issue, therefore art. 11 did not apply. *See Makuchyan & Minasyan*, *supra* note 122, ¶¶ 112–18.

251. U.N. June 2012 Rep., *supra* note 246.

252. Final Rep. of the Group of Experts on the Democratic Republic of the Congo 11, ¶¶ 23, 38–39, U.N. Doc. S/2012/843 (Nov. 15, 2012).

253. ARSIWA, *supra* note 2, art. 4.

254. *Id.* art. 11. *See also* ILC Y.B. 1998 vol. I, *supra* note 17, at 291, ¶ 90.

255. Byers, *supra* note 179, at 408–9; Murphy, *supra* note 179, at 50–51; Dinstein, *supra* note 179, at 261. For a critique of this view, *see* Becker, *supra* note 6, at 225–26.

256. ARSIWA, *supra* note 2, art. 11, cmt. ¶¶ 1–9.; *Makuchyan & Minasyan*, *supra* note 122. *See also supra* sec. 10.2.3.

10.4 ARTICLE 11'S STATUS AND IMPORTANCE WITHIN THE WIDER ATTRIBUTION REGIME

The narrow interpretation of the acknowledgment and adoption thresholds raises questions regarding Article 11's relevance as a means of holding States to account for private conduct that potentially violates their international legal obligations. The preceding analysis reveals that the rule will rarely apply in the absence of an express assumption of responsibility by State officials. This leads to further questions regarding the rule's status and importance within the wider attribution regime.

10.4.1 States' Voluntary Acceptance of Responsibility

When given the opportunity to comment on the rule of attribution reflected in Article 11, States largely declined to do so.[257] The reasons for this are unclear, but they may relate to States' understanding that they retained a choice whether to accept responsibility for another actor's prior conduct. Thus, States were content that if the rule applied, this would be a consequence of their own decision to bear responsibility for the relevant acts; it was unlikely that a State's acknowledgment and adoption would be inferred solely from its conduct.

The preceding analysis demonstrates that if States reached this conclusion regarding the draft article, it was largely correct. This means that States retain discretion whether to assume responsibility for prior conduct, thereby raising the question whether a rule of attribution is necessary at all. Attribution is one of the two elements of an internationally wrongful act, meaning that without attribution, there is no State responsibility and no corresponding obligations on the responsible State, such as a duty to make reparation for any injury or damage caused.[258] Yet States can choose to voluntarily accept responsibility for prior private conduct and compensate victims even in the absence of an internationally wrongful act.[259]

The ARSIWA commentary recognizes this reality, acknowledging that States might "agree to compensate for damage caused as a result of conduct which was not at the time a breach of any international obligation in force for that State."[260] Although this observation relates to conduct that fails to satisfy the "breach" element of an internationally wrongful act, there is no reason why it should not apply

257. 2001 Comments and Observations, *supra* note 20, at 50.

258. ARSIWA, *supra* note 2, arts. 30–31, 34–39.

259. *See generally* Guiding Principles Applicable to Unilateral Declarations of States Capable of Creating Legal Obligations, *in* Int'l Law Comm'n, Rep. on the Work of Its Fifty-Eighth Session, U.N. Doc. A/61/10 (2006), *reprinted in* [2006] 2 Y.B. Int'l L. Comm'n 161–66, U.N. Doc. A/CN.4/SER.A/2006/Add.1 (Part 2) [hereinafter ILC Guiding Principles].

260. ARSIWA, *supra* note 2, art. 13, cmt. ¶ 6.

equally to conduct that does not fulfill the "attribution" element, namely, acts that were private in character at the time of their commission.[261]

Special Rapporteur Ago acknowledged this possibility, noting that a State that puts down an insurrection could agree to assume responsibility for the rebels' acts.[262] He then observed, "[I]n this case it is obviously not a question of attribution to the State, as a source of responsibility, of acts committed earlier by another subject of international law . . . ."[263] Instead, Ago viewed this as "a question of succession by a State to the *ex delicto* obligations which another subject of international law . . . incurred as a result of its actions."[264]

Ago made these comments in the context of insurrectional movements; a specific category of NSA, which he considered had international personality.[265] In the case of NSAs more generally, which are not normally viewed as subjects of international law, the State would not assume the NSA's own obligations. Instead, it would agree to bear responsibility for any harms flowing from the NSAs' conduct, as if the relevant acts had been committed directly by the State.[266]

Although rare, there are examples of States agreeing to assume responsibility for prior private acts. During Mexico's struggle for independence, for instance, Mexican patriots entered contracts with U.S. citizens to obtain supplies for the patriot cause.[267] Once Mexico had gained independence, the government accepted that it was bound by these contracts. The 1849 Mexican-U.S. Claims Commission therefore concluded that Mexico was responsible for breaches of the contracts on the basis that the government "recognised the contracts . . . as binding upon it."[268]

More recently, France agreed to compensate French nationals who suffered damage during the Algerian war of independence, following the refusal by the new State of Algeria to fully implement its obligations under the Évian Accords.[269]

261. *Id.* art. 2.

262. Ago's Fourth Rep. on State Responsibility, *supra* note 8, at 130–31, ¶ 156. *See also* Int'l Law Comm'n, Rep. of the Comm'n to the General Assembly (1975), *in* [1975] 2 Y.B. Int'l L. Comm'n 93 n. 212, U.N. Doc. A/CN.4/SER.A/1975/Add.1.

263. Ago's Fourth Rep. on State Responsibility, *supra* note 8, at 130–31, ¶ 156.

264. *Id.*

265. *See id.* at 129, ¶ 152. For discussion regarding insurrectional movements, *see* ch. 9, sec. 9.5.

266. Michael Akehurst, *State Responsibility for the Wrongful Acts of Rebels–An Aspect of the Southern Rhodesian Problem*, 43 Brit. Y.B. Int'l L. 49, 56 (1968–1969).

267. Kathryn Greenman, State Responsibility and Rebels: The History and Legacy of Protecting Investment Against Revolution 71–75 (2021).

268. *Id.* at 74–75, citing *Parrott's* Case, *in* John Bassett Moore, History and Digest of the International Arbitrations to Which the United States Has Been a Party 3429–30 (vol. 4, 1898).

269. Patrick Dumberry, *New State Responsibility for Internationally Wrongful Acts by an Insurrectional Movement*, 17 Eur. J. Int'l L. 605, 613–14, (2006).

France additionally agreed to compensate a Swiss national for damage caused by an NSA fighting against Algerian independence.[270]

States have also retrospectively agreed to accept responsibility for the conduct of other States. This is evident from the facts of the *Gabčíkovo-Nagymaros* case,[271] which concerned a 1977 treaty concluded between Hungary and Czechoslovakia relating to the construction and operation of a series of locks.[272] Following the 1993 division of Czechoslovakia, Hungary, and Slovakia concluded a Special Agreement relating to the submission of a dispute concerning the implementation and termination of the treaty to the ICJ.[273]

The preamble to the Special Agreement set out the parties' understanding that the Slovak Republic was "the sole successor State in respect of rights and obligations relating to the Gabčíkovo-Nagymaros Project."[274] In light of Slovakia's express agreement to assume responsibility, the court concluded that "Slovakia thus may be liable to pay compensation not only for its own wrongful conduct but also for that of Czechoslovakia . . . ."[275]

In his later work on State responsibility, Crawford referred to the *Gabčíkovo-Nagymaros* case, opining that "the relevant acts of Czechoslovakia could be considered attributable to the Slovakian state" based on the rule of attribution reflected in Article 11 ARSIWA.[276] However, this assertion is questionable. The ICJ concluded that Slovakia was liable to pay compensation for Czechoslovakia's wrongful conduct because Slovakia had agreed that it was Czechoslovakia's sole successor in respect of the Gabčíkovo-Nagymaros Project.[277] Therefore, Slovakia's responsibility arose not due to the operation of a rule of attribution but rather due to its agreement to assume all the rights and obligations related to the project.

As Kress has observed, retrospective attribution is not necessary to achieve the results the ILC envisaged through the rule expressed in Article 11.[278] States are always in the position to accept responsibility for prior conduct, and it is not

270. *Id.* at 614 n. 43.

271. Gabčíkovo-Nagymaros Project (Hungary v. Slovakia), Judgment, 1997 I.C.J. Rep. 7 (Sept. 25) [hereinafter *Gabčíkovo-Nagymaros Project*].

272. Treaty concerning the Construction and Operation of the Gabčíkovo-Nagymaros System of Locks, Sept. 16, 1977, 1109 U.N.T.S. 211.

273. Special Agreement for Submission to the International Court of Justice of the Differences Between the Republic of Hungary and the Slovak Republic concerning the Gabčíkovo-Nagymaros Project, Apr. 7, 1993, 32 I.L.M. 1293.

274. *Id.*; *Gabčíkovo-Nagymaros Project*, *supra* note 271, ¶¶ 118, 151.

275. *Gabčíkovo-Nagymaros Project*, *supra* note 271, ¶ 151.

276. CRAWFORD, *supra* note 4, at 186–87.

277. *Gabčíkovo-Nagymaros Project*, *supra* note 271, ¶ 151. *See also* CRAWFORD, *supra* note 4, at 446–47 (referring to the case as "an example of succession to responsibility by agreement").

278. Kress, *supra* note 64, at 137.

necessary to resort to the legal fiction of attribution to achieve this.[279] In such cases, in accordance with the ILC's *Guiding Principles Applicable to Unilateral Declarations of States Capable of Creating Legal Obligations*,[280] a State's unequivocal adoption of an NSA's prior conduct can generate legal obligations that are binding on the State. This reality raises questions not only regarding the utility of the rule of attribution reflected in Article 11 but also its status in customary international law.

10.4.2 The Rule's Status in Customary International Law

Certain elements of the rule reflected in Article 11 ARSIWA have a firm basis in customary international law. First, it is apparent from the preceding analysis that States can voluntarily choose to assume responsibility for prior private conduct and that a unilateral declaration on the part of a State can lead to binding legal obligations. This aspect of Article 11 is uncontentious and reflects the ILC's conclusions in its *Guiding Principles* referred to above.[281]

Second, it is clear that a State's words or actions can provide proof of the State's involvement in prior conduct on the part of an NSA that violated the State's international legal obligations. The State's subsequent behavior might demonstrate, for instance, that the NSA was acting on the State's instructions, or under its direction or control at the relevant time.[282] It may be that attribution cannot be proven in the absence of these later words or actions. But even if that is the case, the rule reflected in Article 11 does not apply. The conduct remains attributable to the State on the other basis, for example, Article 8 ARSIWA.[283]

Third, it is not in doubt that the status of an NSA can change, meaning that from the time it begins to act as a State organ or agent, its conduct becomes attributable to the State based on another rule, such as Article 4 or Article 8 ARSIWA.[284] This is what happened in *Tehran Hostages*.[285] The initial actions of the militants in taking control of the Embassy were private in character, but their later actions, once authorized by the State, were public and attributable to Iran. This, again, is uncontentious and derives from rules of attribution other than Article 11.[286]

279. *Id.*

280. ILC Guiding Principles, *supra* note 259.

281. *Id.*

282. ARSIWA, *supra* note 2, art. 8.

283. *Id.*

284. *Id.* arts. 4, 8. For discussion regarding these rules of attribution, *see supra* chs. 4, 6.

285. *See supra* sec. 10.2.3.1.

286. *See, e.g.*, ARSIWA, *supra* note 2, arts. 4, 5, 8.

The key aspect of Article 11 that is not grounded in other rules of international law, and is far more open to debate, is the retrospective attribution of prior private conduct to the State in the absence of an express and unambiguous agreement by that State to assume responsibility for the acts concerned. As discussed in section 10.3.2, attribution on this basis might be appropriate if members of the Wagner Group operating in CAR, who later became State organs of Russia, continued to violate IHL in that capacity. However, attribution in such circumstances would depend not only on the facts, but also on the extent to which the relevant adjudicating body agrees that a State's acknowledgment and adoption of prior private acts can be inferred from its continuation of that same course of conduct.

It is questionable whether this element of the rule expressed in Article 11 reflects customary international law. The authorities the ILC cites to support the rule fail to establish an acceptance by States, or by international courts or tribunals, that private conduct is retrospectively attributable to a State based on its acknowledgment and adoption of the same.[287] Despite Crawford's assertion that the rule was "an essential addition" to the other bases of attribution included within ARSIWA,[288] the ILC cites no convincing examples of international practice to sustain the rule's novel effects, namely, the retrospective attribution of prior private conduct to a State in the absence of an express and unequivocal assumption of responsibility by State officials.

Nevertheless, in the years since ARSIWA's adoption, certain States, courts, tribunals, and other international bodies have accepted the customary character of the rule. For instance, the arbitral tribunal in the *Saint-Gobain* case referred to Article 11 as "a rule of customary international law."[289] The ECtHR in *Makuchyan and Minasyan* similarly indicated its belief that the rule forms part of "the existing rules of international law."[290] Ireland echoed this understanding in its *Position Paper on the Application of International Law in Cyberspace.*[291] Citing Article 11 and referring to *Tehran Hostages*, Ireland concluded that "[i]n a cyber context, a malicious cyber-operation conducted by a third party can thus be attributed to a state where it essentially takes ownership of the act, which might be ascertained through acts of support, approval and/or acquiescence."[292] This statement

287. *See supra* sec. 10.2.3. *See also* de Frouville, *supra* note 10, at 275; Condorelli & Kress, *supra* note 64, at 232; Kress, *supra* note 64, at 136–37; Becker, *supra* note 6, at 74–75; Mackenzie-Gray Scott, *supra* note 120, at 130.

288. ILC Y.B. 1998 vol. I, *supra* note 17, at 249, ¶ 58 (comments of Special Rapporteur Crawford).

289. *Saint-Gobain*, *supra* note 146, ¶ 461.

290. *Makuchyan & Minasyan*, *supra* note 122, ¶ 114. *See also id.* Partly Dissenting Opinion of Judge Pinto de Albuquerque ¶ 3.

291. Ireland Dep't of Foreign Affairs, Position Paper on the Application of International Law in Cyberspace, ¶¶ 21, 23 (July 6, 2023), https://dfa.ie/media/dfa/ourrolepolicies/internationallaw/Ireland---National-Position-Paper.pdf.

292. *Id.* ¶ 23.

highlights a relatively loose understanding of the acknowledgment and adoption thresholds that does not accord with the ARSIWA commentary.

The ICRC has additionally concluded that the rule has customary status. However, like the ILC, it cites very limited State practice to support this assertion.[293] Notably, the ICRC does not mention *Tehran Hostages*, or the other cases referred to in the ARSIWA commentary.[294] Instead, it relies principally on two domestic judgments, namely, the *Priebke* and the *J.T.* cases.[295] The import of these judgments is uncertain due to ambiguity regarding the precise basis of attribution in each case. In *Priebke*, for instance, the ICRC referred simply to the attack's attribution to Italy "on the basis that it had encouraged [the partisans'] actions and had officially recognized them after the conflict."[296] The ICRC also refers in this context to the decision of the ICTY Appeals Chamber in the *Tadić* case.[297] But although the ICTY expressly approved the potential attribution of private conduct to a State based on that State's "retroactive approval" of the conduct, the ICTY addressed this possibility only in passing and failed to provide any authority for it.[298]

Meanwhile, the ICJ, in its jurisprudence, has not pronounced upon the customary nature or otherwise of Article 11.[299] Contrary to the assertion made in the *Tallinn Manual 2.0*,[300] the ICJ in *Tehran Hostages* did not recognize the rule reflected in Article 11 as customary international law. The Court did not express a view regarding the status of this or any other rule of attribution.[301] Moreover, as the analysis in section 10.2.3 demonstrates, it is open to debate whether the judgment supports the principle of retrospective attribution at all.[302]

Thus, the State practice in support of Article 11 ARSIWA is extremely thin. It certainly cannot be characterized as "virtually uniform, extensive and representative."[303] There is also an absence of clear *opinio juris*, illustrating States' belief that,

293. Customary IHL: Rules, *supra* note 190, r. 149.

294. Customary IHL: Practice, *supra* note 191, at 3511.

295. Customary IHL: Rules, *supra* note 190, r. 149, *citing* the *Priebke* case, *supra* note 190, and the *J.T.* case, Judgment (District Court of The Hague, 1949).

296. Customary IHL: Rules, *supra* note 190, r. 149.

297. *Id.*, *citing* Prosecutor v. Tadić, Case No. ICTY IT-94-1-A, Appeals Chamber Judgment (Int'l Crim. Trib. for the former Yugoslavia, July 15, 1999) [hereinafter *Tadić Appeals Judgment*].

298. *Tadić Appeals Judgment*, *supra* note 297, ¶ 118. *See also* Kress, *supra* note 64, at 137.

299. The court declined to address the issue in the *Bosnian Genocide* case. *See Bosnian Genocide*, *supra* note 217, at 43, ¶ 414.

300. Tallinn Manual 2.0, *supra* note 31, r. 17, cmt. ¶ 15.

301. *Tehran Hostages*, *supra* note 38.

302. *See infra* sec. 10.2.3.1.

303. Customary IHL: Rules, *supra* note 190, at xlii. *See also* Int'l Law Comm'n, Draft Conclusions on Identification of Customary International Law, with Commentaries (conclusion 8)

as a matter of law, their acknowledgment and adoption of earlier private acts in breach of international law lead to the attribution of that conduct to the State.[304] Ireland's *Position Paper* is significant in this respect, but other States have for the most part remained silent regarding their understanding of the rule.

States' acceptance of ARSIWA via the UN General Assembly[305] and their failure to comment on draft Article 11 when given the opportunity to do so[306] are insufficient to indicate States' acceptance of the attribution standard as a matter of law. Given the limited practical relevance of the rule to date, either during armed conflict or in broader contexts, States' failure to react cannot reasonably be interpreted as evidence of their acceptance of the rule's binding nature.[307]

Accordingly, it appears clear that the core element of Article 11 ARSIWA, relating to the retroactive attribution of prior private conduct to a State, does not currently reflect customary international law. It is nevertheless possible that in view of statements such as that made by Ireland, and relevant judgments such as *Makuchyan and Minasyan*, the rule could crystallize into a binding norm. Whether it does so is likely to depend on the extent to which States invoke the rule in the future. Unless clarity can be gained regarding the types of State conduct that satisfy the acknowledgment and adoption thresholds in the absence of an express assumption of responsibility, the rule's future status and practical import seem unlikely to change.

10.5 CONCLUSION

Article 11 ARSIWA was formulated belatedly by the ILC, and the rule it reflects has little foundation in State practice or the decisions of international courts or tribunals. It rests primarily on the *Tehran Hostages* case, but a close reading of the judgment reveals that the ruling supports only the prospective, not the retroactive, attribution of conduct to the State.[308] The remaining examples that the ILC cites in Article 11's commentary fail to provide sufficient authority for the exceptional step of attributing private acts to a State, with which that State was not initially involved.

(2018), *in* [2018] 2 Y.B. INT'L L. COMM'N 100–102, U.N. Doc. A/CN.4/SER.A/2018/Add.1 (Part 2) [hereinafter Identification of Customary International Law].

304. *See* Identification of Customary International Law, *supra* note 303, at 102–3 (conclusion 9).

305. G.A. Res. 56/83, U.N. Doc A/RES/56/83 (Jan. 22, 2002).

306. 2001 Comments and Observations, *supra* note 20, at 50.

307. *See* Identification of Customary International Law, *supra* note 303, at 103 (conclusion 10, ¶ 3).

308. *See supra* sec. 10.2.3.1.

It is therefore doubtful that the principle of retroactive attribution expressed in Article 11 reflects customary international law.[309] A State's words or actions relating to prior private conduct may be more pertinent as evidence of the State's involvement in the acts at issue, leading to attribution of the conduct to the State on another basis.[310] Alternatively, a State's subsequent endorsement of such acts may indicate the State's voluntary acceptance of responsibility and its willingness to make the necessary reparations.[311] In the latter case, it is questionable whether a rule of attribution is required at all.[312]

From an accountability perspective, the principle of retrospective attribution expressed in Article 11 has the greatest potential value when a State's acknowledgment and adoption can be inferred from its conduct. In these circumstances, the State would bear responsibility for acts that it would otherwise not accept as its own. However, it is clear from the ARSIWA commentary and relevant case law that the acknowledgment and adoption criteria will rarely be satisfied in the absence of an express assumption of responsibility by State officials.[313]

This high attribution threshold is justified as a matter of legal policy, to avoid States bearing responsibility for private conduct based on mere expressions of approval or failures to condemn.[314] Nonetheless, it reduces the rule's utility to a vanishing point, particularly in the context of armed conflict. When States engage with NSAs during conflict, they do not normally demonstrate an intent to accept responsibility for conduct that violates their international legal obligations. As such, the rule reflected in Article 11 not only has a weak basis in law. In situations of armed conflict, it also serves little practical purpose.

309. *See supra* sec. 10.4.2.

310. *See supra* Part III of this book for further discussion in relation to Articles 4, 5, and 8 ARSIWA.

311. *See supra* sec. 10.4.1.

312. *Id. See also* ILC Guiding Principles, *supra* note 259.

313. *See supra* sec. 10.3.

314. Hessbruegge, *Human Rights Violations*, *supra* note 105, at 52; Milanović, *supra* note 123.

PART FIVE

Final Conclusions

11

Conclusion to Parts Three and Four

11.1 INTRODUCTION

The attribution regime examined in the preceding chapters serves an important purpose. It determines when the acts that individuals or entities perform are attributable to a State and can engage that State's international responsibility.[1] If conduct in violation of international law is attributable to a State, this leads to certain legal consequences, including an obligation on the responsible State to make reparation for any damage or injury caused.[2] It also enables other States to call out the State concerned for its harmful conduct and to take countermeasures in response.[3] But if the relevant conduct is not attributable to a State, it remains wholly private in character. That is the case even if a State facilitated the conduct, for example, by providing the means by which the person or entity was able to commit the acts at issue.[4]

The process of attribution thereby regulates the public–private divide.[5] Its consequences are significant due to the position of States as the principal actors on the world stage. Non-State actors (NSA) lack international legal personality, and the law has not yet developed to hold them to account in the same manner as

1. *See supra* ch. 3.

2. Draft Articles on Responsibility of States for Internationally Wrongful Acts, with commentaries, arts. 30–31, 34–39, *in* Int'l Law Comm'n, Rep. on the Work of its Fifty-Third Session, U.N. Doc. A/56/10 (2001), *reprinted in* [2001] 2 Y.B. INT'L L. COMM'N 31, 88 U.N. Doc. A/CN.4/SER.A/2001/Add.1 (Part 2) [hereinafter ARSIWA].

3. *Id.* arts. 49–53.

4. *See supra* ch. 7, sec. 7.2.3.

5. *See id.* sec. 7.2.3.1.

Attribution of Non-State Actor Conduct During Armed Conflict. Jennifer Maddocks, Oxford University Press.
 DOI: 10.1093/oso/9780197842652.003.0011

States.[6] As such, the law of State responsibility is an important means of redress for those harmed by NSAs' conduct. If the acts in violation of international law are not attributable to a State, the victims might have little possibility of seeking reparation in respect of the injury or damage they have suffered.

This is particularly apparent in situations of conflict, when the harms that victims suffer may be especially egregious. While the law of State responsibility is general in its application and relates to all breaches of international law committed in any circumstances, this book focuses on the attribution of conduct to a State during armed conflict. In this context, States have used NSAs to pursue their national security and foreign policy goals for centuries and the practice continues unabated today.[7] It is therefore critical that States should be properly held to account for the conduct of those persons and entities engaged in conflict that act on their behalf.

The focus of this study is the six rules of attribution related to NSA conduct reflected in the Draft Articles on Responsibility of States for Internationally Wrongful Acts (ARSIWA).[8] In each case, the analysis sought to clarify when the rule applies and to evaluate its effectiveness in achieving its object and purpose.[9] In other words, the preceding chapters assess whether each rule attributes conduct to a State in all the circumstances it was designed to address. This is done principally via examples from the three armed conflicts used as case studies.[10] But the conclusions reached have wider implications for conflicts around the world, both today and in the future.

This final chapter draws together the preceding analysis. It first sets out an overview of the six rules of attribution related to NSA conduct. It then assesses the effectiveness of the attribution regime during armed conflict, taking into account the increased role, sophistication, and autonomy of many NSAs. Finally, the chapter assesses the future evolution of the law of State responsibility, including developments that might hold States more effectively to account for the acts of NSAs that violate their international legal obligations.

11.2 THE ATTRIBUTION REGIME REFLECTED IN ARSIWA

During armed conflict, some of the rules of attribution reflected in ARSIWA are of greater importance than others in attributing NSA conduct to a State. The

6. *See, e.g.*, Jan Klabbers, *(I Can't Get No) Recognition: Subjects Doctrine and the Emergence of Non-State Actors, in* Nordic Cosmopolitanism: Essays in International Law for Martti Koskenniemi 365 (Jarna Petman & Jan Klabbers eds., 2003).

7. *See supra* ch. 2, sec. 2.2.

8. ARSIWA, *supra* note 2, arts. 4, 5, 8, 9–11.

9. *See supra*, chs. 4–10.

10. *See supra* ch. 2, sec. 2.4.

most significant rules in this context are those reflected in Articles 4, 5, and 8 ARSIWA.[11] These relate to State organs and agents, in other words, those persons or entities with which a State maintains factual or legal links at the time the relevant NSA acts in a manner that potentially violates international law.[12] The remaining rules, reflected in Articles 9, 10, and 11 ARSIWA, are exceptional in character and invoked only rarely by States, humanitarian actors, and international courts and tribunals.[13] These can apply in the absence of any factual or legal links between the State and the NSA at the time of the latter's conduct in potential breach of international law.[14]

Part Three of this book focuses on the three rules of attribution relating to State organs and agents.[15] The conclusion to this analysis, in Chapter 7, outlines the attribution regime that these three rules represent and how they operate together.[16] It also highlights interpretive concerns regarding all three rules of attribution. These relate to the prevailing interpretation of the rules, which reduces their effectiveness in properly attributing conduct to a State that was clearly performed on its behalf.[17]

Part Four examines the exceptional rules of attribution reflected in Articles 9, 10, and 11 ARSIWA.[18] Here, it is more difficult to draw together overarching conclusions due to the very different scenarios the rules address. Article 9 relates to NSAs' performance of essential public functions when there is a vacuum of State authority, Article 10 relates to the conduct of successful insurrectional movements, while Article 11 concerns NSA conduct that a State subsequently acknowledges and adopts.[19] Considerable ambiguity surrounds each of these rules and their status in customary international law remains open to doubt.[20]

There are, nevertheless, certain commonalities between all six rules of attribution. First, and most importantly, all the rules potentially apply to NSA conduct during armed conflict. Recent conflicts such as those in Syria and Ukraine provide numerous examples of acts on the part of NSAs to which one or more of the rules of attribution reflected in ARSIWA could apply.

11. ARSIWA, *supra* note 2, arts. 4, 5, 8.

12. *See supra* chs. 4–7.

13. ARSIWA, *supra* note 2, arts. 9–11.

14. *See supra* chs. 8–10.

15. *See supra* chs. 4–7.

16. *See supra* ch. 7, sec. 7.2.

17. *Id. See also infra* sec. 11.4.

18. *See supra* chs. 8–10.

19. ARSIWA, *supra* note 2, arts. 9–11.

20. *See supra* chs. 8–10.

Second, it is likely that the rules will retain their relevance to situations of conflict in the future. Regarding the attribution standards examined in Part Three, the factors that encourage States to act via proxy today are only likely to augment.[21] In the years to come, powerful NSAs will continue to undermine the authority of weaker governments, thereby challenging States' monopoly on the use of force.[22] This reality will lead external States to intervene to exert whatever influence they can over the NSAs concerned.[23] Moreover, as competition between the United States, China, and Russia increases, the perceived benefits of acting via proxy may become even more pressing.[24] The rules of attribution reflected in Articles 4, 5, and 8 will therefore retain their importance in determining when States bear responsibility for the conduct of their organs and agents.

Similarly, it is likely that the scenarios envisaged by the rules examined in Part Four will feature in the hostilities of the future. For instance, the conflict in Ukraine provides many examples of NSAs performing essential governmental tasks in the absence or default of the official authorities, leading to the potential attribution of their conduct to the State pursuant to the rule reflected in Article 9.[25] The "total defense" policies of other States also indicate the continued relevance of this basis of attribution.[26] Meanwhile, the success of the Islamist group, Hay'at Tahrir al-Sham (HTS), in toppling the Assad regime in Syria, demonstrates the continued relevance of the rule expressed in Article 10.[27]

A third commonality between the six rules of attribution is the importance of factual assessments when considering the rules' potential application. While legal relationships between a State and an NSA are pertinent to the rules reflected in Articles 4 and 5 ARSIWA, it is the factual situation that is relevant to de facto State organ status, and to attribution on other grounds.[28] In a complex armed conflict, however, the facts may be far from clear, leading to difficult evidential challenges for injured States. Given the covert nature of many relationships between States and NSAs, for example, it may be challenging to prove that an NSA was acting on

21. *See supra* ch. 2, sec. 2.2.

22. *See, e.g.*, Andreas Krieg & Jean-Marc Rickli, *Surrogate Warfare: The Art of War in the 21st Century?* 18 Def. Stud. 113, 119–21 (2018).

23. Eric Robinson, *The Missing, Irregular Half of Great Power Competition*, Modern War Inst. (Sept. 8, 2020), https://mwi.usma.edu/the-missing-irregular-half-of-great-power-competition/.

24. *See generally* Ronald O'Rourke, Cong. Research Serv., Renewed Great Power Competition: Implications for Defense–Issues for Congress (July 8, 2021), https://fas.org/sgp/crs/natsec/R43838.pdf.

25. *See supra* ch. 8.

26. *See, e.g.*, James Kenneth Wither, *Back to the Future? Nordic Total Defence Concepts*, 20 Def. Stud. 61 (2020); Singapore Ministry of Defence, Total Defence, https://www.mindef.gov.sg/defence-matters/defence-topic/total-defence.

27. *See supra* ch. 9.

28. For discussion of attribution based on law and fact, *see supra* ch. 7, sec. 7.2.2.

a State's instructions for the purposes of Article 8,[29] or that a State acknowledged and adopted an NSA's prior conduct so as to satisfy the rule expressed in Article 11.[30] Equally, it may be unclear whether the official authorities were absent or in default for the purposes of Article 9,[31] or whether there is continuity between the structures of an insurrectional movement and the State it comes to govern for the purposes of Article 10.[32] Such factual ambiguities can present difficulties for injured States in providing the evidence necessary to satisfy any of the rules of attribution reflected in ARSIWA.

Finally, legal ambiguities are inherent in all six rules of attribution. There is a lack of clarity, for instance, regarding the precise acts that are governmental in character for the purposes of Articles 5 and 9.[33] There is ongoing uncertainty regarding the meaning of control for the purposes of Articles 4 and 8.[34] And ambiguity surrounds the application of the rule reflected in Article 10, for example, regarding the legal test to establish whether conduct was performed on behalf of an insurrectional movement.[35] As the preceding chapters demonstrate, uncertainties such as these minimize the rules' effectiveness in holding States to account for NSA conduct that violates international law.

11.3 ASSESSING THE ATTRIBUTION REGIME

When assessing the effectiveness of the attribution regime reflected in ARSIWA in situations of armed conflict, the realities of contemporary conflict clearly impact the analysis. Armed groups and other NSAs are gaining in power, authority, and levels of autonomy, and they frequently challenge States for control over their territories and populations.[36] Moreover, while NSAs often benefit from the support of one or more States, it cannot be assumed that the State is always the dominant party in such relationships.[37]

The law of State responsibility, as expressed in ARSIWA, fails to take into account this reality. After half a decade of work by the International Law Commission (ILC), the draft articles were adopted at a time when the power of NSAs was plain to see, shortly after the attacks of September 11, 2001. At that time, the primacy of

29. *See supra* ch. 6, sec. 6.3.

30. *See supra* ch. 10.

31. *See supra* ch. 8, sec. 8.4.

32. *See supra* ch. 9.

33. *See supra* ch. 5, sec. 5.3; ch. 8, sec. 8.3.2.

34. *See supra* ch. 4, sec. 4.4; ch. 6, sec. 6.4.

35. *See supra* ch. 9, sec. 9.5.3.

36. *See supra* ch. 2, sec. 2.2.

37. *Id.*

States was already in decline.[38] Yet the majority of sources the ILC relied on when formulating the rules of attribution date from a much earlier era, pre-1950.[39] It is perhaps unsurprising, therefore, that these rules are State-centric in their focus, they create a strict public–private divide, and they assume that NSAs in receipt of State support will act under a high degree of State control.

ARSIWA's shortcomings in recognizing the enhanced role of NSAs may be understandable, but they are nevertheless problematic. In situations of conflict, the issue is twofold. First, the rules of attribution reflected in Articles 4, 5, and 8 ARSIWA do not properly attribute to a State all the conduct performed on its behalf.[40] Second, there is no mechanism within ARSIWA to hold States to account for their complicity in NSAs' wrongs.[41] Together, these factors allow States to act via proxy in a manner that they could not lawfully act via their own organs. Frequently, the harmful acts committed by NSAs during armed conflict remain private in character and do not engage the responsibility of a State, even if that State clearly facilitated the acts' commission.

The rules of attribution examined in Part Four do not assist in remedying this problem. These are exceptional rules that attribute conduct to a State in very distinct situations, when the State might not be involved in the relevant NSA conduct at the time of its commission. While the rules reflected in Articles 9 and 10 ARSIWA serve a valid purpose in the broader attribution regime,[42] it is questionable whether the attribution standard expressed in Article 11 has any utility at all.[43] In any event, due to their focus on specific scenarios that do not involve States' use of NSAs to achieve their conflict goals, these rules do not help close the accountability gap identified in Part Three.

Potential future developments in armed conflict demonstrate the pressing need to hold States effectively to account when they act through NSAs or contribute to the harms they cause. While the case studies outlined in Chapter 2 demonstrate the critical role played by NSAs in armed conflicts pre-2025,[44] the relative power of NSAs could augment even further in the future as they gain access to new technologies. Drone technology, for instance, will benefit not only States but also NSAs in battlefields across the world.[45] In the years to come, NSAs might

38. Vaughan Lowe, *Responsibility for the Conduct of Other States*, 101 Japanese J. Int'l L. 1, 2 (2002).

39. Richard Mackenzie-Gray Scott, State Responsibility for Non-State Actors: Past, Present and Prospects for the Future 18–20 (2022).

40. *See supra* chs. 4–6; ch. 7, sec. 7.2.2.

41. *See supra* ch. 7, sec. 7.2.3.

42. *See supra* ch. 8, sec. 8.2.3; ch. 9, sec. 9.2.3.

43. *See supra* ch. 10.

44. *See supra* ch. 2, sec. 2.4.

45. Jane Arraf & Eric Schmitt, *Iran's Proxies in Iraq Threaten U.S. with More Sophisticated Weapons*, N.Y. Times (June 4, 2021), www.nytimes.com/2021/06/04/world/middleeast/iran-dro

additionally gain access to more innovative technologies such as robotic and autonomous systems, or those enhanced by artificial intelligence.

Meanwhile, the perceived benefits of using proxies may become yet more compelling in the new era of great-power competition.[46] As the rivalry between Russia, China, and the United States grows, so does the appeal of proxy warfare as a means by which the powers and their allies can compete while avoiding direct confrontation.[47] Irregular methods of operating are therefore likely to feature heavily in the future, with the great powers relying frequently on hackers, private military and security companies (PMSC), and other NSAs to achieve their goals.[48] Moreover, it is unlikely that future conflict will see any diminution in conduct by NSAs that could violate international law. It is therefore imperative that when States facilitate those harms, international law effectively holds them to account.

11.4 ADDRESSING THE GAP IN ACCOUNTABILITY

Chapter 2 explores States' interactions with NSAs during armed conflict and the propensity of NSAs in receipt of State support to act in a manner that violates international law.[49] It is the civilians and persons *hors de combat* who fall victim to abuses by NSAs who experience the most damaging consequences of those interactions. But they equally cause harm to the wider international legal order. States that seek to evade their international obligations by operating through NSAs deprive those obligations of substance and ultimately weaken the entire framework of international law.

To address such concerns, Chapter 7 identifies three potential remedies: a more relaxed interpretation of the rules of attribution examined in Part Three, the development of a complicity rule that holds States to account when they facilitate harmful conduct on the part of NSAs, and a strengthening of relevant primary norms of international law.[50]

Regarding the first of these proposals, the purpose of the rules of attribution expressed in Articles 4, 5, and 8 ARSIWA is to attribute to a State all the conduct

nes-iraq.html; Rhordan Stephens, *How Drones Have Shaped the Nature of Conflict*, Vision of Humanity (last visited Jan. 9, 2025), https://www.visionofhumanity.org/how-drones-have-shaped-the-nature-of-conflict/.

46. O'Rourke, *supra* note 24.

47. C. Anthony Pfaff & Patrick Granfield, *How (Not) to Fight Proxy Wars*, Nat'l Interest (Mar. 27, 2018), https://nationalinterest.org/feature/how-not-fight-proxy-wars-25102.

48. Seth G. Jones, *The Future of Competition: U.S. Adversaries and the Growth of Irregular Warfare*, Ctr. for Strategic & Int'l Stud. (Feb. 4, 2021), www.csis.org/analysis/future-competition-us-adversaries-and-growth-irregular-warfare; Dominic Tierney, *The Future of Sino-U.S. Proxy War*, 4 Tex. Nat'l Sec. Rev. 50 (2021).

49. *See supra* ch. 2, secs. 2.2, 2.3.

50. *See supra* ch. 7, secs. 7.2, 7.3.

that is performed on its behalf.[51] In terms of the rules themselves, these are "broadly speaking, good enough."[52] In other words, there are no other circumstances, outside the rules reflected in ARSIWA, in which attribution is obviously appropriate. There is no requirement, therefore, for a *lex specialis* standard of attribution that applies in conflict situations.[53]

Yet it is apparent from the analysis in Chapters 4 to 6 that in the context of armed conflict, these rules do not attribute NSA conduct to a State in all the appropriate circumstances.[54] In the case of Articles 4 and 8, it is the stringency of the respective control thresholds that presents the greatest difficulties.[55] The tests formulated by the International Court of Justice (ICJ) are so strict as to make the rules practically unworkable.[56] Chapters 4 and 6, therefore, propose a more relaxed interpretation of the applicable control tests that would bring a greater range of private conduct within their scope.[57]

State control, however, is not always the most suitable basis of attribution. That is particularly the case when the NSA concerned is fighting purely for its State sponsor rather than in pursuit of its own goals, as in the case of Russia's use of the Wagner Group[58] and some of the Shi'a militias acting for Iran in Syria.[59] In such cases, the respective States empowered the NSAs to perform combat functions on their behalf, yet they did not obviously do so in a manner that complied with their domestic laws. Thus, on the ILC's interpretation of the rule reflected in Article 5 ARSIWA, their conduct is not attributable to the State.[60]

Chapter 5 argues that the rule expressed in Article 5 would better meet its object and purpose if evidence to satisfy the "empowerment" criterion could be furnished through an assessment of the facts surrounding the State's relationship with the NSA rather than solely via the State's internal law.[61] Given States' increased

51. *See supra* chs. 4–6; ch. 7, sec. 7.2.1.

52. Marko Milanović, *Special Rules of Attribution of Conduct in International Law*, 96 Int'l L. Stud. 295, 386 (2020).

53. For discussion regarding *lex specialis* rules of attribution, *see id.*

54. *See supra* chs. 4–6.

55. ARIWA, *supra* note 2, arts. 4, 8. *See also supra* chs. 4, 6.

56. *See supra* ch. 4, sec. 4.4; ch. 6, sec. 6.4.

57. *See supra* ch. 4, sec. 4.4.3; ch. 6, sec. 6.4.7.

58. *See, e.g.*, Kimberley Marten, *Russia's Use of Semi-State Security Forces: The Case of the Wagner Group*, 35 Post-Soviet Aff. 181 (2019).

59. *See, e.g.*, Michael Knights, *Iran's Foreign Legion: The Role of Iraqi Shiite Militias in Syria*, Wash. Inst. (June 27, 2013), www.washingtoninstitute.org/policy-analysis/view/irans-foreign-legion-the-role-of-iraqi-shiite-militias-in-syria; Farzin Nadimi, *Iran's Afghan and Pakistani Proxies: In Syria and Beyond?* Wash. Inst. (Aug. 22, 2016), www.washingtoninstitute.org/policy-analysis/irans-afghan-and-pakistani-proxies-syria-and-beyond.

60. *See supra* ch. 5, sec. 5.4.

61. *Id.* sec. 5.4.4.

propensity to outsource combat functions to PMSCs and militia groups, this would be a significant development in the law. It would not only lead to State responsibility in a wider range of circumstances but would also disrupt the perverse incentive that the rules of attribution currently promote for States to empower NSAs to act on their behalf but then distance themselves from those NSAs' activities so as not to exercise control.[62]

This more relaxed interpretation of the rule expressed in Article 5 could make State officials think twice before outsourcing combat functions to an undisciplined NSA. If they nevertheless decide to proceed, the increased risk of State responsibility might encourage States to regulate those NSAs' activities more diligently. A State's exercise of control is often the most effective means by which to ensure that an NSA acts with discipline and in accordance with international law.[63] It is therefore a form of behavior that the law should incentivize, not discourage.

A more flexible interpretation of the attribution thresholds relevant to Articles 4, 5, and 8 ARSIWA would therefore assist in narrowing the accountability gap. However, it would not solve the problem entirely. As discussed in Chapter 7, attribution is appropriate only when the conduct at issue is clearly performed on behalf of a State.[64] But States' relationships with NSAs vary considerably and in many instances, States facilitate harmful conduct on the part of NSAs in circumstances where their involvement in those acts is insufficient to justify legal attribution. This scenario may arise more frequently in future as the relative power and autonomy of NSAs continues to increase.

A focus on the rules of attribution alone is insufficient to ensure that States are properly held to account for their contributions to the harms inflicted by NSAs during armed conflict. Chapter 7, therefore, proposes two additional developments to the law.[65] The first is that ARSIWA's complicity provisions should apply to States' aid or assistance to NSAs. Notwithstanding NSAs' lack of legal personality, it makes little sense for the law to prohibit States from assisting other States to violate international law but to allow them to provide equivalent assistance to NSAs. That is particularly the case given the power and autonomy exercised by many NSAs and their growing propensity to act in a State-like manner.[66]

62. *See, e.g.*, Mark Gibney et al., *Transnational State Responsibility for Violations of Human Rights*, 12 Harv. Hum. Rts. J. 267, 286–87 (1999); Oona A. Hathaway et al., *Ensuring Responsibility: Common Article 1 and State Responsibility for Non-State Actors*, 95 Tex. L. Rev. 539 (2017).

63. Erica L. Gaston, Ctr. for the Study of Armed Groups, Regulating Irregular Actors: Can Due Diligence Checks Mitigate the Risks of Working with Non-State and Substate Forces? 56 (May 2021), https://odi.org/en/publications/regulating-irregular-actors-can-due-diligence-checks-mitigate-the-risks-of-working-with-non-state-and-substate-forces/.

64. *See supra* ch. 7, sec. 7.2.

65. *See id.* sec. 7.3.

66. *Id.* sec. 7.3.1.

Primary norms of international law also play an important role in regulating States' associations with NSAs during armed conflict.[67] These norms are wide-ranging and include the prohibition on the use of force and the principle of due diligence.[68] The latter imposes positive duties on States to take feasible steps to suppress wrongdoing by NSAs operating on territory under their control.[69] Importantly, primary norms hold States to account for their own organs' conduct in relation to the NSA concerned, meaning that they regulate States' behavior toward NSAs without requiring injured States to cross the high evidential bar set by the rules of attribution.[70]

When considering States' facilitation of harmful conduct on the part of NSAs, a further advantage of the complicity provisions within primary norms is that they can require States to take positive steps to ensure their proxies' compliance with international law; a type of obligation that the secondary law of State responsibility simply cannot impose.[71] In this context, the analysis in Chapter 7 focuses on the duty to respect and ensure respect for international humanitarian law (IHL) enshrined in common Article 1 to the Geneva Conventions.[72] It argues that when States develop or sustain relationships with NSAs engaged in conflict, they thereby gain an enhanced capacity to influence their behavior. In such circumstances, the duty in common Article 1 should be interpreted to impose both negative and positive duties on States to ensure that the NSAs they support comply with international law.[73] Such a development would represent one potentially significant step forward in the quest to hold States properly to account when they facilitate harmful conduct on the part of NSAs.

11.5 THE FUTURE DEVELOPMENT OF THE LAW

The conclusions outlined in the preceding analysis raise questions regarding how international law should evolve in the manner suggested and where responsibility should lie for implementing such proposals. Clearly, international law is made by States, and it must develop in a manner that is generally acceptable to governments across the globe. It appears unlikely, however, that States would agree to any

67. *Id.* sec. 7.3.2.

68. U.N. Charter, art. 2(4); Riccardo Pisillo-Mazzeschi, *The Due Diligence Rule and the Nature of the International Responsibility of States*, 35 German Y.B. Int'l L. 9 (1992).

69. Pisillo-Mazzeschi, *supra* note 68.

70. *See supra* ch. 7, sec. 7.3.2.

71. For discussion of the distinction between primary and secondary norms, see *supra* ch. 3, sec. 3.2.

72. *See supra* ch. 7, sec. 7.3.2.

73. *Id.*

expansion in the scope of their international responsibility, particularly given the current fragmented international order in which geopolitical tensions abound.

It is still conceivable that the law of State responsibility could be agreed in the form of a Convention.[74] ARSIWA's future status has remained on the agenda of the UN General Assembly since 2001. But despite a growing number of States now advocating in favor of a treaty on State responsibility,[75] the current status quo, involving periodic reconsideration of the issue, appears entrenched.[76] In any event, the likelihood of such a Convention relaxing the rules of attribution or providing for State complicity in the conduct of NSAs appears slim. States, as the gatekeepers of the international system, have little incentive to either expand the remit of their own responsibility or to agree to any changes that would afford NSAs international legal personality or otherwise elevate their status.[77]

In the absence of any treaty on State responsibility, this body of law can nevertheless develop through State practice and expressions of *opinio juris*.[78] Although some States exploit the law's deficiencies when acting through NSAs, States also suffer harm when malign actors push the boundaries of international law through their use of proxies. If States that perceive such harms call out other States for their behavior, it could prompt additional States to follow suit. This can raise the reputational costs to States that choose to act through NSAs. Moreover, if States make clear that they consider the behavior at issue to be internationally wrongful and properly articulate the basis for their assertions, such *opinio juris* might make an important contribution to the development of international law.[79]

States, additionally, could seek to reach agreement regarding certain particularly harmful practices relating to NSAs engaged in armed conflict. For instance, States already supply sophisticated technologies to their proxies, including drones and precision-guided munitions.[80] Weapons such as these can cause egregious

74. Federica L. Paddeu, *To Convene or Not to Convene? The Future Status of the Articles on State Responsibility: Recent Developments*, 21 MAX PLANCK Y.B. U.N. L. 83 (2018); Arman Sarvarian, *The Ossified Debate on a UN Convention on State Responsibility*, 70 INT'L & COMP. L.Q. 769 (2021); Maurizio Arcari, *The Future of the Articles on State Responsibility: A Matter of Form or of Substance?* QUESTIONS OF INT'L L. (June 30, 2022).

75. Paddeu, *supra* note 74.

76. *Id.*; Sarvarian, *supra* note 74.

77. Klabbers, *supra* note 6.

78. *See* Draft Conclusions on Identification of Customary International Law, with commentaries (2018), *in* Int'l Law Comm'n, Rep. on the Work of its Seventieth Session, U.N. Doc. A/73/10 (2018), *reprinted in* [2018] 2 Y.B. INT'L L. COMM'N 89, U.N. Doc. A/CN.4/SER.A/2018/Add.1 (Part 2).

79. *Id.* conclusions 9–10.

80. *See, e.g.*, Itamar Lifshitz & Ayal Meents, *The Paradox of Precision: Nonstate Actors and Precision-Guided Weapons*, WAR ON THE ROCKS (Nov. 17, 2020), https://warontherocks.com/2020/11/the-paradox-of-precision-nonstate-actors-and-precision-guided-weapons/; Agnes Helou, *Flexing Its Muscles, Iran Steps away from Deniability in Arming the Houthis: Analysts*,

harm to civilian populations if used by NSAs in a manner that violates IHL.[81] To address this threat, the international community could seek to implement an arms control regime that prohibits the transfer of sophisticated weaponry, manufacturing capabilities, and know-how to armed groups or other NSAs engaged in conflict.[82] While such a development would address only a small part of the problem, it would nevertheless be a step in the right direction toward an acknowledgment, on the part of States, of the harms that their assistance to NSAs engaged in conflict can cause.

The judgments of international courts and tribunals can also be influential in shaping the law, as the ICJ's key jurisprudence on the issue of State responsibility demonstrates. However, cases raising issues of State responsibility for private conduct in armed conflict are rarely litigated, and when they are, aspects of the ICJ's judgments form part of the problem rather than providing a solution. The court's strict interpretation of effective control relevant to Article 8 ARSIWA is a case in point.[83] While the judgments of other international courts and tribunals are less authoritative on matters of State responsibility and do not apply directly to situations of armed conflict, the more relaxed approach these bodies sometimes take to attribution perhaps may offer some cause for optimism. Arbitral tribunals, for instance, have found entities to qualify as de facto State organs for the purposes of Article 4 ARSIWA based on less stringent criteria than the ICJ's strict test of complete dependence and control.[84] And the European Court of Human Rights has taken a more flexible approach to evidence when considering attribution under the rule reflected in Article 8, drawing adverse inferences and reversing the burden of proof.[85]

Any developments in the law arising from the judgments of international courts and tribunals will, however, take time. In the shorter term, a more effective means to regulate State behavior in connection with NSAs may be through soft law, meaning nonbinding instruments such as principles or codes of conduct.[86] A pertinent example is the Montreux Document, which articulates good

Breaking Def. (June 5, 2024), https://breakingdefense.com/2024/06/flexing-its-muscles-iran-steps-away-from-deniability-in-arming-the-houthis-analysts/.

81. Lifshitz & Meents, *supra* note 80.

82. *Id.*

83. *See supra* ch. 6, sec. 6.4.

84. Emilio Agustín Maffezini v. The Kingdom of Spain, Case No. ARB/97/7, Decision of the Tribunal on Objections to Jurisdiction, ¶¶ 75–89 (Int'l Ctr for Settlement of Inv. Disp., Jan. 25, 2000), www.italaw.com/sites/default/files/case-documents/ita0479.pdf; Flemingo Duty Free Shop Private Limited v. The Republic of Poland, Arbitral Award, ¶¶ 418–35 (Perm. Ct. Arb., Aug. 12, 2016), www.italaw.com/sites/default/files/case-documents/italaw7709_3.pdf.

85. Carter v. Russia, App. No. 20914/07, ¶¶ 166–69 (2021) (ECtHR).

86. Kumaravadivel Guruparan & Jennifer Zerk, *Influence of Soft Law Grows in International Governance*, Chatham House (June 17, 2021), www.chathamhouse.org/2021/06/influence-soft-law-grows-international-governance.

practice for States relating to their use of PMSCs during armed conflict.[87] The International Committee of the Red Cross (ICRC) promotes a similar approach in its work on support relationships, encouraging States with the capacity to influence those engaged in conflict to enhance the protection of civilians.[88]

The use of nonbinding norms to reach consensus is particularly evident in the cyber domain. Here, the UN Group of Governmental Experts agreed to eleven voluntary, nonbinding norms of responsible State behavior, including an acknowledgment that "States must not use proxies to commit internationally wrongful acts using [information and communication technologies]."[89] Although States likely intended this statement to extend no further than the rules of attribution reflected in ARSIWA,[90] it could be interpreted more broadly to encompass States' use of proxies in circumstances where the stringent attribution thresholds would not be satisfied.

States' adoption of domestic laws and policies can also build consensus regarding acceptable State behavior when dealing with NSAs in conflict situations. Some States are required by domestic law or policy to carry out risk assessments prior to engaging with NSAs, or to conduct vetting of their potential partners.[91] The greater the number of States that implement such policies, the stronger the culture of compliance will be, thereby aiding the development of norms regarding responsible State behavior.

Finally, it is important to address the development of primary norms of international law, which evolve independently of the secondary rules of State responsibility. These play a critical role in regulating State behavior toward NSAs during armed conflict and may develop at a faster pace. IHL is shaped not only by States and international courts and tribunals but also by the work of the ICRC and the

87. The Montreux Document on Pertinent International Legal Obligations and Good Practices for States related to Operations of Private Military and Security Companies during Armed Conflict, U.N. Doc. A/63/467-S/2008/636 (Sept. 17, 2008).

88. ICRC, Allies, Partners and Proxies: Managing Support Relationships in Armed Conflict to Reduce the Human Cost of War 23 (Mar. 2021), www.icrc.org/en/publication/4498-allies-partners-and-proxies-managing-support-relationships-armed-conflict-reduce.

89. Group of Governmental Experts on Advancing Responsible State Behaviour in Cyberspace in the Context of International Security 18, ¶ 71(g), U.N. Doc. A/76/135 (July 14, 2021). *See also* Open-Ended Working Group on Developments in the Field of Information and Telecommunications in the Context of International Security, U.N. Doc. A/AC.290/2021/CRP.2 (Mar. 10, 2021); Michael N. Schmitt, *The Sixth United Nations GGE and International Law in Cyberspace*, Just Sec. (June 10, 2021), www.justsecurity.org/76864/the-sixth-united-nations-gge-and-international-law-in-cyberspace/.

90. Schmitt, *supra* note 89.

91. *See, e.g.*, U.S. Dep't of State, About the Leahy Law (Jan. 20, 2021), www.state.gov/key-topics-bureau-of-democracy-human-rights-and-labor/human-rights/leahy-law-fact-sheet/; U.K. Government, Overseas Security and Justice Assistance (OSJA): Human Rights Guidance (2017), https://assets.publishing.service.gov.uk/government/uploads/system/uploads/attachment_data/file/583304/OSJA_Guidance_2017.pdf.

community of IHL scholars.[92] As is evident from the debate regarding the duty to respect and ensure respect for IHL,[93] the latter's views can carry considerable weight in determining the proper construction of IHL norms. Thus, the interpretation of common Article 1 to the Geneva Conventions may continue to evolve in a manner that enhances humanitarian protections and thereby play a greater role in future in regulating States' conduct toward NSAs during armed conflict.

92. Sandesh Sivakumaran, *Making and Shaping the Law of Armed Conflict*, 71 Current Legal Probs. 119 (2018).

93. *See supra* ch. 7, sec. 7.3.2.

SELECT BIBLIOGRAPHY

Books

Helmut Philipp Aust, Complicity and the Law of State Responsibility (2011).

Tal Becker, Terrorism and the State: Rethinking the Rules of State Responsibility (2006).

Ian Brownlie, State Responsibility: Part 1 (1983).

Lindsey Camerouvn & Vincent Chetail, Privatizing War: Private Military and Security Companies Under Public International Law (2013).

James Crawford, State Responsibility: The General Part (2013).

Yoram Dinstein, War, Aggression and Self-Defence (5th ed., 2011).

Yoram Dinstein, Non-International Armed Conflicts in International Law (2014).

Patrick Dumberry, State Succession to International Responsibility (2007).

Patrick Dumberry, Rebellions and Civil Wars (2022).

Katharine Fortin, The Accountability of Armed Groups Under Human Rights Law (2017).

Erica L. Gaston, Illusions of Control: Dilemmas in Managing U.S. Proxy Forces in Afghanistan, Iraq, and Syria (2024).

Andy Greenberg, Sandworm: A New Era of Cyberwar and the Hunt for the Kremlin's Most Dangerous Hackers (2019).

Kathryn Greenman, State Responsibility and Rebels: The History and Legacy of Protecting Investment Against Revolution (2021).

Jörn Griebel, Die Zurechnungskategorie der de-facto Organe im Recht der Staatenverantwortlichkeit (2004).

Rosalyn Higgins, Problems and Process: International Law and How We Use It (1995).

Geraint Hughes, My Enemy's Enemy: Proxy Warfare in International Politics (2014).

Miles Jackson, Complicity in International Law (2015).

Kenneth Katzman, The Warriors of Islam: Iran's Revolutionary Guard (1993).

Robert Kolb, The International Law of State Responsibility (2018).

Vladyslav Lanovoy, Complicity and Its Limits in the Law of International Responsibility (2016).

Matthew Levitt, Hezbollah: The Global Footprint of Lebanon's Party of God (2013).

Kubo Mačák, Internationalized Armed Conflicts in International Law (2018).

Zachariah Cherian Mampilly, Rebel Rulers: Insurgent Governance and Civilian Life During War (2011).

Anna Matveeva, Through Times of Trouble: Conflict in Southeastern Ukraine Explained from Within (2018).

Tim Maurer, Cyber Mercenaries: The State, Hackers, and Power (2018).

Panos Merkouris, Interpretation of Customary International Law (2024).

Marko Milanović, Extraterritorial Application of Human Rights Treaties: Law, Principles, and Policy (2011).

Andrew Mumford, Proxy Warfare (2013).

Michael N. Schmitt (Ed.), Tallinn Manual 2.0 on the International Law Applicable to Cyber Operations (2017).

Frauke Renz, State Responsibility and New Trends in the Privatization of Warfare (2020).

Tilman Rodenhäuser, Organizing Rebellion: Non-State Armed Groups Under International Humanitarian Law, Human Rights Law, and International Criminal Law (2018).

Haig Silvanie, Responsibility of States for Acts of Unsuccessful Insurgent Governments (1939).

Sandesh Sivakumaran, The Law of Non-International Armed Conflict (2012).

Hannah Tonkin, State Control over Private Military and Security Companies in Armed Conflict (2011).

Kimberly N. Trapp, State Responsibility for International Terrorism (2011).

Beth Van Schaack, Imagining Justice for Syria (2020).

Ziaodong Yang, State Immunity in International Law (2012).

Neil Longley York, Turning the World Upside Down: The War of American Independence and the Problem of Empire (2003).

Book Chapters

Dapo Akande, *Classification of Armed Conflicts: Relevant Legal Concepts*, *in* International Law and the Classification of Conflicts 32 (Elizabeth Wilmshurst ed., 2012).

Hazem Atlam, *National Liberation Movements and International Responsibility*, *in* United Nations Codification of State Responsibility (Marina Spinedi & Bruno Simma eds., 1987).

Andrea Bianchi, *The Fight for Inclusion: Non-State Actors and International Law*, *in* From Bilateralism to Community Interest: Essays in Honour of Bruno Simma 39 (Ulrich Fastenrath et al. eds., 2011).

Veronika Bílková, *Establishing Direct Responsibility of Armed Opposition Groups for Violations of International Humanitarian Law?* *in* Responsibilities of the Non-State Actor in Armed Conflict and the Market Place 263 (Noemi Gal-Or et al. eds., 2015).

Gérard Cahin, *Attribution of Conduct to the State: Insurrectional Movements*, *in* The Law of International Responsibility 247 (James Crawford et al. eds., 2010).

Gérard Cahin, *The Responsibility of Other Entities: Armed Bands and Criminal Groups*, *in* The Law of International Responsibility 331 (James Crawford et al. eds., 2010).

David D. Caron, *The Basis of Responsibility: Attribution and Other Trans-Substantive Rules of State Responsibility*, *in* The Iran-United States Claims Tribunal: Its

CONTRIBUTION TO THE LAW OF STATE RESPONSIBILITY 109 (Richard B. Lillich & Daniel B. Magraw eds., 1998).

James Crawford, *State Responsibility*, *in* MAX PLANCK ENCYCLOPEDIA OF PUBLIC INTERNATIONAL LAW ¶¶ 6–15 (Rüdiger Wolfrum ed., 2015).

Luigi Condorelli & Claus Kress, *The Rules of Attribution: General Considerations*, *in* THE LAW OF INTERNATIONAL RESPONSIBILITY 221 (James Crawford et al. eds., 2010).

Olivier de Frouville, *Attribution of Conduct to the State: Private Individuals*, *in* THE LAW OF INTERNATIONAL RESPONSIBILITY 257 (James Crawford et al. eds., 2010).

Christian Dominicé, *Attribution of Conduct to Multiple States and the Implication of a State in the Act of Another State*, *in* THE LAW OF INTERNATIONAL RESPONSIBILITY 281 (James Crawford et al. eds., 2010).

Tatyana Eatwell, *State Responsibility, "Successful" Insurrectional Movements and Governments of National Reconciliation*, *in* NON-STATE ACTORS AND INTERNATIONAL OBLIGATIONS 388 (James Summers & Alex Gough eds., 2018).

Katharine Fortin, *The Relevance of Article 9 of the Articles on State Responsibility for the Internationally Wrongful Acts of Armed Groups*, in NON-STATE ACTORS AND INTERNATIONAL OBLIGATIONS 371 (James Summers & Alex Gough eds., 2018).

Katharine Fortin, *Which Legal Framework Applies to Deprivation of Liberty by Non-State Armed Groups and Do They Address the Particular Challenges When Detention Is Conducted by Non-State Armed Groups?*, *in* DEPRIVATION OF LIBERTY AND ARMED CONFLICTS: EXPLORING REALITIES AND REMEDIES 200 (Giorgio Battisti ed., 2018).

Gilbert Guillaume, *Overview of Part One of the Articles on State Responsibility*, *in* THE LAW OF INTERNATIONAL RESPONSIBILITY 187 (James Crawford et al. eds., 2010).

Knut Ipsen, *Combatants and Non-Combatants*, *in* THE HANDBOOK OF INTERNATIONAL HUMANITARIAN LAW 85 (Dieter Fleck ed., 2008).

Alexander Kees, *Responsibility of States for Private Actors*, *in* MAX PLANCK ENCYCLOPEDIA OF PUBLIC INT'L L. (Rüdiger Wolfrum ed., 2011).

Jan Klabbers, *(I Can't Get No) Recognition: Subjects Doctrine and the Emergence of Non-State Actors*, *in* NORDIC COSMOPOLITANISM: ESSAYS IN INTERNATIONAL LAW FOR MARTTI KOSKENNIEMI 365 (Jarna Petman & Jan Klabbers eds., 2003).

Jann K. Kleffner, *The Collective Accountability of Organized Armed Groups for System Crimes*, *in* SYSTEM CRIMINALITY IN INTERNATIONAL LAW 238 (André Nollkaemper & Harmen Van Der Wilt eds., 2009).

Nikolay Koval, *Revolution Hacking*, *in* CYBER WAR IN PERSPECTIVE: RUSSIAN AGGRESSION AGAINST UKRAINE 55 (Kenneth Geers ed., 2015).

Lucie Laithier, *Private Codification Efforts*, *in* THE LAW OF INTERNATIONAL RESPONSIBILITY 53 (James Crawford et al. eds., 2010).

Franck Latty, *Actions and Omissions*, *in* THE LAW OF INTERNATIONAL RESPONSIBILITY 355 (James Crawford et al. eds., 2010).

Chia Lehnardt, *Private Military Companies and State Responsibility*, *in* FROM MERCENARIES TO MARKET: THE RISE AND REGULATION OF PRIVATE MILITARY COMPANIES 139 (Simon Chesterton & Chia Lehnardt eds., 2007).

Tim Maurer, *Cyber Proxies and the Crisis in Ukraine*, *in* CYBER WAR IN PERSPECTIVE: RUSSIAN AGGRESSION AGAINST UKRAINE 85 (Kenneth Geers ed., 2015).

Djamchid Momtaz, *Attribution of Conduct to the State: State Organs and Entities Empowered to Exercise Elements of Governmental Authority*, *in* THE LAW OF INTERNATIONAL RESPONSIBILITY 237 (James Crawford et al. eds., 2010).

Nwamaka R. Okany, *State Delegation of Functions to Private and Autonomous Entities: A Basis for Attribution Under the Rules of State Responsibility*, *in* State Responsibility and the Individual 327 (Kalliopi Koufa ed., 2006).

Christopher Paul et al., *Angolan Independence, 1961-1974*, *in* Paths to Victory: Detailed Insurgency Case Studies 226 (2013).

Marco Sassòli, *The Legal Qualification of the Conflict in the Former Yugoslavia: Double Standards or New Horizons for International Humanitarian Law? in* International Law in the Post-Cold War World: Essays in Memory of Li Haopei 307 (Sienho Yee & Wang Tieya eds., 2001).

Brigitte Stern, *The Elements of an Internationally Wrongful Act*, *in* The Law of International Responsibility 193 (James Crawford et al. eds., 2010).

Manuel J. Ventura, *Two Controversies in the Lubanga Trial Judgment of the ICC: The Nature of Co-Perpetration's Common Plan and the Classification of the Armed Conflict*, *in* The War Report 2012 (Stuart Casey-Maslen ed., 2013).

Sten I. Verhoeven, *International Responsibility of Armed Opposition Groups*, *in* Responsibilities of the Non-State Actor in Armed Conflict and the Market Place: Theoretical Considerations and Empirical Findings 285 (Noemi Gal-Or et al. eds., 2015).

Articles

Michael Akehurst, *State Responsibility for the Wrongful Acts of Rebels—An Aspect of the Southern Rhodesian Problem*, 43 Brit. Y.B. Int'l L. 49 (1968–1969).

Philip Allott, *State Responsibility and the Unmaking of International Law*, 29 Harv. Int'l L.J. 1 (1988).

William Banks, *State Responsibility and Attribution of Cyber Intrusions after Tallinn 2.0*, 95 Tex. L. Rev. 1487 (2017).

William Banks, *Cyber Attribution and State Responsibility*, 97 Int'l L. Stud. 1039 (2021).

Gregory Raymond Bart, *Special Operations Forces and Responsibility for Surrogates' War Crimes*, 5 Harv. Nat'l Sec. J. 513 (2014).

Veronika Bílková, *Armed Opposition Groups and Shared Responsibility*, 62 Netherlands Int'l L. Rev. 69 (2015).

Daniel M. Bodansky & John R. Crook, *Symposium on the ILC's State Responsibility Articles: Introduction and Overview*, 96 Am. J. Int'l L. 773 (2002).

Alexandra Boivin, *Complicity and Beyond: International Law and the Transfer of Small Arms and Light Weapons*, 87 Int'l Rev. Red Cross 467 (2005).

Bill Boothby, *"And for Such Time As": The Time Dimension to Direct Participation in Hostilities*, 42 N.Y.U. J. Int'l L. & Pol. 741 (2010).

Fernando Lusa Bordin, *Reflections of Customary International Law: The Authority of Codification Conventions and ILC Draft Articles in International Law*, 63 Int'l & Comp. L.Q. 535 (2014).

Francis A. Boyle, *Determining U.S. Responsibility for Contra Operations Under International Law*, 81 Am. J. Int'l L. 86 (1987).

Michael Byers, *Terrorism, the Use of Force and International Law After 11 September*, 51 Int'l & Comp. L.Q. 401 (2002).

Jeremiah Bvirindi, *Angolan Conflict Analysis: A Lesson for Africa's Emerging Leaders*, 3 Int'l J. Res. & Innovation in Soc. Sci. 2454 (July 2019).

David D. Caron, *The ILC Articles on State Responsibility: The Paradoxical Relationship Between Form and Authority*, 96 Am. J. Int'l L. 857 (2002).

Djemila Carron, *When Is a Conflict International? Time for New Control Tests in IHL*, 98 INT'L REV. RED CROSS 1019 (2016).

Antonio Cassese, *The* Nicaragua *and* Tadić *Tests Revisited in Light of the ICJ Judgment on Genocide in Bosnia*, 18 EUR. J. INT'L L. 649 (2007).

Christine Chinkin, *A Critique of the Public/Private Dimension*, 10 EUR. J. INT'L L. 387 (1999).

Luke Chircop, *A Due Diligence Standard of Attribution in Cyberspace*, 67 INT'L & COMP. L.Q. 643 (2018).

Danwood M. Chirwa, *The Doctrine of State Responsibility as a Potential Means of Holding Private Actors Accountable for Human Rights*, 5 MELBOURNE J. INT'L L. 1 (2004).

Gordon Christenson, *Attributing Acts of Omission to the State*, 12 MICH. J. INT'L L. 312 (1991).

Andrew Clapham, *Human Rights Obligations of Non-State Actors in Conflict Situations*, 88 INT'L REV. RED CROSS 491 (2006).

Luigi Condorelli, *The Imputability to States of Acts of International Terrorism*, 19 ISRAEL Y.B. HUM. RTS. 233 (1989).

Geoffrey S. Corn, *Contemplating the True Nature of the Notion of "Responsibility" in Responsible Command*, 96 INT'L REV. RED CROSS 901 (2015).

Olivier Corten, *L'Arrêt rendu par la CIJ dans l'affaire du Crime de génocide (Bosnie-Herzégovine c. Serbie): Vers un assouplissement des conditions permettant d'engager la responsabilité d'un État pour génocide?* 53 ANNUAIRE FRANÇAIS DE DROIT INT'L 249 (2007).

Olivier Corten & François Dubuisson, *Operation "Liberté Immuable": Une Extension Abusive de Concept de Légitime Defense*, 106 REVUE GENERAL DE DROIT INTERNATIONAL PUBLIC 51 (2002).

Olivier Corten & Vaios Koutroulis, *The Illegality of Military Support to Rebels in the Libyan War: Aspects of the Jus Contra Bellum and Jus in Bello*, 18 J. CONFLICT & SEC. L. 59 (2013).

James Crawford, *Revising the Draft Articles on State Responsibility*, 10 EUR. J. INT'L L. 435 (1999).

James Crawford, *The ILC's Articles on Responsibility of States for Internationally Wrongful Acts: A Retrospect*, 96 AM. J. INT'L L. 874 (2002).

James Crawford & Simon Olleson, *The Continuing Debate on a U.N. Convention on State Responsibility*, 54 INT'L & COMP. L.Q. 959 (2005).

Graham Cronogue, *Rebels, Negligent Support, and State Accountability: Holding States Accountable for the Human Rights Violations of Non-State Actors*, 23 DUKE J. COMP. & INT'L L. 365 (2013).

Wladyslaw Czaplinski, *State Succession and State Responsibility*, 28 CANADIAN Y.B. INT'L L. 339 (1990).

Tom Dannenbaum, *Translating the Standard of Effective Control into a System of Effective Accountability: How Liability Should Be Apportioned for Violations of Human Rights by Member State Troop Contingents Serving as United Nations Peacekeepers*, 51 HARV. INT'L L.J. 113 (2010).

Jean d'Aspremont, *Rebellion and State Responsibility: Wrongdoing by Democratically Elected Insurgents*, 58 INT'L & COMP. L.Q. 427 (2009).

Jean d'Aspremont et al., *Sharing Responsibility Between Non-State Actors and States in International Law: Introduction*, 62 NETHERLANDS INT'L L. REV. 49 (2015).

J. Scott Davidson, *The Rainbow Warrior Arbitration Concerning the Treatment of the French Agents Mafart and Prieur*, 40 INT'L & COMP. L.Q. 446 (1991).

André J. J. de Hoogh, *Articles 4 and 8 of the 2001 ILC Articles on State Responsibility, The* Tadić *Case and Attribution of Acts of Bosnian Serb Authorities to the Federal Republic of Yugoslavia*, 72 Brit. Y.B. Int'l L. 255 (2002).

Katherine Del Mar, *The Requirement of "Belonging" Under International Humanitarian Law*, 21 Eur. J. Int'l L. 105 (2010).

Vojin Dimitrijević & Marko Milanović, *The Strange Story of the Bosnian Genocide Case*, 21 Leiden J. Int'l L. 65 (2008).

Patrick Dumberry, *New State Responsibility for Internationally Wrongful Acts by an Insurrectional Movement*, 17 Eur. J. Int'l L. 605 (2006).

Patrick Dumberry, *Turkey's International Responsibility for Internationally Wrongful Acts Committed by the Ottoman Empire*, 42 Revue Générale de Droit 561 (2012).

Pierre-Marie Dupuy, *Dionisio Anzilotti and the Law of International Responsibility of States*, 3 Eur. J. Int'l L. 139 (1992).

Kristen E. Eichensehr, *The Law and Politics of Cyberattack Attribution*, 67 UCLA L. Rev. 520 (2020).

Mohamed A. El-Khawas, *Tunisia's Jasmine Revolution: Causes and Impact*, 23 Mediterranean Q. 1 (2012).

Tristan Ferraro, *The ICRC's Legal Position on the Notion of Armed Conflict Involving Foreign Intervention and on Determining the IHL Applicable to This Type of Conflict*, 97 Int'l Rev. Red Cross 1227 (2015).

Georgio Gaja, *Interpreting Articles Adopted by the International Law Commission*, 85 Brit. Y.B. Int'l L. 10 (2015).

Tom Gal, *Unexplored Outcomes of* Tadić, 12 J. Int'l Crim. Just. 59 (2014).

Eyassu Gayim, *Reflections on the Draft Articles of the International Law Commission on State Responsibility: Articles 14; 15; & 19, in the Context of the Contemporary International Law of Self-Determination*, 54 Nordic J. Int'l L. 85 (1985).

Mark Gibney, *Genocide and State Responsibility*, 7 Hum. Rts. L. Rev. 760 (2007).

Mark Gibney et al., *Transnational State Responsibility for Violations of Human Rights* 12 Harv. Hum. Rts. J. 267 (1999).

Bernhard Graefrath, *Complicity in the Law of International Responsibility*, 29 Revue Belge de Droit Int'l 370 (1996).

Jörn Griebel & Milan Plücken, *New Developments Regarding the Rules of Attribution? The International Court of Justice's Decision in Bosnia v Serbia*, 21 Leiden J. Int'l L. 601 (2008).

Patycja Grzebyk, *Classification of the Conflict between Ukraine and Russia in International Law (Ius ad Bellum and Ius in Bello)*, 34 Polish Y.B. Int'l L. 39 (2015).

Monika Hakimi, *State Bystander Responsibility*, 21 Eur. J. Int'l L. 341 (2010).

Monica Hakimi, *Toward a Legal Theory on the Responsibility to Protect*, 39 Yale J. Int'l L. 247 (2014).

Helena Harrison et al., *Case Study Research: Foundations and Methodological Orientations*, 18 F.: Qualitative Soc. Res. 1 (2017).

Oona A. Hathaway et al., *Ensuring Responsibility: Common Article 1 and State Responsibility for Non-State Actors*, 95 Tex. L. Rev. 539 (2017).

Ezequiel Heffes & Brian E. Frenkel, *The International Responsibility of Non-State Armed Groups: In Search of the Applicable Rules*, 8 Göttingen J. Int'l L. 39 (2017).

Robert Heinsch, *Conflict Classification in Ukraine: The Return of the "Proxy War"?* 91 Int'l L. Stud. 323 (2015).

Jan Arno Hessbruegge, *The Historical Development of the Doctrines of Attribution and Due Diligence in International Law*, 36 N.Y.U. J. INT'L L. & POL. 265 (2004).

Jan Arno Hessbruegge, *Human Rights Violations Arising from Conduct of Non-State Actors*, 11 BUFF. HUM. RTS. L. REV. 21 (2005).

Christian Hillgruber, *The Admission of New States to the International Community*, 9 EUR. J. INT'L L. 491 (1998).

Carsten Hoppe, *Passing the Buck: State Responsibility for Private Military Companies*, 19 EUR. J. INT'L L. 989 (2008).

Michael Hurst, *After Blackwater: A Mission-Focused Jurisdictional Regime for Private Military Contractors during Contingency Operations*, 76 GEO. WASH. L. REV. 1308 (2008).

Terry Hutchinson & Nigel Duncan, *Defining and Describing What We Do: Doctrinal Legal Research*, 17 DEAKIN L. REV. 83 (2012).

Kushtrim Istrefi & Cedric Ryngaert, *Makuchyan and Minasyan v Azerbaijan and Hungary: Novel Questions of State Responsibility, Presidential Pardon, and Due Diligence of Sentencing Transfer Meet in a Rare Case of the Right to Life*, 3 ECHR L. REV. 263 (2021).

Mohamad Ghazi Janaby, *The Legal Status of Hezbollah in the Syrian Conflict: An International Humanitarian Perspective*, 33 ARIZ. J. INT'L & COMP. L. 383 (2016).

Derek Jinks, *State Responsibility for the Acts of Private Armed Groups*, 4 CHI. J. INT'L L. 83 (2003).

Oliver R. Jones, *Implausible Deniability: State Responsibility for the Actions of Private Military Firms*, 24 CONN. J. INT'L L. 239 (2009).

Remy Jorritsma, *Where General International Law Meets International Humanitarian Law: Attribution of Conduct and the Classification of Armed Conflicts*, 23 J. CONFLICT & SEC. L. 405 (2018).

Ilmari Käihkö, *A Nation in the Making, in Arms: Control of Force, Strategy and the Ukrainian Volunteer Battalions*, 18 DEF. STUD. 147 (2018).

Frits Kalshoven, *State Responsibility for Warlike Acts of the Armed Forces: From Article 3 of Hague Convention IV of 1907 to Article 91 of Additional Protocol I of 1977 and Beyond*, 40 INT'L & COMP. L.Q. 827 (1991).

Menno T. Kamminga, *State Succession in Respect of Human Rights Treaties*, 7 EUR. J. INT'L L. 496 (1996).

Dayna L. Kaufman, *Don't Do What I Say, Do What I Mean!: Assessing a State's Responsibility for the Exploits of Individuals Acting in Conformity with a Statement from a Head of State*, 70 FORDHAM L. REV. 2603 (2002).

Emizet F. Kisangani, *Conflict in the Democratic Republic of Congo: A Mosaic of Insurgent Groups*, 20 INT'L J. WORLD PEACE 51 (2003).

Jeppe Mejer Kjelgaard & Ulf Melgaard, *Denmark's Position Paper on the Application of International Law in Cyberspace*, 92 NORDIC J. INT'L L. 446 (2023).

Jann Kleffner, *The Applicability of International Humanitarian Law to Organized Armed Groups*, 93 INT'L REV. RED CROSS 443 (2011).

Alexis P. Kontos, *"Private" Security Guards: Privatized Force and State Responsibility under International Human Rights Law*, 4 NON-STATE ACTORS & INT'L L. 199 (2004).

Michal Kowalski, *Armed Attack, Non-State Actors and a Quest for the Attribution Standard*, 30 POLISH Y.B. INT'L L. 101 (2010).

Claus Kress, *L'Organe de facto en Droit International Public: Réflexions sur l'Imputation a l'État de l'Acte d'un Particulier à la Lumière des Développements Récents*, 105 REVUE GÉNÉRALE DE DROIT INTERNATIONAL PUBLIC 93 (2001).

Andreas Krieg, *Externalising the Burden of War: The Obama Doctrine and U.S. Foreign Policy in the Middle East*, 92 INT'L AFFAIRS 97 (2016).

Andreas Krieg & Jean-Marc Rickli, *Surrogate Warfare: The Art of War in the 21st Century?* 18 DEF. STUD. 113 (2018).

Vladislav Lanovoy, *The Use of Force by Non-State Actors and the Limits of Attribution of Conduct*, 28 EUR. J. INT'L L. 563 (2017).

Herbert Lin, *Attribution of Malicious Cyber Incidents: From Soup to Nuts*, 70 J. INT'L AFF. 75 (2016).

James R. Lisher, *Outsourcing Cyberwarfare: Drawing the Line for Inherently Governmental Functions in Cyberspace*, J. CONT. MGMT. 7 (FALL 2014).

Vaughan Lowe, *Responsibility for the Conduct of Other States*, 101 JAPANESE J. INT'L L. 1 (2002).

Kubo Mačák, *Decoding Article 8 of the International Law Commission's Articles on State Responsibility: Attribution of Cyber Operations by Non-State Actors*, 21 J. CONFLICT & SEC. L. 405 (2016).

Gurpreet Mahajan, *Reconsidering the Private-Public Distinction*, 12 CRITICAL REV. OF INT'L SOC. & POL. PHIL. 133 (2009).

Peter Margulies, *Sovereignty and Cyber Attacks: Technology's Challenge to the Law of State Responsibility*, 14 MELBOURNE J. INT'L L. 496 (2013).

Kimberley Marten, *Russia's Use of Semi-State Security Forces: The Case of the Wagner Group*, 35 POST-SOVIET AFF. 181 (2019).

Jenny S. Martinez, *Understanding Mens Rea in Command Responsibility: From* Yamashita *to* Blaškić *and Beyond*, 5 J. INT'L CRIM. JUST. 638 (2007).

Tim Maurer, *"Proxies" and Cyberspace*, 21 J. CONFLICT & SEC. L. 383 (2016).

Conor McCarthy, *Victim Redress and International Criminal Justice: Competing Paradigms, or Compatible Forms of Justice?*, 10 J. INT'L CRIM. JUST. 351 (2012).

Frédéric Mégret, *Are There "Inherently Sovereign Functions" in International Law?* 115 AM. J. INT'L L. 452 (2021).

Theodore Meron, *International Responsibility of States for Unauthorized Acts of Their Officials*, 33 BRIT. Y.B. INT'L L. 85 (1957).

Theodor Meron, *Classification of Armed Conflict in the Former Yugoslavia: Nicaragua's Fallout*, 92 AM. J. INT'L L. 235 (1998).

Marko Milanović, *State Responsibility for Genocide*, 17 EUR. J. INT'L L. 553 (2006).

Marko Milanović, *State Responsibility for Genocide: A Follow-Up*, 18 EUR. J. INT'L L. 669 (2007).

Marko Milanović, *From Compromise to Principle: Clarifying the Concept of State Jurisdiction in Human Rights Treaties*, 8 HUM. RTS. L. REV. 411 (2008).

Marko Milanović, *State Responsibility for Acts of Non-State Actors: A Comment on Griebel and Plücken*, 22 LEIDEN J. INT'L L. 307 (2009).

Marko Milanović, *Special Rules of Attribution of Conduct in International Law*, 96 INT'L L. STUD. 295 (2020).

Marko Milanović, *Intelligence Sharing in Multinational Military Operations and Complicity Under International Law*, 97 INT'L L. STUD. 1269 (2021).

Marko Milanović & Tatjana Papić, Makuchyan and Minasyan v. Azerbaijan and Hungary, 115 AM. J. INT'L L. 294 (2021).

Robert H. Mnookin, *The Public/Private Dichotomy: Political Disagreement and Academic Repudiation*, 130 U. PA. L. REV. 1429 (1982).

Harriet Moynihan, *Aiding and Assisting: The Mental Element under Article 16 of the International Law Commission's Articles on State Responsibility*, 67 Int'l & Comp. L.Q. 455 (2018).

Sean D. Murphy, *Terrorism and the Concept of "Armed Attack" in Article 51 of the U.N. Charter*, 43 Harv. Int'l L.J. 41 (2002).

Cathy Nangini et al., *Visualizing Armed Groups: The Democratic Republic of the Congo's M23 in Focus*, 3 Int'l J. Sec. & Dev. 1 (2014).

Virginia Newell & Benedict Sheehy, *Corporate Militaries and States: Actors, Interactions, and Reactions*, 41 Tex. Int'l L. J. 67 (2006).

Katja Nieminen, *Rules of Attribution and the Private Military Contractors at Abu Ghraib: Private Acts or Public Wrongs?* 15 Finnish Y.B Int'l L. 289 (2004).

Alan Nissel, *The ILC Articles on State Responsibility: Between Self-Help and Solidarity*, 38 N.Y.U. J. Int'l L. & Pol. 355 (2006).

André Nollkaemper & Dov Jacobs, *Shared Responsibility in International Law: A Conceptual Framework*, 34 Mich. J. Int'l L. 359 (2013).

André Nollkaemper et al., *Guiding Principles on Shared Responsibility in International Law*, 31 Eur. J. Int'l L. 15 (2020).

Georg Nolte & Helmut Aust, *Equivocal Helpers—Complicit States, Mixed Messages and International Law*, 58 Int'l & Comp. L.Q. 1 (2009).

Phoebe Okawa, *Congo's War: The Legal Dimension of a Protracted Conflict*, 77 Brit. Y.B. Int'l L. 203 (2006).

Simon Olleson, *Attribution in Investment Treaty Arbitration*, 31 I.C.S.I.D. Rev. 457 (2016).

Federica L. Paddeu, *To Convene or Not to Convene? The Future Status of the Articles on State Responsibility: Recent Developments*, 21 Max Planck Y.B. U.N. L. 83 (2018).

Martins Paparinskis, *The Once and Future Law of State Responsibility*, 114 Am. J. Int'l L. 618 (2020).

Riccardo Pisillo-Mazzeschi, *The Due Diligence Rule and the Nature of the International Responsibility of States*, 35 German Y.B. Int'l L. 9 (1992).

John Quigley, *State Responsibility for Ethnic Cleansing*, 32 U. California Davis L. Rev. 341 (1999).

Akbar Rasulov, *Revisiting State Succession to Humanitarian Treaties: Is There a Case for Automaticity?* 14 Eur. J. Int'l L. 141 (2003).

Shane R. Reeves & Ronald Alcala, *Five Legal Takeaways from the Syrian War*, Harv. Nat'l Sec. J. 1 (Sept. 30, 2019).

Shane R. Reeves & David Wallace, *The Combatant Status of the "Little Green Men" and Other Participants in the Ukraine Conflict*, 91 Int'l L. Stud. 361 (2015).

Kilian Roithmaier, *Holding States Responsible for Violations of International Humanitarian Law in Proxy Warfare: The Concept of State Complicity in Acts of Non-State Armed Groups*, 14 Eur. J. Legal Stud. 140 (2023).

Robert Rosenstock, *The ILC and State Responsibility*, 96 Am. J. Int'l L. 792 (2002).

Tom Ruys, *Crossing the Thin Blue Line: An Inquiry into Israel's Recourse to Self-Defense Against Hezbollah*, 43 Stan. J. Int'l L. 265 (2007).

Tom Ruys, *Of Arms, Funding and "Non-Lethal Assistance"—Issues Surrounding Third-State Intervention in the Syrian Civil War*, 13 Chinese J. Int'l L. 13 (2014).

Cedric Ryngaert & Sven Sobrie, *Recognition of States: International Law or Realpolitik? The Practice of Recognition in the Wake of Kosovo, South Ossetia, and Abkhazia*, 24 Leiden J. Int'l L. 467 (2011).

Idean Salehyan et al., *External Rebel Sponsorship and Civilian Abuse: A Principal-Agent Analysis of Wartime Atrocities*, 68 INT'L ORG. 633 (2014).

Pol Vila Sarriá & Agon Demjaha, *Kosovo-Spain Relations and the Dilemmas on the Problem of Non-Recognition*, 14 S.E. Eur. U. REV. 69 (2019).

Arman Sarvarian, *The Ossified Debate on a U.N. Convention on State Responsibility*, 70 INT'L & COMP. L.Q. 769 (2021).

Marco Sassòli, *State Responsibility for Violations of International Humanitarian Law*, 84 INT'L REV. RED CROSS, 401 (2002).

Marco Sassòli & Laura M. Olson, Prosecutor v. Tadić (Judgement) *Case No. IT-94-1-A 38 ILM 1518 (1999)*, 94 AM. J. INT'L L. 571 (2000).

Michael N. Schmitt, *Counter-Terrorism and the Use of Force in International Law*, 79 INT'L L. STUD. 7 (2003).

Michael N. Schmitt, *Deconstructing Direct Participation in Hostilities: The Constitutive Elements*, 42 N.Y.U. J. INT'L L. & POL. 697 (2010).

Michael N. Schmitt, *"Below the Threshold" Cyber Operations: The Countermeasures Response Option and International Law*, 54 VA. J. INT'L L. 697 (2014).

Michael N. Schmitt, *"Virtual" Disenfranchisement: Cyber Election Meddling in the Grey Zones of International Law*, 19 CHI. J. INT'L L. 30 (2018).

Michael N. Schmitt & Liis Vihul, *Proxy Wars in Cyberspace: The Evolving International Law of Attribution*, 1 FLETCHER SEC. REV. 54 (2014).

Michael N. Schmitt & Sean Watts, *Beyond State-Centrism: International Law and Non-State Actors in Cyberspace*, 21 J. CONFLICT & SEC. L. 595 (2016).

Michael N. Schmitt & Sean Watts, *Common Article 1 and the Duty to "Ensure Respect,"* 96 INT'L L. STUD. 674 (2021).

Scott J. Shackelford & Richard B. Andres, *State Responsibility for Cyber Attacks: Competing Standards for a Growing Problem*, 42 GA. J. INT'L L. 971 (2010).

Sandesh Sivakumaran, *Making and Shaping the Law of Armed Conflict*, 71 CURRENT LEGAL PROBS. 119 (2018).

Crispin Smith & Jacques Singer-Emery, *Servants of Two Masters: The Risks Inherent in Iraq's Hashd Al-Sha'abi Legislation*, 52 N.Y.U. J. INT'L L. & POL. 167 (2019).

Louis B. Sohn & R.R. Baxter, *Convention on the International Responsibility of States for Injuries to Aliens*, 55 AM. J. INT'L L. 548 (1961).

Marina Spinedi, *On the Non-Attribution of the Bosnian Serbs' Conduct to Serbia*, 5 J. INT'L CRIM. JUST. 829 (2007).

Stefan Talmon, *The Responsibility of Outside Powers for Acts of Secessionist Entities*, 58 INT'L & COMP. L.Q. 493 (2009).

Charles Tiefer, *No More Nisour Squares: Legal Control of Private Security Contractors in Iraq and After*, 88 ORE. L. REV. 745 (2009).

Dominic Tierney, *The Future of Sino-U.S. Proxy War*, 4 TEX. NAT'L SEC. REV. 50 (2021).

Gregory Townsend, *State Responsibility for Acts of De Facto Agents*, 14 ARIZ. J. INT'L & COMP. L. 635 (1997).

Nicholas Tsagourias, *Non-State Actors, Ungoverned Spaces and International Responsibility for Cyber Acts*, 21 J. CONFLICT & SEC. L. 455 (2016).

Nicholas Tsagourias & Michael Farrell, *Cyber Attribution: Technical and Legal Approaches and Challenges*, 31 EUR. J. INT'L L. 941 (2020).

Davis B. Tyner, *Internationalization of War Crimes Prosecutions: Correcting the International Criminal Tribunal for the Former Yugoslavia's Folly in Tadic*, 18 FLA. J. INT'L L. 843 (2006).

Elies van Sliedregt, *Command Responsibility and Cyberattacks*, 21 J. CONFLICT & SEC. L. 505 (2016).

Michael John Volkovitsch, *Righting Wrongs: Towards a New Theory of State Succession to Responsibility for International Delicts*, 92 COLUM. L. REV. 2162 (1992).

Joseph L. Votel & Eero R. Keravuori, *The By-With-Through Operational Approach*, JOINT FORCE Q. 89 (Apr. 12, 2018).

Edith Brown Weiss, *Invoking State Responsibility in the Twenty-First Century*, 96 AM. J. INT'L L. 798 (2002).

Nigel D. White, *Symposium of Frédéric Mégret, "Are There 'Inherently Sovereign Functions' in International Law?" Outsourcing Military and Security Functions*, 115 AM. J. INT'L L. UNBOUND 317 (2021).

Christopher Williams, *Explaining the Great War in Africa: How Conflict in the Congo Became a Continental Crisis*, 37 FLETCHER F. OF WORLD AFF. 81 (2013).

Lindsay Windsor, *James Bond, Inc.: Private Contractors and Covert Action*, 101 GEO. L.J. 1427 (2013).

James Kenneth Wither, *Back to the Future? Nordic Total Defence Concepts*, 20 DEF. STUD. 61 (2020).

Rűdiger Wolfrum & Christiane E. Philipp. *The Status of the Taliban: Their Obligations and Rights Under International Law*, 6 MAX PLANCK Y.B. U.N. LAW 559 (2002).

William T. Worster, *Law, Politics, and the Conception of the State in State Recognition Theory*, 27 B.U. INT'L L.J. 115 (2009).

Xingzhong Yu, *State Legalism and the Public/Private Divide in Chinese Legal Development*, 15 THEORETICAL INQUIRIES IN L. 27 (2014).

Sebghatullah Qazi Zada & Mohd Ziaolhaq Qazi Zaba, *The Taliban and Women's Human Rights in Afghanistan: The Way Forward*, 28 INT'L J. HUM. RTS. 1687 (2024).

SELECT GOVERNMENTAL DOCUMENTS

Ireland Dep't of Foreign Affairs, Position Paper on the Application of International Law in Cyberspace (July 6, 2023), https://dfa.ie/media/dfa/ourrolepolicies/internationallaw/Ireland---National-Position-Paper.pdf.

U.K. Government, Overseas Security and Justice Assistance (OSJA): Human Rights Guidance (2017), https://assets.publishing.service.gov.uk/government/uploads/system/uploads/attachment_data/file/583304/OSJA_Guidance_2017.pdf.

U.K. National Cyber Security Centre, Reckless Campaign of Cyber Attacks by Russian Military Intelligence Service Exposed (Oct. 3, 2018), www.ncsc.gov.uk/news/reckless-campaign-cyber-attacks-russian-military-intelligence-service-exposed.

U.S. Dep't of State, Draft Articles on State Responsibility: Comments of the Government of the United States of America (Mar. 1, 2001), https://2009-2017.state.gov/documents/organization/28993.pdf.

U.S. DEPUTY SECRETARY OF DEF., DIRECTIVE-TYPE MEMORANDUM 18-005 – AUTHORITY FOR SUPPORT OF SPECIAL OPERATIONS FOR IRREGULAR WARFARE (Aug. 3, 2018), https://fas.org/irp/doddir/dod/dtm-18-005.pdf.

NATO DOCUMENTS

Allied Joint Doctrine for the Conduct of Operations, AJP-3 (ed. C, version 1) (Feb. 2019), https://www.coemed.org/files/stanags/01_AJP/AJP-3_EDC_V1_E_2490.pdf.

ICRC Documents

Allies, Partners and Proxies: Managing Support Relationships in Armed Conflict to Reduce the Human Cost of War (Mar. 2021), www.icrc.org/en/publication/4498-allies-partners-and-proxies-managing-support-relationships-armed-conflict-reduce.

Commentary on the Additional Protocols of 8 June 1977 to the Geneva Conventions of 12 August 1949 (Yves Sandoz, Christophe Swinarski & Bruno Zimmermann eds., 1987).

Commentary on the First Geneva Convention: Convention (I) for the Amelioration of the Condition of the Wounded and Sick in the Armed Forces in the Field (2016).

Commentary on the Second Geneva Convention: Convention (II) for the Amelioration of the Condition of the Wounded, Sick and Shipwrecked Members of Armed Forces at Sea (2017).

Commentary on the Third Geneva Convention: Convention (III) Relative to the Treatment of Prisoners of War (2020).

Customary International Humanitarian Law (Jean-Marie Henckaerts & Louise Doswald-Beck eds., 2005).

Nils Melzer, Int'l Committee of the Red Cross, Interpretive Guidance on the Notion of Direct Participation in Hostilities under International Humanitarian Law 38 (May 2009), www.icrc.org/eng/assets/files/other/icrc-002-0990.pdf.

2024 Report on IHL and the Challenges of Contemporary Armed Conflicts (2024), https://www.icrc.org/en/report/2024-icrc-report-ihl-challenges.

The Roots of Restraint in War (Dec. 2018), www.icrc.org/en/publication/4352-roots-restraint-war.

Select Reports, Blogs, and Theses

A.B.A., Ctr. for Hum. Rts. & Rule of L. Initiative, The Legal Framework Regulating Proxy Warfare 16 (Dec. 2019), www.americanbar.org/content/dam/aba/administrative/human_rights/chr-proxy-warfare-report-2019.pdf.

Ali Alfoneh, *Tehran's Shia Foreign Legions*, Carnegie Endowment for Int'l Peace (Jan. 30, 2018), https://carnegieendowment.org/research/2018/01/tehrans-shia-foreign-legions?lang=en.

Amnesty Int'l, Ukraine: Mounting Evidence of War Crimes and Russian Involvement (Sept. 7, 2014), www.amnesty.org/en/latest/news/2014/09/ukraine-mounting-evidence-war-crimes-and-russian-involvement/.

Amnesty Int'l, Ukraine: Abuses and War Crimes by the Aidar Volunteer Battalion in the North Luhansk Region (Sept. 8, 2014), www.amnesty.org/en/documents/EUR50/040/2014/en/.

Amnesty Int'l, Ukraine: Horror of Civilian Bloodshed in Indiscriminate Attacks (Feb. 2, 2015), www.amnesty.org/en/press-releases/2015/02/ukraine-horror-civilian-bloodshed-indiscriminate-attacks/.

Amnesty Int'l, Iraq: Turning a Blind Eye: The Arming of the Popular Mobilization Units (2017), www.amnestyusa.org/files/iraq_report_turning_a_blind_eye.pdf.

Amnesty Int'l, Syria: Damning Evidence of War Crimes and Other Violations by Turkish Forces and their Allies (Oct. 18, 2019), https://www.amnesty.org/en/latest/press-release/2019/10/syria-damning-evidence-of-war-crimes-and-other-violations-by-turkish-forces-and-their-allies/.

Amnesty Int'l, DR Congo: Rwandan-Backed M23 Rebels Perpetrating Summary Killings and Rapes (Feb. 17, 2023), https://www.amnesty.org/en/latest/news/2023/02/dr-congo-rwandan-backed-m23-rebels-perpetrating-summary-killings-and-rapes/.

Amnesty Int'l, Syria: Aftermath: Injustice, Torture and Death in Detention in North-East Syria (Apr. 17, 2024), https://www.amnesty.org/en/documents/mde24/7752/2024/en/.

Maurizio Arcari, *The Future of the Articles on State Responsibility: A Matter of Form or of Substance?* Questions of Int'l L. (June 30, 2022).

Ryan Bauer & Erik E. Mueller, *Ukraine is a Breeding Group for Russian PMCs*, RAND (June 14, 2023), https://www.rand.org/pubs/commentary/2023/06/ukraine-is-a-breeding-ground-for-russian-pmcs.html.

Wolfgang Benedek et al., OSCE, Report on Violations of International Humanitarian and Human Rights Law, War Crimes and Crimes Against Humanity Committed in Ukraine Since 24 February 2022 (Apr. 13, 2022), https://www.osce.org/odihr/515868.

Christopher M. Blanchard & Amy Belasco, Cong. Res. Serv., Train and Equip Program for Syria: Authorities, Funding and Issues for Congress (June 9, 2015), https://fas.org/sgp/crs/natsec/R43727.pdf.

Nicholas Blanford, CTC Sentinel, The Battle for Qusayr: How the Syrian Regime and Hizb Allah Tipped the Balance (Aug. 2013), https://ctc.westpoint.edu/the-battle-for-qusayr-how-the-syrian-regime-and-hizb-allah-tipped-the-balance/.

Paul Bucala & Frederick W. Kagan, Iran's Evolving Way of War: How the IRGC Fights in Syria 12–13 (Mar. 2016), www.criticalthreats.org/wp-content/uploads/2016/07/imce-imagesIrans_Evolving_Way_of_War_IRGC_in_Syria_FINAL-1.pdf.

Daniel L. Byman, *Why Engage in Proxy War? A State's Perspective*, Brookings (May 21, 2018), www.brookings.edu/blog/order-from-chaos/2018/05/21/why-engage-in-proxy-war-a-states-perspective/.

Carter Ctr., Syria: Pro-Government Paramilitary Forces (Nov. 5, 2013), www.cartercenter.org/resources/pdfs/peace/conflict_resolution/syria-conflict/pro-governmentparamilitaryforces.pdf.

Ctr. for Civilians in Conflict, Nigerian Community Militias: Toward a Solution (Nov. 2019), https://civiliansinconflict.org/wp-content/uploads/2019/11/Issue-Brief_Africa_Final_Web.pdf.

Congo Res. Group, The Resurgence of the M23 (Aug. 2024), https://files.ebuteli.org/assets/9152943b-ca84-455d-8c00-a0f3e020cb1a.

Michael Connell & Sarah Vogler, CNA, Russia's Approach to Cyber Warfare (Mar. 2017), www.cna.org/cna_files/pdf/DOP-2016-U-014231-1Rev.pdf.

Counter Extremism Project, Hezbollah's Influence in Lebanon (Apr. 2018), www.counterextremism.com/sites/default/files/Hezbollah%20Influence%20in%20Lebanon_043018.pdf.

Maksymilian Czuperski et al., Atlantic Council, Hiding in Plain Sight: Putin's War in Ukraine (May 2015), www.atlanticcouncil.org/in-depth-research-reports/report/hiding-in-plain-sight/.

Ivo Daalder et al., Brookings, Preserving Ukraine's Independence, Resisting Russian Aggression: What the United States and NATO Must Do (Feb. 2015), www.brookings.edu/wp-content/uploads/2016/06/UkraineReport_February2015_FINAL.pdf.

Melissa Dalton et al., Ctr. for Strategic & Int'l Stud., Civilians and "By, With, and Through": Key Issues and Questions related to Civilian Harm and Security Partnership (Apr. 2018), www.csis.org/analysis/civilians-and-and-through.

Shane Darcy, *Confronting the Collaborators*, Opinio Juris (Nov. 7, 2022), http://opiniojuris.org/2022/11/07/confronting-the-collaborators/.

Marieke de Hoon, *Dutch Court, in Life Sentences: Russia Had "Overall Control" of Forces in Eastern Ukraine Downing of Flight MH 17*, Just Sec. (Dec. 19, 2022), https://www.justsecurity.org/84456/dutch-court-in-life-sentences-russia-had-overall-control-of-forces-in-eastern-ukraine-downing-of-flight-mh17/.

Thomas de Waal, Carnegie Europe, Uncertain Ground: Engaging with Europe's de facto States and Breakaway Territories (Dec. 3, 2018), https://carnegieeurope.eu/2018/12/03/uncertain-ground-engaging-with-europe-s-de-facto-states-and-breakaway-territories-pub-77823.

Tatyana Jane Eatwell, State Responsibility for the Unlawful Conduct of Armed Groups (Ph.D. thesis, University of Cambridge) (2019), www.repository.cam.ac.uk/bitstream/handle/1810/302004/Eatwell%20Thesis%20May%202020%20updated%20Electronic%20Final.pdf?sequence=8&isAllowed=y.

Erica L. Gaston, Ctr. for the Study of Armed Groups, Regulating Irregular Actors: Can Due Diligence Checks Mitigate the Risks of Working with Non-State and Substate Forces? (May 2021), https://odi.org/en/publications/regulating-irregular-actors-can-due-diligence-checks-mitigate-the-risks-of-working-with-non-state-and-substate-forces/.

Ryan Goodman, *Legal Limits on Military Assistance to Proxy Forces: Pathway for State and Official Responsibility*, Just Sec. (May 14, 2018), www.justsecurity.org/56272/legal-limits-military-assistance-proxy-forces-pathways-state-official-responsibility/.

Kathryn Greenman, *The Secret History of Successful Rebellions in the Law of State Responsibility*, 6 ESIL Reflections (2017), https://esil-sedi.eu/post_name-116/.

Tyrone Groh, *The Utility of Proxy War*, Lawfare (Apr. 28, 2019), www.lawfareblog.com/utility-proxy-war.

Kumaravadivel Guruparan & Jennifer Zerk, *Influence of Soft Law Grows in International Governance*, Chatham House (June 17, 2021), www.chathamhouse.org/2021/06/influence-soft-law-grows-international-governance.

Sam Heller, *Turkey's "Turkey First" Syria Policy*, Century Found. (Apr. 12, 2017), https://tcf.org/content/report/turkeys-turkey-first-syria-policy/.

Franklin Holcomb, Inst. for the Study of War, The Kremlin's Irregular Army: Ukrainian Separatist Order of Battle (Sept. 2017), https://www.understandingwar.org/backgrounder/kremlin%E2%80%99s-irregular-army-ukrainian-separatist-order-battle.

Joseph Holliday, Inst. for the Study of War, Syria's Armed Opposition (Mar. 2012), www.understandingwar.org/sites/default/files/Syrias_Armed_Opposition.pdf.

Travis L. Homiak, Joint Special Operations U. Rep. 09-3, Expanding the American Way of War: Working "Through, With, or By" Non-U.S. Actors (Feb. 2009).

Hum. Rts. Watch, M23 Rebels Kill, Rape Civilians (July 22, 2013), https://www.hrw.org/news/2013/07/22/dr-congo-m23-rebels-kill-rape-civilians.

Hum. Rts. Watch, "No One's Left": Summary Executions by Syrian Forces in al-Bayda and Baniyas (Sept. 13, 2013), www.hrw.org/report/2013/09/13/no-ones-left/summary-executions-syrian-forces-al-bayda-and-baniyas.

Hum. Rts Watch, Northeast Syria: Boys, Men Held in Inhumane Conditions (Oct. 8, 2019), www.hrw.org/news/2019/10/08/northeast-syria-boys-men-held-inhumane-conditions.

Hum. Rts. Watch, Central African Republic: Abuses by Russia-Linked Forces (May 3, 2022), https://www.hrw.org/news/2022/05/03/central-african-republic-abuses-russia-linked-forces.

Int'l Crisis Group, Russian and the Separatists in Eastern Ukraine (Feb. 5, 2016), https://www.crisisgroup.org/europe-central-asia/eastern-europe/ukraine/russia-and-separatists-eastern-ukraine.

Int'l Inst. for Strategic Stud., Iran's Networks of Influence in the Middle East (Nov. 2019), https://www.iiss.org/publications/strategic-dossiers/iran-dossier/.

Faysal Itani & Aaron Stein, Atlantic Council, Turkey's Syria Predicament (May 2016), https://www.atlanticcouncil.org/in-depth-research-reports/issue-brief/turkey-s-syria-predicament/.

Brian M. Jenkins, RAND, The Dynamics of Syria's Civil War (2014), www.rand.org/pubs/perspectives/PE115.html.

Donald N. Jensen, NATO Defence College, Moscow in the Donbas: Command, Control, Crime and the Minsk Peace Process (Mar. 2017), www.ndc.nato.int/news/news.php?icode=1029.

Seth G. Jones, *The Future of Competition: U.S. Adversaries and the Growth of Irregular Warfare*, Ctr. for Strategic & Int'l Stud. (Feb. 4, 2021), www.csis.org/analysis/future-competition-us-adversaries-and-growth-irregular-warfare.

Rana Khalaf, Chatham House, Governing Rojava: Layers of Legitimacy in Syria (Dec. 2016), https://www.chathamhouse.org/sites/default/files/publications/research/2016-12-08-governing-rojava-khalaf.pdf.

Michael Knights, *Iran's Foreign Legion: The Role of Iraqi Shiite Militias in Syria*, Wash. Inst. (June 27, 2013), www.washingtoninstitute.org/policy-analysis/irans-foreign-legion-role-iraqi-shiite-militias-syria.

Michael Knights, *The Houthi War Machine: From Guerrilla War to State Capture*, CTC Sentinel (Sept. 2018), https://ctc.usma.edu/houthi-war-machine-guerrilla-war-state-capture/.

Michael Kofman et al., RAND, Lessons from Russia's Operations in Crimea and Eastern Ukraine (2017), www.rand.org/content/dam/rand/pubs/research_reports/RR1400/RR1498/RAND_RR1498.pdf.

Matthew Levitt, *Waking Up the Neighbors: How Regional Intervention is Transforming Hezbollah*, Wash. Inst. (July 23, 2015), www.washingtoninstitute.org/policy-analysis/view/waking-up-the-neighbors-how-regional-intervention-is-transforming-hezbollah.

Itamar Lifshitz & Ayal Meents, *The Paradox of Precision: Nonstate Actors and Precision-Guided Weapons*, War on the Rocks (Nov. 17, 2020), https://warontherocks.com/2020/11/the-paradox-of-precision-nonstate-actors-and-precision-guided-weapons/.

Charles Lister, Brookings, The Free Syrian Army: A Decentralized Insurgent Brand (Nov 2016), www.brookings.edu/wp-content/uploads/2016/11/iwr_20161123_free_syrian_army.pdf.

Robert Lowe, LSE Middle East Centre, Rojava at 4: Examining the Experiment in Western Kurdistan (Aug. 2016), https://eprints.lse.ac.uk/67515/1/Rojavaat4.pdf.

Aron Lund, *Origins of the Syrian Democratic Forces: A Primer*, New Humanitarian (Jan. 22, 2016), https://deeply.thenewhumanitarian.org/syria/articles/2016/01/22/origins-of-the-syrian-democratic-forces-a-primer.

Jennifer Maddocks, *Russia, The Wagner Group, and the Issue of Attribution*, Articles of War (Apr. 28, 2021), https://lieber.westpoint.edu/russia-wagner-group-attribution/.

Jennifer Maddocks, *Does Russia Exercise Overall Control Over the Wagner Group? Expert Q&A from Stockton Center's Russia-Ukraine Conference*, Just Sec. (Apr. 5, 2023), https://www.justsecurity.org/85819/does-russia-exercise-overall-control-over-the-wagner-group-expert-qa-from-stockton-centers-russia-ukraine-conference/.

Jennifer Maddocks, *Putin Admits to Funding the Wagner Group: Implications for Russia's State Responsibility*, Articles of War (June 30, 2023), https://lieber.westpoint.edu/putin-admits-funding-wagner-group-implications-russias-state-responsibility/.

Jennifer Maddocks, *Israel-Hamas 2023 Symposium – Iran's Responsibility for the Attack on Israel*, Articles of War (Oct. 20, 2023), https://lieber.westpoint.edu/irans-responsibility-attack-israel/.

Jennifer Maddocks, *ISIS Detentions in Syria and the Responsibility of Supporting States*, Articles of War (Aug. 16, 2024), https://lieber.westpoint.edu/isis-detentions-syria-responsibility-supporting-states/.

Daniel R. Mahanty & Elias Youssef, Ctr. for Civilians in Conflict, Exception(s) to the Rule(s): Civilian Harm, Oversight, and Accountability in the Shadow Wars (Nov. 2020), www.stimson.org/wp-content/uploads/2020/11/CIVIC_US_Report_ETR-FINAL1.pdf.

Javier Martín, Libya: The First Totally Privatized War in Modern History (2020), www.ohchr.org/Documents/issues/Mercenaries/WG/OtherStakeholders/shockmonitor_submission.pdf.

Sean McFate, Mercenaries and War: Understanding Private Armies Today (Dec. 2019), https://apps.dtic.mil/sti/pdfs/AD1115550.pdf.

Marko Milanović, *The Tricky Question of State Succession to International Responsibility*, EJIL: Talk! (Feb. 16, 2009), www.ejiltalk.org/the-tricky-question-of-state-succession-to-international-responsibility/.

Marko Milanović, *The Netherlands and Australia Attribute the Downing of MH17 to Russia*, EJIL:Talk! (May 25, 2018), www.ejiltalk.org/the-netherlands-and-australia-attribute-the-downing-of-mh17-to-russia/.

Marko Milanović, *Attribution, Jurisdiction, Discrimination, Decapitation: A Comment on Makuchyan and Minsyan v. Azerbaijan and Hungary*, EJIL:Talk! (July 10, 2020), https://www.ejiltalk.org/attribution-jurisdiction-discrimination-decapitation-a-comment-on-makuchyan-and-minasyan-v-azerbaijan-and-hungary/.

Marko Milanović, *Common Article 1 Does Prohibit Complicity in IHL Violations, Through Arms Transfers or Otherwise*, EJIL:Talk! (Apr. 15, 2024), https://www.ejiltalk.org/common-article-1-does-prohibit-complicity-in-ihl-violations-through-arms-transfers-or-otherwise/.

Vincent L. Morelli, Cong. Res. Serv., Ukraine: Current Issues and U.S. Policy (Jan. 3, 2017), https://fas.org/sgp/crs/row/RL33460.pdf.

Moscow Mechanism Mission of Experts, OSCE, Report on Violations of International Humanitarian and Human Rights Law, War Crimes and Crimes Against Humanity Committed in Ukraine (1 April – 25 June 2022) (July 14, 2022), https://www.osce.org/odihr/522616.

Garrett Nada & Mattisan Rowan, *Pro-Iran Militias in Iraq*, U.S. Inst. for Peace (Nov. 10, 2021), https://iranprimer.usip.org/blog/2021/nov/10/profiles-pro-iran-militias-iraq.

Farzin Nadimi, *Iran's Afghan and Pakistani Proxies: In Syria and Beyond?* Wash. Inst. (Aug. 22, 2016), www.washingtoninstitute.org/policy-analysis/irans-afghan-and-pakistani-proxies-syria-and-beyond.

Richard D. Newton, Joint Special Operations U. Rep. 09-3, The Seeds of Surrogate Warfare (Feb. 2009).

Elizabeth O'Bagy, Inst. for the Study of War, The Free Syrian Army (Mar. 2013), www.understandingwar.org/sites/default/files/The-Free-Syrian-Army-24MAR.pdf.

Simon Olleson, Brit. Inst. Int'l & Comp. L., The Impact of the ILC's Articles on Responsibility of States for Internationally Wrongful Acts (Oct. 10, 2007), www.biicl.org/files/3107_impactofthearticlesonstate_responsibilitypreliminarydraftfinal.pdf.

Marcel Plichta et al., *The Wagner Group Lives on in Africa*, Lawfare (July 21, 2024), https://www.lawfaremedia.org/article/the-wagner-group-lives-on-in-africa.

Nadav Pollak, Wash. Inst., The Transformation of Hezbollah by its Involvement in Syria (Aug. 4, 2016), www.washingtoninstitute.org/policy-analysis/transformation-hezbollah-its-involvement-syria.

Rosaria Puglisi, Istituto Affari Internazionali, Heroes or Villains? Volunteer Battalions in Post-Maidan Ukraine (Mar. 8, 2015), www.iai.it/sites/default/files/iaiwp1508.pdf.

Ian Ralby & Hannah Tonkin, Chatham House, Regulation of Private Military Security Companies in Armed Conflict (2011), www.chathamhouse.org/sites/files/chathamhouse/public/Research/International%20Law/071011ralby%26tonkin.pdf.

Nathaniel Reynolds, *Putin's Not-So-Secret Mercenaries: Patronage, Geopolitics, and the Wagner Group*, Carnegie Endowment for Int'l Peace (July 8, 2019), https://carnegieendowment.org/2019/07/08/putin-s-not-so-secret-mercenaries-patronage-geopolitics-and-wagner-group-pub-79442.

Candace Rondeaux, *Decoding the Wagner Group: Analyzing the Role of Private Military Security Contractors in Russian Proxy Warfare*, New America (Nov. 7, 2019), https://www.newamerica.org/future-security/reports/decoding-wagner-group-analyzing-role-private-military-security-contractors-russian-proxy-warfare/.

William Rosenau & Zack Gold, CNA, "The Cheapest Insurance in the World"? The United States and Proxy Warfare (July 2019), www.cna.org/CNA_files/PDF/DRM-2019-U-020227-1Rev.pdf.

Robert Rotberg, *Failed States, Collapsed States, and Weak States: Causes and Indicators*, Wilson Ctr. (July 7, 2011), www.wilsoncenter.org/publication/failed-states-collapsed-states-and-weak-states-causes-and-indicators.

Michael Schmitt & Jeffrey Biller, *The NotPetya Cyber Operation as a Case Study of International Law*, EJIL:Talk! (July 11, 2017), www.ejiltalk.org/the-notpetya-cyber-operation-as-a-case-study-of-international-law/#more-15401.

Phillip Smyth, *Iran's Afghan Shiite Fighters in Syria*, Wash. Inst. (Jun. 3, 2014), https://www.washingtoninstitute.org/policy-analysis/irans-afghan-shiite-fighters-syria.

Jason Stearns, Rift Valley Inst., From CNDP to M23: The Evolution of an Armed Movement in Eastern Congo (2012), https://riftvalley.net/wp-content/uploads/2018/06/RVI-Usalama-Project-1-CNDP-M23.pdf.

Aaron Stein, Atlantic Council, Partner Operations in Syria (July 2017), www.atlanticcouncil.org/in-depth-research-reports/report/partner-operations-in-syria/.

Marisa Sullivan, Inst. for the Study of War, Hezbollah in Syria (Apr. 2014), http://www.understandingwar.org/sites/default/files/Hezbollah_Sullivan_FINAL.pdf.

Igor Sutyagin, Royal United Servs. Inst., Russian Forces in Ukraine (Mar. 2015), https://rusi.org/sites/default/files/201503_bp_russian_forces_in_ukraine.pdf.

Ariane Tabatabai, *The Fruits of Iran's Victory in Syria*, Lawfare (Apr. 15, 2018), www.lawfareblog.com/fruits-irans-victory-syria.

Ariane M. Tabatabai et al., RAND, The Iran Threat Network: Four Models of Iran's Nonstate Client Partnerships (2021), www.rand.org/pubs/research_reports/RR4231.html.

Eneken Tikk et al., International Cyber Incidents: Legal Considerations (2010), https://ccdcoe.org/publications/books/legalconsiderations.pdf.

U. Ctr. for Int'l Humanitarian L., Expert Meeting on Private Military Contractors: Status and State Responsibility for their Actions (Aug. 29–30, 2005), www.ucihl.org/communication/Private_Military_Companies_report.pdf.

Tom Uren, *Russia's GRU Thugs Double Down on Recruiting Cybercrooks*, Lawfare (Oct. 18, 2024), https://www.lawfaremedia.org/article/russia's-gru-thugs-double-down-on-recruiting-cybercrooks.

Constantijn van Aartsen, *The End of the Public-Private Divide*, Maastricht U. (Sept. 14, 2016), www.maastrichtuniversity.nl/blog/2016/09/end-public-private-divide.

Jack Watling, Royal United Servs. Inst., Iran's Objectives and Capabilities: Deterrence and Subversion (Feb. 2019), https://rusi.org/explore-our-research/publications/occasional-papers/irans-objectives-and-capabilities-deterrence-and-subversion.

Jack Watling & Nick Reynolds, Royal United Servs. Inst., War by Others' Means (2020).

Sean Watts, *Are Molotov Cocktails Lawful Weapons?* Articles of War (Mar. 2, 2022), https://lieber.westpoint.edu/are-molotov-cocktails-lawful-weapons/.

Philippa Westling, The Past Is a Foreign Country: An Examination of the Retrospective Attribution of Organized Armed Groups According to Article 10 of ARSIWA (Bachelor's thesis, Swedish Defence University) (2022), https://fhs.diva-portal.org/smash/get/diva2:1636844/FULLTEXT01.pdf.

Jeffrey White, *Hezbollah's Declaration of War in Syria: Military Implications*, Wash. Inst. (May. 29, 2013), www.washingtoninstitute.org/policy-analysis/view/hezbollahs-declaration-of-war-in-syria-military-implications.

Steven Woehrel, Cong. Res. Serv., Ukraine: Current Issues and U.S. Policy (Mar. 24, 2014) https://apps.dtic.mil/dtic/tr/fulltext/u2/a602711.pdf.

Steven Woehrel, Cong. Res. Serv., Ukraine: Current issues and U.S. Policy (Sept. 4, 2014), www.everycrsreport.com/files/20140904_RL33460_ac8f6d5380c670426d952dc39e784d173dac9739.pdf.

Lachezar Yanev, *The MH17 Judgment: An Interesting Take on the Nature of the Armed Conflict in Eastern Ukraine*, EJIL:Talk! (Dec. 7, 2022), https://www.ejiltalk.org/the-mh17-judgment-an-interesting-take-on-the-nature-of-the-armed-conflict-in-eastern-ukraine/.

Engin Yüksel, Strategies of Turkish Proxy Warfare in Northern Syria: Back with a Vengeance (Nov. 2019), www.clingendael.org/sites/default/files/2019-11/strategies-turkish-proxy-warfare-in-northern-syria.pdf.

Diane M. Zorri et al., Joint Special Operations U. Rep. 20-5, Iranian Proxy Groups in Iraq, Syria, and Yemen: A Principal-Agent Comparative Analysis (Dec. 2020), https://apps.dtic.mil/sti/pdfs/AD1146327.pdf.

INDEX

For the benefit of digital users, indexed terms that span two pages (e.g., 52–53) may, on occasion, appear on only one of those pages.